CULTURE AND ORGANISATION

PEARSON

We work with leading authors to develop the strongest learning experiences, bringing cutting-edge thinking and best learning practice to a global market. We craft our print and digital resources to do more to help learners not only understand their content, but to see it in action and apply what they learn, whether studying or at work.

Pearson is the world's leading learning company. Our portfolio includes Penguin, Dorling Kindersley, the Financial Times and our educational business, Pearson International. We are also a leading provider of electronic learning programmes and of test development, processing and scoring services to educational institutions, corporations and professional bodies around the world.

Pearson Custom Publishing enables our customers to access a wide and expanding range of market-leading content from world-renowned authors and develop their own tailor-made book. You choose the content that meets your needs and Pearson Custom Publishing produces a high-quality printed book.

Every day our work helps learning flourish, and wherever learning flourishes, so do people.

To learn more please visit us at: www.pearsoncustom.co.uk

PEARSON CUSTOM PUBLISHING

CULTURE AND ORGANISATION

Compiled from:

Organisational Behaviour and Analysis: An Integrated Approach Fourth Edition
Derek Rollinson

Understanding Cross-Cultural Management Second Edition
Marie-Joelle Browaeys and Roger Price

Organization Theory: Challenges and Perspectives
John McAuley, Joanne Duberley and Phil Johnson

Organizational Theory, Design, and Change Sixth Edition
Gareth R. Jones

International Management: Managing Across Borders and Cultures Seventh Edition
Helen Deresky

Diversity Consciousness: Opening our Minds to People, Cultures and Opportunities Third Edition
Richard Bucher

Managing Across Cultures Second Edition
Susan C. Schneider and Jean-Louis Barsoux

Understanding and Managing Diversity Fifth Edition
Carol Harvey and M. June Allard

Harlow, England • London • New York • Boston • San Francisco • Toronto • Sydney • Auckland • Singapore • Hong Kong
Tokyo • Seoul • Taipei • New Delhi • Cape Town • Sao Paulo • Mexico City • Madrid • Amsterdam • Munich • Paris • Milan

Pearson Education Limited
Edinburgh Gate
Harlow
Essex CM20 2JE

And associated companies throughout the world

Visit us on the World Wide Web at:
www.pearsoned.co.uk

This Custom Book Edition © Pearson Education Limited 2012

Compiled from:

Organisational Behaviour and Analysis: An Integrated Approach
Fourth Edition
Derek Rollinson
ISBN 978 0 273 71114 8
© Pearson Education Limited 1998, 2008

Understanding Cross-Cultural Management
Second Edition
Marie-Joelle Browaeys and Roger Price
ISBN 978 0 273 73295 2
© Pearson Education Limited 2008, 2011

Organization Theory: Challenges and Perspectives
John McAuley, Joanne Duberley and Phil Johnson
ISBN 978 0 273 68774 0
© Pearson Education Limited 2007

Organizational Theory, Design, and Change
Sixth Edition
Gareth R. Jones
ISBN 978 0 13 608731 1
© 2010, 2007, 2004 by Pearson Education, Inc., Upper Saddle River, New Jersey, 07458.

International Management: Managing Across Borders and Cultures
Seventh Edition
Helen Deresky
ISBN 978 0 13 609867 6
© 2011, 2008, 2006, 2003, 2000 Pearson Education, Inc., publishing as Prentice Hall, One Lake Street, Upper Saddle River, New Jersey 07458.

Diversity Consciousness: Opening our Minds to People, Cultures and Opportunities
Third Edition
Richard Bucher
ISBN 978 0 13 507463 9
© 2010, 2004, 2000 by Pearson Education, Inc., Upper Saddle River, New Jersey 07458.

Managing Across Cultures
Second Edition
Susan C. Schneider and Jean-Louis Barsoux
ISBN 978 0 273 64663 1
© International Book Distributors Limited 1997
© Pearson Education Limited 2003

Understanding and Managing Diversity
Fifth Edition
Carol Harvey and M. June Allard
ISBN 978 0 13 255311 7
© 2012, 2009, 2005, 2002, 1995 Pearson Education, Inc., publishing as Prentice Hall, One Lake Street, Upper Saddle River, New Jersey 07458.

All rights reserved. No part of this publication may be reproduced, stored in a retrieval system, or transmitted in any form or by any means, electronic, mechanical, photocopying, recording or otherwise, without either the prior written permission of the publisher or a licence permitting restricted copying in the United Kingdom issued by the Licensing Agency Ltd, Saffron House, 6–10 Kirby Street, London EC1N 8TS.

ISBN 978 1 78134 232 9

Printed and bound in Great Britain by Henry Ling at the Dorset Press Limited, Dorchester, DT1 1HD.

Contents

TOPIC 1 WHAT IS ORGANISATION THEORY? 1

1 An Introduction to the Study of Organisations 2
from *Organisational Behaviour and Analysis: An Integrated Approach* Fourth Edition
Derek Rollinson

TOPIC 2 HOW TO UNDERSTAND ORGANISATIONAL CULTURE 33

2 Organisational Cultures and Climates 34
from *Organisational Behaviour and Analysis: An Integrated Approach* Fourth Edition
Derek Rollinson

TOPIC 3 DIFFERING APPROACHES TO NATIONAL CULTURE 73

3 Determinants of Culture 75
from *Understanding Cross-Cultural Management* Second Edition
Marie-Joelle Browaeys and Roger Price

4 Dimensions of Culture 89
from *Understanding Cross-Cultural Management* Second Edition
Marie-Joelle Browaeys and Roger Price

5 Cultural Dimensions and Dilemmas 112
from *Understanding Cross-Cultural Management* Second Edition
Marie-Joelle Browaeys and Roger Price

6 Cultures and Styles of Management 127
from *Understanding Cross-Cultural Management* Second Edition
Marie-Joelle Browaeys and Roger Price

TOPIC 4 CROSS CULTURAL COMMUNICATION 147

7 Business Communication Across Cultures 149
from *Understanding Cross-Cultural Management* Second Edition
Marie-Joelle Browaeys and Roger Price

8 Barriers to Intercultural Communication 167
from *Understanding Cross-Cultural Management* Second Edition
Marie-Joelle Browaeys and Roger Price

TOPIC 5 THE IMPACT OF CULTURE ON PERCEPTION 185

9 Reflective Organisation Theory: Symbols, Meanings and Interpretations 186
from *Organization Theory: Challenges and Perspectives*
John McAuley, Joanne Duberley and Phil Johnson

TOPIC 6 OFFICE DESIGN, ORGANISATION AESTHETICS AND CULTURE — 235

10 Decision Making, Learning Knowledge Management and IT — 237
from *Organizational Theory, Design, and Change* Sixth Edition
Gareth R. Jones

TOPIC 7 COMMUNICATION IN A MULTICULTURAL CONTEXT — 267

11 Communicating Across Cultures — 269
from *International Management: Managing Across Borders and Cultures* Seventh Edition
Helen Deresky

12 Communicating in a Diverse World — 295
from *Diversity Consciousness: Opening our Minds to People, Cultures and Opportunities* Third Edition
Richard Bucher

TOPIC 8 HR PRACTICES AND CULTURAL DIMENSIONS PART 1 AND 2 — 331

13 Cultural Diversity in Organisations — 333
from *Understanding Cross-Cultural Management* Second Edition
Marie-Joelle Browaeys and Roger Price

14 Culture and Human Resource Management — 351
from *Managing Across Cultures* Second Edition
Susan C. Schneider and Jean-Louis Barsoux

15 The International Manager — 385
from *Managing Across Cultures* Second Edition
Susan C. Schneider and Jean-Louis Barsoux

16 The Global Organisation — 416
from *Managing Across Cultures* Second Edition
Susan C. Schneider and Jean-Louis Barsoux

TOPIC 9 DIVERSITY IN A CULTURALLY CONTESTED ENVIRONMENT — 453

17 Improving Communication in Today's Diverse Workplace — 455
from *Understanding and Managing Diversity* Fifth Edition
Carol Harvey and M. June Allard

TOPIC 10 CULTURE CHANGE — 467

18 Cultural Change in Organisations — 469
from *Understanding Cross-Cultural Management* Second Edition
Marie-Joelle Browaeys and Roger Price

TOPIC 1
WHAT IS ORGANISATION THEORY?

Chapter 1

An Introduction to the Study of Organisations

LEARNING OUTCOMES

After studying this chapter you should be able to:

- define organisations and name the five key features that distinguish an entity as an organisation
- explain why it is important to study organisations
- define Organisational Behaviour (OB) and Organisational Analysis (OA) and briefly trace their origins
- understand the traditional differences in approach to the study of organisations adopted by OB and OA and the case for their integration
- compare and contrast different conceptualisations used for the study of organisations (metaphors) and contrast them with the postmodernist perspective
- describe the characteristics of contemporary Organisational Behaviour and Analysis, together with the approach towards the subjects adopted in this book

INTRODUCTION

This chapter has two purposes: first, to introduce organisations as a field of study; and, second, to explain how this book will deal with the subject. Because the word organisation is often used in a very loose way that means different things to different people, the chapter starts by defining how the word is used in this book. The next section of the chapter deals with the subjects of Organisational Behaviour (OB) and Organisational Analysis (OA).

Traditionally, OB and OA have tended to focus on different levels of organisation. For the most part OB deals with the micro level, which has a focus on the behaviour of individuals and groups within organisations, whereas OA has focused on the macro level and deals with the behaviour of whole organisations. Since the book covers both levels of organisation, OB and OA are defined, their respective approaches to understanding behaviour in organisations and by organisations are compared, and their origins are described. The chapter then argues that while the distinction between macro and micro levels has some convenience, it is artificial. That is, fully understanding behaviour at the micro level requires that we take account of factors at the macro level, a corollary of which is that understanding the behaviour of a whole organisation requires that due account is taken of how individuals and groups behave at the micro level. The chapter then sets out a number of different perspectives that are frequently used as ways of conceptualising an organisation, and it closes with a description of the characteristics of contemporary Organisational Behaviour and Organisational Analysis, together with a statement of the approach towards the study of organisations adopted in this book.

WHAT IS AN ORGANISATION?

Although our lives are dominated by organisations, like many things we take them for granted. Since this book deals with the behaviour of organisations and the people in them, before entering the subject matter it is necessary to define the entities on which it is focused. As will be seen later in the chapter, there are several ways of conceptualising an organisation but here a simpler approach will be used to illustrate that organisations have a number of important features, which are set out in the following list:

- **Organisations are artifacts** They do not exist in nature but are brought into existence by humans.
- **Goal directed** Organisations are created to serve some purpose. However, this does not mean that everyone in a particular organisation has the same common goal and neither does it follow that everybody is aware of the goals pursued by the organisation.
- **Social entities** Organisations usually consist of more than one person and although a one-person business (such as the corner shop) can be conceived of as an organisation, and in legal terms it might well be classified as one, this is not normally what we mean by the word.
- **Structured activity** Achieving the purpose or goals for an organisation normally requires that human activity be deliberately structured and coordinated in some way, thus there will usually be identifiable parts or activities.

- **Nominal boundaries** It is usually possible to identify nominal boundaries for an organisation, which give a degree of consensus about who or what is part of the organisation and who or what belongs elsewhere. However, this does not mean that the organisation is, or can be, completely sealed off from what is outside.

With these features in mind, a basic definition which would encompass all major conceptualisations of an organisation is:

> social entities brought into existence and sustained in an ongoing way by humans to serve some purpose, from which it follows that human activities in the entity are normally structured and coordinated towards achieving some purpose or goals.

TIME OUT

1. Think about a university or college as an organisation. Describe ways in which it qualifies as an organisation in terms of the five characteristics given above. That is: is it an artifact?; does it have goals and what do you feel that they are?; are there many people involved and who are they?; does it have a structure and coordinating mechanisms and, if so, what are the signs that these exist?; can you place nominal boundaries on the institution and, if so, where would you place them?
2. Now do the same for your immediate family; how easy is it to conceptualise this as an organisation?

WHY STUDY BEHAVIOUR IN ORGANISATIONS?

Although organisations are extremely complex entities that are not easily understood without conscious effort, this in itself is no reason why they should be studied. Nevertheless, there are two important reasons why an understanding of organisations and the behaviour of people in them is, or should be, of concern to us all.

First, it takes but a moment's thought to realise that, in one form or another, organisations are the dominant institution in the modern world. The nature of society is shaped (some would assert badly shaped) by them, and in return they are shaped by the world in which they exist. Some things in life can only be accomplished if people come together to apply collective physical and mental effort, and in many cases this enables tasks to be completed in a more effective way. Although organisations exist in many forms, for the last 400 years they have tended to become larger, more complex and more specialised in what they do. The days have long gone when a family could itself do all that needed to be done to remain self-sufficient, and most people today would be incapable of performing all these activities because they have been taken over by organisations. Thus we all occupy specialist niches in a huge jigsaw of roles that makes up a modern society, in which organisations have become the institutions that shape the conditions under which we live. In addition, they have huge amounts of power. Their decisions about where to locate and the activities in which they engage have a huge impact on individuals, communities and even nation states.

They wield immense power with governments, and in certain cases there is more than a suspicion that they control government decisions. Therefore, the life of everyone in modern society is affected by the existence and behaviour of organisations, and this alone is sufficient reason to try to understand them better.

Second, throughout our lives we are inevitably involved in organisations of some sort. In our early years we are members of an immediate family (a special type of organisation), and from then on we are members of other organisations for the remainder of our lives. We are educated by organisations and our livelihoods depend on them, as does a large part of our social contact with other people, and when we approach the end of our lifespan and can no longer care for ourselves, we gyrate to other organisations to live out our remaining years. This book is mainly concerned with work organisations, in which we probably spend well over half of our lives. For most of this time we try to come to terms with how an organisation functions, how it affects our behaviour and how, in turn, we affect the behaviour of others. To understand this context is part of understanding the world in which we live, and this is also sufficient reason for knowing about the behaviour of organisations and the people in them.

In addition to these two reasons, which apply to everyone, there is a third, which applies to a smaller population: those who manage, or even aspire to manage, organisations or parts of them. For these people, a vital part of performing their roles effectively is to understand the behaviour of humans in an organisational context. Organisations are social collectivities and whatever is done in or by them is ultimately the result of human action. Even in the abstract, robotic world of science fiction, it is humans who decide to create and switch on the robot, and so even machine activity is ultimately traceable to some human action. Therefore, if we are concerned about the effective functioning of organisations, or whether they should become a force for good rather than evil, the human element must be considered. In this sense, understanding the behaviour of organisations and the people in them goes to the very heart of the process of management. However, it must be stated at the outset, and this is a theme that pervades the whole book, these subjects are not lessons in how to manage. Neither do they seek to show managers how to manipulate others, or to bend them to their will. This cannot be emphasised too strongly because there is a regrettable tendency to treat these subjects as part of a tool-kit that equips the manager to 'be in charge'. This view can be detected in some European texts, but is much stronger in those published in America, and is probably linked with the American view of organisations, which is highly functionalist and instrumental. That is, organisations are not seen as social entities but, in terms of tasks that need to be completed, functions that need to be performed and objectives that must be achieved. This view gives rise to a strong managerialist perspective, in which managers are seen to have an almost divine right to decide the goals and objectives of other people and, perhaps more significantly, a right to be obeyed. Thus, anything that is official in organisational terms, or is laid down by a manager, is that which is correct, and while American texts are full of platitudes about the need to understand human behaviour, they leave a strong impression that the main purpose of understanding is to enable managers to get their own way.

However, the managerialist perspective is not one that is universally held. Neither is the belief that human behaviour can be easily controlled by the use of structures and rules. Over 40 years ago Philip Selznick (1957) drew attention to the idea that an organisation is first and foremost a collection of human beings. Therefore, while organisations do have formal and officially sanctioned structures, these can never account for the full range of human behaviour. In practice, individuals interact as people who bring their personalities, problems and interests with them into the work situation, and this influences how well they fit into the neat set of boxes that we call work roles.

REPLAY

The main reasons for studying organisations and the behaviour of people in them are:

- everyone in modern society is affected by the existence and behaviour of organisations
- we are all members of organisations of one sort or another for most of our lives
- since all that happens in organisations is ultimately traceable to human action, those who manage organisations need to take account of those factors that affect human behaviour; not, however, to control or manipulate humans but to better understand their behaviour.

TIME OUT

Reflect on an organisation of which you are or have been a member, preferably not your family or the university or college at which you study, but perhaps one where you have worked. Now re-examine the three reasons given in the Replay section for studying organisations and try to answer the questions below.

1. In what ways did the organisation or the people in it affect your behaviour? How did you feel about this?
2. In what ways did you affect the behaviour of the organisation or that part of it in which you were located? How did you feel about this?
3. If you aspire to manage an organisation or a part thereof, how could the conclusions you have drawn by answering questions 1 and 2 be useful to you in the future?

ORGANISATIONAL BEHAVIOUR AND ANALYSIS

Opening Definitions

Since the terms were first coined, a number of competing definitions for Organisational Behaviour and Organisational Analysis have existed. While this book argues that this is somewhat unreal, because both are really part of a wider subject concerned with understanding human behaviour in organisations and the behaviour of organisations themselves, it is necessary to understand how this state of affairs came about. To some extent it is because, in practice, there has always been some tendency for organisations to be studied at one or other of two levels, which itself creates an impression that there are two different subjects: one called Organisational Behaviour and the other Organisational Analysis.

Organisational Behaviour can most succinctly be defined as:

> **the study of individuals and groups in organisations.**
> (Schermerhorn *et al.* 2000, p 3)

This subject is primarily concerned with examining organisations at the micro level and deals with the cognitive and emotional differences between individuals and how individuals interact with each other. To a large extent the subject relies on knowledge drawn from individual psychology, social psychology and, to a far lesser extent, sociology.

Organisational Analysis is much harder to define, mainly because it is still an evolving subject in which there is an ongoing debate about what an organisation is, how it can most appropriately be viewed, and what methods should be used to study organisations. The reader should also be aware that some authors in this subject do not even use the title Organisational Analysis, but instead prefer the older expression Organisation Theory. This can be defined as:

> **the macro level examination of organisations, which uses the whole organisation as the unit of analysis.**
> (Daft 1996, p 26)

The subject is primarily concerned with differences in structure and behaviour at this level of analysis. Since it views the organisation itself (rather than its component parts) as the social system to be examined, it draws heavily on sociological work. This perhaps is the reason for the ongoing debate about what the nature of the subject should be: different schools of sociology can be notorious in 'going their own ways' and distancing themselves from others who approach a phenomenon from a different perspective.

THE EVOLUTION OF ORGANISATIONAL BEHAVIOUR AND ANALYSIS

While humans have worked together in organisations for thousands of years, the serious study of behaviour in organisations is less than 100 years old, and what we know today is just one stage in an evolving body of knowledge. Until the 1940s, Organisational Behaviour and Organisational Analysis tended to be regarded as part of a somewhat ill-defined subject, variously called Industrial Administration or Administrative Studies, and, while the subject was almost exclusively focused on formal aspects of organisations, it had a strong influence on thinking about behaviour in them. However, some of the theories that have evolved and which have had an abiding influence on the subject are much older than this. Therefore, it is convenient to trace the historic emergence of OB and OA as occurring in a number of phases: first, early formative work; second, for OB and OA separately, a precursor phase followed by a maturity phase; and, finally, for OB and OA together, the current phase. This is shown in outline in Figure 1.1 and for convenience the account that follows will deal with matters in this historical order.

Early Formative Work

Long before people began to focus explicitly on the study of organisations and the behaviour of people in them, scholars working in different places and at different times

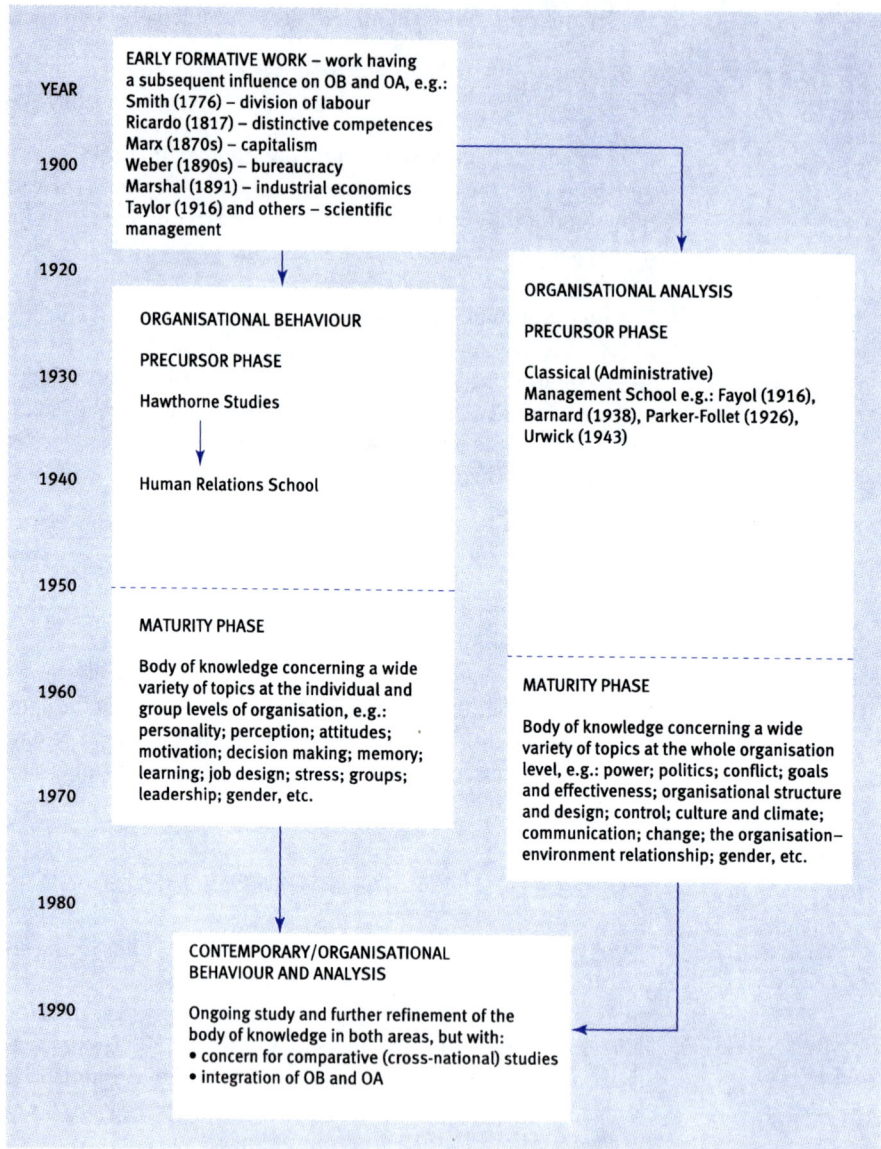

Figure 1.1 An outline of the evolution of contemporary Organisational Behaviour and Analysis

had addressed topics that subsequently shaped the thinking of later workers. The list of these people is almost endless and space precludes mentioning more than a few of the most influential scholars. Among the earliest was an economist, Adam Smith (1776), whose classic description of pin making in Redditch illustrated the effects of specialisation of labour on the economic efficiency of production and this had a lasting impact on theories of organisational structure and the design of jobs. A little later, another economist, David Ricardo (1817), expanded on the work of Smith and developed the concept of 'distinctive competencies', that is, the skills and capabilities that an organisation has over and above its competitors. Later still, another economist, Alfred Marshall (1891) developed Ricardo's ideas even further to explore the competitive advantages of organisations under different market conditions and shortly before this, Karl Marx

(1894) had explained how organisational structure and work design were used as primary mechanisms for subjugating and exploiting workers.

In addition to economic theories, there were early social scientists whose work had a lasting impact on thinking about organisations. One who had a great influence on the next (precursor) phase in the development of OA was the German sociologist Max Weber (1948), who documented the characteristics and workings of bureaucracy, which was influential in later thinking about organisational structure.

All the above work originated from academic sources but, in terms of its enduring impact, the most significant set of ideas came from another source altogether. This appeared early in the twentieth century and, since its effects are still very much in evidence, it deserves a more lengthy description.

Scientific Management

Well before the turn of the nineteenth century, the increasing size and complexity of industrial organisations started to make it more difficult to organise human effort in an effective and efficient way. A diverse but informal collection of American industrial managers, the so-called 'systematic management movement', was formed, which reached the conclusion that the (then) current methods of organising large-scale production were no longer appropriate. The most influential set of ideas to emerge from this movement became known as *scientific management*, a term coined by Frederick Winslow Taylor (1911), but it is also associated with others who later developed his ideas.

Scientific management: a set of techniques for organising work methods to give managers greater control over the labour process, i.e. the exchange of effort for rewards

Scientific management is very different from anything that we would now call Organisational Behaviour. Strictly speaking it is a technique for organising or re-organising work methods to give managers greater control over the labour process; that is, the exchange of effort for rewards. Nevertheless, in management circles, Taylor's ideas were, and still are, very influential, and his work contains a number of behaviourial assumptions. Taylor was an engineer and, to judge from his writings, he had a limitless faith in the application of the principles of physical science and engineering to identify the 'one best way' for an organisation to function. As applied to the matter of obtaining maximum productive effort, this was enshrined in his four key principles: that managers should:

1. Gather together all of the traditional knowledge (the essence of skills, techniques, etc.) which had been acquired and held by workmen in their minds, record and tabulate this information and, wherever possible, reduce it to laws, rules, or even mathematical formulae.
2. Scientifically select workpeople and progressively train and develop them to do the jobs that are required.
3. Bring the scientifically designed job and the scientifically selected workers together.
4. Divide up the actual work of the organisation between management and workers (according to their capabilities and training).

Soldiering: working at a much slower pace than the one of which a person is capable

Taylor had an obsession with combating *soldiering* – the practice of working at a much slower pace than the one of which a person is capable – and he reasoned that there were two basic ways to address this issue. Either close and constant supervision could be given (which adds to the cost of the job), or some incentive to work faster could be provided. The second of these was his preferred option, and his proposed solution is reflected in the first of his four principles, which removes all responsibility for the design and planning of work from the hands of those who perform it, and allows work to be designed by managers to extract the maximum amount of effort from the worker. Taylor recognised that this did not necessarily mean continuous effort, for example obtaining the best effort for a full day would mean that rest pauses would be needed, to permit a measure of recuperation. However, this brought into play the second of his four principles. He openly acknowledged that maximum effort would result in boring and repetitive tasks, which in turn required careful selection of operators with the required physical attributes, but a corresponding lack of aspiration for anything more mentally stimulating. More significantly, he stressed that the most effective way to induce people to follow the laid-down design was to make payment contingent on output. Thus, in basic terms, his theory rests on the assumption that high pay is the main (and perhaps only) thing that people seek to obtain from work.

Taylor's ideas contain a great deal that would be considered controversial, if not downright patronising today. For instance, he asserted that everyone is first class at something, and that being less than first class could only arise for one of two reasons: either the person had been badly selected or trained for the task, or the person was just plain lazy. He also reasoned that since some people are better endowed with mental abilities, and others with physical attributes, efficiency required the separation of 'thinking' from 'doing', with each task allocated to the appropriate people. In Taylor's view, since managers were the (superior) thinking part of an organisation they should provide the mental effort, with the operatives performing the (more menial) physical tasks. Taylor could also be accused of being naive in his thinking. He was convinced that because both parties get the rewards they most desire – for workers, more pay, and for managers a more productive and efficient workforce – scientific management would bring huge benefits to both parties, and lead to a community of interest with an in-built force for cooperation. The truth, of course, turned out to be somewhat different. Managers tended to use the techniques to grind the last ounce of effort from employees and, later, when applied to mass production, they simplified and deskilled work so that cheaper labour could be used. Thus it is not surprising that trade unions saw scientific management as a device to denigrate workers and hasten a return to 'sweated labour' conditions and, as a result, in 1911 there was a wave of strikes against its use in America. Nevertheless, by the 1920s the principles were in widespread use on both sides of the Atlantic and it has become the most widely used set of general principles for organising production.

Although scientific management is a long way from having the same concerns as either Organisational Behaviour or Organisational Analysis, it became the starting point for many fruitful lines of enquiry. For example, it contains an implicit if somewhat oversimplified and crude theory of motivation, an issue which is important in Organisational Behaviour. In the emphasis on task specialisation it also has an outline prescription for the structural design of organisations and this is an important topic in both Organisational Behaviour and Analysis.

Organisational Behaviour

The Precursor Phase: The Hawthorne Studies and Human Relations

Scientific management has attracted a measure of criticism from quite early on, mainly because it seemed to result in an element of dehumanised working conditions, together with physical and psychological strain. A study that did much to highlight its shortcomings, and which became a major turning point in thinking about people in organisations, emerged from a series of investigations in the late 1920s and early 1930s in the Hawthorne plant of West Electric Company in America. This work, which subsequently become known as the Hawthorne Studies, can be thought of as the first, founding step in Organisational Behaviour, and it also gave rise to a new school of management thought, the *human relations movement*.

Human relations movement: a view of the employment situation which holds that employees respond primarily to the social context of the workplace, an important part of which is interpersonal relations at work

The original work, undertaken by industrial engineers in the company, started in the early 1920s and studied female employees engaged in light assembly work, with the aim of uncovering the intensity of lighting conditions that gave the highest level of output. Workers were divided into two groups: an 'experimental' group, where lighting conditions were systematically varied, and a comparison 'control' group, where no changes took place. The experiments took place over a two-year period and resulted in two major findings. First, whenever the intensity of lighting was changed output increased in the experimental group, even when conditions were restored to those pertaining at the start. Second, and perhaps more puzzling, although lighting conditions were only changed for the experimental group, whenever they were changed, output rose in both groups. From this it was concluded that it was probably the change rather than the actual amount of light that influenced output. Moreover, since the control group also responded to the change, it was obviously not the lighting conditions alone that caused the rise in output. There had to be some other factor. Word of these results soon came to the attention of a group of industrial psychologists at Harvard University who, together with employee relations research staff at Hawthorne, conducted experiments for several more years (Mayo 1933; Roethlisberger and Dickson 1939). Since the work is far too extensive to be covered in full, two major experiments, from which significant conclusions were drawn, will be described.

The first is what is now known as the **Relay Assembly Test Room (RATR) Experiments**, in which six female workers engaged in assembling relays for telephone switchboards first had their baseline output accurately measured on the production line, and then were moved into a specially constructed experimental room. The studies on this group took place over a five-year period, and a large number of changes to working conditions was introduced, either singly or in combination. For example, changes were made to working hours, rest periods and physical conditions such as temperature and lighting and also the use of a group financial incentive scheme. These workers were also allowed to make suggestions about conditions in the experimental room, in which a member of the research team was located permanently as an observer, and who virtually took on the role of their supervisor.

Over the five years, output rose to its highest ever recorded level: a 30 per cent increase on the baseline. However, other significant changes were observed in the group. Since the people had much more freedom to control the way that work was done and could interact socially, they welded together as a social entity with its own standards of behaviour and a strong team ethos. Two general conclusions were drawn from this experiment. First, that work satisfaction is strongly dependent on informal social factors, for example friendliness, cooperation between group members, the feeling they were doing something worthwhile and, importantly, relations with the supervisor. Second, that these social factors had a far greater impact on output than physical conditions.

The second set of experiments is generally referred to as the **Bank Wiring Observation Room (BWOR) Studies**, in which 14 men engaged in wiring, soldering and inspecting banks of telephone switchgear, were subject to detailed observation. In time, the men came to ignore the observer, who was able record several interesting features about the group, one of the most important of which was the existence of a distinct group structure. In practice, there were two sub-groups or cliques: one at the back of the room and one at the front, and each had slightly different patterns of behaviour. In addition, there was a certain amount of rivalry between the groups, with the one at the front considering itself to be of slightly higher status, because it was engaged in more difficult work. However, as a whole the 14 men had developed a code of conduct, which was enforced by workers putting pressure on each other, and the most significant item in the code seemed to be a norm about the level of output. No matter what management and supervision deemed to be the required output, the group had established its own criteria for what it considered to be a 'fair day's work'. Therefore, even though management introduced a payment-by-results bonus scheme to boost output, the group made no attempt to maximise production, but aimed for the figure that they had decided was fair. If by chance they did overproduce, this was kept secret from management and used to restore the balance on some future day when there was underproduction. Moreover, this output norm was actively policed by group members, who exerted pressure to conform on the 'chisellers' (those who underproduced), or those who overproduced (the 'rate busters'). This pressure usually took the form of unpleasant but not harmful physical blows, which the men called 'bingeing', together with mild social isolation of the offending colleague. However, the pressure was clearly experienced as significant by those concerned, because there were cases of individuals asking to be transferred to other work.

Output restriction of this type is not unknown and so the Bank Wiring Room results are important in drawing attention to one of the limitations of scientific management. In theory, it is possible to create a formal system of work in which jobs are carefully designed to eliminate non-productive effort. However, alongside, or even as part of, the formal system there exists an informal organisation, which has its own norms, values and expectations, and these informal codes of conduct are sometimes more influential on day-to-day behaviour than the formal rules.

TIME OUT

Look closely at the conclusions drawn by the Hawthorne researchers and compare these with the major assumptions associated with scientific management.

1. To what extent are the two sets of ideas compatible, or does one contradict the other?
2. Can you identify an organisation or an industry in which the principles of scientific management could still be in use?

While the results and conclusions of the Hawthorne Studies have been criticised in terms of the rigour of the research (Yorks and Whitsett 1985), they have had a major impact on the understanding of behaviour in organisations. The most important inference is that people have social needs to be satisfied at work, which can be equally as important as monetary needs. This, it can be noted, is a direct contradiction of one of the tenets of scientific management. Ideas such as this gave rise to the **human relations** school of thought that heralded the emergence of what has eventually become the subject of Organisational Behaviour. Some of the assumptions of human relations theory have a strong influence on certain theories of work motivation. Human relations theory also gave rise to much of the work on groups and leadership.

The Maturity Phase of Organisational Behaviour

From the 1950s onwards, OB rapidy emerged as a mature field of study in its own right. Psychologists were the first in the field, but shortly after this other academic disciplines became involved and it is probably true to say that virtually every aspect of human behaviour in organisations has received some attention, often from several different disciplinary perspectives. Since a great deal of this work is covered in the different chapters of this book, it would be inappropriate to single out any one in particular here.

Organisational Analysis

The Precursors: Classical Organisation Theory

> **Classical organisation theory:** a diverse group of theories which sets out to derive universal rules and guidelines for the design and functioning of organisations

Shortly after scientific management came into widespread use, a complementary set of ideas began to emerge, which subsequently became known as *classical organisation theory*. While scientific management initially focused on the micro level issue of job design, organisation theory attempted to lay down guiding principles for the design and functioning of a whole organisation. In some respects the ideas that emerged are similar to those put forward by the German sociologist Max Weber (1948), whose classic study of bureaucracy laid the foundations for the serious scientific study of formal organisation. However, unlike Weber, whose ideas were based on empirical investigation and focused on the large public sector bureaucracies of Germany, classical management theorists were largely practising managers, who derived their ideas from the practical experience of running large industrial organisations, and who set out what they believed to be guides to good practice. Although these writers differ in detail, they are remarkably similar in terms of basic approach. All give highly prescriptive guidelines, which they claimed were universally applicable. Perhaps the best known is Henri Fayol (1916) who derived a set of 14 principles of organising. Because these will be considered in Chapter 17, details need not concern us here. Suffice it to say that these guidelines set out a highly prescriptive recipe for the design of organisational structures that Fayol claimed was universally applicable, and for this reason the whole approach has been much criticised. For example, it takes no account of interactions between people and, because it underestimates their mental capacities, it has a very naive view of the way they think; in addition it understates the potential for conflict in organisations (March and Simon 1958). Indeed, so prescriptive and mechanical is the approach that it has been called a description of 'organisations without people' (Bennis 1959). Nevertheless, the ideas give a very clear and unambiguous set of guidelines that is easy to understand and apply, and the approach is remarkably resilient in management circles; dressed up in different words it is still common to find the ideas espoused in current management textbooks. So far as current thinking is concerned, the strongest criticism of this school is the assumption that a valid set of universally applicable design principles can be derived from it.

The Maturity Phase of Organisational Analysis

Shortly after OB entered its maturity phase, what has now become known as OA began to emerge as a mature field of study, although the term Organisational Analysis was coined somewhat later. For the most part the first workers in the field were essentially management theorists, many of whom were dissatisfied with the prescriptions of classical management theory with respect to structure and organisational design. As such they abandoned the search for universal prescriptions and, instead, sought to locate structural forms that best fit the specific circumstances of an organisation. In addition, scholars from other academic backgrounds entered the area and, if anything, OA emerged as a more eclectic field than OB. Nevertheless, it is relevant to point out that some of these developments, particularly in terms of work that originated in the USA, are somewhat controversial. Until the early 1960s, the development of organisation theory was mainly located in sociology departments of universities, but from then on in America it was increasingly concentrated in business schools. When this occurred, the purer concerns of social science tended to be replaced by highly managerialist concerns that were almost exclusively focused on promoting the design of more effective, efficient (and sometimes harsher and more exploitative) organisations. As such, many interesting and vital lines of enquiry about the nature and functioning of organisations had a tendency to be regarded as irrelevant (Hinings and Greenwood 2002). This, it can be noted, parallels an earlier change that had occurred in OB, in which the Harvard Business School had effectively hijacked the findings and conclusions of the Hawthorne Studies, to evolve an equally managerialist (and exploitative) version of Human Relations Theory (O'Connor 1999). Once again, since much of this work is covered in later chapters of this book, it would not be appropriate to single out anything for a special mention here.

REPLAY

- Organisational Behaviour and Organisational Analysis originate from two different sources that were focused respectively on micro and macro level aspects of organisations.
- While not in itself Organisational Behaviour, there are assumptions about factors that influence micro level aspects of behaviour contained in scientific management theories. However, the more identifiable origins of Organisational Behaviour lie in the findings of the Hawthorne experiments that gave rise to the human relations movement.
- Organisational Analysis traces its roots to the classical management school of theorists, who attempted to formulate universal principles for the design and functioning of organisations.

The Case for Integration

At first sight it would be all too easy to conclude that Organisational Behaviour and Organisational Analysis are two completely unconnected subjects. They have different names, they are often taught and researched by two different sets of people, who barely communicate with each other. Nevertheless, since both subjects deal with the behaviour of people in organisations, the author of this book views the distinction as more apparent than real. Why then is the distinction so frequently made? To some extent, it is the result of different academic disciplines imposing their own definitions of the most important features of organisations that should be studied. When applied to organisations and the people in them, the word behaviour can refer to a number of different levels:

Level 1: Individual: where the focus is on matters such as values, attitudes, beliefs, aptitudes, intelligence and motivation that influence how people behave as individuals.
Level 2: Group: which is more concerned with social and interactive features such as group dynamics and leadership.
Level 3: Organisational: where the main concern is with the behaviour of an organisation as a whole, for example its relationship with environment and its structure, culture and processes.

This rather arbitrary classification is only possible because different academic disciplines focus their efforts at these different levels. For instance, level 1 exists because this is what individual psychologists do; level 2 exists because this is where social psychologists and, to a lesser extent, sociologists focus their endeavours; and level 3 because this is the area of interest to writers on management, sociologists and economists. This has regrettably led to two distinct views of organisations: the **macro** (level 3) view and the **micro** (levels 1 and 2) view. However, the separation could be very unreal and even downright misleading.

Academically, placing micro level features in one box and calling it Organisational Behaviour and macro level matters into another box and calling it Organisational Analysis is very convenient. It permits the whole body of knowledge to be cut up into manageable chunks and written down as syllabi for courses. Problematically, it also permits different academic disciplines to claim territorial rights over the boxes and sometimes results in an element of unhealthy criticism between the disciplines, and the net result is that there is almost an in-built force that conspires to treat Organisational Behaviour and Organisational Analysis as different bodies of knowledge. However, if we examine one of the first attempts to define the subject of Organisational Behaviour – which, despite its age, is more in keeping with the arguments expressed in this book – we can see that this was never intended:

> the study of the structure, functioning and performance of organisations and the behaviour of groups and individuals within them. (Pugh 1971, p 9)

Note that, in addition to the behaviour of people in organisations at the micro level, it also refers to the behaviour of an organisation as a whole. However, it is important to sound a note of caution here. While people regularly speak of the behaviour of an organisation, organisations can never be said to behave in the same sense that people behave. The word organisation refers to something that is an abstract phenomenon. Therefore, to refer to the behaviour of a person and an organisation in the same sense is *reification*; that is, it treats an abstract idea as something that actually exists. Nevertheless, because this is part of the way that people normally conceive the world, they customarily talk of organisations 'behaving', and to some extent it is meaningful to do so. For example, an organisation behaves as a whole towards its environment, and although this is usually the result of a decision by an individual or group

Reification: to treat an abstract idea as something that actually exists

of individuals, since what behaves is a social collectivity, it is meaningful to speak of the behaviour of the collectivity as a whole. Thus, in this case, reification of the organisation has been argued to be one of organisation theory's most essential and useful tools (Koza and Thoenig 2003). Moreover, it amply justifies why Organisational Behaviour and Organisational Analysis cannot sensibly be considered to be two separate areas of study. Without behaviour by people within an organisation there would be no behaviour of the organisation as a whole. Thus, we need to understand how the behaviour of people influences its actions. Similarly, if we want to know why people behave as they do, we not only need to understand how individual and group factors shape behaviour, but also how the organisation and its interactions with the outside world result in pressures for people to behave in certain ways. Indeed, a review article by Porter (1996) notes that the single most significant failure of Organisational Behaviour (OB) over the last 40 years is to ignore the 'O', and overemphasise the 'B', which tends to result in paying insufficient attention to the impact of the organisational context on the behaviour of individuals and groups. For this reason it is worthwhile examining certain features that the two approaches have in common, and this is considered next.

CONTEMPORARY ORGANISATIONAL BEHAVIOUR AND ANALYSIS

As noted, until comparatively recently, Organisational Behaviour and Organisational Analysis have largely remained apart. However, it is now more widely recognised that they are two aspects of the same overall subject, which can be illustrated by examining some of the characteristics that they have in common.

The Use of Concepts and Theories from Social Science

Both subjects deal with the human element in organisations, with the aim of understanding and explaining the behaviour of organisations and people within them. To do this they draw heavily on concepts and theories from the social sciences and apply them in an organisational setting.

A Multidisciplinary Focus

There are a number of different social science disciplines, which all tend to focus on slightly different aspects of the social world. Therefore, the same phenomenon is sometimes studied by people from more than one discipline, and each one brings its own unique concepts and theories. Thus, there are often several competing explanations of the same phenomenon. However, this does not mean that the findings and explanations stay separate in discrete compartments. Sometimes, scholars working in the same area integrate the work, to produce a more comprehensive explanation and, occasionally, something will be studied by a cross-disciplinary team. The major disciplines involved and their primary areas of focus are shown in Table 1.1.

Theoretical Orientations with Practical Implications

While the whole area uses theory to understand organisational phenomena, this is seldom a matter of 'knowledge for knowledge's sake'. Usually the aim is to inform a

Table 1.1 The major social science disciplines involved in Organisational Behaviour and Analysis

Social science discipline	Typical organisational phenomena of interest
Individual psychology	Individual differences, intelligence, personality, aptitude, motivation, learning, perception
Social psychology	Group dynamics, attitudes, leadership
Sociology	The organisation as a social system, socialisation of organisational members, structures, cultures, communication
Social anthropology	Culture and its effects on behaviour
Politics	Power, decision making, conflict, the behaviour of interest groups, coalitions, control
Economics	Labour markets, product markets and their influence as part of organisational environment

wider audience so that its members will better understand what goes on in organisations. This audience includes other scholars and teachers in the area, and specialist staff and managers in organisations. However, it is important to note that this knowledge is not targeted at any one group in particular. The subject is more frequently taught to students of business and management than to anyone else, and the intention in this is that those who want to make their careers in organisations should better understand the complexities of human behaviour. Having said this, there are differences in approach that reflect the use of the various social sciences, the most notable of which are those that are commonly held in Great Britain and in the USA.

The British position is one that attempts to maintain a neutral and unbiased stance in terms of the uses to which new knowledge are put. At the risk of overstating the position, this broadly entails undertaking research with a view to promoting further understanding and knowledge. Thus, it most definitely is *not* the aim that any new knowledge that is uncovered, should become the sole property of managers so that they become better equipped to control or manipulate the actions of others in a way that takes away their freedom or dignity. One by-product of this is that British academics can be highly critical of management, and their research results feel no compunction to report only the good news, but will often be written in a 'warts and all' style. In the US, however, OB and OA tend to be approached from a very different perspective. Both subjects tend to be far more managerialist in their focus and many books and research papers in the area are unashamedly devoted to providing a toolkit that facilitates the perpetuation of managerial control over others.

Nevertheless, in both countries, the very nature of the work undertaken tends to produces a situation in which knowledge gives rise to technologies; that is, pure knowledge (science) results in a technology for applying the scientific knowledge. At the risk of giving a rather oversimplified picture, Figure 1.2 shows the relationship.

Note that all four cells in Figure 1.2 are connected, which means that the theories connect with practice. Starting with the macro level, organisational development is an organisation-wide strategy for change.

At the micro level, a great deal of the knowledge that emerges gets incorporated into what is now known as human resource management. However, to speak of a 'human

Figure 1.2 Relation of macro and micro level of theory and practice

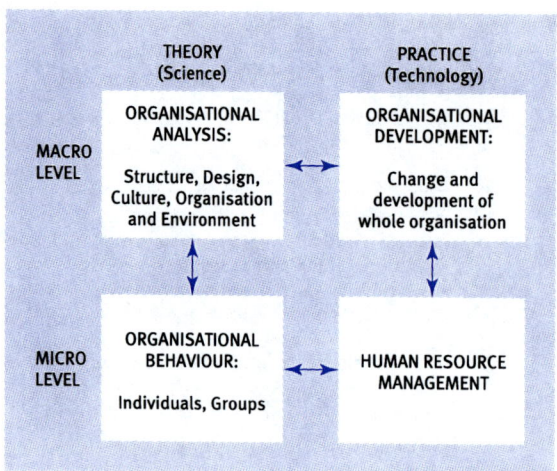

resource manager' is somewhat confusing. Most managers deal with human resources and they need to know something about human behaviour. Nevertheless, in many organisations there are specialists in this area who advise and guide functional managers.

Open Systems Perspectives

Open systems: a system not sealed off from its environment and, therefore, subject to the intrusion of environmental influences

Either consciously or unconsciously, both OB and OA adopt an *open systems* perspective.

This a way of thinking about organisations which contains a recognition that anything on which we focus exists in an environment, by which it can be affected. In its simplest form, an open system can be portrayed, as in Figure 1.3, and the basic principle can be translated into something that is more easily recognised as a commercial organisation in Figure 1.4.

Complex systems have a host of interdependent parts, which contribute to the wellbeing and survival of the whole. The important point about anything that can be classified as a 'system' is that it exists in an environment, to which it must adapt in order to be able to survive. An organisation as a system can often be thought of as a set of sub-systems, all of which interact with each other, and the whole exists in an environment with which it interacts. This is shown in Figure 1.5, where the sub-systems labelled groups A–D can be thought of as departments or functions, although, for convenience, they are simply called groups here. Also note that each group is made up of sub-sub-systems, which can be regarded as individuals.

The first and most obvious point that can be made relates to the focus and concerns of OB and OA as two levels of study. At the micro level the main focus is on

Figure 1.3 Basic open systems model

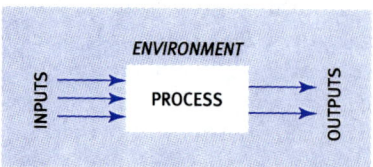

Figure 1.4 Simplified open systems model of a commercial organisation

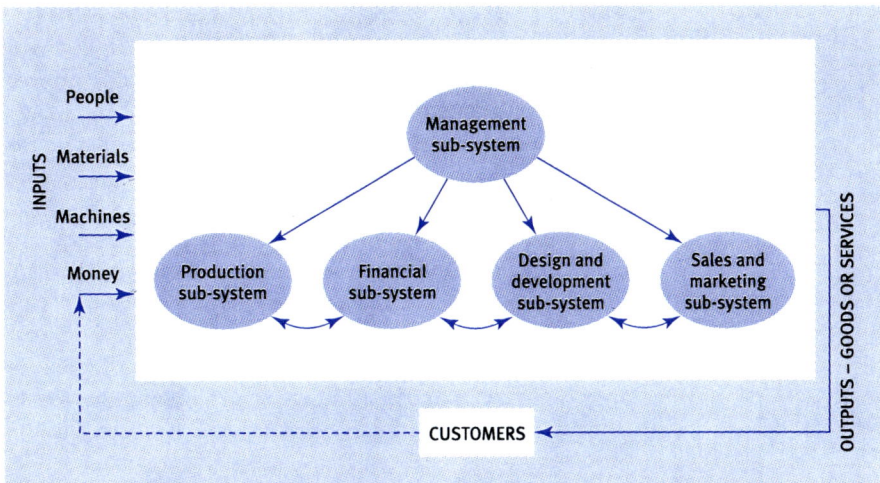

Figure 1.5 The organisation as a system of sub-systems and sub-sub-systems

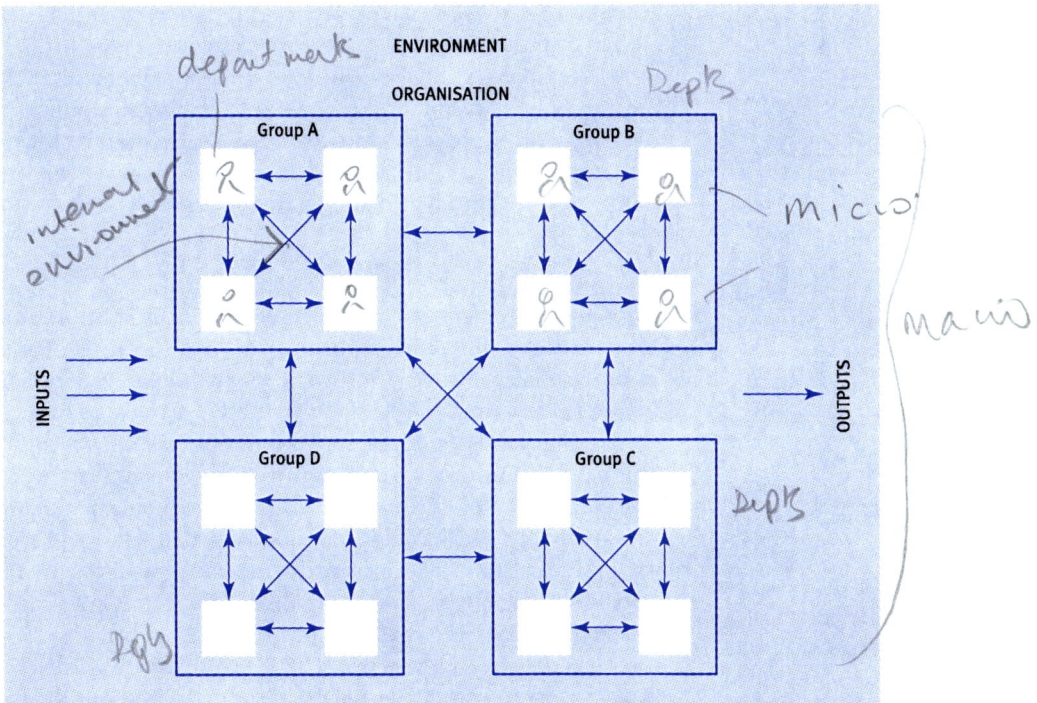

parts (or sub-systems) of an organisation, and so the unit of analysis is the individual or group. The macro level perspective has a focus on the organisation as a whole, that is, the total system made up of all the sub-systems.

A second highly important point that emerges from Figure 1.5 is the idea of system, sub-system and sub-sub-system. At any level, a feature or process that is under consideration can usually be viewed as a system in its own right. Each of the groups in Figure 1.5 is a sub-system made up of individuals that interact with each other, so its characteristics and properties are not simply the sum of its parts; it will have emergent properties that only arise because the individuals interact. Thus, if we reduce one of the groups from four people to three, it would behave differently. Therefore, an individual in one of the groups is affected by being part of the sub-system, and the behaviour of the sub-system is affected by his or her presence, and the sub-system will be affected if he or she leaves. This principle can be applied in the same way at the next level upwards. The system itself (organisation) is made up of interacting sub-systems, and some of its characteristics only exist because sub-systems A–D interact. Moreover, each one is affected by being part of the system, the system is affected because it is there, and the system's characteristics and behaviour will change if it is removed.

The final point concerns environments. Each of the individuals in groups A – D is surrounded by an environment: the other people in the group. Moreover, each of the groups is also surrounded by an environment; and the groups, and the organisation as a whole, are surrounded by an environment external to the firm.

This is a rather elementary use of systems principles. Nevertheless, it illustrates the idea that if we wish to gain a fuller understanding of the behaviour of people in organisations, or the behaviour of an organisation as a whole, there is a need to integrate micro and macro approaches. To some extent, the behaviour of component sub-systems and sub-sub-systems is a result of being part of a bigger system; therefore, to comprehend behaviour of groups and individuals, account needs to be taken of the forces exerted on these systems by the organisation as a whole. Similarly, the behaviour of the organisation as a whole is dependent on the way individuals and groups behave and we can only understand the behaviour of the whole organisation if we take account of behaviour at the lower level.

Contingency Perspectives

Although the precursors of Organisational Behaviour and Analysis sought universal principles and often tried to identify the 'one best way' of addressing problems, this is only possible if there is absolute certainty about what influences a particular piece of behaviour. To some extent this is possible in the physical sciences because they deal with things rather than people. For example, we know that if we heat an iron bar it will expand and so, if we carefully measure its length before it is heated, then raise its temperature by a known amount, we can determine its expansion per degree celsius. From then on we can with certainty assume that if the temperature of the bar is raised by a given number of degrees we can predict its exact length. However, human beings are not like iron bars. They react differently to the same factor and what motivates one individual might not have the same effect on another. For this reason it can be very hard to predict behaviour. Therefore, almost all current work abandons any pretext of being able to derive universal rules that apply everywhere. It usually adopts a *contingency perspective*, which acknowledges that the solution to a problem has to fit the situation in which the problem exists. This, in turn, requires very careful examination of the situation to see what factors are at work, and an equally careful selection of a solution that addresses these factors.

Contingency perspective: an approach to problem solving which assumes that there is no universally applicable solution to a particular type of problem and so remedies have to be tailored to the situation in which the problem exists

Research Orientated and Unprescriptive

Concepts and theories in Organisational Behaviour and Analysis invariably arise out of extensive research. Although this does not mean that students of the subjects need to be experienced researchers, to grasp the strengths and weaknesses of a theory it is sometimes necessary to have an elementary knowledge of the research process. For those who wish to look a little deeper into this matter, the associated website to the book gives a very brief outline of the nature and methods of organisational research, and for the present it is sufficient to note that there are two important features of the theories that result.

First, as theories, they are much more descriptive than predictive. The function of a theory in social science is usually to specify whether there is a relationship between two or more variables and, if possible, to explain the nature of this relationship. However, this does not mean that we can predict with any degree of certainty what change will take place in one variable if there is a change in another. The subject is rich in results that tell us a great deal about the complex nature of behaviour in organisations and also alerts us to the idea that, if one variable should change, changes can be expected in others. In some cases it also provides highly plausible explanations of why these changes occur, but the explanations are seldom strong enough to enable us to predict behaviour with certainty.

Second, although the subject provides information that gives us a better understanding of human behaviour in organisations, in British OB and OA no attempt is made to say what that behaviour should be. This is often a source of acute frustration to students of the subject, particularly if they are managers who feel that they should be able to obtain precise remedies for problems. However, reluctance to be prescriptive does not mean that scholars in the area are evasive, or that they have no opinions. Social scientists are only too painfully aware that when someone asks for prescriptive advice it is because he or she has a reason. All too often this reason is connected with the person's desire to manipulate the behaviour of others to his or her own advantage. Quite simply, British social scientists do not see their purpose in life as serving a particular constituency of interests in this way, and they can be highly critical of those of their number who do. In addition, it is part of a social scientist's training to recognise that he or she has values and to be on guard, lest they influence the way that a social situation is perceived. A natural extension of this is to avoid making prescriptions, because these are almost bound to reflect what the prescriber thinks is right, rather than give an unbiased picture.

Cross-national Perspectives

Organisational Behaviour and Analysis both orginated in the USA and, while considerable contributions have been made by scholars from European nations and elsewhere, overall there has traditionally been a strong bias towards the Anglo-American conceptualisation of organisations and their employees. In recent years, however, perhaps because of the growing prominence of internationalised organisations, there has been a growing awareness that the body of knowledge based on American and British studies should not be regarded as the last word on matters. That is, whatever the body of knowledge tells us about human behaviour in organisations, it might be necessary to accept that matters could be different in other countries. Therefore, wherever possible, there is an increasing tendency to try to incorporate an element of comparative work into topics that are studied, and a cross-cultural perspective is fast becoming an important dimension of the subject in its own right. However, much of this work is still in its infancy and a great deal remains to be uncovered. To a large extent this is because it is much more difficult to undertake comparative work than to study matters in a single country. To start with, the costs incurred in replicating a study of the same phenomenon in several different countries can be significant. In addition, unless the work can be undertaken as a collaborative venture, for example by several universities around the world, the sheer volume of work for a single research team is prohibitive.

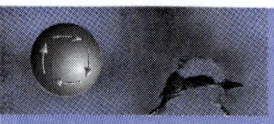

REPLAY

- Contemporary Organisational Behaviour and Analysis reflect a trend towards integrating the two subjects, which is based upon the premise that micro and macro levels are so strongly interconnected that events and behaviour at one level cannot be understood without taking account of matters at the other level.
- Organisational Behaviour and Analysis both use concepts and theories from social science; they usually take an interdisciplinary perspective, have strong practical implications, use open systems perspectives, adopt a contingency (rather than 'one best way') approach and are research orientated and unprescriptive.

DIFFERENT PERSPECTIVES ON ORGANISATIONS

The definition of an organisation given at the start of this chapter is a very general one that purposely avoids singling out anything as the most important characteristic of an organisation. This is only one way of viewing matters and it is often the case that the perspective used to view a particular organisational phenomenon depends on what the person investigating the phenomenon considers to be the most appropriate way to view an organisation. For this reason it is important to make the reader aware that there is no single right way of conceptualising an organisation. Rather, the conceptualisation used tends to depend on what are considered to be the most important characteristics of an organisation, or the reasons for examining a particular phenomenon.

Morgan (1989) draws attention to the idea that there are a number of competing metaphors for organisations. A *metaphor* is a figure of speech in which a term is transferred from the object it ordinarily designates to another object it can designate by an implicit analogy. For example, to refer to the world of business as a jungle implies that it operates on the basis of Kipling's first law of the jungle: 'kill or be killed'. Because metaphors provide a distinct way of perceiving an object and make us aware that some features are considered more important than others, they can be very useful devices. However, because each metaphor provides a different and sometimes competing insight or perspective, none of them is inherently right or wrong. Each one is only a partial view that draws attention to those features of organisations that the user of the metaphor considers to be the most important or interesting. Nevertheless, they can be useful and the four metaphors described by Morgan (he calls them different images of organisations) are: the machine metaphor; the organism metaphor; the (political) systems metaphor and the cultures metaphor. Each of these is now discussed separately.

Metaphor: a figure of speech in which a term is transferred from an object it ordinarily designates to another object it can designate by implicit analogy

The Machine Metaphor

Machines are constructed to do something specific, for example, a kettle turns cold water into hot water. Thus the *machine metaphor* focuses on the purpose and goals of an organisation and how these are achieved by combining its component parts. This view draws attention to such matters as:

- **Purpose or goals**: what is to be achieved.
- **Organisational design**: how the overall task is split down into a set of structured sub-tasks and how these are coordinated.
- **Methods, rules and procedures**: what is done, what behaviour is permitted and what is prohibited.
- **Effectiveness and efficiency**: whether goals are achieved and whether this is done in a way that is economic in the use of resources.

If it is inappropriate for the job, or when a part malfunctions, a machine can fail to serve its purpose. Thus the metaphor is useful if the main reason for studying an organisation is to define what it does and how well it does it. Nevertheless, this view has its shortcomings. Everything is evaluated in terms of technical efficiency and only the functional aspects of organisations are considered. Indeed, people tend to be viewed as merely components of the total machine, which contains two implicit assumptions: that people have a common purpose; and that they should all behave in a predictable way. Since both of these are highly questionable, the metaphor tends to ignore the complexity and diversity of motives that underlie human behaviour.

The Organism Metaphor

Organisms are living entities and so the *organism metaphor* is based on a biological analogy. It also makes use of a concept which in one form or another has come to dominate most current views of organisations – the organisation as a system, which draws attention to:

- **Interaction with environment**: that an organisation exists in, interacts with and is affected by its environment.
- **Sub-systems**: organisations are systems made up of sub-systems.
- **Interconnectedness**: the way that all parts of an organisation are connected, either directly or indirectly.
- **Human element**: implicit recognition that humans are an important organisational component.

The word system is familiar to everyone and most of us use it almost every day. However, it also refers to a whole way of thinking about the world, which originated in biology. Together with Physics, Biology shares the distinction of being highly *reductionist*, because it advances knowledge by studying progressively smaller components of an organism to examine how they work. For example, by progressing from organs down to cells and, these days, down to the fundamental building blocks such as DNA and RNA. This is an extremely powerful approach, but in the 1930s a rather different way of thinking began to emerge in Biology. This was the *holistic* perspective which, expressed in the simplest way, pointed out that cells do not exist in isolation but as parts of organisms. Thus, to understand how cells work in an organism

---

Machine metaphor: organisations regarded as analogous to a machine that is designed for a purpose

Organism metaphor: organisations regarded as analogous to biological organisms

Reductionist: the belief that complex systems can be understood completely by understanding their constituent parts

Holistic: the belief that reality is made up of unified wholes that are greater than the simple sum of their parts

or, indeed, how the organism itself affects the functioning of cells, it is necessary to think in wholes.

Providing certain criteria are met, almost anything can be regarded as a system. For example, we can think of the human body as a total system composed of many sub-systems, all of which interact together: the digestive system, the respiratory system, the nervous system, to name just three. Many people would assert that 'all' systems are open systems, which interact with their environments by taking in inputs and transforming them into outputs. For instance, the human body takes in food and transforms this into usable energy to maintain the body and also exports waste products. Deciduous trees take in nutrients from the ground and their leaves convert sunlight into energy; they also shed their leaves in the autumn and shut down for the winter. The fallen leaves decay, which provides food for a host of smaller organisms that convert the leaves into nutrients so that they can be reingested by the plant. A parallel can be drawn with organisations. Just as a tree absorbs water, nutrients and the sun's energy, organisations take in inputs and use them to survive; and just as a tree sheds its leaves in autumn to protect itself against the harsh winter, an organisation must be managed and controlled to enable it to respond to its environment in an appropriate way. An example of the use of this conceptualisation is given earlier in the chapter where it was used to explain the case for integration of micro and macro level perspectives on organisations.

Since the organism metaphor accepts that all the parts of an organisation are interconnected and have to function in a way that contributes to the whole, it recognises the importance of the human element. However, it still tends to assume that all the component parts of an organisation have a unified, common purpose and, so far as the human element is concerned, this is an oversimplification.

The (Political) Systems Metaphor

Political systems metaphor: organisations regarded as analogous to a political system composed of diverse groups, all of which have their own objectives

The *political systems metaphor* marks a fundamental break with an assumption held by those described above, and draws attention to:

- **Sub-system aims and objectives**: recognition that different parts of an organisation can have their own aims and objectives that they seek to fulfil, rather than all of them subscribing to a single set of organisational goals.
- **Potential for conflict**: the possibility of competition or conflict between sub-systems is acknowledged.

The machine and organisms metaphors both assume that an organisation has a common purpose or goal, whereas this perspective draws attention to the idea that organisations consist of diverse groups that pursue their own aims, some of which are common to all groups, but others can be unique to a particular group. This means that there is always some potential for conflict. However, it does not mean that the metaphor endorses the idea of conflict, merely that a hierarchy of authority and a structure that brings people together into departments and functions will result in groups that have different viewpoints and interests, some of which can give rise to a degree of competition or even conflict. The perspective also focuses on how conflicts are pursued.

The great strength of this metaphor is its recognition of the complex nature of human behaviour in organisations. Instead of assuming a common purpose for everybody, it regards this state of affairs as something that occurs for very special reasons. It also recognises that conflict is not always pursued in an open way, and so political behaviour is regarded as a natural part of organisational life, not just an aberration. Nevertheless, it has its limitations. It all too easily overplays the conflictual aspects of organisations and neglects the idea that if the circumstances are appropriate there is also potential for cooperation.

Organisations as Cultural Systems

Cultural systems metaphor: organisations regarded as analogous to cultural systems in which members have common beliefs, values and shared assumptions

The *cultural systems metaphor* also takes a systemic perspective, but this time the focus is on one of the less tangible features of an organisation: its culture. This metaphor draws attention to such features as:

- **Values and beliefs**: that organisational members usually share a number of values and beliefs that they use to make sense of the world.
- **Effects of culture on behaviour**: the ways in which deep-rooted and largely unstated patterns of belief and values have a pervasive influence on behaviour in an organisation.

In broad terms, a culture is a system of values and beliefs shared by a group of people, and their culture has a very pervasive effect on behaviour. For instance, it helps them to understand why they do certain things and establishes desired patterns of behaviour. Few of us would deny the existence of different national cultures and their influence on behaviour, and, in much the same way, different organisations can also have distinctive cultures. Indeed, in some ways, exploring the culture of a firm can involve viewing it as a society in miniature. However, to identify a culture and its effects it is usually necessary to delve well beneath the surface to try to uncover the social significance that procedures and practices have for organisational members.

In terms of explaining behaviour this can be a very penetrating perspective, but for those not used to this way of thought it has its problems. To start with, each of the three previous metaphors has its own logic or rationality, which is applied to explain organisational activities. For example, the machine analogy uses an engineering logic to decide whether sensible rules have been followed to design and maintain an effective and efficient organisation. The organism metaphor applies its own criteria of rationality to examine whether an organisation is able to adapt internally, to adjust to changing environmental conditions. Finally, the political systems metaphor seeks to explain behaviour by applying the logic of competition for scarce resources. Therefore, if we accept that any of these metaphors is a useful tool for its intended purpose, with practice we can see how each one can be used to explain how certain actions can lead to certain outcomes. However, the cultural metaphor has no overarching rationality, and it casts doubt on whether the word rational can be used to explain human behaviour. It holds that if a person behaves in a certain way because this is the normal way to behave in a certain context, he or she may not even be aware of behaving in that way. Thus, there are probably no universal criteria that can be used to evaluate whether the culturally induced patterns of behaviour are more appropriate in one organisation than another. Indeed, to analyse an organisation it is usually necessary to accept the culture as what it is, and simply try to identify how it affects behaviour.

A second problem stems from the use of the word 'organisational' in conjunction with the word 'culture'. This is sometimes used to imply that everybody in an organisation has the same set of cultural norms. However, different parts of an organisation usually have some differences in outlook, and it is these differences and their behavioural outcomes that give rise to the political systems metaphor. Thus, rather than view an organisation as a cultural system, it might make more sense to think of it as a system of sub-cultures. Finally, as will be seen in Chapter 20, which explores culture in greater depth, although the concept started out as a penetrating way of examining the nature of organisations, certain popular writings have trivialised and watered it down to the extent that in some ways it has become almost worthless.

In summary, each of the four metaphors has its distinctive uses, strengths and weaknesses, and for comparative purposes these are shown in Table 1.2.

Table 1.2 Comparison of organisational metaphors

Metaphor	Analogy	Main focus	Strengths	Weaknesses
Machine Metaphor	Organisation as a machine that is designed to serve a specific purpose	Technical efficiency or fitness for purpose	Strong focus on organisation as a whole and how efficiently it functions	Neglects the human element
Biological System	Organisation as an organism existing in, interacting with and influenced by its environment	Relationship with environment Interrelation of sub-systems in organisation and influence this has on the behaviour of the organisation as a whole	Acknowledges that organisations have a wide variety of component parts (including the human element) which have to play their respective parts if the whole organism is to function well	Tends to assume that all the component parts have a common purpose
Political System	Organisation as a system composed of diverse sub-systems, all of which have their own aims and objectives	Conflict and competition between sub-systems	Accepts that organisations contain different groups whose interests need to be reconciled. Thus conflict and competition are everyday features of organisational life	Some tendency to focus on conflict to the exclusion of all else, and underplay the idea that there are also cooperative features of organisations
Cultural System	Organisations as cultures	Beliefs, values and shared meanings of organisational members and how these result in identifiable patterns of behaviour	Goes well beneath the surface to try to uncover some of the less tangible features of organisations, and their effects on human behaviour	Has a tendency to regard culture as the most important factor, which underplays the impact of other factors external to the person

TIME OUT

Think about the organisation where you work. If you are not in employment, think about your own university or college as an organisation. Identify those aspects and features of the organisation (and the way that it functions) that you would focus on if you were to examine the institution by using:

the machine metaphor
the organism metaphor
the political systems metaphor
the cultural systems metaphor.

A More Recent Development: The Postmodernist Perspective

Postmodernist: either (i) a new era in which the fundamental nature of organisations will be different from hitherto, or (ii) a philosophical stance which questions current assumptions of the nature of reality

Epistemology: a branch of philosophy dealing with the nature and origins of knowledge

Over the last 15 years a more radical view of organisations has emerged: the so-called *postmodernist* perspective. However, the word is used in two very distinct ways. The first defines a new era in which there will be a radical change in the fundamental nature of organisations (Cooper and Burrell 1988). The second use of the word involves epistemological considerations. *Epistemology* is a branch of philosophy dealing with the nature and origins of know-ledge. Postmodernist thought goes to the very root of how an organisation and its activities are conceived, and this results in something much more radical than a new metaphor. Postmodernists are highly critical of conventional ways of conceiving organisations and they would probably reject all four of the metaphors described above as unreal and false. In essence, they argue that current thinking is based on a false notion of scientific rationality, which emphasises rigorous investigation and communication of results to expand the boundaries of knowledge. This is said to hinge on the practice of viewing the world as a set of static, discrete entities and trying to identify causal links between them. For example, phenomena such as individuals, organisations and structures are treated as things which can be separated from the rest of the world, and conventional thought tends to focus on such questions as 'is there a link between culture and structure?', or 'is culture caused by structure or vice versa?' Postmodernists point out that because nothing is static features such as culture and structure have no reality, but are merely temporary states that are treated as fixed and static. This ignores the most important matter of all: the social processes that result in the movement from one state to another. Some postmodernists, for example Bauman (1992), argue that this search for causality is a futile endeavour, based on the false assumption that reality exists and consists of certainty about entities, or what Whitehead (1985) calls the 'fallacy of misplaced concreteness'. Thus the key idea is that everything is in motion, and that what traditional thought views as an object or an entity is only a transitional state, which means that anything that seeks to establish the ultimate truth about entities is a search for the impossible.

Postmodernists argue that to pretend that there is a truth about anything is to deny the essential nature of the world. Their remedy is to regard everything as being in a state of motion, and to reject the idea that anything is real and tangible. So far as studying organisations is concerned, they believe we should shed the intellectual tyranny of thinking in terms of objects, and direct our attention to more important issues. Indeed, they argue that the very term 'organisation' is problematic, because it is not a real entity, simply a label we attach to a very fluid and mobile social configuration (Chia 1995).

These, of course, are very deep philosophical questions, but for anyone who aspires to do more than retreat into a cave and contemplate his or her own navel they are full of problems. For someone who is trying to grasp what makes an organisation tick, postmodernist thought results in more paradoxes than helpful insights. For instance, if nothing is concrete, people can only describe things to each other in terms of their own experience, but postmodernism also asserts that meaning is so personal that it cannot really be communicated. Taken together, these points lead to the inevitable conclusion that it is simply not worth conducting enquiries to try to understand organisations, because we cannot communicate our findings. Therefore, what is portrayed as the leading edge of analytical thought can all too easily start to look like the long discredited doctrine of *nihilism*: that nothing exists, is knowledgeable or can be communicated.

Nihilism: a now discredited doctrine that nothing really exists and thus there can be no knowledge of anything and hence knowledge cannot be communicated

Perhaps the greatest problem is the postmodernist conception of scholarship. Many self-proclaimed postmodernists reject the value of empirical work, favouring instead a seemingly endless stream of *post-hoc* criticism of the empirical work of others. This is a rather particular definition of scholarship, which is less concerned with explanation and verification than with vilifying the explanations produced by other people. Thus postmodernists probably spend more time convincing other postmodernists of the correctness and sanctity of postmodernism than they do in advancing the frontiers of knowledge (Brown 1990). Indeed, one observer has remarked that 'postmodernism' may well end up being nothing more than writers who write about other writers, and address what they write to even more writers: a rather dangerous approach that comes near to turning social science into literary criticism rather than empirical enquiry (Alvesson 1995).

REPLAY

- The machine metaphor likens an organisation to a machine that is designed to serve a specific purpose.
- The organism metaphor likens an organisation to a biological system that exists in conjunction with and must adapt to its environment.
- The political systems metaphor views an organisation as a system of sub-systems, all of which have their own aims and goals, which means that there is always some potential for conflict between sub-systems.
- The cultural systems metaphor views an organisation primarily as a system of values, beliefs and understandings that guide the behaviour of its members.
- The postmodernist perspective is not a metaphor but a philosophical standpoint that strongly questions current assumptions about the nature of organisations.

Although the above critique has some validity, postmodernist thought has matured considerably since the days when early theorists tended to avoid empirical enquiry. Indeed, these days the major focus in the area is in developing new ways of looking at organisations and in this respect postmodernism has made a significant contribution in giving new insights on phenomena that have long been of central concern to OB and OA. To a large extent this has come about through the application of certain concepts that are central to postmodernist analysis, first the concept of *discourse*, which is usually coupled with the allied technique of *deconstruction*.

The very idea of *discourse* alerts us to the idea that language is much more than a useful tool of communication; it can sometimes contain elements (what is said and how it is said) to portray what can be made to seem the essential truth of how things are. This has the effect of limiting the discussion along the lines that the speaker considers legitimate, and disarms any challenges that the listeners might advance to this way of thinking. This can also suppress alternative meanings, by supporting a particular interpretation or conclusions drawn from the discussion. For example, if I state that in the face of the globalisation, all organisations have to be prepared to change to survive. This looks like a statement of common sense wisdom, which on the face of it cannot be challenged.

However, the technique of *deconstruction* could then be applied to this statement to reveal its underlying assumptions about what at first sight appears to be common sense. For instance that:

- there is such a thing as the globalised economy
- it is all powerful and that organisations have to subordinate themselves to these powerful forces
- one of the effects of this is that the organisation must be constantly ready (and able) to change in the way that globalised markets dictate
- failure to do this would be to condemn the organisation to failure
- thus all members of the organisation should willingly embrace change.

The deconstruction can then be taken one stage further to reveal what my motives might be in portraying things in this way, which prompts a whole series of questions about my likely motives for giving this message.

These are very powerful tools of analysis that go well beyond simply trying to uncover the finer nuances of communication. They contain an implicit recognition that communication is almost always underpinned by an agenda, which reflects how the message sender wants her or his audience to interpret the world, so that the audience reacts in a predictable way. For those who might wish to explore the topic further, some suggestions are included in the list of further reading at the end of the chapter.

Discourse: the idea that language is more than just a useful tool of communication because what is said can convey what is seemingly the essential truth about how things are, which has the effect of challenges to an argument, suppressing alternative meanings and supporting particular interpretations or conclusions

Deconstruction: a method used in postmodernist analysis to reveal underlying assumptions in a discourse and challenge them with counter-arguments or alternative interpretations

CONCLUSIONS AND PREVIEW

Summary

From their early beginnings approximately 80 years ago Organisational Behaviour and Organisational Analysis have developed into subjects that contain a wealth of knowledge that seeks to explain the behaviour of humans in an organisational context, and the behaviour of organisations themselves. Although the two subjects have evolved separately, one dealing with micro-level aspects of organisations and the other with macro-level factors, there is now a wider recognition that a more complete understanding of the behaviour of people in organisations, or indeed, the organisation itself is more likely to be obtainable by integrating the two approaches.

The Approach of this Book

There are several ways that could be used to write a text that seeks to explain the behaviour of people in organisations. For instance, it could be written from the perspective of any one of the social science disciplines shown earlier in Table 1.1. Alternatively, it could seek to explain matters by using one of the metaphors contrasted in Table 1.2, or even from a postmodernist perspective. However, since it only draws on these disciplinary and metaphoric approaches where it is felt that it will be helpful for the reader's understanding, perhaps the most appropriate way to describe the general approach is to start by explaining what it is not.

Unlike many books these days, it is not written with the aim of serving the interests of any particular constituency or group in an organisation, either employees or managers. Thus it is most definitely not a textbook on management, nor is it a managerial tool-kit that is designed to give managers the upper hand in bringing employee behaviour under their control. Nevertheless, managers are far from being excluded from the audience at which the book is addressed, if only because as Pfeffer and Sutton (2005) point out, a great deal of management practice is based on very dangerous half-truths promoted by so-called management gurus, and this sometimes results in a host of unintended consequences in organisations. For this reason, although it is hoped that the book will be read by managers, they are not regarded as the primary audience at which it is directed. Rather, there are two reasons why reading the book could have some utility to managers: first, to keep themselves informed, and, second, to encourage them to look critically at some of the ideas they espouse, particularly those that fly in the face of other evidence about factors that affect human behaviour in organisations.

To the extent that it is possible for an individual author to be completely free from his own values and prejudices, the book purposely takes a neutral stance in examining a wide range of factors that impact on humans in an organisational context. These include individual characteristics and processes, because people normally work in settings that are as much social as operational. The book also seeks to be comprehensive by covering topics that are important at all levels, up to that of the whole organisation. For the most part it adopts a critical perspective by seeking to uncover what a particular theory or concept can usefully tell us about human behaviour and, where necessary, to highlight instances where it could have a lack of practical utility. As such, the main aim is describe and explain particular concepts and theories, and at the same time encourage a similarly critical perspective in the reader.

To do this, the book draws extensively on theories and concepts from the social sciences; that is, individual psychology, social psychology, sociology, and more rarely from social anthropology, politics and economics. Some of the theories and concepts that will be explored date from the early, formative stages of development of OB and OA, which involves describing strands of work that are, by now, quite elderly. However, since the book has been written to make it accessible to readers with no prior exposure to the subject, there is no escape from this, because sometimes an understanding of current approaches can crucially depend on understanding the weaknesses in prior work.

Finally, and in keeping with what is said earlier in this chapter, it is considered vital that the reader should never lose sight of the idea that the various chapters in the book are not discrete parcels of knowledge that are divorced from each other. Rather, they are but part of a whole, more complex story and this is particularly true of the need integrate knowledge from Organisational Behaviour and Organisational Analysis.

FURTHER READING

Appignanesi, R and C Garratt (1995) *Postmodernism for Beginners*, Cambridge: Icon Books. An informative, but difficult-to-read book that contains a useful commentary on the use of language to describe what is apparent reality.

Bauman, Z (1992) *Intimations of Postmodernism*, London: Routledge. Not an easy book to read, but an essential text for those wishing to explore postmodernist thought.

Carey, A (1967) The Hawthorne studies: a radical criticism, *American Sociological Review* 32(2): 403–416. As the title suggests, a critique of the findings and conclusions that were drawn from the Hawthorne studies.

Hatch, MJ (1997) *Organisation Theory, Symbolic and Postmodern Perspectives*, Oxford: Oxford University Press. An interesting and clear guide to organisation theory that explores and contrasts three perspectives on organisations: modernist, social constructivist and postmodern.

Hinings, CR and R Greenwood (2002) Disconnects and consequences in organisation theory, *Administrative Science Quarterly* 47(3): 411–421. A review article that traces the origins of organisation theory and how it has been coopted by American business schools in a way that serves managerial ends.

Kvale, S (ed.) (1992) *Psychology and Postmodernism*, London: Sage. A book of readings that explores the implications of postmodernist thought for psychology.

Mayo, E (1933) *The Human Problems of Industrial Civilization*, New York: Macmillan. A work by one of the founding fathers of Organisational Behaviour, which contains ideas that by now read as highly patronising and full of elitism.

Morgan, G (1997) *Images of Organisation*, London: Sage. A very readable book that develops and fully explains the different metaphors for organisations.

O'Connor, ES (1999) The politics of management thought: a case study of the Harvard Business School and the Human Relations School, *Academy of Management Review* 24(1): 117–131. Gives a useful insight describing how early developments in Human Relations theory were hijacked by the Harvard Business School, to serve managerialist ends.

Storey, J, G Salaman and K Platman (2005) Living with enterprise in an enterprise economy: freelance and contract workers in the media, *Human Relations* 58(8): 1033–1054. An interesting paper that illustrates how discourse analysis (a postmodern approach) can be applied in a research study to illustrate how freelance and short-term contract workers can be induced to accept their changed working conditions as normality.

Whitehead, AN (1985) *Science and the Modern World*, London: Free Association Books. An essential, but rather technical, text for those wishing to explore postmodernist thought.

REVIEW AND DISCUSSION QUESTIONS

1. Explain what you take the word 'organisation' to mean and compare your answer with the five key features (given at the beginning of the chapter) which qualify an entity as an organisation.

2. Explain the case for integrating knowledge from OB and OA. To what extent do you feel that failing to integrate knowledge from both areas can result in an incomplete or inaccurate explanation of behaviour in and by organisations?

3. Debate the following statement and state whether, in your collective view, the assertion is a valid one.

> Social science seldom, if ever, produces definitive, irrefutable laws that enable behaviour to be predicted with certainty. Therefore, it is highly questionable whether Organisational Behaviour and Analysis can add much to our understanding of organisations, and even more questionable whether they can provide information that is useful in making organisations more effective.

4. Compare and contrast the main foci and strengths and weaknesses of the following organisational metaphors: the machine metaphor; the organism metaphor; the political systems metaphor; and the cultural systems metaphor. Compare the use of these metaphors with the 'postmodernist' approach to organisations. What do you feel is the practical utility of the postmodernist approach?

TOPIC 2
HOW TO UNDERSTAND ORGANISATIONAL CULTURE

Chapter 2

Organisational Cultures and Climates

LEARNING OUTCOMES

After studying this chapter you should be able to:

- define and understand the nature of organisational culture, its historical roots, how it is maintained and replicated, and how it affects the behaviour of organisational members

- describe a traditional (Peters and Waterman) perspective on organisational culture and contrast this with the more recent (Goffe and Jones) contingency framework

- describe the methodology and techniques that can be deployed in culture change initiatives

- define the nature of organisational climate, describe its antecedents and consequences and its affect on the behaviour of organisational members

- compare and contrast the concepts of organisational culture and organisational climate

INTRODUCTION

Although the visible characteristics of an organisation can reveal much about how it operates, this tells us little of how people experience organisational life. Nevertheless, if we ask them what it is like to work for a particular firm, they often reply in terms of their feelings or emotions; for example by saying that it is very dynamic, or perhaps that it is chaotic. These people would be telling us is something about their perceptions of the atmosphere in the firm, which is one of the less tangible facets of organisational life and is encompassed by the two concepts covered in this chapter: culture and climate.

The first to be considered is culture, a topic that came to the fore in the early 1980s, largely as a result of the appearance of a number of books and articles linking organisational culture with commercial success. Since culture is rather intangible and difficult to define, the discussion commences with a definition, which is followed by an exploration of its nature and the assumed link with commercial success. This is followed by an outline of some of the more influential theories and perspectives on culture and, since these mostly imply that some cultures are more beneficial than others, the topics of culture management and cultural change are examined. To round off the discussion, a brief consideration of the effects of national cultures on organisations is given.

The second topic of the chapter is that of organisational climate. This is a more mature and well-developed concept, which deals with dynamic and changeable organisational features. Climate is defined and distinguished from culture and is then explored in greater depth by examining the nature, origins and outcomes of organisational climates. The chapter concludes by comparing and contrasting the concepts of culture and climate, together with an examination of the organisational implications of both.

ORGANISATIONAL CULTURE

The word culture has been used by many different people to explain a variety of phenomena, and because each one tends to adopt a slightly different perspective, there is no universally accepted definition. As such, the most appropriate way forward is to define how the word will be used in this chapter, which is:

> a pattern of basic assumptions – invented, discovered or developed by a given group as it learns to cope with its problems of external adaption and internal integration – that has worked well enough to be considered valuable and, therefore, to be taught to new members as the correct way to perceive, think and feel in relation to those problems.
> (Schein 1992, p 9)

Culture has been, and still is studied by several different disciplines, all of which have their own distinct approach. The main disciplines include **anthropology**, which can be defined as the study of human cultures and how they influence the structure and functioning of a society. **Sociology** adopts a somewhat different perspective, linking particular sets of values and beliefs to patterns of social action. **Social psychology** explains the internal dynamics of a social situation, focusing especially on how culture produces observable patterns of behaviour and the ways in which people communicate their expectations to each other. For example, the work of Martin and Power (1983) shows that stories and anecdotes are powerful vehicles for communicating the cultural values of an organisation.

THE NATURE OF ORGANISATIONAL CULTURE

The details of an organisation's culture are carried in people's minds, and even though they may not be aware of doing so, they use this information to interpret what surrounds them, and to react to it. If these meanings are shared by all or most of the people in an organisation, it can be said to have a culture, but the details from which the meanings are constructed can exist at different levels of visibility – some are directly observable while others are near invisible. In this respect Schein (1990) conceptualises culture as a 'layered' phenomenon which has three interrelated levels of meaning: *basic assumptions*; *values and beliefs*; and *artifacts and creations*, which is shown diagrammatically in Figure 2.1.

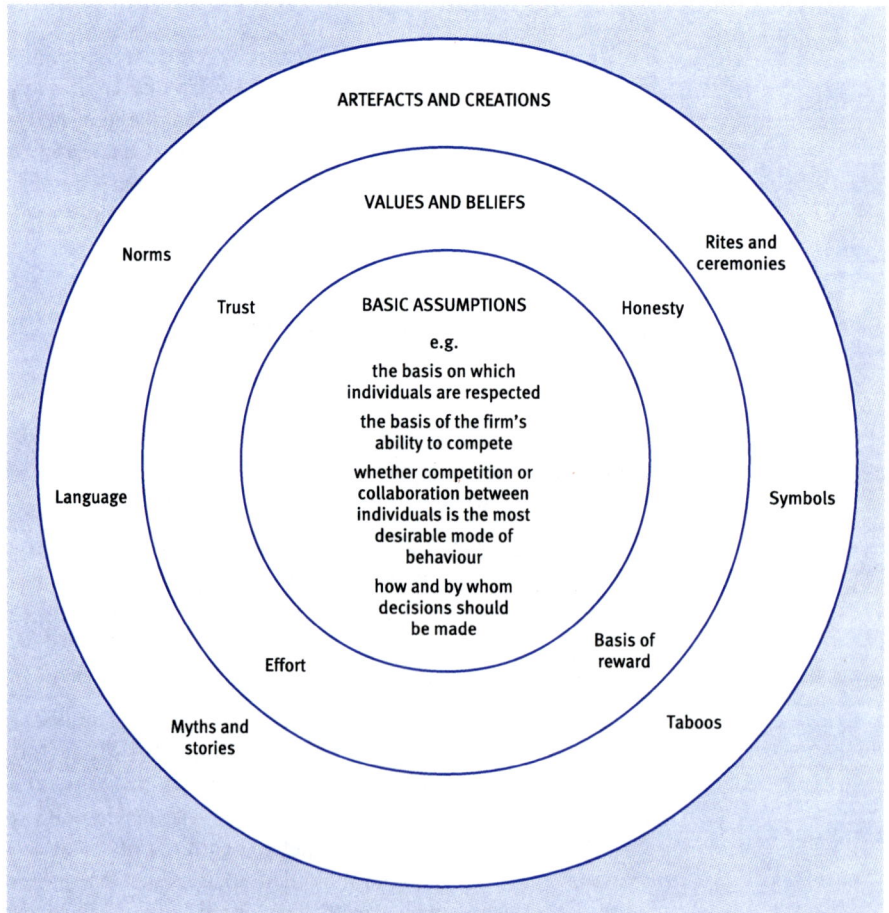

Figure 2.1
Schein's layered conceptualisation of culture

Basic Assumptions

These lie in the innermost core of a culture. In Schein's view they are fundamental and so taken for granted that most people in a cultural unit subscribe to them but not in a conscious way. However, if we dig deep enough, it is not difficult to identify these basic assumptions. For instance, they are quite different in the major political parties in Great Britain. The Labour Party has an assumption that society is or should be a collective body, in which individuals should display a high degree of social responsibility towards each other. Conversely, Conservatives believe that the individual is paramount and their prime responsibility is their own welfare, an idea succinctly expressed in Margaret Thatcher's famous (or infamous, according to one's views) statement 'there is no such thing as society – only individuals'. Business organisations also tend to differ in the basic assumptions contained in their cultures: for example, about whether people deserve respect because of the positions they hold, or because of their skills and abilities; what lies at the root of the firm's ability to compete; or whether competition between individuals is a good thing or should be suppressed.

Values and Beliefs

Values and beliefs exist at the next level of visibility. They consist of consciously held reasons or justifications for people behaving as they do (Sathe 1985) and, are moral or ethical codes that guide behaviour by putting the assumptions into practice. To use the example of British political parties again, values can be seen in their policy guidelines for programmes of legislation. Since Conservatives have a basic assumption about the primacy of the individual, they often express values that dictate how this should be reflected in legislation, for example cutting taxes and encouraging individuals to use the money to make provision for their own health insurance and retirement. Conversely, the Labour Party's basic assumption about collective responsibility strongly advocates the funding of state schemes of social security. Once again there are parallel ways in which values serve as guidelines for action in organisations, such as whether the customers' interests should come first, and whether conflict should be suppressed or is best brought out into the open where it can be handled and resolved.

Artifacts and Creations

These are the most visible manifestations of a culture. They include everything from the physical layout of a building to the way people dress, the way they talk to each other and, often, the things they talk about. Although some of these features are very subtle and it can be dangerous to view them in isolation, they often give vital clues about the underlying values and beliefs (an example of one that is potentially important is given in the OB in Action Box on the next page). It is therefore useful to distinguish between some of these different signs.

Norms

Norms are a code of behaviour brought into being by the underlying assumptions and values, and are perpetuated when people observe the norms. If people only reach high positions by working a 60-hour week, this sets up an expectation that these hours are

OB IN ACTION: The coffee break – an important cultural ritual

Product obsolescence is a familiar phenomenon in workplaces all over the world and 'filter' coffee making machines are rapidy being phased-out and replaced by individualised 'pod' coffee makers. However, as has been pointed out by a number of commentators, the communal coffee-maker encourages people to drink coffee together; it. is a place to have a quick chat with colleagues, catch up on news and gossip, and generally oil the wheels of the organisation. However, current trends force more and more people to make the solitary walk to a machine that does nothing more than provide them with just one cup of coffee and gone is the idea of the [coffee] pot designed for a group; and gone with it are many of the corresponding opportunities for social interaction. As a result, American workers are increasingly rejecting the in-house option altogether.

But why should managers be bothered by any of this? Who cares where staff get their coffee, so long as it helps keep them awake and they are back at their desks working again before too long? Simply because it has to do with workplace culture.

Who your people drink coffee with, and where, is important. You may not think you need to promote the rise of 'café society' internally, but a coffee culture could be beneficial – for collaboration, networking, and cross-fertilisation. As such, the coffee break and its attendant social interaction could be one of the most important rituals or artifacts that exists in many firms.

Source:

Stern, S (2007) Wake up and smell the coffee on your corporate culture, *Financial Times*, 26 March

a criterion for promotion, which permeates downwards and becomes accepted as the normal behaviour for ambitious people.

Language

The language people use can be a valuable indication of culture. For example, how managers talk to subordinates and vice versa can reveal much about the status values at work, and the use of jargon and current 'buzzwords' are often used to signal who is accepted and who is not.

Symbols

Status symbols communicate social position and pecking order in the hierarchy, and their grandness gives a good indication about how much importance is attached to hierarchy as an organising principle.

Rites and Ceremonies

Formal and informal ceremonies abound in most organisations, and these often have important meanings for those involved. Retirement or farewell parties can be used to signal the idea of a happy family or a caring organisation. The ritual of taking a newcomer around and introducing the person to new colleagues is often a way of speeding up the integration process.

Myths and Stories

These are often a way of communicating core values and assumptions to people. Anecdotes are useful for this purpose because they often have an element of drama and are interesting to hear. Myths are stories that are partly fictional and are of questionable accuracy (Ott 1989), but nevertheless convey a central message in a more dramatic form and increase its salience.

Taboos

These signal what should not be done and an example is the story about the junior employee who addressed a director by his first name. This can be used to provide a humorous illustration for a newcomer that respect for someone higher up is a fundamental part of the culture.

Although it has been convenient to describe all these signs separately, it is important to recognise that they complement each other and are often used in combination as reminders of what the culture is and what is expected. For instance, basic assumptions are often expressed in values and, in turn, artifacts, creations and visible behaviour are practical ways of expressing the values.

TIME OUT

Carefully reflect on the organisation in which you work, either full-time or part-time. If you have no experience of being an employee use another organisation of which you are, or have been, a member. Using Schein's layered concept of culture, and starting with the most visible level, try to answer the questions below.

1. What artifacts and creations are there? For example, are there any identifiable norms of behaviour, particular language mannerisms that are encouraged, symbols, rites and ceremonies, myths, stories or taboos?
2. What basic values are indicated by the things you identified in question 1?
3. What are the basic assumptions underpinning the values you identified in question 2?

CHARACTERISTICS OF CULTURES

Pervasiveness or Homogeneity

In some respects the very expression organisational culture is misleading. It conveys the impression that everyone in a particular firm perceives things in the same way. For

> **Integrationist perspective on culture:** culture is an organisation-wide phenomenon which consists of shared values to which all or most employees subscribe
>
> **Fragmentationist perspective on culture:** organisations are so full of ambiguities and inconsistencies that frames of reference are individual and constantly changing so culture is inherently unstable
>
> **Differentiationist perspective on culture:** organisations are made up of different groups with their own sub-cultures

this reason Martin (1992) distinguishes between three distinct perspectives. The *integrationist perspective* (which is the way matters have been discussed so far) views culture as an organisation-wide phenomenon. This is the view that probably appeals most to managers, because it holds out the prospect of using culture as a control mechanism to deliver superior organisational performance. At the other extreme, Martin identifies what she calls the *fragmentationist perspective*, in which organisations are so full of ambiguities and inconsistencies that they cannot be said to have a single culture. Rather, people respond in an *ad hoc* way to constantly changing conditions. Martin also identifies a middle-ground position, which she calls the *differentiationist perspective*. This acknowledges the possibility that within an organisation's overall culture there are variations in which different groups of people have slightly different cultures.

An interesting insight on Martin's ideas is given by Harris and Ogbonna (1998), who show that all three perspectives commonly exist side by side in different parts of the same organisation. Perhaps because they like to view the organisation as one big family, top managers tend to adopt an integrationist view, whereas middle managers, who are more sharply focused on their own functional roles or specialisms, have differentiationist perspectives. At the very bottom of an organisation, where people often have to keep their heads down and focus on their immediate tasks with no sight of a bigger picture, shopfloor workers are prone to take a fragmentationist view.

The evidence for the existence of sub-cultures in anything other than very small firms is overwhelming, and the larger the firm the more likely it is that distinct sub-cultures will emerge. For example, in a study of a large Danish insurance company, Hofstede (1998) identified three highly distinctive sub-cultures (production, administrative and professional) that embraced virtually everyone in the organisation. In the light of this and other evidence, the currently prevailing view is that the differentiation-ist perspective offers the most realistic view of culture in organisations. Moreover, it can be argued that the advantages accruing from having different subcultures outweigh any disadvantages. Sub-cultures give different perspectives, which makes the 'groupthink' phenomenon less likely. In addition, since sub-cultures are associated with the professional expertise and specialist perspectives of different groups, the resulting differences are of great organisational value. For instance, in a marketing department that deals with a very uncertain environment, a dynamic, thrusting sub-culture of risk-taking can be just what is needed. However, to ensure that matters do not get out of hand, it is probably desirable to counterbalance this with the cautious, risk-averting sub-culture that is often found among accountants. After all, this is why specialists are employed – do we really expect accountants to have the same values as marketeers?

Strength of Culture

A recurring theme in popular texts is that strong cultures are associated with superior organisational performance (Deal and Kennedy 1982; Peters and Waterman 1982). Luthans (1995) argues that cultural strength is a function of two factors:

- **Sharedness**, which corresponds to what has been described above as homogeneity and expresses the extent to which all organisational members have the same core values.
- **Intensity**, which corresponds to the degree of commitment of all the people in the organisation to these values.

Taken together these imply that the strength of a culture needs to be assessed in a multidimensional way, which is probably a very sound point. However, Luthans' ideas about the factors that influence these dimensions are open to severe criticism. He states that both are a function of the way that an organisation rewards its members. This implies that culture is totally under management's control and is easily manipulated by the judicious use of rewards and punishments, which grossly overestimates the extent to which deeply held values and beliefs can be controlled by external stimuli. Moreover, Luthans somewhat uncritically accepts that a high degree of sharedness is desirable and, as was pointed out earlier, there are inherent dangers in having an organisational culture that is too homogeneous. The most controversial point, however, is the way that he accepts that a strong culture leads to organisational success. This point will be addressed in detail later, but for the present two brief points can be made. First, a strong culture may only be a predictor of good performance in the short run and, second, it is only safe to assume that a strong culture is an aid to success if it is also an appropriate one, that is, one that is suitable for coping with the conditions faced by an organisation.

Cultural Evolution and Replication

Although it is important to be able to describe an organisation's culture, two questions of equal significance are: how did the culture come to exist?; and what forces are at work to enable it to persist in this state? Both of these will be considered separately.

Cultural Evolution

Schein (1983) argues that the history of an organisation inevitably has a huge impact on its culture and that some cultural elements can be traced back to the values and ideologies of a firm's founder. Those who bring organisations into existence often have a strong entrepreneurial disposition. They can be highly dynamic people who communicate their vision to others and, in the early days of a firm, they tend to attract and recruit a core of like-minded people. What emerges is a key group that has shared assumptions and values and as the firm grows, these people become role models for new entrants.

Cultural patterns such as these can last a long time and may well persist for generations. For instance, certain British firms founded in the nineteenth century were set up by prominent Quaker industrialists who, because of their religious convictions, felt a sense of obligation and duty to their employees and attempted to mitigate many of the harsh industrial conditions of the day by devoting considerable financial resources and effort into improving the lot of the workforce. In these organisations welfare schemes, medical attention and, in one famous case, the building of a whole village that took employees out of the slum conditions of the industrial revolution were put in place and, to some extent, this tradition of welfare paternalism carries on today.

An imprint of the founder is still often encountered in firms, but what remains, however, is seldom identical to the culture that existed in the early years. As firms grow they face new challenges and cope with these by adopting new structural forms and methods (Beekun and Glick 2001). Clearly this is likely to be a slow and continuous process, which is concerned with two generic problems: that of **ensuring survival and external adaptation**; and that of **ensuring internal integration**. These in turn give rise to more specific problems and what emerges from this ongoing process is that the core

Table 2.1 External and internal problems which, when resolved, partially determine organisational culture (adapted from Schein 1983)

Problem orientation	Potential problem
External problems to be resolved: those concerning adaption and survival	1. Developing consensus on the primary task, core mission and latent functions of the group, i.e. strategy 2. Consensus on goals, with goals being a reflection of core mission 3. Developing consensus on the means to be used to achieve goals, e.g. division of labour, organisation structure, reward systems, etc. 4. Developing consensus on the criteria to measure how well the group is performing against its goals and targets, e.g. information and control systems 5. Developing consensus on remedial strategies that may be needed when the group is not achieving its goals
Internal problems to be resolved: those concerning internal integration	6. Common language and conceptual categories need to be derived so that group members can communicate with each other, without which group functioning is impossible 7. Consensus on group boundaries and criteria for inclusion and exclusion needed in order that one of the most important areas of culture (consensus on who is or is not part of the group and what criteria determine membership) are clear 8. Consensus on criteria for the allocation of power and status are needed so that the organisation's pecking order, its rules for obtaining and retaining power, are understood in order that members can manage their own feelings of aggression 9. Consensus on criteria for intimacy, friendship and love so that rules for the way that peers relate to each other and relationships between the sexes are handled, and the degrees of openness and intimacy that will be used in working on organisational tasks are clearly understood 10. Consensus on criteria for the allocation of rewards and punishments so that people in the group know what behaviours are lauded and what are deprecated, what rewards are available, what behaviours are punished by withdrawing rewards, up to and including exclusion from the group 11. Consensus on ideology and religion because, like societies, groups must have ways of giving meaning to 'unexplainable' events so that people are able to respond to them without feeling anxious in the face of the 'unexplainable'

elements of culture (its basic assumptions and values) re-emerge in slightly modified form. Once adopted, these are held at a subconscious level and are so taken for granted that they are taught to new entrants to the organisation as the appropriate way to view things (see Table 2.1).

Cultural Replication

In the short run, cultures are maintained and replicated by the socialisation processes shown in Figure 2.2.

To a large extent, when new organisational members are selected, those who are allowed to enter are the ones who are perceived to fit in with what is already there. In cultural terms new entrants are seldom a perfect match and, almost immediately, another set of processes come into play, which are concerned with inducing these people to adopt the required feelings and behaviour.

- As an immediate measure, those who are already members and have absorbed the organisation's culture pass on their knowledge so that newcomers 'learn the ropes'. Most newcomers view this in a positive way and inducting a new starter

Figure 2.2
Organisational socialisation

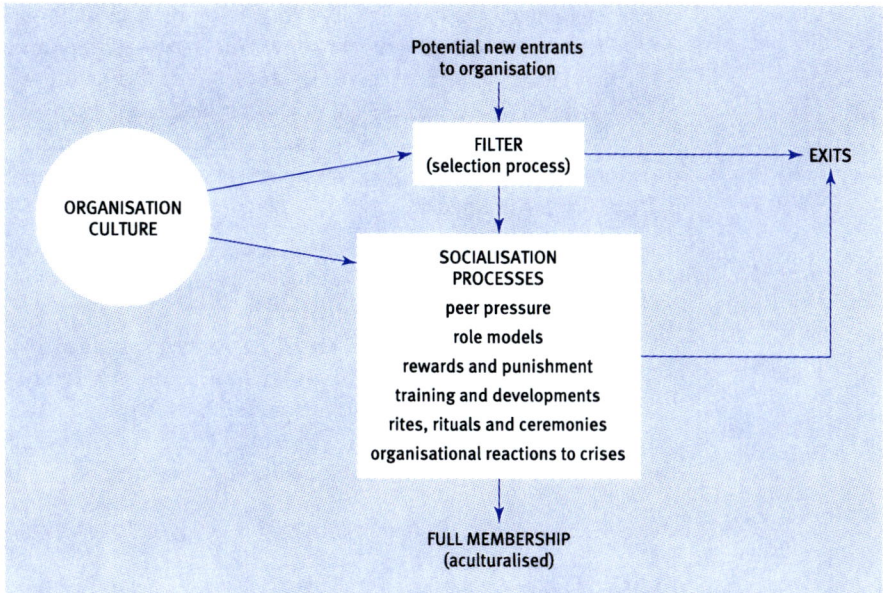

does a great deal to help the person settle in and come to know what is expected (Reichers 1987).

- Most new entrants are also likely to experience a certain amount of **peer pressure**. This can take the form of enquiries about how things were done at the previous place of employment which, if necessary, is followed-up with pointed comments about how the new situation differs.

- Where cultures are very strong and existing members know that the newcomer will find things very different, a new recruit can purposely be put through mildly humiliating experiences. For instance, the person might be given particularly onerous jobs to do, which tends to have the effect of making people question their own prior assumptions, and makes them more open to accepting new norms and values (Pascale 1985).

- It is also common for a new entrant to pick up **role models** early on. For example, newcomers tend to be placed under the wing of a senior, trusted person and it is natural for the newcomer to see this person as someone who fits in well.

- As the newcomer becomes more familiar with the surroundings, he or she also picks up clues about the **criteria for rewards and punishments**. Rewards provide clear indications of the criteria that are used to evaluate performance and, by absorbing this knowledge, the routes to promotion, higher status and prestige can be learned. Conversely, punishment is an indication of behaviour that is viewed as deviating from what is acceptable.

- Newcomers may well be put through **training and development experiences** which, on the face of it, are only designed to teach skills. However, some of these processes also act as a powerful means of transmitting culture. For instance, many organisations use a formal induction course that often contains a strong element of company history, and messages about core values and beliefs.

- The longer a person remains with an organisation the more he or she is likely to witness and come to play an active role in **rites, rituals and ceremonies**. Rites are planned activities that have the power to transmit cultural norms (Beyer and Trice 1987). For example, congratulation gatherings on the promotion of a colleague tell the newcomer what is valued in the culture. Social gatherings emphasise integration and an invitation to attend is often a sign that someone has been accepted.
- **Critical incidents and crises** also signal what culture expects, for instance an 'all hands to the pumps' set of values and behaviours.

Notwithstanding the above, there is always the possibility that someone cannot adapt to the new culture and either exits voluntarily, or is asked to leave. It is also important to recognise that when someone does absorb the culture it does not mean that he or she becomes some sort of a clone. In most organisations there is a degree of tolerance to individuality, so long as core values and beliefs are not violated.

TIME OUT

In an earlier Time Out exercise you examined the culture of an organisation in which you work or, alternatively, the student body at your university or college. Take your analysis one stage further and answer the questions below.

1. How homogeneous is the culture? For example, does everybody seem to be part of the same culture, or are there different groups of people that have their own sub-culture? If so, how different are the sub-cultures?
2. How strong is the culture (and, if they exist, sub-cultures)?

The Effects of Culture on Organisational Performance

Although it is known that culture has a strong effect on people's behaviour, management's interest is less likely to be prompted by curiosity about why this happens, than in its possible bottom-line effects on the commercial or financial performance of an organisation. To a large extent this interest was kindled by the writings of popular authors such as Peters and Waterman (1982) who view culture as a key component in the performance of successful companies. These ideas resulted in an increased awareness among managers of the potential effects of culture but, as is often the case (because these writings conveyed the impression that there is a 'one best culture'), a more dangerous turn of events was set in motion.

Unfortunately, managers have a tendency to look for 'off the shelf' solutions to organisational problems. Therefore, when the cultural characteristics of successful companies were set out in these books in a catchy, marketable and easily grasped way, there was an understandable tendency for some managers to believe that, at last, social science had come up with something of immense practical use – a sure-fire recipe for success.

However, other than in the writings of these popular authors, there is little evidence of a strong association between culture and organisational performance, and none whatsoever for a set of cultural characteristics that are likely to be appropriate in all circumstances. Indeed, when the firms held up as shining examples in the popular works were examined a few years later, no coherent link between culture and performance could be established (Hitt and Ireland 1987). Indeed, several of the firms were in serious financial difficulties (Carroll 1983).

There could be sound reasons why this happens and Miller (1994) notes that, after a period of outstanding success, certain patterns of behaviour can appear in firms, all of which have an adverse impact on future success. For example, a firm can exhibit **inertia**, in which it clings to a past recipe for success, which may no longer be viable. Alternatively it becomes guilty of **immoderation**, in which very bold gambles are made, perhaps because previous success gives a feeling of invulnerability. In addition, the firm exhibits **inattention**, which is similar to a form of institutional 'groupthink', where top managers only pay attention to a very restricted range of environmental signals. Finally, firms show **insularity**, in which there is a failure to adapt to environment, even where the signs that this is necessary are readily available.

It is similarly important to recognise that the idea of a 'one best culture' is over simplistic and is misleading enough to be potentially dangerous. To this end Kilmann *et al.* (1985) reason that there are three features of a culture that could affect performance. These are:

Cultural direction: the extent to which an organisation's culture helps it achieve its goals

Cultural pervasiveness: the homogeneity of an organisation's culture

Cultural strength: the influence of a culture on the behaviour of organisational members

- *Cultural direction*, which broadly corresponds to the extent that a culture actually helps an organisation achieve its goals.
- *Cultural pervasiveness*, which denotes the extent to which an organisational culture is homogeneous. To some extent sub-cultures are probably inevitable, and this has some potential benefits. However, if the sub-cultures are very different and this leads to intergroup conflicts, people can spend more time in internecine warfare than anything else.
- *Cultural strength*, which expresses the influence that a culture has on the behaviour of people. A culture that is positive and strong will clearly have the most beneficial impact, while one that is strong and negative is likely to have adverse consequences. Because it takes time to socialise people into an organisation, one factor that can rapidly dilute cultural strength is staff turnover. Unfortunately, many firms have a regrettable tendency to shed staff when the organisation hits a bad patch and to hire fresh employees when an upturn arrives. Thus they can deprive themselves of the strong culture that they need to take advantage of an upturn, to say nothing of the demoralising after-effects that redundancies have on the culture of those who remain.

In summary, therefore, there are three main conclusions that can be drawn from the above. First, it is all too easy to treat culture as an essential 'must have' to achieve success, whereas if there is a link between culture and success, it could well be a rather tenuous one, and there could be many other factors that produce superior performance. Second, as Killman *et al.* (1985) point out, to have an affect on performance a culture needs to be appropriate to what the organisation seeks to achieve. Finally, Miller's (1994) analysis alerts us to the idea of certain 'perils' of prior success. Thus the characteristics of the culture need to be keyed to future performance, rather than those associated with the past.

REPLAY

- Culture is one of the less tangible features of an organisation and is carried in the minds of organisational members.
- It can be thought of as a layered phenomenon with largely invisible basic assumptions at its core, values that arise out of the basic assumptions as the next level outwards, and visible artifacts and creations that express the culture on the surface.
- Different perspectives exist on whether organisational culture is pervasive throughout a whole organisation or whether sub-cultures exist, but strong cultures, (provided that they are appropriate to an organisation's circumstances) are usually acknowledged to be beneficial in terms of organisational performance.
- The roots of a culture can often be located in an organisation's history, but culture is usually sustained and replicated by socialisation of new organisational members, together with a measure of re-socialisation of people as culture adjusts to changing circumstances.

PERSPECTIVES ON CULTURE

Smircich (1983) distinguishes five different streams of research that link the concepts of culture and organisation. Although these all have their own underlying assumptions, she also points out that they can be divided into two strongly contrasting schools of thought. The first is what will be called here the *key variable or application school*. This makes use of open systems ideas and views an organisation as something that has to acquire appropriate characteristics to remain in balance with its environment. Viewed this way, culture is a property in the same way that structure and size are properties that enable an organisation to cope with environmental demands; that is, culture is something an organisation '*has*'. A key assumption of this school is that culture is a crucial ingredient of organisational success. It allows the firm to marshal the commitment of its members to achieving the firm's goals and so it is similar to Martin's (1992) integrationist perspective. Since this offers the prospect of using culture to influence organisational performance, it is the perspective that has the strongest appeal to managers and has given rise to a considerable volume of work in the area, the vast majority of which has attempted to identify cultures that promote success, and how to obtain these cultural characteristics (Kanter 1995). In non-academic circles this is by far the most influential school and it spawned a growth industry for organisational development practitioners who have long sought to manipulate cultures to serve the interests of management.

Key variable (application) school: culture is viewed as an organisational property (something an organisation has) that can be changed at will

Root metaphor school: culture is assumed to reflect the essence of what an organisation 'is'

The second approach is what Smircich calls the culture as the *root metaphor school*. This views culture as something that an organisation '*is*', which is less concerned with trying to link culture with organisational performance than with trying to understand how cultures are experienced by organisational members, and how this affects the way they behave. While research in this area has great appeal to academics, it finds far less favour with managers, probably because the accounts are difficult to understand and are far too deep and complex for their tastes. Therefore, the better-known perspectives are firmly located in the application school, two of which will be described in what follows. Before giving these descriptions, however, it is important to point out that the first of them appeared nearly 20 years ago, in what could be described as the views of the 'founding fathers' of the cultural movement. In academic circles these are widely acknowledged to be incomplete, if not downright simplistic. Nevertheless, many managers still cling tenaciously to them and it is necessary for the reader to have some appreciation of their origins.

Peters and Waterman: The Characteristics of 'Excellent' Companies

The management interest in organisational culture was greatly stimulated by the publication of Peters and Waterman's (1982) best-seller, *In Search of Excellence*. The two authors, who were management consultants, set out to document management practices that they felt accounted for the superior performance of a number of highly successful American companies (see OB in Action Box on the next page). One of their major conclusions was that these organisations all had similar cultures, the eight most prominent characteristics of which are summarised in Table 2.2.

Bias for Action

Peters and Waterman noted that successful firms have a strong bias for action and outperformed firms where this is absent; for example, managers are expected to make decisions, even in the absence of full information.

Table 2.2 Peters and Waterman – the attributes of excellent companies

Attributes or characteristics	Example
Bias for action	Decisions get made, even in the absence of complete information
Staying close to the customer	The customer is regarded as the source of most of the valuable information the company needs to guide its actions
Autonomy and entrepreneurship	The company is often divided into smaller, more manageable business units to foster innovation and initiative
Productivity through people	People should be treated with dignity and respect and be given opportunities
Hands-on management	Senior managers maintain close contact with operational levels, often by 'walking the floor'
Sticking to the knitting	The company refrains from entering areas of business outside its competence and expertise
Simple form: lean staff	Flat structures with few levels of management and relatively small numbers of headquarters personnel
Simultaneous loose–tight organisation	Tightly knit in terms of common values held by people and at the same time loosely organised in terms of absence of rules and regulations

OB IN ACTION: Corporate culture and the 'excellence' movement

Image is increasingly important to all organisations, which is why companies employ a veritable army of public relations officers, corporate identity consultants, and reputation managers to improve their public perception. Top executives spend vast amounts of time carefully refining their corporate statements and inducting new employees into their corporate culture. Yet a great deal of executives' preoccupation with corporate culture can be traced to the historical influence of elite management consulting firms, which was itself a product of consultants' attempts to establish the professional credibility of their field long before the concept of corporate culture was commonly understood.

For example, consultants in McKinsey & Company have long been careful not to refer to themselves as a business and, instead, call themselves a professional practice. Indeed, McKinsey's training emphasises professional language, professional metaphors, and professional comportment in the firm's socialisation of recruits. This deliberate development and self-conscious codification of McKinsey's professional practice lay behind the concept of 'corporate culture'. This was something that fascinated management theorists during the 1980s and 1990s, and was popularised by Tom Peters and Bob Waterman (both McKinsey consultants) in their best-selling book, *In Search of Excellence*. Importantly the concept of corporate culture emerged from their analysis of McKinsey's past successes and through a gradual process of calculated image building, the success of consulting firms ultimately became the model for their corporate clients.

Today, management consultancies still use metaphorical language to reinforce their image, yet what is most notable is how the rhetorical language of consulting has become less descriptive of the individual consultancies and more evocative of their clients' inner desires. Instead of offering their clients corporate counsel or greater efficiency, firms such as Accenture and Booz Allen now promise to turn their clients into aggressive winners, and there seems to be no shortage of clients who embrace their siren statements.

For the management consultancies themselves, however, two questions remain to be answered. First, whether their professional image and vague formulations of positive management buzzwords are going to continue to be enough? Second, when will the so-called profession of management consulting finally go beyond rhetoric and accept full responsibility for its many implicit promises?

Source:

McKenna, C (2006) In the business of consulting: image is everything, *The Observer*, 20 November

Note: Christopher McKenna, who teaches corporate strategy at the Said Business School, University of Oxford, is the author of *The World's Newest Profession: Management Consulting in the Twentieth Century* (Cambridge University Press, 2006).

Staying Close to the Customer

The authors argue that firms where the customer is valued above all else outperform firms without this frame of reference. Where this viewpoint is held, the customer is seen as a source of information about the quality of current products and a source of ideas about products for the future. Thus meeting and, where necessary, pandering to customers' needs is argued to be an action that leads inevitably to superior performance.

Autonomy and Entrepreneurship

Peters and Waterman argue that while successful firms are often very large, they actively fight tendencies towards bureaucracy and lack of innovation. This is accomplished by dividing the firm into small, manageable units which are encouraged to be independent and creative within their respective areas.

Productivity through People

The authors note that successful firms have a genuine recognition that their most important assets are people at all levels, and this gets translated into committed action.

Hands-on Management

In many large companies, senior managers tend to lose touch with the fundamentals of the firm, but Peters and Waterman note that successful firms purposely try to counter this tendency by encouraging the view that the best way to manage is to stay in contact with what goes on by 'walking the floor' rather than exercising control from behind closed doors.

Stick to the Knitting

Another value that is said to characterise excellent firms is a reluctance to become involved in business outside their spheres of expertise. There is a strong emphasis on relying on the firm's core competencies and doing well what it does best.

Simple Form, Lean Staff

Unlike many organisations where managers measure their status, prestige and importance by the number of their subordinates, Peters and Waterman noted that successful firms have fewer layers of administrative staff, and a relatively small group of headquarters personnel. In what the authors call 'excellent' companies, a person's importance is measured by his or her impact on the organisation's performance rather than the size of his or her empire.

Simultaneously Loose and Tight Organisation

The final attribute identified by Peters and Waterman looks like a contradiction at first sight – how can something be loosely and tightly organised at the same time? What is meant by a loose and tight organisation is connected to the core values. In one sense they are tightly organised because everyone understands and believes in the firm's values, and these provide the glue that holds the firm together. However, in a physical sense they have fewer staff and fewer rules and regulations, which means they are loosely organised. Peters and Waterman argue that the loose physical structure is only possible because of the strong common value system. Thus the tight structure of common cultural values facilitates the loose control structure which is said to encourage innovation and risk taking.

Comments on the Peters and Waterman Contribution

Peters and Waterman's work has attracted strong criticism for its lack of rigour in terms of research methodology, and it has been forcefully argued that the link between cultures, excellence and performance is tenuous and highly fragile. Some of the so-called excellent companies subsequently encountered huge performance difficulties and, in addition, there are severe criticisms of some of the cultural characteristics used by Peters and Waterman. For instance Silver (1987) is particularly scathing about the reality of the 'people orientation' in some of the firms, and in a descriptive parody entitled 'McFactory' cites McDonald's as an example of one of the companies identified as 'excellent'. He notes that McFactory relies heavily on cheap, minimum-wage, non-unionised labour, which is usually made up of teenage workers in part-time employment. Thus behind the façade of what is portrayed as a stimulating work environment, there is a reality of dull monotony, where the emphasis is on deskilling the work by using the principle of scientific management so that the last ounce of effort can be extracted from employees (Silver 1987).

Notwithstanding these criticisms, the Peters and Waterman research played an important part in stimulating interest in organisational culture and this was accompanied by other work in the same style, which for interest is given in the further readings at the end of this chapter. However, things have moved on since then and it is to more recent developments that attention must now be directed.

A Recent Perspective: The Goffee and Jones Contingency Framework

The Peters and Waterman (1982) perspective was firmly part of what is now known as the 'excellence movement', which holds that culture is a key ingredient in the commercial success of an organisation. Because the authors list cultural characteristics that are said to lead to this outcome, it is easy to see why the ideas have an instant appeal to managers. The problem is, however, that this perspective and others like it imply a 'one best culture' suitable for all organisations. This is a rather simplistic idea and, although culture almost certainly has a part to play in organisational performance, it is only likely to have this effect if it helps in coping with the circumstances that confront an organisation. Since different organisations face different circumstances, the most useful approach to the culture–performance relationship is likely to be a contingency perspective, a matter that is addressed in a more recent development by Goffee and Jones (1998), who start with an assumption there is no such thing as a 'right' or 'best' culture for all organisations. Rather, the most appropriate culture for an organisation is the one that best helps it cope with the exigencies of its own business environment.

Goffee and Jones commence their analysis by giving a framework for classifying the characteristics of different organisational cultures. To do this they return to a stream of sociological work by Durkheim (1966), from which they extract two basic dimensions that reflect the way that humans relate to each other: sociability and solidarity.

Sociability

Sociability expresses the degree of friendliness between members of a community or group and where sociability is high, people help each other because they want to, with no thought of favours in return. This dimension of the relationship between people is essentially based on feelings and emotions and where it exists, people tend to value the relationship for its own sake. While those immersed in a relationship of this type sometimes take it for granted, it is usually recognised by a newcomer to an organisation as something special. For instance, if one person has a reason to celebrate they all celebrate; if someone has a reason to feel low, everyone tends to rally around; when people go into hospital they are visited by colleagues, and the people often socialise away from work.

The advantages to an organisation of a high degree of sociability in its culture are said to be:

- high morale, because most people working in these conditions find work a pleasure and work is viewed as fun
- it fosters teamwork, creativity, openness and sharing of ideas, and, because they genuinely want to help each other rather than simply look good, people are likely to go beyond their formal job requirements
- it promotes innovation and uninhibited cross-fertilisation of ideas
- people seldom have a mentality of being there for the shortest possible time, but work until the job is done.

Nevertheless, high sociability can have its downside because:

- strong friendships can mean that poor performance is tolerated and people can be reluctant to disagree with or criticise friends
- in extreme cases it can degenerate into cliques, cabals, in-groups and out-groups which results in behind-the-scenes politicking
- it can be an unpleasant situation for people who value their own personal space and privacy of thought.

Sociability: the degree of friendliness in the relationships between people

Solidarity

This dimension is not so much a reflection of people's feelings and emotions, but their thoughts. It expresses the degree of collectiveness (as opposed to individuality) in the relationship between people. Where solidarity is high, people have a sense of common purpose because they have shared goals, tasks or mutual interests. Thus, even if people do not particularly like or admire their colleagues, they tend to make common cause and work together like a well-oiled machine. Its advantages are said to be:

Solidarity: the degree of collectiveness in the relationship betweem people

- a ruthless commitment to getting done what (by consensus) needs to get done
- many people find it stimulating to work towards and achieve mutually agreed goals and the behaviour of other people is a constant reminder of the behaviours that are considered acceptable
- people are usually very clear about the rewards for good behaviour.

Again, however, solidarity can have its dark side:

- cultures that are high in solidarity can be ruthless in suppressing dissenters, even when they are also innovators
- too strong a focus on group goals can oppress or hurt individuals.

Using high and low values for sociability and solidarity, the two dimensions can be brought together to give a matrix of four cultural types, which Goffee and Jones call the 'Double "S" Cube' (Figure 2.3). Notice that there is a third dimension (depth) to the matrix. This reflects the idea that sociability and solidarity can have positive and negative aspects, the latter being expressed in the far (shaded) end of the cube. The four cultural types and the environmental circumstances for which they are said to be most appropriate are described in what follows.

The Communal Culture

Communal culture: one that is high in sociability and solidarity

While this is most frequently found in thrusting, successful, small to medium-sized organisations, it is occasionally found in larger firms that have taken great care to retain a culture of this type since their early, formative years. Examples cited by the authors are Hewlett-Packard and the pharmaceutical company Johnson and Johnson. Strong sociability results in people working in a highly collaborative, flexible and mutually supportive way, and their high solidarity unites them in a common sense of purpose. Thus there is a strong ethos of people being protective of the organisation and what it stands for, or as Goffee and Jones put it, 'the competition tends to be seen as an enemy that needs to be defeated' (1998, p 29). Since maintaining a communal culture

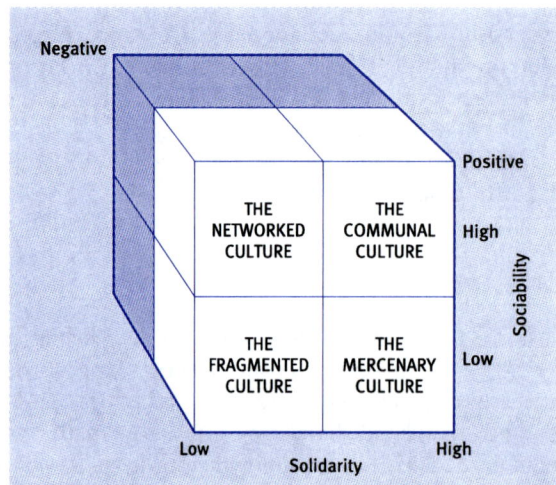

Figure 2.3 'The Double "S" Cube'

Source: Goffe, R and Jones, G (1998) *The Character of a Corporation*, copyright © by Rob Goffee and Gareth Jones. Reprinted by permission of HarperCollins Publishers Ltd and HarperCollins, Inc.

in a large organisation is difficult, a great deal of emphasis is placed on careful selection of new entrants, with only those who are perceived to 'fit in' being admitted. In addition, extensive and somewhat intensive induction programmes are used to inculcate the core values of the organisation and appraisal is not only against performance targets, but adherence to the desired organisational ethos.

The Networked Culture

> **Networked culture:** one that is high in sociability and low in solidarity

This culture, which is high in sociability but low in solidarity, is said to be most appropriate for large organisations that face highly competitive environments. Typically, the critical success factor in these industries is a free and open flow of information across functional, geographic, or even national boundaries and examples cited by the authors are Unilever, Heineken and the international electrical giant Philips. The culture is often found in large, highly successful companies, which perhaps had communal cultures at an earlier stage of development. Because it is hard to retain the right balance of sociability and solidarity to sustain a communal culture, there is a natural transformation to the networked type of organisation. Even so, there is often a strong legacy of sociability and people expect to be friendly with their colleagues.

The Mercenary Culture

> **Mercenary culture:** one that is low on sociability and high on solidarity

Organisations of this type are low on sociability but high on solidarity, and this culture is said to be most beneficial in a fast-changing business environment where competitive pressures are extremely high. In these circumstances, success and even survival can depend on establishing priorities, goals and strategies to beat off the competition, and an ability to move quickly, decisively and cohesively can be all important. Because solidarity is high the culture tends to promote an 'all hands to the pumps' mentality, but this is unencumbered by a compulsion to maintain friendly relations with everybody, which allows the relentless pursuit of effectiveness and efficiency to become the norm. Organisations of this type tend to be highly goal-orientated and goals are usually ambitious and specific – not just improve market share, but improve market share by 10 per cent each year. Here the examples identified by the authors are the confectionery giant Mars, PepsiCo and the financial conglomerate Citicorp. These organisations can be extremely demanding of their employees and the lack of sociability might mean that people only cooperate with each other when they can see a clear personal benefit in doing so. While people are probably well rewarded, the organisation can be merciless and intolerant of those who do not achieve, and so people tend not to remain with the organisation for too long.

The Fragmented Culture

> **Fragmented culture:** one that is low on both sociability and solidarity

This culture is low on sociability and solidarity. It applies to companies in which interdependence between the different activities is low and the critical success factor is having employees who are the star individuals in a particular field. In these circumstances sociability or solidarity are unlikely to have strong effects on performance, and organisations of this type tend to be relatively small in terms of staffing levels, for instance law firms, consultancies or merchant banks. However, this culture is sometimes found in much larger organisations that sub-contract or outsource most of their activities, for example the clothing manufacturer Benetton, or franchised operations such as fast-food chains.

An Appraisal of the Goffee and Jones Framework

The Goffee and Jones framework is an important advance in the study of organisational cultures. Because it is a true contingency theory, it does much to enhance the utility of the culture concept and, since it fits well with other work in the area, it is not a 're-invention of the wheel' but a genuine advance in the body of knowledge. This can perhaps be best illustrated by drawing attention to a number of important implications that arise from the work.

- Although the authors state that an organisation's dominant culture can usually be categorised as one of the four types described above, they also point out that sub-cultures are almost certain to exist in most organisations. Thus they avoid the pitfall of treating culture as an undifferentiated whole, and this is in line with other important work in the area.

- The authors point out that no culture is likely to last forever. Indeed, they put forward the idea that there seems to be a natural life-cycle with three of the four cultural types, which is connected to the changes that inevitably take place as an organisation grows and develops. Companies often start out with communal cultures, which fits well with Schein's (1983) ideas about the effect that the founder of an organisation has on its culture. As it grows, it meets new challenges and for this reason there is probably a natural progression to the networked type in many organisations. Later on, however, complacency can set in and the organisation can come under siege by its competitors. Thus, emergency measures may be needed, which prompts a move to the mercenary culture.

- Goffee and Jones explicitly point out that none of the cultures is inherently good or bad in itself. Sociability and solidarity can both result in human behaviour that is dysfunctional for an organisation in certain circumstances. Thus it is the blend of these two dimensions at a certain point in time that is important. For this reason, the cultural types are more (or less) appropriate at coping with the different environmental exigencies that can be encountered by organisations.

- Although Goffee and Jones do not specifically address the matter of difference in national cultures, they draw attention to the idea that these can have an impact on the cultural type with which an organisation is likely to feel most at ease. For example, in contrasting Procter and Gamble and Unilever, which are direct competitors facing almost identical competitive pressures, they note that the former has long had characteristics typical of the mercenary culture, whereas Unilever has only recently made moves in this direction. The important difference here is that Procter and Gamble is an American organisation, while Unilever is Anglo-Dutch. American organisations are much more likely to be at home with the centralisation of authority, a high task focus, ruthless internal competition and the 'all shoulders to the wheel' ethos of the mercenary culture. European organisations, however, have a much stronger focus on relationships and decentralised authority, both of which characterise the networked culture.

- Finally, although the authors deal with the matter of changing organisational cultures, they avoid the trap of understating the problems involved. Thus, while they view change as possible, which puts them firmly in what has been called earlier the 'application' school, they do not suggest, as do so many others in this school, that culture can be manipulated in an easy way. Indeed, they are at great pains to point out that cultural change is often prompted by a crisis, which itself brings about a degree of modification to culture.

TIME OUT

Before reading the next section, re-examine the culture you explored in the two previous Time Out exercises and answer the questions below.

1. Is the culture an appropriate one from the point of view of:
   (a) the employees (or students)?
   (b) the organisation or institution?
2. If your answer to questions 1(a) and 1(b) is yes, how can this culture be maintained?
3. If your answer to questions 1(a) or 1(b) is no, what changes in culture do you feel the organisation would like to see?
4. How can these changes be brought about?

CULTURE CHANGE AND CULTURE MANAGEMENT

Culture change: modification of an existing culture

Culture management: maintaining or making slight modifications to fine-tune an existing culture

If it is accepted that culture has an important influence on the success of an organisation, managers clearly have a vested interest in being able to influence culture. This can be done in one of two ways: by modifying the existing culture through *culture change*, or using *culture management* to retain one that is felt to be appropriate. However, to regard either of these as a practical possibility it is necessary to assume that culture is something that can be changed at will. This idea still provokes heated debate, and nowhere is it more apparent than in the suggestion that all employees throughout an organisation can be induced to embrace a market-orientated culture; a very fashionable 'must have' in many organisations (Greenley and Foxall 1996). The assumption is that a culture of this type will result in superior organisational performance (Selnes *et al.* 1996). While this may just be a bid for increased power on the part of marketeers in organisations, it can be noted that inculcating a stronger customer focus in employees is also a fundamental part of new control strategies. However, in an extremely penetrating analysis of these ideas, Harris and Ogbonna (1999) conclude that what is proposed is so conceptually and practic-ally flawed that it is doomed to failure because it:

- rests on an integrationist perspective, which assumes that an organisation's culture is common to all its members, whereas the more realistic differentiationist view acknowledges the inevitability of sub-cultures
- assumes that top managers can impose a culture on the rest of an organisation at will, but this is only possible in certain, rarely encountered circumstances

- flies in the face of a substantial body of evidence that cultures perpetuate themselves until such time as culture holders decide that change is desirable.

Many theorists argue that because culture is so deep-rooted, it is highly resistant to manipulation. For example, Ogbonna (1993) points out that while some behaviourial change results from a culture change initiative, it is very unlikely to change deeper values. Thus, all that occurs is a cosmetic impression of culture change. An even stronger position is taken by Ray (1986), who argues that one of the main functions of a culture may well be to enable people to resist changes of this type. For this reason it is not surprising to find that unanticipated consequences and backlash effects often occur in cultural change initiatives. For instance, a study of 530 American companies by Gilmore *et al.* (1997) found that while quality, service levels, competency and productivity often improve, climate, employee morale and work enthusiasm decline considerably. Indeed, Woodall (1996) argues that many attempts at cultural change are so badly conducted that they result in degradation of the workforce and raise questions about the ethics of these initiatives.

In the light of this evidence it is important to understand something of the theory of culture change as it is expressed in most of these change programmes. This will be explained in two stages: first, by giving an overview of the methodology itself and, second, by describing some of the techniques that have been advocated to bring about changes.

The Methodology

Almost all culture change models are derived from the four-step process suggested by Silverzweig and Allen (1976), which is summarised below.

Step 1: Analyse Existing Culture

This usually consists of an extensive survey of organisational members to establish specific objectives for cultural change.

Step 2: Experiencing the Culture

Here organisational members are given the opportunity to examine the existing culture, (hopefully to identify its dysfunctions) and then participate in identifying the culture that is required.

Step 3: System Installation

This is where the actual change process occurs, usually by making use of group discussion workshops. The active participation of organisational leaders is said to be vital in this stage, primarily to provide those lower down with something on which to model their own behaviour. It is usually recognised that if the initiative is not completed effectively, all that is likely to result is superficial surface change, for instance people seeking to please those higher up by displaying signs of the behaviour they believe top people want to see.

Step 4: Ongoing Evaluation

Here the degree of actual change is assessed and, as necessary, other methods are used to bring about or reinforce the desired changes.

Techniques

Most of the techniques described here would probably be deployed in stages 3 and 4 of the above methodology. They are also said to be useful ways of reinforcing existing cultures where they are already considered appropriate.

Taking Advantage of Existing Culture

This is sometimes described as 'working around an existing culture', and requires that a comprehensive understanding of the organisational value system is obtained in stage 1 of the methodology. If this is achieved, the picture can be compared with the cultural values that management would like to see in place and, where necessary, discussion and explanation can be used to correct any discrepancies.

When examined closely, some of the best publicised examples of so-called cultural change probably turn out to be little more than working around an existing culture. One example is given in Ackroyd and Crowdy's (1990) study of slaughtermen, which showed how managers hijacked a culture that was already in place and portrayed the results as something that occurred because of their endeavours.

Socialisation

This has been described earlier and consists of a set of processes that enable employees to learn about their firm's culture and pass on their knowledge and understanding to others. While socialisation seldom brings about a radical change in people's values, it can help them to become more aware of any differences between their own values and those of an organisation, and to develop ways of coping with the differences.

Managing Symbols

As noted earlier, a number of authors suggest that a powerful way to understand a culture is to take note of the values communicated through stories and other symbolic events. This being the case, one way to promote cultural change is to introduce stories and myths that spread the new cultural values.

Change Reward Systems

Behavioural psychologists argue that the behavioural elements of a culture are learned and can just as easily be extinguished. Thus cultural change can be encouraged by changing the organisation's system of rewards and punishments.

Add New Members

New values can sometimes be a lot harder to develop than starting from scratch. Therefore, providing they actually have the desired new culture, adding new organisational members can be a powerful strategy. However, if it is to be effective, there must be enough new people to swamp the existing culture, otherwise they will simply be socialised into what is there.

Implement Culture Shock

Culture shock is something that causes an organisation to take a serious look at its own values and behaviour, for example the loss of a key customer, a scandal of some sort, an unsuccessful lawsuit, or something that threatens its existence. When events like these are attributed to something that is lacking in an organisation's culture, it is often the case that drastic changes are made very quickly.

Change the Top People

As well as having a potential shock value, change at the top can have a major impact on an organisation's culture by sending reverberations throughout an organisation. The person at the top often sets the norms of behaviour and when he or she goes, the next level down soon seems to follow, perhaps because these people are seen as key symbols of the old regime, who will have difficulty in adapting to the new one.

Involve Organisational Members

Strictly speaking, changing a culture involves changing its underlying assumptions, values and beliefs. Therefore, top-down culture change can be interpreted by people below as something that forces them to give up assumptions and values that are almost sacred. Therefore, because people are usually more willing to implement decisions they have helped to make, participative techniques can often be more successful.

What, then, are the general conclusions that can be drawn about the ease of cultural change? There are three in particular that are highly significant:

- Cultures are the result of complex social processes that tend to take place over a long period of time, so a programme of cultural change which becomes a 'quick fix' solution to an organisational problem can do more harm than good.
- All cultures are different, and what can be an effective change strategy in one organisation may be far less effective elsewhere.
- The more deeply ingrained a culture, the more difficult it will be to change, and the more an organisation contains multiple sub-cultures, the more complex and time-consuming will be the change process.

Organisations therefore need to consider very carefully whether they should try to interfere with a culture or simply let other changes that have been put in place give rise to an appropriate culture that emerges at its own pace (Hope and Hendry 1995).

A BRIEF NOTE ON NATIONAL CULTURES

At an intuitive level almost everyone is aware that customs, attitudes and values vary between countries. Indeed, the need to adjust our behaviour can sometimes become very obvious if we travel outside our native country. These days, many organisations operate internationally, with branches or subsidiaries abroad, and there is an increasing realisation that people in organisations need to be aware of cultural differences and adjust their behaviour accordingly. For this reason, an important area of study is now that of cross-cultural differences and how these can influence patterns of behaviour (Adler and Bartholomew 1992). Similarly, it is important to note that the culture of an organisation needs to be compatible with the culture of the country or region in which it is located. If this is not the case, people can find that expected patterns of behaviour in the enterprise clash with what they have been brought up to regard as normal and acceptable.

There is a great deal of evidence to show that national cultures vary considerably in terms of beliefs and values that are held sacred. Importantly, it needs to be noted that these cultural effects are what prompt people in different locations to behave in very different ways.

REPLAY

- Culture is one of the less tangible features of organisational life and, while it is hard to define, there is a growing consensus that it consists of a deeply ingrained set of values that provide people in an organisation with a code of acceptable behaviour.

- A number of different perspectives on organisational culture exist, the most pronounced difference being that between integrationists, who view the phenomena as a relatively homogeneous set of values shared by all organisational members, and differentiationists, who hold that there are different sub-cultures in most organisations.

- While the evidence for a universal 'one best culture' is weak, this is the approach adopted by most popular writers in the area, whose descriptions are often taken as a prescription for an ideal culture. An exception to this, however, is the more recent contingency framework of Goffee and Jones (1998).

- Changing an organisation's culture is likely to be tremendously difficult and, if it can be accomplished, the process will probably take a considerable amount of time and effort.

- Organisational culture nearly always contains elements of the culture of the country in which an organisation is located, which means that a culture that is appropriate for a firm in one country may not be appropriate for a branch or division of the same organisation elsewhere.

ORGANISATIONAL CLIMATE

Although the concept of organisational climate is closely allied to culture, it has existed in a developed form for considerably longer and can be traced back to the work of Kurt Lewin (1951). Like culture, it can be difficult to define precisely, and since some academic definitions can be rather obscure, in the interests of simplicity it is defined here as:

a characteristic ethos or atmosphere within an organisation at a given point in time which is reflected in the way its members perceive, experience and react to the organisational context.

A number of important implications arise from this definition. First, climate is a 'felt' state of affairs, rather than a set of hard, quantifiable attributes. One way to think of it is as the way that people describe relevant features of an organisation to themselves, and interpret what they experience (James and Jones 1974).

Second, climatic conditions can be short-lived (Powell and Butterfield 1978) and this is one of the features that distinguishes climate from culture.

Finally, since climate is experienced by people and affects their attitudes, it gives a basis for the way they will behave (Schneider 1983). This is usually concerned with whether they feel that their membership of an organisation is a psychologically rewarding experience, coupled with the effect this has on their levels of morale, motivation and the desire to remain as organisational members (Litwin and Stringer 1968).

TIME OUT

Carefully consider a group of up to 25 people to which you belong. Preferably this should be a formal group, for instance a section or department at your place of work, or if you choose a group at your university or college, it could be a class or even all the students in your year of the course. You have probably noticed that from time to time there are what seem to be attitude changes in the group. Try to identify some of these that have occurred fairly recently and answer the questions below.

1. What attitudes have you identified? For example, are they attitudes to the organisation as a whole or to a smaller part of it? If you chose an academic location are they attitudes to a course as a whole, a particular subject or class, or towards the institution?

2. What was the nature of these attitude changes? For example, did attitudes become more positive or negative?

3. To what extent do you feel that these attitude changes represent a shift, albeit a temporary one, in climate?

THE NATURE AND ORIGINS OF CLIMATE

The Relation of Climate to Culture

Although there are certain similarities between climate and culture, there are also differences. While both are phenomena that people feel or experience, they tend to be more consciously aware of climate. In addition, although both have effects on behaviour, this occurs in rather different ways. Culture gives people a code of conduct that informs them about the behaviour that is expected, whereas climate tends to result in a set of conditions to which they react. Culture is also more permanent and deeply ingrained. Thus in Smircich's (1983) words it can be regarded as something an organisation '*is*', whereas climate is usually more short-term – a phase that an organisation passes through.

However, one way in which cultures and climates are similar is that both are linked to the value system of organisational members. Values are a fundamental part of a culture and, to some extent, culture itself gives people their values. However, climate is more often a reflection of whether current organisational conditions are in accord with the values that people already hold. Therefore, culture is often a significant background factor to a particular set of climatic conditions.

Before closing this brief contrast, however, it is important to note that this is very much the traditional view of the two concepts. There is another viewpoint that holds that the differences are really much smaller, and that culture and climate may well be the same phenomenon, but measured in different ways (Denison 1996). This is far too important an idea to be ignored or glossed over but, for the present, it is more convenient to use the traditional perspective, and a return to the alternative view will be made at the end of the chapter.

Individual or Group Level Construct?

Although the very expression organisational climate implies that it is an organisation-wide phenomenon, it should be noted that it is something that arises in individual feelings and experiences. This means that it is strongly connected with individual mental processes (Kozlowski and Doherty 1989) and, for this reason, it is necessary to draw a distinction between climate at the individual level and climate at the group level. The individual effect is normally referred to as *psychological climate* (Koys and DeCotis 1991), which reflects how a person experiences and reacts to his or her surroundings. In this book, however, the focus is primarily on *organisational climate*, which is a social phenomenon that affects the behaviour of groups, or even the whole organisation. Nevertheless, there is an important connection between the two levels. Organisational climates are not simply the sum of individual feelings. Rather, when a group of people is exposed to the same organisational conditions, they share their interpretations of the circumstances, and what emerges is a degree of consensus among group members about climate: namely organisational climate.

Psychological climate: how the individual experiences and reacts to his or her surroundings

Organisational climate: how people collectively experience and react to their surroundings

Outcomes or Phenomena?

Climate can have pronounced effects on attitudes and behaviour, but there is sometimes a great deal of confusion about whether it is the phenomenon itself that results

Figure 2.4
Connections between independent, intervening and dependent variables

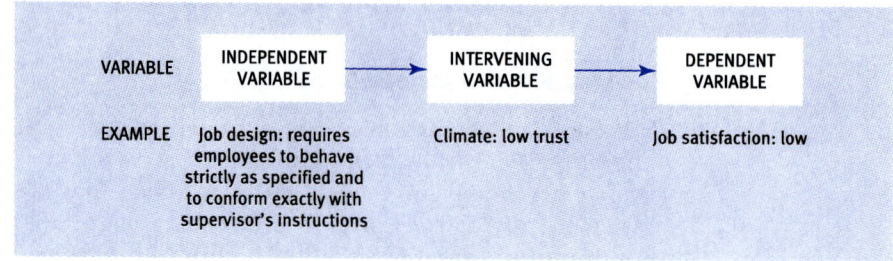

in this effect, or whether what happens is an outcome of something else. Its origins and outcomes will be covered in detail presently, but, for now, it is important to note that most definitions and measures treat climate as something that is both a phenomenon and an outcome; that is, as an intervening variable. This is shown in outline in Figure 2.4.

Note that the independent variable **job design** does not affect the dependent variable **job satisfaction** directly. Rather it influences the climatic dimension of **trust**, which in turn affects **job satisfaction**. The reason for treating climate in this way is largely to provide conceptual clarity; for instance, although we might observe that job satisfaction alters if the design of a job is changed, it is difficult to explain how job design has this effect (cause) on job satisfaction. However, if an intervening variable is placed between the two variables, the causal link is broken down into two stages, and the process can be made much clearer.

TIME OUT

Using the group and its attitude changes that you identified in the previous Time Out exercise, apply the model of cause and effect given in Figure 2.4 and answer the questions below for each attitude.

1. What particular factor (independent variable) prompted the attitude change?
2. What climatic condition (intervening variable) did this create?
3. What was the outcome in terms of attitude?

Hint: You may find it easier to consider matters in the reverse direction; that is, starting with the outcome.

CLIMATE: A MODEL OF ANTECEDENTS AND OUTCOMES

Since climate is usually treated as an intervening variable, it is important to distinguish between the factors that result in climatic conditions and those that are affected by climate. Using some of the results from a diverse range of studies, a model can be constructed which portrays these factors (see Figure 2.5).

Figure 2.5 The origins and outcomes of organisational climate

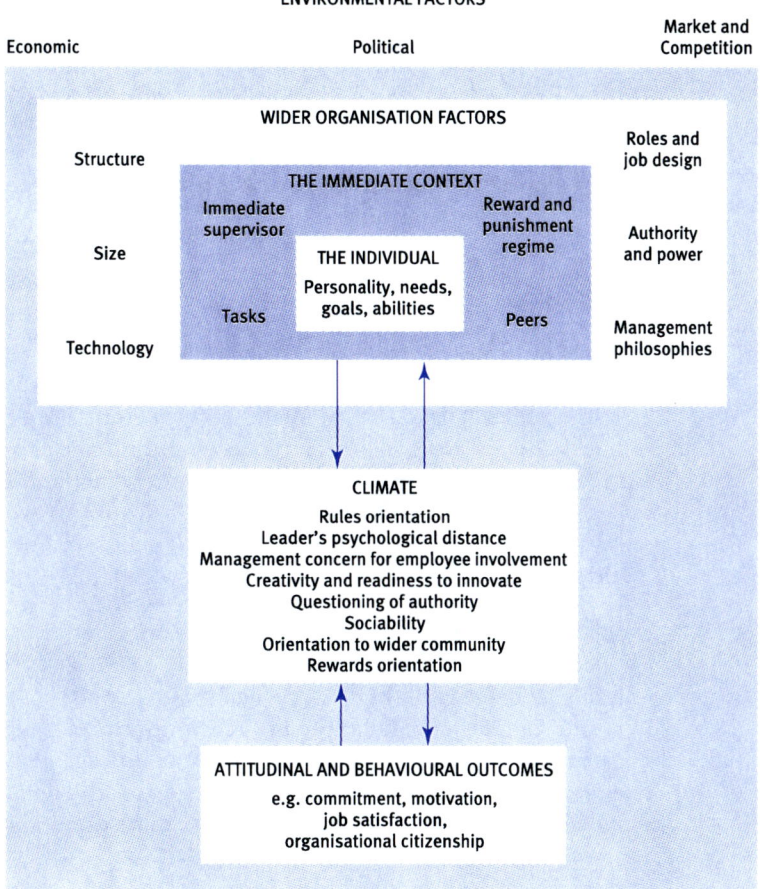

Factors inside and outside an organisation can have an impact on climate. Inside the organisation, influential variables are shown at three levels: the *wider organisation*, the *immediate context* and the *individual*. These can all affect perceptions of climate and, in turn, climate can result in attitudinal and behaviourial outcomes. Before describing the variables in detail it is necessary to emphasise two important points.

- There is an arrow on the model leading from climate to outcomes and another one in the opposite direction. This indicates that climates are often self-reinforcing. That is, poor climatic conditions can result in lowered commitment, motivation and job satisfaction, and these feelings can result in people perceiving that the organisation has a poor climate.
- A similar pair of arrows is shown between climate and the individual. This reflects the idea that some of a person's individual characteristics will shape perceptions of climate, for example needs, goals and personality characteristics. Thus, if there is a poor match between what a person needs or wants and what the organisation provides, there can often be an adverse effect on perceptions of climate. However, people are not totally inflexible, and over a period of time the

climatic conditions can sometimes result in them adjusting their aspirations downwards.

In what follows the different variables and some of their effects are all described separately, but in practice most of them are at work together and they can all affect perceptions of climate. For convenience, the explanation starts by describing the dimensions of climate and then its outcomes. The explanation then proceeds by working from the environment inwards.

Organisational Climate

Since people are usually aware of several organisational characteristics or attributes, they experience life in several different ways at the same time. Thus, climate is a multidimensional phenomenon and the most robust measures evaluate it in this way. Although there are several different measurements that can be used to do this, what is given here is a description of the dimensions used in three of the most prominent scales: Litwin and Stringer (1968), Payne and Phesey (1971) and Dastmalchian (1986). Scales of this type are usually pencil-and-paper questionnaires that are completed by employees of an organisation, and they are used to tap perceptions of:

- **rules orientation**: whether behaviour in the organisation is governed by formal rules and regulations
- **leader psychological distance**: whether those in senior positions emphasise their greater authority and hold themselves apart from subordinates
- **creativity and readiness to innovate**: whether the organisation and its management are seen as receptive to new ideas and ways of doing things
- **questioning authority**: whether it is permissible to question the decision of a senior person
- **sociability**: the extent to which a team spirit exists
- **an orientation to wider community**: whether the organisation and its policies are seen to be sensitive to the needs of a wider community
- **rewards orientation**: whether the organisation and its management are seen to encourage effort with rewards, rather than using punishments for lack of effort.

These dimensions are used by people to describe the organisation to themselves and according to what is perceived, they experience membership as being somewhere between psychologically stimulating and rewarding at one extreme, to stultifying at the other. Predictably, the former is more likely to lead to positive attitudinal and behavioural outcomes.

Outcomes

Outcomes shown in the model are both attitudinal and behavioural. Although the list of outcomes is potentially endless, for simplicity, only four examples are shown. These are: *commitment to organisation, motivation, job satisfaction* and *organisational citizenship*.

It is now time to examine some of the factors that influence climate, and the description starts from the outside and works inwards.

The Environmental Context

Economic Factors

The buoyancy and general health of the surrounding economy can result in management feeling optimistic or pessimistic about the future. Where managers are pessimistic costs might be scrutinised or investment curtailed to hoard reserves for hard times ahead. Employees can be remarkably sensitive about these signs, which often promote a climate of insecurity (Dastmalchian 1986).

Political Factors

In Great Britain, central government policies have forced most public sector organisations to make internal adjustments to comply with legislation that requires them to put work that was hitherto performed by their own employees out to tender. Steps such as this can also prompt structural changes that give rise to insecurity, which is quickly reflected in climate.

Market and Competitive Factors

The market for a firm's products can have a dramatic effect on its prosperity, and market conditions can sometimes threaten an organisation's very existence. Where this occurs, the climate of insecurity can prompt a 'rush to the door' as people look for more secure jobs. However, these conditions can sometimes have surprisingly positive effects. Organisational members can perceive that they are all faced with a common threat, which prompts them to pull together to remedy the situation, which has very positive effects on climate (Dastmalchian 1986).

The Organisational Context

Size, Structure and Authority Patterns

One of the important points to consider is that as organisations get larger they tend to become more formal and bureaucratic, which means that size, structure and authority patterns can conveniently be considered together. Bureaucratic organisations usually have a strong rules orientation and a high emphasis on following established procedures. Moreover, size often goes hand in hand with increased job specialisation, lowered interpersonal communication and a greater centralisation of decision making. All of these characteristics tend to result in climatic conditions in which people feel that there is a lack of freedom to use initiative and skills.

Roles and Job Design

The work of Hackman and Oldham (1975) clearly demonstrates that certain aspects of job design have psycho-gical effects in terms of whether people feel that work is a stimulating and meaningful experience.

Technology

Technology has an impact on the way that jobs are designed, and there is some suggestion that using automation for repetitive and fragmented jobs can enrich work, enhance feelings of worker control and lower feelings of alienation (Crawley and Spurgeon 1979). Conversely, there is also evidence that computerised clerical work results in lowered feelings of personal control and responsibility. However, much seems to depend on the nature of computerisation and the jobs to which it is applied. In some cases it results in more varied, interesting and responsible work with a more positive impact on climate (Oborne 1994).

Management Philosophies

Philosophy is used here to describe the views that managers hold about the roles and functions of subordinates, which often has an impact on the way they are treated and gives rise to climatic effects. One indication of these philosophies is the payment system used within an organisation – too strong an emphasis on incentive payments can create the impression that managers believe that the only thing which motivates subordinates is money (Dastmalchian and Mansfield 1980).

Authority and Power

The way that authority and power are used can also have climatic repercussions. An organisation that is run in a highly autocratic way by a small, powerful clique of executives can be expected to have a climate lacking in employee collaboration but high in fear.

The Immediate Context

The Immediate Supervisor

A person's immediate supervisor can have a strong effect on climate. While some supervisors can mitigate the effects of frustrating organisational policies and practices, others tend to make these features of working life much worse. Therefore, to the extent that a supervisor shields subordinates from these things, there can be a positive effect on climate. In addition, the interpersonal relationships between a supervisor and subordinates can make the overall work experience more pleasant or unpleasant, and this also has climatic repercussions.

Tasks

Some tasks are inherently more psychologically rewarding than others, and so the nature of the work that a person performs is virtually certain to colour his or her experience of an organisation.

Rewards and Punishments

In order to encourage certain behaviours and discourage those that are considered less desirable, organisations usually have a system of rewards and punishments. Most organisational members are aware of this, if only at a subjective level, and this has an effect on how they experience organisational life.

Peers

While climate is an individually experienced phenomenon, people in the immediate context usually share their experiences and interpretations. This enables them to test their perceptions of reality on others and if these perceptions are confirmed as accurate, what has been perceived becomes the reality of the situation.

The Individual

Individual differences are the ways in which people are unique and have their own **personalities**, **abilities**, **needs** and **goals**. An organisation that provides a facility for individuals to satisfy their needs and achieve cherished goals is more likely to be one where membership is perceived as a rewarding experience, which in turn shapes perceptions of climate at the individual level. Nevertheless, as is pointed out above, group effects are also very powerful. Since groups have some capability to shape the views and perceptions of their members, the ensuing climate is more often manifest as a collective phenomenon.

REPLAY

- Because people in organisations take in information about their surroundings and construct personal realities from what they perceive, organisations always have climates of some sort.
- Thus, climate is an experienced phenomenon and, since people in the workplace share their experiences and interpretations, climate tends to emerge as a collectively experienced state of affairs.
- Climate is influenced by a number of organisational features and conditions and, since these can change, climates can also fluctuate.

OVERVIEW AND CONCLUSIONS

The concepts of organisational culture and organisational climate clearly have some similarities. Both deal with intangible aspects of the way that employees relate to and experience an organisation, and both acknowledge that this results in distinctive patterns of employee behaviour. Nevertheless, the traditional view is that culture and climate are different concepts and deal with different facets of organisational life. There are three ways in which they can be contrasted and these are discussed in what follows.

Culture and Climate as Theoretical Constructs

Culture and climate are both abstract constructs, that are used to explain a state of affairs within an organisation. Of the two, culture describes a more ephemeral and intangible state of affairs – the values that are part of what it is, in much the same way that an individual's personality is fundamental to what he or she is. Climate, on the other hand, is much more explicit and precise. It has no pretence of explaining what an organisation is, but expresses the mental reactions of its members to what they perceive it to be.

Although it has long been recognised that organisations have cultures, serious application of the concept is a fairly recent development. The most penetrating work in the area uses an anthropological frame of reference, the output of which usually produces no more than a description of an organisation's culture, perhaps because many anthropologists see the main role of the discipline as describing and documenting. Climate, however, is largely the preserve of social psychologists, who set out to explain how particular sets of climatic conditions arise, and how these have discernible effects on the behaviour of organisational members. Thus, the way the concepts are defined tends to reflect the views of two very different groups of social scientists about ways in which human behaviour in organisations can best be understood. Needless to say, instead of trying to find ways of reconciling their different points of view, researchers from one school are often dismissive of those from the other. Culturalists criticise climatologists for trying to be too precise about measurement, and those who study climate tend to criticise culturalists for adopting an approach which is too strongly focused on producing one-off descriptions that make it impossible to compare organisations. Commenting on this problem, Denison (1996) argues that it is far from clear that culture and climate are concerned with two distinctly different aspects of organisational life. Both, for example, have similar theoretical foundations and, ultimately, they both address the issue of 'How does this affect behaviour?' Indeed, in Denison's view, the apparent difference has resulted in something of a self-fulfilling prophecy. Since culturalist and climatologists come from different academic backgrounds, they tend to use different methods of investigation, the net result of which is that although they can be studying the same phenomenon, the results they produce create the impression that the two phenomena are totally different.

Culture and Climate as Organisational Phenomena

The conventional view about culture and climate is that they exist at different levels. Culture is usually taken to be deeply embedded in subconsciously held values. Conversely, climate tends to be regarded as more of a surface phenomenon, with easily identifiable effects on behaviour. Although sub-cultures are usually found within organisations, until fairly recently there has been a strong tendency to view culture as a pervasive phenomenon, whereas micro climates tend to be regarded as more inevitable because many of the important factors directly influencing climatic conditions are located in a group's immediate context.

Because cultures are taken to be enduring and slow to change it can be difficult to correct a culture that is considered inappropriate. The antecedents of climates are better understood and it is usually assumed that climates change more quickly than cultures. Although this does not mean that climates are any easier to modify, at a theoretical level it probably means that poor climates are more avoidable.

The Utility of Culture and Climate Concepts to Managers

At the present time it is likely that most managers view culture as a more important topic than climate. The rather naive ideas set out in popular texts on the subject have resulted in something of a managerial love affair with the word, perhaps because managers have been encouraged to believe that a universal set of cultural characteristics can be selected as an off-the-shelf recipe for organisational success. These very simplistic ideas probably mean that the concept has less real utility than appears at first sight. This is not necessarily the fault of managers. They are busy people and if they are encouraged by self-styled gurus (many of whom should know better) to believe that culture is a 'quick-fix' solution, it is probably the self-appointed experts who should be blamed. Nevertheless, the idea that an appropriate culture can make a significant contribution to organisational success is an important one, and as the quality of research in the area improves, it is possible that a more definitive picture that tells which cultures are most appropriate for organisations in different circumstances will emerge. In addition, it seems likely that viable methods to move from one set of cultural characteristics to another can be evolved, and when both of these requirements have been satisfied, culture is likely to come into its own as a highly usable concept. Until then, however, its use can sometimes be nothing more than a blind act of faith.

While it has never caught management's imagination in quite the same way as culture, climate has always been important to organisations. There has long been a recognition that work-related attitudes and behaviour are important for organisational performance. In addition it has been known for some time that structure and immediate contextual factors, such as supervisor style and the influence of workgroups, all play a part in shaping attitudes and behaviour. Climate is also a concept that has been exposed to a more rigorous academic exploration and is less plagued with simplistic ideas than culture, so it is, or should be, a concept that has a great deal of practical utility to managers.

FURTHER READING

Cray, D and GR Mallory (1997) *Making Sense of Managing Culture*, Thomson: London. For those who subscribe to the idea that culture can be easily modified, this book gives an interesting 'how to do it' guide.

Deal, TE and AA Kennedy (1982) *Corporate Culture: The Rites and Rituals of Corporate Life*, Reading, MA: Addison-Wesley. A book by two of the 'founding fathers' of the culture movement. Very firmly located in the application school and in its time highly influential in management circles.

Goffee, R and G Jones (1998) *The Character of a Corporation*, London: HarperCollins. The book gives a full description of the authors' more recent contingency application of the culture concept.

Kanter, RM (1995) *The Change Masters: Corporate Entrepreneurs at Work*, London: Allen and Unwin. A highly influential book, written by a management 'guru'. It more about cultural change than anything else and, because it tends to portray culture change as something that is not too difficult to accomplish, it needs to be taken with a pinch of salt.

Martin, J (1992) *Cultures and Organisations: Three Perspectives*, Beverly Hills, CA: Sage. A penetrating analysis of the concept of culture as applied to organisations.

Moore, JD (1997) *Visions of Culture: An Introduction to Anthropological Theories and Theorists*, London: Sage. A book of readings by 21 major theorists on culture and an analysis of their impact on contemporary thought.

Ouchi, WG (1981) *Theory Z*, Reading, MA: Addison Wesley. The author, who was one of the 'founding fathers' of the excellence movement of the 1980s, compares and distinguishes between American and Japanese company cultures. He draws the conclusion that the superior performance of Japanese firms is attributable to their corporate culture.

Parker, M (2000) *Organisational Culture and Identity*, London: Sage. The book takes a critically symbolic perspective on culture, by exploring how organisations shape the identities of their members. It also addresses the important questions of the ethics of this process.

Peters, TJ and RH Waterman (1982) *In Search of Excellence: Lessons from America's Best Run Companies,* New York: Harper and Row. A book which is also by two of the 'founding fathers' of the 'excellence' movement. More than any other book it established culture as a highly fashionable topic in management circles.

Schein, EH (1992) *Organisational Culture and Leadership*, San Francisco, CA: Jossey-Bass. A thorough exploration of organisational culture from a social psychological perspective.

Sackmann, SA (ed.) (1997) *Cultural Complexity in Organisations,* London: Sage. A book of readings in which different authors deal with culture, sub-cultures, and national cultures.

CASE STUDY 2.1: Coca-Cola

Coca-Cola has never found it easy to convince its critics that it runs an ethical business and the anti-Coke website 'thezeromovement.org' claims that the business model of the world's leading soft drinks group involves waste, pollution and questionable nutrition.

However, Dominique Reiniche, president of Coke's European business, argues that the company is developing a more proactive corporate culture to address such issues. 'We are in a time in which we need to change Coke,' Ms Reiniche says. 'I think we have to do more in terms of the environment, and in terms of climate change we have to go even further. I also think we will probably be pushed further on product reformulations.'

Nevertheless, Coke was among the companies praised publicly by the European Commission last year after it, and other soft drinks groups, agreed voluntarily to restrict marketing to children. Drinks companies have moved faster than food companies in altering their marketing practices, with food groups such as Mars, Unilever and Kellogg's a year behind the soft drinks industry in initiating changes. Ms Reiniche claims Coke is working more closely with regulators and other companies than ever before. 'What we have tried to do this time is to influence the industry agenda and bring others with us,' she says. 'It's the end of everybody doing their own thing and creating solutions to the very urgent challenges we are faced with takes collective action.'

Until May 2007, Ms Reiniche was president of the Union of European Beverages Associations, which negotiated the new marketing agreement with the Commission. Of course, Coke also has self-interest at heart: consumers increasingly care about how and where companies make their products, and what they do with their profits, and a survey on Coke in Europe by a Dutch management school found that more than 40 per cent of people canvassed thought the soft drinks group was not making a positive contribution to society.

Ms Reiniche was appointed to her current job by Neville Isdell, Coke's chief executive, who has also become more critical about the company's role in society. He told the Worldwide Fund for Nature's annual conference in Beijing last month that private and non-profit sectors should work together to find answers to global water needs. 'Arguably, we have seen more focus on environmental issues in the past year than the last 20. This has been driven by heightened public awareness of global climate change, and its impact on water, biodiversity, agriculture and human health,' Mr Isdell said. Coke has now enlisted the help of the WWF to find ways to cut back and replenish the 290bn litres of water it uses annually. The company is also working with Greenpeace to develop environmentally friendly beverage coolers and vending machines to cut the hydro-fluorocarbon greenhouse gases released into the atmosphere, as well as considering the agricultural impact of the expansion of its soft drinks portfolio into tea, coffee and juice drinks, which has led it to source ingredients globally. Ms Reiniche says that Coke also aims to convince consumer groups that it is limiting new media marketing to children in order to address concerns that it will use the web instead of television.

Source: Wiggins, J (2007) Coke develops a thirst for sustainability, *Financial Times*, 2 July

Tasks

Working in small groups of three or four students read the above case material, then answer the questions below.

1. According to Dominique Reiniche, the changes Coke envisages are all aimed at developing a more proactive corporate culture. What does this expression mean; is corporate culture the same thing as organisational culture; if not, what is the difference?

2. In your view, what has prompted Coke to embark on the changes it intends to bring about in its culture in the future?

3. To what extent will the changes it envisages require its employees to adopt different values than hitherto; what will these values need to be?

4. To what other things might Coke need to pay attention to bring about these changes?

REVIEW AND DISCUSSION QUESTIONS

1. Using Schien's (1992) conceptualisation of culture as a layered phenomenon that exists at three levels, analyse the culture of an organisation of your own choice and state what you perceive to be its:
   - basic assumptions
   - values and beliefs that reflect these basic assumptions
   - artifacts and creations that reflect its assumptions and value system.

2. Critically evaluate the idea that a strong culture results in commercial success for an organisation.

3. Describe the assumptions of the 'key variable' (application) and 'root metaphor' conceptualisations of organisational culture and distinguish between the ways in which these two schools view the role of culture in an organisation.

4. In outline, describe a four-stage process that could be used to try to change the culture of an organisation and some of the associated techniques that might be used in these stages.

5. Define organisational climate and compare and contrast culture and climate as:
   - theoretical constructs
   - organisational phenomena
   - constructs that have utility for managers in organisations.

TOPIC 3

DIFFERING APPROACHES TO NATIONAL CULTURE

Chapter 3

Determinants of Culture

Culture is an integral part of all human societies. With the advent of globalization, the notion of culture has taken on a broader meaning and has come to be an important element of organizations. These two aspects of culture will be developed in this chapter.

Concept 3.1 will explore the notion of culture in society, while Concept 3.2 will consider the influence of culture on socio-economic realities such as the management of companies.

Learning outcomes

After reading this chapter, you will gain an understanding of:

- The concept of culture and the role of norms and values in determining culture.
- The relationship between culture, organizations and management.
- The concept of culture at various levels, both national and organizational.

Concept 3.1 Facets of culture

According to Fleury (2002), a society is an organized group of individuals who share functional relations. The complexity of present-day societies is increasing the roles for an individual and is, at the same time, diversifying the ways these roles can be interpreted. These roles are determined by culture. Each society defines its own norms and the ways in which they are realized. It can therefore be said that culture is a structure that gives form to behaviour and fixes the framework of exchanges between the people of this group. The function of culture is integration, adaptation, communication and expression. Societies are organized politically into nations, but within this national unity subcultures may exist with specific cultural characteristics. These groups use the society in which they are embedded as their framework of reference, and share their nationality, language and institutions, while being delineated by their socio-economic, historic or geographic characteristics.

What does culture really mean?

One can never use the word 'culture' without being obliged to give a range of definitions that contradict each other! Even if this term had only one meaning, irrespective of whether it was aesthetic, philosophical, national, organizational or managerial, it would only be a form of individual or collective representation. Genelot (1998: 195) stresses that 'men are products of their culture: their representations, their visions of what is good and what is wrong, their behaviour at work, their concepts of organizations are the fruit of the representations carried by their ancestors'. Can one therefore state that a change of culture would only be a change in representations? Anthropologists, sociologists, historians and philosophers have all put forward their definitions, but none of them seems to be sufficiently precise or inclusive.

Rather than look for an exact definition, it may be preferable to look for a meaning that is blurred but which somehow addresses the rather abstract idea of culture. Hofstede (1980: 25) refers to culture as 'the collective programming of the mind which distinguishes the members of one human group from another'. When elaborating on his definition, he says: 'Culture, in this sense, includes systems of values; and values are among the building blocks of culture.' This definition is frequently referred to in cross-cultural literature, probably because it is blurry enough to encompass other definitions, but sharp enough to reflect key elements of a culture.

Consider the implications of Hofstede's definition. Collective programming of the mind implies that members of a group are programmed by that group to perceive the world in a certain way, themselves and others included. In other words, the group shares meanings that hold them together. Furthermore, this definition implies that the group's culture is somehow learned rather than being innate. It is passed down from generation to generation and is the basis of the socialization process in childhood when the norms of behaviour and the values on which these norms are based are learned. Finally, culture is to be seen as relative: no cultural group is 'better' in any absolute sense. There is no cultural standard whereby one group's perception of the world is intrinsically superior to another's.

The building blocks referred to earlier need to be examined more closely: the values that cultural groupings share and the resulting norms of behaviour.

Norms and values

Each culture can be seen as having three layers. The *first*, outer layer is the 'behavioural' or 'explicit' level. It is what you notice immediately when you go abroad for the first time: the language, the food, the architecture, the houses, the buildings and so on. But it is also the communication style: Latin cultures, for example, use exuberant body language and facial expressions. Other, less exuberant cultures, such as those in Nordic Europe consider this sort of behaviour to be 'over the top', but it is really just a matter of comparing the communication styles of one culture with those of another.

The *second* layer contains the 'norms and values'. Every culture has its own system of norms and values. Together, these form the national characteristics of a culture, and act as its framework of reference. Although norms and values are generally presented as a unit, a distinction must be made between the two. Norms are the rules of a society, determining what is good or bad with regard to behaviour. People are, however, allowed a certain individual freedom of choice between what 'you should always do' and what 'you should never do'. Norms are the written and unwritten rules of a society. Values are what is considered important or unimportant, beautiful or not beautiful, right or wrong. A value is something experienced inwardly and which is not up for discussion. The preference or aversion it contains is taken for granted by its bearers.

The *third* and innermost layer, and which lies at the core of 'culture' contains its assumptions and beliefs. These are difficult to describe or explain. When you are asked to justify why you do this or say that, the answer is often: 'I don't know.' Why, for example, do people eat with a knife and fork or with chopsticks? Well, that's the way people eat . . .

The system of values and norms not only varies from culture to culture, but also from one part of a society to another. Not every individual 'operates' from the same basis, nor do subcultures within a society. Moreover, a culture is never static, because norms and values are always changing. However, since every culture is so deep-rooted, the changes are never sudden or extreme and a certain constancy is maintained.

Sociologists who have compared the value systems of countries in terms of the way in which norms and values have developed in society, have concluded that there are four categories (Ruano-Borbalan, 2002: 339):

1. Traditional society, in which religion plays an important role . . . large families are encouraged, conformity is rewarded and individualism rejected. This is, for example, the case in many Arab countries.

2. Rational society, in which the interests of the individual come first, birth control is encouraged and the authority of the state is recognized. Germany . . . is a typical example.

3. A society in which survival is the primary concern, where the people are not happy and rather intolerant, where equality between the sexes has little chance . . . where materialism is predominant. . . . This is often the situation in ex-communist countries.

4. Post-modern society . . . tolerant and democratic, such as those in Scandinavia and the Netherlands.

Politics and norms and values

The influence of politics on norms and values is obvious when it comes to bringing global unity to humanitarian norms and values. These are formally laid down in the 'Universal Declaration of Human Rights'. In a number of countries, however, politics also has a say in education, dress, manners and many other aspects of daily life. Recent reports from Iran, for example, show the degree of political interference in people's lives there. Students from Iranian universities heavily criticized their highest political leaders and the government's vice squad for persistently prescribing how Iranians should dress, how they should do their hair and how they should enjoy themselves.

Conversely, there are degrees of acceptance with regard to what politicians in each country may or may not do; what constitutes a scandal – and what does not. In Nordic Europe, for example, it is acknowledged that there is corruption in political life now and again, but in no way is it regarded as acceptable. If caught out, a politician must resign. In southern Europe, however, involvement in a corruption scandal does not necessarily mean the end of a politician's career. A politician may be involved for several years in corruption proceedings but stay in his/her post, despite being investigated for embezzlement for example. In Surinam, where corruption is regarded as an unavoidable evil, certain limits are nevertheless placed on wayward behaviour. Anyone who attempts to launch a coup d'état there, for example, will be severely punished.

The freedoms a politician may enjoy in his/her private life are also different according to country. When an affair came to light between a US president and an intern working in the White House, there was a call for him to be impeached because he had lied about his relationship with the intern during a formal investigation. The impeachment process stumbled in the Senate and the president was allowed to complete his term of office. In France, however, sex scandals of this nature do not happen. 'Insiders' may have been aware of the double life being led by their country's president (an illegitimate daughter of his eventually emerged at his funeral) but, at the time, his extramarital relationship was regarded as a private matter. Homosexual politicians may not be accepted in many countries, but in the Netherlands, for example, a country where marriage between homosexuals is allowed by law, their sexual orientation is again regarded as a private matter.

Where a certain degree of economic, political and social integration is taking place between countries, can one talk of a movement towards a shared system of norms and values? Referring to the possibility of European countries sharing such a system, the French philosopher Edgar Morin (1987), declared that the creation of a European culture had nothing to do with dominant basic ideas (such as Christianity, humanism, rationalism, or science). It had to do instead with the opposition between ideas. Put another way, what is important in the forming process of European culture is the meeting of diversity, of opposite poles, the complementarity of ideas. This is what Morin calls 'dialogique': the union of two forms of logic, of two different principles, without their duality being lost. The association of contradictory terms or concepts can form one complex phenomenon. He takes mankind as an example: a human is both entirely determined biologically as well as culturally. This 'dialogique' can be found in every culture, but is particularly intensive within the European culture where there is an enormous amount of interaction and interference within areas to do with values, e.g. religion/rationality, mythical thought/critical thought, and humanism/science.

Cultural assumptions in management

After social norms and values comes the third layer of culture: assumptions. This layer is also referred to by Schein when identifying organizational culture. His work is a useful guide in the examination of cultural assumptions in a managerial context, and offers insights into the question of managing relationships. He defines culture as:

> a set of basic assumptions – shared solutions to universal problems of external adaptation (how to survive) and internal integration (how to stay together) – which have evolved over time and are handed down from one generation to the next.
>
> Schein, 2004: 14

In terms of external adaptation, this means, for example, asking: to what extent does management within a culture assume that it can control nature or to what extent is it controlled by nature? This question is allied to that of the nature of human activity: is doing more important than being, acting more important than reflecting? In terms of internal integration, this means asking a question such as: 'Are humans basically assumed to be good or evil', or trying to determine whether relationships at work are more important than the task itself.

The questions raised by Schein on cultural assumptions of organizations imply that management in an international context has not only to take account of the norms and values of the specific culture of a company, but also of its cultural assumptions.

Concept 3.2 Levels of cultures

According to Schein (1999), a culture starts developing in a context where a group of people have a shared experience. Members of a family, for example, share a life together and develop a certain togetherness through undergoing experiences inside and outside the home. Small groups without blood relations can develop the same closeness through sharing a pastime, a hobby or occupation; the experience they share may be rich enough to allow a culture to be formed.

In a business context, culture can develop at different levels – within a department or at the various ranks of a hierarchy. A company or organization can develop its own culture, provided that it has what Schein calls 'sufficient shared history' (1999). This applies also for a collection of companies within a particular business or sector, or for organizations in, say, the public sector. This collective experience can be related to regions of a country, or regions across countries, or a grouping of nations themselves when they share a common experience, be it language, religion, ethnic origins or a shared historical experience in their development. In this concept we will try to distinguish levels at which cultures develop.

Culture and nation

When cross-cultural matters are under discussion, the terms 'culture' and 'nation' should be carefully distinguished, as Tayeb (2003) makes clear. She takes as an example the Kurds. Although they are a people with a distinctive cultural identity, they nevertheless live in three nation states – Turkey, Iraq and Iran. This is an obvious example of one culture straddling the political boundaries of two or more nation states.

This culture/nation distinction can, as Tayeb points out, have a bearing on the way organizations operate. If 'culture' is defined as a set of historically evolved, learned and shared values, attitudes and meanings, then this has an influence on organizations at both macro and micro level.

At the macro level, the nation, in terms of its laws and economic institutions, must be taken into account by organizations going about their business. They have to consider the measures taken by the state to protect its interests and those of its inhabitants. These can range from specific employment laws and safety legislation to general economic and social policies. These macro level considerations are not only subject to change through political changes in government, but also through the desire of the nation's rulers to share legislation at social and economic level with other nations within some kind of association.

At the micro level, the organization is influenced by cultural elements relating to employer–employee relationships and to behaviour among employees. Those wishing to introduce any changes with a view to improving management effectiveness or increasing productivity must take account of these elements when implementing such changes.

National culture

Although cultural make-up has many facets reflecting experience in life and membership of different groupings at different times in various environments, there is, as Tayeb

(2003: 13) says, 'a constant thread . . . through our lives which makes us distinguishable from others, especially those in other countries: this thread is our national culture'. This national culture may be heterogeneous in nature, but it will contain enough elements which together enable a national culture to be created.

Tayeb (2003) gives a list of these elements and considers their effect at both micro and macro level. She starts with two elements that contribute to the building of a nation and the creation of a national culture:

- the physical environment;
- the history the nation has undergone.

She then refers to 'institutions' that contribute to the establishment of a national culture:

a) *Family*. The basic social unit where 'acculturation' takes place, where the culture of a particular environment is instilled in a human from infancy.

b) *Religion*. Religious beliefs can have a significant effect on a person's view of the world. This does not mean that people need to 'believe', but religion has helped in all sorts of direct and indirect ways to shape the environment in which people live.

c) *Education*. The value system on which education is based and the choices it makes in terms of the curriculum both help in the formation of a culture, particularly where educational institutions are well developed. At the micro level, the teaching approach used and the manner of learning can also affect future learning. This, in turn, can determine the quality and versatility of human resources in the labour market.

d) *Mass communication media*. Tayeb pays particular attention to the effect of recent advances in communication on the development of culture. The ever-increasing presence of mass media has given a new meaning to shared experience: newspapers, magazines, television and radio, 'bring people closer together irrespective of their geographical locations, but also in terms of spreading values, attitudes, tastes, meanings and vocabulary – in short, culture' (Tayeb, 2003: 20). She does not, however, regard this as being a threat to the distinctive cultural characteristics of a nation. Instead, the mass media have created a new common dimension in which people can share experiences if they choose to.

e) *The multinational company*. This is a powerful culture-building institution, whose products and services can influence the way people live, whose operations can affect how and where they work. However, the multinational is also influenced by the preferences at national level with regard to product taste and form and the promotion of its goods and services.

Organizational culture

Edgar Schein (1999) refers to the *power* of culture on account of the extent to which it determines our behaviour individually and collectively. In organizational terms he remarks on how cultural elements affect the way strategy is determined, goals are established and how the organization operates. Furthermore, the key personnel involved are influenced by their own cultural backgrounds and shared experience since these have helped shape their own values and perceptions.

Schein (1990: 111) develops his definition of culture when defining organizational culture:

(a) a pattern of basic assumptions, (b) invented, discovered, or developed by a given group, (c) as it learns to cope with its problems of external adaptation and internal integration, (d) that has worked well enough to be considered valid and, therefore (e) is to be taught to new members as the (f) correct way to perceive, think, and feel in relation to chosen problems.

Drawing on this definition, we can say that organizational culture is the acceptance – in a tacit or formal way – of norms of specific behaviour by the members of an organization.

SPOTLIGHT 3.1

Organizational cross-cultural challenges

Setting up joint ventures between East and West European companies has involved a number of cross-cultural challenges. A study made on joint ventures between the Netherlands, the Slovak Republic and Bulgaria revealed some key problems in the following areas:

1. Mutual support climate:

When it comes, for example, to showing concern for colleagues, as well as offering mutual support and understanding, both in solving work and non-work problems, companies in the Slovak Republic appear to be much less supportive than those in Bulgaria and the Netherlands.

2. Innovative climate:

The degree to which employees consider their organization as being innovative is much higher among the Bulgarians and the Dutch than among the Slovakians. Slovak companies are considered to be less flexible, innovative and market-oriented than their Bulgarian or Dutch equivalents. Moreover, they are seen as less open to (self-)criticism and less likely to take risks.

3. Goal-directed climate:

Bulgarian employees consider their companies to be particularly goal-directed, more so than their Slovak and Dutch counterparts. This is apparent in the way Bulgarian companies set clear goals, carefully measure the performance of the company and its employees, as well as monitor the efficient and effective use of materials.

The main conclusion of the study is that, to ensure the success of a joint venture between East and West European companies, the partners need to establish mutual trust as well as develop respect for their mutual differences.

Source: Extract (adapted) from: Browaeys and Göbbels, 1999: 243-251.

Corporate culture

The term 'corporate culture' takes the question of organizational culture a step further. As Meschi and Roger (1994) point out, if an organization develops into a multinational conglomerate, the culture at headquarters may influence that of subsidiaries abroad. In the same way, a firm involved in a joint venture with a company from another country may well find that the presence of the 'foreign' partners influences the underlying culture of the firm. What evolves over time in terms of 'corporate culture' can have as its basis the 'original' organizational culture, or the national/regional culture – or a combination of the two.

The extent of the influence of corporate culture is disputed among experts in the field. Some regard a clearly defined corporate culture as key to a (multi-)national company's success. Others consider a flexible culture to be the key to success because it can adapt to, and respond more effectively to, a local/national environment.

Although it is useful to know where the countries in question lie on the dimensions of national culture when working with other cultures, there are other factors at play, particularly the culture of the company itself. This is determined not just by external cultural factors such as the national and regional cultures, but also by internal cultural factors. The extent of cultural control, through company goals, manuals, instructions and the presence of long-standing employees, is important.

MINI-CASE 3.1

France Telecom

France is particularly sensitive to workplace suicides after patterns of staff taking their lives at Renault, Peugeot and the electricity giant EDF in recent years. Some argue that the remaining public sector workers at the company are having difficulty adapting to the cut-throat ways of a privatised enterprise. But Gaëlle Urvoas, a CGT Brittany union representative, said, 'It's not change, it's the way it's being handled'.

A sociologist, Monique Crinon, said 'management by stress' was not uniquely French, but part of a new trend across Europe. After interviewing a cross-section of France Télécom and Orange staff, she identified feelings of being undervalued and 'low self-esteem' running from directory inquiries, call-centre staff and sales assistants in mobile phone shops, right up to senior managers. Teams were deliberately broken up to leave workers isolated and feeling like failures in a performance-driven system.

Source: Extract from 'Stress and worker suicides mean the future's not bright at Orange', *The Guardian*, 19 September 2009: 25.

The spate of suicides that has rocked France Telecom since the summer has left its managers with a difficult challenge: how to make the former monopoly a better place to work for its 100,000 staff while protecting its long-term performance in an increasingly competitive market.

Didier Lombard, chief executive, sketched out several ideas yesterday for, as he described it, 'putting the human at the heart of our organisation'.

His proposals include giving more autonomy to local managers, reintroducing the culture of team-working, longer postings, fewer compulsory reassignments, and a choice of jobs for employees whose post is scrapped or office closed.

The job of fleshing out and implementing a 'new social contract' for the company's employees falls to Stéphane Richard, the designated successor to Mr Lombard in 2011, who was put in charge of the company's domestic operations on Monday.

France Telecom's senior executives are – belatedly, critics would say – aware of what is at stake. Their priority is to protect the employees. They must also quell the political furore over the crisis, not least because the operator is still 27 per cent owned by the state. And they must act quickly to prevent damage to the company's operational performance.

'It's a serious issue,' said Gervais Pellissier, chief financial officer. 'By bringing it out into the open and addressing it in the proper way, we should become a better, more effective company.'

> The bigger challenge for leadership is to adapt its management practices to accommodate less productive staff – estimated by one insider at 5,000 to 10,000 people – while maintaining the performance of the rest.
>
> Unions and management agree that the combination of a rigid military command structure inherited from the public sector and personal performance targets taken from US practices has destroyed the sense of collective endeavour.
>
> 'The paradox is that we must re-introduce more individualisation to create the collective,' Mr Lombard says. The company hopes that treating its staff more like real people with different contributions to make will, eventually, make France Telecom a stronger business.
>
> By Ben Hall in Paris
>
> Source: from France Telecom in long haul to raise morale and margins, *Financial Times*, 07/10/2009, p. 21 (Hall B.).
>
> ### Questions
>
> 1. Which factors can you distinguish in this case which relate to national culture and corporate culture?
> 2. Which factors do you consider to have been the most influential in this case?

Professional culture

The nature of the line of business the company is in may have an important influence on the corporate culture as well as the professional culture attached to key positions within the organization. Professional culture is essentially to do with the set of values shared by people working together professionally. Schein (1996: 237) talks of three professional cultures in management. First, there are the 'operators' who are directly involved in production of goods or the provision of services. Second, there are the 'engineers', the people who design and monitor the technology behind the production and/or provision of services. Those who share this culture tend to show a preference for solutions where systems rather than people are involved. Third, there are the 'executives', the senior managers who share tacit assumptions regarding 'the daily realities of their status and role'.

The question of how these professional cultures co-exist within an organization preoccupies many scholars. How do the executives handle the 'operators' and 'engineers'? How best to manage conflict constructively? To what extent is delegation and empowerment desirable? What styles of management are appropriate?

Culture and management

At the basis of all the cultures mentioned lies the individual's culture. It is individuals who ultimately form the culture of an organization. The values they embody as members of an organization are formed partially through the family, social and national environment, and partially through the professional, organizational and corporate culture.

It is up to management to take into account the diversity of people in an organization and to manage their cultural differences. In an international context, however, what does cross-cultural management mean?

Nancy Adler (2002: 11) gives a definition of what cross-cultural management is about:

Cross-cultural management explains the behavior of people in organizations around the world and shows people how to work in organizations with employees and client populations from many different cultures. Cross-cultural management *describes* **organizational behavior within countries and cultures;** *compares* **organizational behavior across countries and cultures: and, perhaps most important, seeks to understand and improve the** *interaction* **of co-workers, managers, executives, clients, suppliers, and alliance partners from countries and cultures around the world.**

The importance of cross-cultural management is evident in a world where all kinds of co-operation between companies in many countries is on the increase. Whether these are mergers, takeovers, partnerships or strategic alliances, they all need to be analysed in cultural terms, not only to determine where benefit can be gained, but also where difficulties may be encountered when companies are working together.

Conclusion

This Chapter has shown how difficult it is to give a definition of the word 'culture'. Apart from the multitude of definitions, culture can also be considered at various levels, the deepest of which, according to Edgar Schein contains 'assumptions'. This level, according to Schein, can also be found in the culture of an organization.

This chapter also shows that the individuals in a group form a culture that can be national, organizational or professional. This implies that cross-cultural management has to take into account all of these contexts, not only within organizations, but also in relations with companies of different countries.

Points for reflection

1. The word 'culture' is used in many ways, such as when people talk about 'national culture', 'organizational culture', 'political culture' or 'youth culture'.

   In which ways do the meanings of culture differ?

2. Managing an organization also involves managing human resources. These resources are not static: employees can move to another position, or leave an organization, or be replaced. Ideally, any newcomers will adapt to the culture of the company or at least respect it.

   Give your comments on the statement given above. Then answer the question: Can a corporate culture be managed? If so, explain what needs to be done for it to be managed. If you believe it cannot be managed, explain why.

Further reading

Schneider, S.C. and Barsoux, J.-L. (2003) *Managing Across Cultures*, Harlow: Pearson Education, FT Prentice Hall. This book develops understanding of how culture influences management practice and also guides teams and organizations as to how to be more effective in international business. Theoretical foundations are linked to practical applications.

References

Adler, N.J. (2002) *International Dimensions of Organizational Behavior*, 4th edn, Ohio: South-Western, Thomson Learning.

Browaeys, M.-J. and Göbbels, M. (1999) 'Impact of national business cultures on East and West joint ventures', in Knapp, K., Kappel, B.E., Eubet Kasper, K. and Salo-Lee, L. (eds), *Meeting the Intercultural Challenge*, Berlin: Verlag Wissenschaft & Praxis: 243-251.

Fleury, J. (2002) *La culture*, Paris: Editions Bréa.

Genelot, D. (1998) *Manager dans la complexité*, 2nd edn, Paris: INSEP Editions.

Hofstede, G. (1980) *Culture's Consequences*, London: Sage.

Meschi, P.-X. and Roger, A. (1994) 'Cultural context and social effectiveness in international joint-ventures', *Management International Review*, 34 (3): 197-215.

Morin, E. (1987) *Penser l'Europe*, Paris: Gallimard.

Ruano-Borbalan, J.-C. (2002) 'Valeurs et cultures: allons-nous devenir post-modernes?', in Journet, N. (ed.), *La culture*, Auxerre: Sciences Humaines Editions: 335-342.

Schein, E.H. (1990) 'Organizational culture', *American Psychologist*, 42 (2): 109-119.

Schein, E.H. (1996) 'Culture: the missing concept in organization studies', in *Administrative Science Quarterly*, 41 (2): 229-240.

Schein, E.H. (1999) *The Corporate Culture Survival Guide*, San Francisco, CA: Jossey-Bass.

Schein, E.H. (2004) *Organizational Culture and Leadership*, 3rd edn, San Francisco: Jossey-Bass.

Schneider, S.C. and Barsoux, J.-L. (2003) *Managing Across Cultures*, Harlow: Pearson Education: FT Prentice Hall.

Tayeb, M. (2003) *International Management*, Harlow: Pearson Education.

Chapter 3 Activities

ACTIVITY 3.1

Defining an organizational culture

Schein's definition of organizational culture, as quoted in Concept 3.2, is as follows:

> (a) a pattern of basic assumptions, (b) invented, discovered, or developed by a given group, (c) as it learns to cope with its problems of external adaptation and internal integration, (d) that has worked well enough to be considered valid and, therefore (e) is to be taught to new members as the (f) correct way to perceive, think, and feel in relation to chosen problems.
>
> Schein, 1990: 111

Using Schein's definitions, do the following tasks.

Task 1

Select an organization you are familiar with (i.e. one where you have worked or where you would like to work). If you have access to the Internet, you could examine the annual report of a company, its mission statement, its directors and possibly the way it is organized, to try to answer the following questions.

1. What are the basic assumptions within the organization?
2. Where do you think these assumptions come from?
3. To what extent could the national culture have an influence on the organizational behaviour of this company?

Examples

- If you look at the website of **Marks & Spencer**, for example (www.marksandspencer.com), you can click on 'The Company' section for the annual report and read through the section on 'Governance'.
- **Shell** is another example. If you look at its corporate website (www.shell.com), you can click on 'About Shell', then 'who we are' to discover the company's vision, values and leadership.

Task 2
Compare your findings with those of your peers.

ACTIVITY 3.2

Foreign influences: Expats force locals to ask who they are

By Nada El Sawy

The UAE is unique in that expatriates constitute more than 80 per cent of the population. As the country continues to grow and accept foreigners at an astounding pace, Emiratis worry that their national identity and culture are at stake. The issue has become so pressing that President Sheikh Khalifa Bin Zayed al-Nahyan declared 2008 UAE national identity year.

'People here have the feeling that we are losing our own country if this double-digit [expatriate percentage of population] growth continues and if the government does not address the problem and address it squarely and urgently,' says Abdulkhaleq Abdulla, a professor of political science at United Arab Emirates University in Al Ain.

Issues such as the demographic imbalance, the disappearance of the Arabic language, competition over jobs, lagging education and a lack of sensitivity towards Emirati cultural and religious values, have been discussed in the past, but are now taking centre stage.

Last month, a two-day forum on national identity took place in Abu Dhabi to debate such issues openly for the first time. The conference, organized by the Ministry of Culture, Youth and Community Development, featured more than 30 high-level government and private-sector speakers.

Participants spoke their minds. Ahmad al-Tayer, chairman of the National Human Resources Development and Employment Authority (Tanmia), said: 'Today, an Emirati student is being taught Islamic studies in English by a Pakistani. This is the state of our nation.'

Meanwhile, Dubai's police chief, Lieutenant General Dahi Khalfan Tamim, warned that there would be serious security issues if demographic balance was not restored. He advocated reducing foreign workers from any single country to a maximum 25 per cent of the population, according to press reports. He also suggested that property ownership be opened mostly to Emiratis and Arabs, and that increased childbearing should be a national strategy.

The UAE is a young country, created in 1971, but it attracted foreigners early on due to its strategic trade location and with the discovery of oil. During the period 1975 to 2004, the population of nationals increased 4.5 times while the expatriate population increased almost tenfold.

'We had this problem before. There were voices that were asking since the mid-70s [about the loss of national identity] when the country started construction,' says Ebtisam al-Katbi, also a professor of political science at UAE University.

Prof al-Katbi says several factors have exacerbated this problem. First, most foreigners coming to the UAE were initially Arab or Muslim, or from similar cultures. Today, more are coming from the west, Russia or the Balkan countries, where the cultural values are markedly different.

'It's not their fault. They come, they are not aware of the people's values, the culture, what should be done and what should not be done,' she says. 'But they have misused their freedom here. I've never seen people who go to work or malls with this kind of dress. I'm not calling for conservative action, but this is still a Muslim country.'

'It's not a matter now of labour. You can limit labour. The problem now is that we are selling properties to expatriates. You cannot limit that,' says Prof al-Katbi. Foreigners should be welcomed on a temporary basis, not as permanent residents, she says. 'We are giving 99 years for those who are buying the properties to stay here. Why 99? Five years is enough.'

Some Emiratis, especially among the younger generation, say that expatriates are a part of the equation. Mishaal al-Gergawi, a 27-year-old, wrote an opinion piece in Abu Dhabi's *The National* headlined: 'If we Emiratis don't adapt, we'll become extinct', warning that there was a need for integration and dialogue between expatriates and locals.

He suggested promoting national culture through such activities as desert camps, traditional dance, fishing and diving trips, and visits to elders. Long-term residency should be open to foreigners who have made a strong contribution to the UAE and, ideally, have familiarized themselves with its values.

Other Emiratis advocate making Arabic the main language for communication, and improving the public education system so Emiratis do not feel the need to attend private international schools.

'We ought to note that we are not opposed to foreign nationalities and not opposed to the English language,' says Bilal al-Bodour, assistant undersecretary at the Ministry of Culture. 'But this must not be instead of our nationality, and our language, and our identity.'

Several initiatives are already in place to help preserve national identity. Watani, a UAE social development programme, works with schools and universities to strengthen Emirati identity among youth. In March, students from more than 20 universities across the UAE participated in a conference on national identity at the University of Sharjah.

Source: FT.com, 15 May 2008 (abridged).

Questions

1. How would you describe the national identity of the UAE. How do they distinguish themselves from other Arab countries?
2. What do you think the inhabitants there need to do to 'preserve their own identity'?

Chapter 4

Dimensions of Culture

This chapter explores the conceptualization of culture in terms of 'dimensions'. These are concepts that allow variations between the attributes of cultures to be quantified. Attention will be given to the reflection of these cultural dimensions in the business environment.

Concept 4.1 will first outline a model of value orientations drawn from social anthropology that has proved to be influential in the development of a dimensional approach to cross-cultural comparisons. It will then summarize the dimensions developed by Geert Hofstede, paying particular attention to the fifth dimension (short-term/long-term orientation). The concept will finally pinpoint some criticisms of Hofstede's model.

Concept 4.2 takes the notion of cultural dimensions a stage further by considering the more recent projection of cultural dimensions developed by the GLOBE project, as well as the methods used in the research to determine values and practices at both organizational and societal level. The concept gives particular attention to GLOBE's findings with regard to the 'Power Distance' dimension. The notion of culture clusters is introduced, using the metaconfiguration proposed by the GLOBE project.

Learning outcomes

After reading this chapter you will:

- Understand the concept of cultural dimensions.
- Be familiar, in particular, with the five-dimensional model developed by Hofstede as well as the culture construct definitions of more recent research by the GLOBE project.
- Be acquainted with criticisms of Hofstede's concept.
- Have some insight into the relationship between societal values and practices and the culture of organizations working within a society.
- Become familiar with the idea of clustering cultures according to their similarities, particularly the metaconfiguration of clusters devised by the GLOBE project.

One important hypothesis underlying much research into culture is the stability of a culture's characteristics. Although cultural groupings all undergo change over time according to the ways they deal with the challenges laid down by their environment, they each remain constant in the sense that they maintain certain notions about the world and attitudes towards their fellow humans.

The characteristics that define each cultural group can offer international managers considerable insights when it comes, for example, to co-operating with companies from other cultural backgrounds. If awareness of cultural differences is consciously raised, then the ability to analyse the effectiveness of employing business policies in differing cultural environments is considerably improved.

A model from social anthropology

Before examining cultural differences in the business context, it is worthwhile considering a comparative model developed in the early 1960s that has been influential in other, more recent models relating to cross-cultural management. Kluckholn and Strodtbeck (1961) devised a model based on responses to questions concerning the human condition. An adapted version of this is given in Table 4.1, together with the possible range of responses.

This model, drawn from the field of social anthropology, suggests that a particular cultural grouping will display a certain orientation to the world in response to questions relating to those given in the table. It does not claim, however, that all individuals within a particular grouping will respond in the same way. Moreover, it does not account for so-called sub-cultural groupings or for the way organizations in a particular cultural environment respond to the questions. Nevertheless, it does enable a comparison to be made along certain dimensions of different cultures. Moreover, the model has proved to be the source of inspiration for many other researchers into cross-cultural matters, including Trompenaars (see Chapter 5) and Hofstede. These value orientations influence not only attitudes to work, but also to other concerns in life. As Diana Robertson (2002) suggests, if a culture has the future as its time focus, then it is likely to put more emphasis on the preservation of the environment for the sake of future generations than a culture that focuses on the past or present.

Table 4.1 Variations in value orientations

Basic questions	Range of responses		
What is the character of human nature?	Good	A mixture of good and evil	Evil
What is man's relationship to nature?	Man dominates	Harmony between man and nature	Nature dominates
What is the time focus of human activity?	Past	Present	Future
What is the modality of human activity?	Spontaneous expression of desires	All-round development of self	Achieving measurable goals
What is the relationship of man to man?	Hierarchical	Collectivist	Individualist

Source: adapted from Kluckholn and Strodtbeck (1961): 11-12.

Concept 4.1 National cultural dimensions in the business context

Hofstede's dimensions

Geert Hofstede's research in the area of culture and management is known worldwide. His theories are not only frequently quoted and applied in cross-cultural research, but also used (often indiscriminately) in prescriptive works on dealing with other cultures. Despite, or maybe because of, its prominence, his work has provoked much criticism from theorists and practitioners alike, as we will see later. Nevertheless, consideration of Hofstede's work is indispensable to any study on culture and management.

Hofstede developed a dimensional approach to cross-cultural comparisons through his pioneering studies into how management is affected by differences between cultural groupings. He conducted extensive studies into national cultural differences, the first being across employees working in subsidiaries of a multinational corporation (IBM) in 64 countries. Hofstede, who had founded and managed the personnel research department of IBM Europe, took a database of scores resulting from attitude surveys among IBM employees worldwide and re-analysed the figures. The surveys had been developed as a management tool to examine issues relating to the work situation (determined beforehand through interviews with personnel). The original respondents in these surveys were matched groups (Hofstede, 1980) in seven occupational categories, five of them being non-managerial and two managerial.

The research set-up, as well as the statistical methods used by Hofstede, was applied by other researchers to other groups, including students in 23 countries, commercial airline pilots in 23 countries and civil service managers in 14 countries. These studies together identified and validated the first four dimensions of national culture differences described in this concept. Hofstede later developed a fifth dimension to account for value orientations that emerged from research carried out from a Chinese perspective.

Hofstede used the results of his research to produce a comparison between cultures on four and eventually five dimensions:

- Power distance (high/low): attitudes to authority, the distance between individuals in a hierarchy.
- Uncertainty avoidance (high/low): the degree of tolerance for uncertainty or instability.
- Individual versus group orientation: independence and interdependence, the loyalty towards oneself and towards a group.
- Masculine versus feminine orientation: importance of work goals (earnings, advancement) compared with personal goals (co-operation, relationships).
- Short-term versus long-term orientation: fostering virtues related to the past and present or virtues related to the future.

It should be stressed that these dimensions form a general model and are not necessarily applicable in specific circumstances. They describe tendencies within a certain cultural grouping; they present orientations adopted by the majority of members of a cultural grouping in normal situations. They do not account for cultural differences in absolute terms but in relative terms.

In the second edition of his publication *Cultures and Organizations* (2005), which he wrote with his son, Hofstede examines differences between cultures not only at society level, but also in terms of the family, education and the workplace. When examining these cultural dimensions this book will focus on the workplace, i.e. the business context.

Low/high power distance

'Power distance' refers to the extent to which members of a culture expect and accept that power is unequally distributed in society. It was developed by Hofstede on the basis of earlier research concerning preferences for power among different cultures and, in particular, on research identifying centralization as a characteristic of organizations (Pugh, 1976).

As the Hofstedes' book says: 'Power and inequality, of course, are fundamental facts of any society and anybody with some international experience will be aware that all societies are unequal, but some are more unequal than others' (Hofstede and Hofstede, 2005: 137). Essentially, this dimension reflects how a culture relates to authority of one form or another. In relational terms, the comparisons made between cultures on this dimension convey the extent to which subordinates are dependent on their bosses. The extremes of this cultural dimension are characterized in Table 4.2.

How subordinates view their superiors depends on a combination of factors, and this combination can vary considerably from one culture to another. In some cultures the status of superiors is important: their position in the hierarchy, their age, their family and their connections. In others, greater importance is attached to a person's competence and experience. In short, it may be that who you are is more important than what you do – or vice versa.

This leads to the question of how subordinates deal with their superiors, regardless of how the latter are chosen. If they show great respect for status and life experience, they may be reluctant to show initiative and prefer to be given instructions instead, which are then accepted without question. If they consider their superior to be more of a first among equals, they will consider that person's judgements, decisions and instructions to be subject to discussion and may even challenge them.

Table 4.2 Extremes of Hofstede's 'power distance' dimension

Low power distance	High power distance
There should be a minimum of inequality since it can exploit others	Inequality is unavoidable and everyone has the place they deserve
If there is a hierarchy in an organization it is only for the sake of convenience	Hierarchy in an organization reflects natural differences
People who are superiors or subordinates are all the same	Superiors or subordinates are different kinds of people
Everyone should enjoy the same privileges; there should be no status symbols	Power-holders are entitled to privileges and status symbols
Subordinates should be consulted	Subordinates should be told what to do
Individuality is to be respected	Authority is to be respected
The manager should be a resourceful democrat	The manager should be a benevolent autocrat

In high power distance cultures, effective managers are essentially benevolent autocrats who are focused on the task. They are inaccessible and enjoy privileges their power gives them. If things go wrong, the subordinates – who are dependent on their superiors – are usually to blame. In low power distance cultures, on the other hand, effective managers are more oriented towards the people in an organization and allow them to participate more in making decisions. The relations between subordinates and superiors are more horizontal than vertical: superiors are accessible and try to make out they are less powerful than they are. If anything goes wrong, the system is more to blame rather than the individuals involved.

Individualism/collectivism

This dimension concerns itself with the relationship between the individual and the group. To what extent are individuals in society autonomous and to what extent are they embedded in the group? This particular construct, apparent in ancient civilizations and to be found at the heart of much philosophical thought about the nature of the state and the individual, continues to be given much attention in many disciplines, particularly sociology, anthropology and psychology. It was Hofstede who subjected this construct to empirical investigation on a large scale and eventually produced a ranking of societies in individualistic/collectivistic terms.

The extremes of this dimension are characterized in Table 4.3.

This dimension is essentially about the importance that a cultural grouping attaches to relationships. Some cultures place more importance on personal relationships rather than the task to be performed or the deal to be completed. These relationships may well be within an extended family, so that blood-ties guarantee trust and loyalty. Relations outside the family need to be built on face-to-face social encounters. Loyalty to those within the circle of relations and friends is considered essential and is rewarded in many ways. Collective achievement is the focus, rather than the attainment of individual goals and careers. Indeed, some form of personal sacrifice may be necessary for the sake of the common good. In individualist cultures, the focus is more on rights and the achievements of the individual. Individuals are expected to achieve their own goals and to do so are willing, if necessary, to undergo contractual obligations. Managers expect employees to fulfil the terms of a contract and vice versa. Close ties may develop between the two, but this does not diminish

Table 4.3 **Extremes of Hofstede's 'collectivist/individualist' dimension**

Collectivist	Individualist
'We' mentality	'I' mentality
Identity is based on one's social group	Identity is based on the individual
Decisions are primarily made according to what is best for the group	Decisions are based primarily on individual needs
Relationships prevail over task	Tasks prevail over relationships
Focus is on belonging to an organization	Focus is on individual initiative and achievement
Values differ according to the group (particularism)	Value standards apply to all (universalism)

the value of the contractual arrangements. Within this sort of environment, competition between individuals is encouraged, thus allowing them to meet their goals and needs, as long as these are in line with those of the organization within which they are working.

Masculinity/femininity

From his initial studies at IBM, Hofstede developed a dimension whereby certain societies could be characterized as being either assertive and competitive (masculine in nature), or more caring and therefore more feminine. Hofstede does stress rather traditional roles of the sexes: masculine values such as achievement and exercise of power are used to characterize cultures along this dimension as are feminine values: caring for others, being less self-centred. Nevertheless, when a culture is examined in terms of the work environment, this dimension allows clear distinctions to be made between cultures in terms of their attitude to work. The characterization of the two extremes of this dimension show how dramatic these distinctions can be (Table 4.4).

Highly masculine cultures see work as a challenge, offering the possibility of high rewards and recognition. The stress is on performance, on competing with others to achieve goals. Highly feminine cultures give more attention to the broader picture, particularly to relationships with others in the workplace. Quality of life is a prime concern, not just in terms of how the work is performed but also in terms of what the work achieves.

This dimension is one that Hofstede (1998: 11) himself characterized as 'taboo' since he saw the 'duality of male versus female' as a problem always under discussion, and answers to which cause wide-ranging discussion. The taboo was greatest, he felt, amongst 'masculine' countries where there was considerable stress on political correctness and concern about sexual harassment. Perhaps the very explicit use of the term masculine/feminine exacerbated matters, as evidenced in the tendency of other researchers exploring the phenomenon to talk of 'gender egalitarianism' (House et al., 2004) or to incorporate features of this dimension into one relating to assertiveness.

Table 4.4 Extremes of the 'masculine/feminine' dimension

Masculinity	Femininity
Distinct gender roles	Fluid gender roles
Men are assertive, women are nurturing	Men and women in nurturing roles
Stress on competition and performance	Stress on co-operation and environmental awareness
Acquisition of wealth	Quality of life
Ambition motivates	Service motivates
Live to work	Work to live
Sympathy for the successful achiever	Sympathy for the unfortunate
Independence ideal	Interdependence ideal
Managers are expected to be decisive and assertive	Managers use intuition and strive for consensus

Uncertainty avoidance

This fourth dimension measures the extent to which people in a certain culture avoid uncertainty. To what extent do they feel threatened by ambiguous, risky situations? To what extent do they prefer predictability in their lives, clearly prescribed rules and procedures in their work? Uncertainty-avoiding cultures perceive life as a battle against anxiety and stress. They may be willing to accept familiar risks but not the danger of the unknown. To that end they tend to resist innovation or anything that deviates from the known. They appreciate authorities who have the 'right' answers, who lay down rules to prevent ambiguities. Cultures with low uncertainty avoidance are not disconcerted by ambiguity, and tolerate differences generally. They perceive that there are not always answers to problems and that laws are not always effective or necessary in dealing with deviation – they may be changed if deemed ineffective.

The two extremes of this dimension are characterized in Table 4.5.

Managers in uncertainty-avoiding cultures would be expected to maintain the rules and regulations of an organization, to have precise answers to questions and to give exact instructions. Managers in cultures with low uncertainty avoidance would be expected to uphold or establish rules only as absolutely necessary (most problems can be resolved without strict rules anyway); managers cannot possibly be the source of all wisdom and may need to draw others into their decision-making who are more competent.

Hofstede's initial four dimensions have had an enormous influence on the development of management theories in many management areas, particularly those focusing on relations between the leader and the led. Two dimensions, power distance and uncertainty avoidance, are particularly important in this respect. As Hofstede and Hofstede themselves say:

> Both dimensions help answer two fundamental questions:
> Who should have the power to decide what?
> What rules or procedures should be followed in order to attain the desired ends?
>
> Hofstede and Hofstede, 2005: 63

Table 4.5 Extremes for Hofstede's 'uncertainty avoidance' dimension

Low uncertainty avoidance	High uncertainty avoidance
Uncertainty is a fact of life: take things as they come	Uncertainty in life is threatening and must be reduced
Deviance is not a threat	Intolerant of deviant persons and ideas
Ambiguity is tolerated	Predictability and clarity are preferable
Readiness to take risks	Concern about security
Toleration of innovation	Resistance to change
The fewer rules there are the better	Formal rules and regulations are necessary
Competition and conflict can be constructive	Consensus is better than conflict
Belief in generalists and common sense	Belief in experts and their knowledge
Hard work as such is not a virtue	There is an inner urge to work hard

Table 4.6 summarizes the influence of the four dimensions on issues of management and business.

Table 4.6 The effect of Hofstede's four dimensions on issues in management and business

Power distance	Low	High
Organizational structure	Relatively flat	Hierarchical pyramid
Status symbols	Relatively unimportant	Very important
Importance of 'face'	Face-saving less important	Face-saving Important
Participative management	Possible	Not possible
Role of manager	Facilitator	Expert
Uncertainty avoidance	**Low**	**High**
Corporate plans	Seen as guidelines	Seen as important to follow
Competition	Seen as advantageous	Seen as damaging
Budgeting systems	Flexible	Inflexible
Control systems	Loose	Tight
Risk	Take	Avoid
Individualism	**Collectivist**	**Individualist**
Decision-making	Group consensus	Individual
Reward systems	Group-based	Individual/Based on merit
Ethics/values	Particularism	Universalism
Organizational concern	Look after employees	Employees look after selves
Masculinity/Femininity	**Masculine**	**Feminine**
Valued rewards	Money, performance	Quality of life
Networking	Important for performance	Important for relationships
Interpersonal focus	Getting the task done	Maintaining relationships
Basis for motivation	Ambition – getting ahead	Service to others

Source: http://homepage.psy.utexas.edu/homepage/class/Psy365M/Merritt/HOFcharts.html, accessed 8 April 2007.

The fifth dimension: short-term versus long-term orientation

The dimensions outlined above were supplemented by this, fifth, dimension. Hofstede (2001) maintains that this dimension was not found in the data used to determine the original dimensions because the questions used in the surveys were designed by Westerners. Only when an investigation was made into values suggested by researchers with what Hofstede calls 'Eastern minds' did this additional dimension come to the fore.

This fifth dimension emerged from a survey, carried out around 1985, among students from 23 countries. This was initiated by Michael Bond and associates who were attempting to measure value orientations from a Chinese perspective. The instrument which they developed – the Chinese Values Survey (CVS) – contained an element called the Confucian dynamism scale, reflecting those values upheld by Confucius and his followers.

Confucius, born in 551 BC in the province of Lu, China, was a political figure, educator and philosopher. He lived during a time when China was divided into small states locked in endless conflicts and power struggles. He spent many years travelling from state to state, speaking for peace and universal love among humankind. His teachings, preserved by his followers, form the basis of subsequent Chinese thought on how the ideal man should live and interact, as well as how society and government should be formed. Humans, Confucius believed, could eventually reach a state of perfectibility through learning from the Chinese past and attain a state of orderliness and peace by adopting the traditional values of their forefathers. It was these forefathers who had a perfect understanding of the order in heaven and on earth: by following their rituals, humans could create within themselves the same wisdom.

The principles of Confucian teaching are summarized by Hofstede (2001: 354) as follows:

1. The stability of society is based on unequal relationships between people.
2. The family is the prototype of all social organizations. A person is not primarily an individual; rather, he or she is a member of a family.
3. Virtuous behaviour towards others consists of not treating others as one would not like to be treated oneself (the Chinese golden rule is negatively phrased!).
4. Virtue with regard to one's tasks in life consists of trying to acquire skills and education, working hard, not spending more than necessary, being patient and persevering.

The fifth dimension from Bond's studies is defined by Hofstede as the short-term versus long-term orientation. Although all the values to be found along the dimension are taken from the teachings of Confucius, those deemed short-term in nature are oriented towards the past and present and are more static; whereas those deemed to be long-term are oriented towards the future and are more dynamic. It should be noted that one end of the dimension is not to be considered better or worse than the other – they are simply orientations towards life.

A *short-term* orientation includes fostering virtues related to past and present, especially respect for tradition, preservation of face and fulfilling social obligations. A *long-term* orientation includes fostering virtues oriented towards the future, especially perseverance and thrift, ordering relationships by status, and having a sense of shame.

In relation to the business context, this dimension can be characterized as in Table 4.7.

In his study of overseas Chinese, Gordon Redding (1990) shows how Confucian dynamism works and how the values in this continuum are reflected in the way the Chinese run their businesses outside China. The companies are owned by the family and usually run by one dominant family member. They are kept small to enable this family control to persist since non-family employees are unlikely to have the necessary loyalty to the enterprise. If such companies decide to co-operate with other companies they do so through a network of personal relations based on (extended) family members, village, clan or ethnic group within the Chinese population. The Confucian virtues of thrift and persistence are

Table 4.7 Hofstede's fifth dimension

Short-term orientation	Long-term orientation
Need for achievement, self-determination	Need for accountability, self-discipline
Loyalty towards others can vary according to the needs of business	Develop and maintain lifelong personal networks
People should be rewarded according to their abilities	Large social and economic differences should not be tolerated
Stress is on short-term profits	Stress is on future market position
Managers and employees are in different camps	Owner-managers and workers share the same aspirations

evident in their cost-conscious approach and in their patient accumulation of wealth. The two virtues are combined in the way the Chinese move their capital round the world to take advantage of low risk and high profitability.

Bond (1988) chose to label these values as Confucian since they generally reflect the teachings of Confucius. Hofstede prefers not to use the Confucian label since, in his view, the majority of the countries where the fifth dimension was found are 'unfamiliar with Confucius's teachings, and anyway, *both* opposing poles of the dimension contain Confucian values' (2001: 315). Confucius nevertheless permeates the values of a number of countries in Asia.

The fifth dimension may be less categorical than Hofstede's original four dimensions, yet it offers insight into values which the latter do not account for.

Criticism of Hofstede's model

The very simplicity of Hofstede's framework of analysis is seductive: he has come up with a minimum number of dimensions to enable cultural observers and analysts to pinpoint features to which they and their readers can relate. The fact that the results of replicated research often reflect those of Hofstede's original research has helped to increase his stature in the field.

However, since the publication in 1980 of his major work, *Culture's Consequences*, Hofstede has been subject to criticism from fellow researchers and from humble mortals who are wrestling with day-to-day problems arising from cross-cultural co-operation in an increasingly global world. As criticism has grown, so has the robustness of Hofstede's reactions to them, aided and abetted by the results of many follow-up research projects and the employment of facts and figures produced by economic institutions to back up his findings. Possibly tired of the occasional but persistent criticism of his work, Hofstede even lists a number of the reservations made about his work in the second edition of *Culture's Consequences* in 2001. These deal with the criticism that using surveys to measure culture is unsuitable, that using nations as units of analysis is not the most appropriate, that using only surveys at one company – IBM – as the basis of his research cannot yield information about entire national cultures. Finally, he responds to the reproach made that culture cannot be boiled down to so few dimensions.

Hofstede counters these criticisms with authority. Surveys are suitable, he maintains, but should not be the only method used. He agrees that nations are not always appropriate units of analysis, but they are the only sort of unit available. When it comes to the criticism concerning the use of data from IBM, he reminds his critics of the detailed and thorough research methods used, the well-matched samples obtained and the correlations with other data, including many replications of his research. As for the reproach made that his five dimensions cannot possibly tell the whole story, his reaction is, basically: if others can find more dimensions that are independent of those he has devised and which can be validated – fine. As he puts it: 'Candidates are welcome to apply' (Hofstede, 2001: 73).

Doubts remain, however, concerning a number of aspects of Hofstede's research in terms of reliability and validity. A number of critics point out that the respondents could not be called representative because they were taken from only one location in each country and from only one company (IBM) and its carefully selected employees. Hofstede, however, considered this to be an advantage to his research because the company is homogeneous in nature, and this allowed a comparison to be made of cultural values across the subsidiaries. By ensuring that respondents to his questionnaires shared one organizational culture as well as one occupational culture (if their responses were matched), Hofstede believed he had been able to isolate nationality:

The only thing that can account for systematic and consistent differences between national groups within such a homogeneous multinational population is nationality itself . . .
Hofstede, 1991: 252

To make the assumption that there is homogeneity within IBM is, for many critics, a questionable one, particularly if, as Hofstede maintains, you can separate its organizational and occupational cultures from the national cultures present. Can one really talk of one organizational culture at IBM? Hofstede had not investigated this question carefully and acknowledged in his later work that organizations could contain different types of organizational culture. Even if the idea is accepted of one organizational culture within IBM, is such a culture, as Hofstede maintains, to do with perceived common practices rather than the values of the employees concerned? (This issue is discussed further in Concept 4.2.) Even if Hofstede has matched the results of the survey at IBM on an occupational basis, can one talk of a homogeneic occupational culture in the company?

McSweeney is one of Hofstede's staunchest critics. Pursuing Hofstede's notion that 'occupational values . . . are learned through socialization at school or university' (Hofstede, 1991: 182), McSweeney wonders whether employees from different nations who share the same occupation can really be said to share uniformity of culture: courses purporting to deliver similar qualifications can differ considerably between countries as well as within a country. As for someone in marketing at IBM, McSweeney (2002: 98) remarks that that person 'was just as likely to have studied zoology, or anthropology, or French, as "marketing" itself'.

As for cultural homogeneity, McSweeney argues that if it is important for there to be a sameness in organizational and occupational terms, then the national culture should display a similar homogeneity. However, the results of the surveys show considerable variation within the samples in each country. Therefore, according to McSweeney, rather than talking of cultural uniformity whereby each inhabitant of a nation embodies the same cultural values, Hofstede can only resort to using cultural average tendencies when comparing nations.

If we therefore add to this criticism the points made concerning the source of Hofstede's data, its representative nature and the questions around the homogeneity of organizational cultures, then McSweeney's words below are particularly pertinent:

> If somehow the average tendency of IBM responses are assumed to be nationally representative then, with equal plausibility, or rather equal implausibility, it must also be assumed that this would be the same as the average tendency in every other company, tennis club, knitting club, political party, massage parlour, socialist party and fascist party within the same country.
>
> McSweeney, 2002: 101

The dimensions Hofstede uses to delineate cultural differences have also undergone many critical reviews. Apart from questioning whether just five dimensions can really encapsulate all the complexities of a national culture, critics cast doubt on the independent nature of each of Hofstede's dimensions: how can we be sure, they argue, that these dimensions do not interact? There is also doubt expressed about the way Hofstede differentiates between cultures on each dimension according to their position on a continuum. Although this position reflects an 'average tendency', it does not account for which situations cause cultures to emphasize one extreme of a continuum rather than the other. McSweeney (2002) takes up this point and refers to the work of scholars who maintain that the opposite ends of any dimension – such as individualism and collectivism – co-exist in all of us. Situations cause one or the other end to come to the fore.

Finally, there are questions about Hofstede's notion that cultures are territorially bound. Even though Hofstede himself acknowledges that this unit of measurement is not perfect, objections continue to be raised about the validity of national cultural profiles, particularly in the light of recent world developments. What is the status of Hong Kong's profile now that it has become part of China? Is it now to be regarded as a subculture within a much larger entity? What about the cultural profile of (former) Yugoslavia? Do all the independent states that once comprised the country now 'deserve' separate full-blown cultural profiles? Then there is the question of Belgium. This very small country has recently received much attention within Europe because of the political tensions there. This is a country where Dutch-speaking Flemings, French-speaking Walloons and German-speaking

SPOTLIGHT 4.1

Fake news

Belgium's public television broadcaster RTBF was in hot water yesterday after running a hoax news show declaring that the powerful Flemish region had declared independence, breaking up the nation. The 30-minute programme, in which a reporter outside the royal palace claimed the king had fled the country, fooled thousands of viewers, who besieged the French-language channel with phone calls.

But Guy Verhofstadt, the (Flemish) prime minister, was unamused, branding the show a bad joke. Some ambassadors were also said to have been fooled, sending news of the 'split' to their home countries. There were even comparisons to Orson Welles' *War of the Worlds* broadcasts. One frustrated official said: 'The frightening thing is that, with all the tension, things like this could become self-fulfilling prophecies.'

Source: from Observer: Fake News, *Financial Times*, 15/12/2006, p. 12.

Belgians live side-by-side with their distinct identities, languages, cultural bodies and regional parliaments, as well as one federal parliament. What is the value of a set of statistics that waters down crucial differences between the 'subcultures' of Belgium and presents itself as a cultural profile of 'Belgium'? What would happen to this cultural profile if Flanders (the Flemish region of Belgium) or Wallonia (the French-speaking region) actually declared independence from the rest of Belgium (see Spotlight 4.1)?

In short, the validity and applicability of Hofstede's model is called into question by a number of critics, not only by scholars, but also by practitioners in the field of cross-cultural management training who feel uneasy when applying Hofstede's dimensions to 'the real world'.

We will return to criticism of Hofstede's work in Chapter 5 when comparing Hofstede's dimensions with those devised by Trompenaars.

Concept 4.2 Cultural dimensions according to GLOBE

Many of Hofstede's findings have been confirmed by those of the Global Leadership and Organizational Behaviour Effectiveness research programme, in short, the GLOBE project. GLOBE is a long-term programme designed to conceptualize, operationalize, test and validate a cross-level integrated theory of the relationship between culture and societal, organizational and leadership effectiveness. The first two phases of the project are described in House et al. (2004).

Dimensions of societal cultural variation

During the first phase of the project, the investigators developed a range of dimensions of societal cultural variation, a number of which have their origins in those identified by Hofstede. The nine dimensions which GLOBE developed are given in the first column of Table 4.8, along with the definition of each. The dimensions were used to examine the practices/values construct at industrial, organizational and societal level. This was done by asking respondents questions as given in the second column of Table 4.8. These questions were first phrased in terms of 'is' and 'are', so that the responses would indicate actual practice, i.e. 'the way we do things'. The same questions were later rephrased using 'should' and put to the respondents at a later stage to enable a response that indicated the value(s) held by each respondent (i.e. 'the ideal way of doing things').

Table 4.9 gives some of the scores on these dimensions for those countries that feature in the follow-up GLOBE publication by Chhokar et al. (2008) entitled *Culture and Leadership Across the World: The GLOBE Book of In-Depth Studies of 25 Societies*. These studies examine the historical, social and economic development of twenty-five countries which took part in GLOBE's extensive research. The chapter featuring India includes Table 4.9 where the scores of the country are compared with the highest and lowest scores from the original list of countries under investigation (as listed in Table 4.10).

One point worth noting from the table is that India's scores in terms of 'As Is' are high for all dimensions except for Gender Egalitarianism and Assertiveness. Another point

Table 4.8 Culture construct definitions and sample questionnaire items

Culture construct definitions	Specific questionnaire item
Power distance: the degree to which members of a collective expect power to be distributed equally	Followers are (should be) expected to obey their leaders without question
Uncertainty avoidance: the extent to which a society, organization, or group relies on social norms, rules and procedures to alleviate the unpredictability of future events	Most people lead (should lead) highly structured lives with few unexpected events
Humane orientation: the degree to which a collective encourages and rewards individuals for being fair, altruistic, generous, caring and kind to others	People are generally (should be generally) very tolerant of mistakes
Collectivism 1 (institutional collectivism): the degree to which organizational and societal institutional practices encourage and reward collective distribution of resources and collective action	Leaders encourage (should encourage) group loyalty even if individual goals suffer
Collectivism 2 (in-group collectivism): the degree to which individuals express pride, loyalty and cohesiveness in their organizations or families	Employees feel (should feel) great loyalty towards this organization
Assertiveness: the degree to which individuals are assertive, confrontational and aggressive in their relationships with others	People are (should be) generally dominant in their relationships with each other
Gender egalitarianism: the degree to which a collective minimizes gender inequality	Boys are encouraged (should be encouraged) more than girls to attain a higher education (scored inversely)
Future orientation: the extent to which individuals engage in future-oriented behaviours such as delaying gratification, planning and investing in the future	More people live (should live) for the present rather than for the future (scored inversely)
Performance orientation: the degree to which a collective encourages and rewards group members for performance improvement and excellence	Students are encouraged (should be encouraged) to strive for continuously improved performance

Source: House et al. (2004): 30.

emerging from this table is the considerable discrepancy between the 'As Is' score and the 'Should Be' score for Power Distance.

Such discrepancies come to the fore in many of GLOBE's findings, as exemplified in the second illustration taken from Chhokar et al. (2008). In Figure 4.1, the scores of societies on one particular dimension, that of Power Distance, are visualized.

The reader will see that all the scores in Table 4.9 show that the 'As is' scores were higher than 'Should Be' scores in all countries. All the societies covered, it appears, want more equality than there actually is. This goes particularly for China. The discrepancy between this society's 'As Is' (5.04) score and its 'Should Be' (3.10) is the highest discrepancy of all the scores for China. Although Chinese managers show themselves to be very tolerant of inequality of power in society, they consider that power should be spread more equally. Chhokar et al. (2008) consider this to be a possible reflection of the two forces – one internal and one external – that are at play in Chinese society. Upholding traditional values entails superiors being held in great respect, which in turn can hold

Table 4.9 Societal Culture 'As Is' and 'Should Be'

Societal Culture 'As Is' and 'Should Be'			
Societal culture 'As Is'	India (Rank)	Highest (Country)	Lowest (Country)
Assertiveness	3.73 (53)	4.80 (Albania)	3.38 (Sweden)
Institutional Collectivism (Collectivism I)	4.38 (25)	5.22 (Sweden)	3.25 (Greece)
In-Group Collectivism (Collectivism II)	5.92 (4)	6.36 (Philippines)	3.53 (Denmark)
Future Orientation	4.19 (15)	5.07 (Singapore)	2.88 (Russia)
Gender Egalitarianism	290 (55)	4.08 (Hungary)	2.50 (South Korea)
Humane Orientation	4.57 (9)	5.23 (Zambia)	3.18 (Germany)
Performance Orientation	4.25 (23)	4.94 (Switzerland)	3.20 (Greece)
Power Distance	5.47 (16)	5.80 (Morocco)	3.89 (Denmark)
Uncertainty Avoidance	4.15 (29)	5.37 (Switzerland)	2.88 (Russia)
Societal culture 'Should Be'	India (Rank)	Highest (Country)	Lowest (Country)
Assertiveness	4.76 (7)	5.56 (Japan)	2.66 (Turkey)
Institutional Collectivism (Collectivism I)	4.71 (32)	5.65 (El Salvador)	3.83 (Georgia)
In-Group Collectivism (Collectivism II)	5.32 (50)	6.52 (El Salvador)	4.94 (Switzerland)
Future Orientation	5.60 (29)	6.20 (Thailand)	4.33 (Denmark)
Gender Egalitarianism	4.51 (36)	5.17 (England)	3.18 (Egypt)
Humane Orientation	5.28 (44)	6.09 (Nigeria)	4.49 (New Zealand)
Performance Orientation	6.05 (26)	6.58 (El Salvador)	4.92 (S. Africa Black Sample)
Power Distance	2.64 (38)	3.65 (S. Africa Black Sample)	2.04 (Colombia)
Uncertainty Avoidance	4.73 (29)	5.61 (Thailand)	3.16 (Switzerland)

Source: Chhokar et al. (2008): 993.

104 Differing Approaches to National Culture

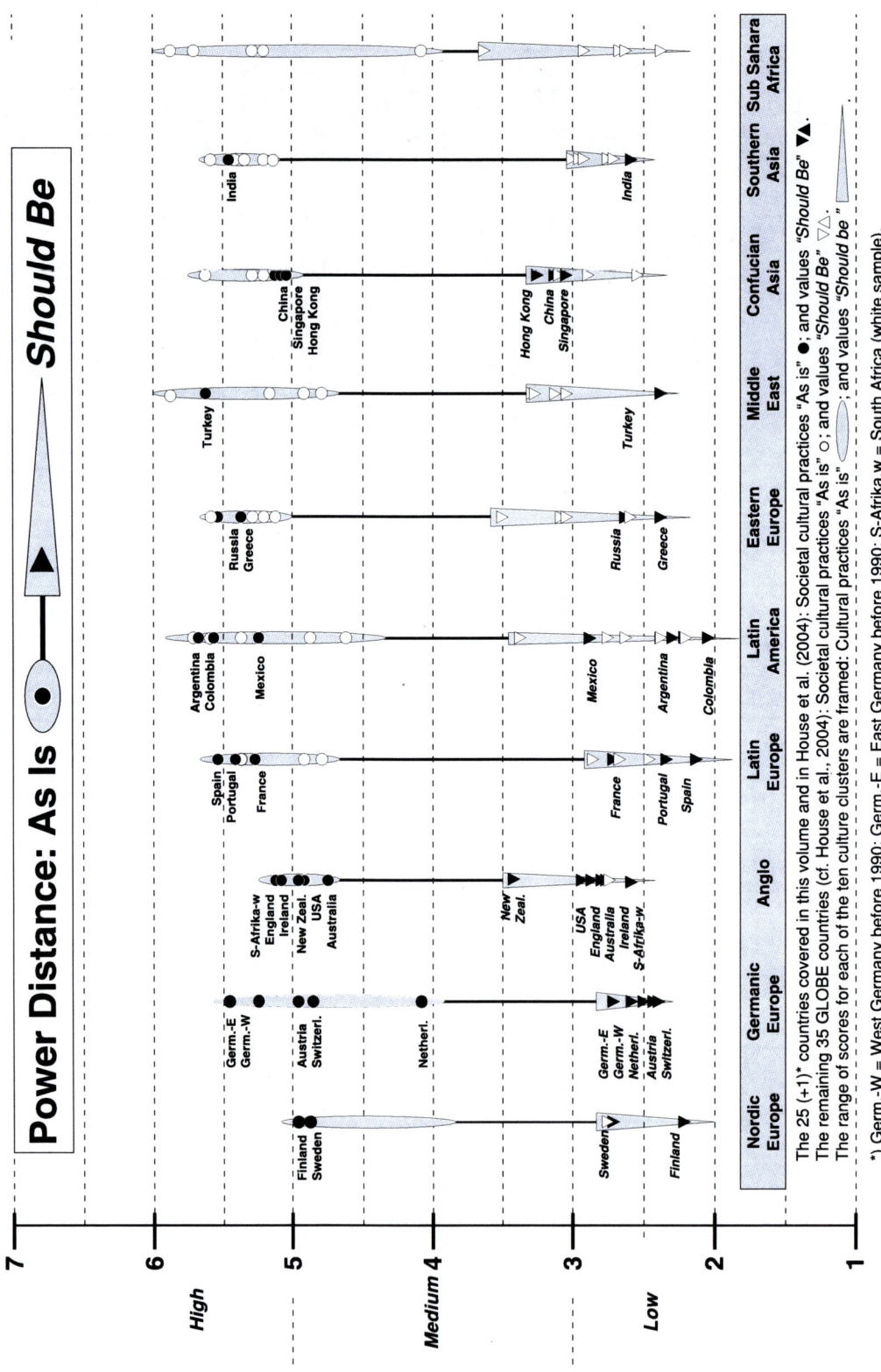

Figure 4.1 GLOBE dimension of societal culture practices ('As Is') and values ('Should Be'): Power Distance

Source: Chhokar et al. (2007): 108.

superiors being held in great respect, which in turn can hold Chinese leaders back in their attempts to promote economic efficiency. Pressures from outside China, on the other hand, are forcing these leaders to become even more competitive, to consider merit rather than superiority of age or position. This question of competing values will be examined further in Concept 10.2 with regard to changing corporate culture.

This particular finding with regard to China reflects those of the GLOBE project generally: societal values and practices had a significant effect on organizational culture on all nine dimensions of organizational cultural practice. This went for all three industrial sectors and all the medium to large companies being investigated.

One reservation concerning GLOBE's findings should be mentioned. Although a large number of respondents were involved in the project, multinational employees were not involved in the surveys. They were excluded in order to ensure that responses came only from representatives of the country in question.

Despite the praise given to the GLOBE project for the scale and thoroughness of its efforts, there has been criticism of the constructs devised, criticism which echoes some of the doubts described earlier concerning Hofstede's model. Even Hofstede (2006) himself is critical of GLOBE's need to use nine dimensions. When re-analysing their scores he found a significant correlation between the dimensions. After using factor analysis, he was able to reduce their number to five.

From dimensions to clusters

When faced with a cornucopia of cultures, it is natural to try to establish some sort of order that allows cultures to be clustered in terms of their similarities. Doing so enables those involved in multicultural operations to gain a perspective, be it a very general one, of similarities and differences between cultures. House et al. (2004) have followed in the footsteps of Ronen and Shenkar (1985) and Hickson and Pugh (2001) by devising a 'metaconfiguration' (Figure 4.2). They have used the findings of the GLOBE project, in

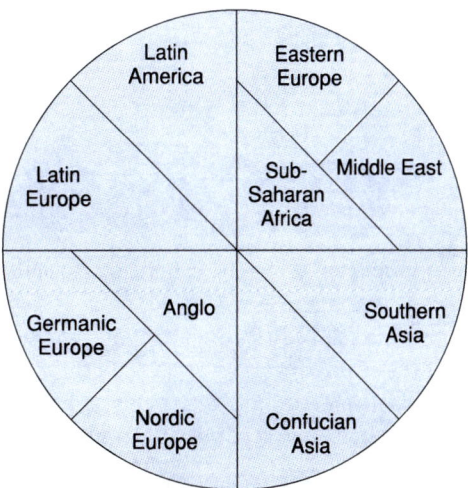

Figure 4.2 **Clusters of cultures**
Source: House et al. (2004): 2001.

Table 4.10 The countries composing each cluster

Anglo	Latin Europe	Nordic Europe	Germanic Europe
Australia Canada England Ireland New Zealand South Africa (White sample) United States	France Israel Italy Portugal Spain Switzerland (French-speaking)	Denmark Finland Sweden	Austria Germany (Former East) Germany (Former West) Netherlands Switzerland (German speaking)
Eastern Europe	**Latin America**	**Sub-Saharan Africa**	**Middle East**
Albania Georgia Greece Hungary Kazakhstan Poland Russia Slovenia	Argentina Bolivia Brazil Colombia Costa Rica Ecuador El Salvador Guatemala Mexico Venezuela	Namibia Nigeria South Africa (Black sample) Zambia Zimbabwe	Egypt Kuwait Morocco Qatar Turkey
Southern Asia	**Confucian Asia**		
India Indonesia Iran Malaysia Philippines Thailand	China Hong Kong Japan Singapore South Korea Taiwan		

Source: Chhokar et al. (2008): 13.

particular the nine dimensions referred to earlier, as well as the results of previous empirical research projects. Religion, languages, geography and ethnicity are considered relevant factors, as are work-related attitudes and values. Historical developments and economic similarities are also seen as playing a crucial role in the clustering. The result is a configuration on an East–West axis, with the clusters arranged according to calculations relating to the average distance in societal culture dimensions The Anglo and Sub-Saharan clusters are placed in the centre since they show mid-level scores on the nine dimensions used. The countries featuring in the clusters are given in Table 4.10.

Conclusion

This chapter has explained the cultural dimensions of Hofstede and the relationship between national cultural values and those of organizational cultures. It has also outlined the many criticisms of Hofstede's research method, particularly the reliability and applicability of the findings. The chapter has also explained how the researchers involved in the GLOBE project have expanded this five-dimension model to eighteen and used a survey method which allows for a better understanding of the relations between organizational practices and social values.

The significance of Hofstede's fifth dimension – short-term and long-term orientation – has also been described. This dimension is of special significance bearing in mind the increasing importance in current business of the relations between the Western countries and those in the East, especially China.

Points for reflection

1. This chapter has described cultural dimensions that can give insight into differences between national cultures.

   What are the advantages and limitations when using these dimensions to describe organizational cultures?

2. Hofstede's cultural dimensions were characterized in this chapter in relation to the business environment.

   Which of these dimensions – and the others referred to in this chapter – do you consider to be most relevant to the study of culture in the business context? Explain your choice.

3. Hofstede supplemented his dimensions with a fifth one arising from research carried out by researchers with 'Eastern minds'.

   What added value does this extra dimension give to measuring the effect of culture in the business context?

4. One criticism of Hofstede's work is that the scores on each dimension reflect only an 'average tendency' of a particular country, and therefore inadequately reflect the wide range of responses given within a country to the survey, particularly from subcultures.

   Look up the profile of your country, as given on the Geert Hofstede website (www.geert-hofstede.com) and consider its analytical value, particularly with regard to any subcultures that you are aware of within your country.

Further reading

Burns, R. (1998) *Doing Business in Asia: A cultural perspective*, Melbourne, Australia: Addison Wesley Longman. This book provides a reference point for Western business people visiting Asian countries. Burns gives assistance in determining the nuances of cultural behaviour, expectations and values, and the effect of these issues on business activities.

Hofstede, G. and Hofstede, G.J. (2005) *Cultures and Organizations: Software of the Mind*, 2nd edn, London: McGraw-Hill. The book describes and analyses Geert Hofstede's research. It has been completely rewritten. His co-author, his son Gert Jan, has hands-on experience teaching the subject to students and practitioners.

McSweeney, B. (2002) 'Hofstede's model of national cultural differences and their consequences: a triumph of faith – a failure of analysis', *Human Relations* 55 (1): 89-118. This article is a detailed and passionate critique of Hofstede's national culture research. McSweeney questions the assumptions underlying Hofstede's research method and findings, and contains many useful references to other critics of Hofstede's work. Hofstede responded to McSweeney in the following article: **Hofstede, G. (2002)** 'Dimensions do not exist: a reply to Brendan McSweeney', *Human Relations* 55 (11): 1355-1361. McSweeney in turn reacted to Hofstede's response in the same edition of the journal: **'The essentials of scholarship: a reply to Geert Hofstede'**, *Human Relations*, 55 (11): 1363-1372.

References

Bond, M.H. (1988) 'Finding dimensions of individual variation in multicultural studies of values: the Rokeach and Chinese value surveys', *Journal of Personality and Social Psychology*, 55 (6): 1009-1115.

Chhokar, J.S., Brodbeck, F.C. and House, R.J. (eds) (2008) *Culture and Leadership Across the World: The GLOBE Book of In-Depth Studies of 25 Societies*, New York, NY: Lawrence Erlbaum Associates.

Hickson, D.J. and Pugh, D.S. (2001) *Management Worldwide*, London: Penguin.

Hofstede, G. (1980) *Culture's Consequences*, 1st edn, Beverly Hills: Sage.

Hofstede, G. (1991) *Cultures and Organizations: Software of the Mind*, London: McGraw-Hill.

Hofstede, G. (1998) *Masculinity and Femininity: The Taboo Dimension of National Cultures*, Thousand Oaks, CA: Sage.

Hofstede, G. (2001) *Culture's Consequences*, 2nd edn, Thousand Oaks, CA: Sage.

Hofstede, G. (2006) 'What did GLOBE really measure? Researchers' minds versus respondents' minds', *Journal of International Business Studies*, 37: 882-896.

Hofstede, G. and Hofstede G.J. (2005) *Cultures and Organizations: Software of the Mind*, 2nd edn, London: McGraw-Hill.

House, R.J., Hanges, P.J., Javidan, M., Dorfman, P.W. and Gupta, V. (eds) (2004) *Leadership, Culture and Organizations: The GLOBE study of 62 societies*, Thousand Oaks, CA: Sage.

Kluckhohn, F. and Strodtbeck, F. (1961) *Variations in Value Orientations*, Evanston, IL: Row, Peterson.

McSweeney, B. (2002) 'Hofstede's model of national cultural differences and their consequences: a triumph of faith – a failure of analysis', *Human Relations*, 55 (1): 89-118.

Pugh, D.S. (1976) 'The "Aston" approach to the study of organizations', in Hofstede, G. and Kassem, M.S. (eds), *European Contributions to Organization Theory*, Assen, The Netherlands: Van Gorcum: 62-78.

Redding, G. (1990) *The Spirit of Chinese Capitalism*, Berlin and New York: Gruyter.

Robertson, D. (2002) 'Business ethics across cultures', in Gannon, M.J. and Newman, K.L. (eds), *Blackwell Handbook of Cross-Cultural Management*, Oxford: Blackwell: Chapter 18.

Ronen, S. and Shenkar, O. (1985) 'Clustering countries on attitudinal dimensions: a review and synthesis', *Academy of Management Review*, 10 (3): 435-454.

Chapter 4 Activities

ACTIVITY 4.1

Masters of collaboration

By Tom Lester

Read the article below and answer the questions

Ants, those masters of collaboration, have made their species some of the most successful on the planet. In contrast, tigers walk alone, and are in grave danger of extinction. The message for business is this: in the modern world, we must collaborate or die.

Too often, however, in many UK companies, successful collaboration – both internal and external – happens by accident rather than design, contrasting vividly with many overseas rivals.

There are good reasons why effective collaboration is growing rapidly. Business operations are becoming steadily more flexible at every level of the organization. Non-core activities are outsourced, and procurement has become a worldwide activity centred on China. Satisfying customers at home demands an unprecedented level of co-operation unimpeded by rigid hierarchies and departmental boundaries.

Flatter organizations depend not on authority but on teamwork for effective action, and networks of individuals may stretch halfway round the globe and connect only electronically. The truly multinational executive, able to work effectively anywhere in the world with any nationality, remains a rare beast, and ordinary staff therefore need to understand and learn from different cultures to achieve the right level of collaboration.

A foreign joint venture or alliance, for example, may be agreed in Mumbai with great enthusiasm at board level, but the hoped-for results will only materialize if operating staff at all levels in Birmingham are ready and able to work with their opposite numbers.

Nationality, religion or corporate culture may be the big hurdle, but it is important to also realize that even within the same organization wider cultural gaps can exist between, say, R&D and finance as between the R&D teams of two partners. Wherever it occurs, the failure to understand can be disastrous. Rover is a tragic example. Back in the 1980s, when shop-floor collaboration in the UK car industry was near zero, Rover nonetheless managed to form a partnership with the Japanese group Honda to fill its vital new model programme.

But the arrogance of the Rover managers and the lack of a learning culture prevented them from obtaining the real benefits of the relationship, according to Professor Lord Bhattacharyya, head of the Warwick Manufacturing Group. Later, in 1992, when BMW bought the Rover business, communication with the German managers was even worse (exacerbated by political infighting on the German side).

Failure was the inevitable and bitter result. No doubt, ex-Rover patriots today will see the somewhat similar collapse of the DaimlerChrysler link as salve for wounded pride. Rather like Rover, DaimlerChrysler was dogged by poor collaboration and infighting, which stemmed in part from national cultural differences and traditions between German and US managers.

The outcome in both cases will have come as no surprise to Professor Geert Hofstede, who 30 years ago pioneered the study of cultural diversity in 56 countries using IBM's worldwide database. He has since been joined by others, notably a fellow Dutchman, Fons Trompenaars, and the American Craig Storti.

Interest in their work is currently reviving after some big companies, including IBM, found that trying to impose a single corporate culture around the globe did not lead to better collaboration.

Two of the five 'cultural dimensions' that Prof Hofstede derived from his database go some way to explaining the difficulties faced by Honda, BMW and Daimler-Benz managers in collaborating with their opposite numbers at Rover and Chrysler respectively.

One is individualism, defined as the degree to which ties between individuals – family as well as business colleagues – are loose or tight. The UK score as assessed by Prof Hofstede is 89 out of a possible 100, indicating a high degree of individualism, exceeded only by the US with 91. Germany is a little above the European average at 67, but Japan scores 46.

On another dimension, uncertainty avoidance – the degree to which individuals feel uncomfortable in unstructured environments – the Japanese score 92, the Germans 65, the Americans 46 and the Brits 35. In real terms, the lack of precise rules and procedures at Longbridge, Rover's main factory, may have made the BMW team uncomfortable from the outset.

The cultural guru's great contribution may lie less in detailed analysis of deeply held cultural attitudes and more in helping companies anticipate and understand behaviour patterns that their foreign managers may display in their home territory, and the different patterns that they display when transferred to the UK.

As immigration grows, and London expands even further as an international financial centre, it becomes an important skill to be able to work effectively with and through executives of widely different backgrounds. Nationality, however, is not the only cause of non-communication, and not even the main cause, points out Kris Wadia, Accenture's executive partner for global sourcing.

'Put five English-speakers in a room to agree a set of tasks, and each will come away with a slightly different perspective,' he says. Add in personal fiefdoms, ancient IT systems and complex and inappropriate organization and reward structures, and effective collaboration will sink rapidly.

Accenture's Mr. Wadia finds that with modern technology, companies can set up the infrastructure and telecommunications links between units relatively easily. What is more difficult and time-consuming are the soft issues, such as training UK managers to work together, and with foreign counterparts, and vice-versa.

The more sophisticated the communications systems, the more room there is for misunderstanding. Ants have no such problems.

Source: adapted from Masters of collaboration *Financial Times*, 29/06/2007, p. 8 (Lester T.).

Questions

1. 'Individualism' and 'Uncertainty Avoidance' are the two dimensions proposed by Hofstede which are mentioned in the text as influential factors in international collaboration. The text gives the 'scores' of the UK, USA, Germany and Japan on these dimensions to illustrate the differences.

    a) Look up the scores of these same countries on the remaining cultural dimensions on www.geert-hofstede.com

    b) How could score differences on these other dimensions also influence collaboration between the four cultures mentioned? Give concrete examples, if possible.

2. The text mentions that within the same organization wider cultural gaps can exist between, say, R&D and finance as between the R&D teams of two partners.

    To what extent can Hofstede's cultural dimensions be used to explain such cultural gaps?

ACTIVITY 4.2

Read the case study and answer the questions below.

Pulling out all the stops

A Canadian packaging company wished to extend its activities in the area of convenience foods. It had pinpointed one particular area where it could supply pizza boxes to half a dozen chains of pizza restaurants which operated home delivery services. These chains relied on local suppliers for their pizza boxes and were unhappy with the products supplied, the irregular delivery and, above all, the cost.

Through intensive online research and consultation with the commercial section of the embassy of the People's Republic of China, the Canadians had managed to find a packaging manufacturer near Shanghai that could provide pizza boxes at a very reasonable price in line with the specifications and quantities required – and deliver them within the deadlines set.

Negotiations by email and phone had taken place and a deal seemed imminent. Before contracts could be signed, however, it was agreed that both the Chinese and Canadians should visit each other's headquarters and meet face-to-face to establish complete confidence in their venture and to settle final details. The Chinese were to visit Canada and the Canadians were to fly to China two weeks later.

The Canadian company decided to pull out all the stops to give their visitors a reception they would never forget. They arranged an elaborate welcome ceremony in a five-star hotel, to be followed by an authentic Chinese dinner. Considerable attention was paid to all the details involved – some of the ingredients for the meal had even been specially imported for the occasion.

Eventually the big day came and the Chinese guests were whisked by limousine to the hotel where they were greeted by the Canadian company's president and management team. Despite the lavish words of praise from the Canadians in front of the hundred guests present, and the bonhomie everyone tried to engender, the Chinese remained reticent and very formal in their behaviour. During the meal the Chinese did not seem to appreciate the effort put into the food they were served. Moreover, they said very little and the attempts by the Canadians to keep the social conversation going eventually ended in silence on both sides. Despite being promised an exotic Chinese floor-show after the dinner, the delegation made their excuses (they were tired after their journey) and quietly retired to their rooms. The Canadians were surprised and disappointed. What had gone wrong?

Questions

1. Why were the Canadian hosts surprised by the behaviour of the Chinese? How do you think the Canadians expected the Chinese to behave?
2. Why do you think the Chinese behaved the way they did?
3. If you had to choose a word to describe Chinese culture, what would that word be?
4. Read the information on the fifth dimension one more time. Try to explain the Chinese author's analysis by using the values described in Concept 2.1.

Chapter 5

Cultural Dimensions and Dilemmas

Figure I.2 in the introduction to Part One mentioned the names of two social scientists, Kluckholn and Strodtbeck. Their book, *Variations in Value Orientations* (1961), has served as a primary source of reference for many researchers into culture and management, including Schein, Adler, Hall, Hofstede and Trompenaars. These researchers developed cultural value orientations when investigating the phenomenon of culture and developed cross-cultural management models for a business context.

Some insight was given in Chapter 4 into the relationship between national cultural values and management. Trompenaars also developed dimensions to measure cultural differences and gain further understanding about cultural diversity in business. What is particularly original about his work is that he presents opposing cultural values in the form of dilemmas.

Concept 5.1 gives an overview of Trompenaars' dimensions and the ensuing dilemmas which a manager may encounter in an intercultural environment. It also highlights some of the differences between Trompenaars' and Hofstede's dimensions.

Concept 5.2 explains the method and the process for reconciling the dilemmas outlined in Concept 5.1.

Learning outcomes

After reading the chapter you should:

- Understand the concept of value orientations.
- Have gained insight into Trompenaars' seven dimensions.
- Have explored some cultural dilemmas in business.
- Have learned how cultural differences can be reconciled.

Concept 5.1 Value orientations and dimensions

The concepts of cultural theory have inspired researchers, particularly those relating culture to management, to examine the effect of the norms and values of a society on the individual.

Parsons, an American sociologist who attempted to integrate all the social sciences into a science of human action, argued in his ground-breaking work, *The Structure of Social Action* (1937), that the action of the individual is totally integrated into a social system.

Individuals passively follow the rules of conduct of the specific society in which they are living. The norms of the society are institutionalized and internalized by the individuals in it through a process of socialization. These norms steer their actions and subordinate individuals to the social order, reducing the uncertainty they experience when interacting. Without this social mechanism, interaction would be much less predictable, the motives and reactions of those involved much less certain.

The value-orientation concept

Kluckholn and Strodtbeck (1961: 4) define value orientations as being complex principles that are the result of interaction between three elements: the cognitive, the affective and the directive. This final element is of particular interest since it orders and conducts human thoughts and actions 'as these relate to the solution of "common human" problems'.

They put forward a classification of the universal components of value orientations, including some intra-cultural variations. To enable this classification to be made, Kluckholn and Strodtbeck (1961: 10) formulate three assumptions:

1. 'There are a limited number of common human problems for which all peoples at all times must find some solution'. This forms the essentially universal nature of value orientations.
2. There are many ways of solving problems.
3. Societies have different preferences when it comes to choosing solutions.

These assumptions allow them to determine five problems common to all human groupings. On the basis of these problems they established the variations in five orientations, which have been integrated into the concept in Chapter 6 dealing with cultural values in management.

To enable a clearer understanding of these value orientations, Kluckholn and Strodtbeck (1961: 11–20) illustrate their definitions with examples, many of which relate to the culture prevailing in the US.

1. *Human nature orientation* (goodness or badness of human nature): 'Some in the United States today incline to the view that human nature is a mixture of Good and Evil. These would say that although control and effort are certainly needed, lapses can be understood and need not always be severely condemned'.
2. *Man–nature orientation* (harmony-with-nature and mastery-over-nature): 'In the conceptualization of the man–nature relationship is that of harmony; there is no real separation of man, nature and supra-nature . . . The mastery-over-nature position is the first-order (that is, the dominant orientation) of most Americans. Natural forces of all kinds are to be overcome and put to the use of human beings'.
3. *Time orientation* (past, present and future): 'Americans place an emphasis upon the future – a future which is anticipated to be bigger and better . . . The ways of the past are not considered good just because they are past, and truly dominant . . . Americans are seldom content with the present. This view results in a high evaluation of change, providing the change does not threaten the existing value order – the American way of life'.
4. *Activity orientation* (being, being-in-becoming and doing): 'The doing orientation is so characteristically the dominant one in American society . . . "Getting things done" and "Let's do something about it" are stock American phrases'.

5. *Relational orientation* (man's relation to other men): 'The Lineal, the Collateral and the Individualistic 'relational' alternatives are analytical concepts for the purpose of making fine distinctions both within and between systems rather than generalizing concepts for the specification of the gross differences between systems'.

The US, with its many ethnic groups, serves as an ideal example to illustrate the degrees of variation in value orientations. These variations result from the presence of subgroups in every society whose behaviour is more or less patterned according to the value orientations of the dominant group. These subgroup variations contribute to the creation of what Kluckhohn and Strodtbeck (1961: 28) call a 'web of variation' in a society.

SPOTLIGHT 5.1

Ubuntu

This term, which refers to the spirit of community in Africa, comes from traditional African culture. It can be translated in several ways, but means essentially 'I am because you are'. It reflects a way of life in which collective responsibility is considered more important than individual concerns. It is the group which ensures the survival of the individual as long as the individual remains loyal to the collective cause. In the many squatter camps in South Africa *ubuntu* means that those in need are helped by others who have the means, without any obligation to give in return.

Trompenaars follows the same line of reasoning as Kluckhohn and Strodtbeck by proposing dimensions based, in particular, on the orientation of societies with regard to their relations with other people, with time and with nature. However, he goes beyond the framework of anthropology and sociology to show how these dimensions also affect the process of managing across cultures.

Trompenaars' seven dimensions

The standpoint of Fons Trompenaars is that each culture has its own specific solutions for universal problems. In his surveys he presented his respondents with a number of dilemmas and asked them to choose one of a number of solutions. In the first edition of his book, *Riding the Waves of Culture* (1993), Trompenaars attempts to show the effects of culture on management by describing different cultural orientations based on academic and field research carried out in several countries. He rejects the notion that there is one 'best way' of doing business and advocates a better understanding of the cultural dilemmas faced by international companies. Furthermore, if there is a large number of products and services on world markets, attention should be given to 'what they mean to the people in each culture' (1993: 3). Trompenaars examines culture within seven dimensions divided into three main categories: people, time and environment. Some of the dimensions produced reflect those of the authors mentioned above – Parsons (1951), Kluckhohn and Strodtbeck – and these are relevant to business.

Five of the seven dimensions of culture as presented by Trompenaars in *Riding the Waves of Culture* are outlined in Table 5.1. This first set of dimensions is based on the five relational orientations borrowed from Parsons which describe 'the ways in which human beings deal with each other' (Trompenaars, 1993: 8).

Table 5.1 Relations to the other people

1. *Universalism versus particularism*: • societal versus personal obligation	*Universalism*: absolute rules apply, irrespective of circumstances and situations *Particularism*: circumstances and relationships are more important considerations than absolutes Example in business: the role of the contract
2. *Individualism versus collectivism (communitarianism)*: • personal versus group goals	*Individualism*: personal welfare and fulfilment *Collectivism*: social concern and altruism Example in business: goals of negotiating and decision-making
3. *Neutral versus affective relationships*: • emotional orientation in relationships	This dimension concerns the contexts and ways that cultures choose to express emotions. Should emotion be exhibited in business relations?
4. *Specific versus diffuse relationships*: • contact versus contract • rapport versus report	*Specific*: company employees are hired in contractually to be part of a system which performs efficiently *Diffuse*: company employees are members of a group working together. Their relations with each other and the organization determine how the company functions
5. *Achievement versus ascription (doing/being)*: • legitimating power and status	In achievement-oriented cultures, business people are evaluated by how well they perform an allocated function. In ascriptive cultures, status is attributed, for example, to older people, those who are of good family or highly qualified

Source: adapted from Trompenaars (1993: 8-11) and his other publications.

Let us have a look at an example, which could be analysed with the dimensions: 'relations to other people'.

MINI-CASE 5.1

Statements of commitment

One of my tasks as financial manager was to implement a customer profitability system at a Swedish company located in Amsterdam. The system required a team of people from different parts of the company to aggregate and analyze information related to customer activities. Under my direction, this team of workers had created all the necessary processes and analyses for the customer profitability model. The new system had already succeeded in helping the company's account managers to derive more profits from their existing customers.

Pleased with the results of my team's customer profitability system, the Swedish head of the branch asked me to ensure that the system remained in place even after I had returned to the US. With this in mind, I wrote a formal document that stated the individual commitments of everyone on the team in terms of the profitability system over the next year. My intention was to have each member of the team individually sign up to these commitments. My Swedish branch head believed that the idea to have all the team members agree to their commitments on paper was an excellent one because he believed that the project might otherwise fall apart after I had left Amsterdam.

> Upon presenting my commitment document to one Dutch manager with whom I had worked closely, I was surprised by his unease when signing the document. He said that having individuals sign a document in this manner was very 'un-Dutch'. However, if I failed to gain some kind of formal commitment to the project, I felt sure that my Swedish manager would be dissatisfied.
>
> Source: adapted from Browaeys and Trompenaars (2000): case 7.

Questions

1. What do you think the financial manager should do to get the team's formal commitment?
2. How can this situation be analysed using Trompenaars' dimensions as given in Table 5.1?

Trompenaars added two dimensions of particular interest to management and business. The dimensions he delineated are to do with time (monochronic/polychronic) and the environment (Table 5.2).

Table 5.2 **Relations to time and the environment**

6. Sequential versus synchronic time (monochronic/polychronic)	*Sequential:* time is tangible and divisible. Only do one activity at a time
	Synchronic: time is flexible and intangible. Appointments are approximate and subject to 'giving time' to significant others
7. Inner versus outer directed • Internal or external control to the environment	*Internal control:* one's personal conviction is the starting point for every action and this may result in conflict with others and resistance to nature
	External control: Sensitive to the environment and seeks harmony. Often flexible attitude, willing to compromise

Source: see Table 5.1.

Although it is important to know the dimensions based on value differences in societies to compare cultures, it is nevertheless necessary for management to define what these dimensions mean in concrete terms, the differing attitudes that result. A useful way of demonstrating these differences is by examining the ways in which dilemmas are approached. Details of these dimensions and the related cultural dilemmas are presented below.

A framework for the new millennium manager

These seven dimensions were essentially the result of Trompenaars' research based on the question 'Where are you coming from?' Are the value-systems of a person predominantly universalistic or particularistic; is that person an individualist or communitarian person? Does the status of that person derive from what (s)he does or who (s)he is? This approach:

> helps to identify and model the source of not only national cultural differences, but related issues of corporate culture as well as dealing with a diverse work force. This has served to help managers structure their real world experiences. The Trompenaars' database of 50,000 managers worldwide continues to be a rich source of social constructs for identifying and explaining and predicting culture clash.
>
> Trompenaars and Woolliams, 2000: 22

Trompenaars and Woolliams (2000: 25–27) developed a framework for the 'millennium manager' by combining these seven dimensions with a range of dilemmas. By using a factor analysis, they reduced the variety of behaviours to seven core competencies that categorize a range of dilemmas. These competencies are defined on the basis of seven dimensions on which the values of diverse cultures vary. The same framework can be used to consider many business dilemmas (Table 5.3). These concepts are abstract but all exhibit bifurcation. Effective behaviours can be defined for each dimension.

Table 5.3 A framework for the 'millennium manager'

1. Universalism-particularism

A high-performing manager recognizes, respects and reconciles allegiance to rule-bound activity or unique circumstances.

In practice, dilemmas are typically between:

- Legal contracts and loose interpretations;
- Emphasis on globalism or localism;
- Human rights or special relationships;
- Low-cost strategies or premium strategy; and
- Extending rules or discovering exceptions.

Thus, effective management lies not in the values of rule-making or exception-finding, but between these. How else can the rules be improved except by noting each exception and revising the rules accordingly? In complementarity, how else can exceptional abilities be developed than by noting the highest defined standards and exceeding them?

To their annoyance, managers promulgate a rule only to discover an exception. A scientist would believe he had failed. A boss would feel defied. A moralist would be against the sinfulness of it all. A 'millennium manager' would learn from it!

2. Individualism-communitarianism (collectivism)

A high-performing manager recognizes, respects and reconciles the individual employee's development, enrichment and fulfilment or the extent to which the corporation and customers should be the beneficiaries of personal efforts.

In practice, dilemmas are typically between:

- Profit or market share strategy;
- Rights or duties;
- Egoism or altruism;
- Responsibility for self or others; and
- Originating ideas or refining useful products.

3. Neutral or affectivity

A high-performing manager recognizes, respects and reconciles the legitimacy of showing or controlling emotions.

Dilemmas can arise from:

- Being detached or enthusiastic;
- Long pauses or frequent interruptions; and
- Being professional or engaged.

4. Specific-diffuse

A high-performing manager recognizes, respects and reconciles the tendency to analyse and break down the field of experience or to synthesize, augment and construct the experience.

Dilemmas can arise from:

- The bottom line or general good will;
- Data and codification or concepts and models;
- Being results-oriented or process-oriented; and
- Facts or relationships.

Table 5.3 (*continued*)

5. Achieved or ascribed status
A high-performing manager recognizes, respects and reconciles why status is conferred on people. Dilemmas can arise from: • Pay for performance or vindication for worth; • Status following success or status preceding success; • Head-hunting or developing in-house; and • Learning at school or learning through life.
6. Sequential or synchronic time
A high-performing manager recognizes, respects and reconciles different meaning and priority given to time passing in sequence or coming around and around. Dilemmas can arise from: • Highly rational, standardized production or just-in-time production; • Keeping to schedule or being easily distracted; and • Winning the race or shortening the course.
7. Inner or outer directed
A high-performing manager recognizes, respects and reconciles whether the locus of control is inside or outside the people involved. For the latter, it is the environment to which people must adapt. Dilemmas can arise from being: • Driven by conscience or responsive to outside influence; • Strategically oriented or fusion-oriented; and • Dauntless entrepreneur or public benefactor.

Source: adapted from Trompenaars and Woolliams (2000): 25-27.

Mini-case 5.2 is a typical example of the cultural dilemma of achievement versus ascription.

MINI-CASE 5.2

In search of status

An English friend of mine had finished her studies in the most famous 'Grande Ecole' of commerce in France. She did both her undergraduate and her MBA studies there and then she was hired by a well-known consulting firm in London.

She worked there for four years and reached the level of senior consultant by the age of thirty-three. She was then given an assignment with an oil company based in Saudi Arabia. Until then she had had no problems in communicating with the client's team-members and had always produced successful results. However, with this particular client, she had enormous difficulties.

She worked as hard as she could to figure out the structure of the company, its problems and possible solutions. Despite her efforts, however, she could feel that her opinions were not being taken seriously, and that senior managers of the client usually tried to avoid discussing issues with her. Moreover, she had difficulty in getting vital information from employees lower down in the hierarchy, so she was unable to come up with the analyses she wanted.

Although she felt she could really help the company with her knowledge and experience, she found it difficult to persuade the client to put her ideas into practice. In fact, the better and more innovative her ideas were, the more difficult it was to get them over to the managers in Saudi Arabia.

Source: adapted from Browaeys and Trompenaars (2000): case 5.

Questions

1. Which particular aspects of status relate to the consultant and to the company for whom she was working?
2. How do you think the consultant can try to improve her situation?

Trompenaars' dimensions versus Hofstede's dimensions

Fons Trompenaars, a compatriot of Geert Hofstede's – but with a French mother – has on several occasions acknowledged his indebtedness to Hofstede. The seven dimensions he has developed may, at first glance, even look as if they are 'more of the same'. However, as this concept has shown, the nature of these dimensions is different and reflects irreconcilable differences in approach between these two Dutch stalwarts. This is very clear from the response which Trompenaars and co-author Charles Hampden-Turner (1997) gave to the review made by Hofstede (1996) of Trompenaars' model of national culture differences.

Having carried out an empirical analysis of Trompenaars' own data, Hofstede (1996) comes to the conclusion that the questionnaire used by Trompenaars is essentially measuring Hofstede's own individualism dimension by using dimensions that are interrelated. Hofstede questions Trompenaars' research method, claiming among other things that the latter had started his research using preconceived notions taken from mid-twentieth century US literature and had not changed these concepts using the database Trompenaars compiled. Hofstede had concluded his review by implying that Trompenaars was less interested in scholarship, more in commerce: 'He tunes his messages to what he thinks the customer likes to hear.'

In their measured response to Hofstede's review, Hampden-Turner and Trompenaars (1997) concede that Hofstede has taught them a lot and that they basically respect the results of his research. They staunchly defend their approach by giving a detailed account of the statistical methods used and which, they say, Hofstede should consider more carefully. They insist that he does not have the right when assessing their results to view his 'independent variables' as sovereign and to claim that other cultural concepts are derived from them. As for the question of 'preconceived notions' and implied lack of rigour, Hampden-Turner and Trompenaars strongly defend the US research literature, rejecting the idea that the many researchers whose work they drew on did no empirical research. If anything, it is continental Europe that is more concerned with 'an excess of rationalism and grand theories'. They then turn to the questions Hofstede himself uses in his questionnaires: these are, they argue, borrowed from (or disguised versions of) questions used in various psychological profile tests used during the 1950s and 1960s in the US, a time when personality research was extremely popular.

As for the dimensions themselves, they consider Hofstede's pursuit of the least number of dimensions to account for observed differences to be 'one dimensional thinking' (1997: 158). Hampden-Turner and Trompenaars see cultures as 'dancing' from one preferred end of a dimension to another when encountering various dilemmas. In that sense, cultures are more like circles with 'preferred arcs joined together' rather than being Hofstede's linear forms where cultures are positioned high or low or in the middle. Faced with dilemmas, they argue, cultures attempt to integrate and reconcile values to come up with a satisfactory response. Their dimensions, they believe, are essentially 'heuristic devices' or speculative formulations that serve as a guide when investigations are being made into 'family resemblances' between cultures when they are faced with dilemmas.

Rather than being 'the perfect model', which Hofstede is still seeking, Hampden-Turner and Trompenaars see theirs as a 'model-to-learn-with'. They can learn from their respondents – and vice-versa. Hofstede's search for perfection has, they maintain, slowed his learning and hindered renewal. Hampden-Turner and Trompenaars say they have moved on, as can be seen in Trompenaars' recent publications, including '*Riding the Whirlwind* (2007)' (see Further reading).

Reconciling dilemmas

The dilemmas outlined in Trompenaars' seven-dimensional model of culture, require some kind of resolution. Hampden-Turner has explored and conceived a methodology which aims to reconcile what appear to be opposing values within each of the dimensions. This will be explained in the next concept of this chapter.

Concept 5.2 Reconciling cultural dilemmas

In his article, 'The practice of reconciliation', Trompenaars (2000: 29–33) gives more consideration to the question of cultural dilemmas in the business context. He proposes a model that can be used to reconcile what appear to be values that conflict with each other:

A model of reconciliation

When businesses cross cultures there are many potential situations in which the reconciliation of differences may be both desirable and necessary. The success of the business being conducted may depend on it. Reconciliation is part of building transcultural competence. There are three essential components of transcultural competence: awareness, respect and reconciling cultural differences.

Especially important are the processes of reconciliation. Without the confidence that reconciliation is possible, awareness can bring pain and frustration can emerge from respect. However, awareness and respect are necessary foundations for reconciling cultural differences. If people lack sufficient awareness of the differences that may exist between cultures, they may easily damage a relationship without intending to do so.

Cultural awareness is understanding states of mind, your own and the person being encountered. You can never be fully informed, since the permutations of options are countless. The seven-dimensional model of culture provides with frames of reference for analyzing ways in which people attribute meaning to the world.

Respect is most effectively developed once people recognize that most cultural differences are in themselves, but they have not recognized most of them. One could say that Westerners think the Japanese are mystics, at times even unreliable. It is difficult to know what they feel or think, they always say 'yes', even in cases where they might feel or think negatively about it. Yet, consider the case where a child has given a nervous and halting performance in her first solo in a school concert. She must go on again after the interval. Might her father not say 'Wonderful, darling' to give her confidence, although he did not actually believe her performance was good?

To sum up, both awareness and respect are necessary steps toward developing transcultural competence. But even their combined powers may not always suffice. People often ask questions such as: 'Why should only we respect and adapt to the other culture? Why don't they respect and adapt to ours?' Another, perhaps more interesting problem is that of mutual empathy (Bennett, 1979). What happens when one person attempts to shift to another culture's perspective when at the same time the other person is trying to do the same thing?

Motorola University recently prepared carefully for a presentation in China. After considerable thought, it was entitled: 'Relationships do not retire.' The gist of the presentation was that Motorola had come to China to stay and help the economy to create wealth. Relationships with Chinese suppliers, sub-contractors and employees would constitute a permanent commitment to building Chinese economic infrastructure and earning hard currency through exports.

The Chinese audiences listened politely to the presentation, but were quiet when invited to ask questions. Finally, one manager put up his hand and said: 'Can you tell us about pay for performance?'

What was happening here is very common. Even as the Americans moved towards the Chinese perspective, the Chinese started to move towards theirs, and the two sides passed each other invisibly, like ships in the night. Remember that the Chinese who turn out for a presentation by a Western company, may already be pro-Western and see Western views as potentially liberating. This dynamic is especially strong when a country is small and poor. When a drug salesman from a US company meets with a health minister from Costa Rica, the former's salary may be ten times the latter's. The temptation to 'sell out' one's own culture is overwhelmingly strong and, of course, such encounters only harden prejudices. 'See, they all want to be like us.'

However, foreign cultures have integrity, which only some of its members will abandon. People who abandon their culture often become weakened and corrupt. Companies need foreigners to be themselves if partnership is to work. It is this very difference that makes the relationship valuable. This is why people need to reconcile differences, to be themselves, but at the same time see and understand how the other's perspectives can help their own.

Once one is aware of one's own mental models and cultural predispositions, and once one can respect and understand that those of another culture are legitimately different, then it becomes possible to reconcile differences. Why do this? Because business people aim to create wealth and value, not just for themselves, but also for those who live in different cultural worlds. People need to share the value of buying, selling, of joint venturing, of working in partnership.

How does reconciliation work?

In essence, the process of reconciliation leads to a dynamic equilibrium between seemingly opposed values, which make up a dilemma. In fact, reconciliation results in the integration of values through synergy. There are many ways of achieving synergy. The first one is *processing*, the activity in which a dilemma is made into two processes. So if the dilemma is central versus decentral it has to be turned into centralizing versus decentralizing. It is easier to reconcile verbs than nouns.

The second approach is called *contextualizing*. Here, one has to decide what is text and what is context. For example, compare the names of two luxury hotels located in Amsterdam:

| Le Meridien | AMSTEL HOTEL |
| Apollo Hotel | InterContinental |

The Apollo Hotel is a member of the Le Meridien hotel group and uses the group's name as its main logo. The Amstel Hotel uses its name in capital letters, and shows its membership of the InterContinental hotels group after its name. Text and context change.

A third option is *sequencing*. You can first centralize and later decentralize. Every process of reconciliation is also a sequence. Finally, the process of *synergizing* is a way to reconcile. Synergizing is best explained by adding the word 'through' between the two opposite orientations. It is the answer to the question: 'How can we increase the quality of our central offerings through better learning from our decentralized operations?'

Reconciliation is preferred over other methods for dealing with cultural differences such as conflict, in which both parties may not benefit. Even compromise has its problems, because in a compromise both parties may still not get what they expected. Reconciliation permits both parties to maintain what is important to them, yet recognize the needs of the other.

Source: adapted from Trompenaars, 2000: 29-33.

The reconciliation process

Marion Estienne (1997) see five stages to the reconciliation process as developed by Trompenaars. These are given in Table 5.4, as well as the methods she proposes for moving from one stage to the next. The first mandatory stage involves the relevant parties showing their commitment to developing their relationship. There then follows a rigorous search for clear difference and similarities among the parties during which dialogue plays a key role. Those involved discuss openly not only the conflict itself but also their relationship.

The skills mentioned in Table 5.4 will be elaborated upon in later chapters, particularly in Part Three, but these go hand-in-hand with knowledge of the cultures involved.

As Estienne (1997) indicates, going through these stages is itself a way of developing skills for global business. Those involved need to maintain a rapport despite all the cultural differences encountered. The focus needs to be not on getting things done, but rather on developing and maintaining a rapport, despite the tensions involved, which eventually enables effective action to be undertaken by the parties involved.

Table 5.4 Framework for the reconciliation of cross-cultural conflict

	STAGES OF THE RECONCILIATION PROCESS	METHOD EMPLOYED TO ARRIVE AT NEXT STAGE
1	Reaffirm our commitment to the ongoing relationship and its benefit to both parties	Think 'win-win' and concentrate on the benefits of collaboration to each culture
2	Recognize where and how we differ	Develop a global mindset Legitimise diversity Acquire knowledge of other cultures Display 'acceptance' when appropriate
3	Continue by searching for similarities	Employ dialogue
4	Synthesize our solutions or create outcomes which utilize the most appropriate elements of the opposing cultural dimensions	Practise creative thinking Demonstrate a willingness to learn Dialogue
5	Review the learning process, capture it, and make available for the future	Practise experience-based learning Articulate what has been seen and known Act on learning at a later stage

Source: Estienne (1997): 17

The reconciliation approach opens the door to a third dimension, unblocks in some way the duality of the dilemma. In an intercultural business context, recourse to reconciliation may well avoid a situation ending in an impasse. Getting to know the cultural framework of reference of one's interlocutors seems to be the best way of adapting to their culture(s) and their way of working. Chapter 6 offers an instrument to assist in this exploration.

Conclusion

This chapter has outlined the cultural dimensions devised by Trompenaars. These allow cultures to be classified according to certain values, as expressed in the way they confront dilemmas. These dimensions reflect the value-orientation concept proposed by Kluckholn and Strodtbeck since they take into account the relations with others, with nature and with the environment. These dimensions serve not only to distinguish national cultures, but also to show how the values they reflect can affect relations in business and management.

The cross-cultural manager has to face dilemmas. Dilemmas are universal, but the way they are resolved is determined culturally. Chapter 5 gives examples to demonstrate this point as well as the means to resolve them through the principle of reconciliation. The approach to dilemmas by means of reconciliation remains an interesting approach, especially since it takes into account the dynamics of cultures, i.e. the interaction between the interlocutors. Rather than the dimensions themselves, it is the model of reconciliation that distinguishes the work of Trompenaars and Hampden-Turner from that of Hofstede.

Points for reflection

1. Many researchers in the area of cross-cultural management refer to authors whose disciplines are in the field of social sciences. These researchers appear to rely more on cultural theory than theories of management.

   Why do you think this is the case?

2. In their response to Hofstede, Trompenaars and Hampden-Turner consider their dimensions to be essentially 'heuristic devices' or speculative formulations that serve as a guide for investigations into 'family resemblances' between cultures when faced with dilemmas. Their perception of dimensions contrasts with what they term the linear nature of Hofstede's dimensions.

   In what other ways do the two sets of dimensions differ? To what extent do they resemble each other?

3. For cultural dilemmas in business, Trompenaars proposes the reconciliation method as a way of dealing with opposing values. If the definition of 'dilemma' is taken as 'a situation that requires a choice between options that are or seem equally unfavourable or mutually exclusive' (www.thefreedictionary.com/dilemma), **to what extent do you believe the reconciliation method can be used to resolve all dilemmas?**

Further reading

Trompenaars, F. (2007) *Riding the Whirlwind*, Oxford: Infinite Ideas Limited. Inspired by the humour and John Cleese's vision of creativity, Trompenaars describes in his book how connecting people (individuals and teams) and organizations in a culture of innovation.

Trompenaars, F. and Hampden-Turner, C. (1997) *Riding the Waves of Culture*, 2nd edn, London: Nicholas Brealey. Fons Trompenaars first published this book in 1993. Additions to the second edition are significantly influenced by Charles Hampden-Turner's way of thinking. The authors added three new chapters: one on methodology for reconciling cultural dilemmas and two where they discuss diversity within, rather than between, countries.

Trompenaars, F. and Woolliams, P. (2003) *Business Across Cultures*, Chichester, England: Capstone. The aim of this book is to provide executives with a cross-cultural perspective on how companies meet the diverse needs of customers, investors and employees.

Website

Trompenaars Hampden-Turner, Culture for Business, www.thtconsulting.com, website of the firm run by Trompenaars and Hampden-Turner. The firm provides consulting, training, coaching and (un)learning services to help leaders and professionals manage and solve their business and culture dilemmas.

References

Bennett, M.-J. (1979) 'Overcoming the golden rule: sympathy and empathy', in Nimmo, D. (ed.), *Communication Yearbook 3*, Austin, TX: International Communication Association.

Browaeys, M.-J. and Trompenaars, F. (eds) (2000) *Case Studies on Cultural Dilemmas*, Breukelen, Netherlands: Nyenrode University Press.

Estienne, M. (1997) 'The art of cross-cultural management: an alternative approach to training and development', *Journal of European Industrial Training*, 20 (1): 14-18.

Hampden-Turner, C. and Trompenaars, F. (1997) 'Response to Geert Hofstede', *International Journal of Intercultural Relations*, 21 (1): 149-159.

Hofstede, G. (1996) 'Riding the waves of commerce: a test of Trompenaars', *International Journal of Intercultural Relations*, 20 (2): 189-198.

Kluckhohn, F. and Strodtbeck, F.L. (1961) *Variations in Value Orientations*, Connecticut: Greenwood.

Parsons, T. (1937) *The Structure of Social Action*, New York, NY: McGraw Hill.

Parsons, T. (1951) *The Social System*, New York, NY: Free Press. Quoted in Trompenaars, F. (1993) *Riding the Waves of Culture*, London: Economist Books, p. 8.

Trompenaars, F. (1993) *Riding the Waves of Culture*, London: Economist Books.

Trompenaars, F. (2000) 'The practice of reconciliation', in Browaeys, M.-J. and Trompenaars F. (eds), *Case Studies on Cultural Dilemmas*, Breukelen, Netherlands: Nyenrode University Press, pp. 29-33.

Trompenaars, F. (2007) *Riding the Whirlwind*, Oxford: The Infinite Ideas.

Trompenaars, F. and Hampden-Turner, C. (1997) *Riding the Waves of Culture*, 2nd edn, London: Nicholas Brealey.

Trompenaars, F. and Woolliams, P. (2000) 'Competency framework for the millennium manager', in Browaeys, M.-J. and Trompenaars, F. (eds), *Case Studies on Cultural Dilemmas*, Breukelen, Netherlands: Nyenrode University Press, pp. 21-28.

Chapter 5 Activities

ACTIVITY 5.1

Individual and group bonus plans: a case for reconciliation

The dilemma below explores the issue of reconciling a cultural dilemma in a business environment (adapted from Trompenaars, 2000: 31–32).

Jeff Mate was the human resources director of an Australian company in household appliances. In the last couple of years, Matehold had internationalized its operations. First, some activities had been transferred to the Mid-West of the USA and some research and development work was being done in the UK because of its excellent education system. Sales were promising, especially in the Pacific Rim markets. A subsidiary had been set up in Japan to develop operations there.

During an international human resources meeting, Jeff raised the question of the need for greater consistency among his colleagues. In the past, the Japanese had worked in Japan and the Americans had worked in the US. Now, however, multicultural teams were slowly being formed, with US, British, Japanese and Australian employees working together. The US HR manager and Jeff proposed an individual incentive system worldwide that would increase the staff's productivity. Mr Kataki from Japan saw big difficulties in implementing the individualized bonus system in the light of the predominantly team-oriented value system of the Japanese. This led to a heated discussion involving all the HR directors present.

In the evening, Jeff was asked to make a decision that would be respected by all.

Question

What would you do if you were in Jeff's position? Choose one of the options given below. Check your answer with your instructor.

1. I would implement the individual incentive programme. After all, everyone responds to individualized monetary rewards. The programme would be based on the success of the Australian employees who produced more effort since they had been recognized for their individual work. And it would improve consistency between the international operations.

2. a) I would recognize that the individual incentive programme alone would not be effective, given the communitarian orientation of some Asian staff.

    b) I would allow the company employees in Asia to choose a group-oriented incentive system in Asia and those working in the more individualistic parts of the world to choose a system based on individual incentives.

3. I would discuss the idea further with the HR staff, asking them to tell me what aspects of the incentive programme they thought would be worthwhile. I would then implement a worldwide programme in which one of the major individual incentives is based on how people support the group.

4. I would introduce a consistent plan worldwide that rewards the group, but which makes the team responsible for looking after individuals either who do not optimally support the group's production goals or who support individual inventiveness.

ACTIVITY 5.2

Read the following case and answer the questions that follow.

Expatriate's first job in Switzerland

Marcus, an American whose parents had been born in India, arrived in Zurich with his Swiss wife. They were both excited about starting a new chapter in their life together. After spending four years in San Diego, they were keen for a change, although Marcus had mixed feelings about job prospects for himself in Switzerland. Four months into their new environment they were elated when Marcus found a challenging new position at Kraft Jacobs Suchard, managing its international assignments programme.

Though this was now a US company (Jacobs Suchard having been acquired three years before) and quite a few expatriates of varying backgrounds worked in the Zurich regional head office where Marcus was posted, there were nevertheless some strong Swiss work attitudes that pervaded the work environment, much to the confusion and chagrin of Marcus.

One area of confusion and some conflict had to do with teamwork and the boundaries of job descriptions. A newcomer to a function or a department, as Marcus was, will have a rather steep learning curve for the first few months on the job. From this perspective, Marcus presumed that his new Swiss colleague Heidi would help with the vast amount of learning that he faced, particularly as there was no formal training for this posting. This was a natural assumption given that this is what he had experienced in various jobs in the US.

However, this was not to be the case in Zurich. Although Heidi did lend some assistance to Marcus (by telling him, for instance, when she normally had lunch), she made it plain that she considered giving any sort of training to Marcus to be beyond her job description. And she stuck to this position adamantly. This left Marcus in a quandary. How could he gain the knowledge he needed to be effective in this new job?

Another point of contention was overtime. Since the Zurich regional head office was in frequent contact with the head office in New York, Zurich staff had to stay later because of the time difference (Zurich is seven hours ahead of New York). During Marcus' interviews for the position, it was made clear that overtime would be required because of this time difference. Marcus did not feel this was unusual for someone in a salaried position, particularly since he had had similar experience dealing with different time zones when working in the US. Heidi, however, did not feel the same way. Her work responsibilities, she felt, ended at 5pm, prompt. Naturally, this left Marcus having to deal most evenings with the less uptight (relatively speaking of course) New Yorkers.

But was this fair? And how could Marcus achieve a more equitable work balance while at the same time build a working relationship with Heidi, whose knowledge he needed to become proficient in his job?

Source: Browaeys and Trompenaars (2000): case 9.

Questions

1. After reading the case, refer to Concept 5.1 and try to identify in which of the seven dimensions you can categorize the dilemma in question. Justify your choice.
2. Using the model of reconciliation, how can Marcus and Heidi resolve the dilemma in order to enable them to work together efficiently and effectively?

Chapter 6

Cultures and Styles of Management

In this chapter cultural values are presented that have been extracted from the dimensions examined in earlier chapters. These values are each characterized in bipolar terms and their influence on everyday business activities discussed.

The cultural values are presented as a model of culture that the reader will be asked to apply in one of Part One's final activities. Therefore, by the end of Part One you will be expected to be able to establish your own cultural profile, as well as to sketch the profiles of (future) business partners and colleagues from other cultures.

Learning outcomes

After reading this chapter you should:

- Gain a clearer appreciation of the effect cultural values have on the way managers work.
- Understand how a number of management practices are shaped according to the cultural preferences of the managers concerned.

Concept 6.1 Management tasks and cultural values

There are many managerial activities performed across all societies on which cultural values have a considerable effect. The activities chosen below will be discussed in the light of cultural values.

Management tasks

The following management tasks and Table 6.1 to 6.8 are based on material in the participant workbook of *Doing Business Internationally* (1992):

1. **Planning**. This has to do with how the goals and objectives of a company or department are established, as well as determining what actions are needed to achieve them.
2. **Organizing**. This is a big responsibility of managers. They need to decide how the work involved is to be divided up and how it is to be co-ordinated. The use of the resources involved also requires careful organization to ensure effectiveness and efficiency.

3. **Staffing.** The task of allocating employees to particular positions within a company is demanding, is hiring suitable employees for particular responsibilities. Consideration must also be given to they show for enabling people to fulfil their potential within the company.
4. **Directing.** This has to do with leading the organization and its employees towards its goals. How do managers relate to the employees, how they do they communicate with them, how do they supervise them?
5. **Controlling.** Monitoring the performance of a company or department is a task for which different cultures may use different systems and approaches. This goes also for the ways used to prevent problems or to resolve them. The differences reflect the relations between managers and employees as well as the way performance is perceived.

The way the above tasks and responsibilities are performed will be examined in the light of cultural values.

The effect of cultural values on management

A number of cultural values have emerged in previous chapters when cultural dimensions were being presented and discussed. Since the terminology used often varied, we have used the value concepts presented so far to compile our own list of cultural value orientations which we judge as having a considerable influence on the way managers perform their activities. This list has been supplemented by other value orientations based on the works of other scholars, Hall in particular, whose ideas on time, space and communication have proved to be especially relevant to management activities.

Figure 6.1 presents the value orientations and characterizes the related values in bipolar terms to clarify the differences. It is intended to be used as a framework of reference when readers are attempting to understand some of the differences they may encounter when doing business internationally and when managing across cultures. This framework will also be used in the Final activity A1.1 of Part One, an activity aimed at developing cross-cultural effectiveness in an international context.

The eight cultural value orientations featured in the model will now be examined in turn.

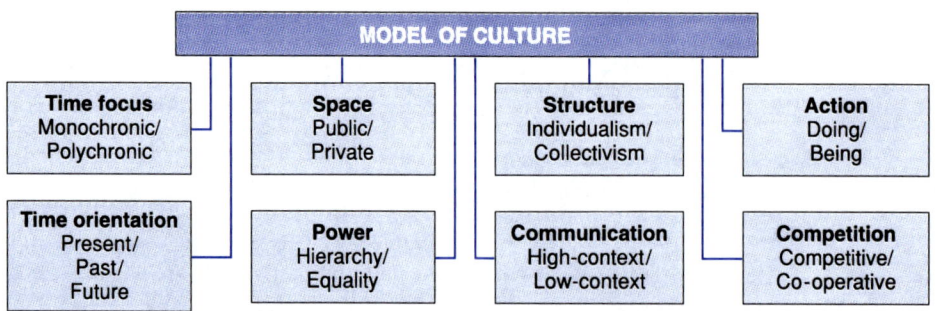

Figure 6.1 A model of culture
Source: adapted from *Doing Business Internationally*, Participant Workbook: 2.3.

1. Time focus (monochronic and polychronic)

Time is related to the rhythm of nature. Different cultures have different perceptions of time according to their environment, history, traditions and general practices. Time, therefore, is one of the fundamentals on which all cultures rest and around which all activities revolve.

Hall and Hall (1990) analyse differences in time systems among cultures. These authors distinguish two prominent time systems of particular relevance to management: monochronic and polychronic. In cultures where a monochronic perception of time prevails, time is experienced and used in a linear way. People tend to do one activity at a time and dislike having to move away from a schedule. They are more focused on information than people, and their relations with others may suffer because they do not fit into the schedule of things to be done. In cultures where polychronic time is preferred, people tend to focus on several tasks and are less dependent on detailed information when performing these tasks. Schedules, if kept, are much more approximate and may be changed at any time. What is more important is involvement with other people – they take priority over schedules. That explains why polychronic cultures may well have problems respecting timings within the working environment.

SPOTLIGHT 6.1

Keeping time

When asked about her experiences working in small multicultural groups at a European business school, an Indian student, Ali, spoke euphorically about the joys of getting to know other nationalities. However, there was one issue which she and her colleagues from the Indian subcontinent and South America found a real challenge, one which often overshadowed the many positive experiences from being exposed to other cultures, and that was punctuality.

Arriving in time for the start of group meetings was still a problem for her, even after several months into the programme. Those who regularly arrived promptly showed a certain understanding during the first few meetings as she and her fellow latecomers walked apologetically into the room, but their goodwill soon turned into frustration. Angry words were spoken and the latecomers promised to be more 'business-like' and to do everything to arrive on time. Their punctuality had improved, Ali admitted: they often arrived late, but no later than five minutes after the offical start of the meeting. This margin of time now seemed to have been accepted by those who always arrived on time.

Outside working hours, however, the punctuality rule didn't seem to apply so rigidly. On the residential campus life was generally chaotic and social events Ali had attended often began well after the official starting-time. Initially, she and the other habitual latecomers had arrived just a few minutes after the start to discover they were the only ones present. The others attending arrived up to thirty minutes late.

The differences in time focus as characterized in Table 6.1 can be seen in the role given to formal meetings. These may be used more to determine action points and deadlines or more as an opportunity to reflect on the company generally and to sound each other out on the way things are going or should be going. Actual decisions may come later through further (informal) consultation.

Cultures can also be categorized according to another aspect of time, namely a culture's orientation towards the past, present and future.

Table 6.1 Characteristics of two attitudes to time

	Monochronic cultures	Polychronic cultures
1. Planning	The focus of activity is more on the task itself and making schedules	The focus of activity is more on relationships when planning
2. Organizing	The approach used is structured, linear and task-focused	The approach is a less structured one, more holistic in nature and people-focused
3. Staffing	Concerns are focused on the shorter term, meeting immediate needs and requirements	The focus is on the longer term, with concern for building relationships over time
4. Directing	The emphasis is on making and following plans, managing the inflow and distribution of detailed information	The emphasis is on being flexible, reacting according to (changed) circumstances, giving priority to people over plans, relying more on the sharing of implicit knowledge and information
5. Controlling	Tendency to use control systems that depend on detailed information and involve strict deadlines	Tendency to use more flexible control systems involving people as well as information

2. Time orientation (past, present and future)

Cultures focused on the past value the upholding of tradition. Changes and plans are made according to whether or not they are in line with the history of the company and the way it usually does things. Those cultures concerned with the present are out for quick results and short-term gain. Those with a view towards the future are more likely to give up short-term gains when there is the prospect of more substantial long-term benefits. Any changes or plans are therefore assessed in the light of expected future benefit.

SPOTLIGHT 6.2

How to plan your time

'Without planning, you'll never have the time for anything. Yes, initially, you may have to spend even more time to make time – but that is a sensible, positive investment. You have to take control of the time at your disposal and decide how you want to spend it. Time is a resource to be husbanded in the same way as you would treat raw materials or finished goods or stock in the business. Time also costs money. So if you have only a finite amount of time, and that time is expensive, it is crucial to plan out how it's going to be spent to most effect. This means clarifying the main purpose of your job.

Ask yourself: what am I here for? Those whose answers identify or match the purpose of the organization for which they work can award themselves several gold stars. Yes. Your purpose is to assist the organization in achieving its objectives, regardless of whether your job function is that of data processing manager, senior welfare officer, sales director or typing pool supervisor. Being organized will help you to achieve those objectives. Having a plan is the first step on the way to that achievement.'

Source: Video Arts (1984) *So You Think You Can Manage?* London: Methuen: 20.

Table 6.2 Time orientation and management skills

	Past orientation	Future orientation
1. Planning	The emphasis is on continuing traditions and building in long-term time frames if the plan is for a change process	The emphasis is on longer-term plans and long-term results
2. Organizing	Organizational decisions are made within the context of the customs of the society. Past goals and precedents guide the process of organizing	Work and resources are divided and co-ordinated to meet longer-range goals and projections for the future
3. Staffing	Management are slower in adapting the criteria by which they select and train employees	Management select and train employees to meet long-term business goals
4. Directing	Tendency to develop vision and mission statements that emphasize the continuation of the company's values and reputation	Tendency to develop vision and statements which focus on achieving long-term benefits
5. Controlling	Tendency to develop performance objectives in keeping with customary goals	Tendency to develop performance objectives in the context of long-term goals

Hall and Hall (1990) emphasize the importance of knowing which parts of the time frame are given prominence in which areas of the world. They see that countries in the Far East, as well as India and Iran, have cultures oriented towards the past. On the American continent, however, they consider the culture of the urban US to be more oriented towards the present and short-term future, while the cultures of Latin America, are both past and present-oriented.

These differences in values (Table 6.2) can be perceived in many activities, particularly when it comes to negotiations. Those who are 'past-oriented' may be more intent on compensating for previous losses or regaining past successes rather than aiming for a resolution that all those involved find acceptable. Plans for the future will tend to be based on past experiences rather than expectations whereby employees are entrusted with responsibility for what happens in the future.

3. Power (hierarchy and equality)

The power value orientation is to do with the extent to which the less powerful members of a society expect and accept that power is distributed unequally. As Mead indicates (1994: 66) it is in this area that a culture shows the extent to which it 'tolerates and fosters pecking orders, and how actively members try to reduce them'.

In some cultures, inequality is a given and no attempt is made to make any compensations on a socio-economic level for intellectual or physical inequalities. In other cultures, inequality is regarded as undesirable, necessitating some form of correction through legal, political and economic means.

At work, the level of power and authority are strictly marked out by cultures oriented to hierarchy. There, the employees do their work according to the directives of their boss. In their eyes, the role of the manager is to allocate tasks and to take decisions. During

Table 6.3 Effects of hierarchy

	Hierarchy	Equality
1. Planning	More autocratic or paternalistic planning is displayed, in which managers make decisions without consulting employees	Employees may implement the plan in the way they believe is the most appropriate. More participative planning is displayed
2. Organizing	The organizational structure is tightly controlled. Authority and responsibility are centralized	The organizational structure encourages individual autonomy. Authority is decentralized to the lowest possible level
3. Staffing	Subordinates expect bosses to take the initiative to train, develop and promote them	Work relationships should not be strictly prescribed in terms of appropriate/inappropriate behaviours and roles
4. Directing	Leaders are expected to behave in ways that reinforce their importance. Employees like being closely supervised and feel comfortable with a directive supervisor	Managers exhibit participative or consultative styles. In boss-subordinate communications, employees are not afraid to disagree with their managers
5. Controlling	Employees prefer the personal control of superiors over impersonal control systems	Subordinates tend to like working with their bosses to develop, implement, monitor and alter performance objectives

negotiations, title, status and formal position have less influence in cultures oriented towards equality. There, the hierarchy exists essentially to facilitate the relations between the people in an organization. Managers see their role as more participative than directive. They are more likely to consult employees before taking decisions (Table 6.3).

In companies oriented towards equality there will be more informal structures based on expertise or focused on certain projects. However, hierarchy may still be there below the surface. When risks have to be taken or when there is a budgetary crisis, those with formal authority may well re-assert their power. An organization with a formal hierarchy that adopts certain features of equality in the way it is run will always feel the tension between control and empowerment.

SPOTLIGHT 6.3

Culture and airline safety

The controversial Canadian journalist, Malcolm Gladwell, dedicates a chapter of his recent book 'Outliers' (2008) to an examination of the role of culture in air crashes. He focuses in particular on one crash involving Colombian pilots and another involving pilots from South Korea. He maintains that, apart from the weather conditions and fatigue, the pilots in question were struggling with a cultural legacy: the hierarchical relationship between the crew members. In both cases, the subordinates had to be deferential towards the captain and felt unable to warn him that the plane was about to crash. Planes such as those built by Boeing and Airbus, Gladwell argues, must be flown by two equals because of their complex nature.

4. Competition (Competitive and co-operative)

Management may well encourage competition in an organization, particularly where the environment is that of a 'free market'. It encourages employees to take responsibility for the organization's survival and can be crucial in stimulating innovation and developing markets. When competitiveness is valued, the culture is focused on acquiring wealth, performing well and achieving ambitions. The success of a project is determined only by the profit it makes. In other cultures, however, job satisfaction has less to do with making money and more to do with working in a pleasant environment. Here, competition is not so highly valued and not considered to be the main purpose of business. Instead, co-operation is preferred, with the stress on the quality of life, relationships and consensus (Table 6.4).

Table 6.4 Co-operation and competition

	Competitive	Co-operative
1. Planning	The emphasis is on speed and task performance when implementing plans	Emphasis is on maintaining relationships in plan implementation
2. Organizing	Individual achievement is allowed and encouraged in organizing the work. Managers have more of a leadership role	Group integration is permitted, together with maintenance of a positive working environment and convenient schedules. Managers have more of a facilitating role
3. Staffing	Employees are selected on their ability to act independently	Employees are selected for their ability to work well in groups
4. Directing	The leader's role is to track and reward achievement. The stress involved in the work is generally higher	The leader's role is to facilitate mutually beneficial relationships
5. Controlling	Systems that are predominantly performance-based are preferred	Task performance is recognized as a standard for success; however, other standards are also considered important, including team effectiveness

SPOTLIGHT 6.4

Co-operating competitively

Despite the fierce competition between carmakers, there are many examples where rivals decide to work together to promote their individual interests. Autolatina SA is one such example – a joint venture set up in the 1980s by Ford and Volkswagen in Brazil and Argentina.

According to Yoshino and Rangan (1995), the creation of Autolatina allowed the two companies to address the difficulties of doing business in a small, fragmented market, but one which both considered to have considerable potential growth.

The two companies shared design and marketing facilities but still marketed their cars separately. The co-operation lasted for eight years until 1994 when Brazil opened up its car market to foreign car importers. Differing views on how to deal with Autolatina's new competitors led to the joint venture being dissolved.

A company operating in a competitive, dynamic market, but which is keen to maintain or develop co-operation among its staff, will experience a tension between opposing values similar to that felt during other management activities mentioned earlier. Nevertheless, the company will wish to promote creativity among its employees through competition while, at the same time, encouraging co-operation between its employees to ensure effective running of the organization.

5. Action (activity: doing and being)

Kluckholn and Strodtbeck (1961) place 'activity' in their value orientation system because they consider this to be one of the universal human problems. They see every method of human expression as resulting in some form of activity (not in the active or passive sense) which, in turn, shows a preference towards a 'being' or 'doing' orientation (Table 6.5).

If the orientation is towards being, then this is 'a spontaneous expression of what is conceived to be "given" in the human personality'. The 'doing' orientation, on the other hand, prefers 'a kind of activity which results in accomplishments that are measurable by standards conceived to be external to the acting individual'.

The stress in 'doing' cultures is placed on action and achieving personal goals. Prime motivators are recognition of achievement and promotion. In 'being' cultures, the stress is placed on working for the moment and living the experience rather than achievement itself. The prime motivator is the promise of future rewards while maintaining social harmony.

Table 6.5 Two approaches to 'action'

	Doing cultures	Being cultures
1. Planning	Tends to be done by developing measurable, time-framed action steps	Tends to be done with a strong focus on the vision or ideal a company wishes to attain
2. Organizing	Involves developing action-oriented documentation for project management in which task responsibilities are clearly spelled out	Based more on the assumption that implementation is not so much dependent on action steps as on common vision and personal trust
3. Staffing	Account is not necessarily taken of a person's worth beyond his or her ability to carry out organizational tasks	Career development is usually based not only on performance but also on other standards, such as personal or social criteria
4. Directing	Managers are considered to be effective if they have the necessary expertise and competence	Managers are considered to be effective if their personal philosophy, values and style are seen as compatible
5. Controlling	The focus is not only on the tasks to be done, but also on the ways in which they are done. Management of performance is carried out systematically	The focus is less on efficiency and more on effectiveness and adaptability. Management of performance measurement tends to be less systematic

> **SPOTLIGHT 6.5**
>
> ### The meeting
>
> The contrast between these two types of culture can come clearly to the fore when decisions are being taken during meetings. In a 'being' culture, the status of the 'boss' is unquestioned: it is he who makes the decision. In a 'doing' culture, everybody attending the meeting has a role to play, and these roles can change according to the type of decision, the expertise and experience available. The 'boss' may take the final decision on the basis of the information and analysis emerging during the meeting, or may even delegate the decision to those he considers more competent.

6. Space (private and public)

One aspect of space orientation relates to what is to be regarded as private and public space (Table 6.6). In some cultures, a house, car or refrigerator is not open to public view, in others some or all of these are. Another aspect relates to the invisible boundary around every person, a 'comfort zone'. If this zone is encroached upon, people feel uneasy or even under threat. In some cultures, this zone is much narrower than in others. The proximity of people in conversation, for example, may be much closer in one culture than in another.

This concept of space can be seen in terms of personality, as Hoecklin (1995: 44) notes when reviewing Trompenaars' dimension of 'specific versus diffuse relationships':

> Every individual has various levels to their personality, from a more public level to the inner, more private level. However, there can be cultural differences in the relative size of people's public and private 'spaces' and also in the degree to which they feel comfortable sharing those parts of their personality with other people.

Table 6.6 The influence of personal space at work

	Private	Public
1. Planning	Tendency to use more individualistic or systematic forms of planning	Public space cultures tend to use more group-oriented or authoritative forms of planning
2. Organizing	The approaches used tend to centre on tasks	The approaches used tend to be more centred on relationships
3. Staffing	The information about how staff are to be employed is more explicit	The information about how staff are to be employed is more implicit
4. Directing	Managers and employees do not share the same office	The location or size of the place where an employee works does not necessarily reflect that person's rank in the company
5. Controlling	Since managers are separated spatially from their employees, they need to use more explicit measures of performance	Managers can use more informal checks on performance

> **SPOTLIGHT 6.6**
>
> **Private business**
>
> A European manager may find himself getting invited by his Chinese business partner to the latter's home, his private space. By doing so, the Chinese is hoping to get to know his partner well with a view to establishing a close relationship. This can prove to be an important basis for (more) business deals.

In cultures that are more specific in nature, there are large public spaces or spheres where personal matters are openly discussed, where family worries and individual failings are revealed for all to comment on. Private spheres, however, are very small and not easily penetrated.

In more diffuse cultures, public spaces are smaller and more formal, access to which is not easy for strangers. However, once a member of a diffuse culture accepts someone, then that person will be given access to a larger private sphere.

7. Communication (high-context and low-context)

When investigating communication between different cultures, Hall introduced the concept of context and described the role it plays in the communication process (Table 6.7). Context relates to the framework, background and surrounding circumstances in which communication or an event takes place. He distinguishes between high-context and low-context messages:

Table 6.7 Communication and context

	Low-context	High-context
1. Planning	Low-context cultures develop plans that are explicit, detailed, quantifiable and information-based	High-context cultures develop plans that are more implicit and less detailed in terms of instructions
2. Organizing	Task-responsibility guidelines are explicit: they are detailed and understood through verbal or written instruction	Job descriptions and responsibilities are implicit and understood according to the context
3. Staffing	Detailed contracts of employment and explicit performance appraisals	The criteria and methods for recruitment, selection, pay and firing are not explicit, nor is the appraisal process
4. Directing	Managers get work done through others by outlining specific goals and ways to achieve them. Communication is explicit and conflict is depersonalized	In high-context cultures, managers get work done through others by giving attention to relationships and group processes. Conflicts must be resolved before work can progress
5. Controlling	Control is more task-driven in accordance with monitoring and control procedures used to ensure performance objectives	Control is more process-driven. Information regarding the various aspects of control is embedded in the cultural context

> A high context (HC) communication or message is one in which most of the information is already in the person, while very little is in the coded, explicit, transmitted part of the message. A low context communication (LC) is just the opposite; i.e., the mass of the information is vested in the explicit code.
>
> Hall and Hall, 1990: 6

When applying this concept to cultures, he sees the US as a low-context country, because the messages conveyed generally, and in business in particular, are usually clear and explicit. Japan, however, is a high context country, where the most important part of any information is 'hidden' in the text; the situation in which the communication takes place carries most of the information.

SPOTLIGHT 6.7

The office

To illustrate the contrast between the two ends of this context spectrum, Hall and Hall (1990) describe a typical routine in a US office and compare it with one in a French or Japanese office. When an American company director is in his office, he has to work through a stream of pre-arranged appointments, with visitors usually entering the office one at a time. The information needed to do the job comes from a small group of people seen through the day as well as from memos and reports he reads. The flow of information is controlled by supervisors and assistants. According to Hall and Hall (1990), the equivalent office day in a high-context country such as France or Japan is very different. People are constantly entering and leaving the office, both requesting and passing information on. The organization itself is dependent on the collection and distribution of information so that everyone in the business knows about every aspect and who is the best informed about which subjects.

Although Hall does not rank countries in terms of their degree of LC or HC, Figure 6.2 reflects the qualitative insights of Hall himself as well as of other scholars in cross-cultural communication as to where certain countries lie on the context dimension. At one end

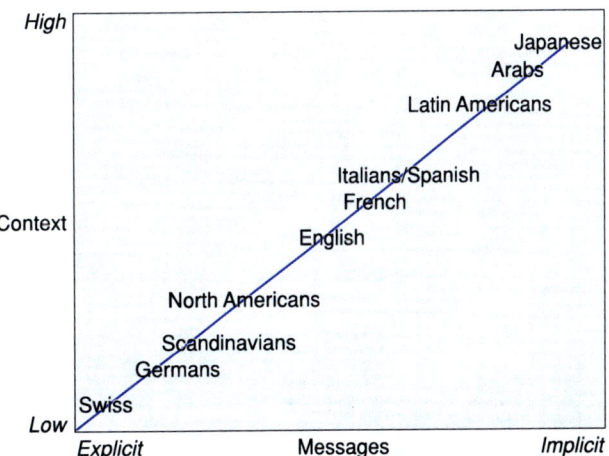

Figure 6.2 **Messages and context (adapted from Hall)**
Source: Usunier (1993): 103.

of the dimension are a number of countries in Asia, at the other a number of Northern European countries, as well as the US.

Part Three of this book will deal with this high/low context orientation in more detail.

8. Structure (individualism and collectivism)

The term 'structure' refers to a social structure or, in business terms, an organizational structure, which allows management to distinguish uncertain situations, ambiguity, stress and risk (Table 6.8). This particular value orientation concerns the relation between the individual and the group.

According to Kluckholn and Strodtbeck (1961), individualism shows the extent to which cultures elevate the role of the individual over the role of the group. When individualism is valued, the 'I' predominates over the 'We'. Individual goals, initiative and achievement are most important and people are encouraged to be independent and self-reliant. There is less need to conform to a group and less distinction made between in-groups and out-groups. Individuals frequently acquire and change their friends and do not hesitate to establish preferred relationships among family relatives.

Collectivism shows the extent to which the interests of the group prevail over individual interests. Each person in a collectivist society is encouraged to conform, to do what is best for the group and to avoid expressing opinions or beliefs that go against it. Reluctance to co-operate within the group or eagerness to stand out is frowned upon. Clearer distinctions are made between in-groups and out-groups. Relationships are more constant both within and outside the family.

Table 6.8 **Structure and business activities**

	Individualism	Collectivism
1. Planning	It is expected that those involved in planning will take the initiative to present their views	Plans are developed within the shared values used for measuring and justifying activities in the organization
2. Organizing	Organizational structures emphasize the individual in tasks assignments and resources allocation	Organizational structures emphasize the group; the team is assigned tasks and resources
3. Staffing	Organizations are not expected to look after their employees' career development	Promotion is based primarily on seniority. Managers are evaluated according to how well they conform to organizational or group norms
4. Directing	Leaders expect employees to meet or exceed their responsibilities and defend their own interests. Management entails managing individuals	Leaders expect loyalty in exchange for protection. Group or top-down decisions are the norm, with the leader in quiet control
5. Controlling	Control tends to be exerted by individual standards of excellence. Fear of losing self-respect discourages deviance from standards	Deviation from standards and expectations is discouraged through group-oriented pressure

> **SPOTLIGHT 6.8**
>
> **An in-tray task**
>
> Christopher Earley, a US management researcher, gave 48 management trainees from southern China and a matched group of 48 management trainees from the US an 'in-tray task' consisting of 40 items requiring between two and five minutes each (Earley, 1989). The task involved such activities as writing memos evaluating plans and rating job candidates' application forms. Half of the participants from each country were given an individual goal of 20 items; the other half were given a group goal of 200 items to be completed in one hour by 10 people. In addition, half of the participants from either country, both from the group and from the individual goal subsets, were asked to mark each item with their name; the other half turned them in anonymously. The Chinese, collectivist, participants performed best when operating with a group goal and anonymously. They performed worst when operating individually and with their name marked on their work. The individualist US participants performed best when operating individually and with their work attributed to them personally, and performed very poorly when operating as a group and anonymously.
>
> Source: Hoecklin (1995): 37.

This concept has led to a number of cultural value orientations and presented extreme differences between the values within each orientation. Sometimes, of course, the differences between (some) cultural values may not be as extreme as the differences presented here, so that some sort of accommodation can be made between the representatives of the cultures in question. On the other hand, the contrasts may be such that co-operation is extremely difficult.

Concept 6.2　Other views on values

The previous concept outlined the cultural values and the way they are reflected in management. Values are what people essentially share in a particular culture, what helps them co-exist. Hofstede (1991) emphasizes their durability, as does Trompenaars. The latter's dilemma approach, however, acknowledges that in dealing with foreign cultures it may be necessary to talk of reconciliation whereby the parties involved recognize each other's needs while maintaining their own values. As seen in Chapter 5, this process may, according to Trompenaars, entail the development of a third dimension in which the values of the parties concerned are integrated through close synergy. This is a much more productive way of addressing the either/or nature of a cultural dilemma than trying to resolve it through making weak compromises.

This idea of integrating values is much less clear-cut in nature than that of trying to find a trade-off of values during cultural collisions. The complex and unpredictable nature of this integration process, however, seems to reflect much more faithfully the nature of present-day international business and the increasing interdependence between countries and business sectors across the globe.

This interdependence between cultures has led some cross-cultural scholars to question the stability of cultures generally and cultural values in particular. Søderberg and Holden

(2002), for example, refer to a recent dynamic approach to the way culture is conceptualized in terms of relations between people rather than in terms of stable sets of values. The cultural identity of people is determined by the context:

> **This relational approach to culture and to cultural complexity and the idea of cultural complexity suggest that every individual embodies a unique combination of personal, cultural and social experiences, and thus that ultimately any communication and negotiation is intercultural.**
>
> Søderberg and Holden, 2002: 112

The consequence of this standpoint is that making a standard cultural profile is impossible because it ultimately reflects only constructs based on 'the practitioners' and the researchers' own cultural thought patterns, and the concepts and categories to which they are socialized.

Increasing consideration is therefore being given to the notion of culture as a sharing of 'patterns of meaning and interpretation' (Søderberg and Holden, 2002: 112) resulting from interaction with others. Rather than there being stable cultural communities, there are groups sharing such patterns who, when interacting with others whose patterns they can identify with, may take them on board, be it in adapted form, and/or negotiate a shared meaning and interpretation.

Managers who are involved in globalization may relate to this concept much more readily than to the fixed dimensions of culture as described in Part One. They will see their role as more to do with ensuring that the interaction within multicultural teams is effective and reaping synergetic rewards. Rather than being a matter of dealing with cultures in isolation, their work is 'the management of multiple cultures' (Søderberg and Holden, 2002: 110), thereby ensuring that 'knowledge, values and experience are transferred into multicultural domains of implementation'.

Earley (2006) is another scholar who sees the concept of culture as being related to the context, to interaction with others. He is adamant about wanting to avoid what he calls the 'cultural quagmire' of the cultural dimension construct whereby cultural values are an aggregate of individual perceptions and therefore contradict the construct itself. 'Culture', Earley claims, 'is not a value or set of values; culture is the meaning which we attach to aspects of the world around us'. Values as culture remains what Earley calls the 'obsession' of cross-cultural research. They should, he maintains, be more focused on meaning as culture. Values are only one element allowing meaning to be attached to the environment. Rather than developing even more value-based classifications on a grand scale, he proposes (more) research based on the concept of culture as a psychological construct whereby an individual is subject to a number of influences. Earley shows how this ties in with a definition of culture made by Rohner (1984: 119–120):

> **The totality of equivalent and complementary learned meanings maintained by a human population, or by identifiable segments of the population, and transmitted from one generation to the next.**

What is needed, Earley says, is the development of theories and framework that 'link culture to action', which can be used to understand 'the linkage among cultures, perceptions, actions, organizations, structures, etc.' (Earley, 2006: 928). At the heart of this lies the individual, not societies and their 'average tendencies' (the term used by Hofstede to describe the nature of cultural dimension scores).

After reviewing work done to establish the linkage described above, Earley (2006) points to the work done by several authors, including Earley himself, on the 'cultural intelligence' construct. This approach to studying cultural differences examines the extent to which individuals are able to adapt to cultural settings. The focus moves from the context of interaction (such as shared values and meanings) to the behaviour of the individual and the (meta-) cognitive processing involved. Earley admits this approach needs considerable development, but believes it offers a promising way to examine how individual actions are affected by culture.

One final activity in Part One provides you with the opportunity to reflect on your own cultural values as well as those of others. This reflection will, it is hoped, allow you to develop a clear definition of your own style of working.

Conclusion

This chapter has shown the link between theory and practice. Definitions based on research in the field of culture and management have enabled a model of culture to be developed. This model has been applied to the world of international business and the daily tasks of a manager examined in terms of cultural values. The assumption underlying this study is that an individual's framework of cultural preferences influences the way in which their tasks are executed. The case given in Activity 6.1 will demonstrate this influence.

Such cultural models, however, may well be too constrictive in nature, particularly when applied to management. By giving the viewpoints of several writers who question the validity of such models, this chapter has given its readers food for thought concerning the application of cultural values to management behaviour, particularly since they do not take account of what may happen when (different) cultures interact.

Points for reflection

1. The concept gives a range of eight cultural values that could affect five management skill areas.

   Can you suggest other cultural value ranges that could be applied? Are there other management skill areas to which these values could apply?

2. There are those who think that when doing business internationally it is necessary to follow certain professional codes of behaviour, such as keeping to deadlines, meeting delivery dates and obeying terms of contract. There are others, however, who consider that business culture rather than business convention has a greater influence on the way people work internationally or otherwise. Managers operating internationally therefore need to take cultural differences into account.

   Which standpoint do you support? Explain why and give examples on the basis of your experience or analysis.

3. You have seen how culture can affect management.

    Apart from being aware of this, what else do you think is needed to perform successfully in a cross-cultural context?

4. Earley argues that culture has less to do with determining values and more to do with meanings. When doing so, he refers to Rohner's definition of culture: 'The totality of equivalent and complementary learned meanings maintained by a human population, or by identifiable segments of the population, and transmitted from one generation to the next.'

    Compare this definition of culture with that made by Hofstede (Chapter 1): 'The collective programming of the mind which distinguishes the members of one human group from another'.

    In which ways do you consider these definitions to be complementary and/or oppositional in nature?

Further reading

Earley, P.C. and Mosakowski, E. (2004) 'Cultural intelligence', *Harvard Business Review*, 82 (October): 139-146. This article describes what the authors claim to be the three sources of cultural intelligence. After giving six cultural intelligence profiles to enable readers to assess which one describes them, the authors suggest ways in which cultural intelligence can be cultivated.

Hall, E.T. and Hall, M.R. (1990) *Understanding Cultural Differences*, Maine: Intercultural. Although this book was written primarily for business people, it is oriented towards interpersonal relations with foreigners. It is therefore useful for many other people whose lives involve contact with foreign nationals, either in their personal or professional lives.

Hoecklin, L. (1995) *Managing Cultural Differences: Strategies for Comparative Advantage*, Wokingham: Addison-Wesley. The book explores the effect of culture on each business area and provides a framework for considering cultural factors. The research findings help to clarify what can go on in international management.

References

Doing Business Internationally: The Cross-cultural Challenges (1992) Participant Workbook, Princeton, NJ: Princeton Training Press.

Earley, C.P. (1989) 'Social loafing and collectivism: a comparison of the United States and the People's Republic of China', *Administrative Science Quarterly*, 34: 565-581.

Earley, P.C. (2006) 'Leading cultural research in the future: a matter of paradigms and taste', *Journal of International Business Studies*, 37: 922-931.

Gladwell, G. (2008) *Outliers: The Story of Success*, London: Penguin.

Hall, E.T. and Hall, M.R. (1990) *Understanding Cultural Differences*, Yarmouth, ME: Intercultural Press.

Hoecklin, L. (1995) *Managing Cultural Differences: Strategies for Comparative Advantage*, Wokingham: Addison-Wesley.

Hofstede, G. (1991) *Cultures and Organizations: Software of the Mind*, London: McGraw-Hill.

Kluckholn, F. and Strodtbeck, F.L. (1961) *Variations in Value Orientations*, Westport, CT: Greenwood.

Laurent, A. (1983) 'The cultural diversity of western conceptions of management', *International Studies of Management and Organization* 13 (1-2): 75-96.

Mead, R. (1994) *International Management: Cross-cultural Dimensions*, Oxford: Blackwell Business.

Rohner, R.P. (1984) 'Toward a conception of culture from cross-cultural psychology', *Journal of Cross-Cultural Psychology*, 15 (2): 111-138.

Søderberg, A.-M. and Holden, N. (2002) 'Rethinking cross cultural management in a globalizing business world', *International Journal of Cross Cultural Management*, 2 (1): 103-121.

Usunier, J.C. (1993) *Marketing Across Cultures*, Hernel Hempstead: Prentice-Hall: 103.

Video Arts (1984) *So You Think You Can Manage?* London: Methuen.

Yoshino, M.Y. and Rangan, U.S. (1995) *Strategic Alliances: An Entrepreneurial Approach to Globalization*, Cambridge, MA: Harvard Business School Press.

Chapter 6 Activities

ACTIVITY 6.1

Read the case study below, based on the experiences of Larry Zeenny in the Lebanon. It concerns a football agent's attempt to make a deal for his client. When you have read it, answer the questions that follow.

An own goal

The taxi arrived at the impressive mansion in Faqra and I made my way through the blistering sun towards the entrance. I was met by two servants and directed to Mr. Haider's room. He had faxed me a contract, the terms of which were ridiculously low, and I was determined to get a better deal for my client.

A peek at my watch revealed it was 11.30. I'd arrived just in time, despite the flight delays at Frankfurt and the queues at Beirut airport. In front of Haider's door I cleared my throat, tightened my tie, gathered all my courage and entered the room. 'Mr. Haider, I am delighted to meet you', I said, rather too exuberantly. 'Ahlan Wilhelm, welcome my friend,' said Haider. 'I just have to say goodbye to my important visitors. Please make yourself at home while you're waiting.'

A servant led me to a large room where there were two men and, in the far corner, a beautiful oriental woman. I sat down in a chair and waited for Mr. Haider. An elaborate clock chimed twelve, but there was still no sign of him. By now the other three were thoroughly enjoying their lunch, which I had refused out of politeness. To keep my nerves steady I had only accepted a glass of arak. By 12.15 my patience had started to desert me. I was going to be too late for my next meeting. How could I trust Mr. Haider if he had already broken his promise beforehand?

Eventually, at 12.30, Mr. Haider entered the room. He looked extremely relaxed in his traditional dress and I jumped up to greet him. Before approaching me he first kissed both men and had a brief conversation with the woman. I had prepared myself well for this moment. I gave him a firm handshake and seated myself.

'Ahlan Wilhelm, welcome to Lebanon,' he said. Looking at the table, he added: 'I hope you enjoyed your delicious lunch with my beloved sons, Alain and Elie, and of course with my habibi, Charlotte.'

'Mr. Haider,' I replied, 'Thank you for your warm reception, but I ate on the plane. My client is extremely pleased about your interest and he is looking forward to playing for such an illustrious club as Al Ansar. Shall we come to terms as quickly as possible so we can finalize this matter in the best interest of both parties?'

'Shouf Wilhelm,' he retorted. 'Please call me Hashem. But why the rush? We have the time for business until the sun walks out on us! When will your client arrive?'

I told him that my client, a goalkeeper who had played for German, Italian and British teams, as well as for his home country, Denmark, would be unable to attend the negotiations. 'The thing is . . .' (I hesitated: how could I call him by his first name and show my total respect?) 'It's usual for a player to leave such dealings to his agent.'

Mr. Haider seemed disgruntled, but agreed to talk. He called his two sons over while his wife quietly headed for the door. As she passed by I respectfully looked her in the eye and wished her a pleasant day.

The bargaining process began and, quite disconcertingly, Mr. Haider's sons joined in. Was he hoping to get the upper hand through force of numbers? Could I trust his sons to honour the confidentiality aspect of the negotiation? I was concerned details would leak out to the predators from the international press. After an hour we had reached an impasse, but I couldn't really understand why. Mr. Haider refused to provide me with a bank guarantee with respect to my client's salary and signing-on fee. In fact, Mr. Haider persistently refused to go into financial matters. These could be discussed the next day, he insisted, since they would not be a problem as far as he was concerned.

But for me they *were* the problem. And that was why we had reached a stalemate.

Questions

1. What is the significance of the title of this case?
2. How would you define the problem from your perspective?
3. What do you think has caused the so-called stalemate? Refer to the cultural values outlined in this chapter that have had an impact on the way the agent handled his encounter with Mr. Haider. Mention, in particular, issues relating to:
   - time focus;
   - competitiveness;
   - activity;
   - space;
   - communication; and
   - structure
4. How do you think Wilhelm can rescue the deal?
5. How can Wilhelm best prepare for any future negotiations in the Middle East on behalf of his football clients?

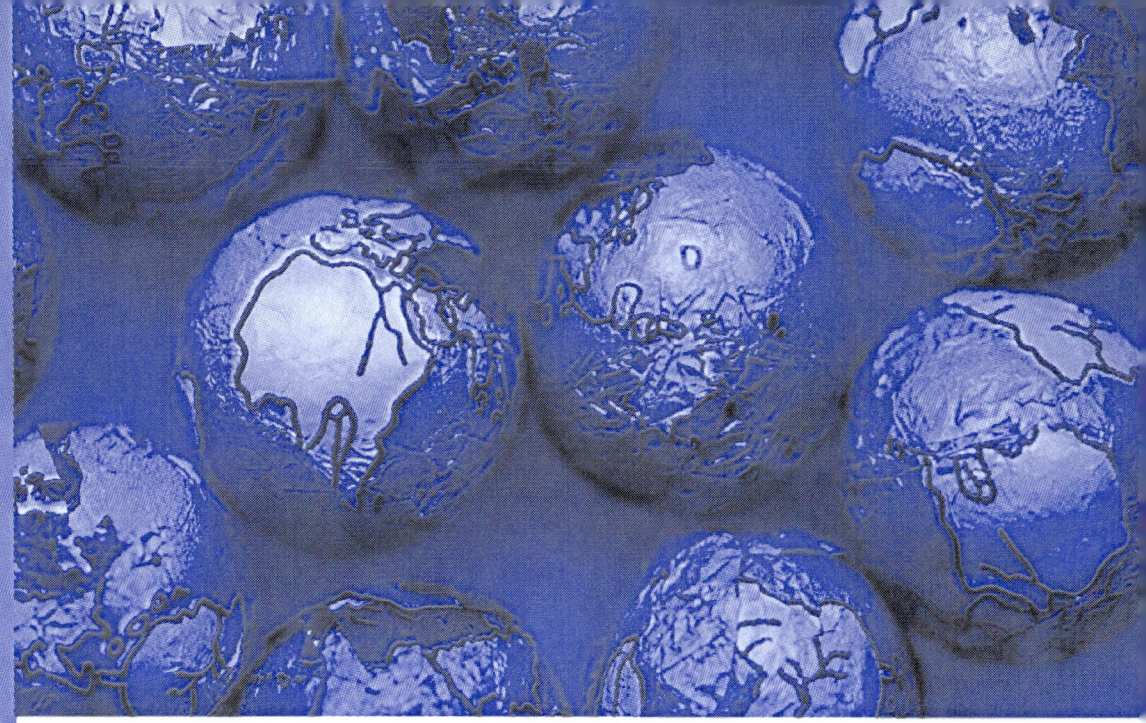

TOPIC 4
CROSS CULTURAL COMMUNICATION

Chapter 7

Business Communication Across Cultures

As seen in Part Two, the development of globalization in business has compelled managers, employees and customers to take increasing account of intercultural relations. The increasingly global nature of business and the growing interaction between cultures is adding to the complexity of doing business.

The composition of staff and clientele is changing as companies start up operations in countries across the globe. Managers in such companies must therefore be able to operate on an international level and deal with other cultures. It is no longer enough for them to be aware of the existence of cultural differences; they must also be able to communicate, negotiate and work together with business partners from other cultures.

These requirements go far beyond the standard recipes for management from early business studies where the emphasis was very much on a universal approach, one which took no account of relativity or diversity. New management skills are necessary, particularly in the area of communication skills.

The concept in Chapter 7 first examines the elements involved in inter- and intracultural communication before looking at communication in business. Chapter 8 follows on with an analysis of a number of barriers, both verbal and non-verbal, to intercultural communication.

Learning outcomes

After reading this chapter you will gain an understanding of:

- The different components that have an influence on the process of communication.
- The role of communication in business practices.

Concept 7.1 Communicating in and between cultures

As discussed in the introduction to Part Three, intercultural communication comprises all forms of communication both within and between cultures. This concept should be considered not just in terms of comparisons between cultures, but also in terms of the process of interaction and exchange between different cultures. As Ladmiral and Lipiansky (1989) indicate, the term 'intercultural communication' could imply that it is the cultures and identities that are in contact. This is not really the case. Instead, it is individuals who are interacting and it is they who bring their culture's way of thinking, feeling and living into the interaction. These authors therefore consider that intercultural communication can be seen as a 'fabric of relations', a fabric created by the individuals or groups from different cultures and woven from the perceptions they have of each other, as well as the values, codes, lifestyles and thought processes belonging to their respective cultures.

Intercultural communication can be better defined as an interactive phenomenon rather than one involving comparisons between cultures. These cultures are non-homogeneous social groups that are forever evolving. Their interaction should not just be seen in terms of a set of relations between the cultures, but also as a dynamic process (therefore one implying change) whereby the cultures are defined both through their own characteristics as well as through their interaction with each other. This definition therefore takes both a systemic perspective (involving sets of interrelations between individuals) and a dynamic one (whereby the interrelations can change).

This approach to communication brings us to the model which we presented in the introduction to Part Three (Figure III.1).

A model of communication

The schematic representation of the model in the introduction emphasizes the actors involved in the communication, namely the addresser and the addressee. When they communicate, they unconsciously make use of a frame of reference which, in general terms, consists of:

- knowledge (about the subject under discussion);
- experience (in professional or individual terms);
- norms (i.e. the norms of the society in which they live); and
- prejudices (with regard to each other).

However, according to a model proposed by researchers known as the Palo Alto Group, human communication does not emphasize the addresser and the addressee. These researchers, who were based at the Mental Research Institute in Palo Alto in the US, collaborated in the 1950s and 1960s on the theory of communication and the relationship between the individuals. They maintained that since both addresser and addressee are in perpetual interaction, they cannot be isolated. The emphasis is not on the message, but on the whole system of communication involved, including a network of relations that cannot be broken up. Everybody is involved in a network of relations woven by the cultural group (the ethnic group or society in question). Communication does, of course, require a message (form and content), but more important than the message in the exchange between protagonists is the interaction, i.e. the relation between the persons communicating and the context of the communication. This determines the information exchanged. Furthermore, the information in the message does not have an absolute value; it is subject to interpretation due to the interaction itself. That is why in human communication – and even more so in intercultural communication – the question of interpretation remains crucial (Donnadieu and Karsky, 2002).

Without going more deeply into the concepts of the theory of communication, it can be concluded that not only are the relations between those communicating an important factor, but also the role of context. It is this role, to which this chapter now turns, with particular reference to the business environment.

The role of the 'context' in communication

Context can be defined as the environment in which the communication process takes place and which helps to define the communication. Knowing the physical context, one can predict much of the communication to a high degree of accuracy. The choice of the environment, the context, helps assign the desired meaning to the words communicated. Culture is also context. Every culture has its own world view; its own way of thinking of activity, time and human nature; its own way of perceiving self; and its own system of social organization. Knowing each of these helps people assign meaning to the symbols. The component of context helps identify the extent to which the source and receiver have similar meanings for the communicated symbols. Similar understandings of the culture in which the communication takes place is critical to the success of the communication.

Hall and Hall (1990) established two groups of cultures, called *high-context* and *low-context*. The difference between them was the degree of importance attached to the context of any message. In low-context cultures, the information of any message is contained in the message itself, i.e. in the words used. The message is explicit. In high-context cultures, most of the information is contained in the context where the message is being sent, i.e. in the relationships between the people involved and the situation where people are communicating. The message is implicit.

When representatives of high-context and low-context cultures are doing business, the one may have a very different idea as to what is important in their communication. For example, when the Swiss and the Japanese meet, the former may prefer to come quickly to the point and get down to business. The Japanese, on the other hand, prefer not to talk directly about the business at hand; they are inclined to talk generally about this and that, about life in general, and to do so in order to get to know each other.

As Figure 6.2 in Chapter 6 shows, Hall and Hall place the Swiss in the low-context group and the Japanese in the high-context group. These two cultures lie at the extreme ends of a continuum.

Another aspect of the process of communication raised by Hall, one often neglected but also important in the relation between cultures, is what he called 'proxemics'.

Proxemics and cultures

The term **proxemics** was coined by Hall (1966) to describe the study of how people perceive their social and personal space. Hall maintains that awareness of the differences between cultures with regard to proxemics is indispensable when interacting with other cultures. This entails being able to work out the 'silent' messages being communicated through the distance separating people when they are interacting, as well as in terms of the senses (touch, smell, sight and sound). Different cultural frameworks define the information received by our physical senses, not only in terms of what can be perceived, but also in terms of what can be eliminated. According to Hall, individuals learn from childhood which types of information they need to retain and which they can dispense with. As soon as these perceptive models have been developed, they appear to be fixed for life.

Personal space is characterized by an invisible zone with distinct boundaries. When an intruder enters this zone, people may feel uncomfortable. This space is a sort of personal territory, a zone of protection or even of defence. The main factors influencing personal space are: gender, age, personality, the degree of sympathy towards the individuals concerned, the situation in which the individuals are confronted and also the culture(s) involved.

Corraze (1988) reports on investigations made by Hall (1966, 1969) and Watson (1970) into the differences between cultures with regard to the notion of 'personal space'.

Hall postulates that the distance between individuals is related to the preferences each culture has with regard to the sensory inputs used. Each culture has a preference for certain sensory receptors. Take, for example, the differences in personal space between Arabs and Americans: Arabs, it seems, prefer a smaller personal space than Americans because the former are more susceptible to the olfactory dimension, including skin odour. Hall, in fact, makes a link between smell and a person's disposition in the Arabic-speaking world.

> When couples are being matched for marriage, the man's go-between will sometimes ask to smell the girl, who may be turned down if she doesn't 'smell nice'.
>
> Hall, 1969: 149

Watson compares the distances between people in conversation in different cultures and makes a ranking according to the differences in the size of their personal space. The ranking, from small to large is illustrated in Figure 7.1. Research supports the hypothesis that if someone's personal space is violated, this can impair communication because of an increase in anxiety.

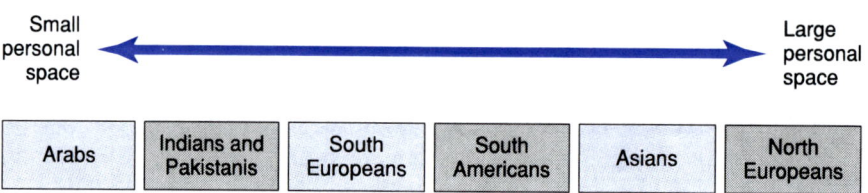

Figure 7.1

Proxemics also relates to the places where people move and the places where they work. If tables in a restaurant are placed in a way that does not respect personal space, the occupants may well apologize to their neighbours for sitting so close, or display non-verbal behaviour (such as deliberately looking away). If managers do not take the concept of personal space into account when seeing to the organization of offices and arrangement of desks, the ensuing anxiety among staff can hamper communication and thus the efficient running of a business. This is a non-verbal aspect of communication in the working environment to which managers pay little attention.

Communication also refers to the meaningful exchange process by which verbal and nonverbal information is shared through messages, and it can take many forms. Even if managers use all these forms in their business practices, they each have different perceptions of the effectiveness of these forms of communication and may therefore prefer some over others. The question of which forms of communication to use is one that should receive more attention in business as well as in research into communication generally.

Forms of communication in business practice

Many channels of communication are available to managers. Electronic mail, for example, is becoming the most common form of written communication within many companies.

Table 7.1 Channels of business communication

Medium	Oral	Written	Electronic/digital
(Telephone) conversations	✗		
Conference calls	✗		
(Online) meetings	✗		✗
Online forums/blogs/social networks		✗	✗
Voice mail (asynchronic)	✗		✗
Video teleconferences (synchronic)	✗		✗
Electronic mail (asynchronic)		✗	✗
Instant Messaging (synchronic)		✗	✗
Training sessions	✗	✗	✗
Presentations, speeches	✗	✗	✗
Press conferences	✗	✗	✗
Press releases		✗	
Memos		✗	
Proposals		✗	
Letters		✗	
Reports		✗	
Fax		✗	

NB: any of the written documents listed above, if attached to emails, could also be considered as communication by means of the electronic channel.

The email used for many purposes, both externally and internally: managers use it to call a meeting, or give their colleagues and subordinates feedback and instructions, or correspond with customers and clients. Some managers, however, prefer to communicate by talking face-to-face in a meeting or informally, by making phone calls (including conference calls), or by using video teleconferences. These ways of communicating in turn involve the use of some or all of the non-verbal elements of communication, such as gestures, tone of voice, facial expressions, and body language generally.

Table 7.1 summarizes the main channels of business communication.

Culture and choice of communication mode

The choice of communication mode can be influenced by cultural factors. Mead (1990: 84) gives an example with regard to telephoning. A US businessman would consider it quite normal to make a 'cold call', to phone a stranger with whom he thinks he could do business. A Japanese businessman, on the other hand, would consider this to be intrusive or aggressive, preferring instead to find a third party who can 'vouch for your credibility and make a formal introduction'.

This is, of course, related to the cultural dimensions discussed in earlier chapters. A business from an 'individualist' culture, for example, may be intent on what it considers 'efficient' communication when dealing with a business in a 'collectivist' culture. It puts forward a comprehensive business proposal and expects a similar response. If the company asked to respond is not accustomed to such direct approaches, it may well decide not to deal with the proposal directly in writing, but to request instead a face-to-face meeting with representatives of the company concerned. In this way, a good relationship can be established before any discussion of the proposal is entered into since, in the eyes of the possible business partner, efficiency and speed are less important than establishing trust and confidence. The oral mode is used to set the conditions for co-operation, whereafter the written mode can be considered as a means of communication, provided the relationships established are scrupulously maintained.

Computer (or mobile)-mediated communication (CMC)

As was said earlier, electronic mail is being increasingly used as a way of sending documents, requests and information generally to colleagues and (potential) clients. However, even though it offers many advantages in terms of speed and efficiency, it can also contain many pitfalls when used interculturally. Problems of comprehension may arise, of course, through inaccurate language and poorly structured text. (These points are discussed in the next sub-section with reference to using English as the medium of communication.) Also, cultural issues can lead to misunderstanding and even antagonism. The recipient of an email may consider its style too formal or informal depending on what their expectations are. They may take offence, for example, if they are not addressed at the start of the email or if the style of the message is too direct or casual, particularly if it contains careless language. Others who consider emails to be more conversational in nature may dislike the distancing effect of a formal written style and the lack of explicit information or opinion, particularly if direct answers are not given to direct questions. As with any written form of communication, there are no facial expressions to mitigate or clarify messages.

It could be argued that the use of email, just as other forms of computer-mediated communication (CMC), blurs the distinction between the oral and written messages for many of its users. A sender or recipient may expect an email to be the equivalent of a letter or memo, meeting the formal requirements of language accuracy and text cohesion of a written text. Another sender/recipient, however, may regard the message sent as being the start (or continuation) of a conversation in writing, of a thread of messages. The style will reflect more the spoken word with its slips of the tongue, false starts, hesitations and inaccuracies. Any resulting misunderstanding or incomprehension can be communicated and dealt with in later messages.

Such differing expectations, be they intra- or inter-cultural, need to be recognized and managed by the communicating parties. However, CMC can help to alleviate discrepancies because both sender and receiver have, in theory, time to reflect upon and discuss the process as they are communicating.

Differences in expectation and resulting behaviours in both the intra- and inter-cultural context are discussed in a literature review, in which Waldvogel (2001) found that many of the gender differences in face-to-face interaction were carried over into CMC and even accentuated:

> There is evidence that women and men communicate in different ways on the net. A study of two academic groups conducted by Herring (1996) reveals that 'Both men and women structure their messages in an interactive way and that for both, the pure exchange of information takes second place to the exchange of views. Significant gender differences are found in how electronic messages are oriented... Although messages posted by women contain somewhat more interactional features they are also more informative, in contrast with male messages which most often express (critical) views.'
>
> Herring found that while women value politeness, men operate in accordance with competitive values which result in violations, including flaming, of conventional politeness norms. Men dominated the 'talking' time. They participated at a higher rate than their numerical representation justified, and their messages were considerably longer. They took little interest in what women had to say, which seems to have resulted in a decline of female participation. In this supposedly liberal academic environment, CMC was found to be male-dominated, power-based and hierarchical.
>
> Waldvogel, 2001: 7-8

Language during business encounters

The previous discussion assumes that the two business representatives are able to communicate even though their native languages are different. When this is not possible, a number of options present themselves:

- Both sides could insist on using their native language when communicating, necessitating the use of an intermediary to translate. This may remove the obligation of managers to learn their counterpart's language and ensure that communication runs efficiently. However, apart from practical problems (including the availability of interpreters and the cost involved), there is always the question of reliability: is the translation accurate? Is the interpreter able to convey the full nuance of what is being said? Moreover, the presence of an intermediary can hamper the establishment of a relationship between the parties. Interaction is necessarily delayed and the role of non-verbal communication reduced. The focus of interaction may well become the interpreter who, in a way, is controlling the whole exchange without bearing the responsibility for the outcome.

- One interlocutor uses the mother tongue of the other. Many regard this as the best solution: by becoming truly bilingual, the manager is able to 'tune into' the other's culture, pick up all the nuances, understand the cultural references and respond appropriately. An 'expat' manager who has worked and lived for a long time in one country or region may well be in a position to perform this role optimally. However, managers who are operating across many cultures and making forays into new countries cannot be expected to acquire the language of every culture with which they are (about to be) involved.

It is worthwhile mentioning here problems experienced by interlocutors who share the same language, whether they come from different cultures or not. Within an English-speaking country, such as the UK, there can be enormous differences in the level of expression in both written and spoken language, and this can affect communication generally. Between English-speaking countries, such as the UK and the US, there may be a shared language, but British and US managers must sometimes check the meanings of words that their counterparts use. Differences in pronunciation can also add confusion. This goes also for speakers of other dialects of English such as Indian-English, Singapore-English and South African-English.

Spotlight 7.1 shows how native speakers of English in the UK can be confused by the plethora of business terms taken from American-English.

English: a neutral language?

A third possibility for managers who cannot communicate with each other through their mother tongues is for them to share a neutral foreign language. History shows how the use of a 'lingua franca' (common language) has been indispensable to the development of trade in many parts of the world. Nowadays, English frequently serves as a means of communication between companies whose managers have acquired the language as part of their education and have been exposed to it through various media. This language is often referred to as 'international English', but is difficult to define exactly because it has evolved organically on the basis of how non-native speakers use English. It is said to contain words and phrases that are generally understood across the world. It appears to be devoid of complex grammar constructions and of all but the most common idiomatic phrases. Those using it may often need to readjust their use of the language while using it to accommodate

SPOTLIGHT 7.1

Meeting-room jargon: just fuel for buzzword bingo?

By Michael Quinion

If you can't understand half of what your colleagues are saying in meetings, take heart – you are not alone.

A survey of a thousand office workers in Britain was published last week by the firm of recruitment consultants Office Angels. It reported that two-thirds of office staff used unnecessary jargon terms, for the usual reasons of wanting to confuse opponents and seem superior. But 40 per cent of those surveyed found it irritating and distracting, and 10 per cent thought it made the most frequent users sound pretentious and untrustworthy. Nothing very new or startling so far. But the list of buzz phrases that were reported as being at the same time most common and least understood was intriguing:

Low-hanging fruit, e-tailing, talk off-line, blue-sky idea, win-win situation, think outside the box, holistic approach, level playing field, sanity check, put to bed, whole nine yards, helicopter view, gap analysis, touch base, rain check, sing from the same hymn sheet, finger in the air, get in bed with, big picture, benchmark, ball park, ticks in all the right boxes, strategic fit, bread and butter.

It's clear that jargonisers in British offices are picking up terms from American-English, some from the standard language, but mostly from business jargon. The survey suggests they are doing so because more business people have access to the American-dominated internet.

You can see that phrases like rain check, ball park and touch base could confuse hearers in Britain, because we literally don't play the game. (But one supermarket in Britain uses rain checks as its name for the vouchers it gives out when special offers are in short supply, so some of us have been exposed to it.)

Some terms are odd and would stop almost anybody for a moment – low-hanging fruit, for a target that's easy to reach, helicopter view, for an overview, and gap analysis, for assessing untapped opportunities. But several – such as level playing field, benchmark, and blue-sky – have been in British-English for many years. And are strategic fit or bread and butter really so hard to figure out, in context? It would seem so, from the survey.

Jargon is all right in its place. But what the survey shows is that people are easily confused by the unfamiliar, good enough reason for sticking to plain English the rest of the time. Giving bored attendees at meetings the chance to play buzzword bingo is hardly a substitute.

Source: www.worldwidewords.org/articles/jargon.htm, accessed 1 September 2010.

differences in knowledge and understanding between the speakers concerned. The differences in pronunciation may also need to be considered, especially when it is heavily influenced by that used for the mother tongue.

Even here, however, there are problems. A speaker using English as a neutral foreign language may well suffer similar problems to native speakers using English to communicate with non-native speakers. This is particularly the case when the speaker in question is from a country where English is used as the second language of communication in, for example, education and business. The speaker may not be aware of the breadth of his vocabulary compared with that of his counterpart, and may be unable to modify his pronunciation since it is part and parcel of the way English is used in his country of origin.

Some observers regard international English as a move towards cultural neutrality, a way of shedding the cultural connotations of British- or American-English. However, as a sort of default language, it has considerable limitations: discussion can be superficial and communicating thoughts difficult. The basic problem is that language is the very expression of a culture, be it Canadian-English, Hong Kong-English, Caribbean- or African-English. Stripping culture off any language, let alone a particular sort of English, can impoverish the semantics of the language and reduce its whole power of expression. There may be less room for nuance and subtlety, for saying something that expresses much more than the words used. The language can be deprived of its deeper meaning.

This goes equally for written English. A report in writing in a 'stripped down' English – particularly one using 'bullets' of information – may not in itself prove easy to understand by a non-native speaker of English. A noble attempt to simplify English may cause more problems than those it was intended to solve. The connections between thoughts, ideas and information may become more diffuse or even non-existent. Deprived of proper cohesion, clear context and any oral explanation, the adapted text may have lost a good deal of the intended meaning of the original. Such problems frequently occur during exchanges of emails when messages sent in simplified telescopic form can result in misunderstandings or incomprehension. This goes particularly for emails written in idiomatic, telegram-style language that may be appropriate for an office colleague, but not for a client in Bangladesh.

Over and above such problems, there is, of course, the question of language as a potent way of expressing cultural identity. How motivated are people to use a language that is not theirs and which does not allow them to assert their own personal or cultural identity? Mini-case 7.1 shows what can happen when a company, which was once a Chinese state-owned enterprise, adopts English as its official language.

MINI-CASE 7.1

Straight-talking, English-speaking culture brings communication problems

By Justine Lau

When a Hong Kong-based analyst recently called computer-maker Lenovo's Beijing office and asked for an employee by the English first name on her business card, he got a puzzling response. The operator told him the person did not exist.

Baffled, he called back and asked for the same person in her Chinese name. He was put through to her office immediately.

> What the analyst encountered was a Lenovo in flux where the transformation of a corporate culture has yielded occasional moments of confusion even within the company.
>
> Some employees at Lenovo, which acquired IBM's PC unit last year, now receive internal emails from a 'John' or 'Mary' whom they struggle to identify until they find out their Chinese names.
>
> 'In the past, we used to call each other by Chinese names. But now since a lot of our communications involve our US colleagues, some people may find it easier to have an English name,' says one Lenovo employee.
>
> The spontaneous move by staff to adopt English names may be causing slight confusion, but it underlines broader changes in the company's culture that analysts see as key to its success in managing the acquisition of the IBM unit.
>
> Shortly after the deal, Lenovo hired Bill Amelio, a former Dell executive, to be its chief executive. It moved its headquarters from Beijing to North Carolina and changed the official company language from Chinese to English. It is also establishing a straight-talking culture inside the company.
>
> 'Lenovo used to behave like any state-owned enterprise. [But] it has realised that in order to become a true global company, the first step is to drop some of the old habits,' said Randy Zhou, an analyst at Bank of China International.
>
> Source: from Straight-talking, English-speaking culture brings communication problems, *Financial Times*, 09/11/2006, p. 31 (Lau, J.).

Questions

1. How do you think the adoption of English by the company would help establish a 'straight-talking culture'?
2. What else do you think would need to be done for this new culture to be established?

Face-to-face management relations

This brings us to the question of face-to-face business encounters. Whatever the language chosen, encounters occur in situations and contexts where the expectations of the interlocutors may be very different, where the pressure of differing social norms can disturb the communicative relationship.

The first encounter

The way different cultures pursue the formality mode indicated earlier reflects tendencies within the cultures concerned. The very start of an encounter can indicate clear differences, even if it takes place in a shared language. A formal first meeting between a US manager and a German manager, for example, may show how the one is intent on establishing an open, friendly and eventually informal relationship whereas the other is more reserved in exchanging information, particularly with regard to their respective positions and responsibilities. The very exchange of names ('Hi! I'm Ron Smith.' – 'Hello. Stoldt, Dr Peter Stoldt.') can be the start of a precarious scenario, particularly when English is being used: using 'you' goes hand-in-hand with informality for the American, whereas the German may use 'you' as the equivalent of 'Sie', the formal version of 'you' in German which establishes a certain distance between speakers. Two conflicting functions of the meeting (cultivating social ties and exchanging information) may well be pursued with growing unease by the two parties. The German possibly does not share the optimism and (superficial) friendliness of the other; he is more intent on establishing the other's credentials and clarifying the potential of a business deal. Any attempt by the American to break through what he considers to be the rather cold reserved manner of his counterpart could have an adverse effect, with the German developing an antipathy towards persistent affability.

The context of meetings can determine the nature of such encounters. For example, it will become apparent to any foreign visitor in a Japanese setting that addressing a Japanese manager by his first name is inappropriate: office relationships retain a formality not experienced in many Western business cultures. Any attempt to counter this can result in extreme embarrassment for the Japanese manager and his colleagues. In another (Western) setting, however, first-name terms may be the norm and insistence on using a title and surname may prove a barrier to establishing trust and confidence in that setting.

Conversational styles

If a business relationship develops, some kind of negotiated communication mode may be established, whereby the context involved plays a decisive role. Once the Japanese manager has deemed it appropriate for business with his Western counterpart to be pursued, then he may be prepared to drop his guard and enter into a less formal style of communication. However, if other, less involved, Japanese colleagues are present, the more formal style will be retained, and the American will adapt his (verbal) behaviour correspondingly. On the other hand, the Japanese may well be prepared to communicate (and possibly behave) more informally in a Western setting – as long as his authority is not questioned.

Once the relationship between managers from different cultures has been established, the maintenance of such a relationship can be fraught with difficulty, particularly when different styles of conversation are used. One interlocutor may expect those involved in a meeting, for example, to be able to take turns when speaking, the other may assume it is his right to interrupt as and when necessary; one interlocutor may be focused on his particular take on matters, the other may involve his 'ego' much less; one may tend to make assertive, conclusive statements, the other may prefer to make more negotiable contributions and be less conclusive; one may consider pauses in the conversation to be appropriate for reflection, the other may shy away from silence and fill up a gap as soon as it appears.

Listening is, of course, a crucial element of any conversation: understanding not only what is being said but evaluating the meaning of what is being said. Taking turns to speak, rather than interrupting each other, may certainly ease the process of understanding, as will asking questions to check on understanding. The use of a shared second language will probably necessitate a check on the intended meaning of words or phrases used, and possibly a rephrasing of statements to clarify understanding. Listening carefully to what is not said is just as important. As Mead (1990: 118) indicates in his list of habits a good listener needs to develop:

Listen for what is *not* said; that is, for what the sender thinks is so obvious as to be redundant or what is so new as to be outside his or her experience. This means processing the message in terms of the differences between your and the speaker's personal and cultural priorities.

Another element to take into account when evaluating the contributions of other interlocutors is their facial expressions.

Facial expressions during interaction

Facial expressions have been analysed more frequently in terms of the emotions expressed than in terms of their effect on human relations. However, such expressions give important signals in social and business interaction. They are totally linked to the context and differ according to whether the context is clear or ambiguous. A persistent look can make the interlocutor feel like escaping or responding with signals of aggression. Such looks are therefore often associated with feelings (unease, embarrassment) which, according to the context, will express attitudes that are diametrically opposed (such as aggression and friendliness).

Facial expressions are also connected to the status of the interlocutors. In social and business encounters they can play an important role when expressing the degrees of dominance between people with different levels of status. Any perceived degree of status can, however, have causes unrelated to a person's actual social position. We sometimes arbitrarily attribute a dominant status to someone because they are able to talk very fluently and knowledgeably during a discussion.

Cultural differences can play a significant role in the way facial expressions function. The length of visual contact, for example, depends to a great extent on the cultural origin of the interlocutors. When someone actually averts their gaze, this can be interpreted differently. In some cultures this act can have a negative connotation, but in others it may be seen simply as a sign that the speaker is changing direction in the discussion. The act of smiling might be assumed to have a similar function across the world as a signifier of happiness. Trumble's (2004) book *A Brief History of the Smile* reveals many of the nuances attached to this physiological process. Through his enlightening account Trumble shows that smiling intersects not just with happiness, but also with piety, sex and corruption. Here is an account of how a Russian smile can be interpreted (Sauer, 2007: 13):

> Anyone who has been to Russia knows how unbelievably sullen the people look. They hardly ever smile but instead give all the signs that life for most Russians is just hell. I maintain that a smile actually has another function – an observation that has been scientifically corroborated. My teacher of Russian, Maria, obtained her doctorate from Moscow University with a dissertation entitled: 'A comparison between the function of the smile in Russia and its function in Western cultures, together with the historical background.' My teacher spent over three years researching the subject and interviewed hundreds of Russians and non-Russians. A smile in Russian culture, sends a totally different message to that sent by a smile in the West. According to Maria, a smile in Russia – when shown to a stranger – has a negative connotation: 'He's pulling my leg!', or 'He's criticizing me!' In Russian, the word 'smile' often evokes a negative feeling. Maria: 'We use the phrase "Enough smiling!" meaning "Cut it out!", while in English you say "Keep smiling" – which means the opposite.'

Interaction through interpreters

English may be the working language during many international encounters, but many executives still rely on interpreters to explore and develop business opportunities abroad particularly in regions of the world where local companies have not yet been able to develop sufficient English language skills within their workforce.

Having a third party involved in encounters with (potential) agents or clients is fraught with difficulty. An interpreter is essentially an outsider who is most probably not familiar with the company for whom he/she is working, nor with its culture, nor with its expertise in the area under discussion. Moreover, at a personal level, the interpreter may end up becoming the focus of any interaction between parties; rather than establishing eye contact and developing a rapport with each other, they may well tend to concentrate on the interpreter who is speaking directly to them. Even if the interpreter manages to translate expertly, the actual communication may still be unsuccessful because signals in a translated utterance may not be picked up by the receiver since he/she is unaware of the cultural context, of the 'loading' which the words contain.

SPOTLIGHT 7.2

Dealing with a Japanese subsidiary

In her article 'A matter of interpretation'[1], Alicia Clegg gives an account of the problems which Gaelle Olivier, vice president of Axa, the French insurance group, encountered when dealing with a Japanese subsidiary which was struggling to survive in the market.

'Ms Olivier was sometimes told that a task would be "muzukashii". Her interpreter translated this as "difficult", which Ms Olivier took to mean tough but do-able. Only when her team repeatedly missed deadlines did she begin to understand that muzukashii is a cultural euphemism for saying "It is impossible and we cannot do it".

Misunderstandings prompt the question of whether it is better to work with interpreters who translate word for word or with those who sacrifice literal accuracy to get across the spirit of what is being said. Ms Olivier, who has since learned Japanese, prefers the literal approach. She believes that relying on the interpreter's potted version is risky and makes you even more of an outsider. "If you are living in a country, it is important to make yourself knowledgeable about its culture," she adds'.

[1] From A matter of interpretation, *Financial Times*, 02/02/2010, p. 16 (Alicia Clegg).

This concept has presented the main forms of communication exchange and addressed some of the issues involved in the choice of language in business encounters. The management of relations during such encounters has also been examined and this has shown the many facets of communication that people from different cultures need to be mindful of during face-to-face meetings.

The tendency to use stereotyping is also ever-present during such encounters and these will be discussed in Chapter 8.

Conclusion

This chapter has given a brief outline of the theory of communication, which is indispensable to a better understanding of intercultural communication. Even if language remains the dominant factor in communication situations, there are other elements that come into play, including the context, proxemics and facial expressions.

Even if they share a common language (English being increasingly used in business by non-native speakers), interlocutors may still experience problems because of their cultural backgrounds. Developments in computer (or mobile)-mediated communication in particular are changing the way people communicate. The numerous examples given in this chapter allow a better understanding of the new framework of intercultural business communication.

Points for reflection

1. The concept examined three possibilities with regard to the use of language during a business encounter. A fourth possibility is for the manager in question to learn the target language and employ translators.

   What advantages does this combination afford those involved?

2. When two people from different cultures meet in a business situation, the interaction, which is specific to each situation, does not allow the protagonists to be certain of the outcome of their encounter.

   What, in your opinion, are the factors that can influence the outcome of an intercultural interaction? Explain how these factors can influence the outcome.

Further reading

Gudykunst, W.B. (ed.) (2004) *Cross-Cultural and Intercultural Communication*, **Thousand Oaks, CA: Sage.** In his role as editor, W.B. Gudykunst has chosen to classify the contributions from experts in the field into two distinct categories: cross-cultural communication and intercultural communication. The difference lies essentially in the subject area being researched. Intercultural communication includes all aspects of the study of culture and communication. Cross-cultural communication research tends to be comparative and focuses on cultural communication – the role of communication – and cultural identities. The book covers such topics as: language and verbal communication across cultures; nonverbal communication across cultures; cultural influences on the expression and perception of emotions; identity and intergroup communication; communication in intercultural relationships; and adapting to an unfamiliar culture.

References

Corraze, J. (1988) *Les communications non-verbales*, 4th edn, Paris: Presses Universitaires de France.

Donnadieu, G. and Karsky, M. (2002) *La systémique*, Rueil-Malmaison, France: Editions Liaisons.

Hall, E.T. (1966) *The Hidden Dimension*, New York, NY: Bantam Doubleday Dell.

Hall, E.T. (1969) *The Hidden Dimension: Man's Use of Space in Public and Private*, London: Bodley Head.

Hall, E.T. and Hall, M.R. (1990) *Understanding Cultural Differences*, Yarmouth, ME: Intercultural Press ANC.

Herring, S. (1996) *Computer-Mediated Communication: Linguistic, Social and Cross-cultural Perspectives*, Amsterdam: John Benjamins. Quoted in: Waldvogel, J. (2001): 7-8.

Ladmiral, J.R. and Lipiansky, E.M. (1989) *La communication interculturelle*, Paris: Armand Colin.

Mead, R. (1990) *Cross-Cultural Management Communication*, Chichester: John Wiley.

Sauer, D. (2007) 'Gimlach', *Het Parool*, 16 June: 13.

Trumble, A. (2004) *A Brief History of the Smile*, New York, NY: Basic.

Waldvogel, J. (2001) 'Email and workplace communication: a literature review,' Wellington, New Zealand: Victoria University of Wellington, accessed 1 June 2008, www.vuw.ac.nz/lals/research/lwp/docs/ops/op3.htm.

Watson, O.M. (1970) *Proxemic behavior*, The Hague: Mouton. Quoted by Corraze, J. (1988) *Les communications non-verbales*, 179.

Chapter 7 Activities

ACTIVITY 7.1

English names catch on among Chinese: Young bridging a gap with West

By Jehangir S. Pocha

Di, Chao, Xu and Wentao now answer to Eddy, Super, Promise and Wendy

For pragmatic Chinese, adopting English names has long represented a way for them to bridge the linguistic and cultural gap. Now, as China widens its reach abroad and as the number of foreigners living in mainland China swells, picking an English name has become a rite of passage for most young, urban Chinese.

When students enrol in Chinese universities, they routinely are required to pick English names as a way to prepare themselves for life in their increasingly Westernized world. Students race to snap up the 'best' English names on a list the schools circulate.

'Popular names like Michael and Alex go quite fast, and Eddie was already gone before I could choose it,' said Eddy Wu, 19, a student at Beijing Forestry University, explaining that he wanted the name because it sounded like his Chinese name, Di. 'So I said "OK, let me take Eddy with this other spelling."'

People usually adopt only English first names and retain their Chinese family name. The practice is informal and has no legal significance. Sometimes, the results can be quirky, with Chinese names that potentially mystify foreigners often being replaced with English aliases that amuse them.

Super Zhang, 25, a paralegal in Beijing, said he chose his English name because it is a literal translation of his Chinese one, Chao. 'I like to see myself as a great and extraordinary person,' Super said. 'People wonder about my name all the time and are always asking me to explain it. But I still enjoy having it.'

Most Chinese take their English name – its meaning, its sound, and its associations with historic figures – very seriously. Promise Hong, a 30-year-old writer in Beijing, said her English name was a rough translation of her Chinese one, Xu, and that she saw a philosophical connotation in it.

'Promise has more profound meanings especially with the biblical background of the promised land,' she said. 'I began to use it when I was a freshman in college, twelve years ago, and some people I've met have expressed their kind appreciation and curiosity about my choice.'

In nineteenth-century China, choosing an English name was the privilege of only a handful of elites. Possessing one was a status symbol indicating that a person had been to college and rubbed shoulders with the 'laowai', the Puntonghua word for foreigner. The process of picking the name often involved weeks of discussions between the person, English tutors and foreign friends. Chinese sages would then vet the short list of names for their tonal qualities and astrological powers.

That English names are now ubiquitous in urban China is a sign of the country's progress, Eddy said. 'My parents tell me how once any foreigner on the street would be stared at, they were so unusual,' he said. 'Now, China is developing very fast and Chinese are becoming very modern.'

While most Chinese with English names reserve their use for times when they are in the company of foreigners, Eddy said more people, especially young women, prefer using their English names. This is particularly true for Chinese immigrants in the US and other English-speaking countries, who use their Western names to help them fit into their new world.

Wentao Zhang, 40, began calling herself Wendy while living in New Jersey for 15 years. 'It just makes things easier,' she said. 'People (in the US) used to find it really hard to say my name, so I began saying "Just call me Wendy" and it worked really well.'

This phonetic approach, picking a new name that sounds like your original one, sidesteps the pitfalls of trying to find English translations of Chinese names.

Of course, not every Chinese person has an English name. In the sleepy hamlets that dot the countryside, farmers and workers look surprised at the thought of taking an English name. And sometimes, name-changes alone are not enough to bridge the cultural gap.

Apple Li, 21, a travel agent in Beijing, said she chose her English name because her Chinese name is Ping and the Mandarin word for apple is 'pingguo'. But one problem remains: her business card reads Li Ping, since the Chinese write their family name first and given name second.

Many foreigners accustomed to the Western format assume that Li means apple in Mandarin, she said. Adding to the confusion is that Li, when written using a certain character, means pear.

Source: *Boston Globe*, 1 October 2006, accessed 1 June 2008, www.boston.com/news/world/asia/articles/2006/10/01/english_names_catch_on_among_chinese.

Questions

1. What are the reasons given for young Chinese adopting an English first name?
2. Do you think that this custom can help to improve communication between China and Western countries? Explain why.
3. What changes, if any, do you think the use of English names brings to the Chinese way of doing business? Explain your point of view.

ACTIVITY 7.2

The text below highlights the problem of cultural identity by describing developments in France, a country proud of the historical importance of French as the language of politics and culture. The behaviour of Jacques Chirac, born in 1932, president of France at the time, provoked many discussions on the role of English in French society.

Why English is de rigueur in many French boardrooms

By Tom Braithwaite in Paris and Chris Smyth

When Jacques Chirac stormed out of a meeting at the European Union summit, he said it was because he had been 'profoundly shocked' to hear a French industrialist speaking in English. On this basis, the French president may wish to stay away from a number of his nation's boardrooms.

Mr. Chirac's outrage was all too visible on Thursday night when he heard Ernest-Antoine Seillière, the head of the Unice employers' organization, explain he had decided to deliver his speech in English because it was 'the language of business'.

But in the boardroom of Air Liquide, the French industrial gases group, meetings are usually held in English. So too at the media group Thomson, once chaired by Thierry Breton, the French finance minister, who joined his president in boycotting Mr. Seillière's meeting. At France Telecom – where Mr. Breton was also once chairman – English is commonly used in internal memos.

French companies choose English because they do most business outside France and because of an increased foreign presence on their boards. Meetings at Total, the oil group, regularly take place in English, even when only Frenchmen are present. 'It's the language of the oil industry,' explains a spokeswoman. English is also the lingua franca at Thales and EADS – the French government has stakes in both defence groups.

Air France-KLM holds meetings of 'the strategy management committee' in English, while competence in the language is compulsory for managerial recruits at Renault. Mike Quigley, the chief operating officer and heir apparent at the telecoms equipment maker Alcatel, is an Australian who does not speak French. 'The English language has connotations of liberalism,' said Jean-Louis Muller, the director of Cegos, a management training school. 'The defence of the French language by politicians and unions is the defence of the French social model.'

Mr. Muller said the rise of English in French boardrooms appeared unstoppable: 'I witnessed a meeting at [engineering group] Alstom where there were only French managers in the room but English was still the language.'

Source: from Why English is de rigueur in many French boardrooms, *Financial Times*, 25/03/2008, p. 8 (Baithwaite, T. and Smith, C.).

Questions

1. What may explain the sudden departure by the president of France when a French industrialist used English to address the summit meeting?
2. Why, according to the interviews, is English used more and more in French boardrooms?
3. What, according to Jean-Louis Muller, do French and English seem to represent in terms of cultural identity?

Chapter 8

Barriers to Intercultural Communication

Apart from the framework of reference examined in Chapter 7 and the context of the communication, other elements play an important role in intercultural communication. These are essentially barriers to the communication process, as described in Figure III.1 in the Introduction to Part Three. When the sender and receiver in this figure are from different cultures, the communication process may be impaired through misunderstandings and may eventually break down. The barriers involved will be examined in the concept of this chapter.

Concept 8.1 examines the obstacles preventing the effective flow of information within an organization. These obstacles relate to either the failure of individuals to communicate effectively, or the failure of systems to make effective communication possible. The breakdown in communication is often to do with either too much information (information overload) or too little information, or it can be caused by communication that is misplaced, inaccurate or incomplete. It may also involve the context: personal and environmental factors can impair the quality of the information received. The context of communication is often complicated by the question of culture, with misunderstandings occurring when the sender and receiver do not share similar meanings for the communicated symbols.

Learning outcomes

After reading this chapter you will gain an understanding of:

- Those components of communication that can create obstacles in intercultural communication.
- The importance of the effects that barriers have on communication in business.

Concept 8.1 Barriers in cross-cultural management communication

What are communication barriers?

Ideally, for communication to take place, the frameworks of reference being used – with regard to norms and values, for example – should not be in conflict. However, since a framework of reference is to a considerable degree culturally determined, it is to be expected that the communication between individuals from two different cultures will be disturbed.

Some problems of this nature can occur when doing business with foreign partners, working with foreign colleagues in the same company, or within a joint venture with a foreign company. Communication problems may happen not only during meetings or negotiations, but also during informal situations. A barrier can lead to a business opportunity falling through and/or a business relationship ending on the rocks.

Such disturbing factors between cultures are many in number and nature (see Figure III.1 in the Introduction). Breakdowns in communication commonly occur when the context of the message being communicated between the sender and receiver is unclear. Some barriers to communication originate from cultural misunderstandings between the speaker and receiver and these can clearly be of great importance for communication in business. Before looking at these barriers in detail, this chapter will discuss some notions that offer insights into the causes of misunderstandings in communication between cultures.

Non-verbal behaviour as barrier

Is non-verbal behaviour natural or cultural? Is it productive (monologue) or communicative (dialogue)? Is it done voluntarily or spontaneously? We know from the many researchers who have investigated this phenomenon that antiquity was also fascinated by it and, moreover, that non-verbal communication plays an important role in communication as a whole. What this term encompasses is so large that this discussion must confine itself to gestures, facial expression (including affective expressions such as laughter or showing anger), posture and the distance between sender and receiver. These are all closely allied to, or indeed replace, verbal communication in terms of producing messages. They may even contradict the accompanying verbal messages. In short, all these also have a communicative value over and above verbal communication.

Meta-communication and non-verbal behaviour

In its basic form, a meta-communication is an act of communication between two protagonists that also communicates something about the communication itself, or about the relationship between the two protagonists, or both.

In terms of non-verbal behaviour, meta-communicative functions can also include:

- making gestures to complete messages when information is missing (e.g. when gesturing to indicate someone's height or size);
- making hand gestures and modulating the voice by adding rhythm and emphasis to reinforce the verbal message;
- replacing spoken language when it is impossible for some reason (physical barriers, the dominance of other sounds, unknown foreign language).

The nature of this meta-communicative behaviour is determined by personal, social, relational and cultural factors. The nature of the interaction itself may be modified by the intended character of the non-verbal signal of the sender on the one hand, and by the way the receiver reacts to the signal on the other.

The cultural dimension of non-verbal behaviour is apparent once the body language used by interlocutors from different cultures is compared and contrasted. The interactional nature of face-to-face communication therefore takes on an intercultural dimension. All cultures use forms of body language to communicate, but the meaning of these forms is subject to different interpretations according to the cultural background of the interpreter.

Non-verbal interaction

Although facial expressions communicating anger, sadness and fear are considered to be universal, the causes of these expressions may be different. Other gestures, however, may not be so universal: a nod of the head may well be expected to indicate affirmation and a shake negation, but some cultures nod to negate and shake to affirm (for example the Greeks give a shake of the head to say 'yes'). When a speaker raises his shoulders, this could convey indifference, resignation or ignorance, depending on the cultural context. Furthermore, to convey the idea that someone is stupid can be conveyed in several ways, depending on the cultural context. If the gesture or expression made is unknown in another culture, then its meaning will not be understood. Communication could be interrupted or, if an incorrect meaning is applied by the 'receiver', diverted.

When those interacting come from different cultures, the non-verbal signals used in a certain context may therefore not only differ but also necessarily influence other consequent non-verbal signals. Furthermore, the question of the intention behind non-verbal language must also be addressed. How is it possible to determine whether the sender (if from another culture) has intentionally chosen to transmit a non-verbal message with an exact purpose or whether he is pretending to do so? The receiver is expected to respond to the signal given by the sender who in turn may need to re-adjust his communicative goal, vary the non-verbal messages so that the desired goal is eventually reached. Non-verbal behaviour therefore can be crucial in face-to-face interaction.

Those communicating across cultures therefore must be careful not to assume that certain gestures have the same meaning as in their own culture. In France, for example, pulling one's eyelid down with the forefinger means 'I don't believe you!' In Italy, however, the same gesture means something very different: 'I'm keeping an eye on you!'

Since gestures are a purely cultural acquisition, they also reveal certain characteristics of a culture's collective mentality. Let us compare the expression 'to be fed up with . . .' or 'have had enough of . . .' in France and the Netherlands (Figure 8.1).

Figure 8.1 'I've had enough!'

The gesture for these words is made in the same way by raising one's hand to the head. However, there is a crucial difference as to where the hand movement stops. In France, the hand stops at the top of the head but in the Netherlands it stops earlier – at the neck. Therefore, in this example, it is more than only a difference of gesture: the gesture represents a cultural attitude that here expresses either the limit of exasperation or loss of patience.

We can only make tentative explanations about how certain gestures and body language generally came into being. This is due to the unstable nature of the values of gestures associated with a language. If, for example, we look at the past with Cresswell (1968), he reminds us that in the eighteenth century there was disapproval of the tendency of the English to use gestures when speaking. A century later, however, the English were characterized for their 'phlegm', their calm self-possession!

Non-verbal communication barriers in business

Although verbal communication is essential in business contacts and can be the main source of misunderstandings between cultures, language differences can be a dominant factor in any communication barrier and can even be an insurmountable one. Just as with translating from one language to another, it can be difficult to convey the full meaning and nuances of expression. As seen in Chapter 7, using English as a means of communication can make the situation easier when doing business, but this does not mean, of course, that misunderstandings do not occur. This applies even to native speakers of English who come from different countries.

However, non-verbal communication can also be a source of misunderstanding and irritation. For example, research carried out into the use of body language by Dutch and French people from a similar business environment showed how great the differences were. When using gestures, for example, the French are very expressive and use the whole upper part of their body. The Dutch, on the other hand, usually limit gestures to the use of their arms – or just one arm – to emphasize the rhythm of their speech. When the Dutch are interacting with the French they can easily come to the conclusion that their interlocutors are very emotional and excited since, in their culture, such 'exaggerated' use of gestures is only witnessed when very strong emotions are at play (Browaeys, 1989).

Silence can also be a cause of misunderstandings, particularly between Western and Asian cultures. In Western cultures, silence marks pauses in a discourse. These pauses must not last too long, unlike those in oriental cultures where any time without a word being spoken is an integral part of communication. In Thailand, for example, silence is not only a sign of respect, of agreement or disagreement, but it is also highly appreciated as a style of discourse. Asian cultures discourage verbalization since it contradicts the principle of modesty. In Korea, silence is preferable to the improper use of words. Japan, however, appears to be the exception: even if silence is preferred to verbalization, it can also be considered as being impolite in situations where active participation by the interlocutors is expected. This is especially the case where an interlocutor is a stranger; remaining silent 'is considered more negative than it is in America' (Tae-Seop Lim, 2003: 62).

It should be said at this point that such examples of non-verbal communication are simply styles of communication and do not indicate that a particular culture experiences more or less emotion. However, the way all sorts of feelings are expressed can be so different between cultures that it can result in representatives of one culture having negative feelings towards another. The creation of such prejudices is not the differences in themselves but the way in which the differences are interpreted.

Assumptions and culture

Cultural assumptions evolve as basic human responses to fundamental problems. Usunier and Lee (2005) provide a framework for the evaluation of the problems and combine three dimensions. Assumptions may have: a cognitive dimension, related to presumptions as to how people think that things work; an affective dimension, related to the presumed likings of people; and a directive dimension related to the presumed choices of people.

Cultural assumptions can be related to time, space or identity. Time-related cultural assumptions relate to four common questions:

- Is time considered as a scarce good (economy of time)?
- Are tasks performed simultaneously or one after the other (monochronic versus polychronic)?
- Is life seen as a continuity or as cyclic episodes?
- Is the orientation in time towards the past, the present or the future?

Cultural assumptions that are space-related have to do with being 'in' or 'out'; being a member or not; belonging or not belonging. The strict opposition defines the content of the 'out-group' and 'in-group' whereby the group space includes – or excludes – families, nations and cultures. Out-group orientation is based on the assumption that there is a unity of mankind beyond the borders of in-group spaces. In-group orientation does not completely exclude out-group orientation. This can be seen, for example, in Nordic European cultures, where a strong sense of national identity goes along with a strong commitment to the development of the poorest nations and international organizations.

Identity-related assumptions relate to self and others and are about the ideal conduct in certain social contexts. They are related to the main socio-demographic categories (age, sex, social class), as well as to particular roles in society (such as the perfect politician, or successful businessman).

Cultural assumptions are difficult for foreigners to detect because they are not easily expressed and are, for the most part, hardly understood by the insiders. As seen in Part One, statements may be given about values and ideas, but the underlying assumptions are generally unclear. There is a gap between the explanations that people give for their behaviour and the real motives for the behaviour. In the same way, there is a difference between what people say and what people want to say (Schneider and Barsoux, 2003). That is why assumptions can generate a lack of understanding and misunderstandings when people from different cultures are communicating.

Barriers

Apart from a system of values, every culture has assumptions that are seldom tested for their justifiability. These are affirmations, mostly normative in nature, about what is true and what is not. To be accepted in a culture or subculture, one has to respect these assumptions.

What 'should be done' is generally close to what is believed to be the 'nature of things'. However, assumptions about 'how things are' are often disguised suppositions about 'how they should be'. Moreover, once the values of a group are institutionalized and assimilated, they acquire a kind of existential validity for the members of the group. Sometimes, a value acts as a self-fulfilling prophecy and causes behaviour that complies with the idea, e.g. 'men don't cry' (Oomkes, 1987).

As such, assumptions can create all kinds of problems. A simple example from the business world shows how they can even lead to conflict (Spotlight 8.1). Imagine you receive an order confirmation from a supplier stating that the delivery date of the order will be two weeks. The question is: what does a Dutch supplier mean by 'delivery date' compared with a French supplier?

SPOTLIGHT 8.1

Delivery date: two weeks

Paul had recently begun working as the purchasing manager of a French-owned company in the Netherlands. He was in a bad mood because of a delay resulting from a bottle-neck. His mood worsened when he read a memo on his desk. The memo informed him that an order to be supplied by the parent company had not yet been delivered, although it should have arrived two weeks previously.

Delivery delays had almost become a routine problem in his dealings with the parent company. He sent a very business-like reply stating briefly, in English, that he had not yet received the goods on order and that they must be delivered as soon as possible, otherwise he would have to turn to an outside supplier.

The reply came by email, three pages of it, written in French by Jacques, the production manager. His tone was friendly:

We have done everything possible, but you see – what with the renovation of the production area and the holiday period, as well as the specifications of your order – there has been a delay. But don't worry: it's only a question of time now – a little patience and all will be fine.

Paul was flabbergasted by what he considered to be French arrogance. His reaction was as follows:

Firstly, I don't understand French, and secondly, the delivery date had been clearly indicated in the order, namely in two weeks' time. The two weeks have elapsed and now it's a simple matter of whether the goods are here or not. That's the only thing that counts here.

A Dutch supplier will in all likelihood think that the product must be delivered within two weeks: he feels contractually bound to this delivery time. A French supplier, however, may well think that he will do everything he can to dispatch the goods by the date given. For him this date is a promise that is still subject to negotiation.

This problem of interpretation is not a language issue but a cultural one. The words are clear, but the assumptions underlying the words may differ from culture to culture. This can also be seen in the use of words describing time such as 'soon' or 'straightaway'. Does that mean in one minute or an hour? These words can have a very different meaning in Indonesia than in Germany.

Table 8.1 Who is saying what about whom?

Who/About whom?	What?
Germans	They're pretentious
British	They've got no sense of humour
Americans	They're chauvinist
Spaniards	They're hypocritical
Dutch	They're arrogant
French	They're individualistic

Source: Based on Gruère and Morel (1991).

Perceptions and stereotypes

Table 8.1 is an example of an introduction to the question of stereotypes. In the right hand column is a list of stereotypical remarks made by or about a number of Western cultures given in the left hand column. Can you work out which nationality says what about whom?

The French could be the subject of all the stereotypical remarks in Table 8.1. The Germans consider the French to be showy, the Americans see them as chauvinistic, the Spanish as hypocritical, and the Dutch view them as the embodiment of arrogance. The British may even see them as having no sense of humour. And the French see themselves as individualistic.

However, all the comments given on the right could be applied to each other by all the nationalities in question. Some generally perceived stereotypical characteristics may well emerge from such an exercise: the British could consider that the Germans have no sense of humour. They are very serious and any humour a German displays does not fit into the British concept of what is funny. The Dutch could well consider the French as chauvinist. They see themselves as being much more tolerant of other nationalities than the French and do not so readily express their feelings of superiority. All the European nationalities could well consider the Americans to be arrogant. In their eyes the Americans may come over as people who wish to impose on others what they think is best for them. Europeans may consider themselves superior to the Americans, but do not express their feelings of superiority so crassly.

Every culture sees its own system of values in a positive light. So when asked to apply a stereotypical characteristic to itself, every culture listed above could, for example, refer to itself as being individualistic because in the West this is generally considered to be a positive trait.

However, if individuals of a specific nationality within a multicultural group are confronted with negative rather than positive stereotypes of themselves by other nationalities, these individuals will, according to Lipianski (1992), not recognize themselves in the profile made. They will react strongly because they feel personally under attack and deny belonging to the group being characterized. They will defend their own personal identity and see their national identity more in terms of 'them' rather than 'us'.

Identity as an obstacle to communication

National identity therefore appears first as a compulsory image imposed by the outside world. It may characterize people with the same nationality, but it is an identity that the people may not recognize in themselves. In intercultural encounters, this identity dimension influences communication. Indeed, there is no communication without identity and identification of the persons present. According to Ladmiral and Lipianski (1989: 145), when people meet for the first time it is difficult to avoid asking and answering questions to do with identity (Who are you? Where do you come from?). For these authors: 'It is a question of knowing at the same moment the identity of my interlocutor and what elements of my own identity (sexual, social, professional, national, ideological) are going to be required during our exchange.'

However, identity can also appear as an obstacle to communication because the identity of both interlocutors defines and sets the limits of the exchange. The conflicts of ideas, opinions and interpretations – also in the interpersonal relations between individuals of different nationalities – refer to identity conflicts: on the one hand there is the alter ego, namely the double who reflects our own image, and on the other hand the opponent for whom we feel aversion (Ladmiral and Lipianski, 1989). The perception of the other always has a projective nature and can only have one's own culture as base and reference. This phenomenon is called **ethnocentrism** and refers to the values of one's own culture even when dealing with others who cannot share these values.

> **Likewise, the tendency exists to describe and judge the value systems and dominant practices of other cultures from the standpoint of one's own. Such an attitude has connections with the stereotyping of others.**
>
> Edgar and Sedgwick, 2002: 133

Ethnocentrism is inherent to any membership of a socio-cultural, ethnic or national group. It is the intrinsic mechanism of distinction separating mine from yours, relatives from foreigners, people here from people elsewhere. Ethnocentrism is both a cultural feature and a psychological phenomenon. It leads to any perception being made through a barrier that is unconsciously made up of our own values. Ethnocentrism, in its most simplified and elementary form, is responsible for forming prejudices and stereotypes – 'ready-for-use judgments' (Ladmiral and Lipianski, 1989: 138).

Consumer attitudes and perceptions about foreign products are highly influenced by ethnocentrism, the belief in the superiority of one's own ethnic group. Usunier and Lee (2005) report that highly ethnocentric consumers, who are usually older people, are likely to believe that purchasing imported products harms the domestic economy and causes unemployment. Younger consumers, they found, were less affected by ethnocentricity. This means that domestic companies may benefit to a certain extent from ethnocentrism. However, they also found that the resistance experienced by foreign companies to their products depends on the product category (e.g. wine, cars) and the consumers targeted.

Stereotyping in advertising

Stereotypes can be a disturbing factor not only in communication, but also in other areas of management. It is advisable in marketing to tread very carefully when it comes to stereotyping across consumer nationalities.

MINI-CASE 8.1

'Unleash the power of the Hispanic market by avoiding these pitfalls'

By Mary Baroutakis

While writing this article, I tried to narrow down the number of pitfalls that marketers encounter when advertising to the Hispanic market. There are many, but for the sake of brevity, I will address the three that I come across most frequently:

- overusing Hispanic traits in ads;
- cloning a general market strategy for use in the Hispanic market; and
- keeping Hispanic advertising less ambitious and far more conservative than that aimed at the general market.

Overusing Hispanic traits

We have all heard again and again that Hispanics are very family-oriented; that they are very close to their extended family; that they take care of their elders; that children tend to live at home after they reach 18. We've also heard that Hispanics tend to be emotional and sentimental. They listen to their hearts a lot and value relationships. This brings me to the first common mistake: the overuse of the above traits in Hispanic advertising and how this can sometimes weaken or cloud a selling message.

A few years ago, a telecommunications company aired a commercial introducing a new plan for international callers to Latin America. The commercial was absolutely beautiful. It was shot on location in many parts of Latin America and the scenery was breathtaking. It showed vignettes of people abroad receiving calls from their family in the US. The background music score was very nostalgic.

The research company that pre-tested this commercial uncovered very positive findings for the client. After a couple of months on the air, however, the amount of calls to the free phone number in the commercial seeking more information was very disappointing. The client was perplexed. What happened? Why was there was so little interest?

The client contacted us because they wanted another firm to re-test the spot. We did so and found, to the client's and agency's amazement, that the first research company had misread the results. Even though the target audience understood the main message and liked the spot, all they retained were the bittersweet images of the people back home, the beautiful scenery and the feeling of nostalgia for their family and country. The execution had gone overboard using warm-and-fuzzy family scenes and nostalgia to sell its product. After people saw this commercial at home, they made a call – but not to the free number to inquire about the calling plan. Instead, they called their mother, or their grandmother or their sister in Latin America. They had been distracted by these warm scenes and completely forgot about the calling plan!

Our client decided to start from scratch. A new commercial was shot based on our findings and recommendations. In this new spot, the calling plan was 'the hero' – not the family or the scenery. It was a happy commercial but also one that provided factual information about the calling plan. This new commercial broke all previous records in number of calls received and new subscribers to the plan.

Cloning the general market

The next pitfall is using a general market strategy for the Hispanic market. Generally, marketers like to do this because it keeps everything nice and organized. It is also the path of least resistance: upper management will buy into their plans faster and it's easier to deal with one strategy.

Using a general market strategy may be effective but this can only be determined after testing various options. I can't count the number of times that marketers have decided to use a general market approach before any testing has been conducted among the intended Hispanic target.

Before taking this step, advertisers must be sure that this will be the most compelling strategy. It isn't that the general market strategy is plain wrong, it's just not the one that will attract most Hispanic consumers. An even worse scenario is forcing the use of a general market commercial (re-shot with Hispanic actors) to target Hispanics.

Here's an example of both pitfalls. A while back, we tested a commercial for a drink that was being sold as 'offbeat and wacky' in the general market. The client wanted to define the brand the same way in the Hispanic market, so a number of commercials were produced using this strategy. By the way, this was the first time this client had advertised to the Hispanic market and this was the first piece of Hispanic research it had conducted. In other words, without knowing if this wacky, offbeat personality would sell in the Hispanic market, the client and the agency had already produced five radio commercials, which we were going to test.

The focus group participants rejected this strategy. Unfamiliar with this drink's general market spots, Hispanics had their own image of the product – they saw it as fun and friendly – and what was being presented went against that perception. They felt that this product, as presented in the radio executions, was for weird, confused people!

We also tested a commercial for an ice-cream brand that was a word-for-word adaptation of the general market spot. In this case, the spot used humour to make its point – American humour translated into Spanish.

The spot features a couple of vignettes. One tested well, the other did not. It shows a little boy telling his father that he's going to wash the family car. What he neglects to say is that he intends to use a scouring pad. When the father finds out, the announcer comes on and tells him: 'Relax, and enjoy some of our ice cream.' No one saw the situation as funny. And, everyone agreed that this would not be the right time to enjoy this product.

Inordinate caution

Another mistake advertisers make quite frequently is 'holding back their horses', in other words, running more 'in-the-box,' less ambitious advertising in the Hispanic market. Hispanic consumers complain about this phenomenon all the time.

Why does this happen? Many reasons are cited. The one we hear most often from Hispanic agencies is that Hispanic production budgets are much lower than those allocated for the general market. But we all know that big budgets don't always lead to great commercials nor do low budgets result in poor advertising.

There is another possible reason, however, for creating less-ambitious Hispanic ads – the idea that simplistic, innocuous commercials are good enough for the Hispanic market or even worse, that 'out-of-the-box' commercials do not appeal or are not understood by Hispanic consumers. How many times have we heard the phrase 'Hispanics take everything literally'? This is generally true in instances where the audience is looking for concrete information. It should not be used as an excuse, however, to lower standards in the Hispanic market.

Less ambitious, more run-of-the-mill advertising falls short of achieving goals, especially with Hispanic teenagers and young adults who are bilingual and also watch American TV and tend to compare the Spanish with the English language ads.

For example, we tested some commercials for a sports drink that strongly appeals to Hispanic male teens and young adults. They complained that the Hispanic commercials for this product constantly showed young males like themselves playing different sports (basketball, soccer, baseball) in different venues (the park, the beach, the gym). These commercials may be new but they always come across as old and tired. These consumers couldn't help comparing them with the general market commercials, which they described as cutting-edge. And the question remains: why does a leading-edge product use tired, run-of-the-mill commercials to attract its Hispanic target?

Unfortunately, the root of many of these marketing mistakes is the result of preconceived notions or impressions about ethnic markets. When it comes to the general market, no client expects its agency or researchers to be experts on Americans and the American way of life. Think for example what you would say as an American if someone asked you 'What are Americans like?' You probably wouldn't even know where to start or what to say. The American market is not a static market. New things happen all the time and that's why studies are conducted every day. You would never ask such a general question of your agency or researchers. Yet this question is asked every day of Hispanic agencies, consultants and primary researchers. What is odd is that there are people who answer this question, ignoring the fact that things are constantly changing in the Hispanic market as well.

Source: *Quirk's Marketing Research Review*, April 2000, article 20000402, accessed 1 September 2010, http://www.quirks.com/articles/a2000/20000402.aspx?%20searchID=2071341.

Questions

1. How would you summarize the suggestions made by the author for avoiding the three pitfalls mentioned?
2. Regarding your own country, give some principles for avoiding cultural mistakes in situations similar to those described in the case.

Having seen how stereotypes can be a disturbing factor in marketing as well as communication, we need to examine the way stereotypes are formed.

Building stereotypes

In specifically cultural terms, the starting-point for building stereotypes is the norms and values of the culture concerned. When someone from that culture judges someone from another culture, the tendency is for that person to do so using these norms and values. If the person being judged does not conform to these in some way through their behaviour – or simply appearance – then a negative judgement will probably be made.

A stereotype is a series of images created in our minds with regard to a group or groups of people, in this context: cultural groups. These images are over-generalizations made through selective perceptions (self-perceptions) and information that corresponds with our beliefs. The development of prejudices, which are a 'distinct combination of feelings, inclinations to act and beliefs' (Myers, 2005: 333), is supported or provoked by our cultural environment: family, friends and the media can fill us with stereotyping images of all kinds. A stereotype is therefore a confirmation of prejudices rather than the result of accurate observations of reality.

Comments, jokes, commercials and anecdotes can create and perpetuate stereotypes, categorize nationalities in a way that sustains a culture's norms and values.

Spotlight 8.2 illustrates how a prejudice can lead to unjustifiable behaviour of one group towards another.

SPOTLIGHT 8.2

The misunderstood marketing manager

A Dutch company wanted to introduce a new product into its range. On-site production would be too costly and, besides, there was a US company already manufacturing this product.

The marketing manager decided to phone this supplier. 'Yes' was their reaction, but only if a large quantity were to be ordered. The minimum amount they stated was much more than the Dutch market would warrant. When told this, the US manufacturer suggested the Dutch company contact a partner of theirs operating in France.

So the marketing manager phoned the French company. Talking in French to the manager of the production department, he gave the name of this company in the usual way, explaining that he would like to buy this product because the US company was unable to supply the small amount which they required. The Dutchman was told to put his request in writing.

The Dutchman was really shocked by this reaction and accused the French of being odd. Why could they not simply give him the information he required over the phone?

The French manager had asked for a request in writing because the Dutch marketing manager had put forward his query without any preliminaries, and had not fully introduced his company. The Frenchman could not therefore 'place' the person on the other end of the phone. He needed to know exactly which company he was doing business with, and the identity of the man proposing the co-operation in the first place.

After he had put down the phone, the Frenchman wondered: 'Who the hell was this guy with the funny accent?'

To summarize the building process of stereotypes, it can be said that prejudices, which may be positive or negative in nature, are basic, irrational reactions that depend simply on how someone views the group in question in terms of their own cultural preferences. People may be classified in some way socially on the basis of a perception of common attributes: people may perceive them as members of an 'in-group', sharing a system of values or as members of an 'out-group' whose values counter theirs in some way. As prejudices are confirmed over and over again through such selective perceptions, people develop stereotypical images that come quickly to mind and which serve to legitimize the statements people make about another culture. However, as indicated earlier, cultural stereotypes may also display positive traits, particularly when people perceive that there are aspects of another culture's norms and values that reflect their own and in an exemplary way.

This issue of prejudices and stereotypes is illustrated in Spotlight 8.3. Most people regard the information and computer technology (ICT) sector to be a male preserve. This is indeed the case, since the majority of ICT workers in most countries are male. Malaysia, however, is an exception.

SPOTLIGHT 8.3

Delete stereotypes!

ICT is a male profession! In Malaysia, such a statement raises smiles. In the faculty of information technologies of Kuala Lumpur, the capital, all those in positions of responsibility in the department are women, including the dean. In Penang, 65 per cent of the ICT students and seven of the ten ICT professors are women, as well as the dean. The head of the department says she has never considered ICT as a male discipline: 'I do not see anything male in ICT!'. The reasons she gives are that ICT is clean work, does not require much physical strength, is an activity exercised in the service sector, and allows those employed in it to work at home. In contrast, outside Malaysia, ICT is a very masculine sector. In France, it is the only scientific profession where there has been a very large fall in the proportion of females employed.

Source: extract from Isabelle Collet (2007), 'L'informatique a-t-elle un sexe?', *Le Monde Diplomatique*, June: 3.

However, stereotypes are not always based on prejudices. A stereotype may have an intrinsic quality as shown in the passage below on the perception of Confucianism in the world of business.

Stereotypes in the Confucian business world

Cazal (1993) raises the question of stereotypes in business relating to Confucianism. This system of thought was referred to in Chapter 4 when the importance of loyalty in Chinese business relations was being discussed. Cazal wonders how present-day Confucianism, which he defines as 'a specific discourse constructed to maintain the economic development and performance of [Asian-run] companies' (Cazal, 1993: 188), is perceived in the West and in Asia. He reminds us of an important characteristic of Confucianism whereby formal value is attached to status in the sense that a person in a subordinate position must behave in a way that conforms to that of his interlocutor. Nowadays, however, a subordinate is not expected to adhere to these Confucian principles.

Foreigners, especially those who have lived in South Korea, observe that Confucianism still survives in social relations, such as those within the hierarchy based on age, gender and qualifications. Although these people still see that it reflects a philosophy that rests on the principle of harmony, they consider the majority of the stereotypes resulting from it as being negative in nature. Some Asians are critical of Confucianism, seeing it as a 'cultural alibi for political, social and managerial abuses' (Cazal, 1993: 190). Cazal ends up by questioning whether present-day Confucianism is itself a stereotype since its principles are far from the founding precepts in the teachings of Confucius. Even if classic Confucianism serves as a reference, this doctrine as applied in countries such as China, South Korea and Japan lacks unity and homogeneity.

Several articles have commented on and misrepresented Confucian thought. And that explains why doubt can be cast on the unity of Confucianism as a doctrine in countries such as China, South Korea and Japan, even if this unity is to be found at a practical level.

Dealing with stereotypes

The question remains: what is the best way of dealing with prejudices and stereotypes? Is it best to try and suppress them, fight against them or simply ignore them? The best route may lie in the views of those anthropologists (including Caroll (1987) and Hall (1983)), who approach the question of cultural differences without battling against stereotypes or without creating stereotypes to replace the old ones. It is better when dealing with other cultures not to fight against stereotypes and prejudices. A stereotype is, after all, the first stage in the process whereby the existence of another culture is acknowledged.

Furthermore, it can be argued that stereotypes are a necessary way of establishing one's own cultural identity. If a cultural group cannot compare itself with other groups then it cannot become aware of what it is. All its characteristics must be perceived in terms of those characteristics of others. In this context, a stereotype can be seen as an articulation of this differentiation, even though it is based on prejudices and imperfect information.

Moreover, if stereotypes were to be somehow set aside, the vacuum created would inevitably be filled by those who had set them aside. In other words, the culture of these people would be perceived as the one and only culture in the world – the worst of all prejudices.

Nevertheless, cross-cultural researchers are attempting to find perception areas that cultures share, rather than the differences. In the best of all possible worlds, people would be able to place another culture in its own context and so avoid judging a culture on the basis of their own. Only then would stereotypes eventually disappear.

Finally, it should be noted that there is a dynamic element present when two people are communicating, namely interaction. Not only do the specific characteristics of the speakers play a role, but also the structure of the situation and the context, as well as time and space (see Chapter 7). If you are aware of the barriers when communicating with your interlocutor, this does not mean that you are unable to conduct the conversation well. The variable nature of the interaction makes every communicative situation unique and therefore unpredictable.

Every culture proposes a structure which, even if it is not unchanging, forces its members to conform to it, and it is by the process of communication that it succeeds in doing so. Furthermore, as seen in this chapter, the encounters between cultures often destabilize the process of communication, create barriers and lack of understanding between the interlocutors. At the same time, thanks to these intercultural contacts, the expression of a culture – and thereby the way it communicates – evolves without any loss of identity. On the contrary, this identity is maintained because, according to Todorov (1986: 16), 'what happens between cultures is per se an element of culture'.

The concepts described in Chapters 7 and 8 can be used as a basis for any form of communication in the professional domain.

Conclusion

This chapter has elaborated the model of communication given in the introduction by looking at barriers to intercultural situations in general and in those in business in particular. The culture of the interlocutors filters the information and interprets it according to their own reference framework. Barriers can build up at various levels: badly interpreted gestures, a smile expressing the opposite of satisfaction, concrete words having an implicit meaning. Stereotypes, however, remain the most important barrier in communication. They are very difficult to deal with since they are formed by the identity and the perceptions of individuals.

Points for reflection

1. Stereotypes appear in all cross-cultural situations. When you are doing business with other cultures, stereotypes particularly arise in meetings and negotiations. If you are aware of the stereotypes of the group you are dealing with, it may help you at the beginning of the interaction.

   What is your opinion of this statement?

2. You have just read about barriers to communicating with other cultures. Some of these can lead to misunderstandings, others can degenerate into conflict.

   Which of these barriers, in your opinion, can lead to misunderstandings and which of them can lead to conflict? Explain your choice.

Further reading

Mead, R. (1990) *Cross-Cultural Management Communication*, **Chichester: John Wiley.** This book explores the many aspects and problems of cross-cultural communication encountered by managers. It focuses on understanding management cultures, and explores how situations within the context of different cultures and markets can be interpreted accurately. The author shows how management priorities are decided and communicated in different cultures and examines the organizational problems managers may face when operating in other cultures. Despite its age, this book remains a useful reference.

References

Browaeys, M.-J. (1989) *Les gestes conversationnels et les différences culturelles en France et aux Pays-Bas*, Amsterdam: Universiteit van Amsterdam.

Browaeys, M.-J. and Trompenaars, F. (eds) (2000) *Cases Studies on Cultural Dilemmas*, Breukelen, Netherlands: Nyenrode University Press.

Caroll, R. (1987) *Evidences invisibles*, Paris: Editions du Seuil.

Cazal, D. (1993) 'Ethique et management interculturel: le cas du confucianisme d'entreprise', in Bosche, M. (ed.), *Le management interculturel*, Paris: Editions Nathan: 181-192.

Cresswell, R. (1968) 'Le geste manuel associé aux langages', *Langages*, 10: 119-127.

Edgar, A. and Sedgwick, P. (eds) (2002) *Cultural Theory: The Key Concepts*, London: Routledge.

Gruère, J.-P. and Morel, P. (1991) *Cadres français et communications interculturelles*, Paris: Editions Eyrolles.

Hall, E.T. (1983) *The Dance of Life*, New York, NY: Anchor Press/Doubleday.

Ladmiral, J.R. and Lipianski, E.M. (1989) *La communication interculturelle*, Paris: Armand Colin.

Lipianski, E.-M. (1992) 'Identité, communication interculturelle et dynamique des groupes', in *Interculturel: groupe et transition*, Toulouse: Editions Erès: 59-70.

Myers, D.G. (2005) *Social Psychology*, 8th edn, New York, NY: McGraw-Hill.

Oomkes, F.R. (1987) *Communicatieleer*, Amsterdam: Boom Meppel.

Schneider, S.C. and Barsoux, J.-L. (2003) *Managing Across Cultures*, 2nd edn, Harlaw: Pearson Education.

Tae-Seop Lim (2003) 'Language and verbal communication across cultures', in Gudykunst, W.B. (ed.), *Cross-Cultural and Intercultural Communication*, Thousand Oaks, CA: Sage: 53-71.

Todorov, T. (1986) 'Le croisement des cultures', *Communications*, 43: 5-24.

Usunier, J.-C. and Lee, J.A. (2005) *Marketing across cultures*, 4th edn, Harlow: Pearson Education.

Chapter 8 Activities

ACTIVITY 8.1

Read the text below which describes how Germany tried to improve its image during the 2006 World Cup which was held in Germany. Answer the questions that follow the text.

Germans aim to spring a World Cup surprise: they're fun

Soft power: The nation long seen as dull is plotting an image overhaul that could help it punch its weight on the international stage

By Hugh Williamson

For the host country Germany, next month's football World Cup is about a lot more than its (pretty slim) chances of lifting the trophy. An image overhaul for Europe's largest economy is the prize in its sights.

Robert Rode, a Berlin bus driver, understands the scale of the challenge. A stocky man with a strong local accent who speaks little English, he was one of 4,000 drivers who recently struggled through a 'World Cup language course'. Taking a break from learning how to guide fans through Berlin, he says that, despite the tongue-twisting, the course was worth it. 'When people arrive in Berlin, say at the airport or main station, and the first German they talk to is a bus driver who either cannot understand them or tells them to go and ask someone else, then that doesn't create a very good impression.'

Mr. Rode is in good company. True to the tournament motto 'A time to make friends', chancellor Angela Merkel and her government, leading companies and cultural organizations and dozens of local authorities, have planned thousands of initiatives in the most ambitious attempt by a country to alter the way it is viewed. Ms Merkel heralded the tournament as 'a unique chance for Germany to present itself as a welcoming, tolerant and modern country, bursting with ideas'.

But as teams arrive in Germany this week ahead of kick-off on June 9, a senior German official is disarmingly candid. 'The world generally sees us in a positive, but one-sided way. A bit like the cars and household goods for which we are famous, Germans are seen as efficient, reliable but a touch boring. We need to show we are more than this: friendly, surprising and fun.' At stake is more than national *amour propre*. The transformation is seen as vital if Berlin is to maximize the country's post-reunification potential on the world stage.

The business community alone has invested more than €10m ($12.8m, £6.8m) to promote Germany as a 'Land of Ideas'. 'An opportunity of this kind will not return for another 50 years,' says Franz Beckenbauer, president of the German tournament organizing committee.

Since 1990, Germany has stepped up its public diplomacy, as it has increased its role in international peacekeeping operations and intensified efforts to gain a permanent United Nations Security Council seat. Its World Cup campaign marks not only a new milestone in its engagement with the world but also a form of laboratory experiment in whether image offensives work.

Many are sceptical. A German ambassador, who declined to be named, argues: 'You can't market a country like a washing powder. To believe you can just tell others that, all of a sudden we [Germans] have become funny and good looking, is wrong. You can't deceive people.'

Germany's endeavour, which started three years ago, includes a €30m arts programme linking soccer and culture: a 'friendly service campaign' involving handbooks on how to welcome foreign guests; and giant sculptures in Berlin of football boots and aspirins to illustrate the wonders of German creativity.

Attempts to stir national pride raise some discomfiting parallels, however. 'You can't conquer history, or wash it away by just being happy,' says Ulrich Maly, mayor of Nuremberg, the city infamous for Hitler's Nazi party rallies where England is due to play one of its games.

Meanwhile, Volker Perthes, director of Berlin's Institute for International and Security Affairs, points out that in twenty years, (*former*) West Germany went from post-war international pariah to economic beacon – only to see its attempt to present a more open face to the world go 'terribly wrong' when Israeli athletes were murdered at the 1972 Munich Olympics.

Germany's campaign is part of a broader debate on the value of public diplomacy and 'soft power' – the tools increasingly used by national governments to deepen their influence without resorting to economic and military might.

Joseph Nye, a Harvard professor and author of *Soft Power: The means to success in world politics*, argues that it can be used to complement traditional diplomacy. 'Tangible threats or payoffs' are replaced by initiatives to influence stereotypes about a country, for example.

According to an internal German government strategy paper seen by the *Financial Times*, this approach was partly behind the decision to use the World Cup to alter Germany's image abroad. 'States are increasingly in competition for markets, tourists ... value systems and political influence', and in this context 'Germany must take a position', the paper argues. It notes that foreigners' images of Germany often 'lack emotion' and 'exclude the [country's] more dynamic developments over the last 20-30 years'. 'Emotional aspects, such as street cafes in Munich ... [German] lifestyle brands such as Adidas and Boss, and the happiness of reunification in 1989/90' need to be emphasized, the paper concludes. In a section on 'Germany's Image Abroad', Michael Reiffenstuel of the foreign office enthuses that the World Cup provides a 'unique communications opportunity'.

Germany is not the first country to attempt a national makeover. Britain tried – with limited success – to repackage itself as 'Cool Britannia' early in Tony Blair's premiership. Japan, co-host with South Korea of the 2002 World Cup, ran a less elaborate image campaign than Germany's. But visitors were surprised to find a country more vibrant and accessible than many had expected. The Japanese government has since deployed 'soft power' to exploit the popularity of manga cartoons and Japanese design and fashion. The number of tourists has noticeably increased – in part the result of an official tourism campaign but also reflecting a 'word-of-mouth' effect from the World Cup.

In Germany the jury is out on the campaign's impact. Nathalie Thiemann-Huguet, of the business-led Land of Ideas programme, says the giant sculptures in Berlin have become a 'major tourist attraction', while about 2,000 foreign journalists have registered to use pictures and TV footage on 'positive aspects of Germany's economy and society'.

Yet a series of organizational and other problems that have blighted tournament preparations have brought negative media coverage. Most recently, Ms Merkel was forced to allay concerns in the United States Congress that Germany was ignoring an alleged rise in illegal trafficking of prostitutes for the tournament. Worst of all was last month's apparent racist attack that left a young Ethiopian man in a coma. Experts argue that such incidents are unlikely to undermine Germany's broader campaign, but that this must in turn be seen as only one element in reshaping its image. Ulrich Sacker of the Goethe-Institut, Germany's overseas cultural agency, says the World Cup will remain in the minds of tens of millions of global television viewers. 'We have to surprise people, make them think: "Germany is different to the country I imagined",' he says.

Mr. Perthes believes government campaigns can only ever have a modest impact, given the post-Cold War complexity of public diplomacy. But rhetorically posing the question 'will the country's image after the

World Cup return to the cliché about the ugly German?', he provides his own, upbeat answer: 'I don't think so. At least something from the campaign will stick.'

Source: from Germans aim for a World Cup surprise: they're fun *The Financial Times*, 22/05/2006, p. 19 (Williamson, H.), Copyright © The Financial Times Ltd.

Questions

1. Referring to Concept 8.1, comment on the statement made in the text: 'You can't market a country like a washing powder.'
2. Find expressions in the text that characterize the Germans. Consider whether each of these reflects your own individual perception or rather stereotypes of German culture.

ACTIVITY 8.2

Read the following account of an Indian's experiences when inspecting a local bank in India. Then answer the questions below.

Meeting a brick wall

I was working in the inspection department of the Central Bank of India and was given an assignment a few years ago to inspect a branch of a private commercial bank. I was assisted by a junior officer. One of our main tasks was to get some important information about a fraud, determine the chain of events, establish accountability and pass on the information to the team which was inspecting the head office of the bank.

The branch was in a small town which was very different to what I was used to: they spoke a different language there, ate different food and enjoyed a very different climate. The people working there were very old compared to employees of other banks I had visited and they behaved towards me in an indifferent and uncooperative manner. They claimed they had no idea how the fraud was committed and were reluctant to show me the relevant records.

Many of the staff members had been working in the branch for decades and had developed close relationships with each other. Their former branch manager had already been suspended for his suspected involvement in the fraud. My colleague, who was from the same region and of a similar age, managed to mix with the staff but was unable to get hold of the information needed. Eventually he also became rather reluctant to get items of information requested, giving delays and unavailability as reasons for their non-appearance.

I was proud of my experience in inspections, my analytical skills, my management education and my past success in meeting deadlines. I followed the code of behaviour expected of someone in my position and kept the staff at a distance. I declined offers of lunch or even tea or coffee so that these should not be considered as some sort of bribe. I felt that the local staff were making one excuse after another not to come up with the right information. Were they perhaps trying to protect their colleagues, or were they afraid of being reprimanded by their bosses? The information I needed was crucial and could be obtained only from this branch. The days passed, but nothing substantial emerged. Time was running out.

Source: adapted from Browaeys and Trompenaars (2000): case 11.

Questions

1. To what extent is the problem presented in the case a communication problem?
2. How do you think the author could try to get hold of the information needed?

TOPIC 5
THE IMPACT OF CULTURE ON PERCEPTION

Chapter 9

Reflective Organisation Theory: Symbols, Meanings and Interpretations

Introduction

Imagine that you have been at a meeting of the executive team of your organization to discuss some issue of great importance to yourself, to the others at the meeting and to the organization. During its course, many controversial issues are raised, but by the end, agreements are made and differences are left for later. Afterwards you talk about the meeting with others who were there. You realize that you have agreement with some of them about what happened. With others, however, it is almost as if they were at a different event. As far as they are concerned, that meeting has a different meaning from yours. They have interpreted incidents in ways that are radically different from your interpretation. What you heard as a deep and damaging argument during the meeting they understood as constructive debate. When the managing director intervened to make a decision, you felt her interruption as a symbol of her power and need to control; others thought her contribution as a symbol of her admirable qualities of quiet decision making.

The underlying theme of this chapter is: how do we give meaning to the complex events that confront us in organizational life? When we see objects, hear stories, smell perfumes, taste food, touch materials, how do we interpret them so that they mean something to us? How do we create and communicate our understanding of 'reality' in organizational settings? What are the processes by which we seek to negotiate with others the different meanings that we give to events and processes in everyday organizational life? In this chapter, we will look at a number of theories and perspectives that explore these issues.

The development of understanding of meaning and interpretation is related to two key issues in contemporary organizational theory. The first is concerned with the ways we make meaning through symbols that capture our understanding of reality. The study of this ability to make meaning through the interpretation of symbols has given the body of theories to be explored in this chapter the title of *interpretavist* theories. The second key idea is that members of organizations can find profound value in *reflection* about the deeper issues of organizational life. The development of reflective approaches to life and work in organizations requires the ability to stand apart from the rush and crisis of everyday life and develop intellectual and emotional understanding.

Learning outcomes

- Define what is meant by 'reflective' organization theory.
- Compare and contrast how different strands of interpretavist, reflective organization theory sheds light on how organization members give meaning to their lives at work.
- Discuss the ways individuals develop a sense of self in organizations.
- Assess how these theories provide insights into how individuals and groups create their organizational identities.
- Explore how these different theories enrich our understanding of organizational culture.
- Examine the ways these theories challenge our understandings of the design of organizations.

Structure of the chapter

- In this chapter, we discuss two approaches to the interpretation and understanding of organizations, both of which have had an important impact on the development of organization theory. Although we shall, in this chapter, discuss ways these themes are interrelated, historically they come from quite different traditions; the implications of difference and interrelationship will be developed as the chapter progresses. Both these approaches emphasize the ways readers can use these theories of organization in order to *reflect* on their own circumstances, both personal and organizational.

What it means to be reflective

There has been a tradition in organization theory, especially when it has been aligned to management theory, of *prescriptive* outcomes so that managers can be presented with a clear, well-defined set of approaches that gives them the 'best way' to manage people and organizations. A different tradition in the development of organization theory has been that of the *reflective* attitude.

At its heart, the reflective attitude is important to those who research organizations, those who develop organization theory and those who are members of an organization (and many of us are all three of these, formally or informally). It is a belief that organization theory and research in organizations should enable the researcher, the theorist and organization members (individuals and groups) to achieve a full understanding of their situations through the process of reflection. This involves the development of a self-critical consideration of assumptions and consistent exploration of alternative interpretative frameworks. This has major implications:

1. Understanding the link between 'empirical information' (the facts and figures) and the interpretation of that information. This relates to the idea that the same

Ideas and perspectives

The reflective attitude

One of the first writers on the reflective attitude was the highly influential writer Donald A. Schön in his book *The Reflective Practitioner* (1991, originally published in 1983). He explores some of the key dilemmas that face professionals – doctors, scientists, engineers, lawyers, managers and so on – in their organizational activity and in their role in society. He argues that by the 1980s, the very idea of 'the professional', at one time the pillar of society, had come under profound question and that professionals were suffering a crisis of confidence. At the heart of this, he argues, was the problem that the 'knowledge base' – what the doctor learns in medical school, for example – of the traditional profession is not sufficient to meet the new complexities of contemporary life. It is too specialized, too focused on the development of technical expertise.

Schön suggests that one of the key ways of dealing with this profound problem is through the development of 'reflection in action.' It is through reflection, he suggests, that the professional can 'surface and criticize the tacit understandings that have grown up around the repetitive experiences of a specialized practice, and can make new sense of the situations of uncertainty or uniqueness which he may allow himself to experience' (p. 61).

What this means for the manager is that as she undertakes her MBA and then works in an organization, her whole approach to management typically becomes a matter of accepted 'common sense'. She no longer thinks deeply about the ways she deals with staff, with the ways she makes decisions and so on; it has become her routine. Undertaking reflection as part of her everyday life causes her to think about these routine ways of doing things without disabling her ability to act. Reflection slows her down and enables her to deal more effectively with new and uncertain situations.

'information' can be given many interpretations. For the organization theorist, this multiplicity of meaning means that the researcher needs to possess the ability to capture the complexity of interpretation in the development of theory; for the organization member, it means understanding that many features of the situation are not what they seem to be.

2. **Understanding that the language that people use is typically not as straightforward as it might seem.** As organizations develop, members characteristically build up 'common sense' ways of talking about events and processes.

> ### Example: The managing director talks
> This is an excerpt from comments made by the managing director of a division of a professional services organization. He was talking to the executive at their weekly formal meeting. The six monthly financial figures had just been received, and they were disappointing:
>
>> We've not done at all well although not as badly as some of the other divisions; they've got real problems. We need to develop quite rapidly our recovery plan. We need to have a post-mortem with people, investigate what's gone wrong with your areas and we need to develop a recovery plan. You know we've got a clear vision of where we want to get to and we've got to stick with it.
>
> As we shall discuss as the chapter unfolds, our language is pervaded by metaphor. The image of 'the vision' points the group to something to which it can aspire; the word suggests the nobility of the enterprise. The common sense language that members use relates to specific contexts that they all 'understand' as organizational members. The members of the executive know that in *this* organization, the metaphors 'recovery plan' and 'post-mortem' indicate that there is going to be some 'blaming' of the failure onto specific groups of staff. The way people talk is embedded in the history of the organization. The references to how other divisions have fared is 'understood' by members of the executive to refer to past rivalries and conflicts with other divisions. The managing director is appealing to a sense of *schadenfreude*, that perverse pleasure that members can take in the downfall of others.

The language we use is geared toward creating an image of how we understand the truth rather than the truth itself. For the researcher and organization theorist, this involves the understanding of the language-in-use in its context; for the organization member, this involves development of understanding of the deeper issues of language and communication in the organization (Alvesson and Deetz, 2000) so they can act in an informed manner. In the example given above, one of the members of the executive, later in the meeting, discussed with the managing director the way that he had talked of undertaking a 'post-mortem'. There was a useful discussion of the need to avoid 'blame' and focus on the issues – and indeed, that the very term 'post-mortem' was inappropriate. This modest clarification of the common sense understanding of the language proved fruitful.

The development of reflection is closely linked to contemporary ideas that explore the development of emotional and spiritual intelligence to improve the quality of leadership and management. This involves the development of self-awareness, self-control, motivation of self and others, and skill in dealing with social situations (Goleman, 1998). At an organizational level, this is a recognition that emotions are an important aspect of the ways people at all levels relate to organizational tasks and processes and that there is a need to develop approaches that understand the emotional aspects of work and issues of organizational change (Huy, 1999). Underpinning this need to be reflective about our lives in organizations is an understanding that organizational life can be dysfunctional and problematic for its members. The development of reflective emotional intelligence means that managers can develop the ability to identify aspects of organizational life that are emotionally toxic, that 'drains vitality from individuals' and that need to be handled in 'healthy and constructive ways' (Frost, 2004, p. 111).

From the point of view of organizational theory, then, the reflective approach is one that gets the researcher closer to deeper, more truthful, understanding of the ways organization members develop and understand their organizational world. From the point of view of the organizational member, this reflective attitude provides people with a richer understanding of core issues of organizational life. In a practical manner, it enables members to act in organizational life in ways that are considered and thought through.

In the following sections, we shall look at a number of theories and perspectives that have informed and contributed to the development of reflective organizational theory. These approaches are concerned with the ways humans can act together, collectively; can give meaning to their lives in organizations; and develop and interpret symbols, metaphors and stories that enable them to develop meaning and share understandings of the world. The first of these approaches developed in the United States and is known as symbolic interactionism.

Working and acting together: symbolic interactionism

A couple talking together, a group of people undertaking a task, an organization committed to producing goods and services are all examples of collective action. How this ability to act in a collective way happens is the core subject matter of symbolic interactionism.

What is important about this is that it emphasizes that organization members can be purposive in the ways that we make meaning and work together to achieve that shared definition of the situation – or fail to reach an agreement. It takes us away from any view of the human being that we are essentially passive actors tossed about by the vicissitudes of fate. It also emphasizes that we can choose to *reflect* on our actions and our situation.

The origins of symbolic interactionism in the early years of the twentieth century are strangely reminiscent of the growth of the neo-modernist human relations school in Harvard, in that both developed from a particular university and both had formidable leaders in the development of the approach.

> **Ideas and perspectives**
>
> ### Symbolic interactionism
>
> These are some of the key issues that symbolic interactionism seeks to answer. They are taken from one of the key writers on symbolic interactionist theory, Becker (1977):
>
> The theory of symbolic interaction takes as its central problem this question: How is it possible for collective human action to occur? How can people come together in lines of action in something we can call a collective act? By collective act we should understand not simply cooperative activities in which people consciously strive to achieve some common goal, but any activity involving two or more people in which individual lines of activity come to have some kind of unity and coherence with one another (p. 290).

'The Chicago school'

Although the symbolic interactionist movement developed in other American universities (so that the term 'Chicago school' is more about a movement than an actual geographical location), its most famous home was the department of sociology at the University of Chicago.

In the early years of the twentieth century, distinguished scholars were appointed to the department. One of these was Robert E. Park. His interest, developed from working with the great German sociologist Georg Simmel, was in the meanings that we give to everyday life – what might be called the ignored, common sense, 'trivial' (but enduring) aspects of living. These include the ways humans are 'sociable', create relationships, hold conversations and shape their actions. His interest in the processes of everyday behaviour led to a consideration of the relationship between the individual and the society. Park began to analyse the processes by which we take on and shape, by virtue of our own qualities and personalities, the roles that we occupy. This eventually led to a third interest – the idea that institutions (e.g., religious groups, business organizations) develop because of internal and environmental changes (Matthews, 1977). These interests were taken on by later generations of academics within the department.

Another key member in these early years was George Herbert Mead, who came to Chicago with a somewhat different perspective from Park's. For our purposes, his key contribution was his concern with the notion that human consciousness emerges from interaction and that the high level of human development comes from a synthesis of the biological, psychological and sociological circumstances that surround our development. These features that differentiate the human from other species enable us to reflect on our experiences and to give them meaning – the reflective process (Meltzer et al., 1975).

A second wave of scholars in the 1960s and 1970s developed the earlier interests of Park and his colleagues into the various forms of symbolic interactionism that will be discussed in this chapter. Writers such as Erving Goffman, Howard Becker, Anselm Strauss and many others to be discussed later in the chapter came to prominence. Unlike the neo-modernist academics in Harvard Business School whose focus was entirely on organizations, the symbolic interactionists were sociologists with a wide interest in society and its institutions. However, Everett Hughes' seminal work *Men and Their Work* (and note the gender specificity – so typical of its time) published in 1958 focused attention on organizations and began work towards an organization theory derived from symbolic interactionism.

Although there were many other influences on the Chicago school as it developed, this interest in the everyday construction of life endured. Although the world in which we live is one of 'change, movement, instability and conflict', the mystery is that it 'never quite fell apart; beneath the disorder lurked "natural" principles of organization which kept it, if not healthy, at least functioning and a certain natural vitality which kept it alive and lively, lurching from one state of disequilibrium to another' (Matthews, 1977, p. 120). It is that mystery that sociologists who wish to 'understand the social world from the point of view of the social actor' (Bulmer et al., 1997, p. 251) would want to uncover.

An important aspect of the development of the Chicago school is that it can be seen to be particularly American in its development. It has within it an understanding that people live in an 'open society' that is not constrained by deep and enduring class divisions. In many respects, it captures aspects of the fondly held myth of the 'American way of life' – respect for the individual and a belief in flexibility and mobility (Shaskolsky, 1970, quoted in Meltzer et al., 1975). Despite this American flavour, the Chicago school has developed a theoretical perspective on organizations that is deeply influential and has universal appeal. Some of the key issues that emerge from the Chicago school and their contribution to organization theory are discussed in later sections of this chapter. In what follows, we explore some of the core ideas, the basic assumptions, that lie behind symbolic interactionism.

The processes of making and sharing meaning

The symbolic interactionists developed a network of ideas and propositions about the ways we make and share meaning. They emphasized the ways we as human beings are able to actively construct and create symbols of the world in which we live. This construction of the world is *individual* to the extent to which we have different personalities and experiences that filter experiences in particular ways, but it is also *social* in the sense that we share (or fail to share) meanings and interpretations.

The aim of symbolic interactionism is not to penetrate to the depths of *individual* thought and action. As a social science, its aim is instead to develop an understanding of the statements made by actors acting collectively, in small or large groupings, based upon specific interactions. It explores the ways members give meaning to situations and from this, to develop insights that can be related to other interactive situations so that an overall theory of social interaction can be developed (Cossette, 1998).

The basic assumptions of symbolic interactionism

Symbolic interactionists make a number of assumptions about the nature of the individual, how individuals interact with others and how we undergo processes of change. These core principles – the ontological underpinning – were captured by the

> **Ideas and perspectives**
>
> ## The symbol
>
> The Swedish academics Mats Alvesson and Per Olof Berg see symbols as 'instruments to create order out of chaos' (1992, p. 85). They say that a symbol always represents something different from or something more than itself so that:
>
> - *The corporate logo* is more than just a sign; it is a symbol of the way 'the organization' would like to be seen. The logo is an expression of 'the brand' that characterizes the organization; it is a symbol of its identity.
> - *Special parking spaces for top management* are more than just parking spaces; they are a symbol of power and authority.
> - *The ways formal meetings are handled* are more than just places where decisions are made; they are symbols of social relationships and, at a deep and often hidden level, the values and priorities of members.
> - *Corporate plans* are more than a plan for the next period; they are symbols of the organization's sense of its place in the world.
> - *Offices in which colleagues pile papers around them where there is officially a 'tidy desk' policy* are more than just untidiness; they can be a symbol of discontent or indifference to the 'petty rules' of the organization.
> - *Architecture, statues, interior design and decoration* are all symbols that, in different organizational contexts, have different meanings. In the United Kingdom, for example, there have been occasions where expensive contemporary statues have been erected on hospital grounds. For some, they symbolize the notion that hospitals can be aesthetically pleasing places; for others, they symbolize the ways health care can be wasteful of money.
>
> Symbols are the objects, stories, sayings, tastes and smells that give us (as couples, groups, organizations) a sense of identity, that give us meaning and structure. We do not always agree about the *interpretation* of the symbol (and this can be a source of profound and deep conflict), but we recognize its power to capture meaning.

American sociologist Norman Denzin (1971). The model in Figure 9.1 captures the essence of these assumptions and we then discuss why these ideas are important in contemporary organization theory. These assumptions can also be looked at as *a process* by which individuals and groups learn and develop through their interaction. The symbolic interactionists refer to a process such as this as a 'career' with the idea that if all goes well, any interaction or sharing of meaning has a beginning, a middle and an end. It is important to note, however, that although the model is presented in a linear fashion, the everyday processes of making meaning and communicating do not necessarily happen in this orderly way.

As the individual grows and develops and communicates with others, he or she:

1. **Is capable of self-reflective thought and action:** This refers to the idea that it is part of our human capability to be *reflective*. In organizational terms, this

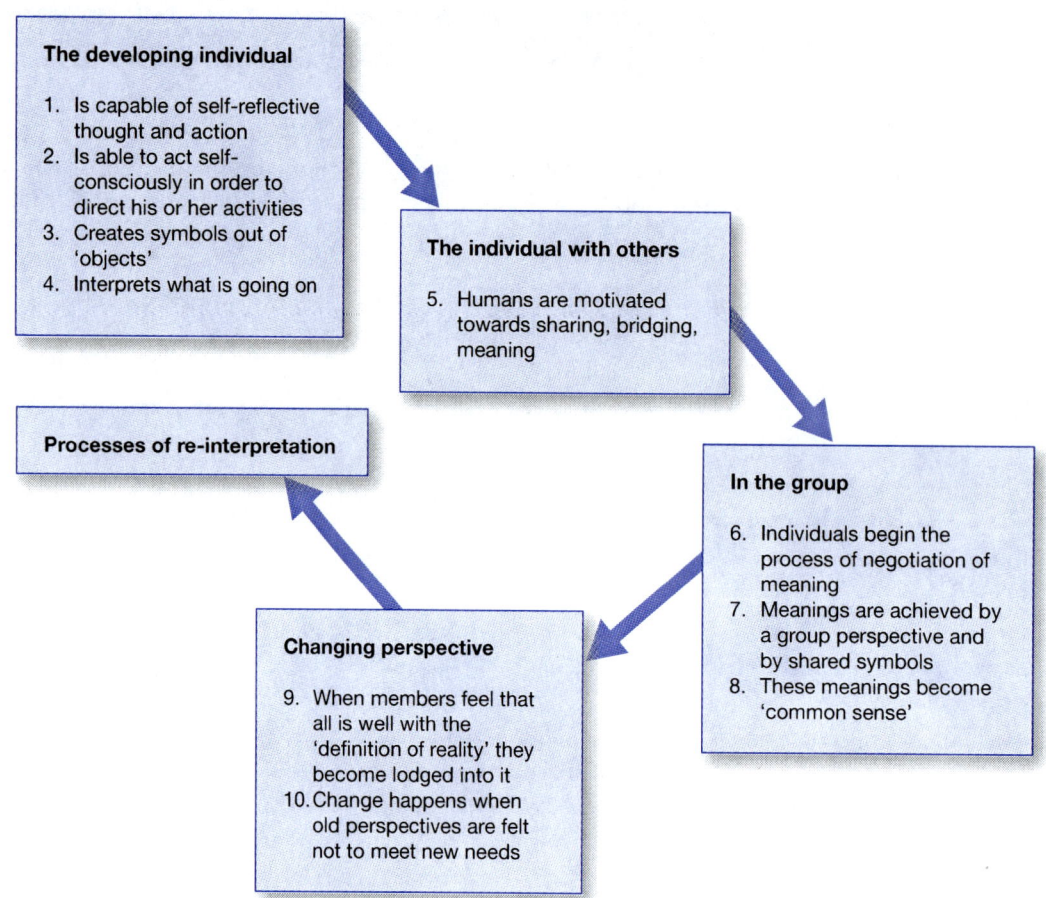

Figure 9.1: The processes of making meaning – a symbolic interactionist approach. (*Source:* Based on Denzin, 1971.)

means that *all* members of the organization *are capable of* making sense of their own actions, both as individuals and as members of their group. The implication of this is that in organizations, there are different understandings of what is happening. This view contrasts with the view in modernist thinking that most members of organizations are driven by the desire for individual economic success. It also contrasts with the view that managers are 'superior beings' who need to harness the commitment of employees to the values and purposes of the organization.

2. **Is able to act self-consciously in order to direct his or her activities:** Not only are we capable of reflective thought, but we can also consciously choose to act in certain ways. We are not corks tossed hither and thither by the vicissitudes of fate or by our genetic inheritance. In organizational terms, this points toward the idea that organizations are pluralistic, with different ways of acting and behaving. Pluralist perspectives in organization theory say that in any one organization, we can find many different ways of thinking and acting amongst individuals and groups. This is an important theme that is discussed in later sections

of the chapter. This contrasts with unitarist theories that suggest that thinking and acting in organizations is uniform and directed to organizational goals so that people who do not behave in this way are regarded as *deviants*.

3. **Creates symbols out of 'objects':** Denzin suggests that an 'object' is anything toward which action can be organized. This may be illustrated by an example. At one time, spaces in the car park of the office in which the author[1] works were 'allocated' on the basis that any employee could use the car park until it was full. Then there was a change in policy so that allocation was based on strict criteria. This meant, as it worked out, that most occupants of it were senior management. There were various reactions to this from the somewhat embarrassed pleasure of those who had a guaranteed space to the deep resentment of those who saw the new policy as 'yet another' symbol of what they saw as the increasing split between 'management' and 'staff'.

   In organizational terms, this implies that such 'objects' as business plans, vision statements, the spaces in which people work, the technologies of everyday life such as the PC (or Apple Mac) and the modes of dress adopted, are all symbols to which different groups (or individuals) give different meanings.

4. **Interprets what is going on:** As we go about our everyday business, doing what we do, we interpret our own actions and the actions of others. The interpretations that we give to events and people can be quite different as between different individuals and groups and this can lead to conflicts. It should be added that awareness of the self and of others is not evenly distributed across the population; we may have colleagues whose interpretive ability is to all organizational intents and purposes minimal (they are 'insensitive') yet others whose awareness of the other is somewhat overwhelming (oversensitive).

As individuals work with others:

5. **Humans are motivated toward sharing, bridging meaning:** Human beings are interested in the process of discovering the meanings that others give to 'objects' and situations and are frequently engaged in the process of working toward understanding the other.

As the group develops:

6. **Individuals begin the process of negotiation of meaning:** As we work together, we negotiate the 'meaning' of other members of the group and the 'objects' that are part of the group's life. After a while, we develop a group consensus as to the meaning. In this process, the language that people use becomes 'a dynamic reality that is shaped by events which it, in turn, helps shape' (Cossette, 1998, p. 1368). An example of this is the way members of a committee may initially have a struggle to develop a shared understanding of the purposes and processes of their committee. They negotiate over the meaning and significance of 'the agenda', what should or should not be included as 'standing items' and so on. Over a period, however, there is characteristically the development of shared, stable definitions of the key issues.

---

[1] During the course of this chapter, the author has deliberately chosen to give examples that relate to his professional and managerial organizational life. This is in the spirit of the reflective tradition and is done in the hope that it will illustrate the issues that are discussed in the chapter.

7. **Meanings are achieved through the development of a group perspective – joint action rests on ability to grasp direction of the act of others:** If things are going well, individuals develop through interaction a group understanding of the situation. Because of this, they can act together toward a joint effort at understanding and action. The development of the group perspective and the processes leading to joint action are likely to have within it a degree of conflict and disturbance. A conflict-free group would have difficulty in establishing a clear identity and consciousness of itself; it would not be able to develop a distinctive group structure (Denzin, 1971). The absence of conflict leads to collusion and the destruction of the group – the Abilene paradox (Harvey, 1988).

8. **These meanings become the group's common sense:** As soon as the group has achieved this level of shared perspective, the core issues that are its business become part of the group's common sense. There is acceptance of the meaning of, for example, 'the agenda', the importance of 'the finances', the significance of 'thinking strategically' and so on. When the meanings become shared, they become 'symbols'. The group also develops 'rules' and 'codes' that are taken-for-granted aspects of the interaction. These rules and codes relate to the roles of the members of the group, who has 'the right' to talk most (and who is regarded as marginal, whose voice does not count), the relative formality or informality of conduct in the group and so on.

As time goes by, the group may begin to go through change:

9. **When members feel that all is well with the 'definition of reality', it becomes the 'truth':** Both as individuals and groups, we can become very comfortable with the way we are. As individuals, we can think that our understanding of reality and of ourselves is one that is true and correct. As a group, we may believe that we are doing our business efficiently and effectively. There is no need to change; we have our lives sorted. This can be an important feature of organization life in the sense that it can be important, even in periods of major change, to be able to identify those quiet areas in the midst of the storm that are undertaking their business effectively because they know what they are supposed to be doing. On the other hand, groups (and individuals) can become complacent, unable to see that there is stormy weather on the way.

10. **Change takes place when old perspectives fail to meet new needs:** But then there are occasions when our way of looking at the world no longer fits the circumstances in which we find ourselves; we are motivated to change. In organizational terms, this means that we are capable of developing new understandings of social objects and our environment.

As change takes place, so there are processes of reinterpretation. This takes us through to the developing individual.

As you read these assumptions that underpin symbolic interactionism, it is important to remember that although they are all part of a process of reflective learning, they do not happen in the straightforward, sequential manner presented. As we go through everyday life, we encounter many groups and situations, and this leads to complex patterns of learning and development. In addition, even when we enter a group for the first time, we carry into that group meanings and definitions that come from our previous history and experience (Knights and Willmott, 1999).

> **Stop and think**
>
> As you look through these assumptions and processes that the symbolic interactionists associate with learning and development, how do they fit with your experience? Do you think the core assumptions hold true to you? Can you think of occasions when the development of a shared meaning has gone wrong? Could you identify from the model above where problems and issues that caused things to go wrong arose?

Strengths and weaknesses of the symbolic interactionist understanding of organizations

Strengths

Symbolic interactionist theory suggests that human beings are capable of applying reason and logic to situations, capable of intentional action and of reflecting on their circumstances. In this sense, the ideas that lie behind symbolic interactionism help us to develop understanding of the ways members place themselves within their organization.

Beyond this, symbolic interactionism gets us to explore key organizational issues of the nature of organizational reality. They suggest that our understanding of reality is 'mediated through symbols' so that our 'taken for granted sense of reality and selfhood is seen to be held together by a precarious set of symbols with which we just happen to have identified' (Knights and Willmott, 1997, p. 74). The importance of this is that it points to the way meaning in organizational life is constantly the subject of negotiation and that beneath the apparently solid exterior of the organization, there lie the shifting sands of a constantly changing understanding of organizational 'reality'.

Weaknesses

The British organization theorists David Knights and Hugh Willmott (1999) suggest that in its interest in the processes of the achievement of consensus, the symbolic interactionists ignore the deeper contradictions that the person (or the group) can encounter in the development of its identity. Symbolic interactionism presents a model of 'self-consciousness' that 'appears overly abstracted and detached from the "lived experience" of human beings with bodily desires' (p. 73). They suggest that this smoothes people out so that the symbolic interactionists avoid discussion of deep and enduring conflict. They also claim, along with many other writers, that symbolic interactionism ignores the deeper, more emotional aspects of the self. Although symbolic interactionists acknowledge that the constructions of reality created by individuals and groups may not be rational and that interaction may have hidden aspects as well as the overt 'purpose', it deals with the surface aspects of interaction rather than the emotional content of it.

As an example of this, from a symbolic interactionist perspective, activities such as 'accomplishing a task, exchanging a greeting, eating a meal or making love' are regarded as processes by which individuals act together. They negotiate, fit together 'disparate, conflicting and often incomplete plans of action into a package of meanings that, at least for the moment of activity, provides a basis for interaction. This feature of the joint action suggests that interaction may have a variable career' (Denzin, 1971, p. 264) – it can fail as well as succeed. Although this provides a plausible account of the development of the ways people act together to accomplish their work, it is interesting to note the way that Denzin brackets together 'accomplishing a task' with 'making love' – as if they were of the same emotional content (which, of course, they may be for some).

As we shall see in later sections, despite these weaknesses, the symbolic interactionist perspective provides a powerful body of theory for the reflective exploration of key organizational issues. In the next section, we turn to theories that take us to another depth in this journey of reflective organization theory. Although, as we saw in the discussion of the rise of the Chicago school, symbolic interactionism had its roots in nineteenth century European sociological thought, it developed as a particularly American approach to understanding the ways we create and share meaning through the symbols of everyday life. Within European thought in organization theory, interest in the way that we symbolize organizations came initially from a different intellectual set of sources, although in recent years there has been a degree of synthesis of these perspectives, both in the United States and in Europe.

The chapter so far

As the chapter has unfolded, we have discussed a core theme in the theories to be discussed here. This is the idea that habits of reflection can be an important part of the members' lives in organization. Reflection is the ability to stand apart from everyday organizational life in order to understand some of the deeper issues that confront it. One of the key issues that confront organizational members lies in the ways we understand and interpret the actions and communications of others. To initiate an exploration of this issue, we looked at one of the key theoretical perspectives that throws light on the processes by which we communicate and collaborate – symbolic interactionism. We discussed the ways this theory has developed a number of strands and that at the heart of the theory is the idea of the 'symbol.' We have seen that although there is much in symbolic interactionism that helps us to understand, in a reflective way, the ways we communicate, it says little about the ways we can understand the emotional aspects of life. In the next section, we look at an approach that claims to give insight into emotional understanding.

Phenomenology reaches the emotions

The British organization theorist Yannis Gabriel (2000) suggests that symbolic interactionists believe that myths, stories and symbols gives *clues* about the nature of social reality in organizations; phenomenologists see stories everywhere. Such things

> **Ideas and perspectives**
>
> ## Phenomenology
>
> The literature on phenomenology is vast and highly complex. This definition is meant to give just an indication of phenomenology in organizational life.
>
> **Phenomenological approaches** are concerned with the description and understandings of the everyday experience of organizational members without imposing on these experiences theories or presuppositions – letting the experience 'speak for itself'. The great German phenomenologist Husserl's slogan was – 'Back to the things themselves'. Underpinning phenomenology are processes of reflection in order to achieve understanding of the ways members make sense of their organizational life. In phenomenology, there is no such thing as 'the truth' as something out there, external from human experience. Instead of searching for 'the truth', phenomenologists explore perceptions, fantasies, stories, myths, sagas and so on in order to develop understanding of the meanings that members give to everyday and extraordinary features of their lives.
>
> This means that we can reach a deeper 'truth' – an understanding of the ways members' structure and communicate the meaning that they give to their organizations. Although 'meaning' starts with the individual shaping his or her world, phenomenologists are interested in the ways we share meaning – intersubjectivity.
>
> (Based on Urmson and Rée, 1991.)
>
> As we shall see later in this chapter, phenomenologists are 'scientific' in the sense that they have procedures and processes for developing an understanding of everyday experience.

as strategies, business plans, performance appraisals, all the artefacts of organizational life are stories. Phenomenology claims to give a reflective understanding of organizations because of its approach to the ways members give meaning to their organizations through conversation, metaphor and storytelling.

A phenomenological approach to organizations provides an understanding of 'interior', deeper meanings, the emotions and values that are part of the person's experience of organizational life. The roots of phenomenology's claim for a deeper understanding of human experience lies in its development as a philosophy and as a key theoretical position in sociology that can be applied to organization theory. The core thinkers in the development of phenomenology were, in Europe, the German philosopher Edmund Husserl (1859–1938), and in the United States, the philosopher George Herbert Mead (1863–1931). The key aspects that underpin phenomenology are that it illuminates the nature of human experience and as a method it provides a detailed description of human experience. What it does is to take 'the individual human being as the centre of a system of coordinates on which the experience of the world is mapped' (Luckman, 1978, p. 8). It is also 'reflective' in that it makes human experience the core of all our understanding of the world. In this sense, 'objects' – the things that surround us such as telephones, the desk at which we work – are given meaning through our consciousness. This means that 'reality' is something that is represented by our minds – the meaning of the telephone does not exist without our consciousness of it. However, because of the physical existence of reality, we can confirm its existence by looking at it on the desk and see it as a telephone (Strati, 1999).

Example: The room is prepared for the important visitor

In the intervening hours the castle had come to life like a device whose mechanism has been wound up and reset: not only the furniture, chairs and sofas liberated from their linen shrouds, but also the paintings on the walls. . . . Logs were piled on the hearth ready for a fire for it was the end of summer and after midnight the cold mist spread a damp breath through the rooms. *All of a sudden the objects seemed to take on meaning, as if to prove that everything in the world acquires significance only in relation to human activity and human destiny* (from Sándor Márai's novel *Embers* originally published in Hungary in 1942).

Stop and think

This is clearly a romantic way of depicting the way we give meaning to the objects in our environment. Can you think of places in your own experience that have achieved this kind of meaning and significance? Or are most of the offices and places where we work so anonymous that it is difficult to give them any significance? Why do some people like to bring into their workplace photographs and other objects and display them on their desks?

In this sense, organizations can be seen as places in which members are capable of making meaning, capable of cooperation and able to choose. As organizations develop, Strati suggests, there are intertwining aspects of the 'formal' organization (its structures and its rules) and the informal in which 'customs, cognitions, social norms, ideals, folklore and institutions' (p. 87) play an enduring part. These informal aspects of members' organizational lives give the formal aspects meaning and significance so that the formal is embedded in the informal and the informal embedded in the formal.

Case study: Phenomenology in action

In this case study, the writers on organizations Anne Wallemacq and David Sims were acting as organizational facilitators to a small group of managers. They wrote of this experience of using a phenomenological approach in a paper published in 1998.

Three managers from small business organizations came for help to the authors of this case study. These managers came from organizations that had gone through significant change – in one case, a merger; in another, product diversification; and in the third, an internal crisis – and they were looking for improved ways of managing change. During the change process, things had gone wrong, and the vision of their organizations that they held in their heads seemed no longer very appropriate.

The facilitators believed that the best way forward was to undertake with the managers a process of sense making. Their aim was to enable the managers to achieve an 'operating vision' of their firm that would allow them to understand what was going on and to cope with the major changes. The facilitators' core task was to act as a 'mirror' to the managers, reflecting their *way* of saying what they said. They also discovered, through the language in use and the physical features of the organizations (e.g., the design of offices) the basic images that members relied on to think about and act in their organizations.

The facilitators then offered a number of concepts – as for example presentation of different forms of organization structure – that helped the managers to begin to surface a number of the basic beliefs they held about organizational life. This helped members to uncover the 'hidden metaphors' – the aspects of organizational life that are normally hidden beneath the 'rational' order of things.

One of the managers gave an example of this. She had founded a small firm that provided intensive training in information technology. The firm grew rapidly, and as it grew, she created new branches in different parts of Europe. Thinking it through in a rational manner, each branch was structurally 'a copy' of the original company. As time went by, the number of branches grew, but the founder felt increasingly marginalized as all the new branches went their own way. As the managers discussed this situation with each other and with the facilitators, it became clear that there was, beneath the rational story of the development of new branches, another story. This second story was a 'hidden metaphor'. This 'hidden metaphor' was that the owner had been going through the biological process of cellular division. The 'mother cell' (the owner) had duplicated itself, and in doing so, had replicated the new cells in exactly the same form as the original. For her, the problem was that these new 'cells' all asserted their independence; they were her 'children' who had 'grown up'. When they visited the company, this image of the owner as 'mother' was reinforced. She tried to create a family atmosphere: when she visited the branches she insisted on tidying up and so on.

These two stories – the rational story of the successful company opening new branches modelled on the original company structure and the story of the founder as 'mother' – sit alongside each other. They do not exist without each other. As each of the managers talked through their issues, it was realized that all of them had various stories operating at different levels.

The outcome of this reflective way of looking at their understanding of themselves as managers and their organization was they were able to look at their situations from a very different perspective. By the end of the process, they no longer felt trapped in the processes of change but rather felt that they could manage themselves – and others – through the process in a more proactive manner.

Stop and think

This account looks at the way people experience their organizational life at a number of layers. There is the layer of everyday reality in which people make rational decisions. There are also deeper stories expressed as 'hidden metaphors'. Reality is composed of many different stories that we tell about our organizations, some on the surface and some hidden from view. What would you see as the advantages and disadvantages of this approach within organizations known to you?

The phenomenological view of organization involves the development of an understanding that 'exterior' aspects of behaviour and 'interior' emotions and values are interlinked. It also implies that the stories that we tell about organizations, those aspects of organizational life that are rational and those that are irrational, are at some deep level all integrated and intersect with each other. This complexity means that 'knowledge' about our organizations 'has to be perpetually created and re-created in social, symbolic and interactive relationships' (Røyrvik and Wulff, 2002, p. 155).

So, in everyday life, there is this level of perpetual creation and recreation as we talk to each other and create new symbols and meanings, retell the stories in new contexts and reveal 'hidden metaphors' in different ways. Lying alongside this is another everyday world – the world of 'common sense' reality. This is the part of our organizational world that we 'take for granted'. This study of the everyday world of common sense takes us to another perspective, ethnomethodology.

Ethnomethodology: understanding organizational 'common sense'

The origins of ethnomethodology were primarily in the United States with its key author Harold Garfinkel. The tradition of this kind of study has been developed in the United Kingdom by a group of writers influenced by Wes Sharrock and his colleagues at the University of Manchester.

In his original and highly influential studies, Garfinkel (1976) got his students to engage in a variety of activities in which the taken-for-granted common sense assumptions were put under question. In one situation, for example, he asked his students to:

> . . . engage someone in conversation and to imagine and act on the assumption that what the other person was saying was directed by hidden motives which were his real ones. They were to assume that the other person was trying to trick them (p. 51).

When he discussed this with the students, the vast majority found the assignment difficult and actually found the conversation very difficult to handle – because it ran

Ideas and perspectives

Ethnomethodology

At its heart, ethnomethodology is the study of the 'common sense' methods that members use to solve problems, make decisions, make sense of their situations and undertake fact finding in their everyday lives. They are the 'quite ordinary, familiar, unsurprising ways that people enquire into and determine the reality of various things' (Cuff et al., 1998, p. 163). In this perspective, 'the study of an organization must begin with the study of its use by members' in the sense that when we become a competent member of organizations we display, adhere to and develop a sense of order that enables us to conduct our everyday business (Manning, 1971, p. 244).

so directly against their common sense assumptions about the nature of trust in conversation. In another situation:

> Students were asked to spend from fifteen minutes to an hour in their homes imagining that they were boarders and acting out this assumption. They were instructed to conduct themselves in a circumspect and polite fashion. They were to avoid getting personal, to use formal address, to speak only when spoken to (p. 47).

The reactions of the families to this varied considerably. In some cases, they took the student's behaviour as a joke or that the student 'wanted something'. However, in the vast majority of cases, family members were astonished and bewildered by this change in behaviour. The general feeling was that the student's polite behaviour had disturbed the 'common sense' assumptions that family members make of each other.

This exploration of the common sense assumptions that members make about the ways they make decisions and about the ways we interact with each other helps us to understand three key issues that are central to ethnomethodology.

1. The first of these, according to the Swedish writers on organizational research Mats Alvesson and Kaj Sköldberg (2000), is concerned with *membership*. This is the ability to speak the 'natural language' of the group. When the students were using formal address with their families, they were no longer using the natural language of the family; to be a competent member is to show that you can 'speak the speech' of the group.

2. The second of these concepts is *accountability*. This is concerned with the way we recount our actions reflectively in a common sense way. When we describe to colleagues what happened in a meeting, for example, we tell it as a story with a beginning, middle and end. If we construct the meeting as 'serious', we tell the story of the meeting in a 'serious' manner.

3. The third of these concepts is to do with the way that in most organizational situations, we are able to create and sustain 'rules of conduct' that are common sense ways of enabling conversations to take place – although there can be occasions where we cannot 'find the rules' and the interaction ends up in embarrassment and difficulty.

One of Sharrock's doctoral students, Alex Dennis (2001), provides an interesting example of this kind of study in an organizational setting. He explores detailed transcripts of interactions between different members of staff concerning the everyday decision making of staff in a hospital stroke unit. He examines the way that staff make decisions about patients, how they weave their way through formal 'operating procedures' that may conflict with what is happening before them, how one member of staff who is a doctor reconciles his 'doctorly' background with being a member of a multidisciplinary team.

The intellectual roots of ethnomethodology come from phenomenology in the sense that ethnomethodology explores the ways we develop our understanding of the world from the microprocesses of everyday interaction from which come our common sense knowledge and understanding of the world. The last of the perspectives is the way these common sense understandings are captured in the symbols, myths and stories of organizational life.

Organizational symbolism

Since the mid 1970s, the development of understanding of the ways in which symbols lie at the heart of organizational life has become an important strand of organizational theory through the concept of organizational symbolism. The development of this approach came particularly from Scandinavia. The first major text on the topic was written by Gunnar Westerlund and Sven-Erik Sjöstrand in 1979. The Swedish organization theorists Alvesson and Berg (1992) write that the supporters of this approach claim that it creates a new understanding of organizational 'reality' that is far different from the sorts of approach that the modernists or the neo-modernists put forward. Indeed, some of the organization symbolists regard themselves as to be firmly placed within the postmodern movement, although Alvesson and Berg are sceptical of this claim.

The organizational symbolists share with the symbolic interactionists and the phenomenologists the idea that within any organization, there are many versions of 'reality' as individuals and groups develop different symbols or use the same symbols but give them different meanings. What is different, however, is that whereas the symbolic interactionists tend to assert that members create symbols in specific organizational settings to meet specific needs, the organizational symbolists believe that individuals and groups import into the organization symbols and meanings from their wider society. An example of this is the way that we look at 'leadership' as a symbol. For the organizational symbolist, the way we look at the 'leaders' in the organization as a symbol is an outcome of our prior experience of 'leaders' from other organizations, from literature and movies, from our everyday social life. These issues are taken up in the discussion of culture in a later section of this chapter.

The organizational symbolists are also interested in the idea of looking at organizations as an aesthetic experience. The Italian organization theorist Antonio Strati (1999) writes of the way we use our senses of hearing, sight, touch, smell and taste and our capacity to make aesthetic judgements in order to 'assess whether something is pleasant or otherwise, whether it matches our taste or otherwise, whether it "involves" us or leaves us indifferent or even repelled' (p. 2).

The chapter so far

As this chapter has developed, we have looked at a number of perspectives that are concerned with the ways we symbolize the world around us. We looked in particular at the worldview of the symbolic interactionists and the ways they suggest we explore and develop meaning in organizational life. We then looked at a somewhat different approach, that of phenomenology. Here the claim is that in developing understanding, there is an exploration of the meaning-in-context of members and that lying alongside the surface 'reality' there lie other stories. We also looked at the ideas that underpin ethnomethodology as an approach to uncovering the common sense everyday realities of organizational life. We concluded with a brief review of 'organizational symbolism' as a perspective that focuses on these issues as they relate to organizations.

There is some evidence that many (but by no means all) writers within these perspectives are developing an understanding of each other. For the purposes of this chapter and the development of an understanding of the ways these interpretavist, reflective perspectives and theories present challenges to organizational theory, we shall deal with them together unless the approaches present conflicts that are particularly useful to explore.

The ways in which individuals develop a sense of self in organizations

During the twentieth century, there was ambivalence amongst writers on organizations about the nature of the individual in organizational life. At one end of the scale, there is the sternly modernist view that the individual was a sophisticated machine devoid of emotion and sentiment. Then there emerged the view that individuals are emotional and sentient beings with a longing to 'belong' to the organization that would give their lives meaning and commitment. In other chapters of this text, you will find many other versions of the relationship of the self to the organization. In this section, we explore an understanding of the self in organizations based on the idea that the 'self' emerges out of an existing understanding of the 'self' (who I am) *and* out of interaction with others.

The self as dramatic artful creation

Within the symbolic interactionist movement, Goffman perhaps best developed this sense of self as artful creation. He looks at interaction as a form of drama in which we undertake impression management – the process by which we wish to impress others that we are worth listening to and that our ideas and beliefs are valid and truthful. At the heart of this aspect of his work is the notion that whenever 'I' am in interaction

Biography — Erving Goffman (1922–1982)

Erving Goffman was born in Canada in 1922 and died in Philadelphia in 1982. He studied at the University of Edinburgh and started his academic career at the University of Chicago, where he spent a brief period and then had a distinguished career at a number of universities in the United States. Although his work falls within the symbolic interactionist tradition, he is generally regarded as something of a maverick member. His work relies strongly on his observation of people in their ordinary settings. The book that first brought him to the attention of a wider public was *The Presentation of Self in Everyday Life* (1959). His fascination with the ways people make sense of their everyday lives was reflected in a number of works, including *Frame Analysis* (1974) and in *Forms of Talk* (1981). His interest in the nature of organizations was reflected in *Asylums* (1974), a study of organizations such as prisons, convents and monasteries, and psychiatric hospitals that exist as closed communities. He believed that the study of these organizations had implications for 'open' organizations in which most of us work.

with others, 'I' engage in a constant process of discovering information about them, and they are also in a constant process of discovering information about me. This is done in a context of prior knowledge about each other; prior knowledge of where we come from, socially speaking; the rules that we have about gender; and so on.

When 'I' am in communication with others there are, Goffman (1959) suggests, two key elements. At one level is what 'I' provide as the conscious performance that 'I' am controlling carefully to manage an impression of myself. This is the presentation of myself as a credible, competent person. 'I' need to project an image of myself so that 'you' will find me to be a person in whom you can put your trust, so that 'you' can believe that my account of reality is one that you will find to be plausible. On the other hand, 'you' will be searching for the 'given-off' signals – those features of my performance that present me as not quite the person I wish to present. We are like actors in a drama – except that the 'script' is constantly improvised and much more liable to break down or to take unexpected directions than in the theatre.

Example: Given and given off signals in a meeting

This is an account of an incident during a meeting in a professional services organization:

The other day, I was in a meeting where I really wanted to present the case that a particular programme I lead was truly marvellous, but at the back of my mind was a sense of doubt about it. I started the presentation in fine voice. All was in control. However, a minute or so into my presentation, I realized that there were hesitations, little contradictions, unexpected lowering of the voice as I lost a degree of confidence in what I was saying. If *I* noticed my 'given offs', I am sure that the others, who I wished to impress, did, thus discrediting the confidence of the 'given' performance.

Goffman's model of interaction as drama has rich implications for organizational theory and the ways we conduct ourselves in organizational life. This includes the way we arrange the setting in which our performance takes place. This not only relates to the ways status is symbolized in the organization through the physical surroundings but also the ways we present ourselves. This can relate, for example, to issues of who works in shared offices and who works in their own office – and in the case of the latter, who gets an office with a good view and who gets an office with a view of the back of the building. It can also relate to forms of dress. In many organizations, it seems to be the case that staff can dress relatively informally, but when they reach a certain level (which varies from organization to organization), they are expected to dress more formally (they become 'a suit' – or even more pejoratively, a 'grey suit').

Negotiating the way between the self and the organization's rules

In most organizations, there is a negotiation between the ways the individual wishes to present himself or herself and the norms of the organization, although some organizations are stricter than others. Goffman suggests that there are important ways that these fronts are negotiated, especially when people are working in team or group situations.

> ### Example: 'Mohican worker can return to airport job'
>
> A Stansted Airport worker has been told his job is safe after facing the axe over his Mohican-style haircut. Ryanair check-in clerk John Graham, 22, breathed a sigh of relief yesterday when Swissport bosses told him he could return to work. . . . 'We have agreed to negotiate a much more transparent dress code policy'. Mr. Pearce (the Trade Union representative) said there was some confusion over how much hair gel employees were allowed to use and that he would be meeting Swissport bosses to devise a clearer definition next week.
>
> *Source:* © *Essex Chronicle,* 25 February, 2005.
>
> This example from an airport near London that is primarily geared toward economy flights to Europe illustrates that in the presentation of 'front', there can be interesting flashpoints between what the individual considers 'fashionable' and what the organization considers respectable.

The development of the front, in organizational and everyday life, involves understanding the rules of conduct that are embedded in the situations we encounter. A rule of conduct is a 'guide for action that is recommended not because it is pleasant, cheap or effective, but because it is suitable or just' (Goffman, 1972, p. 48). The rules of conduct become part of our common sense, and when we are committed to them, they also become an important part of our self-image, our organizational identity. This development of the front and the organizational identity can, for some members, be easily attained so that they enter the organization seamlessly, as if to the manner born. For others, the transition into the organization is arduous as they go through a difficult process of socialization into it (a process to be discussed in a later section). And of course, there is the extent to which we choose to go into organizations that suit our own understanding of what we want from organization life. In some cultures, there is a sense that we can match aspiration to organization; in other cultures, the sense of choice is much more restricted.

> ### Example: To be a 'good professor'
>
> This is an account of his everyday life given by a university professor who lectures and manages a group of research colleagues:
>
> > If I wish to be seen as a 'good (or competent) lecturer' I would wish to be seen as someone who fulfils not only the overt *obligations* of a lecturer (e.g., marking assignments on time) but also the covert aspects. These include the implicit rules of conduct shared by colleagues in relation to 'how we behave towards' students and colleagues in relation to degrees of intimacy and distance. Additionally, if I am performing those obligations, I will have an *expectation* that others will reciprocate
>
> *(Continued)*

Example: (Continued)

so that they display a conception of me that agrees with my self-image as one who 'buys into' the rules of conduct.

When I was giving a lecture to a final year undergraduate group the other day I tried to fulfil the overt obligations through presenting the lecture in a straightforward manner, gave each member of the group a handout, provided them with a PowerPoint presentation. In terms of the implicit rules of intimacy and distance – well, I greeted students who were late with a teasing amiability, during the lecture invited comments and discussion (which did not happen but it was my attempt to engage with them), at times engaged in 'tiny chats' with members of the group, and made a few asides that were designed to be 'spontaneous' humorous reflections on what was going on. The management of 'distance' came in part from the formal set-up of the lecture situation and from the observation of clear boundaries – when the lecture finished I (and the students) switched off attention to each other, I (and they) became anonymous.

As the lecture started at 0900 hours the students were passive but seemed to 'buy in' to my performance. They would, from time to time, acknowledge what was happening in relation to my little attempts to enliven the scene without it disturbing their conception of the lecture (at that time of the day) as a place in which they could 'quietly learn' or gently slumber (but not *show* that they were asleep since that might be taken to show contempt for the situation).

As I go through my organizational day I notice that I go through these performances – as colleague to other academic colleagues, as manager in meetings, as member of academic staff talking through issues with administrative colleagues. There are also moments of 'informality' when I have a 'moment of flirtation' (in a deeply respectful way) with someone I rather like. Some of the serious meetings are handled in a deeply serious manner. In other meetings there can be quite 'personal' but humorous comments and teasing in the midst of the seriousness. In other meetings I can put on an impression of submission as a means of impressing management. This is a way of conveying that I am listening to the other's every word although some interpret this behaviour on my part as ironic, a comment on the other's seriousness. In all these performances there is a mixture of me as the 'professional' and my idiosyncratic interpretation of the extent to which I can bring a fondly held impression of my 'self' into the situation.

Of course as I write this I realize that all may be delusion – that instead of seeing these as credible performances students and colleagues see laid before them something rather pathetic – or menacing. In the performance of the drama but in the absence of critical reviews one can never be sure. . . .

Stop and think

This issue of impression management and the display of competence is an important topic. What are the ways that people known to you undertake this impression management? Have you noticed people who apparently are utterly careless of these issues of impression management and displays of competence? Do they 'get away with it', or is their utter carelessness *their own* form of impression management? How do you manage the impression you make on others?

Developing the organizational identity

Although the literature on the development of identity in the symbolic interactionist movement is rich and complex, four themes are of particular significance. What follows is a summary of some of the key issues.

Theme 1: Role making and role taking

The first of these is concerned with a bundle of issues about the *nature and development of the concept of role* in organizations. In modernist literature, the idea of the role tended to be something rather fixed. For example, the role of 'manager' was circumscribed in an official definition, the role description, from which departures would be regarded as a deviation. Within symbolic interactionism, however, the concept becomes much more fluid. No role can exist without other roles to which the particular role is orientated, and roles are negotiated around a set of implicit rules. That is to say, within the organization, there may well be a generalized concept of 'the manager', and this may be captured in such documents as the 'role description' but on a day-to-day basis, enactment of the role of 'manager' is a performance that is based (to a greater or lesser extent) upon the basis of an understanding of:

1. the way the individual 'manager' wishes to perform the role
2. the way the other person (as role holder) wishes the role of 'manager' to be performed
3. the way the other person wishes to perform his or her own role.

In this sense, the performance of a role is a combination of 'role taking' and 'role making'. In role taking, the person acts 'in the perspective supplied in part by his [sic] relationship to others whose actions reflect roles that he must identify' (Turner, 1962, p. 23). What happens when 'I get it right' when I am role taking is that 'I' am properly orientated to the role performance of the other and their expectations of me; my performance matches the expectations of the other, and the other's performance matches my expectations. When I get it wrong, I miscalculate either the other's understanding of his or her role performance or of his or her role relationship with me.

Ideas and perspectives

Getting it wrong, organizationally speaking

One of the roles taken by the writer is that of a relatively senior middle manager. In terms of personal style, I have developed over many years a self-presentation that is somewhat self-deprecating with a love for irony. Soon after I was appointed to my management role, I became engaged in conversation with a very senior manager. The meeting went seriously wrong. The feedback I received later was that my self-deprecating presentation was taken seriously as a sign of lack of competence, and my sense of irony was taken as a sign that I was not committed as strongly as I should be to the purposes of the meeting. There was also a hint that my treatment of the senior manager of the university as an equal was inappropriate. What I had to learn (take on in the role) was a more serious manner, to display commitment and to observe the (unwritten) protocols of deference and demeanour that are important in dealing with senior managers.

Stop and think

Can you think of a situation in which you presented yourself in a manner that did not meet the expectations of the other, even though you felt sure that it was a credible self-presentation? Were there any consequences of this? Typical organizational situations you might like to think about are interviews, undertaking a presentation or interaction with a colleague or manager.

The other side of the coin – role making – is the process by which the person constructs the role. Turner (1962) suggests that most roles:

> ... 'exist' in varying degrees of concreteness and consistency, while the individual confidently frames his behavior as if they had unequivocal existence and clarity. The result is that in attempting from time to time to make aspects of the role explicit he is creating and modifying roles as well as merely bringing them to light' (p. 22).

In this sense, role making is akin to improvization in jazz. There is a core theme that is capable of variation, but within boundaries. In jazz and in organizational settings, performances can run along an axis from 'safe' (and possibly with an implication that the performance is somewhat boring) through to 'developmental' (in which the performance is seen to be fresh, providing a novel interpretation of the role) through to the 'bizarre' (in which the performance is seen as 'too idiosyncratic' to be 'reliable').

Example: A psychiatrist does some role making

During the 1970s, Dr Mendoza was a distinguished consultant psychiatrist who worked at a psychiatric hospital with an international reputation. He had been thinking deeply about his medical practice. He came to realize that something that alienated him and his colleagues from the patients was the use of specialist psychiatric language. He decided to undertake some extreme role making. This took the form of 'talking' with the patients and with colleagues using ordinary, lay language. Initially, this was greeted with a degree of shock. Many of his psychiatrist colleagues saw the behaviour as bizarre – indeed, some thought that he was going through a psychiatric disturbance. Eventually, however, others began to see that this was a useful way of interacting with patients. Some 20 years later, a profound change in medical training in the United Kingdom is that doctors have the development of effective communication with patients as part of their core curriculum. That which was at one time regarded as bizarre role making is now embedded within the role.

In organizational terms, these concepts of role making and role taking throw considerable light on issues of interpersonal relationships. An example of this, to be developed further in the discussion of culture below, is the ways that managers develop understandings of the needs to collaborate. The author of a number of texts on organizations as dramas, James Bryant (2002) suggests that on the one hand, managers face the challenge of working effectively with others in order to benefit their customers and to cope with challenges in their global marketplace. In Goffman's terms, the *character* of management is collaborative. However, the enactment of collaboration involves many tensions at many different levels. Bryant suggests that an understanding of these tensions – the 'conditions of performance' in Goffman's terms – needs to be understood if networks of collaboration are to be truly developed.

The ability of organization members to undertake role making and role taking is intimately bound up with the ways members see themselves and others as 'competent'. In this sense, members of organizations have some concern to display their competence. A presentation of the self that leads to the person to be seen as a 'competent member' generally leads to an assessment of that person which concludes that continued investment in him or her is worthwhile or that he or she is placed for promotion or at the very least is placed to maintain employment in the organization (McAuley, 1994). The Swedish academic Jörgen Sandberg (2000) researched the ways that some 50 engineers in the department of engine optimization at the Volvo Car Corporation understood what constituted 'competence' amongst this group of highly skilled personnel. What he found was that 'workers' knowledge, skills, and other attributes used in accomplishing work are preceded by and based on their conceptions of work' so that competence is assigned on the basis of members' understanding of the nature of their work. What Sandberg is suggesting is that although formal role descriptions may have sets of attributes in them that describe what it is to be a 'competent' manager, doctor, scientist and so on, what counts is the way members construct in their everyday lives attributes of competence in assessing their own and others' activities.

Theme 2: Socialization into the organization or profession

A second key theme is the ways members are socialized into an organizational role or identity. Within symbolic interactionism, this interest in the ways that people become organizational members or members of their profession arose out of a preoccupation with personal and group change in adult life. You may remember that when we introduced symbolic interactionism at the start of the chapter, we suggested that people begin to change, as individuals and groups, when old perspectives and ways of understanding no longer fit new situations. In the development of understanding of the processes of socialization, the sociologist Howard Becker suggested that there are two key questions.

The first is the consideration of the organizational context of personal change:

> What kinds of situations do the socializing institutions place their new recruits in, what kinds of responses and expectations do recruits find in these situations, and to what extent are these incorporated into the self? (Becker, 1977).

Biography | **Howard S. Becker (1928–)**

Howard S. Becker was born in Chicago, Illinois in 1928. He studied for his doctorate at the University of Chicago and worked there at the same time as Erving Goffman and Anselm Strauss. He currently divides his time between San Francisco and France. In addition to his academic career, he was a jazz musician and an exhibition-rated photographer.

His range of publications was enormous. For many people, one of his most famous books is *Outsiders* (1963). This was a key study in the ways that people and social groups become labelled as 'deviants' and the consequences that this has for them and for those who apply the labels. He also wrote extensively on the processes of socialization into professions and on the nature of professions as well as on the development of sociological theory.

In many organizations, some of the overt signals and situations that are used to socialize members include:

- **Mentoring and coaching:** These are the processes by which newcomers to the organization are placed with more senior members in order to enable the newcomer to develop understanding of the ways the organization 'does things' (coaching) and develops its understanding of the core processes of the organization (mentoring).
- **Management development:** These are the processes by which 'new' managers are developed into the role.
- **Appraisal and performance review:** Formal appraisal sessions are often a process by which members can feel rewarded for undertaking tasks and processes in an organizationally appropriate way and be reminded when they have strayed from the path of appropriate behaviour.

In addition, in covert ways, the sorts of situations that socialize members include both at the organizational and the group levels:

- Signals of approval or disapproval that are given in informal settings. This might include on the one hand a smile or friendly gesture or on the other a frown or 'being ignored' when the normal behaviour from the other is a greeting.
- The 'quiet word' that 'We don't do things the way you just did that'.
- Nicknames, especially when they are used to indicate that the person named is in some way or other a deviant or politically powerful.

The second question that Becker suggests is of crucial importance in this process of socialization to understand the inner processes of organizational socialization: what is happening to the individual as he or she is 'going through' the socialization process? The sorts of features that are important here include:

- What *meaning* do I give to the sorts of covert and overt situations and signals mentioned above? Do I see them as indicative of an organization that meets my own self-ideal, an organization in which I would really like to work? Do they indicate that I should be suspicious? Do the ways that these socialization efforts are conducted indicate that 'they are a bunch of idiots'?
- How do the 'official' overt situations fit in with what I see happening within the group that I feel closest to, and *their* 'culture'?
- To what extent do the 'socialization situations' that I am encountering fit with my own desire for autonomy or conformity?

Stop and think

You might like to think how these issues of 'personal preference' in the socialization process are important to you. For example, the extent to which one wants to 'fit in' to the organization (or that part of the organization one is entering) and the extent to which one wishes to preserve autonomy from it can lead to interesting tensions. Can you think of situations in which you have been in conflict with efforts to socialize you into organizational values you have thought to be ridiculous?

In relation to the issue of the organizational context, Becker suggests that we can infer from the symbolic interactionist literature a basic model of how members are socialized into the organization. Although the process of socialization may appear to be relatively straightforward, the outcomes are likely to be complex.

The ways that socialization happens in organizations are related to the social networks that are part of organizational members' lives. An example of this is the case of information technology professionals working for large information technology-based organizations. From an organizational perspective, it was desirable to retain these professionals on long-term contracts in order to maintain a degree of stability. However, within the social networks of these professionals, the general view was that they owed no loyalty to the organization and that it was preferable to 'follow the money'. In some respects, this 'freelance' view was entirely rational; in other respects, it was a shared value of the network not entirely borne out by the evidence. Longer term commitment to the organization could yield rewards in relation to salary, status and security.

The process of socialization is likely to be a collective experience rather than an entirely individual one. In organizational terms, this means that in terms of the 'socialization situations', members of the organization go through these either as groups (as in management development) or as individuals experiencing a shared, institutionalized process (as in mentoring). Amongst the local group of colleagues, the individual is entering into the 'group culture', the shared experience of 'becoming' a competent member.

An example of the way these three issues are interrelated may be found in leadership development programmes that are designed to socialize senior members of organizations into an approach to leadership roles that is seen by the organization to be desirable. Selected personnel attend a series of modules provided by organizations that provide 'leadership development'. Many of these organizations undertake this process through exercises that take place out of doors that are then discussed and processed by an experienced facilitator indoors. An example of this approach is given in the box below.

Example: Leadership development

The Leadership Trust

The Leadership in Management (LM) programme is an intensive five-day course aimed at identifying and exploring the fundamental aspects of good leadership, communication and team building.

Through a combination of project work and review, central presentations, activities (climbing, caving or sub-aqua diving) and personal feedback, the LM programme recreates the complex challenges and changing context of the business world in the 'safe' environment of The Leadership Trust.

In order to ensure maximum benefit from attending, delegates are encouraged to consider their own personal and corporate learning objectives. Upon receipt of a booking, all delegates will be directed to our web-based pre-course briefing service.

(Continued)

> **Example: (Continued)**
>
> **Delegate Profile**
>
> The LM programme is designed to develop the personal leadership skills of those at director and middle-senior management levels.
>
> Delegates are grouped into teams of six to nine individuals from different organizations, facilitated by course tutors and led by the overall course director.
>
> *Source:* www.leadership.co.uk

It is interesting to observe the complexity of response to attendance on the programme when members return to their organization. For some, it is either the confirmation of 'what they already knew' – that the concept of leadership espoused by the programme (and endorsed by the organization) is entirely legitimate and one to which they would wish to adhere. For others, the programme is the beginning of a journey of enlightenment as they attempt to relate the issues from the programme into their lives at work. For others, the programme is 'interesting' but not experienced as particularly relevant to their lives. In addition, there are those for whom the programme is a form of indoctrination into a particular 'way of being' that is the opposite of their identity as a member of the organization. Paradoxically, for some members of the group, the stressful environment of the programme and the novelty of the situation may reinforce existing behaviours and attitudes rather than changing them (Grant, 1996) – they re-enter their organization with an enhanced conviction that their way of 'being a leader' was the right way all along.

Theme 3: The career

These themes of role and socialization are closely connected with the concept of the *career*. This is based on the idea that as we go through the process of 'being' in the organization (or in life generally), we go through a continuing series of experiences, each of which has a cycle or trajectory.

Ideas and perspectives

The trajectory

The sociologists Anselm Strauss and Juliet Corbin (1990) write about the processes of 'managing' patients who have chronic illnesses as they go through the trajectory of their condition.

This trajectory can be brief or extended; each of the stages may well have quite different timelines. It starts with the patient's growing awareness that all is not well, to the diagnosis of the condition, to a state of crisis for the patient, to the stage of acute (i.e., not long lasting) illness, from stability of the condition to instability, to deterioration and ultimately the death of the patient. Strauss' work was very influential in the development of understanding amongst medical and nursing staff of appropriate care interventions at each of these stages.

The idea of the trajectory has found wide use. Figure 9.2 is an example of a 'trajectory of change' that looks at the different stages that a person (or group or even organization) can go through in the process of change.

Although these depictions of the trajectory can appear to be quite mechanistic, the timelines for the various stages are not predetermined. In addition people, can become 'stuck' at any one stage of the process. We can work with colleagues who are 'stuck' in depression from changes that took place many years ago.

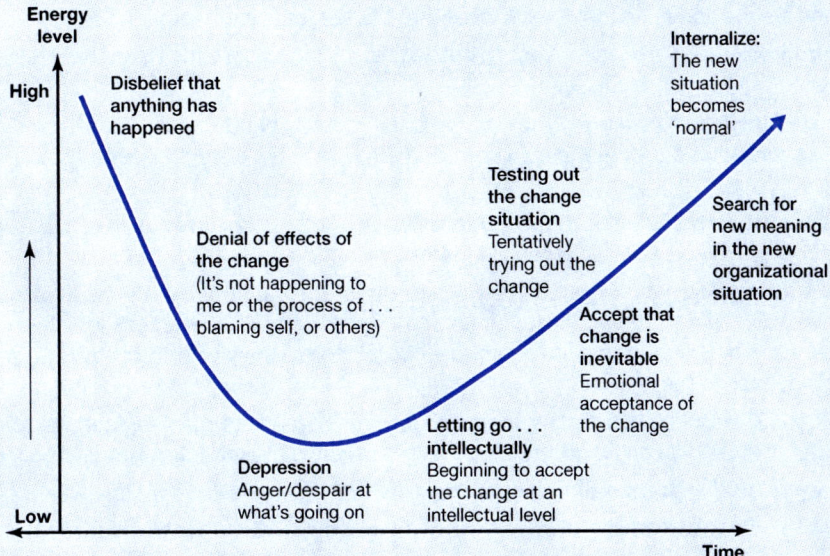

Figure 9.2: A trajectory of change. (*Source:* From Hayes, J., *The Theory and Practice of Change Management*, 2002, Palgrave, reproduced with permission of Palgrave Macmillan.)

Within symbolic interactionist research, there was a fascination with the ways that professionals become socialized into their profession, with studies, particularly in the 1950s through to the 1980s, of the development of medical and nursing students in particular. This research is a way of thinking about the challenges of the development of organizational and professional identity that continues to be influential.

Example: Was it like this for you?

During the 1960s, the sociologist Fred Davis (1968) studied student nurses in a nursing college in the United States. At that time, all the students were women and they lived a fairly enclosed existence. They had many rituals and ceremonies to symbolize the stages of their career as students. The stages of the career were, in broad outline:

- **Initial innocence:** They came into college with a view that they would be 'curing' sick patients. They had high ideals about the nature their career.

(*Continued*)

> ### Example: (Continued)
>
> - **Their experience was different from their expectations:** They were spending a lot of time in class; they had not seen patients. There was a discrepancy between their high ideals and what was going on. Initially, this was not talked about amongst them, but after a while this became a shared pain.
> - **'Psyching out':** This was a period of adjustment when the students experienced lack of fit between goals and the means of achieving the goals. This state is known as *anomie*. The American sociologist R.K. Merton suggests that when people are in this state, they go through a number of responses to it. These are the sorts of *anomic responses* that the students went through:
>   - **Conformed:** Despite the discomfort, they stuck to their studies in the hope that things would get better.
>   - **Ritualized their performance:** Some of the students continued to attend the classes, handed in their assessments, but were there more in body than in mind, essentially detached and alienated from the college.
>   - **Retreated from the college:** Some students actually left the college because it was not meeting their goals and they could not reconcile themselves to the means.
>   - **Innovated:** A pattern of behaviour was that some of the students set themselves out to be the 'lecturers' pet'. In befriending the lecturers, they learnt the route to success in achieving what the college wanted. Some of these secrets they would communicate to their struggling colleagues; some they kept to themselves.
>   - **Rebellion:** Some of the students adopted a position of constant questioning, of demanding that 'things should be different' in the college and in the way that their training was developing.
> - **Preliminary role taking and making:** For those who stayed in the college, this was a period when they began to take on the role of 'student nurse', although this does not mean that they all conformed to the same pattern of behaviour – the role making involved bringing in aspects of themselves into the performance. They began to use the 'language of nursing' but often with joking gestures that this language was not *their* language. They were beginning to take on a new 'common sense' understanding of what it is to be a nurse.
> - **Sustained role taking and making:** At this stage, they began to adopt in a sustained way the language of nursing and the 'professional demeanour' expected of the nurse that was a graduate from the college.
>
> ### Stop and think
>
> If at some stage in your life, you have been a 'student' or undergone induction into a profession, how does the above compare with that experience? Does this concept of the career ring true in your experience, or is the actual experience much more ambiguous and uncertain?

Theme 4: The power of the professional symbol

In the 1960s Howard Becker produced a seminal paper called *The Nature of a Profession*. In this paper, he takes up a number of themes that come from the thinking of previous writers on the nature of the professionals, and he captures many of the issues that were around in the Chicago school at the time. These preoccupations came to be known as the 'professional project', an explanation of the ways that the label 'professional' is a means to the acquisition of power and influence (Macdonald, 1995); these same considerations could be applied to the 'management and leadership projects'.

Becker suggests that there had been a long tradition in the social sciences of attempts to define the nature of the professional. Traditionally, they are depicted as people who possess specialized skills that require prolonged training and study. Success as a professional was measured by quality of service rather than financial reward. In this traditional view, the work of professionals is regulated by a professional body in order to maintain the professional service and to enforce a code of ethics. However, Becker suggests, these traditional definitions are fraught with ambiguity.

Becker's (1977) crucial suggestion is, in understanding the nature of the profession, that we 'view *profession* as an honorific symbol in use in our society and analyse the characteristics of that symbol' (p. 93). He suggests that when we look at the 'great professions' (medicine and the law) we do so with a sentimental gaze; we attribute to them an idealism that is not realistic given our everyday experience of the way in which they work. This is why so many groups, including management, wish to achieve professional status. They wish to bask in the glory of the label 'professional'. As far as the professional is concerned, the collective possession of the symbolic label of 'professional' gives them a justification for their claims to autonomy in the conduct of their work and a remit to control the activities of others. This is because no outsider can judge their work or their assessments of the situation because outsiders have not been exposed to the prolonged training of the professional.

The prizes of autonomy and control have been two of the key drivers for occupational groups to achieve professional status, especially in the context where they practise in large organizations rather than in small professional practices. The way that professionals of all sorts – medical practitioners, lawyers, accountants, scientists and engineers, marketing and human resources, to name but a few – assert their professional status on the one hand and 'fit into' the organizations in which they practise their profession continues to be an issue of considerable importance.

Stop and think

Becker's key thinking on this issue of professionals was written in the 1970s. To what extent do you think these issues regarding the place of professionals in organizations have changed since he wrote that article? On the one hand, there are ways in which our 'respect' for professionals has declined – but maybe there are ways in which we are now, given the advances in technology and knowledge that are part of professional life, even more deferential to them. What do you think?

Throughout this chapter, we have tried to show how these insights from reflective organization theory can help us to develop understanding of the self, the group and the organization. This proposition can be taken a step further in the sense that we can understand identity as being not only about reflection and self-examination. These are the processes by which individuals and the organization can come to question key issues about their identities – who they are and what they stand for. It is through these processes, according to the writers on organization culture Mary Jo Hatch and Majken Schultz (2002), that members can engage in active processes of change. They suggest that these issues of personal, group and organizational identity need to be explored in the context of understandings of the organization culture. This provides a useful link with the next section.

> **The chapter so far**
>
> **Characters in search of an identity**
>
> In this section, we have explored some of the ways that key issues of identity in organization are shaped and developed. We have discussed the ways we construct our identities and conduct ourselves in organizational life. We have suggested that our identities are lodged in the performances that we give in organizational and everyday life and that the development of these performances (and their interpretation by others) involves understanding the rules of conduct that are embedded in the situations we encounter. We explored a bundle of issues about the *nature and development of the concept of role* in organizations and suggested that the performance of a role is a combination of 'role making' and 'role taking'. We also discussed the ways people become organizational members or members of their profession through socialization via direct and indirect processes.

Understanding organization culture through symbols

Introduction – two ways of exploring culture

As discussed elsewhere in this book, there are, within organization theory, radically different approaches to the exploration of organization culture. At one end of the spectrum, there is the view that an organization *has* a culture or organizational climate at the postmodern end of the spectrum, there is a view that within the organization, 'culture' is highly fragmented and dispersed.

The perspective on culture discussed in this section is the *subjectivist* or *interpretavist* perspective. In this approach, culture is that which is conceptualized, understood, by either the organizational member or the researcher through his or her subjective experience. What this means is that 'organization members, as social actors, actively participate in the construction of organizational reality through organizational symbolism, in its various forms' (Mumby, 1988, p. 12). At its most radical, this subjectivist approach dissolves the whole concept of organization culture so that it becomes, as an idea, problematic. The theories and perspectives discussed in this section, however, enable us to understand the ways that organization members develop meaning and significance in their organizational lives, the ways that they develop symbols that capture the essence of their organizational lives.

Communicating cultures

As suggested earlier in this chapter, the claim of writers in the phenomenological tradition is that it can 'write meaning, and its close relative emotion, back into the study of organizations' (Gabriel, 1991, p. 857). The key interest in this approach is in the nicknames, jokes, stories, myths and sagas that pervade organizational life. According to organization theorist Yannis Gabriel, different forms of communication represent members' attempts to 'humanize organizations and strengthen the individual in his/her daily engagement with them'. For those who feel that they have power in the organization, these stories and myths provide a means of preserving their sense of authority; for those who feel powerless, they help, Gabriel suggests, to make organizational live bearable. This conceptualization of culture as serving a function for organizational members separates it from the postmodern view of culture. The postmodern view sees culture as emergent text 'involving authors, readers, texts and other texts' (Linstead and Grafton-Small, 1992, p. 350) that is concerned with difference rather than shared meaning.

Many writers have developed understanding of the role of nicknames, jokes, stories, myths and sagas in the development and communication of cultures. In the following, we mention some of the core ideas.

1. **Jokes and nicknames:** The psychoanalyst Sigmund Freud suggested, in a book written in 1916, that there are two kind of jokes. The first is what he called 'innocent jokes'. These are jokes that do not make any particular point and where the joke is an end in itself. The second type of joke has a purpose, it is 'tendentious', to use Freud's (1976) term. Such jokes can run the risk of offending listeners and 'run the risk of meeting with people who do not want to listen to them' (p. 132), but they can bring great pleasure as well. Purposive jokes enable people to express difficult emotions or their anger in a way that is more acceptable than the straightforward expressions of feelings. Wherever there are purposive jokes, there are usually three parties involved. These parties to the joke are the teller of the joke, the listener to the joke and the person who is the focus of the joke.

   It is interesting to observe the ways that these general principles, especially with regard to jokes that are purposive, are acted out in organizations. Phiup Bougen (1994), an academic at Madrid Business School, writes of the way that accountants are the subject of stereotypes and humour. In many organizations, the accountant is seen to be a stern figure who exercises control through the budgets, and the jokes and stereotypes are ways of dealing with the perceived threat that they pose; the jokes are essentially hostile. Bougen also shows the ways that the humour changes over time as perceptions of the character of 'the accountant' as professional change. In her study of young managers studying for a qualification the academic, Irena Grugulis (2002) found that they used humour as a way of dealing with the stress of assessment and the possibility of failure. At a deeper level, humour allows them to criticize the course and the qualification so that their hostility to the situation is not 'personal'. They use humour to deal with the complexity of the situation without committing themselves to any serious action. In this sense, humour acts as a defence against the anxiety that they found in the situation.

   In many ways, nicknames are jokes captured in a word. They may, in Freud's terms, be innocent or purposive. In a paper on the use of nicknames in organizations, the American academic Bruce Fortado (1998) suggests that their use has a number of functions that can be interpreted from their context. Nicknames can be used to identify character defects in senior people; they help to bond colleagues together. In particular, they can be a form of bonding for people who feel that they are 'deviants' from the 'normal' order in the organization. The nickname, for these people, is a way of gaining some feeling of control in difficult situations. Nicknames serve the function, Fortado argues, of developing members' social control of situations, of developing camaraderie amongst the group, of socialization into the group. They are an important aspect of labelling and identifying others and creating and sustaining negative or positive images of the other.

> ### Example: Joking nicknames
>
> Because jokes and nicknames are understood in a particular context, they can be difficult to explain. But an example that comes to mind is this from the author's experience.
>
> One of our senior male managers was nicknamed 'the fat controller'. This name comes from a series of books for children written by the Reverend Wilbert Awdry about a mythical railway. The nickname captured feelings that some of his colleagues had about him as a somewhat dominating person. In a similar vein, one of the senior female managers was known as 'the head girl'. Again, this image goes back to children's books about schools and the way in which the 'head girl' was seen as a somewhat dominating person.
>
> What is perhaps interesting is the ways in which these names could be used with affection for most of the time but could sometimes be used with an edge of aggression when these characters were experienced as being *too* bossy or imperious.

2. **Stories, myths and sagas:** The range of what is meant by the term 'stories' is considerable. It ranges from 'corridor gossip' to tales told about victories or defeats within the organization, to accounts of meetings through to public proclamations by the chief executive on the future of the organization. In his study of storytelling, Gabriel (2000) created a detailed taxonomy of stories. His main classifications included:

   1. Comic stories in which the teller of the story is a deserving victim or comes out of the story as a foolish person. This includes incidents in which the teller made a mistake.
   2. Comic stories in which the teller of the story is a survivor, shows a good sense of humour in adversity or plucks victory out of adversity.
   3. Romantic stories in which the teller talks of love and affection. Sometimes these stories were 'romantic' in the sense that customers or hospital patients had expressed great appreciation for the care that they had received. They were also more directly 'romantic' in that there were stories of love and affection between members of the organization.

   We would add, however, another type of story. These are the 'serious stories' that can be spoken or written that represent the different representations of the different groups in the organization – management, trades and professional unions that advocate their different perspectives. From a management perspective, these can take the form of rules and procedures, business plans or strategic documents. When senior management of an organization works toward the development of a corporate culture, that emphasizes the idea that all members share a set of core values, they are developing a story, a 'grand narrative' about the organization.

A major theme in the study of stories has been to understand them as ways that members give their work and their lives meaning. The idea of the corporate culture can have great appeal for the kind of person who wants to work for an organization that 'provides' strong core values. Their story is more or less the same as the corporate story. On the other hand, some members may gain meaning from their work by constantly complaining about the organization and its ways. Their 'stories' are, organizationally speaking, tales told by dissidents. Between the 'true believer' and 'the dissident', there are likely to be many shades of organizational story, including 'innocent' stories told just for the fun of it. As Gabriel (1991) points out, stories are not 'the truth' but are there to be interpreted, their deeper meaning to be discerned from the context of the story.

One of the most important areas of study in the interpretavist approach to organization culture has been into the idea of the *myth*. A myth can be regarded as a 'bundle' of stories that when taken together make some overall sense, although it is often the case that we do not realize until we have moments of reflection that we have created a 'myth'. They are best looked at as explanations of core aspects of organizational life that people hold to be 'good enough'. Myths can be complex and interwoven, and as new myths develop, they become deeply interwoven with the existing 'mythic reservoir' (Røyrvik and Wulff, 2002). They are stories with a veiled meaning that people tell to each other in the organization. The myth sustains people in the belief that their version of the organizational story is correct. This approach to culture has particular appeal in the Scandinavian countries (Czarniawska and Sköldberg, 2003). Myths provide 'sign posts' that can lead organization members and theorists toward the ways that relationships are structured in organizations; understanding myths and rituals can help organizations develop.

Case study — Pervasive myths in an engineering consulting company

Scandiaconsult, a Scandinavian consulting engineering company, had been going through a period of rapid growth after it had undertaken a number of mergers and acquisitions. As a consulting company, its aim was to provide sophisticated solutions to large engineering projects. The authors of a case study, Emil Røyrvik and Egil Wulff (2002), worked with top management and project workers in project situations and through interviews to develop understanding of their stories and the everyday issues and problems. In the course of their work, they uncovered two key myths that pervaded the organization:

- **How the company initiated new projects:** A key activity for a consulting organization such as Scandiaconsult is the ability to acquire and generate new projects; they are the life blood of the organization. In this case, there were pervasive 'myths' held by people responsible for getting new projects. On the one hand, there was the myth that the company could only get projects through pure and 'objective' invitations for tender. This is the idea that when the company received an invitation to submit a tender for a project, those responsible for submitting the tender would design the document so that it would be of high quality but also be the most competitive tender. On the other hand, there was a myth that new projects were best gained through the development of long-term relationships and networks with organizations that needed the services of Scandiaconsult. The issues that

(Continued)

> **Case study** (Continued)
>
> were contained within these two myths are very complex. Through the uncovering of the myths and discussion of them, members of the organization developed a new understanding of these myths and developed improved approaches to making choices as to how new projects should be approached.
>
> - **The ideal form of organization for the company:** In this case, there were again two basic 'myths' (with many positions between). On the one hand, there was the 'myth' that the company should be organized around the geographical location of its regional branches. In this way of organizing, the teams of consultants would be multidisciplinary and able to provide an immediate service to clients within the region. On the other hand, there was a prevailing myth that the company should be organized around the different professional and technical disciplines. This was on the basis that the work that they performed required a high level of expertise and the constant development of professional knowledge and that this was best achieved by the co-location of the different disciplines. The issues and dilemmas that were contained within the myths of organization were complex and involved many dilemmas for organizational members. As in the first example, uncovering the myths led to a better understanding of the dilemmas and choices that could be made.
>
> *Source: Based on Røyrvik and Wulff (2002)*

What is important in the myths is that they contain rational and non-rational elements *and* that within them there are elements about core values and the emotional commitments of members to the organization, their professions and their own sense of being. Strati (1999) suggests that organizations are not pervaded by a single myth that is well defined but rather the outcome of each member's account of the relationship between the individual and the organization; the myths display the intensity of their feelings with regard to their everyday organizational life that they construct and reconstruct.

Myth making occurs not only at the local organizational level; within organization and management theory there have developed myths about organizations and organizational life. With perhaps a hint of mischief, the Swedish organization theorist Barbara Czarniawska-Joerges (1992) reports of the way in which writers on corporate culture such as Deal and Kennedy (1982), convey a 'myth' of organizational life. This mythology tells heroic stories of leaders who succeeded against all the odds, of the American dream of heroic entrepreneurial leadership *and also* paradoxically, talks of organizations as places in which values are shared within a view of 'corporate culture'. These myths provide managers and leaders with a sense of aspiration, an emotional buzz that ultimately, the organization can be 'managed'.

> **Case study** Contrasting myths of an organization
>
> An interesting feature of the growth of the 'guru academic' has been the extent to which they can extol the virtues of organizations that exemplify the approach to organizational success that they advocate. One of the leading guru academics is Gary Hamel. He is founder and chair of an international management consultancy company, visiting professor of strategy and international management at

London Business School and the Thomas S. Murphy Distinguished Research Fellow at Harvard Business School.

An example of the way a myth of organization can be created was Hamel's text *Leading the Revolution* (2000) in the course of which he mythologized the now disgraced energy and communications organization, Enron. The underpinning set of beliefs that this myth of Enron supports is that the American approach to conducting business is the very engine of change and progress. It is interesting to look at just some of the images and metaphors that Hamel uses to construct the myth:

- Enron . . . has '*again and again reinvented*' themselves.
- It '*revolutionized* international power plant development.'
- 'Enron's leaders know that you can't *pioneer* new markets without taking some risks.'
- 'Enron's *pro-entrepreneur* culture.'
- Building teams depended on the 'willingness of top-notch Enron people to *uproot* their careers *almost overnight*' (p. 219).
- Most Enron workers have '*self directed careers*' (p. 220).
- 'You can't build a *forever restless, opportunity seeking company* unless you're willing to hire *forever restless, opportunity seeking individuals*' (p. 221).
- 'There's also a chance for *some serious wealth creation*' (p. 259).
- The company has '*out-sized aspiration*' (p. 221).
- Enron had 'a *passion* to make markets . . . more efficient . . . a *vibrant* internal market . . . Highly motivated *entrepreneurs*.
- *Fluid organizational boundaries* (Hamel's emphasis, p. 222).

Hamel's mythology may be contrasted with this alternative 'myth' (written by a journalist, Madeleine Bunting, for the *Guardian* newspaper in 2002) that is highly critical of Enron and celebrates its demise. In this version, the underpinning core values that support the myth is that advanced capitalism is essentially corrupt and corrupting.

'Enron provides a *textbook case* of how *corporate power* subverts the political process. . . . It's *mucky stuff*, and *heads will roll*, but it's also a very familiar theme'. The Enron story 'spells the end not just to some nasty *pork-barrel politics* but to an *ideologically driven vicious corporate model*. . . . This vision of a *Darwinian dog-eat-dog market*' drove Enron. The company relied on 'a *near fundamentalist faith*' in the market so that '*true believers*' claimed there were simply no limits to its application.

Enron became the example par excellence of how, in the late 90s US corporate culture *highjacked and inverted* 60s radicalism. *Business guru* Gary Hamel praised Enron's activists (who) lived the rule of 'creative destruction' in which all conventional assumptions were to be challenged. . . . *It bred a culture of breathtaking arrogance* that Enron could do the impossible.

(In both of the extracts, the emphases, unless otherwise indicated, are from this chapter's author.)

From the interpretavist perspective jokes, nicknames, stories and myths are core aspects of organizational life. The ways in which they interrelate, sustain and create change to the rich and complex cultures of organizations. They tell us of important issues that members confront on a daily basis, about power and influence (or the lack of it), decision making (or feelings of impotence), issues about control (or lack of it) and so on.

Negotiation of meaning influences organizational design

In this last section, we will discuss the ways that interpretive understandings of organizations illuminate the ways organizations are designed. In conventional organizational theory the structure of organizations is something that comes from formal processes of organizational design. An interpretive perspective shows, however, that lying alongside the formal structure, members can develop very different understandings of organizational design. We shall explore one particular perspective – the Arena concept developed by Strauss et al. (1964). This concept demonstrates how members use language and symbols in order to create a shifting design of their organization.

At the core of the concept of *negotiated order* is the idea that although the official structure of the organization is based upon a hierarchical or network or matrix model, what *actually* happens is significantly based upon processes of *negotiation*.

Strauss and his colleagues initially developed the idea of the negotiated order from their seminal study of seven psychiatric units in hospitals in the United States. At one extreme were units in which the emphasis was psychotherapeutic, where all members of the unit – doctors, patients, nurses, physiotherapists and so on – were strictly equal in their rights and there was no hieratical distinction made about the mode of care. At the other extreme were units in which the hierarchy was strictly defined as between doctors, nurses and patients. Other units occupied positions between these extremes. The issue that interested Strauss and his colleagues was: why is it that, given that each unit has the same types of staff and the same types of patient, they had such different structures and arrangements for the treatment of patients?

Ideology, rhetoric and negotiation

Strauss and his colleagues were deeply aware of the nature of power and politics in organizations. They observed that in many organizations, position in the hierarchy was important and that position could be used as part of the process of negotiation. In many (but not all) of the psychiatric units, the medical staff were able to impose their definition of the situation onto the situation. They used their professional

---

Biography — Anselm Strauss (1916–1996)

Anselm Strauss was born in 1916 and died in San Francisco in 1996. He studied at the University of Chicago for both his masters degree and his PhD but spent most of his academic career (from 1960) at the University of California. Much of his writing was within the symbolic interactionist tradition. Indeed, he believed that, with due modesty, the ideas discussed in this section represented an extension of the Chicago school. He was one of only a few members of the Chicago school who took a direct interest in organizations. His interests in sociology were extensive, although for a time he tended to concentrate on the sociology of medicine and the medical system. It was from this that he developed the theories of negotiation and negotiated order that became central to his thinking. His interest was also in the development of methodologies for social science research. In 1967, he wrote with Barney Glaser a text on qualitative research, *The Discovery of Grounded Theory*, which is still in print. He developed his approach to research methods (with Juliet Corbin) in a number of influential texts.

> **Ideas and perspectives**
>
> ### Professional ideologies, professional rhetoric: the negotiated arena
>
> The key to this issue lies in what Strauss calls the different *professional ideologies* held by the staff. Professional ideologies are derived from the type of training and subsequent experiences that the professional has had. The psychiatric and nursing staff placed themselves into well-defined ideological camps, and their identities were firmly lodged in those ideologies. Strauss uses the term 'professional' in a broad sense to include any member of staff who has a particular understanding of the issues.
>
> For example, some psychiatrists have a 'medical' ideology. By this, they would believe that the only way to treat patients effectively would be by giving them the right drugs, and when appropriate, the administration of electric shock treatment. Holding this ideology, with its emphasis on accurate diagnosis, means that the psychiatrists see themselves as having absolute control over the fate of the patient and the right to issue precise instructions to staff. This ideology also involves the dismissal of other forms of treatment, such as psychotherapy, as being unscientific.
>
> At the other extreme are the psychiatrists who believe in psychotherapeutic methods of treatment. This involves an ideology that involves concepts of equality as between the parties involved in treatment and may regard the 'medical' model as not getting to the roots of the patient's problems (the psychotherapeutic psychiatrist believes the medical model to be relatively good at treating symptoms but poor at treating causes). Nurses and others also hold to treatment ideologies, and these can be very powerful in determining the pattern of care given to patients.
>
> This professional ideology is expressed through the *professional rhetoric*. This term is used to describe the specialist language (the jargon) that members learn during the course of their training and socialization into the role. In the psychiatric units, all the different professionals had their own professional rhetoric. Staff who trained in schools where there was an emphasis on the medical model had a professional rhetoric that was different from those trained in schools where there was an emphasis on psychotherapeutic approaches.
>
> When the nurses, psychiatrists, physiotherapists and others work together in order to discuss problems and issues they enter the *professional arena* in which the different groups of staff use their rhetoric in order to promote their particular ideology. This idea of the professional arena can be extended to any working group. If you take, for example, a board meeting of a manufacturing organization, the professional arena would consist of such professionals as marketing, production, sales, human resource and so on.

> **Stop and think**
>
> Take an organization (or department) known to you. What would you see as the key ideologies in relation to the tasks that need to be undertaken? In the situation you are exploring, are there conflicts that make work difficult, or do the different ideologies and rhetorics make for an exciting life? If you think that there is little or no ideological difference between members, what are the consequences?

rhetoric (their esoteric, specialized language) to achieve that definition. However, as a rule, in order for the professional rhetoric to be effective, it needs to be accompanied by careful presentation of self. If the person's language is too esoteric, too much bound up in the language of the profession, he or she runs the danger of being thought of as narrow, not having the broad picture. If on the other hand, the person's language it too 'popular', he or she may be thought of as being 'incompetent' in the performance of their professional tasks and therefore unreliable as a colleague.

In some of the units that Strauss and his colleagues studied, the doctors did not have it all their own way. There were occasions when the nursing staff exercised the dominant ideology. They used their professional rhetoric to push the medical staff into methods of treatment with which the latter did not entirely agree. Typically, what happened in a case of this sort was that the medical staff, for career reasons, tended to work in some of the units for a shorter period than the nursing staff. In these cases, the nurses had a high degree of 'local knowledge' of the patients and their circumstances. In this situation, the nurses could bring their experience to bear as part of their professional rhetoric to counter the proposals of the doctors. Because members with high local knowledge *tended* to be more conservative in their ideas about therapy (largely because they had become insulated to the conditions on the ward), they would use arguments such as: 'We tried that before, and it didn't work then' if the doctors introduced new ideas.

This process of negotiation can also be seen in other aspects of work, characteristically, in terms of task allocation. Generally, people in work organizations have such documents as job descriptions that describe the nature of their contribution to the organization. However, it is typically the case that these descriptions are somewhat fuzzy around the edges; they rarely if ever describe exactly the sort of rights and responsibilities to be allocated to the various types and grades of people in the organization. They usually set a minimum level of performance, and the sociologist is generally interested in the ways in which people use these rules in order either to restrict or improve their work situations. Amongst the sorts of activities and negotiations in this area that Strauss discusses we find:

1. **Task gaining:** This is when a staff group would actively search out new tasks to perform because the task would give them, for example, prestige or a place nearer the 'centre of things'.

2. **Task offering:** A staff group would offer tasks because it enables them to be rid of irksome duties or it might mean that they are not inconvenienced. When there is offering, there might also be *task refusal*. Relevant people have recourse either to the rules of the organization or to legal constraints to prevent them either from being obliged to take on a task they do not want to perform or to deny the possibility of a person's taking on a task they would want to undertake.

3. **Task stripping:** This occurs when a person wants to take away a task from another. This could be because the first person wants to perform the task himself or herself, feeling that it is rightly his or hers. Alternatively, it could be because the first person feels that the second is performing the task incompetently.

4. **Task maintenance** is the attempt by the person who is threatened by the task stripper to maintain stability in the tasks performed. Again, this may be done either by recourse to the rules or by claiming that 'It has always been the case that I perform this task'.

These activities are undertaken because organizational members want to control the various aspects of their work and negotiate to make this possible. They stake claims and counterdemands and engage in 'games' of give and take in order to achieve satisfactory outcomes for themselves and their groups.

Arenas and games

The idea that organizations can be looked at as arenas is analogous to the view that they can be looked at as an 'ecology of games'. Many years ago, the American sociologist Norton Long (1958) argued that the activities that people undertake in any particular situation could be looked at as a serious and profound game. The game provides the players with a set of goals that give them a sense of success or failure in their activities. These evolving games also provide members with clear roles and help them to develop strategies and political tactics. The ability to understand the behaviour of an individual or group depends upon the ability to understand the game in which that person or group is involved. The important issue here at all levels from individual to corporate is the development of competence in the games.

Example: The rules of the game

This is from a conversation with a senior divisional manager:

> When we have meetings of the senior management group, it is interesting to observe the way things get played out. I noticed the other day how neatly Lindsey, who looks after research and development, got for herself quite a useful place on the marketing group. But then it's fascinating how they all play their roles. I love the way the executive tries to dominate the senior managers on the board and then the way that the senior managers create alliances with different members of the executive. And then it's interesting who has a voice and who is ignored. I have a feeling that the human resources guy will not be a member of the group much longer; he's such a wimp. The other thing I notice is the way we talk about head office, the way we feel we've always got to do it their way and if someone gets too rebellious about that way they get stamped on by the others.

The negotiated arena approach to organizational design does not deny the power of hierarchy or other forms of authority in organizations. It is fascinating to look at the ways in which people *use* their position in the hierarchy (whether senior or junior), *use* their 'job descriptions', *use* their professional rhetoric, *use* their understanding of their personal power and so on in order to attempt to influence their place and the place of others in the organization.

Organizational members work together in webs of negotiation. At the start of this chapter, we discussed the idea that one of the fundamental assumptions behind symbolic interactionism was that when members of a group (or a department or even an organization) feel that all is well with the current definition of reality, they become 'lodged' into it. Change happens when old perspectives are believed not to meet new needs. In this sense, aspects of the everyday design of the organization can be seen as an emergent structure. If members come to believe that the game is not one that is yielding the results, or as people leave the organization and newcomers join, then the arena itself has the potential for change.

Conclusions

In this chapter, we have looked at the ways that key theories and perspectives from sociology have made major contributions to organizational theory and provide challenges to other theories of organization. These perspectives challenge modernism and neo-modernism in the sense that they get beneath the prescriptive approaches to organizations that ultimately pervade these theories. They challenge postmodernism in the sense that these perspectives do not deny the reality of organizational life; they enable people to reflect in practical ways on the nature of their experience in organizations. The symbolic interactionists and the phenomenologists took a lead in the development of interpretative methodologies in the social sciences generally and in organizations in particular.

Interpretivists, particularly in the later Chicago school, were not interested in the development of a 'grand theory' that explains everything in the social world. Rather, their interest was in the development of theories that were empirically grounded and that provided ideas and propositions about the ways we create and communicate meaning. According to the sociologist Martin Bulmer (Bulmer et al., 1997), the perspectives presented in this chapter bring theoretical ideas and empirical data together so that the theory and the data illuminate each other – and sometimes sparked new directions of investigation through their confrontation.

Crucially, however, what the perspectives and theories presented in this chapter do is to present organizational members with propositions and methods that enable them to reflect deeply on issues of personal and organizational identity, on the nature of organizational purposes and the ways we give meaning to organizational life. These processes of reflectiveness and self-examination are there to enable the organization to develop and undergo change in intellectually rigorous and thoughtful ways. Some of these issues are summarized below where we match the learning outcomes of the chapter against the challenges these represent to organizational members.

Concluding grid

Learning outcomes	Challenges to the contemporary organization
Define what is meant by 'reflective' organization theory.	The development of reflective ability enables deeper understanding of key organizational issue and it enables informed action.
Compare and contrast how different strands of interpretavist, reflective organization theory sheds light on how organization members give meaning to their lives at work.	Enables us to understand the ways that members give diverse and complex meanings to their organizational world.
Discuss the ways individuals develop a sense of self in organizations.	Enables us to develop deeper insights into the ways that members actually experience the world of their organizations.

Assess how these theories provide insights into how individuals and groups create their organizational identities.	The challenge that these perspectives give is to develop our understanding of the ways that members structure their organizational lives.
Explore how these different theories enrich our understanding of organizational culture.	Develops a deeper understanding of the underlying cultural beliefs that members hold about the organization.
Examine the ways these theories challenge our understandings of the design of organizations.	Enable organizational members to reflect on the ways that the patterns of negotiation actually help the organization develop or may be dysfunctional.

Annotated further reading

The key ideas and perspectives that lie behind 'reflection' as an important organizational activity are contained in Donald Schön (1991). Although this book concentrates on the significance of reflection for members of professions such as medicine and engineering, it also has profound lessons for the practice of management.

If you are interested in the development of the Chicago school and in the work of Howard Becker visit his web page at http://home.earthlink.net/~hsbecker/

If you find the ideas of Goffman interesting, you might find the American film *Primary Colors* (director, Mike Nichols, 1998) both entertaining and instructive. It is a satirical study in impression management as it explores the fictionalized experiences of a candidate for the US presidency.

Goffman's book, *The Presentation of Self in Everyday Life* (1959), gives a very good insight into his overall approach to the development of identity and the processes by which we manage meaning.

Gabriel's (2000) *Storytelling in Organizations: Facts, Fictions, and Fantasies* is an authoritative account of stories in organizations. In particular, his classification of the types of story told by members in organizations provides very useful insights.

Discussion questions

1. At the start of the chapter, we developed a model that underpins symbolic interactionism. This model took us through a number of 'stages' in the processes of individual and group meaning making and the ways we develop symbols. What do you see as the strengths and weaknesses of this model?
2. Some describe the work of Goffman as 'cynical' in its emphasis on impression management and its absence of notions of the 'true self'. Others feel that in his exploration of 'impression management', Goffman is actually describing key human abilities in making and communicating meaning. What do you think?

3. If you look at your own experience and those of colleagues, what are the key features that lie behind the development of your identity as, for example, a student or manager?
4. In our discussion of culture in this chapter, we have explored the reflective, interpretavist approach to this important topic. We ended the section, however, by putting forward the view that all the different perspectives on culture presented in this text have value. From what you have read so far in this chapter and others, do you think that this synthesizing view is useful, or do you prefer a purist view that one of the perspectives is superior to others? What influenced your preference?
5. In the section on 'design of organizations', we expressed the view that the negotiated order can be as important as the formal structure of the organization (e.g., hierarchy, network or matrix) in determining the ways that people and organizations undertake their work. Do you think that this view is useful?

References

Alvesson, M. and Berg, P.O. (1992) *Corporate Culture and Organizational Symbolism: An Overview*, Berlin: Walter de Gruyter.

Alvesson, M. and Deetz, S. (2000) *Doing Critical Management Research*, London: Sage.

Alvesson, M. and Sköldberg, K. (2000) *Reflexive Methodology. New Vistas for Qualitative Research*, London: Sage.

Becker, H.S. (1963) *Outsiders: Studies in the Sociology of Deviance*, New York: The Free Press.

Becker, H.S. (1977) *Sociological Work: Method and Substance*, New Brunswick, NJ: Transaction Books.

Bougen, P.D. (1994) 'Joking apart: The serious side to the accountant stereotype', *Accounting, Organizations and Society* 19(3):319–335.

Bryant, J. (2003) *The Six Dilemmas of Collaboration*, Chichester: John Wiley.

Bulmer, M., Thomas W.I. and Park, R.E. (1997) 'Conceptualizing, theorizing and investigating social processes', in C. Camic (ed.), *Reclaiming the Sociological Classics: The State of the Scholarship*, Oxford: Blackwell Publishers.

Bunting, M. (2002) 'Fall of the arrogant', *The Guardian*, 28 January.

Cossette, P. (1998) 'The study of language in organizations: A symbolic interactionist stance', *Human Relations* 51(11):1355–1379.

Cuff, E.C., Sharrock, W.W. and Francis, D.W. (1998) *Perspectives in Sociology*, 4th edn, London: Routledge.

Czarniawska, B. and Sköldberg, K. (2003) 'Tales of organizing: Symbolism and narration in management studies', in B. Czarniawska and G. Sevón (eds), *The Northern Lights – Organization Theory in Scandinavia*, Copenhagen: Copenhagen Business School Press.

Czarniawska-Joerges, B. (1992) *Exploring Complex Organizations: A Cultural Perspective*, Newbury Park, CA: Sage.

Davis, F. (1968) 'Professional socialization as subjective experience', in H. Becker (ed.), *Institutions and the Person*, New York: Aldine.

Deal, T.E. and Kennedy, A.A. (1982) *Corporate Cultures: The Rites and Rituals of Corporate Life*, Reading, MA: Addison Wesley.

Dennis, A. (2001) *Making Decisions About People: The Organizational Contingencies of Illness*, Aldershot: Ashgate Publishing Ltd.

Denzin, N.K. (1971) 'Symbolic interactionism and ethnomethodology', in J.D. Douglas (ed.), *Understanding Everyday Life: Toward the Reconstruction of Sociological Knowledge*, London: Routledge & Kegan Paul.

Fortado, B. (1998) 'Interpreting nicknames: A micropolitical portal', *Journal of Management Studies* 35(1):14–34.

Frost, P.J. (2004) 'Handling toxic emotions: New challenges for leaders and their organization', *Organizational Dynamics* 33(2):111–128.

Freud, S. (1976) *Jokes and their Relation to the Unconscious*, Harmondsworth: Penguin Books.

Gabriel, Y. (1991) 'Turning facts into stories and stories into facts: A hermeneutic exploration of organizational folklore', *Human Relations* 44(8):857–875.

Gabriel, Y. (2000) *Storytelling in Organizations: Facts, Fictions, and Fantasies*, Oxford: Oxford University Press.

Garfinkel, H. (1976) *Studies in Ethnomethodology*, New York: Prentice Hall.

Glaser, B. and Strauss, A.L. (1967) *The Discovery of Grounded Theory: Strategies for Qualitative Research*, New York: Aldine.

Goffman, E. (1959) *The Presentation of Self in Everyday Life*, New York: Doubleday.

Goffman, E. (1972) *Interaction Ritual: Essays on Face-to-Face Behaviour*, Harmondsworth: Penguin University Books.

Goffman, E. (1974) *Asylums*, Harmondsworth: Penguin Books.

Goffman, E. (1974) *Frame Analysis: An Essay on the Organization of Experience*, Harmondsworth: Penguin Books.

Goffman, E. (1981) *Forms of Talk*, Oxford: Basil Blackwell.

Goleman, D. (1998) 'What makes a leader?' *Harvard Business Review* 76(6):92–102.

Grant, D. (1996) 'Metaphors, human resource management and control', in C. Oswick and D. Grant (eds), *Organization Development: Metaphorical Explorations*, London: Pitman Publishing.

Grugulis, I. (2002) 'Nothing serious? Candidates' use of humour in management training', *Human Relations* 55(4):387–406.

Hamel, G. (2000) *Leading the Revolution*, Cambridge, MA: Harvard Business School Press.

Hatch, M.J. and Schultz, M. (2002) 'The dynamics of organizational identity', *Human Relations* 55(8):989–1018.

Harvey, J.B. (1988) 'The Abilene paradox: The management of agreement', in J.B. Harvey (ed.), *The Abilene Paradox and other Meditations on Management*, San Francisco: Jossey-Bass.

Hayes, J. (2002) *The Theory and Practice of Change Management*, Basingstoke: Palgrave.

Hughes, E. (1958) *Men and Their Work*, Glencoe, IL: Free Press.

Huy, Q.N. (1999) 'Emotional capability, emotional intelligence, and radical change', *Academy of Management Review* 24(2):325–345.

Knights, D. and Willmott H. (1999) *Management Lives; Power and Identity in Work Organizations*, London: Sage.

Linstead, S. and Grafton-Small, R. (1992) 'On reading organizational culture', *Organization Studies* 13(3):331–355.

Long, N.E. (1958) 'The local community as an ecology of games', *American Journal of Sociology* 64(3):251–255.

Luckman, T. (1978) 'Preface', in T. Luckman (ed.), *Phenomenology and Sociology: Selected Readings*, Harmondsworth: Penguin Books Ltd.

Macdonald, K.M. (1995) *The Sociology of the Professions*, London: Sage.

McAuley, J. (1994) 'Exploring issues in culture and competence', *Human Relations* 47(4): 417–430.

Manning, P.K. (1971) 'Talking and becoming: A view of organizational socialization', in J.D. Douglas (ed.), *Understanding Everyday Life: Toward the Reconstruction of Sociological Knowledge*, London: Routledge & Kegan Paul.

Márai, S. (2002) *Embers*, London: Penguin Viking.

Matthews, F.H. (1977) *Quest for an American Sociology: Robert E. Park and the Chicago School*, Montreal: McGill-Queen's University Press.

Meltzer, B.N., Petras, J.W. and Reynolds, L.T. (1975) *Symbolic Interactionism: Genesis, Varieties and Criticism*, Boston: Routledge & Kegan Paul.

Mumby, D.K. (1988) *Communication and Power in Organizations: Discourse, Ideology, and Domination*, Norwood, NJ: Ablex Publishing Corporation.

Røyrvik, E.A. and Wulff, E. (2002) 'Mythmaking and knowledge sharing: Living organizational myths and the broadening of opportunity structures for knowledge sharing in a Scandinavian engineering consultant company', *Creativity and Innovation Management* 11(3):154–164.

Sandberg, J. (2000) 'Understanding human competence at work: An interpretative approach', *Academy of Management Journal* 43(1):9–2.

Schön, D.A. (1991) *The Reflective Practitioner: How Professionals think in Action*, Aldershot: Ashgate Arena.

Shaskolsky, L. (1970) 'The development of sociological theory in America – A sociology of knowledge interpretation', in L.T. and J.M. Reynolds (eds), *The Sociology of Sociology*, New York: McKay.

Strati, A. (1999) *Organization and Aesthetics*, London: Sage.

Strati, A. (2000) *Theory and Method in Organization Studies: Paradigms and Choices*, London: Sage.

Strauss, A., Bucher, R., Ehrlich, D. and Sabshin, M. (1964) *Psychiatric Institutions and Ideologies*, Glencoe, IL: Free Press.

Strauss, A. and Corbin, J. (1990) 'Trajectory framework for management of chronic illness', in A. Strauss (ed.), *Creating Sociological Awareness: Collective Images and Symbolic Representation*, New Brunswick, NJ: Transaction Publishers.

Turner, R.H. (1962) 'Role-Taking: Process versus Conformity' in A.M. Rose (ed.), *Human Behaviour and Social Processes: An Interactionist Approach*, London: Routledge and Kegan Paul.

Urmson, J. and Rée, O.J. (1991) *The Concise Encyclopedia of Western Philosophy and Philosophers*, London: Routledge

Wallemacq, A. and Sims, D. (1998) 'The struggle with sense', in D. Grant, T. Keenoy, and C. Oswick (eds), *Discourse and Organization*, London: Sage.

Westerlund, G. and Sjöstrand, S.-E. (1979) *Organizational Myths*, New York: Harper & Row.

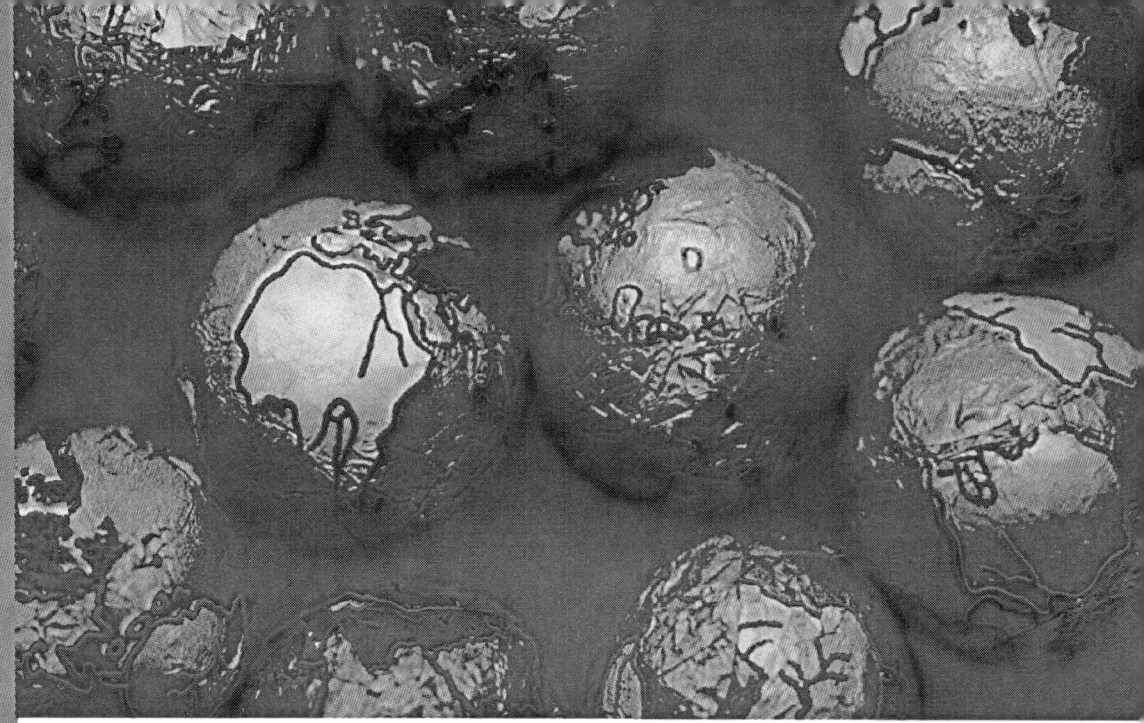

TOPIC 6

OFFICE DESIGN, ORGANISATION AESTHETICS AND CULTURE

Chapter 10

Decision Making, Learning, Knowledge Management, and Information Technology

Learning Objectives

Decision making results in choices that determine the way an organization operates and how it changes or transforms itself over time. Organizations must continually improve the way decisions are made so managers and employees can learn new, more effective ways to act inside the organization and respond to a changing environment.

By the end of this chapter you should be able to:

1. Differentiate among several models of decision making that describe how managers make decisions.
2. Describe the nature of organizational learning and the different levels at which learning occurs.
3. Explain how organizations can use knowledge management and information technology to promote organizational learning to improve the quality of their decision making.
4. Identify the factors, such as the operation of cognitive biases, that reduce the level of organizational learning and result in poor decision making.
5. Discuss some techniques that managers can use to overcome these cognitive biases and thus open the organization up to new learning.

ORGANIZATIONAL DECISION MAKING

In previous chapters, we discussed how managers design a structure and a culture that match the organization's environment, choose a technology to convert inputs into outputs, and choose a strategy to guide the use of organizational skills and resources to create value. In making these choices, managers are making decisions. Indeed, everything that goes on in an organization involves a decision of some kind. Clearly, an organization is not only a value-creation machine but a decision-making machine as well. At every level and in every subunit, the members of an organization continuously make decisions, and how well they make them determines how much value they create.

Organizational decision making is the process of responding to a problem by searching for and selecting a solution or course of action that will create the most value for organizational stakeholders. Whether the problem is to find the best inputs, to decide on the right way to provide a service to customers, or to figure out how to deal with an aggressive competitor, in each case managers must decide what to do. To make the best choices, managers must make two kinds of decisions: programmed and nonprogrammed.

Organizational decision making
The process of responding to a problem by searching for and selecting a solution or course of action that will create value for organizational stakeholders.

Programmed decisions
Decisions that are repetitive and routine.

Nonprogrammed decisions
Decisions that are novel and unstructured.

Programmed decision making involves selecting the most effective—easy, repetitive, and routine—operating procedures to handle an organization's ongoing value-creation activities.[1] Typically, the routines and procedures that result in the best or most effective way of operating are formalized in advance in an organization's rules and standard operating procedures (SOPs) and are reflected in the values and norms of its culture.

Nonprogrammed decision making involves striving to create and implement the most effective—creative, novel, and unstructured—solutions to allow an organization to adapt to changing and uncertain conditions. No rules, routines, or SOPs can be developed to handle these problems in advance for they are unique or unexpected. So solutions must be found after problems have arisen.[2]

Nonprogrammed decision making requires much more search for information, and active cooperation between managers, functions, and divisions to find a solution than does programmed decision making. This is because in making unprogrammed decisions it is impossible to know in advance if these decisions are the right ones—unlike with programmed decisions that are based on the results of past experience and so can be improved over time.

For example, nonroutine R&D is based on nonprogrammed decision making by scientists and engineers who must continually experiment to find a solution to a problem and often fail in the attempt. Similarly, the creation of an organization's strategy involves nonprogrammed decision making by managers who cooperate to find the best way to use an organization's skills and resources to create value, but they can never tell if they have made the best decision in advance.

So, nonprogrammed decision making forces managers to rely on judgment, intuition, and creativity to solve organizational problems; they cannot rely on rules and SOPs to provide nonprogrammed solutions. *Nonprogrammed decisions* lead to the creation of a new set of rules and procedures that would allow organizational members to make appropriate *programmed* decisions that can be improved on over time (by using TQM, for example).

All organizations have to develop the capacity to make both programmed and nonprogrammed decisions. Programmed decision making allows an organization to increase its efficiency and reduce the costs of making goods and services. Nonprogrammed decision making allows the organization to change and adapt to its environment and to generate new ways of behaving so it can effectively take advantage of its environment. Programmed decision making provides stability and increases predictability. Nonprogrammed decision making allows the organization to change and adapt itself so it can deal with unpredictable events. In the next section, we examine several models of organizational decision making.

MODELS OF ORGANIZATIONAL DECISION MAKING

In the past, organizational decision making was portrayed as a rational process in which all-knowing managers make decisions that allow organizations to adjust perfectly to the environment in which they operate.[3] Today, we recognize that decision making is an inherently uncertain process in which managers grope for solutions that may or may not lead to outcomes favorable to organizational stakeholders.

The Rational Model

According to the *rational model*, decision making is a straightforward three-stage process (see Figure 10.1).[4] At stage 1, managers identify problems that need to be solved. Managers of an effective organization, for example, analyze all aspects of their organization's specific and general environments to identify conditions or problems that call for new action. To achieve a good fit between an organization and its environment, they must recognize the opportunities or threats it presents. At stage 2, managers seek to design and develop a series of alternative courses of action to solve the problems they have identified. They study ways to take advantage of the

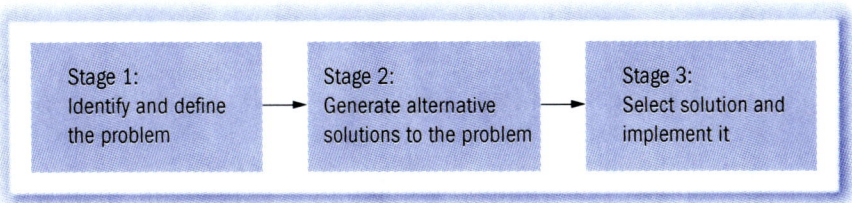

Figure 10.1 The Rational Model of Decision Making
This model ignores the uncertainty that typically plagues decision making.

organization's specific competences to respond to opportunities and threats. At stage 3, managers compare the likely consequences of each alternative and decide which course of action offers the best solution to the problem they identified in stage 1.

Under what "ideal" circumstances can managers be sure they have made a decision that will maximize stakeholders' satisfaction? The ideal situation is one in which there is no uncertainty: Managers know *all* the courses of action open to them. They know the exact effects of all alternatives on stakeholders' interests. They are able to use the same set of objective criteria to evaluate each alternative. And they use the same decision rules to rank each alternative and thus can make the one best or right decision—the decision that will maximize the return to organizational stakeholders.[5] Do such conditions exist? If they did, managers could always make decisions that would perfectly position their organizations in the environment to acquire new resources and make the best use of existing resources.

This ideal state is the situation assumed by the rational model of organizational decision making. The rational model ignores the ambiguity, uncertainty, and chaos that typically plague decision making. Researchers have criticized as unrealistic or simplistic three assumptions underlying the rational model: (1) the assumption that decision makers have all the information they need, (2) the assumption that decision makers have the ability to make the best decisions, and (3) the assumption that decision makers agree about what needs to be done.

Information and Uncertainty

The assumption that managers are aware of all alternative courses of action and their consequences is unrealistic. For this assumption to be valid, managers would have access to all the information necessary to make the best decision, could collect information about every possible situation the organization might encounter, and would possess accurate knowledge about how likely it is that each situation would occur.[6]

The assumption that it is possible to collect all the information needed to make the best decision is unrealistic.[7] Because the environment is inherently uncertain, every alternative course of action and its consequences cannot be known. Furthermore, even if it were possible to collect information to eliminate all uncertainty, the costs of doing so would be as great as, or greater than, any potential profit the organization could make from selecting the best alternative. Thus nothing would be gained from the information.[8]

Suppose a fast-food company thinks that some new kind of sandwich has the potential to attract large numbers of new customers. According to the rational model, to identify the right kind of sandwich, the company would do extensive market research, test different kinds of sandwiches with different groups of customers, and evaluate all alternatives. The cost of adequately testing *every* alternative for *all* possible different groups of customers would be so high, it would swallow up any profit the new sandwich would generate from increased sales. The rational model ignores the fact that organizational decision making *always* takes place in the midst of uncertainty, which poses both an opportunity and a threat for an organization.

Managerial Abilities

The rational model assumes that managers possess the intellectual capability not only to evaluate all the possible alternative choices but also to select the optimum solution. In reality, managers have only a limited ability to process the information required to make decisions, and most do not have the time to act as the rational model demands.[9] The intelligence required to make a decision according to the rational model would exceed a manager's mental abilities and necessitate the employment of an enormous number of managers. The rational model ignores the high level of managerial costs.

Preferences and Values

The rational model assumes that different managers have the same preferences and values and will use the same rules to decide on the best alternative. The model also assumes that managers agree about what are the most important organizational goals. These "agreement assumptions" are unrealistic.[10] Managers in different functions are likely to have different subunit orientations that lead them to make decisions that favor their own interests over those of other functions, other stakeholders, or the organization as a whole.

To sum up, the rational model of decision making is unrealistic because it rests on assumptions that ignore the information and managerial problems associated with decision making. The Carnegie model and other newer models take these problems into consideration and provide a more accurate picture of how organizational decision making takes place.

The Carnegie Model

In an attempt to better describe the realities of the decision-making process, researchers introduced a new set of assumptions that have come to be called the Carnegie model of decision making.[11] Table 10.1 summarizes the differences between the Carnegie and the rational models of decision making. The Carnegie model recognizes the effects of "satisficing," bounded rationality, and organizational coalitions.

Satisficing

Satisficing
Limited information searches to identify problems and alternative solutions.

In an attempt to explain how organizations avoid the costs of obtaining information, the Carnegie model suggests that managers engage in **satisficing**, limited information searches to identify problems and alternative solutions.[12] Instead of searching for all possible solutions to a problem, as the rational model suggests, managers resort to satisficing. That is, to save time and cost, they choose a set of problem-specific criteria or measures they will use to evaluate a range of possible solutions.[13] They then work together to develop several best alternative solutions and select the one that best satisfies the criteria

Table 10.1 Differences Between the Rational and the Carnegie Models of Decision Making

Rational Model	Carnegie Model
Information is available	Limited information is available
Decision making is costless	Decision making is costly (e.g., managerial costs, information costs)
Decision making is "value free"	Decision making is affected by the preferences and values of decision makers
The full range of possible alternatives is generated	A limited range of alternatives is generated
Solution is chosen by unanimous agreement	Solution is chosen by compromise, bargaining, and accommodation between organizational coalitions
Solution chosen is best for the organization	Solution chosen is satisfactory for the organization

they have previously chosen. Thus satisficing involves a much less costly information search and puts far less of a burden on managers than does the rational model.

Bounded Rationality
The rational model assumes that managers possess the intellectual ability to evaluate all possible alternatives. The Carnegie model assumes that managers' ability is restricted by **bounded rationality**, meaning they only have limited capacity to process information about alternatives. But even though they only have limited information-processing capacity, managers can improve their decision making by sharpening their analytical skills.[14] Managers can also make use of use of technology like computers to improve their decision-making skills.[15] Thus bounded rationality in no way implies lack of ability or motivation. The Carnegie model recognizes that decision making is subjective and that decision-making quality depends on managers' prior experience, knowledge, beliefs, and intuition.

Bounded rationality
A limited capacity to process information.

Organizational Coalitions
The rational model ignores the variation in managers' preferences and values and assumes different managers will evaluate different alternatives in the same way. The Carnegie model, in contrast, explicitly recognizes that the preferences and values of managers differ and that disagreement and conflict between different managers is inevitable.[16] The Carnegie model views an organization as a coalition of different interests, in which decision making takes place by compromise, bargaining, and negotiation between managers from different functions and areas of the organization. Any solution chosen must be approved by the *dominant coalition*, the collection of managers or stakeholders who have the power to decide which solution is chosen and can commit resources to implement it.[17] Over time, as the interests and preferences of managers change, so the makeup of the dominant coalition changes and so does decision making. The Carnegie model recognizes that decision making is not a rational "neutral" process driven by objective decision rules, but a subjective process in which managers formulate decision rules that allow them to achieve their personal goals and interests.

To sum up, the Carnegie model recognizes that decision making takes place in an uncertain environment where information is often incomplete and ambiguous. It also recognizes that decisions are made by people who are limited by bounded rationality, who satisfice, and who form coalitions to pursue their own interests. The Carnegie model offers a more accurate description of how decision making takes place in an organization than does the rational model. Yet Carnegie-style decision making is rational because managers act intentionally to find the best solution to reach their desired goal, despite uncertainty and disagreement over goals. In the nearby Organizational Insight box, the response of GE to the question of whether it should continue to make its own washing machines or buy machines made by other companies illustrates decision making in accordance with the Carnegie model.

The Incrementalist Model
In the Carnegie model, satisficing and bounded rationality curb the number and complexity of alternatives that can be selected for analysis. According to the *incrementalist model* of organizational decision making, when selecting a set of new alternative courses of action, managers tend to choose those that are only slightly, or incrementally, different from those used in the past, thus lessening their chances of making a mistake.[18] Often called the science of "muddling through," the incrementalist model implies that managers rarely make major decisions that are radically different from decisions they have made before.[19] Instead, they correct or avoid mistakes through a succession of incremental changes, which eventually may lead to a completely new course of action. During the muddling-through process, organizational goals and the courses of action for achieving them may change, but they change very slowly so that corrective action can be taken if things start to go wrong.

Organizational Insight 10.1

Should GE Make or Buy Washing Machines—or Exit the Business?

In the 1990s, GE faced a major decision. GE's appliance division, maker of well-known products such as dishwashers, ranges, refrigerators, and washing machines, was experiencing declining profitability. Its technologically outdated washing machine operations contributed significantly to this loss, and GE had to evaluate two alternative courses of action: Should GE spend $70 million and make a major investment in new technology to bring the washing machine operations up to date so GE could compete into the next century, or should GE close down its own washing machine operations and buy washing machines from another manufacturer that it would sell under its own brand name?

To evaluate each alternative, GE's managers had to decide which one would result in the best long-term outcome. They used criteria such as manufacturing costs, quality, and product development costs to evaluate each alternative. One of the factors that GE was most concerned about was whether the unions in its Appliance Park operations would agree to flexible work arrangements that would reduce labor costs. At the same time, managers talked to companies like Maytag and Whirlpool to determine what it would cost GE to have them make a washing machine according to GE specifications.[20]

If GE could buy another manufacturer's washing machine for less than it would pay to make its own, then it seemed to make sense to choose the less costly alternative. However, GE's managers had to evaluate the effects of other factors. For example, if GE stopped making washing machines, it would lose a core competence in washing machine production that it would be unable to recover. Suppose the company that GE chose to make its GE machines deliberately made inferior machines that were lower in quality than the machines it produced for itself? Then GE would be at the mercy of its supplier. Or suppose the unions reneged on the contract and refused to cooperate after GE had made the investment in modernizing the washing machine plant? The situation was further complicated by appliance division managers who were lobbying for the investment because it would protect their jobs and the jobs of 15,000 workers. The division managers championed the advantages of the investment for improving the competitive advantage of the division. Corporate managers, however, had to evaluate the potential return of the investment to the entire organization.

Because of uncertainty, GE's managers had a very difficult time evaluating the pros and cons of each alternative; they could not accurately predict the consequences of any decision they made. In the end they decided that GE should make the investment and continue to produce its own washing machines. New lines of modern washing machines were introduced throughout the 2000s. GE tripled the amount it spends on R&D to produce appliances that never break down and which "delight" its customers.[21] By the mid-2000s, GE's appliance division was once again profitable and it was making innovative new products such as front-loading, water-saving washing machines and energy-efficient appliances.

But in 2008, GE's top managers had to debate a new alternative because the company as a whole was now experiencing declining profitability. Analysts claimed the reason was that GE was operating in too many different industries (it has 150 different product divisions) and that it needed to sell off those divisions that had the poorest future prospects. The alternative on the table was that GE should get out of the appliance business by selling it to the highest bidder. Then it would invest the money from the sale to improve the competences of its other divisions.

Just as managers had debated the question of whether to make or buy washing machines, now they had to go through a new round of decision making and debate whether to keep or sell the appliance division. As before, using a set of relevant criteria they made the choice, and in the spring of 2008, they put the division up for sale. LG, the Korean appliance maker, expressed strong interest in the appliance division, and in June, LG's managers were examining its accounts to decide if their company should buy the division or not.

The incrementalist model is very different from the rational model. According to the rational model, all-knowing decision makers weigh every possible alternative course of action and choose the best solution. According to the incrementalist model, managers, limited by lack of information and lack of foresight, move cautiously one step at a time to limit their chances of being wrong.

The Unstructured Model

The incrementalist approach works best in a relatively stable environment where managers can accurately predict movements and trends and so make the incremental decisions that will lead to higher effectiveness. In an environment that changes suddenly or abruptly, an incrementalist approach would prevent managers from changing quickly enough to meet new conditions and so cause the organization to go into decline. The *unstructured model* of decision making, developed by Henry Mintzberg and his colleagues, describes how decision making takes place when uncertainty is high.[22]

The unstructured model recognizes that decision making takes place in a series of small, incremental steps that collectively have a major effect on organizational effectiveness over time. Incremental decisions are made within an overall decision-making framework consisting of three stages—identification, development, and selection—that are similar to the stages shown in Figure 10.1. In the *identification* stage, managers develop routines to recognize problems and to understand what is happening to the organization. In the *development* stage, they search for and select alternatives to solve the problems they have defined. Solutions may be new plans or modifications of old plans, as in the muddling-through approach. Finally, in the *selection* stage, managers use an incremental selection process—judgment and intuition, bargaining, and to a lesser extent formal analysis (typical of the rational model)—to reach a final decision.[23]

In the unstructured model (unlike the incrementalist model), however, whenever organizations encounter roadblocks, they rethink their alternatives and go back to the drawing board. Thus decision making is not a linear, sequential process but a process that may evolve unpredictably in an unstructured way. For example, decision making may be constantly interrupted when uncertainty in the environment alters managers' interpretations of a problem and thus casts doubt on the alternatives they have generated or the solutions they have chosen. Now, managers must generate new alternatives and solutions, for example, find new strategies to help the organization adapt to its environment.

In essence, Mintzberg's approach emphasizes the unstructured nature of incremental decision making: Managers make decisions in a haphazard, intuitive way, and uncertainty forces them to reexamine their decisions continuously to find new ways to behave in a constantly changing environment. They strive to make the best possible decisions, but uncertainty forces them to adopt an unstructured approach to decision making. Thus the unstructured model explains why and how managers make *nonprogrammed* decisions, and the incrementalist model explains why and how managers can improve their *programmed* decision making over time.

The Garbage-Can Model

The view of decision making as an unstructured process is taken to its extreme in the *garbage-can model* of organizational decision making.[24] This model turns the decision-making process around and argues that managers are as likely to start decision making from the *solution side* as from the *problem side*. In other words, decision makers may propose solutions to problems that do not exist; they create a problem they can solve with solutions that are already available.

Garbage-can decision making arises in the following way: An organization has a set of solutions deriving from its competences and skills with which it can solve certain problems—for example, how to attract new customers, how to lower production costs, or how to innovate products quickly. Possessing these organizational competences, managers seek ways to use them and so they create problems—or decision-making opportunities—for them to solve. Suppose a company has skills in making custom-designed furniture. The head of the marketing department persuades the company president that the organization should take advantage of these skills by expanding internationally. Thus a new problem—how to manage international expansion—is created because of the existence of a solution—the ability to make superior custom-designed furniture.

While an organization's managers must tackle new problems of their own making, at the same time they must also generate alternatives and find solutions to problems that have arisen because of shifts in the environment or strains and stresses that stem from the way it operates. To further complicate decision making, different coalitions of managers may champion different alternatives and compete for resources to implement their own chosen solutions. Thus decision making becomes like a "garbage can" in which problems, solutions, and the preferences of different managers and coalitions all mix and contend with one another for organizational attention and action. In this situation, an organization becomes an "organized anarchy" in which the decision about which alternative to select depends on which manager or coalition has the most influence or power to sway other decision makers at that moment.[25] Chance, luck, and timing also come into play in determining which alternative is selected. Often, the problem that is currently generating the most uncertainty for the organization is the one that has the best chance of being acted on, and this may change from week to week. Decision making becomes fluid, unpredictable, and even contradictory as the preferences and priorities of decision makers change.

The garbage-can approach to organizational decision making is clearly the opposite of the approach described by the rational model. Instead of benefiting from the wisdom of all-knowing managers who can generate all possible solutions and unanimously agree on the best one so decisions can be programmed over time, in reality managers are forced to make unprogrammed decisions in an unstructured, garbage-can-like way to deal with the uncertainty that surrounds them. The way in which Microsoft dealt with the Netscape challenge is instructive in this respect, as discussed in the nearby Organizational Insight box.

Organizational Insight 10.2

Microsoft Is Not All-Seeing After All

The success of Microsoft might lead to a belief that Bill Gates and his managers possess some superhuman ability to predict the future and thus make the choices that will lead it to dominate in most segments of the computer market in which it competes. Although there is no doubt that Microsoft has many talented managers, indeed it employs several "futurists" whose only job is to try to predict how the future of the software industry will evolve, it has nevertheless found itself caught unaware by changes in the environment at several points in its history. The way in which it confronted the challenge from Netscape in the Internet browser market is one of these.

Microsoft, like most other large computer companies, was aware of developments in the Internet and the importance of the growing World Wide Web in the 1990s. Indeed, it began its MSN Internet service to provide consumers access to the Web and to provide information and entertainment content for customers. However, Microsoft's managers believed, as the PC software leader, they could control access to the Internet and the development of the content of the Web through its MSN network. This belief proved totally erroneous because of the speed at which the Web was growing and changing and the emergence of many different entry points or portals through which customers could gain access to the Internet and its content.

But what shocked Microsoft most was the introduction, by Netscape, of the first Web browser at the end of 1994, which made it simple for ordinary Internet users to surf the Web and explore its potential. The Netscape browser was hugely popular and by the summer of 1995, it enjoyed an 80% market share. Microsoft had no such product under development, although it had been warned by two low-level programmers of the threat Netscape's browser posed for Microsoft proprietary MSN service because now users would not need to access its services.

In a classic example of garbage-can thinking, in the fall of 1994 Bill Gates decided that the future of Microsoft hung on its ability to develop its own Web browser to keep PC users loyal to its Windows platform—this was the solution to its survival. He mobilized over half of the company's software engineers to counter Netscape's threat. Hundreds of teams of programmers were created and were instructed to take apart the Netscape browser; each was to focus on developing one part of the new browser software. Their task was to produce a Microsoft browser clone that would be compatible with its new Windows 95 operating system, due for release in 1995.

At record-breaking speed these teams worked to develop the new Web browser; cost was no object—Microsoft's survival was the goal. In August 1995, less than one year after the Netscape revolution, Microsoft had its own browser, Internet Explorer, and thereafter Microsoft used its enormous market power to promote its browser and to crush Netscape. Microsoft's decision to give its browser away free, something made possible because of its control of the PC operating and applications software market, effectively made it impossible for Netscape to become profitable. Internet Explorer's market share increased rapidly, and Netscape was bought and integrated into AOL in November 1998.

Nevertheless, the speed at which new uses for the Web were being found, such as search and video, and the speed at which Internet software applications were being developed in the 2000s once again took Microsoft by surprise. As discussed elsewhere, the rapid growth of companies such as Yahoo and Google, which offer customers all forms of Web applications such as email, messaging, and phone calls but receive their revenues not directly from customers but from advertising revenues, shocked Microsoft. Its focus on the desktop PC once again blinded it to the potential uses of the Internet. Beginning in 2005, Microsoft once again marshaled its enormous resources to catch up and improve the quality of its online applications such as search, communication, gaming, and video. It made a bid to buy Yahoo in 2008 to merge their strengths to combat Google, and Gates announced to the world that his goal was to make Microsoft's search engine the world leader.

In summary, decision making determines the way an organization operates. At the core of every organization is a set of decision-making rules and routines that bring stability and allow the organization to reproduce its activities, core competences, and structure over time. These routines provide the organization with a memory and provide managers with programmed solutions to problems, which in turn increase organizational effectiveness.[26] However, routines also can give rise to inertia. If an organization gets in a rut and managers cannot make the decisions that allow it to change and adapt to its environment, it may fail and die. To prevent this from happening, managers need to encourage organizational learning.

THE NATURE OF ORGANIZATIONAL LEARNING

Because decision making takes place in an uncertain environment, it is not surprising that many of the decisions that managers and organizations make are mistakes and end in failure. Other decisions, of course, allow the organization to adapt to the environment and sometimes result in outcomes that exceed managers' wildest dreams—such as those that resulted in the Apple iPod or Research in Motion's Blackberry cell phone. Organizations survive and prosper when managers make the right decisions—sometimes through skill and sound judgment, but sometimes through chance and good luck. If managers are to make successful decisions over time, they must put in place a system that helps organizational members improve their ability to learn new adaptive behaviors and unlearn inefficient, outdated ones.

One of the most important processes that helps managers to make better nonprogrammed decisions—decisions that allow them to adapt to, modify, and change the environment to increase an organization's chances of survival—is organizational learning.[27] **Organizational learning** is the process through which managers seek to improve organization members' desire and ability to understand and manage the organization and its environment so they make decisions that continuously raise organizational effectiveness.[28] Today, organizational learning is a vital process for organizations to manage because of the rapid pace of change affecting every organization.

As previous chapters have discussed, managers must strive to develop new and improved core competences that can give them a competitive advantage and fight off the competitive challenge from low-cost overseas competitors. To do this, they search for every opportunity to use advanced materials technology and IT to pursue their strategies and manage their structures more effectively. Indeed, the need for managers continually to restructure and reengineer their organizations is motivated by the realization that today, only those organizations that learn new ways to operate more efficiently will survive and prosper. Consequently, managers must understand how organizational learning occurs and the factors that can promote and impede it.

Types of Organizational Learning

James March has proposed that two principal types of organizational learning strategies can be pursued: exploration and exploitation.[29] **Exploration** involves organizational

Organizational learning
The process managers use to improve organization members' capacity to understand and manage the organization and its environment so they can make decisions that continuously increase organizational effectiveness.

Exploration
Organizational members' search for and experimentation with new kinds or forms of organizational activities and procedures.

members searching for and experimenting with new kinds or forms of organizational activities and procedures to increase effectiveness. Learning that involves exploration might involve finding new ways to manage the environment—such as experimenting with the use of strategic alliances and network organizations—or inventing new kinds of organizational structures for managing organizational resources—such as product team structures and cross-functional teams.

Exploitation involves organizational members learning ways to refine and improve existing organizational activities and procedures to increase effectiveness. Learning that involves exploitation might involve implementing a total quality management program to promote the continuous refinement of existing operating procedures, or developing an improved set of rules to perform specific kinds of functional activities more effectively. Exploration is therefore a more radical learning strategy than exploitation, although both must be used together to increase organizational effectiveness.[30]

A **learning organization** is an organization that purposefully designs and constructs its structure, culture, and strategy so as to enhance and maximize the potential for organizational learning (explorative and exploitative) to take place.[31] How do managers create a learning organization, one capable of allowing its members to appreciate and respond quickly to changes taking place around it? By increasing the ability of employees, at every level in the organization, to question and analyze the way an organization currently performs its activities and to experiment with new ways to change them to increase effectiveness.

Levels of Organizational Learning

To create a learning organization, managers need to encourage learning at four levels: individual, group, organizational, and interorganizational[32] (Figure 10.2). Some principles for creating a work setting at each level that encourages learning have been developed by Peter Senge and are discussed next.[33]

Individual

At the individual level, managers need to do all they can to facilitate the learning of new skills, rules, norms, and values so individuals can increase their own personal abilities and, in doing so, help build an organization's core competences. Senge has argued that for organizational learning to occur, each of its members needs to develop a sense of *personal mastery*, by which he means that organizations should

Figure 10.2 Levels of Organizational Learning

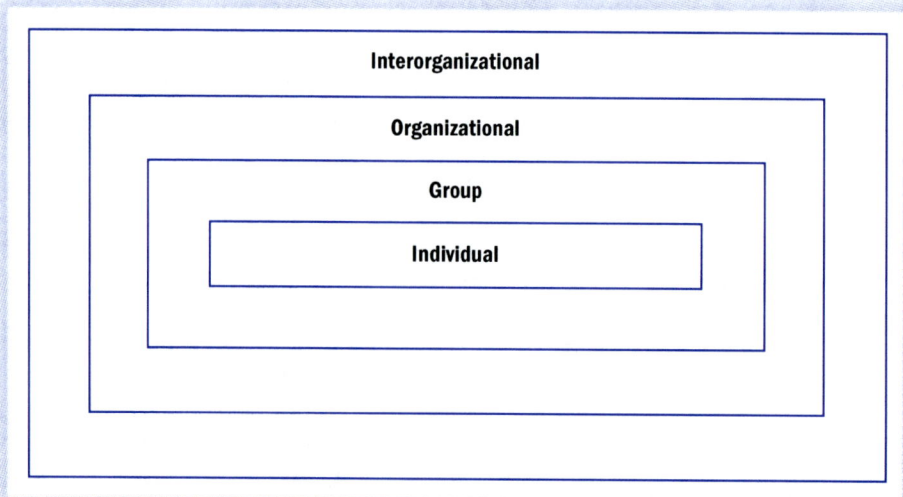

To create a learning organization, managers must use systems thinking and recognize the effects of one level of learning on another.

Exploitation
Organizational members' learning of ways to refine and improve existing organizational activities and procedures.

Learning organization
An organization that purposefully designs and constructs its structure, culture, and strategy so as to enhance and maximize the potential for organizational learning to take place.

empower all employees and allow them to experiment and create and explore what they want. Google, for example, allows its employees to spend 30% of their time on projects of their own choosing to free them to "think out of the box."[34] The goal is to give employees the opportunity to develop an intense appreciation for their work that will translate into new distinctive competence for the organization, as it has for Google where employees suggested new applications such as Google Gadgets.

To help them achieve personal mastery, and to give employees a deeper understanding of what is involved in performing a particular activity, organizations need to encourage employees to develop and use complex *mental models* that challenge them to find new or better ways of performing a task. To give an analogy, a person might mow the lawn once a week and treat this as a chore that has to be done. However, suppose the person decides to study how the grass grows and to experiment with cutting the grass to different heights and using different fertilizers and watering patterns. Through this study, he or she notices that cutting the grass to a certain height and using specific combinations of fertilizer and water promote thicker growth and fewer weeds, resulting in a better-looking lawn that needs less mowing. What has been a chore may become a hobby, and the personal mastery achieved from the new way of looking at the task may become a source of deep personal satisfaction. This is the message behind Senge's first principle for developing a learning organization: Organizations must encourage each individual member to develop a similar commitment and attachment to their job so they will develop a taste for experimenting and risk taking.[35]

A learning organization can encourage employees to form complex mental models and develop a sense of personal mastery by providing them with the opportunity to assume more responsibility for their decisions. This can be done in a variety of different ways. Employees might be cross-trained so they can perform many different tasks, and the knowledge that they gain may give them new insight into how to improve work procedures. Or perhaps a work procedure that was performed by several different workers can be redesigned or reengineered so only one worker, aided by advanced IT, is needed to perform the procedure. Again, the result may be an increase in the level of organizational learning as the worker finds new ways to get the job done. Recall that one of the aims of reengineering is fundamentally to rethink basic business processes. Reengineering is about promoting organizational learning.

Group

At the group level, managers need to encourage learning by promoting the use of various kinds of groups—such as self-managed or cross-functional teams—so that employees can share or pool their skills and abilities to solve problems. Groups provide a setting for synergy to develop—the idea that the whole is much more than the sum of its parts—which can enhance performance. In terms of Thompson's model of task interdependence, for example, the move from a pooled, to a sequential, to a reciprocal form of task interdependence increases the potential for synergy and group-level learning to develop because there is more opportunity for group members to interact and learn from one another over time. "Group routines" and "shared pools of collective meaning" that enhance group effectiveness may develop from such group interactions.[36] Senge refers to this kind of learning as *team learning* and argues that team learning is even more important than individual learning in promoting organizational learning because most important decisions are made in subunits such as groups, functions, and divisions.

The ability of teams to bring about organizational learning was unmistakable when Toyota revolutionized the work process in the former GM factory discussed in Organizational Insight 6.1. Large performance gains were achieved in the factory when Toyota's managers created work teams and empowered team members to take over the responsibility for measuring, monitoring, and controlling their own behavior to find ways continuously to increase performance. The power of teams to bring about organizational learning is also revealed in another of Toyota's attempts to increase effectiveness.

Experimenting with ways to increase technical efficiency, Toyota decided to produce cars in fully roboticized factories embodying the latest, most advanced manufacturing technology. As a result, when it built a new manufacturing plant in Kyoto, Toyota's engineers focused on perfecting the plant's materials technology, and workers became simply an "appendage to the machines." Within a few years it became clear to Toyota's managers that the new technology had not resulted in the large performance gains they had expected. Why? According to Toyota, the new factories had eliminated the opportunity for team learning; workers were neither asked nor expected to contribute their ideas for improving operating efficiency. Computers are only as good as the people who program them, and programmers were not the ones working on the production line. Toyota has since junked its fully roboticized factories, and in its new factories it makes sure that people in teams can contribute their knowledge and skills to increase effectiveness. Yet Toyota is the first to admit it is not perfect and that it is constantly trying to learn and improve as the nearby Organizational Insight box suggests.

Organizational Insight 10.3

Toyota Is a Learning Organization

Although Toyota is regarded as a world leader in total quality management and continually strives to learn better ways to perform its activities, it would be a mistake to believe its record is perfect—or anything close to it. Over the years it has made many mistakes and errors as it seeks to learn new and better ways to improve its functional activities and increase innovation, quality, and operating efficiency. The issue, however, is that Toyota always seeks to learn from its mistakes and it keeps tackling a problem until it finds a solution.

On the innovation front, for example, Toyota's Japanese engineers have often failed to understand the needs of its global customers because they did not listen to and learn from their managers, employees, and customers overseas. As a result, the first generation of many of its new vehicles such as pickup trucks, minivans, and SUVs were flops. For example, its first pickup truck was too small for the U.S. market, its first minivan was clumsy compared to Chrysler's, and its first SUV was underpowered and lacked the comfort and features of competitors such as Ford and Land Rover. Over time, Toyota's engineers have learned from their mistakes, and today using the skills of its U.S. and European designers its new generation of pickup trucks, minivans, and SUVs have become the market leaders.[37]

On the quality front, for which it is best known, it has also made many mistakes. On several occasions its engineers designed parts such as air conditioning and brake systems that proved defective and led to many recalls. But they have learned from their mistakes and most problems have been corrected. Even so, it was only in 2007 that Toyota realized it could find even more ways to improve quality if it started to collect repair information on what kinds of repair problems its vehicles suffered *after* their warranty had expired. If it had taken such a long-term view earlier, its engineers could have focused their attention on the specific problems that led to poor parts quality.[38]

On the efficiency front, cars have become more difficult to assemble because both components and work processes have become more complex. Although the world leader in the mid-2000s, Toyota, which has been rapidly expanding around the globe, found the number of recalls increasing. Since 2004, for example, Toyota has recalled 9.3 million vehicles in the United States and Japan—almost three times the previous rate. The reason for this problem was that in its concern to grow, managers had failed to increase the amount of work training employees receive to allow them to make its increasingly complex vehicles.[39] To solve this problem Toyota has delayed the introduction of some of its new models by several months while it trains its workforce in the many intricate procedures that must be followed to achieve the high quality it demands. Indeed, to allow it to regain its high-quality standards, it opened "global production centers," learning centers, in Kentucky, England, and Thailand to permit its engineers to train production supervisors in the advanced techniques, such as welding and painting, needed to maintain state-of-the-art production quality.

In 2007, Toyota's president Katsuaki Watanabe publicly apologized for these increasing errors and affirmed that Toyota was now back on the right track—even though it is almost always on top of the quality list of the best global carmaker.[40] Even the best companies have to strive to learn how to maintain—let alone exceed—their high standards.

Organization

At the organizational level, managers can promote learning through the way they create its structure and culture. An organization's structure can be designed to inhibit or facilitate communication and cooperation between functions or divisions, for example, and so affects their ability to learn from each other. Similarly, mechanistic and organic structures encourage different approaches to learning. The design of a mechanistic structure facilitates exploitative learning; the design of an organic structure facilitates explorative learning. Indeed, organizations need to strike a balance between a mechanistic and an organic structure to take advantage of both types of learning.

Cultural values and norms are also an important influence on learning at the organizational level. Another of Senge's principles for designing a learning organization emphasizes the importance of *building shared vision*, by which he means creating an ongoing mental model that all organizational members can use to frame problems or opportunities and that binds them to an organization. At the heart of this vision is likely to be the set of terminal and instrumental values and norms that guide the way employees interact and so which affect how they learn from one another. Thus yet another important aspect of organizational culture is its ability to promote or inhibit organizational learning and change.

Indeed, in a study of 207 companies, John Kotter and James Heskett distinguished between adaptive cultures and inert cultures in terms of their ability to facilitate organizational learning.[41] **Adaptive cultures** are those that value innovation and encourage and reward experimenting and risk taking by middle and lower-level managers. **Inert cultures** are those that are cautious and conservative, do not value middle and lower-level managers taking such action, and, indeed, may actively discourage such behavior. According to Kotter and Heskett, organizational learning is higher in organizations with adaptive cultures because managers can quickly introduce changes in the way the organization operates that allow the organization to adapt to changes occurring in the environment. This does not occur in organizations with inert cultures. As a result, organizations with adaptive cultures are more likely to survive in a changing environment and should have higher performance than organizations with inert cultures—exactly what Kotter and Heskett found.

Adaptive cultures
Cultures that value innovation and encourage and reward experimentation and risk taking by middle and lower-level managers.

Inert cultures
Cultures that are cautious and conservative and do not encourage risk taking by middle and lower-level managers.

Interorganizational

Organizational structure and culture not only establish the shared vision or framework of common assumptions that guide learning inside an organization, they also determine how learning occurs at the interorganizational level. Organizations with organic, adaptive cultures, for example, are more likely to actively seek out new ways to manage linkages with other organizations, whereas mechanistic, inert cultures are slower to recognize and to take advantage of new linkage mechanisms, often preferring to go it alone.

In general, interorganizational learning is important because organizations can improve their effectiveness by imitating each other's distinctive competences. Mimetic, coercive, and normative processes encourage organizations to learn from each other to increase their legitimacy, but this can also increase their effectiveness. In the car industry, for example, Japanese carmakers came to the United States after World War II to learn U.S. manufacturing methods and took this knowledge back to Japan where they improved on it. This process was then reversed in the 1980s when struggling U.S. carmakers went to Japan to learn about the advances that Japanese carmakers had pioneered, took this knowledge back to the United States, and improved on it.

Similarly, organizations can encourage explorative and exploitative learning by cooperating with their suppliers and distributors to find new and improved ways of handling inputs and outputs. Enterprise-wide IT systems, business-to-business networks, strategic alliances, and network organizations are important vehicles for increasing the speed at which new learning takes place because they open up the organization to the environment and give organizational members new opportunities to experiment and find new ways to increase effectiveness.

In fact, Senge's fifth principle of organizational learning, *systems thinking*, is that to create a learning organization, managers must recognize the effects of one level of learning on the others. For example, there is little point in creating teams to facilitate team learning if an organization does not also take steps to give employees the freedom to develop a sense of personal mastery. Similarly, the nature of interorganizational learning is likely to be affected by the kind of learning going on at the organization and group levels.

By encouraging and promoting organizational learning at all four levels—that is, by looking at organizational learning as a system—managers can create a learning organization that allows an organization to respond quickly to changes in the environment. Managers need to promote both explorative and exploitative learning and then use this learning in ways that will promote organizational effectiveness. In the next section an important technique for promoting organizational learning, knowledge management, is discussed. Then the many factors that may impede learning are examined.

KNOWLEDGE MANAGEMENT AND INFORMATION TECHNOLOGY

As we have seen in previous chapters, new IT has had a major impact on the way an organization operates. IT-enabled organizational structure allows for new kinds of task and role relationships among electronically connected people that promote superior communication and coordination. One type of IT-enabled organizational relationship that has important implications for both organizational learning and decision making is **knowledge management**, the sharing and integrating of expertise within and between functions and divisions through real-time, interconnected IT.[42] To understand the importance of knowledge management, consider how Accenture, profiled in the nearby Organizational Insight box, has developed a knowledge management system to improve the ability of its consultants to acquire the vital new knowledge that allows them better to serve the needs of their clients.

Knowledge management
A type of IT-enabled organizational relationship that has important implications for both organizational learning and decision making.

As the example of Accenture suggests, one important benefit from using a knowledge management system is the development of synergies between people and groups that may result in competitive advantage in the form of product or service differentiation. Unlike more rigid bureaucratic organizing methods, IT-enabled organizations can respond more quickly to changing environmental conditions such as increased global competition.

What kind of knowledge management system should managers design for their organizations? Is the same kind of system suitable for all kinds of organizations? Or would we expect organizations with a more mechanistic or organic orientation to develop and adopt different kinds of systems?

Knowledge Management: Codification Versus Personalization

One solution to this question has been proposed by Hansen, Nohria, and Tierney, who argue that organizations should choose between a codification or personalization approach to creating an IT-based knowledge management system.[43] With a *codification approach*, knowledge is carefully collected, analyzed, and stored in databases where it can be retrieved easily by users who input organization-specific commands and keywords. Essentially, a codification approach results in collection of standardized organization best practices, rules, and SOPs that can be drawn on by anyone who needs them. It is a form of bureaucratic control than can result in major gains in technical efficiency and allow an organization better to manage its environment. For example, Dell uses an advanced in-house codification approach to manage its transactions with its global suppliers. All suppliers have access to Dell's knowledge management system, which gives them real-time access to its changing input demands, and it allows them to forecast demand for their products months in advance and to redesign their products so they will fit better with Dell's future needs. The result has been tremendous cost savings.

Organizational Insight 10.4

Accenture's Knowledge Management System

Accenture, the biggest global management consulting company, has been a pioneer in using IT to revolutionize its business practices. As it grew to employ over 70,000 employees in more than 46 countries by 2001, its CEO, Joe Forehand, realized a new way to organize and control an army of global consultants was needed. Because only each of Accenture's consultants in the field could diagnose and solve client problems, however, Forehand realized a control system that facilitates creative, on-the-spot, decentralized decision making was needed. Moreover, to increase effectiveness, Accenture also needed to find a way to allow consultants to share each others' firsthand knowledge and expertise, which, after all, is the source of its competitive advantage.

To accomplish both these goals, Accenture decided to create a knowledge management system and substitute direct control by managers with control through a sophisticated in-house IT system.[44] First, they restructured the managerial hierarchy, eliminating many levels of managers. Then they went about setting up an organization-wide information management system to allow consultants to make their own decisions while providing them with access to an expert knowledge system that provided advice when they needed to solve client problems.[45]

The change process began by equipping every consultant with a laptop computer. Using sophisticated in-house IT, each consultant was linked to all of the company's other consultants and became a member of a specific group that specialized in the needs of a particular kind of client, such as consumer product firms or brokerage companies. The group therefore possessed collective expert knowledge about a particular kind of client. To find a solution to a problem, the members of a specific group could email others in the group working at different client sites to see if they had faced similar client problems.

If group members still couldn't solve the problem, consultants communicated with members of other groups by tapping into Accenture's company-wide knowledge management database containing volumes of potentially relevant information. In this way different groups could share state-of-the-art business practices because it was likely another group had encountered the same problem in a different context and thus a solution did exist. Consultants who found clues using the electronic knowledge management system then communicated directly with consultants in other groups through a combination of phone, voice mail, email, and videoconferencing to gain access to the most current information being gathered and applied at existing client sites.[46] By using these resources, consultants kept abreast of the innovative practices within their own firm and within client firms. Remember that Accenture's consulting contracts with individual clients run into the millions of dollars; the enhancement in learning gained through an electronic knowledge management system is vital.

Accenture has found that its knowledge management system, by flattening its structure, decentralizing authority, and enlarging and enriching roles, has increased its consultants' creativity and performance. By providing employees with more information to make a decision and enabling them to coordinate easily with other people, IT has given consultants much more freedom to make decisions. And senior managers can easily manage what their consultants do by monitoring their progress electronically and taking corrective action as necessary. The end result is that by 2008, Accenture had grown to be the biggest and most profitable global consulting company.[47]

A codification approach, however, is only suitable when the product of service being provided is itself quite standardized so best practices can continually be discovered and entered into the knowledge management system to be used by others in the organization. It works best when the different functions in the organization are able to provide standardized information—about changing customer demands or product specifications, for example—that provides vital input to other functions so the level of mutual adjustment and learning between functions increases, resulting in major gains in effectiveness. In this sense, a knowledge management system allows an organization with a more mechanistic structure to react in a more "organic" fashion, albeit the flexibility is provided by new, sophisticated IT protocols based on the codification of standardized organizational knowledge.

By contrast, a *personalization approach* to knowledge management is pursued when an organization needs to provide customized products or solutions to clients, when technology is changing rapidly, and when employees rely much more on know-how, insight, and judgment to make decisions. In these cases, it is very difficult (often impossible) to write down or even verbalize a course of action that leads to a solution. Often, the solution results from mutual adjustment between people and groups when intensive technology, is employed.

In a personalization approach, information systems are designed to show employees who in the organization might possess the knowledge they might need or who might have confronted a similar problem in the past. In a management consulting company such as Accenture, for example, individual consultants will write up synopses of the ways they have solved client problems, and the nature of these problems, so others in the organization can gain a sense of what they are doing. Working in teams, consultants can also spread their knowledge across the organization, often globally, and IT is used to facilitate direct interactions between people and the exchange of know-how by informing employees about upcoming seminars and visiting internal experts, for example.

Over time, as an organization like Accenture confronts more examples of a similar type of problem, consultants can increasingly codify this informal know-how into best practices that can be shared more widely throughout the organization. An organization's information system plays an especially crucial role, for competitive success depends on the speed with which it can provide clients with a state-of-the-art solution to their problems. And given that software is advancing all the time, such solutions change continually. An organization's ability to provide a quick, customized solution, and to translate this rapidly into best practices, often depends on the degree to which it is *specialized*, for example by industry or product or service, and therefore deals with a narrower and deeper range of problems. That is why so many small specialized software and consulting computer companies exist.

Knowledge management is therefore an important tool for increasing the level of integration inside an organization, among people, functions, and even divisions. In the 2000s, many companies have moved to develop knowledge management systems to speed learning and decision making, and for many of them, it has resulted in success. It is important to remember, however, that knowledge management is expensive; people must be employed to help codify knowledge and disseminate it throughout the organization. Today, so much information is available to managers through IT that they can be swamped in it, and the process of discovering best practices and solutions requires a lot of search and judgment in its own right. Companies like HP, Chevron, and Texas Instruments have saved hundreds of millions of dollars by implementing knowledge management systems; they also are spending hundreds of millions to maintain these systems. Organizations must always compare the benefits and costs of using IT and knowledge management to facilitate learning.

FACTORS AFFECTING ORGANIZATIONAL LEARNING

Whereas knowledge management can enhance organizational learning, several factors may *reduce* the level of learning over time. A model developed by Paul C. Nystrom and William H. Starbuck illustrates how problems may arise that prevent an organization from learning and adapting to its environment and so result in an organizational crisis, a situation that seriously threatens an organization's survival.[48]

According to Nystrom and Starbuck, as organizations learn to make decisions they develop rules and SOPs that facilitate programmed decision making. If an organization achieves success by using its SOPs, this success may lead to complacency and deter managers from searching for and learning from new experiences![49] Thus past (successful) learning may inhibit new learning and lead to organizational inertia. In essence, if programmed decision making drives out nonprogrammed decision making, the level of organizational learning falls. Blindness and rigidity in organizational decision making may then set in and lead to a full-blown crisis.

Managers often discount warnings that problems are impending and do not perceive that crises are developing. Even if they notice, the source of the problems is often attributed to temporary disturbances in the environment. So managers implement "weathering-the-storm strategies," they postpone investments, downsize the workforce, and centralize decision making and reduce autonomy at lower levels in the organization. Managers adopt this incrementalist approach to decision making because sticking to what they know is much safer than setting off in new directions where consequences are unknown. Managers continue to rely on the information obtained from their existing operating routines to solve problems—information that does not reveal the real nature of the problems they are experiencing.

Another reason why past learning inhibits new learning is that managers' mindsets or cognitive structures shape their perception and interpretation of problems and solutions. A **cognitive structure** is the system of interrelated beliefs, preferences, expectations, and values that a person uses to define problems and events.[50] In an organization, cognitive structures reveal themselves in plans, goals, stories, myths, and jargon. Cognitive structures shape the way top managers make decisions—and determine the degree to which forces in the environment are perceived as opportunities and threats. Often top managers cling to outdated ideas and use inappropriate cognitive structures to interpret events and problems—something that leads to faulty learning. To explain why, it is necessary to examine some factors that distort managers' perceptions and flaw organizational learning and decision making.

Cognitive structure
The system of interrelated beliefs, preferences, expectations, and values a person uses to define problems and events.

Organizational Learning and Cognitive Structures

As noted earlier, cognitive structures are the systems of beliefs, preferences, and values that develop over time and predetermine managers' response to and interpretations of a situation. When managers confront a problem, their cognitive structures shape their interpretation of the information at hand; that is, the way managers view a situation is shaped by their prior experience and customary ways of thinking.[51] That view, however, might be distorted or wrong because of the operation of cognitive biases.

Types of Cognitive Biases

Several factors may lead managers to develop a cognitive structure that causes them to misperceive and misinterpret information. These factors are called **cognitive biases** because they systematically bias managerial decision making and so lead to poor organizational learning and decision making (see Figure 10.3). Cognitive dissonance, illusion of control, and several other cognitive biases that influence organizational learning and decision making are discussed next.[52]

Cognitive biases
Factors that systematically bias cognitive structures and affect organizational learning and decision making.

Cognitive Dissonance

Cognitive dissonance is the state of discomfort or anxiety that a person feels when there is an inconsistency between his or her beliefs and actions. According to cognitive dissonance theory, decision makers try to maintain consistency between their images of themselves, their attitudes, and their decisions.[53] Managers seek or interpret information that confirms and reinforces their beliefs, and they ignore information that does not. Managers also tend to seek information that is only incrementally different from the information they already possess and therefore supports their established position.

Cognitive dissonance theory explains why managers tend to misinterpret the real threats facing an organization and attempt to muddle through even when it is clear to many observers that the organization is in crisis. The desire to reduce cognitive dissonance pushes managers to adopt flawed solutions.

Cognitive dissonance
The state of discomfort or anxiety a person feels when there is an inconsistency between his or her beliefs and actions.

Illusion of Control

Some people, like entrepreneurs, seem able to bear high levels of uncertainty; others prefer the security associated with working in established organizations. Regardless of one's tolerance for ambiguity, however, uncertainty is very stressful. When an organization's environment or future is uncertain, managers do not know whether they have made the right choices, and considerable organizational resources are often at stake. Managers can reduce the degree to which they fear uncertainty by strengthening their

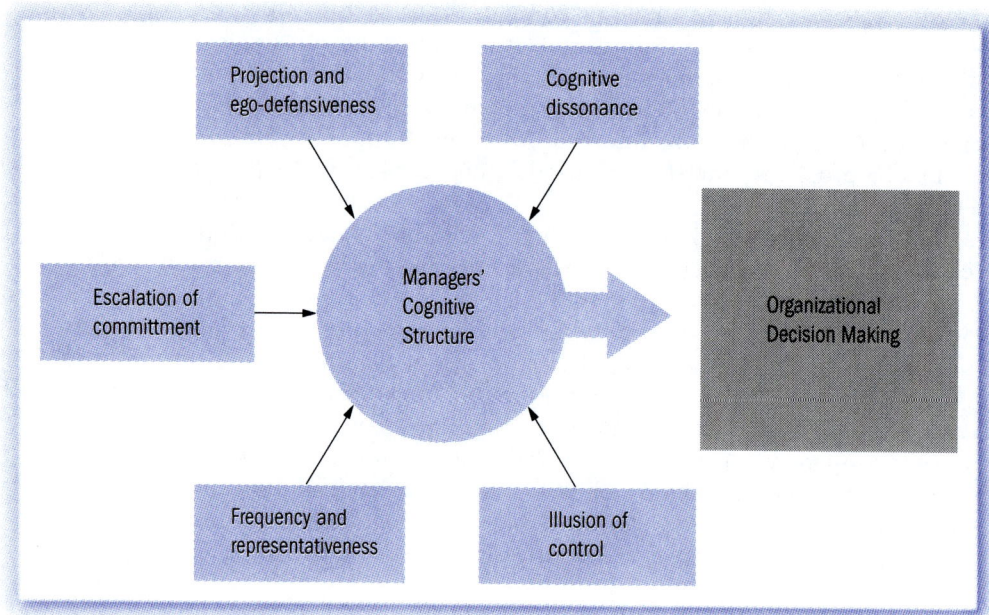

Figure 10.3 The Distortion of Organizational Decision Making by Cognitive Biases

Cognitive dissonance and other cognitive biases affect managers' information-processing abilities and distort managers' interpretation of a problem.

perception that they have the personal abilities to control the situation.[54] However, the more managers perceive they can control a situation, the more likely is the cognitive bias known as illusion of control to arise.

Illusion of control is a cognitive bias that leads managers to overestimate the extent to which they can control a situation because they have the skills and abilities needed to manage uncertainty and complexity.[55] In uncertain situations in which their ability and competence are really being tested, managers may develop irrational beliefs about their personal ability to manage uncertainty. They may, for example, overestimate their skills to enter new industries and embark on a huge acquisition program. Soon, however, they encounter problems and realize they lack the ability to manage the more complex organization effectively, but it is too late.

Frequently, when top managers lose control they move to centralize more authority, in the mistaken belief that this will give them greater control and allow them to solve their problems. But because their perception of control is an illusion, the organizational crisis deepens. It is not uncommon for a strong CEO or the members of an entrenched top-management team to develop the illusion that only they have the ability to manage the uncertainty facing the organization and to lead the organization to success—even when it is in crisis.

Frequency and Representativeness

Frequency and representativeness are tendencies that often lead managers to misinterpret information.[56] **Frequency** is a cognitive bias that deceives people into assuming that extreme instances of a phenomenon are more prevalent than they really are. Suppose purchasing managers have had a particularly bad experience with a supplier that has been shipping them large quantities of defective goods. Because of severe manufacturing problems caused by the defective parts, the managers decide to sever relations with that supplier. The frequency bias may cause them to become very fearful of relying on other suppliers for their inputs. They may instead decide to integrate their operations vertically so they control their inputs, even though vertical integration will increase costs. Although there is no rational reason to believe a new supplier will be as bad as, or worse than, the rejected supplier, the managers jump to an expensive solution to avoid the risk, and faulty learning has occurred.

Illusion of control
A cognitive bias that causes managers to overestimate the extent to which the outcomes of an action are under their personal control.

Frequency
A cognitive bias that deceives people into assuming that extreme instances of a phenomenon are more prevalent than they really are.

Representativeness is a cognitive bias that leads managers to form judgments based on small and unrepresentative samples. Exposure to a couple of unreliable suppliers, for example, prompts managers to generalize and believe that all suppliers are untrustworthy and unreliable, again leading to faulty learning.

Frequency and representative biases can also work in the opposite direction. A company that has great success with a new product may come to believe this product is the wave of the future and devote all its resources to developing a new product line for which there actually is little demand. FedEx, for example, believed that the demand for international express delivery would increase dramatically as companies became increasingly global. It came to this conclusion because it had been receiving more and more requests for international delivery. FedEx thus decided to invest a huge amount of resources to buy and operate a global fleet of planes and overseas facilities to handle worldwide express delivery. The decision was a disaster. The volume of express packages shipped to Europe turned out to be only half of that shipped in the United States, and the cost of operating the new global structure was enormous. After major losses, FedEx decided to form strategic alliances with foreign delivery companies to deliver the mail (rather than go it alone), and this new strategy has been successful. As this example shows, a bad decision can be made because top managers overgeneralize from a limited range of knowledge and experience.

> **Representativeness**
> A cognitive bias that leads managers to form judgments based on small and unrepresentative samples.

Projection and Ego-Defensiveness

Projection is a cognitive bias that allows managers to justify and reinforce their own preferences and values by attributing them to others.[57] Suppose a top-management team is dominated by managers who are threatened by a deteriorating economic situation and doubt their ability to manage it. Feeling threatened and powerless, the team may accuse other lower level managers of being unable to control the situation or of lacking the ability or desire to do so. Thus top managers project their own feelings of helplessness onto others and blame them. Obviously, when projection starts to operate, it can become self-reinforcing: Everybody blames everybody else, and the culture of the organization deteriorates.

Ego-defensiveness also affects the way managers interpret what is happening in the organization. **Ego-defensiveness** is a cognitive bias that leads managers to interpret events in such a way that their actions appear in the most favorable light. If an organization is employing more and more managers but profitability is not increasing, managers may emphasize that they are positioning the organization for future growth by putting in place the infrastructure to support future development. Ego-defensiveness results in little organizational learning, and faulty decision making ultimately leads to a manager's replacement or an organization's failure.

> **Projection**
> A cognitive bias that allows managers to justify and reinforce their own preferences and values by attributing them to others.

> **Ego-defensiveness**
> A cognitive bias that leads managers to interpret events in such a way that their actions appear in the most favorable light.

Escalation of Commitment

The bias toward escalation of commitment is another powerful cause of flawed learning and faulty decision making.[58] According to the Carnegie model of decision making, managers generate a limited number of alternative courses of action, from which they choose one that they hope will lead to a satisfactory (if not optimum) outcome. But what happens if they choose the wrong course of action and experience a negative outcome, such as when FedEx found itself losing enormous amounts of money as a result of its international express delivery venture? A logical response to a negative outcome would be a reevaluation of the course of action. Research, however, indicates that managers who have made an investment in a mistake tend to persist in the same behavior and increase their commitment to it, even though it is leading to poor returns and organizational ineffectiveness.

Escalation of commitment is a cognitive bias that leads managers to remain committed to a losing course of action and to refuse to admit they have made a mistake, perhaps because of ego-defensiveness or because they are gripped by the illusion of control. In later decision making, they try to correct and improve on their prior (bad) decision rather than acknowledge that they have made a mistake and turn to a different

> **Escalation of commitment**
> A cognitive bias that leads managers to remain committed to a losing course of action and refuse to admit they have made a mistake.

course of action. At FedEx, for example, the CEO realized the error and quickly moved to redeploy resources to make the international express delivery venture viable, and he succeeded. The bias toward escalation of commitment is clearly reinforced by an incrementalist approach to decision making. Managers prefer to modify existing decisions to make them fit better with new conditions rather than to work out new solutions. Although this method of decision making may work in stable environments, it is disastrous when technology or competition is rapidly changing.

The net effect of all of the cognitive biases is that managers lose their ability to see new problems or situations clearly and to devise new responses to new challenges—and the level of learning falls. The flawed decision making that results from these biases hampers an organization's ability to adapt and modify its environment. By hampering organizational learning, biased decision making threatens an organization's ability to grow and survive. What can an organization do to develop a less incremental and more unstructured approach to decision making? How can managers be encouraged to be receptive to learning new solutions and to challenging the assumptions they use to make decisions?[59] Research has suggested several ways to increase organizational learning and promote organizational change.

IMPROVING DECISION MAKING AND LEARNING

Organizational inertia and cognitive biases make it difficult to maintain the quality of organizational decision making and promote organizational learning over time. How can managers avoid using inappropriate routines, beliefs, and values to interpret and solve problems? Organizations can use several means to overcome the effect of cognitive biases and promote learning and change: implement strategies for organizational learning, increase the breadth and diversity of the top-management team, use devil's advocacy and dialectical inquiry, use game theory, and develop a collateral organizational structure.

Strategies for Organizational Learning

Managers must continuously unlearn old ideas and test their decision-making skills to confront errors in their beliefs and perceptions. Three ways in which they can unlearn old ideas (and learn new ones) are by listening to dissenters, by converting events into learning opportunities, and by experimenting.[60]

Listening to Dissenters

To improve the quality of decision making, top managers can choose to surround themselves with people who hold different and often opposing points of view. By doing so they can collect new information to evaluate new alternatives generated by dissenters and so find the best solution. Unfortunately, research shows that many top managers do not listen to their subordinates and surround themselves with flatterers who distort the information they provide and enhance good news and suppress the bad.[61] Moreover, because of bounded rationality, managers may be reluctant to encourage dissent because dissent will increase the amount of information they have to process—and this is a burdensome, stressful activity.

Converting Events into Learning Opportunities

Nystrom and Starbuck discuss one unidentified company that appointed a "Vice President for Revolutions," whose job was to step in every four years and shake up the organization by transferring managers and reassigning responsibilities so that old taken-for-granted routines were reexamined and people could bring new points of view to various situations. It did not make much difference what specific changes were made. The objective was to make them large enough so people were forced to make new interpretations of situations. After each shakeup, productivity increased for two years and then declined for the next two, until the organization was shaken up again.[62]

In general, an organization needs to redesign its structure and culture—in ways discussed in previous chapters—to motivate managers to find better ways to respond to a situation. TQM is based on the idea of having employees continuously examine their tasks to discover whether improvements that increase quality and productivity can be made. Also, different kinds of organizational structure and culture, for example, mechanistic or organic structures, can encourage or discourage organizational learning. An interesting study conducted in California of hospitals that experienced an environmental jolt caused by a doctor's strike shows the influence of organizational structure in decision making. The study found that responses by hospitals to this crisis were strongly influenced by the way in which each hospital typically made decisions in uncertain situations.[63] Hospitals that had organic structures characterized by decentralized decision making and frequently redesigned their structures were accustomed to both learning and unlearning. As a result, these hospitals dealt with the strike much better than did hospitals with centralized, mechanistic structures and a formalized, programmed approach to decision making.

Experimenting

To encourage explorative learning, organizations must encourage experimenting, the process of generating new alternatives and testing the validity of old ones. Experimenting can be used to improve both incremental and garbage-can decision-making processes. To test new ways of behaving, such as new ways to serve customers or to manufacture a product, managers can run experiments that deviate only slightly from what the organization is currently doing. Or, taking a garbage-can approach, managers can brainstorm and come up with new solutions that surprise even themselves. Managers who are willing to experiment avoid overcommitment to previously worked-out solutions, reduce the likelihood of misinterpreting a situation, and can learn from their failures.

Using Game Theory

As we have already discussed, organizations are in a constant competitive struggle with rivals in their industry to secure scarce resources. In understanding the dynamics of decision making between competitors in the environment, a useful tool that can help managers improve decision making and enhance learning is *game theory*, in which interactions between organizations are viewed as a competitive game. If companies understand the nature of the competitive game they are playing, they can make often make better decisions that increase the likelihood of their obtaining scarce resources.[64]

From a game theory perspective, companies in an industry can be viewed as players that are all simultaneously making choices about which decisions to make that will maximize their effectiveness. The problem that managers face is the potential effectiveness of each decision they make, for example of which competitive strategy they select, is not some "fixed or stable amount." What value they will get from making a certain choice—the payoff—will vary depending on the strategies that rivals also select. There are two basic types of games: sequential move games and simultaneous move games. In a *sequential move game*, such as chess, players move in turn, and one player can select a strategy to pursue after considering its rival's choice of strategies. In a *simultaneous move game*, the players act at the same time, in ignorance of their rival's current actions.

In the environment both sequential and simultaneous move games are commonplace as managers compete for scarce resources. Indeed, game theory is particularly useful in analyzing situations where a company is competing against a limited number of rivals in its domain and they are highly interdependent—something very common in most environments. In such a setting, the value that can be created by making a certain choice—for example, to pursue a low-cost or differentiation strategy—depends critically on the strategies pursued by rivals. The basic principles that underlie game theory can be useful in determining which choices to make and strategies to select to manage the environment.

A fundamental premise of game theory is that when making decisions, managers need to think in two related ways. First, they need to look forward, think ahead, and anticipate how rivals will respond to whatever might be their competitive moves. Second, managers need to reason backward to determine which moves their company should pursue today given their assessment of how their rivals will respond to various future moves. If managers do both these things, they should be able to make the decision that will lead to the best choice—to make the move that will lead to the greatest potential returns. This cardinal principle of game theory is known as *look forward and reason back:* To understand its importance, consider this scenario.

UPS and FedEx, which specialize in the next-day delivery of packages, dominate the U.S. air express industry. They have very high costs because they need to invest in a nationwide capital-intensive network of aircraft, trucks, and package-sorting facilities. For these companies, the key to increasing their effectiveness is to attract more customers, growing volume so they can reduce the average cost of transporting each package. Suppose a manager at UPS calculates that if UPS cuts prices for their next-day delivery service by 10%, the volume of packages they ship will grow by over 25%, and so will UPS's total revenues and profits. Is this a smart choice? The answer depends on whether the manager has remembered to look forward and reason back and think through how FedEx would respond to UPS's price cuts.

Because UPS and FedEx are competing directly against each other, their choices are interdependent. If UPS cuts prices, FedEx will lose market share, its volume of shipments will decline, and its profits will suffer. FedEx is unlikely to accept this. Rather, if UPS cuts prices by 10%, FedEx is likely to follow, make the same choice and cut its prices by 10% to hold on to its customers. The net result is that the average level of prices in the industry will fall by 10%, as will revenues, and both players will see their profits decline and the environment will become poorer. To avoid this situation, and make better decisions, managers need always to look forward and reason back—an important principle of learning.

Decision trees can be used to help in the process of looking forward and reasoning back. Figure 10.4 maps out the decision tree for the simple game just analyzed from the perspective of UPS. (Note that this is a sequential move game.) UPS moves first, and then FedEx must decide how to respond. Here you see that UPS has to choose between two strategies, cutting prices by 10% or leaving them unchanged. If it leaves prices unchanged, it will continue to earn its current level of profitability, which is $100 million. If it cuts prices by 10%, one of two things can happen: FedEx matches the price cut, or FedEx leaves its prices unchanged. If FedEx matches UPS's price cut (FedEx decides to fight a price war), profits are competed away and UPS's profit will

Figure 10.4 A Decision Tree for UPS's Pricing Strategy

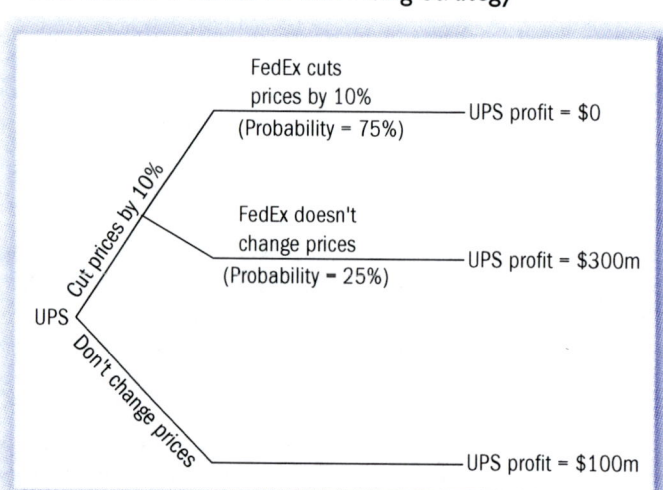

be $0. If FedEx does not respond, however, and leaves its prices unaltered, UPS will gain market share and its profits will rise to $300 million. So the best pricing strategy for UPS to pursue depends on its assessment of FedEx's likely response.

You will note that Figure 10.4 assigns probabilities to the different responses from FedEx. Specifically there is a 75% chance that FedEx will match UPS's price cut and a 25% chance that it will do nothing. These probabilities come from each company's assessment of the other's likely decision based on their past history of making decisions in the environment—from looking at the history of FedEx's responses to UPS's price moves and vice versa. Although both sets of managers cannot calculate exactly what the profit impact and probabilities would be, they make an informed decision by collecting information and devoting resources to learning about their rivals and about the environment. This illustrates a second basic principle of game theory: Know thy rivals! To improve learning, managers must put themselves in the position of a rival to answer the question of how that rival is likely to act in a particular situation. If a company's managers are to be effective at looking forward and reasoning back, they must have a good understanding of what their rival is likely to do under different scenarios, and they need to be able to extrapolate their rival's future behavior based on this understanding.

Nature of the Top-Management Team

The way the top-management team is constructed and the type of people who are on it affect the level of organizational learning.[65] There are various ways to construct a top-management team, and each has different implications for the processing of information, organizational learning, and the quality of decision making.[66] Figure 10.5 shows two top-management configurations, each of which has different implications for the level of learning taking place. In the wheel configuration, organizational learning is decreased because managers from the different functions report separately to the CEO. Rather than coordinate their own actions as a team, they send all information to the CEO, who processes this information, arrives at a decision, and communicates the decision back to the top managers. Research suggests that the wheel works best when problems are simple and require minimal coordination among top team members.[67] When problems are complex and nonprogrammed decision making is required, the wheel configuration slows organizational learning because all coordination takes place through the CEO.

In the circle configuration, top managers from different functions interact with each other and with the CEO. That is, they function as a team, which promotes team and organizational learning. Research has suggested that the circle works best for

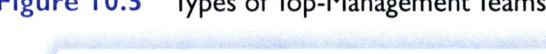

Figure 10.5 Types of Top-Management Teams

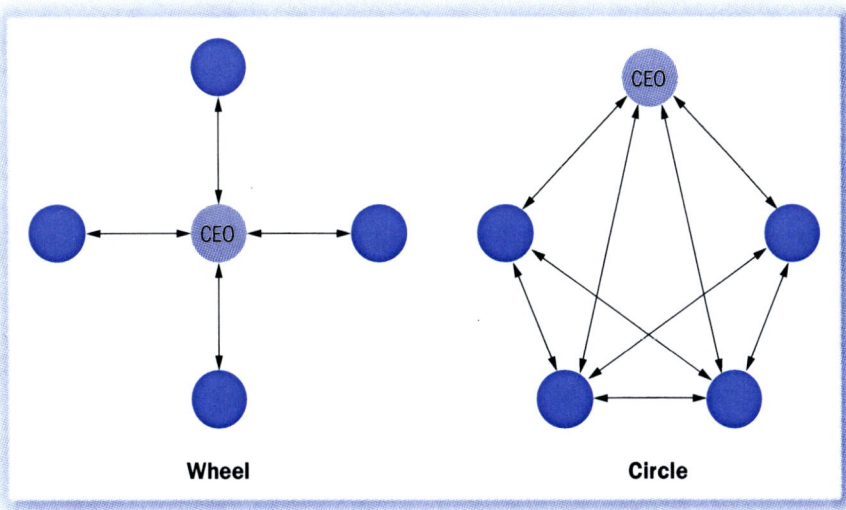

complex problems requiring coordination among group members to arrive at a solution. The circle design solves complex problems much more quickly than the wheel arrangement: Communication around the circle takes less time because there is more opportunity for team and organization learning between all top managers.[68]

The level and quality of organizational learning and decision making by the top-management team is also a function of the personal characteristics and backgrounds of team members.[69] An organization that draws its top-management team from many different industries and different functional backgrounds can promote organizational learning and decision making. Diversity in the top-management team also exposes managers to the implications and consequences of many alternative courses of action. Such exposure may cause managers to examine their own expectations and assumptions more closely.

It has been found that the most learning takes place when there is considerable heterogeneity among team members and when managers from different functions have an opportunity to express their views. When managers bring different information and viewpoints to bear on a problem, the organization can avoid **groupthink**, the conformity that emerges when like-minded people reinforce one another's tendencies to interpret events and information in similar ways.[70] It has also been found that top-management teams function most effectively when their membership is stable and there is not too much entry into or departure from the team.[71] When team membership is stable, group cohesiveness increases and promotes communication among members and improved decision making.[72]

Designing and managing the top-management team to promote organizational learning is a vital task for a CEO.[73] Often, an organization picks as CEO the person who has the functional and managerial background needed to deal with the most pressing issues facing the organization. Caterpillar, PepsiCo, Ford, and Wal-Mart are some of the many companies that have chosen CEOs from managers who have had extensive experience in international business because their major problems center on the challenge of global expansion and competition.[74] Sometimes the only way to promote organizational learning is to change the CEO or the top-management team. Removing and changing top managers can be the quickest way to erase organizational memory and thus poor programmed decision making, allowing an organization to develop successful new routines.

Devil's Advocacy and Dialectical Inquiry

A **devil's advocate** is the person willing to stand up and question the beliefs of more powerful people, resist influence attempts, and who work to convince others that new ideas or plans may be flawed or wrong and harmful. Devil's advocacy and a related technique, dialectical inquiry, are ways of overcoming cognitive biases and promoting organizational learning.[75] Figure 10.6 shows how these strategies differ from one another and from the rational approach to decision making. The goal of both is to improve decision making.

An organization that uses devil's advocacy institutionalizes dissent by assigning a manager or management team the role of devil's advocate. The devil's advocate is responsible for critiquing ongoing organizational learning and for questioning the assumptions the top-management team uses in the decision-making process. 3M makes excellent use of devil's advocacy. At 3M, product managers submit proposals for a new product to a product development committee composed of top managers. The committee acts as devil's advocate. It critiques the proposal and challenges assumptions (such as the estimated size of the market for the product or its cost of manufacturing) to improve the plan and verify its commercial viability. 3M directly attributes its product development successes to the use of devil's advocacy.

An organization that uses dialectical inquiry creates teams of decision makers. Each team is instructed to generate and evaluate alternative scenarios and courses of action and then recommend the best one. After hearing each team's alternatives, all of the teams and the organization's top managers sit down together to cull the best parts of each plan and synthesize a final plan that offers the best chance of success.

Groupthink
The conformity that emerges when like-minded people reinforce one another's tendencies to interpret events and information in similar ways.

Devil's advocate
A person who is responsible for critiquing ongoing organizational learning.

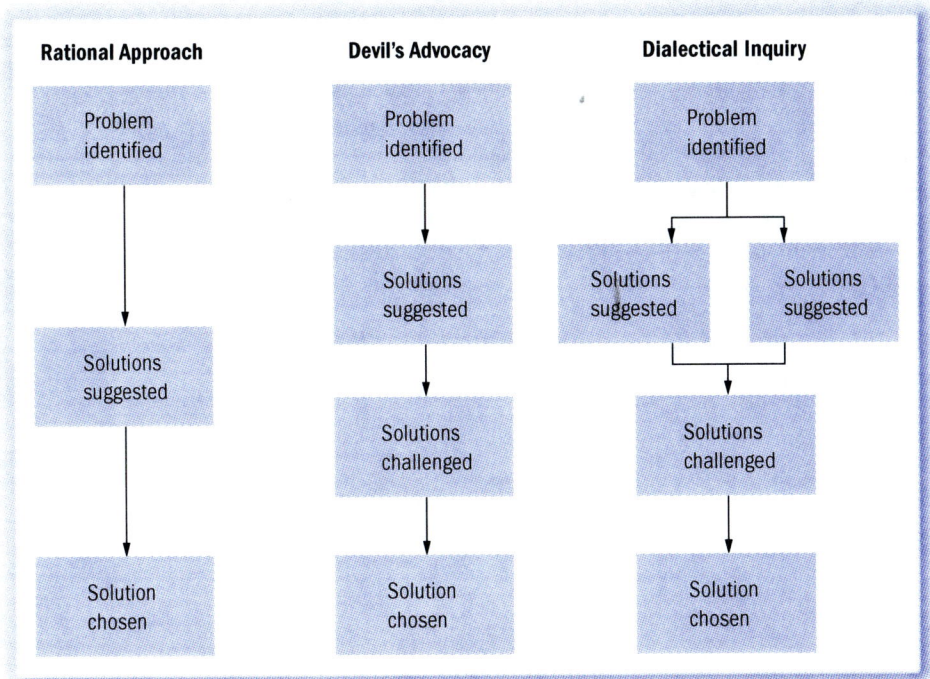

Figure 10.6 How Devil's Advocacy and Dialectical Inquiry Alter the Rational Approach to Decision Making

Devil's advocacy and dialectical inquiry improve decision making by making managers aware of several possible solutions to a problem and by encouraging the analysis of the pros and cons of each proposed solution before a final decision is made.

Collateral Organizational Structure

Finally, an organization can attempt to improve learning and decision making by establishing a *collateral organizational structure*—that is, an informal organization of managers set up parallel to the formal organizational structure to "shadow" the decision making and actions of managers in the formal organization.[76] Managers in the formal structure know that their decisions are being evaluated by others and become used to examining the assumptions that they use to test alternatives and arrive at a solution. An organization establishes a collateral structure to improve the organization's ability to learn and adjust to new situations, and to enhance its ability to make decisions in an unstructured way. A collateral organizational structure allows an organization to maintain its capacity for change at the same time it maintains its stability.

MANAGERIAL IMPLICATIONS
DECISION MAKING AND LEARNING

1. Try to guard against blindness and rigidity in decision making, be on the lookout for new problems, and be open to new solutions.
2. Develop a questioning attitude, and never discount warnings that problems are impending.
3. Analyze the cognitive structures through which you and your subunit define problems. Question whether these beliefs or values reflect the realities of the situation.
4. Examine your decision making to determine whether cognitive biases are affecting the quality of your decisions.
5. To protect the quality of your decision making, develop strategies to enhance organizational learning. For example, listen to your opponents, experiment with new solutions, encourage diversity, and use dialectical inquiry.

SUMMARY

The problems that many established companies encounter are a warning about the need to encourage organizational learning so organizations have the ability to continuously adapt to and modify their environments. Strategy and structure are the tools that an organization uses to fashion its future; the decisions about strategy and structure that an organization makes now will determine its fate years from now. Too often, managers view strategy and structure as unchangeable and not as factors to be experimented with and altered to move the organization forward. When strategy and structure are viewed as something to be protected at all costs, they can become a source of organizational inertia that may bring an organization to its knees. Managers need to understand how an organization's current strategy and structure can constrain organizational learning, and they need to prevent the emergence of cognitive biases that reduce learning and distort the decision-making process. Chapter 10 has made the following main points:

1. Organizational decision making is the process of responding to a problem by searching for and selecting a solution or course of action that will create value for organizational stakeholders.
2. Managers make two basic types of decisions: programmed and nonprogrammed. Programmed decisions provide an organization with stability and increase efficiency. Nonprogrammed decisions allow an organization to adapt to changes in its environment and find solutions to new problems.
3. The rational model of decision making outlines how decision making takes place when there is no uncertainty. It ignores the effects of information costs and managerial costs.
4. Newer models of decision making recognize the effects of uncertainty, information, bounded rationality, satisficing, and bargaining by coalitions on the decision-making process. The Carnegie, incrementalist, unstructured, and garbage-can models provide a more realistic picture of how organizational decision making takes place.
5. Organizational learning is the process through which managers seek to improve organization members' desire and ability to understand and manage the organization and its environment so they can make decisions that continuously raise organizational effectiveness. There are two main kinds of learning—explorative and exploitative—and both are necessary to raise the quality of decision making.
6. The routines and procedures that an organization uses to make programmed decisions can cause organizational inertia. When programmed decision making drives out nonprogrammed decision making, the level of organizational learning drops. To encourage organizational learning, managers can act at the individual, group, organizational, and interorganizational levels.
7. Information technology and knowledge management systems can be developed to improve decision making and enhance organizational learning. The two main approaches to knowledge management are codification and personalization.
8. Cognitive structures (sets of interrelated beliefs, preferences, expectations, and values) affect the way managers interpret the problems facing an organization and shape the way they make decisions.
9. Cognitive biases may distort the way managers process information and make decisions. Common cognitive biases include cognitive dissonance, the illusion of control, frequency and representativeness, projection and ego-defensiveness, and escalation of commitment.
10. An organization can counter the effect of cognitive biases and raise the level of learning and decision making in several ways. It can implement strategies for organizational learning, use game theory, increase the breadth and diversity of the top-management team, use devil's advocacy and dialectical inquiry to evaluate proposed solutions, and develop a collateral organizational structure.

DISCUSSION QUESTIONS

1. What are the critical differences between the rational and the Carnegie approaches to decision making? What are the critical differences between the incrementalist and the garbage-can models? Which models best describe how decision making takes place in (a) a fast-food restaurant and (b) the research and development laboratory of a major drug company?
2. What is organizational learning? In what ways can managers promote the development of organizational learning by acting at various levels in the organization? By using knowledge management?
3. How can knowledge management promote organizational learning? What determines which kind of knowledge management system a company should adopt?
4. How do cognitive biases affect organizational learning and the quality of decision making? What can be done to reduce their negative impact?

ORGANIZATIONAL THEORY IN ACTION

Practicing Organizational Theory:
Store Learning

Form groups of three to five people and discuss the following scenario:

You are a group of top managers of a major clothing store who are facing a crisis. Your establishment has been the leading clothing store in your city for the last 15 years. In the last three years, however, two other major clothing store chains have opened up in your city, and they have steadily been luring away your customers—your sales are down 30%. To find out why, you have been surveying some of your former customers and have learned that they perceive, for whatever reason, that your store is just not keeping up with changing fashion trends and new forms of customer service. In examining the way your store operates, you have come to realize that over time the ten buyers who purchase the clothing and accessories for your store have been buying increasingly from the same set of clothing suppliers, and they have become reluctant to try new ones. Moreover, your salespeople rarely, if ever, make suggestions for changing the way your store operates. Your goal is to shake up store employees and turn around store performance.

1. Devise a program to increase the level of organizational learning.
2. In what specific ways can you promote the level of learning at all levels?

Making the Connection #12
Find an example of an organization that has been using information technology to change the way it makes decisions or increase its level of learning. Why is the organization making these changes? What is it doing to stimulate new learning?

The Ethical Dimension #12
Managers' desire or willingness to act ethically and make ethical decisions can be affected by any cognitive biases that are operating in a particular context.

1. Discuss how the various cognitive biases can lead managers to behave unethically. Do you see any theme or pattern in how these biases operate on ethics?

2. Which kinds of techniques or tools discussed in this chapter, for example, a knowledge management system, can be best used to combat the problem of cognitive biases?

Analyzing the Organization: Design Module #12
This module focuses on organizational decision making and learning and on the way your company has changed its strategy and structure over time.

Assignment

1. Given the pattern of changes your organization has made to its strategy and structure over time, which of the decision-making models best characterizes the way it makes decisions?
2. At what hierarchical level does responsibility for nonprogrammed decision making seem to lie in your organization? What problems do you see with the way your company makes decisions?
3. Characterize your organization's ability to learn over time. Evaluate its capacity to adapt itself to and modify the environment.
4. Can you pinpoint any cognitive biases that may have affected the way managers made decisions or influenced their choice of strategy or structure? What was the effect of these cognitive biases?

Case for Analysis
E-Retailing Mistakes in Hong Kong

Jimmy Lai (黎智英) is a maverick among businesspeople in Hong Kong. During the 1980s, he started a clothing retailer with a unique style. In a city that is notoriously tough on small retailers, Lai's clothing chain, Giordano, grew rapidly and created a standard for quality mid-range retail service in Hong Kong and around East Asia. Building on the success of Giordano, Mr. Lai created his trendy Chinese language magazine, *Next*, and the popular newspaper *Apple Daily*, modeled loosely after *USA Today* with color pictures and charts. Readers liked the entertainment gossip and Lai's challenging of the political establishments in Hong Kong and Beijing. Foreigners liked calls for democratic change and accountability from government officials, though this also made enemies for him in high places in China.

Given the success of Giordano and the Next Media publications, Mr. Lai rode the dot com boom into e-retailing. He started an online grocer in 1999 called Admart. It did well at first, phone lines were always jammed, and deliveries were slow because of the popularity. But as with many online retailers, low margins limited the service. Goods often arrived late, and many major brands would not supply Admart for fear of alienating Hong Kong's retail oligopoly—two of the big property firms dominate retailing in Hong Kong through their flagship stores Park N Shop and Wellcome. Suppliers and small retailers do not want to take on these major retailers, because of their buying power and the ability to freeze products out of Hong Kong (collusion on price and purchasing is not uncommon among retail firms in Hong Kong and many other parts of East Asia). In addition, the large property companies collaborated to keep Admart's delivery trucks out of their property developments. That meant that Admart's trucks had to stop outside of the gates of the housing estates (often 5 to 10 high rise buildings make up one housing estate in Hong Kong, the entrance to which is controlled by a guard station). People had to come outside to pick up their deliveries. Finally, Park N Shop and Wellcome started promoting their own delivery services aggressively, costing Admart many customers. Admart lost $140 million in six months trying to sell groceries over the Internet and in spite of early success and positive reviews, Admart had to exit the grocery delivery business. Mr. Lai sought some help from the Hong Kong government in opening up the delivery rules, but none was forthcoming.

In addition to making the big property developers angry, Mr. Lai had also criticized some important Mainland Chinese government officials in his Next Media publications and this did not sit well with Hong Kong and Beijing government officials or the property developers who depend heavily on favorable relations with governments. As a result of these political and image problems as well as losses from e-retailing, Mr. Lai divested his holdings in retailing and moved much of his media and advertising business to Taiwan where he says the competition is much fairer than in Hong Kong's oligopolistic environment. Online grocery service has succeeded primarily in markets with large and concentrated populations, which facilitates delivery. But securing proper distribution is the downfall of many businesses—even those with a very good product and solid business model. Mr. Lai did not have the connections to pry open Hong Kong's tight grocery market and did not help his case by alienating major property developers, Hong Kong officials, and top politicians in Beijing. ∎

Source: Ng, Isabella. 2001. "Taipei's Next" *Time Asia*, vol. 157 (3), January 22, p. 46.

DISCUSSION QUESTIONS

1. Illusion of control is a cognitive bias that leads managers to overestimate their control over a situation. Do you think Jimmy Lai exhibited this cognitive bias in his decision-making? What actions and statements illustrate this bias? Why might this bias been a more difficult problem for a successful entrepreneur like Jimmy Lai?
2. If you had been assisting Mr. Lai at that time with his businesses (successful clothing stores in Hong Kong, South China, and Southeast Asia, Next Media magazines and newspaper, and Admart), how would you have advised him in managing the relationships with the government officials and property developers? Does it seem like there was any behavior that he had to 'unlearn' in getting Admart—a very different business than clothing retailing or newspapers—successfully launched?

REFERENCES

1. H. A. Simon, *The New Science of Management Decision* (New York: Harper & Row, 1960), p. 206.
2. Ibid.
3. S. Keiser and L. Sproull, "Managerial Response to Changing Environments: Perspectives on Sensing from Social Cognition," *Administrative Science Quarterly*, 27 (1982), 548–570; G. T. Allison, *The Essence of Decision* (Boston: Little, Brown, 1971).
4. Simon, *The New Science of Management Decision*.
5. H. A. Simon, *Administrative Behavior* (New York: Macmillan, 1945).
6. Ibid.; J. G. March and H. A. Simon, *Organizations* (New York: Wiley, 1958).
7. J. G. March, "Decision Making Perspective," in A. Van De Ven and W. Joyce, eds., *Perspectives on Organizational Design and Behavior* (New York: Wiley, 1981), pp. 205–252.
8. J. G. March, "Bounded Rationality, Ambiguity, and the Engineering of Choice," *Bell Journal of Economics*, 9 (1978), 587—608.
9. Simon, *Administrative Behavior*.
10. R. M. Cyert and J. G. March, *A Behavioral Theory of the Firm* (Englewood Cliffs, NJ: Prentice Hall, 1963).
11. P. D. Larkey and L. S. Sproull, *Advances in Information Processing in Organizations*, vol. 1 (Greenwich, CT: JAI Press, 1984), pp. 1–8.
12. March and Simon, *Organizations*.
13. H. A. Simon, *Models of Man* (New York: Wiley, 1957); A. Grandori, "A Prescriptive Contingency View of Organizational Decision Making," *Administrative Science Quarterly*, 29 (1984), 192–209.
14. Simon, *The New Science of Management Decision*.
15. H. A. Simon, "Making Management Decisions: The Role of Intuition and Emotion," *Academy of Management Executives*, 1 (1987), 57–64.
16. Cyert and March, *A Behavioral Theory of the Firm*.
17. Ibid.
18. C. E. Lindblom, "The Science of Muddling Through," *Public Administration Review*, 19 (1959), 79–88.
19. Ibid., p. 83.
20. Z. Schiller, "GE's Appliance Park: Rewire, or Pull the Plug?" *Business Week*, February 8, 1993, p. 30.
21. J. Ward, "GE Center Makes Things Fail So It Can Make Them Better," *The Courier Journal*, September 12, 1999, p. 1.
22. H. Mintzberg, D. Raisinghani, and A. Theoret, "The Structure of Unstructured Decision Making," *Administrative Science Quarterly*, 21 (1976), 246–275.
23. Ibid., p. 257.
24. M. D. Cohen, J. G. March, and J. P. Olsen, "A Garbage Can Model of Organizational Choice," *Administrative Science Quarterly*, 17 (1972), 1–25.
25. Ibid.
26. G. P. Huber, "Organizational Learning: The Contributing Processes and the Literature," *Organizational Science*, 2 (1991), 88–115.
27. B. Hedberg, "How Organizations Learn and Unlearn," in W. H. Starbuck and P. C. Nystrom, eds., *Handbook of Organizational Design*, vol. 1 (New York: Oxford University Press, 1981), pp. 1–27.
28. P. M. Senge, *The Fifth Discipline: The Art and Practice of the Learning Organization* (New York: Doubleday, 1990).
29. J. G. March, "Exploration and Exploitation in Organizational Learning," *Organizational Science*, 2 (1991), 71–87.
30. T. K. Lant and S. J. Mezias, "An Organizational Learning Model of Convergence and Reorientation," *Organizational Science*, 5 (1992), 47–71.
31. M. Dodgson, "Organizational Learning: A Review of Some Literatures," *Organizational Studies*, 14 (1993), 375–394.
32. A. S. Miner and S. J. Mezias, "Ugly Duckling No More: Pasts and Futures of Organizational Learning Research," *Organizational Science*, 7 (1990), 88–99.
33. P. Senge, *The Fifth Discipline: The Art and Practice of the Learning Organization* (New York: Doubleday, 1990).
34. www.google.com, 2008.
35. P. Senge, "The Leader's New Work: Building Learning Organizations," *Sloan Management Review* (Fall 1990): 7–23.
36. Miner and Mezias, "Ugly Ducking No More."
37. Press release, www.toyotausa.com, November 12, 2007.
38. I. Rowley, "Even Toyota Isn't Perfect," www.businessweek.com, January 22, 2007.
39. "Toyota Blames Rapid Growth for Quality Problems," www.iht.com, March 13, 2008.
40. I. Rowley, "Katsuaki Watanabe: Fighting to Stay Humble," www.businessweek.com, March 5, 2007.
41. J. P. Kotter and J. L. Heskett, *Corporate Culture and Performance* (New York: The Free Press, 1992).
42. Ibid.
43. M.T. Hansen, N. Nohria, and T. Tierney, "What's Your Strategy for Managing Knowledge?" *Harvard Business Review* (March–April 1999): 3–19.
44. A. Williams, "Arthur Andersen IT Initiatives Support Shifts in Business Strategy," *Information Week*, September 11, 2000, 14–18.
45. T. Davenport and L. Prusak, *Information Ecology* (New York: Oxford University Press, 1997).
46. www.accenture.com, 2007.
47. www.accenture.com, 2008.
48. P. C. Nystrom and W. H. Starbuck, "To Avoid Organizational Crises, Unlearn," *Organizational Dynamics*, 12 (1984), 53–65.
49. Y. Dror, "Muddling Through—Science or Inertia?" *Public Administration Review*, 24 (1964), 103–117.
50. Nystrom and Starbuck, "To Avoid Organizational Crises, Unlearn."
51. S. T. Fiske and S. E. Taylor, *Social Cognition* (Reading, MA: Addison-Wesley, 1984).
52. See G. R. Jones, R. Kosnik, and J. M. George, "Internalization and the Firm's Growth Path: On the Psychology of Organizational Contracting," in R. W. Woodman and W. A. Pasemore, eds., *Research in Organizational Change and Development*, vol. 7 (Greenwich, CT: JAI Press, 1993), pp. 105–135, for an account of the biases as they operate during organizational growth and decline.
53. L. Festinger, *A Theory of Cognitive Dissonance* (Stanford, CA: Stanford University Press, 1957); E. Aaronson, "The Theory of Cognitive Dissonance: A Current Perspective," in

54. L. Berkowitz, ed., *Advances in Experimental Social Psychology*, vol. 4 (New York: Academic Press, 1969), pp. 1–34.
54. J. R. Averill, "Personal Control over Aversive Stimuli and Its Relationship to Stress," *Psychological Bulletin*, 80 (1973), 286–303.
55. E. J. Langer, "The Illusion of Control," *Journal of Personality and Social Psychology*, 32 (1975), 311–328.
56. A. Tversky and D. Kahneman, "Judgment Under Uncertainty: Heuristics and Biases," *Science*, 185 (1974), 1124–1131.
57. R. De Board, *The Psychoanalysis of Organizations* (London: Tavistock, 1978).
58. B. M. Staw, "The Escalation of Commitment to a Course of Action," *Academy of Management Review*, 6 (1978), 577–587; B. M. Staw and J. Ross, "Commitment to a Policy Decision: A Multi-Theoretical Perspective," *Administrative Science Quarterly*, 23 (1978), 40–64.
59. Nystrom and Starbuck, "To Avoid Organizational Crises, Unlearn."
60. Ibid.
61. L. Porter and K. Roberts, "Communication in Organizations," in M. Dunnette, ed., *Handbook of Industrial and Organizational Psychology* (Chicago: Rand McNally, 1976).
62. Nystrom and Starbuck, "To Avoid Organizational Crises, Unlearn."
63. A. D. Meyer, "Adapting to Environmental Jolts," *Administrative Science Quarterly*, 27 (1982), 515–537; A. D. Meyer, "How Ideologies Supplant Formal Structures and Shape Responses to Environments," *Journal of Management Studies*, 7 (1982), 31–53.
64. For a basic introduction to game theory, see A. K. Dixit and B. J. Nalebuff, *Thinking Strategically* (London: WW Norton, 1991). Also see A. M. Brandenburger and B. J. Nalebuff, *The Right Game: Using Game Theory to Shape Strategy*, Harvard Business Review (July–August 1995): 59–71; and D. M. Kreps, *Game Theory and Economic Modeling* (Oxford, UK: Oxford University Press, 1990).
65. D. C. Hambrick, *The Executive Effect: Concepts and Methods for Studying Top Managers* (Greenwich, CT: JAI Press, 1988).
66. D. G. Ancona, "Top-Management Teams: Preparing for the Revolution," in J. S. Carroll, ed., *Applied Social Psychology and Organizational Settings* (Hillsdale, NJ: Lawrence Erlbaum Associates, 1990).
67. M. Shaw, "Communications Networks," in L. Berkowitz, ed., *Advances in Experimental Social Psychology*, vol. 1 (New York: Academic Press, 1964).
68. Ibid.
69. S. Finkelstein and D. C. Hambrick, "Top-Management Team Tenure and Organizational Outcomes: The Moderating Role of Managerial Discretion," *Administrative Science Quarterly*, 35 (1990), 484–503.
70. I. L. Janis, *Victims of Groupthink*, 2nd ed. (Boston: Houghton Mifflin, 1982).
71. K. M. Eisenhardt and C. B. Schoonhoven, "Organizational Growth: Linking Founding Team, Strategy, Environment, and Growth Among U.S. Semiconductor Ventures, 1978–1988," *Administrative Science Quarterly*, 35 (1990), 504–529; L. Keck and M. L. Tushman, "Environmental and Organizational Context and Executive Team Structure," *Academy of Management Journal*, 36 (1993), 1314–1344.
72. A. J. Lott and B. E. Lott, "Group Cohesiveness and Interpersonal Attraction: A Review of Relationships with Antecedent and Consequent Variables," *Psychological Bulletin*, 14 (1965), 259–309.
73. D. L. Helmich and W. B. Brown, "Successor Type and Organizational Change in the Corporate Enterprise," *Administrative Science Quarterly*, 17 (1972), 371–381; D. C. Hambrick and P. A. Mason, "Upper Echelons: The Organization as a Reflection of Its Top Managers," *Academy of Management Journal*, 9 (1984), 193–206.
74. R. F. Vancil, *Passing the Baton* (Boston: Harvard Business School Press, 1987).
75. C. Schwenk, "Cognitive Simplification Processes in Strategic Decision Making," *Strategic Management Journal*, 5 (1984), 111–128.
76. D. Rubenstein and R. W. Woodman, "Spiderman and the Burma Raiders: Collateral Organization Theory in Practice," *Journal of Applied Behavioral Science*, 20 (1984), 1–21; G. R. Bushe and A. B. Shani, *Parallel Learning Structures: Increasing Innovations in Bureaucracies* (Reading, MA: Addison-Wesley, 1991).

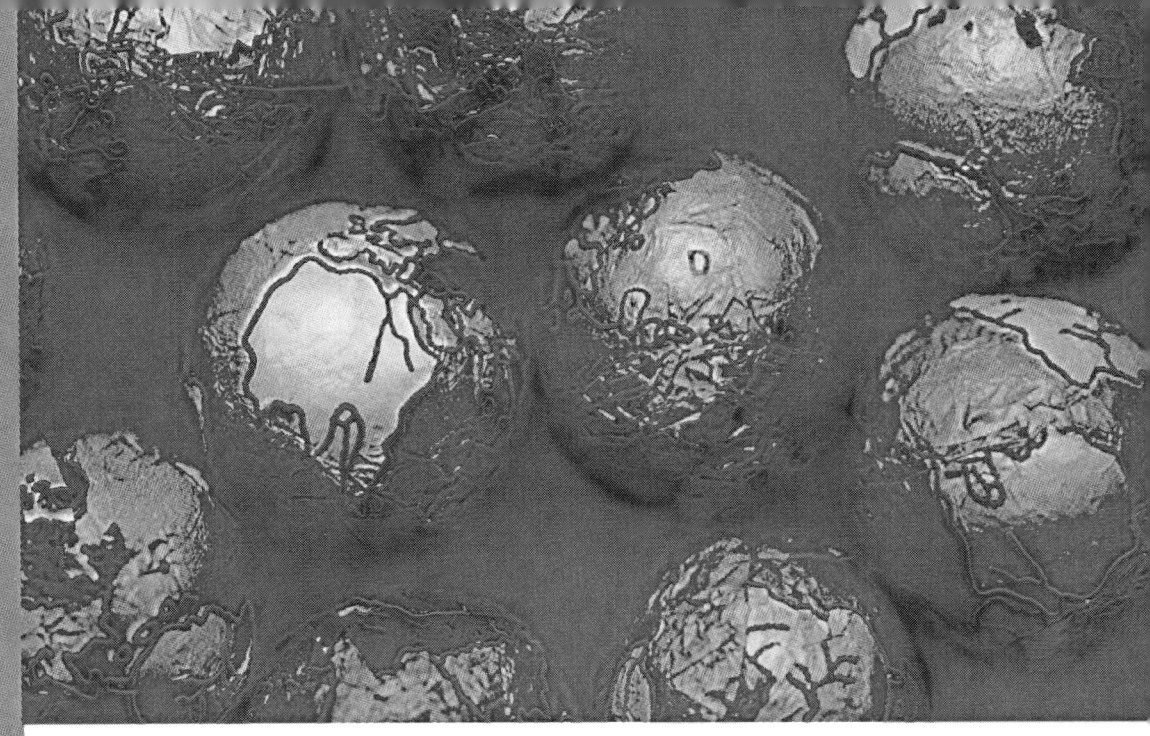

TOPIC 7

COMMUNICATION IN A MULTICULTURAL CONTEXT

CHAPTER 11

Communicating Across Cultures

Outline

Opening Profile: Google's Internet Communications Clash with European Culture

The Communication Process
Cultural Noise in the Communication Process

The Culture–Communication Link
Trust in Communication
The GLOBE Project
Cultural Variables in the Communication Process
Context

Management Focus: Oriental Poker Face: Eastern Deception or Western Inscrutability?

Comparative Management in Focus: Communicating with Arabs
Communication Channels

Information Technology: Going Global and Acting Local

Managing Cross-cultural Communication
Developing Cultural Sensitivity
Careful Encoding
Selective Transmission
Careful Decoding of Feedback
Follow-up Actions

Conclusion
Summary of Key Points
Discussion Questions
Application Exercises
Exercise Questions
Experiential Exercise
Internet Resources
Case Study: Elizabeth Visits GPC's French Subsidiary

OBJECTIVES:

1. To recognize the cultural variables in the communication process and what factors can cause "noise" in that process.
2. To develop an awareness of differences in non-verbal behaviors, context, and attitudes and how they affect cross-cultural communication.
3. To understand the complexities of Western-Arab communications.
4. To be aware of the impact of IT on cross-border communications.
5. To learn how to successfully manage cross-cultural business communications.

Opening Profile: Google's Internet Communications Clash with European Culture[1]

Google has been expanding into European markets for five years and now has a headquarters in Dublin, large offices in Zurich and London, and smaller centers in countries like Denmark, Russia and Poland. However, Google is now getting caught in a cultural web of privacy laws that threaten its growth and the positive image it has cultivated.

The latest clash is over Google's plan to introduce "Street View," a mapping service that provides a vivid, 360-degree, ground-level photographic panorama from any address. However, data protection officials in Switzerland are pressing Google to cancel those plans, since "Street View" would violate strict Swiss privacy laws that prohibit the unauthorized use of personal images or property. In Germany, where Street View is also not available, simply taking photographs for the service violates privacy laws. At the same time, the EU Article 29 Data Protection Working Group, which is a collaboration among all the information and data protection watchdogs within the European Union, is also contesting Google's practices. The EU Justice Commissioner, Franco Frattini, was backing the investigation. Google, the world's largest search engine, provoked a debate about internet privacy in May 2008, when it announced it would institute changes to its policies on holding personal information about its customers. The policy change related to Google's server logs (the information a browser sends back to Google when somebody visits a site). At present, the search engine retains a log of every search indefinitely, including information—such as the unique computer address, browser type and language—which could be traced back to a particular computer. The policy change was to reduce how long that information was retained to 18–24 months.

Peter Schaar, chair of Article 29, who is also Germany's federal commissioner for freedom of information, developed a report on the relationship between search-engine business models and European privacy laws. The draft report concluded that IP addresses are personal information because they can help identify a person. Europeans fiercely protect their privacy and trust that the government enforces it in law. Mr. Schaar has challenged Peter Fleischer of Google's global privacy law team to explain why such a long storage period was chosen and to give a legal justification for the storage of server logs in general. Google's response so far, from founders Sergei Brin and Larry Page, was to identify others as the bigger threat to internet users' privacy. They stated that information posted on social networking sites, such as photographs of young people at drunken parties, are a greater privacy concern. They defended the value of users' information for refining search results, and blamed the way some companies have used that information for privacy problems in the industry. The outcome of this cross-cultural internet communication clash remains to be seen. One thing that is clear is that the European Union (EU) has fired a warning shot across the bows of the search-engine companies.

Cultural communications are deeper and more complex than spoken or written messages. The essence of effective cross-cultural communication has more to do with releasing the right responses than with sending the "right" messages.

HALL AND HALL[2]

Multi-local online strategy . . . is about meeting global business objectives by tuning in to the cultural dynamics of their local markets.

"THINK GLOBALLY, INTERACT LOCALLY,"
New Media Age[3]

As the opening profile suggests, communication is a critical factor in the cross-cultural management issues discussed in this book, particularly those of an interpersonal nature, involving motivation, leadership, group interactions, and negotiation. Culture is conveyed and perpetuated through communication in one form or another. Culture and communication are so intricately intertwined that they are, essentially, synonymous.[4] By understanding this relationship, managers can move toward constructive intercultural management.

Communication, whether in the form of writing, talking, listening, or via the Internet, is an inherent part of a manager's role and takes up the majority of a manager's time on the job. Studies by Mintzberg demonstrate the importance of oral communication; he found that most managers spend between 50 and 90 percent of their time talking to people.[5] The ability of a manager to effectively communicate across cultural boundaries will largely determine the success of international business transactions or the output of a culturally diverse workforce. It is useful, then, to break down the elements involved in the communication process, both to understand the cross-cultural issues at stake and to maximize the process.

THE COMMUNICATION PROCESS

The term **communication** describes the process of sharing meaning by transmitting messages through media such as words, behavior, or material artifacts. Managers communicate to co-ordinate activities, to disseminate information, to motivate people, and to negotiate future plans. It is of vital importance, then, for a receiver to interpret the meaning of a particular communication in the way the sender intended. Unfortunately, the communication process (see Exhibit 11-1) involves stages during which meaning can be distorted. Anything that serves to undermine the communication of the intended meaning is typically referred to as **noise.**

The primary cause of noise stems from the fact that the sender and the receiver each exist in a unique, private world thought of as her or his life space. The context of that private world, largely based on culture, experience, relations, values, and so forth, determines the interpretation of meaning in communication. People filter, or selectively understand, messages consistent with their own expectations and perceptions of reality and their values and norms of behavior. The more dissimilar the cultures of those involved, the more the likelihood of misinterpretation. In this way, as Samovar, Porter, and Jain state, cultural factors pervade the communication process:

> *Culture not only dictates who talks with whom, about what, and how the communication proceeds, it also helps to determine how people encode messages, the meanings they have for messages, and the conditions and circumstances under which various messages may or may not be sent, noticed, or interpreted. In fact, our entire repertory of communicative behaviors is dependent largely on the culture in which we have been raised. Culture, consequently, is the foundation of communication. And, when cultures vary, communication practices also vary.*[6]

Communication, therefore, is a complex process of linking up or sharing the perceptual fields of sender and receiver; the perceptive sender builds a bridge to the life space of the receiver.[7] After the receiver interprets the message and draws a conclusion about what the sender meant, he or she will, in most cases, encode and send back a response, making communication a circular process.

The communication process is rapidly changing, however, as a result of technological developments, therefore propelling global business forward at a phenomenal growth rate. These changes are discussed later in this chapter.

Cultural Noise in the Communication Process

> *In Japanese there are several words for "I" and several words for "you" but their use depends on the relationship between the speaker and the other person. In short, there is no "I" by itself; the "I" depends on the relationship.*[8]

EXHIBIT 11-1 The Communication Process

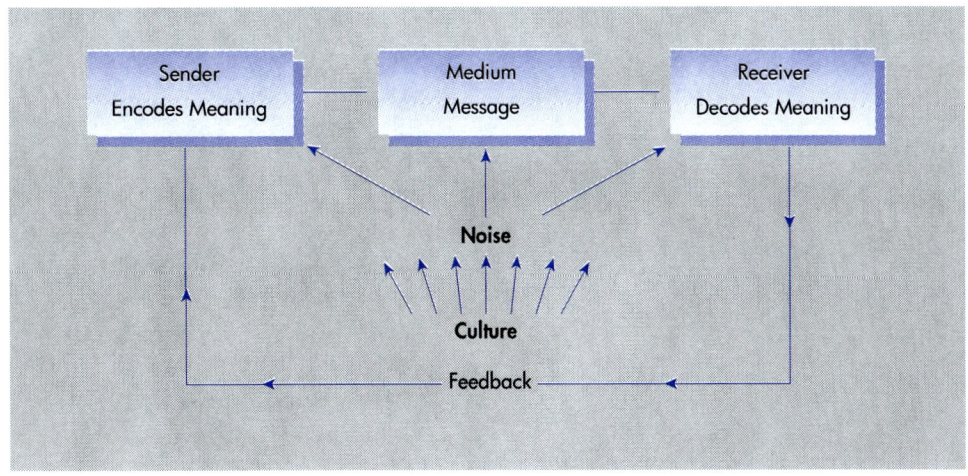

Because the focus in this text is on effective cross-cultural communication, it is important to understand what cultural variables cause noise in the communication process. This knowledge of **cultural noise**—the cultural variables that undermine the communications of intended meaning—will enable us to take steps to minimize that noise and so to improve communication.

When a member of one culture sends a message to a member of another culture, **intercultural communication** takes place. The message contains the meaning intended by the encoder. When it reaches the receiver, however, it undergoes a transformation in which the influence of the decoder's culture becomes part of the meaning.[9] Exhibit 11-2 provides an example of intercultural communication in which the meaning got all mixed up. Note how the attribution of behavior differs for each participant. **Attribution** is the process in which people look for an explanation of another person's behavior. When they realize that they do not understand another, they tend, say Hall and Hall, to blame their confusion on the other's "stupidity, deceit, or craziness."[10]

In the situation depicted in Exhibit 11-2, the Greek employee becomes frustrated and resigns after experiencing communication problems with his American boss. How could this outcome have been avoided? We do not have much information about the people or the context of the situation, but we can look at some of the variables that might have been involved and use them as a basis for analysis.

EXHIBIT 11-2 Cultural Noise in International Communication[11]

Behavior		Attribution	
American:	"How long will it take you to finish this report?"	*American*:	I asked him to participate.
		Greek:	His behavior makes no sense. He is the boss. Why doesn't he tell me?
Greek:	"I don't know. How long should it take?"	*American*:	He refuses to take responsibility.
		Greek:	I asked him for an order.
American:	"You are in the best position to analyze time requirements."	*American*:	I press him to take responsibility for his actions.
		Greek:	What nonsense: I'd better give him an answer.
Greek:	"10 days."	*American*:	He lacks the ability to estimate time; this time estimate is totally inadequate.
American:	"Take 15. Is it agreed? You will do it in 15 days?"	*American*:	I offer a contract.
		Greek:	These are my orders: 15 days.
In fact, the report needed 30 days of regular work. So the Greek worked day and night, but at the end of the 15th day, he still needed to do one more day's work.			
American:	"Where is the report?"	*American*:	I am making sure he fulfills his contract.
		Greek:	He is asking for the report. (Both attribute that it is not ready.)
Greek:	"It will be ready tomorrow."		
American:	"But we agreed it would be ready today."	*American*:	I must teach him to fulfill a contract.
		Greek:	The stupid, incompetent boss! Not only did he give me the wrong orders, but he doesn't even appreciate that I did a 30-day job in 16 days.
The Greek hands in his resignation.			The American is surprised.
		Greek:	I can't work for such a man.

THE CULTURE–COMMUNICATION LINK

The following sections examine underlying elements of culture that affect communication. The degree to which one is able to effectively communicate largely depends on how similar the other person's cultural expectations are to our own. However, cultural gaps can be overcome by prior learning and understanding of those variables and how to adjust to them.

Trust in Communication

The key ingredient in a successful alliance is trust.

JAMES R. HOUGHTON,
Former Chairman, Corning, Inc.[12]

Effective communication, and therefore collaboration in alliances across national boundaries, depends on the informal understandings among the parties that are based on the trust that has developed between them. However, the meaning of trust and how it is developed and communicated vary across societies. In China and Japan, for example, business transactions are based on networks of long-standing relationships based on trust rather than on the formal contracts and arm's-length relationships typical of the United States. When there is trust between parties, implicit understanding arises within communications. This understanding has numerous benefits in business, including encouraging communicators to overlook cultural differences and minimize problems. It allows communicators to adjust to unforeseen circumstances with less conflict than would be the case with formal contracts, and it facilitates open communication in exchanging ideas and information.[13] From his research on trust in global collaboration, John Child suggests the following guidelines for cultivating trust:

- Create a clear and calculated basis for mutual benefit. There must be realistic commitments and good intentions to honor them.
- Improve predictability: Strive to resolve conflicts and keep communication open.
- Develop mutual bonding through regular socializing and friendly contact.[14]

What can managers anticipate with regard to the level of trust in communications with people in other countries? If trust is based on how trustworthy we consider a person to be, then it must vary according to that society's expectations about whether that culture supports the norms and values that predispose people to behave credibly and benevolently. Are there differences across societies in those expectations of trust? Research by the World Values Study Group of 90,000 people in 45 societies provides some insight on cultural values regarding predisposition to trust. When we examine the percentage of respondents in each society who responded that "most people can be trusted," we can see that the Nordic countries and China had the highest predisposition to trust, followed by Canada, the United States, and Britain, while Brazil, Turkey, Romania, Slovenia, and Latvia had the lowest level of trust in people.[15]

The GLOBE Project

Results from the GLOBE research on culture, provide some insight into culturally appropriate communication styles and expectations for the manager to use abroad. GLOBE researchers Javidan and House make the following observations:[16] For people in societies that ranked high on performance orientation—for example, the United States—presenting objective information in a direct and explicit way is an important and expected manner of communication; this compares with people in Russia or Greece—which ranked low on performance orientation—for whom hard facts and figures are not readily available or taken seriously. In those cases, a more indirect approach is preferred. People from countries ranking low on assertiveness, such as Sweden, also recoil from explicitness; their preference is for much two-way discourse and friendly relationships.

People ranking high on the "humane" dimension, such as those from Ireland and the Philippines, make avoiding conflict a priority and tend to communicate with the goal of being supportive of people rather than of achieving objective end results. This compares to people from France and Spain whose agenda is achievement of goals.

The foregoing provides examples of how to draw implications for appropriate communication styles from the research findings on cultural differences across societies. Astute global managers have learned that culture and communication are inextricably linked and that they should prepare themselves accordingly. Most will also suggest that you carefully watch and listen to how your hosts are communicating and to follow their lead.

Cultural Variables in the Communication Process

On a different level, it is also useful to be aware of cultural variables that can affect the communication process by influencing a person's perceptions; some of these variables have been identified by Samovar and Porter and discussed by Harris and Moran, and others.[17] These variables are as follows: attitudes, social organization, thought patterns, roles, language (spoken or written), nonverbal communication (including kinesic behavior, proxemics, paralanguage, and object language), and time. Although these variables are discussed separately in this text, their effects are interdependent and inseparable—or, as Hecht, Andersen, and Ribeau put it, "Encoders and decoders process nonverbal cues as a conceptual, multichanneled gestalt."[18]

Attitudes We all know that our attitudes underlie the way we behave and communicate and the way we interpret messages from others. Ethnocentric attitudes are a particular source of noise in cross-cultural communication. In the incident described in Exhibit 11-2, both the American and the Greek are clearly attempting to interpret and convey meaning based on their own experiences of that kind of transaction. The American is probably guilty of stereotyping the Greek employee by quickly jumping to the conclusion that he is unwilling to take responsibility for the task and the scheduling.

This problem, **stereotyping,** occurs when a person assumes that every member of a society or subculture has the same characteristics or traits. Stereotyping is a common cause of misunderstanding in intercultural communication. It is an arbitrary, lazy, and often destructive way to find out about people. Astute managers are aware of the dangers of cultural stereotyping and deal with each person as an individual with whom they may form a unique relationship.

Social Organization Our perceptions can be influenced by differences in values, approach, or priorities relative to the kind of social organizations to which we belong. These organizations may be based on one's nation, tribe, or religious sect, or they may consist of the members of a certain profession. Examples of such organizations include the Academy of Management or the United Auto Workers (UAW).[19]

Thought Patterns The logical progression of reasoning varies widely around the world and greatly affects the communication process. Managers cannot assume that others use the same reasoning processes, as illustrated by the experience of a Canadian expatriate in Thailand:

While in Thailand a Canadian expatriate's car was hit by a Thai motorist who had crossed over the double line while passing another vehicle. After failing to establish that the fault lay with the Thai driver, the Canadian flagged down a policeman. After several minutes of seemingly futile discussion, the Canadian pointed out the double line in the middle of the road and asked the policeman directly, "What do these lines signify?" The policeman replied, "They indicate the center of the road and are there so I can establish just how far the accident is from that point." The Canadian was silent. It had never occurred to him that the double line might not mean "no passing allowed.[20]

In the Exhibit 11-2 scenario, perhaps the American did not realize that the Greek employee had a different rationale for his time estimate for the job. Because the Greek was not used to having to estimate schedules, he just took a guess, which he felt he had been forced to do.

Roles Societies differ considerably in their perceptions of a manager's role. Much of the difference is attributable to their perceptions of who should make the decisions and who has responsibility for what. In the Exhibit 11-2 example, the American assumes that his role as manager is to delegate responsibility, to foster autonomy, and to practice participative management. He prescribes the role of the employee without any consideration of whether the employee will understand that role. The Greek's frame of reference leads him to think that the manager is the boss and should give the order about when to have the job completed. He interprets the

American's behavior as breaking that frame of reference, and therefore he feels that the boss is "stupid and incompetent" for giving him the wrong order and for not recognizing and appreciating his accomplishment. The manager should have considered what behaviors Greek workers would expect of him and then either should have played that role or discussed the situation carefully, in a training mode.

Language Spoken or written language, of course, is a frequent cause of miscommunication, stemming from a person's inability to speak the local language, a poor or too-literal translation, a speaker's failure to explain idioms, or a person missing the meaning conveyed through body language or certain symbols. Even among countries that share the same language, problems can arise from the subtleties and nuances inherent in the use of the language, as noted by George Bernard Shaw: "Britain and America are two nations separated by a common language." This problem can exist even within the same country among subcultures or subgroups.[21]

Many international executives tell stories about lost business deals or lost sales because of communication blunders:

> *When Pepsi Cola's slogan "Come Alive with Pepsi" was introduced in Germany, the company learned that the literal German translation of "come alive" is "come out of the grave."*
>
> *A U.S. airline found a lack of demand for its "rendezvous lounges" on its Boeing 747s. They later learned that "rendezvous" in Portuguese refers to a room that is rented for prostitution.*[22]

More than just conveying objective information, language also conveys cultural and social understandings from one generation to the next. Examples of how language reflects what is important in a society include the 6,000 different Arabic words used to describe camels and their parts and the 50 or more classifications of snow used by the Inuit, the Eskimo people of Canada.

Inasmuch as language conveys culture, technology, and priorities, it also serves to separate and perpetuate subcultures. In India, 14 official and many unofficial languages are used, and over 800 languages are spoken on the African continent.

Because of increasing workforce diversity around the world, the international business manager will have to deal with a medley of languages. For example, assembly-line workers at the Ford plant in Cologne, Germany, speak Turkish and Spanish as well as German. In Malaysia, Indonesia, and Thailand, many of the buyers and traders are Chinese. Not all Arabs speak Arabic; in Tunisia and Lebanon, for example, French is the language of commerce.

In North Africa—Morocco, Tunisia, Algeria, Libya, Egypt—people are used to doing business with Europe and the United States. People in Morocco, Algeria, and Tunisia, with their history of French rule, are familiar with the business practices in Europe—they speak French and use the metric system, for example. Egypt has a similar history with the British and so its citizens commonly speak English as their second language. Egypt also has a close political relationship and business ties with the United States.[23]

International managers need either a good command of the local language or competent interpreters. The task of accurate translation to bridge cultural gaps is fraught with difficulties, as Joe Romano, a partner of High Ground, an emerging technology-marketing company in Boston, found out on a business trip to Taiwan, how close a one-syllable slip of the tongue can come to torpedoing a deal. He noted that one is supposed to say 'au-ban,' meaning 'Hello, No.1. Boss.' But instead he said 'Lau-ban ya," which means 'Hello, wife of the boss." Essentially Mr. Romano called him a woman in front of twenty senior Taiwanese executives, who all laughed; but the boss was very embarrassed, because men in Asia have a very macho attitude.[24]

Even the direct translation of specific words does not guarantee the congruence of their meaning, as with the word "yes" used by Asians, which usually means only that they have heard you, and, often, that they are too polite to disagree. The Chinese, for example, through years of political control, have built into their communication culture a cautionary stance to avoid persecution by professing agreement with whatever opinion was held by the person questioning them.[25]

Sometimes even a direct statement can be misinterpreted instead as an indirect expression, as when a German businessman said to his Algerian counterpart, "My wife would love something like that beautiful necklace your wife was wearing last night. It was beautiful." The next day the Algerian gave him a box with the necklace in it as a gift to his wife. The Algerian had interpreted the compliment as an indirect way of expressing a wish to possess a similar necklace. The German was embarrassed, but had to accept the necklace. He realize he needed to be careful how he expressed such things in the future—such as asking where that kind of jewelry is sold.[26]

Politeness and a desire to say only what the listener wants to hear creates noise in the communication process in much of the world. Often, even a clear translation does not help a person to understand what is meant because the encoding process has obscured the true message. With the poetic Arab language—replete with exaggeration, elaboration, and repetition—meaning is attributed more to how something is said rather than what is said.

Businesspeople need to consider another dimension of communication style that can cause noise whether in verbal or non-verbal language—that of *instrumental versus expressive communicators*. Expressive communicators—such as those from Russia, Hungary, Poland—are those who make their communications personal by showing their emotions openly or using emotional appeals to persuade others. This compares with instrumental communicators—whom we find as one moves west and north, such as in the Czech Republic, Slovenia; emphasis is on the content of the communication, not personal expressions.[27]

For the American supervisor and Greek employee cited in Exhibit 11-2, it is highly likely that the American could have picked up some cues from the employee's body language, which probably implied problems with the interpretation of meaning. How might body language have created noise in this case?

Nonverbal Communication

Behavior that communicates without words (although it often is accompanied by words) is called **nonverbal communication.** People will usually believe what they see over what they hear—hence the expression, "A picture is worth a thousand words." Studies show that these subtle messages account for between 65 and 93 percent of interpreted communication.[28] Even minor variations in body language, speech rhythms, and punctuality, for example, often cause mistrust and misperception of the situation among cross-national parties.[29] The media for such nonverbal communication can be categorized into four types: (1) kinesic behavior, (2) proxemics, (3) paralanguage, and (4) object language.

The term **kinesic behavior** refers to communication through body movements— posture, gestures, facial expressions, and eye contact. Although such actions may be universal, often their meaning is not. Because kinesic systems of meaning are culturally specific and learned, they cannot be generalized across cultures. Most people in the West would not correctly interpret many Chinese facial expressions; sticking out the tongue expresses surprise, a widening of the eyes shows anger, and scratching the ears and cheeks indicates happiness.[30] Research has shown for some time, however, that most people worldwide can recognize displays of the basic emotions of anger, disgust, fear, happiness, sadness, surprise, and contempt.[31]

Visitors to other countries must be careful about their gestures and how they might be interpreted. In the United States, for example, a common gesture is that for "O.K."—making a circle with the index finger and the thumb. That is an obscene gesture to the Brazilians, Greeks and Turks. On the other hand people in Japan may point with their middle finger, considered an obscene gesture to others. To Arabs, showing the soles of one's feet is an insult; recall the reporter who threw his shoe at President Bush in late 2008 during his visit to Iraq. This was, to Arabs, the ultimate insult.

Many businesspeople and visitors react negatively to what they feel are inappropriate facial expressions, without understanding the cultural meaning behind them. In his studies of cross-cultural negotiations, Graham observed that the Japanese feel uncomfortable when faced with the Americans' eye-to-eye posture. They are taught since childhood to bow their heads out of humility, whereas the automatic response of Americans is "look at me when I'm talking to you!"[32]

Subtle differences in eye behavior (called *oculesics*) can throw off a communication badly if they are not understood. Eye behavior includes differences not only in eye contact but also in the use of eyes to convey other messages, whether or not that involves mutual gaze. Edward T. Hall, author of the classic *The Silent Language*, explains the differences in eye contact between the British and the Americans. During speech, Americans will look straight at you, but the British keep your attention by looking away. The British will look at you when they have finished speaking, which signals that it is your turn to talk. The implicit rationale for this is that you can't interrupt people when they are not looking at you.[33]

It is helpful for U.S. managers to be aware of the many cultural expectations regarding posture and how they may be interpreted. In Europe or Asia, a relaxed posture in business meetings may be taken as bad manners or the result of poor upbringing. In Korea, you are expected to sit upright, with feet squarely on the floor, and to speak slowly, showing a blending of body and spirit.

Managers can also familiarize themselves with the many different interpretations of hand and finger signals around the world, some of which may represent obscene gestures. Of course, we cannot expect to change all of our ingrained, natural kinesic behavior, but we can be aware of what it means to others. We also can learn to understand the kinesic behavior of others and the role it plays in their society, as well as how it can affect business transactions. Misunderstanding the meanings of body movements—or an ethnocentric attitude toward the "proper" behavior—can have negative repercussions.

Proxemics deals with the influence of proximity and space on communication—both personal space and office space or layout. Americans expect office layout to provide private space for each person, and usually a larger and more private space as one goes up the hierarchy. In much of Asia, the custom is open office space, with people at all levels working and talking in close proximity to one another. Space communicates power in both Germany and the United States, evidenced by the desire for a corner office or one on the top floor. The importance of French officials, however, is made clear by a position in the middle of subordinates, communicating that they have a central position in an information network, where they can stay informed and in control.[34]

Do you ever feel vaguely uncomfortable and start moving backward slowly when someone is speaking to you? This is because that person is invading your "bubble"—your personal space. Personal space is culturally patterned, and foreign spatial cues are a common source of misinterpretation. When someone seems aloof or pushy, it often means that she or he is operating under subtly different spatial rules.

Hall and Hall suggest that cultural differences affect the programming of the senses and that space, perceived by all the senses, is regarded as a form of territory to be protected.[35] South Americans, Southern and Eastern Europeans, Indonesians, and Arabs are **high-contact cultures,** preferring to stand close, touch a great deal, and experience a "close" sensory involvement. Latin Americans, for example, have a highly physical greeting such as putting their arms around a colleague's back and grabbing him by the arm. On the other hand, North Americans, Asians, and Northern Europeans are **low-contact cultures** and prefer much less sensory involvement, standing farther apart and touching far less. They have a "distant" style of body language. In France, a relationship-oriented culture, good friends greet members of the opposite sex with a peck on each cheek; a handshake is a way to make a personal connection.

Interestingly, high-contact cultures are mostly located in warmer climates, and low-contact cultures in cooler climates. Americans are relatively nontouching, automatically standing at a distance so that an outstretched arm will touch the other person's ear. Standing any closer than that is regarded as invading intimate space. However, Americans and Canadians certainly expect a warm handshake and maybe a pat on the back from closer friends, though not the very warm double handshake of the Spaniards (clasping the forearm with the left hand). The Japanese, considerably less **haptic (touching),** do not shake hands; an initial greeting between a Japanese and a Spanish businessperson would be uncomfortable for both parties if they were untrained in cultural haptics. The Japanese bow to one another—the depth of the bow revealing their relative social standing.

When considering high- and low-contact cultures, we can trace a correlation between Hofstede's cultural variables of individualism and collectivism and the types of kinesic and proxemic behaviors people display. Generally, people from individualistic cultures are more remote and distant, whereas those from collectivist cultures are interdependent: They tend to work, play, live, and sleep in close proximity.[36]

The term **paralanguage** refers to how something is said rather than the content—the rate of speech, the tone and inflection of voice, other noises, laughing, or yawning. The culturally aware manager learns how to interpret subtle differences in paralanguage, including silence. Silence is a powerful communicator. It may be a way of saying no, of being offended, or of waiting for more information to make a decision. There is considerable variation in the use of silence in meetings. While Americans get uncomfortable after 10 or 15 seconds of silence, Chinese prefer to think the situation over for 30 seconds before speaking. The typical scenario between Americans and Chinese, then, is that the American gets impatient, says something to break the silence, and offends the Chinese by interrupting his or her chain of thought and comfort level with the subject.[37] Graham, a researcher on international negotiations, taped a bargaining session held at Toyota's U.S. headquarters in California. The U.S. executive had made a proposal to open a new production facility in Brazil and was waiting for a response from the three Japanese executives, who sat with lowered eyes and hands folded on the table. After about 30 seconds—an eternity to Americans, accustomed to a conversational response time of a few tenths of a second—the American blurted out that they were getting nowhere—and the meeting ended in a stalemate. More sensitivity to cultural differences in communication might have led him to wait longer or perhaps to prompt some further response through another polite question.[38]

The term **object language, or material culture,** refers to how we communicate through material artifacts, whether architecture, office design and furniture, clothing, cars, or cosmetics. Material culture communicates what people hold as important. In the United States, for example, someone wishing to convey his important status and wealth would show guests his penthouse office or expensive car. In Japan, a businessman presents his business card to a new contact and expects the receiver to study it and appreciate his position. In Mexico, a visiting international executive or salesperson is advised to take time out, before negotiating business, to show appreciation for the surrounding architecture, which is prized by Mexicans. The importance of family to people in Spain and much of Latin America, would be conveyed by family photographs around the office and therefore an expectation that the visitor would enquire about the family.

Time   Another variable that communicates culture is the way people regard and use time. To Brazilians, relative punctuality communicates the level of importance of those involved. To Middle Easterners, time is something controlled by the will of Allah.

To initiate effective cross-cultural business interactions, managers should know the difference between *monochronic time systems* and *polychronic time systems* and how they affect communications. Hall and Hall explain that in **monochronic cultures** (Switzerland, Germany, and the United States), time is experienced in a linear way, with a past, a present, and a future, and time is treated as something to be spent, saved, made up, or wasted. Classified and compartmentalized, time serves to order life. This attitude is a learned part of Western culture, probably starting with the Industrial Revolution. Monochronic people, found in individualistic cultures, generally concentrate on one thing at a time, adhere to time commitments, and are accustomed to short-term relationships.

In contrast, **polychronic cultures** tolerate many things occurring simultaneously and emphasize involvement with people. Two Latin friends, for example, will put an important conversation ahead of being on time for a business meeting, thus communicating the priority of relationships over material systems. Polychronic people—Latin Americans, Arabs, and those from other collectivist cultures—may focus on several things at once, be highly distractible, and change plans often.[39]

The relationship between time and space also affects communication. Polychronic people, for example, are likely to hold open meetings, moving around and conducting transactions with one party and then another, rather than compartmentalizing meeting topics, as do monochronic people.

The nuances and distinctions regarding cultural differences in nonverbal communication are endless. The various forms are listed in Exhibit 11-3; wise intercultural managers will take careful account of the role that such differences might play.

What aspects of nonverbal communication might have created noise in the interactions between the American supervisor and the Greek employee in Exhibit 11-2? Undoubtedly, some cues could have been picked up from the kinesic behavior of each person. It was the responsibility of the manager, in particular, to notice any indications from the Greek that could have prompted him to change his communication pattern or assumptions. Face-to-face communication permits the sender of the message to get immediate feedback, verbal and nonverbal, and thus to have some idea as to how that message is being received and whether additional information is needed. What aspects of the Greek employee's kinesic behavior or paralanguage might have been evident to a more culturally sensitive manager? Did both parties' sense of time affect the communication process?

EXHIBIT 11-3 Forms of Nonverbal Communication

- Facial expressions
- Body posture
- Gestures with hands, arms, head, etc.
- Interpersonal distance (proxemics)
- Touching, body contact
- Eye contact
- Clothing, cosmetics, hairstyles, jewelry
- Paralanguage (voice pitch and inflections, rate of speech, and silence)
- Color symbolism
- Attitude toward time and the use of time in business and social interactions
- Food symbolism and social use of meals

Context

East Asians live in relatively complex social networks with prescribed role relations; attention to context is, therefore, important for their effective functioning. In contrast, westerners live in less constraining social worlds that stress independence and allow them to pay less attention to context.

RICHARD E. NISBETT,
September 2005[40]

A major differentiating factor that is a primary cause of noise in the communication process is that of context—which actually incorporates many of the variables discussed earlier. The **context** in which the communication takes place affects the meaning and interpretation of the interaction. Cultures are known to be high- or low-context cultures, with a relative range in between.[41] In **high-context cultures** (Asia, the Middle East, Africa, and the Mediterranean), feelings and thoughts are not explicitly expressed; instead, one has to read between the lines and interpret meaning from one's general understanding. Two such high-context cultures are those of South Korea and Arab cultures. In such cultures, key information is embedded in the context rather than made explicit. People make assumptions about what the message means through their knowledge of the person or the surroundings. In these cultures, most communication takes place within a context of extensive information networks resulting from close personal relationships. See the following Management Focus for further explanation of the Asian communication style.

In **low-context cultures** (Germany, Switzerland, Scandinavia, and North America), where personal and business relationships are more compartmentalized, communication media have to be more explicit. Feelings and thoughts are expressed in words, and information is more readily available. Westerners focus more on the individual, and therefore tend to view events as the result of specific agents, while easterners view events in a broader and longer-term context.[42]

In cross-cultural communication between high- and low-context people, a lack of understanding may preclude reaching a solution, and conflict may arise. Germans, for example, will expect considerable detailed information before making a business decision, whereas Arabs will base their decisions more on knowledge of the people involved—the information is present, but it is implicit. People in low-context cultures, such as those in Germany, Switzerland Austria, and the United States, convey their thoughts and plans in a direct, straightforward communication style, saying something like "we have to make a decision on this today." People in high-context cultures, such as in Asia, and, to a lesser extent, in England, convey their thoughts in a more indirect, implicit manner; this means that someone from Germany needs to have more patience and tact and be willing to listen for clues—verbal and nonverbal—as to their colleagues' wishes.

People in high-context cultures expect others to understand unarticulated moods, subtle gestures, and environmental clues that people from low-context cultures simply do not process. Misinterpretation and misunderstanding often result.[43] People from high-context cultures

MANAGEMENT FOCUS

Oriental Poker Face: Eastern Deception or Western Inscrutability?

Among many English expressions that are likely to offend those of us whose ancestry may be traced to the Far East, two stand out quite menacingly for me: "Oriental poker face" and "idiotic Asian smile." The former refers to the supposedly inscrutable nature of a facial expression that apparently reflects no particular state of mind, while the latter pokes fun at a face fixed with a perpetually friendly smile. Westerners' perplexity, when faced with either, arises from the impression that these two diametrically opposed masquerading strategies prevent them from extracting useful information—at least the type of information that at least they could process with a reasonable measure of confidence—about the feelings of the person before them. An Asian face that projects no signs of emotion, then, seems to most Westerners nothing but a facade. It does not matter whether that face wears an unsightly scowl or a shining ray; a facial expression they cannot interpret poses a genuine threat.

Compassionate and sympathetic to their perplexity as I may be, I am also insulted by the Western insensitivity to the significant roles that subtle signs play in Asian cultures. Every culture has its unique modus operandi for communication. Western culture, for example, apparently emphasizes the importance of direct communication. Not only are the communicators taught to look directly at each other when they convey a message, but they also are encouraged to come right to the point of the message. Making bold statements or asking frank questions in a less than diplomatic manner (i.e., "That was really a very stupid thing to do!" or "Are you interested in me?") is rarely construed as rude or indiscreet. Even embarrassingly blunt questions such as "President Clinton, did you have sexual intercourse with Monica Lewinsky?" are tolerated most of the time. Asians, on the other hand, find this direct communicative communication style quite unnerving. In many social interactions, they avoid direct eye contact. They "see" each other without necessarily looking directly at each other, and they gather information about inner states of mind without asking even the most discreet or understated questions. Many times they talk around the main topic, and, yet, they succeed remarkably well in understanding one another's position. (At least they believe they have developed a reasonably clear understanding.)

To a great extent, Asian communication is listening-centered; the ability to listen (and a special talent for detecting various communicative cues) is treated as equally important as, if not more important than, the ability to speak. This contrasts clearly with the American style of communication that puts the utmost emphasis on verbal expression; the speaker carries most of the burden for ensuring that everyone understands his or her message. An Asian listener, however, is prone to blame himself or herself for failing to reach a comprehensive understanding from the few words and gestures performed by the speaker. With this heavier burden placed on the listener, an Asian speaker does not feel obliged to send clearly discernible message cues (at least not nearly so much as he or she is obliged to do in American cultural contexts). Not obligated to express themselves without interruption, Asians use silence as a tool in communication. Silence, by most Western conventions, represents discontinuity of communication and creates a feeling of discomfort and anxiety. In the Orient, however, silence is not only comfortably tolerated but is considered a desirable form of expression. Far from being a sign of displeasure or animosity, it serves as an integral part of the communication process, used for reflecting on messages previously exchanged and for carefully crafting thoughts before uttering them.

It is not outlandish at all, then, for Asians to view Americans as unnecessarily talkative and lacking in the ability to listen. For the Asian, it is the American who projects a mask of confidence by being overly expressive both verbally and nonverbally. Since the American style of communication places less emphasis on the act of listening than on speaking, Asians suspect that their American counterparts fail to pick up subtle and astute communicative signs in conversation. To one with a cultural outlook untrained in reading those signs, an inscrutable face represents no more than a menacing or amusing mask.

Source: Dr. Jin Kim, State University of New York–Plattsburgh. Copyright © 2003 by Dr. Jin Kim. Used with permission of Dr. Kim.

EXHIBIT 11-4 Cultural Context and Its Effects on Communication[45]

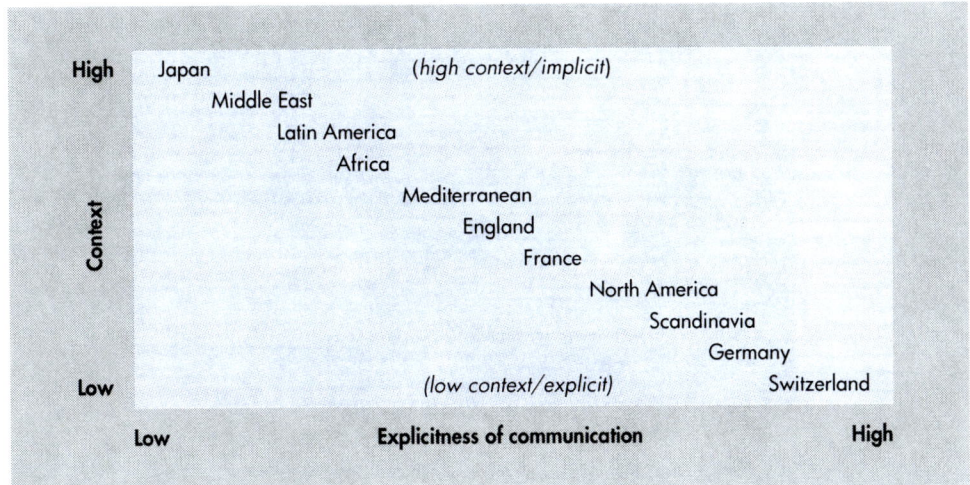

perceive those from low-context cultures as too talkative, too obvious, and redundant. Those from low-context cultures perceive high-context people as nondisclosing, sneaky, and mysterious. Research indicates, for example, that Americans find talkative people more attractive, whereas Koreans, high-context people, perceive less verbal people as more attractive. Finding the right balance between low- and high-context communications can be tricky, as Hall and Hall point out: "Too much information leads people to feel they are being talked down to; too little information can mystify them or make them feel left out."[44] Exhibit 11-4 shows the relative level of context in various countries.

The importance of understanding the role of context and nonverbal language to avoid misinterpretation is illustrated in the Comparative Management in Focus: Communicating with Arabs.

 **COMPARATIVE MANAGEMENT IN FOCUS**
Communicating with Arabs

In the Middle East, the meaning of a communication is implicit and interwoven, and consequently much harder for Americans, accustomed to explicit and specific meanings, to understand.

Arabs are warm, emotional, and quick to explode: "sounding off" is regarded as a safety valve. In fact, the Arabic language aptly communicates the Arabic culture, one of emotional extremes. The language contains the means for overexpression, many adjectives, words that allow for exaggeration, and metaphors to emphasize a position. What is said is often not as important as *how* it is said. Eloquence and flowery speech are admired for their own sake, regardless of the content. Loud speech is used for dramatic effect.

At the core of Middle Eastern culture are friendship, honor, religion, and traditional hospitality. Family, friends, and connections are very important on all levels in the Middle East and will take precedence over business transactions. Arabs do business with people, not companies, and they make commitments to people, not contracts. A phone call to the right person can help to get around seemingly insurmountable obstacles. An Arab expects loyalty from friends, and it is understood that giving and receiving favors is an inherent part of the relationship; no one says no to a request for a favor. A lack of follow-through is assumed to be beyond the friend's control.[46]

Because hospitality is a way of life and highly symbolic, a visitor must be careful not to reject it by declining refreshment or rushing into business discussions. Part of that hospitality is the elaborate system of greetings and the long period of getting acquainted, perhaps taking up the entire first meeting. While the handshake may seem limp, the rest of the greeting is not. Kissing on the cheeks is common among men, as is hand-holding between male friends. However, any public display of intimacy between men and women is strictly forbidden by the Arab social code.

Women play little or no role in business or entertainment; the Middle East is a male-dominated society, and it is impolite to inquire about women. Other nonverbal taboos include showing the soles of one's feet and using the left (unclean) hand to eat or pass something. In discussions, slouching in a seat or leaning against a wall communicates a lack of respect.

Westerner Meeting with Arab Businessmen.
Source: Getty Images/Digital Vision

The Arab society also values honor. Harris and Moran explain: "Honor, social prestige, and a secure place in society are brought about when conformity is achieved. When one fails to conform, this is considered to be damning and leads to a degree of shame."[47] Shame results not just from doing something wrong but from having others find out about that wrongdoing. Establishing a climate of honesty and trust is part of the sense of honor. Therefore, considerable tact is needed to avoid conveying any concern or doubt. Arabs tend to be quite introverted until a mutual trust is built, which takes a long time.[48]

In their nonverbal communication, most Arab countries are high-contact cultures. Arabs stand and sit closer and touch people of the same sex more than Westerners. They do not have the same concept of "public" and "private" space, or as Hall puts it, "Not only is the sheer noise level much higher, but the piercing look of the eyes, the touch of the hands, and the mutual bathing in the warm moist breath during conversation represent stepped-up sensory inputs to a level which many Europeans find unbearably intense. On the other hand, the distance preferred by North Americans may leave an Arab suspicious of intentions because of the lack of olfactory contact."[49]

The Muslim expression *Bukra insha Allah*—"Tomorrow if Allah wills"—explains much about the Arab culture and its approach to business transactions. A cultural clash typically occurs when an American tries to give an Arab a deadline. "I am going to Damascus tomorrow morning and will have to have my car tonight," is a sure way to get the mechanic to stop work," explains Hall, "because to give another person a deadline in this part of the world is to be rude, pushy, and demanding."[50] In such instances, the attitude toward time communicates as loudly as words.

In verbal interactions, managers must be aware of different patterns of Arab thought and communication. Compared to the direct, linear fashion of American communication, Arabs tend to meander: They start with social talk, discuss business for a while, loop round to social and general issues, then back to business, and so on.[51] American impatience and insistence on sticking to the subject will "cut off their loops," triggering confusion and dysfunction. Instead, westerners should accept that there will be considerable time spent on "small talk" and socializing, with frequent interruptions, before getting down to business.

Exhibit 11-5 illustrates some of the sources of noise that are likely to interfere in the communication process between Americans and Arabs.

For people doing business in the Middle East, the following are some useful guidelines for effective communication:

- Be patient. Recognize the Arab attitude toward time and hospitality—take time to develop friendship and trust, for these are prerequisites for any social or business transactions.
- Recognize that people and relationships matter more to Arabs than the job, company, or contract—conduct business personally, not by correspondence or telephone.
- Avoid expressing doubts or criticism when others are present—recognize the importance of honor and dignity to Arabs.
- Adapt to the norms of body language, flowery speech, and circuitous verbal patterns in the Middle East, and don't be impatient to "get to the point."
- Expect many interruptions in meetings, delays in schedules, and changes in plans.[52]

EXHIBIT 11-5 Miscommunication Between Americans and Arabs Caused by Cross-cultural Noise

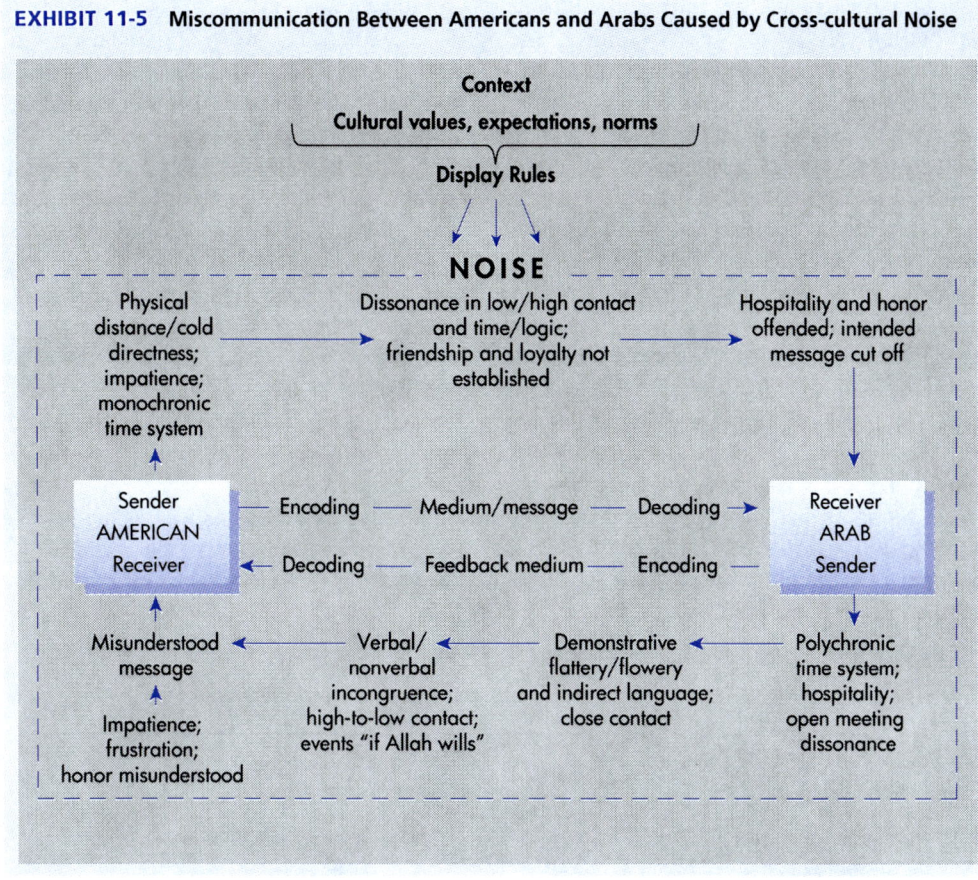

Communication Channels

In addition to the variables related to the sender and receiver of a message, the variables linked to the channel itself and the context of the message must be taken into consideration. These variables include fast or slow messages and information flows, as well as different types of media.

Information Systems Communication in organizations varies according to where and how it originates, the channels, and the speed at which it flows, whether it is formal or informal, and so forth. The type of organizational structure, the staffing policies, and the leadership style will affect the nature of an organization's information system.

As an international manager, it is useful to know where and how information originates and the speed at which it flows, both internally and externally. In centralized organizational structures, as in South America, most information originates from top managers. Workers take less responsibility to keep managers informed than in a typical company in the United States, where delegation results in information flowing from the staff to the managers. In a decision-making system in which many people are involved, such as the **ringi system** of consensus decision making in Japan, the expatriate needs to understand that there is a systematic pattern for information flow.

Context also affects information flow. In high-context cultures (such as in the Middle East), information spreads rapidly and freely because of the constant close contact and the implicit ties among people and organizations. Information flow is often informal. In low-context cultures (such as Germany or the United States), information is controlled and focused, and thus it does not flow so freely.[53] Compartmentalized roles and office layouts stifle information channels; information sources tend to be more formal.

It is crucial for an expatriate manager to find out how to tap into a firm's informal sources of information. In Japan, employees usually have a drink together on the way home from work, and this becomes an essential source of information. However, such communication networks are based on long-term relationships in Japan (and in other high-context cultures). The same information may not be readily available to "outsiders." A considerable barrier in Japan separates strangers from familiar friends, a situation that discourages communication.

Americans are more open and talk freely about almost anything, whereas Japanese will disclose little about their inner thoughts or private issues. Americans are willing to have a wide "public self," disclosing their inner reactions verbally and physically. In contrast, the Japanese prefer to keep their responses largely to their "private self." The Japanese expose only a small portion of their thoughts; they reduce, according to Barnlund, "the unpredictability and emotional intensity of personal encounters."[54] Cultural clashes between the public and private selves in intercultural communication between Americans and Japanese result when each party forces its cultural norms of communication on the other. In the American style, the American's cultural norms of explicit communication impose on the Japanese by invading the person's private self. The Japanese style of implicit communication causes a negative reaction from the American because of what is perceived as too much formality and ambiguity, which wastes time.[55]

Cultural variables in information systems and context underlie the many differences in communication style between Japanese and Americans. Exhibit 11-6 shows some specific differences. The Japanese *ningensei* ("human beingness") style of communication refers to the preference for humanity, reciprocity, a receiver orientation, and an underlying distrust of words and analytic logic.[56] The Japanese believe that true intentions are not readily revealed in words or contracts but are, in fact, masked by them. In contrast to the typical American's verbal agility and explicitness, Japanese behaviors and communications are directed to defend and give face for everyone concerned; to do so, they avoid public disagreements at all costs. In cross-cultural negotiations, this last point is essential.

EXHIBIT 11-6 Difference Between Japanese and American Communication Styles

Japanese Ningensei Style of Communication	U.S. Adversarial Style of Communication
1. Indirect verbal and nonverbal communication	1. More direct verbal and nonverbal communication
2. Relationship communication	2. More task communication
3. Discourages confrontational strategies	3. Confrontational strategies more acceptable
4. Strategically ambiguous communication	4. Prefers more to-the-point communication
5. Delayed feedback	5. More immediate feedback
6. Patient, longer-term negotiators	6. Shorter-term negotiators
7. Uses fewer words	7. Favors verbosity
8. Distrustful of skillful verbal communicators	8. Exalts verbal eloquence
9. Group orientation	9. More individualistic orientation
10. Cautious, tentative	10. More assertive, self-assured
11. Complementary communicators	11. More publicly critical communication
12. Softer, heart like logic	12. Harder, analytic logic preferred
13. Sympathetic, empathetic, complex use of pathos	13. Favors logos, reason
14. Expresses and decodes complex relational strategies and nuances	14. Expresses and decodes complex logos, cognitive nuances
15. Avoids decision making in public	15. Frequent decision making in public
16. Makes decisions in private venues, away from public eye	16. Frequent decision in public at negotiating tables
17. Decisions via *ringi* and *nemawashi* (complete consensus process)	17. Decisions by majority rule and public compromise is more commonplace
18. Uses go-betweens for decision making	18. More extensive use of direct person-to-person, player-to-player interaction for decisions
19. Understatement and hesitation in verbal and nonverbal communication	19. May publicly speak in superlatives, exaggerations, nonverbal projection

EXHIBIT 11-6 *(Continued)*

20. Uses qualifiers, tentativeness, humility as communicator	20. Favors fewer qualifiers, more ego-centered
21. Receiver/listening-centered	21. More speaker- and message-centered
22. Inferred meanings, looks beyond words to nuances, nonverbal communication	22. More face-value meaning, more denotative
23. Shy, reserved communicators	23. More publicly self-assertive
24. Distaste for purely business transactions	24. Prefers to "get down to business" or "nitty gritty"
25. Mixes business and social communication	25. Tends to keep business negotiating more separated from social communication
26. Utilizes *matomari* or "hints" for achieving group adjustment and saving face in negotiating	26. More directly verbalizes management's preference at negotiating tables
27. Practices *haragei* or "belly logic" and communication	27. Practices more linear, discursive, analytical logic; greater reverence for cognitive than for affective

Source: Reprinted from A. Goldman, "The Centrality of 'Ningensei' to Japanese Negotiating and Interpersonal Relationships: Implications for U.S. Japanese Communication," *International Journal of Intercultural Relations* 18, no. 1 (1994), with permission from Elsevier.

The speed with which we try to use information systems is another key variable that needs attention to avoid misinterpretation and conflict. Americans expect to give and receive information very quickly and clearly, moving through details and stages in a linear fashion to the conclusion. They usually use various media for fast messages—letters or emails giving all the facts and plans up front, faxes, and familiar relationships. In contrast, the French use the slower message channels of deep relationships, culture, and sometimes mediators to exchange information. A French written communication will be tentative, with subsequent letters slowly building up to a new proposal. The French preference for written communication, even for informal interactions, echoes the formality of their relationships—and results in a slowing down of message transmission that often seems unnecessary to Americans. Jean-Louis Reynal, a plant manager at Citröen, explains that "it wouldn't be too much of an exaggeration to say that, until they are written, until they are entrusted to the blackboard, the notepad, or the flip chart, ideas have no reality for the French manager. You could even say that writing is an indispensable aid to 'being' for us."[57]

In short, it behooves Americans to realize that, because most of the world exchanges information through slower message media, it is wise to schedule more time for transactions, develop patience, and learn to get at needed information in more subtle ways—after building rapport and taking time to observe the local system for exchanging information.

We have seen that cross-cultural misinterpretation can result from noise in the actual transmission of the message—the choice or speed of media. Interpreting the meaning of a message can thus be as much a function of the transmission channel (or medium) as it is of examining the message itself.

INFORMATION TECHNOLOGY: GOING GLOBAL AND ACTING LOCAL

All information is local; IT systems can connect every corner of the globe, but IT managers are learning they have to pay attention to regional differences.

COMPUTERWORLD[58]

Deploying B2B e-commerce technology [globally] . . . becomes exponentially more difficult because systems must address concerns not germane to domestic networks, such as language translation, currency conversion and even cultural differences.

INTERNETWEEK[59]

Using the Internet as a global medium for communication has enabled companies of all sizes to quickly develop a presence in many markets around the world—and, in fact, has enabled them to "go global." However, their global reach cannot alone translate into global business. Those companies are learning that they have to adapt their e-commerce and their enterprise resource planning (ERP) applications to regional idiosyncrasies beyond translation or content management issues; even asking for a name or an email address can incur resistance in many countries where people do not like to give out personal information.[60] While communication over the Internet is clearly not as personal as face-to-face cross-cultural communication, those transactions must still be regionalized and personalized to adjust to differences in language, culture, local laws, and business models, as well as differences in the level of development in the local telecommunications infrastructure. Yet, if the Internet is a global medium for communication, why do so many U.S. companies treat the Web as a U.S.-centric phenomenon? Giving preference to some geographic regions, languages, and cultures is "a short-sighted business decision that will result in diminished brand equity, market share, profits and global leadership."[61] With an annual predicted growth rate of 70 percent in non–English-language sites and usage, this soon puts English-language sites in the minority.[62]

It seems essential, then, that a global online strategy must also be multilocal. The impersonal nature of the Web must somehow be adapted to local cultures to establish relationships and create customer loyalty. Effective technological communication requires even more cultural sensitivity than face-to-face communication because of the inability to assess reactions and get feedback, or even to retain contact in many cases. It is still people, after all, who respond to and interact with other people through the medium of the Internet, and those people interpret and respond according to their own languages and cultures, as well as their local business practices and expectations. In Europe, for example, significant differences in business cultures and e-business technology have slowed e-business progress there. However, some companies are making progress in pan-European integration services, such as *leEurope*, which aims to cross language, currency, and cultural barriers. Specifically, *leEurope* is building a set of services "to help companies tie their back-end e-business systems together across European boundaries through aseries of mergers involving regional e-business integrators in more than a dozen countries."[63]

MANAGING CROSS-CULTURAL COMMUNICATION

Steps toward effective intercultural communication include the development of cultural sensitivity, careful encoding, selective transmission, careful decoding, and appropriate follow-up actions.

Developing Cultural Sensitivity

When acting as a sender, a manager must make it a point to know the receiver and to encode the message in a form that will most likely be understood as intended. On the manager's part, this requires an awareness of his or her own cultural baggage and how it affects the communication process. In other words, what kinds of behaviors does the message imply, and how will they be perceived by the receiver? The way to anticipate the most likely meaning that the receiver will attach to the message is to internalize honest cultural empathy with that person. What is the cultural background—the societal, economic, and organizational context—in which this communication is taking place? What are this person's expectations regarding the situation, what are the two parties' relative positions, and what might develop from this communication? What kinds of transactions and behaviors is this person used to? Cultural sensitivity is really just a matter of understanding the other person, the context, and how the person will respond to the context. Americans, unfortunately, have a rather negative reputation overseas of not being culturally sensitive. One not-for-profit group, called Business for Diplomatic Action, has the following advice for Americans when doing business abroad, in its attempts to counteract the stereotypical American traits such as boastfulness, loudness, and speed:

- **Read a map:** Familiarize yourself with the local geography to avoid making insulting mistakes.
- **Dress up:** In some countries, casual dress is a sign of disrespect
- **Talk small:** Talking about wealth, power, or status—corporate or personal—can create resentment.
- **No slang:** Even casual profanity is unacceptable.

- **Slow down:** Americans talk fast, eat fast, move fast, live fast. Many cultures do not.
- **Listen as much as you talk:** Ask people you're visiting about themselves and their way of life.
- **Speak lower and slower:** A loud voice is often perceived as bragging.
- **Religious restraint:** In many countries, religion is not a subject for public discussion.
- **Political restraint:** Steer clear of this subject. If someone is attacking U.S. politicians or policies, agree to disagree.[64]

Careful Encoding

In translating his or her intended meaning into symbols for cross-cultural communication, the sender must use words, pictures, or gestures that are appropriate to the receiver's frame of reference. Of course, language training is invaluable, but senders should also avoid idioms and regional sayings (such as "Go fly a kite" or "Foot the bill") in a translation, or even in English when speaking to a non-American who knows little English.

Literal translation, then, is a limited answer to language differences. Even for people in English-speaking countries, words may have different meanings. Ways to avoid problems are to speak slowly and clearly, avoid long sentences and colloquial expressions, and explain things in several different ways and through several media, if possible. However, even though English is in common use around the world for business transactions, the manager's efforts to speak the local language will greatly improve the climate. Sometimes people from other cultures resent the assumption by English-speaking executives that everyone else will speak English.

Language translation is only part of the encoding process; the message also is expressed in nonverbal language. In the encoding process, the sender must ensure congruence between the nonverbal and the verbal message. In encoding a message, therefore, it is useful to be as objective as possible and not to rely on personal interpretations. To further clarify their messages, managers can hand out written summaries of verbal presentations and use visual aids, such as graphs or pictures. A good general guide is to move slowly, wait, and take cues from the receivers.

Selective Transmission

The type of medium chosen for the message depends on the nature of the message, its level of importance, the context and expectations of the receiver, the timing involved, and the need for personal interaction, among other factors. Typical media include email, letters or memos, reports, meetings, telephone calls, teleconferences, videoconferences, or face-to-face conversations. The secret is to find out how communication is transmitted in the local organization—how much is downward versus upward or vertical versus horizontal, how the grapevine works, and so on. In addition, the cultural variables discussed earlier need to be considered: whether the receiver is from a high- or low-context culture, whether he or she is used to explicit or implicit communication, and what speed and routing of messages will be most effective.

For the most part, it is best to use face-to-face interaction for relationship building or for other important transactions, particularly in intercultural communications, because of the lack of familiarity between parties. Personal interactions give the manager the opportunity to get immediate verbal and visual feedback and to make rapid adjustments in the communication process.

International dealings are often long-distance, of course, limiting the opportunity for face-to-face communication. However, personal rapport can be established or enhanced through telephone calls or videoconferencing and through trusted contacts. Modern electronic media can be used to break down communication barriers by reducing waiting periods for information, clarifying issues, and allowing instant consultation. Global telecommunications and computer networks are changing the face of cross-cultural communication through the faster dissemination of information within the receiving organization. Ford Europe uses videoconferencing for engineers in Britain and Germany to consult about quality problems. Through the video monitors, they examine one another's engineering diagrams and usually find a solution that gets the factory moving again in a short time.

Careful Decoding of Feedback

Timely and effective feedback channels can also be set up to assess a firm's general communication about the progression of its business and its general management principles. The best means for getting accurate feedback is through face-to-face interaction because this allows the manager to hear, see, and immediately sense how a message is being interpreted. When visual feedback on important issues is not possible or appropriate, it is a good idea to use several means of attaining feedback, in particular, employing third parties.

Decoding is the process of translating the received symbols into the interpreted message. The main causes of incongruence are (1) the receiver misinterprets the message, (2) the receiver encodes his or her return message incorrectly, or (3) the sender misinterprets the feedback. Two-way communication is thus essential for important issues so that successive efforts can be made until an understanding has been achieved. Asking other colleagues to help interpret what is going on is often a good way to break a cycle of miscommunication.

Perhaps the most important means for avoiding miscommunication is to practice careful decoding by improving one's listening and observation skills. A good listener practices projective listening, or empathetic listening—listening without interruption or evaluation to the full message of the speaker, attempting to recognize the feelings behind the words and nonverbal cues, and understanding the speaker's perspective.

At the multinational corporation (MNC) level, avenues of communication and feedback among parent companies and subsidiaries can be kept open through telephone calls, regular meetings and visits, reports, and plans, all of which facilitate cooperation, performance control, and the smooth running of the company. Communication among far-flung operations can be best managed by setting up feedback systems and liaison people. The headquarters people should maintain considerable flexibility in cooperating with local managers and allowing them to deal with the local context as they see fit.

Follow-up Actions

Managers communicate through both action and inaction. Therefore, to keep open the lines of communication, feedback, and trust, managers must follow through with action on what has been discussed and then agreed upon—typically a contract, which is probably the most important formal business communication. Unfortunately, the issue of contract follow-through is a particularly sensitive one across cultures because of the different interpretations regarding what constitutes a contract (perhaps a handshake, perhaps a full legal document) and what actions should result. Trust, future communications, and future business are based on such interpretations, and it is up to managers to understand them and to follow through on them.

The management of cross-cultural communication depends largely on a manager's personal abilities and behavior. Those behaviors that researchers indicate to be most important to intercultural communication effectiveness (ICE) are listed here, as reviewed by Ruben:

1. Respect (conveyed through eye contact, body posture, voice tone, and pitch)
2. Interaction posture (the ability to respond to others in a descriptive, nonevaluative, and nonjudgmental way)
3. Orientation to knowledge (recognizing that one's knowledge, perception, and beliefs are valid only for oneself and not for everyone else)
4. Empathy
5. Interaction management
6. Tolerance for ambiguity
7. Other-oriented role behavior (one's capacity to be flexible and to adopt different roles for the sake of greater group cohesion and group communication)[65]

Whether at home or abroad, certain personal capabilities facilitate effective intercultural communication; these abilities can help the expatriate to adapt to the host country and enable productive working relations to develop in the long term. Researchers have established a relationship between personality traits and behaviors and the ability to adapt to the host-country's cultural environment.[66] What is seldom pointed out, however, is that communication is the mediating factor between those behaviors and the relative level of adaptation the expatriate achieves. The communication process facilitates cross-cultural adaptation, and, through this process, expatriates learn the dominant communication patterns of the host society. Therefore, we can link those personality factors shown by research to ease adaptation with those necessary for effective intercultural communication.

Kim has consolidated the research findings of these characteristics into two categories: (1) **openness**—traits such as open-mindedness, tolerance for ambiguity, and extrovertedness; and (2) **resilience**—traits such as having an internal locus of control, persistence, a tolerance of ambiguity, and resourcefulness.[67] These personality factors, along with the expatriate's cultural and racial identity and the level of preparedness for change, comprise that person's potential for adaptation. The level of preparedness can be improved by the manager before his or her assignment by gathering information about the host country's verbal and nonverbal communication patterns and norms of behavior. Kim explains that the major variables that affect the level of communication competence achieved between the host and the expatriate are the adaptive predisposition of the expatriate and the conditions of receptivity and conformity to pressure in the host environment. These factors affect the process of personal and social communication, and, ultimately, the adaptation outcome. Explains Kim, "Three aspects of strangers' adaptive change—increased functional fitness, psychological health, and intercultural identity—have been identified as direct consequences of prolonged communication-adaptation experiences in the host society."[68]

In identifying personal and behavioral specifics that facilitate ICE, however, we cannot lose sight of the whole picture. We must remember the basic principle of contingency management, which is that managers operate in a system of many interacting variables in a dynamic context. Studies show that situational factors—such as the physical environment, time constraints, degree of structure, feelings of boredom or overwork, and anonymity—are strong influences on intercultural communication competence.[69]

It is this interdependence of many variables that makes it difficult for intercultural researchers to isolate and identify factors for success. Although managers try to understand and control up front as many factors as possible that will lead to management effectiveness, often they only find out what works from the results of their decisions.

CONCLUSION

Effective intercultural communication is a vital skill for international managers and domestic managers of multicultural workforces. Because miscommunication is much more likely to occur among people from different countries or racial backgrounds than among those from similar backgrounds, it is important to be alert to how culture is reflected in communication—in particular through the development of cultural sensitivity and an awareness of potential sources of cultural noise in the communication process. A successful international manager is thus attuned to these variables and is flexible enough to adjust his or her communication style to best address the intended receivers—that is, to do it "their way."

Cultural variables and the manner in which culture is communicated underlie the processes of negotiation and decision making. How do people around the world negotiate: What are their expectations and their approach to negotiations? What is the importance of understanding negotiation and decision-making processes in other countries?.

Summary of Key Points

1. Communication is an inherent part of a manager's role, taking up the majority of the manager's time on the job. Effective intercultural communication largely determines the success of international transactions or the output of a culturally diverse workforce.
2. Culture is the foundation of communication, and communication transmits culture. Cultural variables that can affect the communication process by influencing a person's perceptions include attitudes, social organizations, thought patterns, roles, language, nonverbal language, and time.
3. Language conveys cultural understandings and social norms from one generation to the next. Body language, or nonverbal communication, is behavior that communicates without words. It accounts for 65 to 93 percent of interpreted communication.

4. Types of nonverbal communication around the world are kinesic behavior, proxemics, paralanguage, and object language.
5. Effective cross-cultural communication must take account of whether the receiver is from a country with a monochronic or a polychronic time system.
6. Variables related to channels of communication include high- and low-context cultures, fast or slow messages and information flows, and various types of media.
7. In high-context cultures, feelings and messages are implicit and must be accessed through an understanding of the person and the system. In low-context cultures, feelings and thoughts are expressed, and information is more readily available.
8. The effective management of intercultural communication necessitates the development of cultural sensitivity, careful encoding, selective transmission, careful decoding, and follow-up actions.
9. Certain personal abilities and behaviors facilitate adaptation to the host country through skilled intercultural communication.
10. Communication via the Internet must still be localized to adjust to differences in language, culture, local laws, and business models.

Discussion Questions

1. How does culture affect the process of attribution in communication? Can you relate this to some experiences you have had with your classmates?
2. What is stereotyping? Give some examples. How might people stereotype you? How does a sociotype differ from a stereotype?
3. What is the relationship between language and culture? How is it that people from different countries who speak the same language may still miscommunicate?
4. Give some examples of cultural differences in the interpretation of body language. What is the role of such nonverbal communication in business relationships?
5. Explain the differences between monochronic and polychronic time systems. Use some examples to illustrate their differences and the role of time in intercultural communication.
6. Explain the differences between high- and low-context cultures, giving some examples. What are the differential effects on the communication process?
7. Discuss the role of information systems in a company, how and why they vary from country to country, and the effects of these variations.

Application Exercises

1. Form groups in your class—multicultural groups, if possible. Have each person make notes about his or her perceptions of (1) Mexican-Americans, (2) Native Americans, (3) African-Americans, and (4) Americans of European descent. Discuss your notes and draw conclusions about common stereotypes. Discuss any differences and why stereotyping occurs.
2. Invite some foreign students to your class. Ask them to bring photographs, slides, and so forth of people and events in their native countries. Have them explain the meanings of various nonverbal cues, such as gestures, dress, voice inflections, architecture, and events. Discuss with them any differences between their explanations and the attributions you assigned to those cues.
3. Interview a faculty member or a businessperson who has worked abroad. Ask him or her to identify factors that facilitated or inhibited adaptation to the host environment. Ask whether more preparation could have eased the transition and what, if anything, that person would do differently before another trip.

Experiential Exercise: Script for Juan Perillo and Jean Moore

Scene I: February 15, San Juan, Puerto Rico

JUAN: Welcome back to Puerto Rico, Jean. It is good to have you here in San Juan again. I hope that your trip from Dayton was a smooth one.

JEAN: Thank you, Juan. It's nice to be back here where the sun shines. Fred sends his regards and also asked me to tell you how important it is that we work out a firm production schedule for the next three months. But first, how is your family? All doing well, I hope.

JUAN: My wife is doing very well, but my daughter, Marianna, broke her arm and has to have surgery to repair the bone. We are very worried about that because the surgeon says she may have to have several operations. It is very difficult to think about my poor little daughter in the operating room. She was out playing with some other children when it happened. You know how roughly children sometimes play with each other. It's really amazing that they don't have more injuries. Why, just last week, my son . . .

JEAN: Of course I'm very sorry to hear about little Marianna, but I'm sure everything will go well with the surgery. Now, shall we start work on the production schedule?

JUAN: Oh, yes, of course, we must get started on the production schedule.

JEAN: Fred and I thought that June 1 would be a good cutoff date for the first phase of the schedule. And we also thought that 100 A-type computers would be a reasonable goal for that phase. We know that you have some new assemblers whom you are training, and that you've had some problems getting parts from your suppliers in the past few months. But we're sure you have all those problems worked out by now and that you are back to full production capability. So, what do you think? Is 100 A-type computers produced by June 1 a reasonable goal for your people?

JUAN: (hesitates a few seconds before replying): You want us to produce 100 of the newly designed A-type computers by June 1? Will we also be producing our usual number of Z-type computers, too?

JEAN: Oh, yes. Your regular production schedule would remain the same as it's always been. The only difference is that you would be producing the new A-type computers, too. I mean, after all, you have a lot of new employees, and you have all the new manufacturing and assembling equipment that we have in Dayton. So, you're as ready to make the new product as we are.

JUAN: Yes, that's true. We have the new equipment, and we've just hired a lot of new assemblers who will be working on the A-type computer. I guess there's no reason we can't meet the production schedule you and Fred have come up with.

JEAN: Great, great. I'll tell Fred you agree with our decision and will meet the goal of 100 A-type computers by June 1. He'll be delighted to know that you can deliver what he was hoping for. And, of course, Juan, that means that you'll be doing just as well as the Dayton plant.

Scene II: May 1, San Juan, Puerto Rico

JEAN: Hello, Juan. How are things here in Puerto Rico? I'm glad to have the chance to come back and see how things are going.

JUAN: Welcome, Jean. It's good to have you here. How is your family?

JEAN: Oh, they're fine, just fine. You know, Juan, Fred is really excited about that big order we just got from the Defense Department for 50 A-type computers. They want them by June 10, so we will ship them directly to Washington from San Juan as the computers come off your assembly line. Looks like it's a good thing we set your production goal at 100 A-type computers by June 1, isn't it?

JUAN: Um, yes, that was certainly a good idea.

JEAN: So, tell me, have you had any problems with the new model? How are your new assemblers working out? Do you have any suggestions for changes in the manufacturing specs? How is the new quality control program working with this model? We're always looking for ways to improve, you know, and we appreciate any ideas you can give us.

JUAN: Well, Jean, there is one thing . . .

JEAN: Yes? What is that?

JUAN: Well, Jean, we have had a few problems with the new assemblers. Three of them have had serious illnesses in their families and have had to take off several days at a time to nurse a sick child or elderly parent. And another one was involved in a car accident and was in the hospital for several days. And you remember my daughter's surgery? Well, her arm didn't mend properly, and we had to take her to Houston for additional consultations and therapy. But, of course, you and Fred knew about that.

JEAN: Yes, we were aware that you had had some personnel problems and that you and your wife had had to go to Houston with Marianna. But what does that have to do with the 50 A-type computers for the Defense Department?

JUAN: Well, Jean, because of all these problems, we have had a few delays in the production schedule. Nothing serious, but we are a little bit behind our schedule.

JEAN: How far behind is "a little bit"? What are you trying to tell me, Juan? Will you have 50 more A-type computers by June 1 to ship to Washington to fill the Defense Department order?

JUAN: Well, I certainly hope we will have that number ready to ship. You know how difficult it can be to predict a precise number for manufacturing, Jean. You probably have many of these same problems in the Dayton plant, don't you?

Source: L. Catlin and T. White, *International Business: Cultural Sourcebook and Case Studies* (Cincinnati, Ohio: South-Western, 1994), used with permission.

Exercise Questions

1. Drawing from this chapter, explain in detail what went wrong for Jean in Puerto Rico. Could this have been avoided? What should she have done differently?

2. Replay the role of Jean and Juan during their conversation, establishing a more constructive communication and management style than Jean did previously.

Internet Resources

Visit the Deresky Companion Website at www.pearsonhighered.com/deresky for this chapter's Internet resources.

CASE STUDY

Elizabeth Visits GPC's French Subsidiary

Elizabeth Moreno is looking out the window from her business-class seat somewhere over the Indian Ocean on Thai Air en route to Paris's Orly International Airport from the Philippines, where she has just spent a week of meetings and problem solving in a pharmaceutical subsidiary of the Global Pharmaceutical Company (GPC).

GPC has the lion's share of the worldwide market in ethical pharmaceutical products. Ethical drugs are those that can be purchased only through a physician's prescription. In the United States, GPC has research and manufacturing sites in New York, New Jersey, Pennsylvania, and Michigan. The company also has subsidiaries in Canada, Puerto Rico, Australia, the Philippines, Brazil, England, and France. GPC has its administrative headquarters in Pennsylvania.

Because of the geographically dispersed locations of its subsidiaries, GPC's top scientists and key managers log thousands of jet miles a year visiting various offices and plants. Its top specialists and executives regularly engage in multisite real-time video and telephone conferences, and they also use electronic mail, faxes, modems, and traditional mail to keep in touch with key personnel.

Despite these technological advances, face-to-face meetings and on-site consultations are used widely. In the case of the French subsidiary, nothing can take the place of face-to-face consultations. The French manager is suspicious of figures in the balance sheet, of the telephone, of his subordinates, of what he reads in the newspaper, and of what Americans tell him in confidence. In contrast, the American trusts all these. This is the reason GPC regularly sends its scientists and executives to France.

Elizabeth Moreno is one of the key specialists within GPC. Her expertise in chemical processing is widely known not only within her company but also in the pharmaceutical industry worldwide. She has been working at GPC for more than twelve years since finishing her advanced degree in chemistry from a university in the Midwest. While working for GPC, she has been given more and more responsibilities leading to her current position as vice president of chemical development and processing.

From a hectic visit in the Philippines, her next assignment is to visit the French subsidiary plant for one week to study a problem with shelf-life testing of one of its newest anti-allergy capsules. It seems that the product's active ingredient is degrading sooner than the expiration date. During her stay, she will conduct training for chemists in state-of-the-art techniques for testing and for training local managers in product statistical quality control. These techniques are now currently used in other GPC locations.

To prepare for her foreign assignments, Elizabeth attended a standard three-hour course given by her company's human resource management department on dealing with cross-cultural issues. Moreover, she recalls reading from a book on French management about the impersonal nature of French business relations. This was so much in contrast with what she just has experienced during her visit to the Philippine subsidiary. The French tend to regard authority as residing in the role and not in the person. It is by the power of the position that a French manager gets things done. With this knowledge, she knows that her expertise and her position as vice president will see her through the technical aspects of the meetings that are lined up for the few days she will be in Paris.

French managers view their work as an intellectual challenge that requires application of individual brainpower. What matters to them is the opportunity to show one's ability to grasp complex issues, analyze problems, manipulate ideas, and evaluate solutions.

There are a few challenges for Elizabeth on this assignment. She is not fluent in French. Her only exposure to France and the language was a two-week vacation with her husband in Paris a couple of years ago. However, in her highly technical field, the universal language is English. Thus, she believes she will not have much difficulty communicating with the French management to get her assignment successfully completed.

Americans place high value on training and education. In the United States, the field of management has principles that are generally applicable and can be taught and learned. In contrast, the French place more emphasis on the person who can adapt to any situation by virtue of his intellectual quality. Expertise and intellectual ability are inherent in the individual and cannot be acquired simply through training or education.

It appears that Elizabeth will be encountering very different ways of doing business in France. While she thought about the challenges ahead, her plane landed at Orly International Airport. She whisked through customs and immigration without any delays. No limousine was waiting for her curbside at the arrival. Instead she took the train to downtown Paris and checked into an apartment hotel that was reserved for her in advance of her arrival.

After a week in Paris, she is expected back in her home office to prepare reports to GPC management about her foreign assignments.

Case Questions

1. Drawing from your understanding of verbal and nonverbal communication patterns from this chapter, explain what Elizabeth Moreno can do to establish her position in front of French managers. How can she get them to help her accomplish her assignment in five days?
2. What should Elizabeth know about high-context versus low-context cultures in Europe? How can this knowledge help her be successful there?
3. What should Elizabeth include in her report, and what should be the manner in which it is communicated, so that future executives and scientists avoid communications pitfalls?
4. How can technical language differ from everyday language in corporate communications? Explain.

Source: This case was prepared by Edwin J. Portugal, MBA, Ph.D., who teaches multinational management at State University of New York–Potsdam. It is intended to be used as a basis for discussion on the complexity of multicultural management and not to illustrate effective versus ineffective management styles. Copyright © 2004 by Edwin J. Portugal.

12 Communicating in a Diverse World

Learning Objectives

Upon completion of this chapter, you will be able to:

- Explain how communication and culture interrelate.
- Discuss the effects of electronic communication.
- Explain the relationship between diversity consciousness and communication.
- List and give examples of barriers to effective communication.
- Define and give examples of "hot buttons."
- Describe at least five strategies for communicating inclusively.

I think that people within my culture and from other cultures may mistake my lack of eye contact for dishonesty. I feel that staring into someone's eyes lets them see into my soul so instead I focus on something else when speaking.

I usually fold my arms and I don't walk around smiling. People always comment to me "Is it that bad?" or "Smile; there is nothing to be sad about." I have been told that I look unapproachable because of my stance and facial expressions, but I think I am one of the most approachable people on the streets.

One day, a man called my house taking a survey and he started asking me questions. Before I got a chance to tell him my race, he was already writing down that I was White. I interrupted and told him that I was Black and he apologized and told me that I sound White. I was wondering what Whites sound like.

A communication style I have that other cultures may find offensive is my openness about personal feelings or experiences. I have to be careful not to overwhelm people with "too much information" about a certain subject. This tends to make many people feel uncomfortable. I have learned to think before I speak; however, it is sometimes difficult.

(continued)

> *(continued)*
>
> When I smile, there are men who think I'm "coming on to them." All I'm trying to do is be friendly.
>
> I have felt like I have represented all Kenyans in all my classes since I'm the only one from that part of the world, standing out sometimes when I dress in African dress or when I speak. There is pin drop silence every time I begin to speak. All eyes are on me when a dub of British is detected in my accent. I wonder what goes through their minds, from my pronunciation to the spelling of certain words. After the first day of class when I introduce myself I face questions about Africa on a daily basis—questions often of places and things I don't even know.
>
> —Other perspectives

Communication takes place whenever meaning is attached to a message. The meaning may be intended or unintended. By developing our diversity consciousness and, in particular, our communication skills, we become more aware of the messages we are sending and receiving. This empowers us and enriches our lives. However, poor communication skills can make it difficult for us to achieve our goals and can alienate, confuse, and hurt others. Communication skills are one specific form of diversity skills.

COMMUNICATION AND CULTURE

Communication and culture interrelate. Culture is reflected in the way we communicate, and the way we communicate shapes our culture. Because of our upbringing, we attach specific meanings to what people say and do. These meanings may vary within and between cultures. As our work, school, and community environments become more multicultural, it is increasingly important to become more conscious of our cultural differences as well as our similarities. This, in turn, will enable us to become more sensitive to the cultural context of one's words and more proficient in using language precisely and sensitively.

Communication is the process by which people transfer information, ideas, attitudes, and feelings to each other. The word *communicate* comes from the Latin verb *communicare*, which means to share. When people use and share symbols with others who can understand their meanings, they are communicating. A **symbol** is anything that represents something else. Symbols take many forms. Spoken and written words probably come to mind, but we also communicate with nonverbal symbols. Examples of nonverbal communication, or what we refer to as body language, include gestures, facial expressions, body positioning, touching, and eye movements.

People throughout the world send messages by a vast array of body language. In *Gestures: The Do's and Taboos of Body Language Around the World,* author Roger Axtell discusses **kinesics,** the study of body movements as a means of communication. He cites studies by a number of researchers, including Mario Pei and Ray Birdwhistell. Pei estimates that humans can produce approximately 700,000 physical

FIGURE 12.1 What might this gesture mean?
Source: © Brooks Kraft/Corbis.

signs. According to Birdwhistell, the face alone is capable of 250,000 expressions.¹ By studying the kinesics of different cultures, anthropologists have determined that people from different cultures may signal each other in very different ways.

Body language throughout the world is culturally specific. If a gesture is **culturally specific,** it may mean one thing to one culture but something quite different to another. During his presidency, former President Bush, a native of Texas, made a "hook 'em horns" gesture that is well known among University of Texas fans (see Fig. 12.1).

Unfortunately, the gesture is culturally specific, and carries different meanings in other regions of the world. Some Norwegians saw this gesture as the president of the United States making the "sign of the devil." Some people in Central and South America were shocked. To them, the president was indicating someone's wife was unfaithful. A Rand Corporation report, commissioned by the U.S. Joint Forces Command, cited this gesture as one example of how misinterpreted symbols have negatively impacted the U.S. government's credibility elsewhere.

Communication allows us to dialogue and feel a sense of togetherness. Also, it can illustrate our differences and drive a wedge between us. This is especially true of intercultural communication. **Intercultural communication** refers to a process in which messages created in one culture must be processed and interpreted in another culture. Misunderstandings can also occur between people who may be different in other ways. Maybe they have different styles of communication. Perhaps differences in gender, age, marital status, or social class make it difficult to connect with someone.

Miscommunication often results because we attach different meanings to the same symbol. As an example, a few years ago Nike marketed some of its products by displaying their logo, the word *Air*, in stylized letters. They soon discovered that the logo resembles the Arabic word for Allah. Under threat of a worldwide boycott of its product by Muslims, Nike agreed to recall and stop selling any shoes with this logo. Muslims found this logo to be offensive, especially when it appeared on shoes. By communicating a totally different message than they intended, Nike learned a costly and important lesson. According to one spokesperson for Nike, "Our company has to be more vigilant and work more with communities on issues of sensitivity."[2]

Men and Women, Divided by Language

Deborah Tannen is a professor of *linguistics*, the science of language. In her research, Tannen focuses on the different communication styles of men and women. She has written extensively on this subject. Her books, entitled *You Just Don't Understand*, *That's Not What I Meant*, and *Talking from 9 to 5* offer some examples of gender differences.

- Men engage in report talk, women in rapport talk. *Report talk* is a way of showing one's knowledge and skill. *Rapport talk* allows one to share with others and develop relationships.
- When making requests, women tend to be indirect. A female supervisor might ask, "Could you do this by 5 P.M.?" Something more direct and to the point is more typical of a male supervisor: "This needs to be done by 5 P.M."
- Women have a greater *information focus*. They do not hesitate to ask questions in order to understand something. Men have more of an *image focus*. Even though men may be unclear about an issue, they may forgo asking questions to preserve their image or reputation.
- Women often say "I'm sorry" to express concern about something. Men, however, may interpret this to mean that women are accepting blame or responsibility. This is not at all what women have in mind.
- People tend to judge men for what they say and do, and women by how they look and dress.

Tannen makes the point that these differences do not apply to all men or women in all situations. Furthermore, she states that no one's communication style is absolute. Each person's style may change in response to social context and others' styles. By realizing that differences such as these may exist, we lessen the chances of miscommunication and conflict.

Most of us think of ourselves as literate. Because of our educational background, we can read and write. But we are literate only in a particular cultural environment. In another setting within our society or abroad, we may have no idea how to communicate ideas and feelings.

There are a lot of beautiful, favorite places in any language in which you feel yourself at home. In English, I don't have such a place yet. All phrases come out from my mouth, rough and heavy . . . the words fall with plops on the floor, like ugly frogs. And I am so waiting for the butterfly.

—Another perspective

FIGURE 12.2 Students at Gallaudet University communicate with each other between classes.

Source: Courtesy of the Office of Public Relations, Gallaudet University, Washington, D.C.

Imagine sitting in a classroom at Gallaudet University in Washington, D.C., the world's only accredited four-year liberal arts university for deaf and hard-of-hearing people. In *Seeing Voices: A Journey Into the World of the Deaf,* Oliver Sacks describes his first visit to Gallaudet. "I had never before seen an entire community of the deaf, nor had I quite realized (even though I knew this theoretically) that Sign might indeed be a complete language—a language equally suitable for making love or speeches, for flirtations or mathematics. I had to see philosophy and chemistry classes in Sign . . . I had to see the wonderful social scene in the student bar, with hands flying in all directions as a hundred separate conversations proceeded."[4] (see Fig. 12.2).

Sign language, a visual form of communication using hand shapes and movements to talk or to express an idea, is not uniform or universal. Contrary to popular thought, deaf people all over the world cannot communicate with each other. Sign languages, which have been around since the beginning of recorded history, are as distinct and differentiated as spoken languages. Hundreds of different sign languages exist, including American, British, Mayan, French, and Chinese.

Linguistic diversity refers to the many languages spoken in the United States and throughout the world. Some people speak only one language; others speak more than one. We refer to people who are able to speak two languages fluently as **bilingual,** and those capable of speaking more than two as **multilingual.** Language differences and the way we view these differences affect our achievement. Although proficiency in English is critically important, more and more research shows that fluency in more than one language can enhance one's marketability and job performance.

Perhaps this explains why the CEO of General Motors Corporation asked his director of Diversity Marketing and Sales to modify the beginning of her presentation to a large gathering of car dealers. The director, who is bilingual, was asked to speak in Spanish for the first five minutes. None of the dealers spoke Spanish fluently.

Think of those situations in which coworkers, customers, or acquaintances do not speak "your language." How do you feel, and how do you think they feel? In circumstances such as this, we are apt to feel a range of emotions, including inadequacy, humiliation, and frustration. These are not feelings that make you want to do business with someone. Clearly, the CEO wanted these dealers to experience what it is like when people do not reach out to you and adjust to language differences.

Individuals who speak a language other than English may encounter **linguicism,** a relatively new term that refers to discrimination based on language. How do you feel when you enter a particular class for the first time and you are met by an instructor or teaching assistant who is bilingual and speaks English with an unfamiliar accent? When you are in a group with a number of ESL (English as a Second Language) students, do you take the time to listen carefully and encourage full participation from everyone? Do you accept responsibility for making sure that you understand what is being communicated? When you don't understand, are you comfortable asking people to repeat themselves until you do?

Some of us are apt to view situations such as these as problems rather than challenges. Although communication with the teacher or students just described might be difficult for a period of time, persistence as well as good listening skills can help a great deal. Also, consider what they have to offer. Studies show that people who speak more than one language have higher levels of *cognitive flexibility,* meaning they can adjust more easily to different situations. Someone who is bilingual or multilingual may be better able to share a variety of world perspectives.

> *Students tell me I have an accent. I usually tell them they have an accent too.*
>
> —Another perspective

ELECTRONIC COMMUNICATION

Electronic communication is the imparting or interchange of information through technology, such as cell phones and computers. The capabilities of electronic communication are expanding rapidly. Computer technology is transforming electronic communication. College professors use the Internet to post syllabi, class notes, related links, and other necessary information. At a number of universities, lectures given in the classroom are almost immediately available on handheld media players and personal computers. Some professors have launched "virtual office hours," enabling them to help students anywhere and at any time, via text or microphone.

In the workplace, employees telecommute from home or any other location. Unlike the office setting of the past, they communicate by fax, e-mail, cell phones, PDAs, and smartphones. Wherever work takes place, advances in technology have improved communication for people with disabilities. For instance, texting has the benefit of being interactive as well as 100 percent visual. Thus, many deaf and hard-of-hearing people prefer texting because it is more practical and faster than a text pager or TTY (Text Telephone), an electronic device providing text communication via a telephone line.

As more and more people throughout the world learn to use new technologies, new communication problems arise. Because Internet communication relies primarily on text, such as e-mail, blogs, and texting, people cannot rely on other cues, such as tone of voice or gestures. We do not necessarily know anything about who is sending the message and his or her position, cultural background, or even the person's mood. In fact, an individual is free to create a new identity or a number of different identities. A person can create a new virtual self by becoming another race, age, or profession, assuming a whole new personality, and keeping his or her personal data hidden from others. For instance, people can communicate through sites where they represent themselves using an avatar that may not look anything like them. In his book, *Interaction Ritual: Essays on Face to Face Interaction,* Erving Goffman calls this **impression management,** the ways in which people attempt to control the impressions they make on others and how others see them.[5]

Electronic messages may result in misunderstandings, name calling, and hard feelings if people are unfamiliar with certain rules of etiquette and cyber shorthand. For example, Internet etiquette defines communicating in all capital letters as YELLING. Some people, who like using "all caps" because they find it easier, do not realize that they may be offending others. Abbreviated messages, such as g2g ("got to go"), lol ("laughing out loud"), and btw ("by the way") may not be understood by others. Uncertainties also arise because rules governing electronic communication differ depending on the organization or group. As an example, some workplaces permit personal messages while others do not. Many organizations review every message for inappropriate material.

What are the implications of new forms of electronic communication? Consider the networking that took place in the immediate aftermath of the Virginia Tech shootings, far ahead of coverage by news organizations. The college community and friends, families, and others used cell phones, instant messaging, Facebook, and other means to obtain and relay information. Use of this technology allowed so many to communicate instantaneously and give comfort to one another.

The Internet offers a diversity and wealth of information as well as misinformation. Distinguishing between accurate information and hoaxes, scams, lies, and other inaccurate information is difficult. On the Internet, information travels so quickly and so much information gets produced. Anyone and any group, for example, can write a blog and consciously or unconsciously inject their biases or points of view. In spite of the Web's capacity for spreading misinformation, it also can be used to verify information. When confronted with a "fact" that seems "too good to be true," we can use the Web to authenticate what we find, by checking sources and gathering additional information from around the world.

Some see this form of communication as a vehicle for breaking down barriers, expanding social networks, and promoting the diffusion of language and culture in general. **Cultural diffusion** refers to the spread of objects and ideas from one culture to another. Each year, the Internet is becoming more multicultural. Browsers now allow for instant translation of Web pages written in almost any foreign language. As mentioned earlier, Web developers have discovered a tremendous market for multilingual websites. To see some of the Web's most innovative multicultural and multilingual sites (Best Global Website Award winners), visit http://www.bestglobalwebsiteaward.com. Others view the impact differently. According to former Brown University president Vartan Gregorian, "What is being created is . . . the ability to retreat to small communities of the like-minded, where we are safe not only from unnecessary interactions with those whose ideas and attitudes are not like our own, but also from having to relate our interests and results to other communities."[6] Blogs allow people with similar interests or agendas to gravitate to each other. This can have positive or negative consequences. As an example, the Net can bring together people who are looking for support and current information about a particular disease or disability. It can also serve as a safe haven for hate groups. Therefore, the Internet is a tool we can use to access other perspectives and worlds or isolate ourselves even further.

> ### E-Mail Privacy?
>
> Many employees converse casually by e-mail each day. In many instances, they mistakenly assume that their messages are private. Consequently they often say things they would not communicate in writing or discuss in public. This includes racist, sexist, and other derogatory messages. Many companies routinely save all e-mail messages. These saved messages are now being used to provide evidence in lawsuits.
>
> Experts say that e-mail is a matter of official record. It is no different than a memo written on company letterhead. Consequently, jokes or other offensive messages circulated through a company's e-mail system may constitute evidence of discrimination.
>
> Energy giant Chevron paid a $2.2 million settlement to employees who sued, claiming that sexually harassing e-mails created a hostile work environment. A Washington, D.C., police investigation turned up hundreds of vulgar, racist, and homophobic e-mail messages written by officers. Officers' remarks were cross-referenced with civilian complaints to determine whether any of the messages indicated illegal actions. Increasingly, organizations are responding to inappropriate e-mail by creating policies regarding e-mail usage and monitoring messages with a variety of software capable of scanning offensive words and phrases.

Business and educational publications describe the effects of communicating via computers using terms such as *empowerment* and *inclusiveness*. There are a number of reasons for this. When conferencing through the Internet, a person with relatively little status can be empowered. This same person's status may be much more of a consideration in a face-to-face meeting. In face-to-face groups, higher-status people tend to talk more, and what they say is assumed to be more important. However, numerous research studies show that the flow of communication online is more evenly distributed and respected, regardless of who occupies what status.

In their book, *Connections: New Ways of Working in the Networked Organization,* Sproull and Kiesler describe a study of decision making by college students: "When pairs of graduate students and undergraduates met face-to-face to decide their joint project, the pairs were likely to choose the topic preferred by the graduate student." When the decision was made via computers, each person's choice was equally likely to be chosen.[7]

Taking a course online may offer a number of advantages. Students who are for any reason unable to attend school physically can continue their studies. Online courses facilitate lifelong learning regardless of age (see Fig. 12.3). In general, students taking

FIGURE 12.3 Computer literacy has become a necessity for workers of all ages.

these courses have more time to ask and respond to questions. Discussion boards, where members of a class can communicate freely with each other at their own pace, promote inclusive communication. Learning is *asynchronous,* meaning students can interact in the "classroom" at any time. Consequently, they never have to miss a class. Much of their identities remain hidden or anonymous. As a result, people ask questions online that they would not ask face to face. People may project themselves in any way they want. In this kind of communication, race, gender, and other dimensions of diversity become less relevant. The message is more important than the messenger.

DIVERSITY CONSCIOUSNESS AND COMMUNICATION

The development of diversity consciousness occurs in six areas. These areas help us understand the communication process. For example, if we are to communicate effectively, we need to have a sense of who we are individually and culturally. Additionally, we need to broaden our perspectives and develop an understanding of people from a variety of backgrounds. Finally, we need to apply and improve those skills that allow us to connect with others.

> *Knowledge of languages helps us to extend our circle of friends.*
> —Another perspective

Areas of Development: Diversity Consciousness and Communication

Your communication skills will improve as you become more conscious of diversity. As discussed earlier, there are six areas of development: (1) examining ourselves and our world, (2) expanding our knowledge of others and their worlds, (3) stepping outside of ourselves, (4) gauging the level of the playing field, (5) checking up on ourselves, and (6) following through. Each of the areas, and its implications for effective communication, follows.

Examining Ourselves and Our World

Before we begin to make sense of communication outside our culture, we need to develop awareness of our own communication style and why we communicate the way we do. Our individual and cultural backgrounds profoundly influence the way we communicate. The most obvious example is the language we learn and use. It is easy to take our own language for granted and assume that everybody interprets words and gestures in the same way. What about the words *you* use? If you are majoring in computers, your vocabulary consists of terms such as *gigs* and *terrabytes, OS, motherboard,* and *cards*. When you use these terms with people who are not familiar with computers, how do they react? In general, is communication problematic between people who are and are not computer savvy?

Even material culture can be interpreted in many ways. **Material culture** is that which we create and can see, touch, or feel. Consider the clothes you wear. What do they communicate to different people in different settings? How do they connect to your culture? For example, what does a pair of $200 jeans symbolize? Does it symbolize the same thing to people of varying ages?

International events can alter the meaning of material culture. The hijab or head scarf, worn by some Muslim women as an expression of female modesty, has taken on added significance in the aftermath of the terrorist attacks on the World Trade Center and the Pentagon. As evidenced by the following comments made by middle school students who attended a Muslim school in the United States, the hijab took on new meaning after September 11, 2001.

> "Before September 11, when we wore scarves, they made us feel special. Now we're just paranoid."
>
> "People, because of our scarves, they think we're something we're not."
>
> "Under our scarves, we're just like other girls. We like to do our hair, and we like to go shopping."[8]

Since September 11, a number of Muslim women's websites have blogs to discuss those who are considering wearing the hijab. Some Muslim women have found themselves researching their own religion and reexamining their spiritual development. For those who feel misunderstood or under attack because of their faith, putting on the hijab may be a way of standing up for their religion and showing pride in being Muslim. Madeline Zilfi, a professor of Middle Eastern history, says, "It's like when you go to a foreign country as an American and you don't feel patriotic until someone starts attacking your country. Then you find yourself standing up for the good things about it . . . the interesting thing is that the American forum is very open to this kind of expression."[9]

Sometimes, we are ineffective communicators because we fail to realize that everyone does not share our interpretation(s). Furthermore, we may find it difficult to examine our own ways of communicating. In her book *Ways with Words*, Shirley Brice Heath describes a technique that we can use to stand back and look at ourselves. She suggests that we put ourselves "under a microscope" and take the role of an **ethnographer,**[10] a person who spends time living with people in order to research their customs. Using this method, we assume the role of a neutral observer and observe our own communication systematically. We record even the smallest details and try to discover patterns. As an ethnographer, you might focus on how you communicate with others in a variety of settings. What about the tone and volume of your voice? How might your body gestures influence how your message comes across to others? How do you react to people whose accent is markedly different from yours?

Expanding Our Knowledge of Others and Their Worlds

Do we even recognize the presence of others and their capacity or right to communicate? Sometimes, we view women, men, children, lower-class persons, and people with disabilities as unable to speak for themselves in certain situations. Raymond Bingham recounts the assumptions he made one morning while working as a nurse in a newborn intensive care unit. A child with a heart defect needed emergency surgery. The nurse vividly recalls meeting the child's father for the first time. He was "a large Black man, with unkempt clothes, somewhat slurred speech, and at 8 o'clock in the morning a hint of beer on his breath."

The nurse's first impression was not to expect too much from this man. He was soon proven wrong. The father showed a great deal of caring and compassion for his son. When he needed to explain the procedure to the child's mother on the phone, he gave a complete and thorough description of the surgery and why it was necessary. Finally, the nurse remembers the father sitting at the child's bedside and crying. Toward the end of his shift, the nurse reflected back on this experience. "This man, of whom I had thought so little at first glance, who had been so strong, so calm, so resolved throughout a tumultuous day, who had so many things to worry about and take care of . . . had handled them all."[11]

THINKING THROUGH DIVERSITY

If students sit in the same classroom, read the same assignments, and hear the same lectures, are they all receiving the same education? Might these students interpret the same lesson differently because of the social worlds in which they live?

Frequently, we are unaware of different patterns of cultural differences and the pivotal role they play in communication. Depending on the cultural setting, it may or may not be appropriate to be frank about emotions, to delegate decision making, or to deal directly with conflict in face-to-face meetings. Awareness regarding these differences can help to avoid or resolve misunderstandings or even apologize (see Fig. 12.4).

When you encounter cross-cultural communication difficulties, are you mindful of how your cultural background may be influencing your own reactions? Do you listen intently and try extra hard to understand? Are there times when you refuse to accommodate or even acknowledge differences? When you go to school or work, are you likely to encounter different communication styles? What do you assume when:

FIGURE 12.4 A Personal Apology in Tokyo

Citigroup Inc. CEO Charles Prince (right) and Citigroup Japan CEO Douglas Paterson make a deep bow of apology. Under their leadership, the company failed to comply with legal and regulatory requirements in Japan. As a first step toward restoring Citigroup's reputation in Japan, the leaders observed Japanese norms by traveling to Japan to apologize in person. Source: Courtesy of japantoday.com.

- *People converse with their faces only a few inches apart?* Among some cultures, this is the norm. In others, people like to keep their distance and are uncomfortable if someone stands closer than a couple of feet.
- *A student or a coworker takes a long time to answer a question?* According to researchers who study language, short wait times put some people at a disadvantage. For example, the cultures of many Native Americans emphasize deliberate thought. Before making a decision, they learn to consider all possible implications.
- *People do not look at you when you talk to them?* Among many African, Asian, and Latin American cultures, it is rude to establish direct eye contact with elders or people in authority.
- *People talk informally for a period of time before "getting down to business"?* In many cultures, this is considered good manners. Many Middle Easterners, for example, see this type of "small talk" as a necessary part of business. It is not at all unusual for Asians or Latinos to view the process of getting to know each other as important as the message itself. To many U.S. businessmen and women, it is simply a waste of time.
- *People answer a question with "yes"?* In many East Asian cultures, it is rude to answer a question in the negative. In such situations, people may say "yes" even though they mean "no." It is a way of showing respect or "saving face," saving someone from embarrassment.
- *You see two people verbally challenging each other?* If your cultural background is Greek, Italian, or Israeli, you might view it positively, as a sign of intimacy. If you are from certain Hispanic or Asian cultures, you would probably view this kind of verbal sparring differently. Because expressing anger in this way is frowned upon, you might consider it more appropriate to repress feelings and simply smile or change the subject.

When you meet people on the way to class, on the street, in a store, or wherever, they say "Hi" plus they ask "How are you doing?" or "How are you?" even if you are a complete stranger to them. I like when they say "Hi" to me, but what really doesn't make sense is that they add "How are you feeling?" even though they don't care whether I am well or not. I feel like Americans ask this just because they are obliged to do it. In fact, if I answered "I am not OK," nobody would care. In a certain way, this is like a movie where the actors have to say what is written in the script. To the question, you feel obliged to answer you are well no matter whether it is the truth or not. Considering this point, I prefer Italians who just say "Hi" or nothing to the people they have never met before. They don't even think to ask about their health. It could appear colder, but it is certainly less hypocritical.

—Another perspective

We cannot be familiar with all variations in communication. Furthermore, we cannot assume that all people from a given culture will communicate in the same way. However, it is important to be open to the possibility that communication differences exist. Keep in mind that despite our differences, we all want people to listen to, acknowledge, and respect us.

A Profile In Diversity Consciousness

Curtis Cook was ready to take on a new challenge. After completing some graduate work in linguistic studies in the mid-1960s, he traveled to the Zuni reservation in New Mexico. There, he turned his attention to creating a Zuni version of the Bible. Because the Zuni language is not written; he took it upon himself to talk to the Zuni elders and storytellers, some of whom were 100 years or older. By living with the Zuni Indians, he developed a genuine awareness and understanding of Zuni people and their culture.

Initially, he spent a year learning the Zuni language and developing an alphabet. He approached the Zuni Tribal Council, suggesting that many of the tribe's stories be recorded. The council agreed, and by the time Cook left some 15 years later, 300 reel-to-reel tapes had been produced. Moreover, Cook's work allowed Zunis to teach their written language and pass it on to their children.

Now, as he nears 70 years of age, Cook makes sure he visits the reservation each year. As he says, "They see me as a novelty, a white man who speaks Zuni."[12] His transcriptions of Zuni stories, biblical translations, photos, and other materials are now part of the *Curtis Cook Collection*, housed in the Library of Congress's American Folklife Center archives in Washington, D.C.

Stepping Outside of Ourselves

One of the most important skills needed for effective communication is the ability to process and understand another person's point of view. This skill allows us to step outside of ourselves and become more open and sensitive to others, although it does not necessarily mean that we will fully comprehend or agree with their thoughts and feelings. Certain experiences may teach students the importance of putting themselves in the shoes of friends, family, and others.

Ashley is a high school senior whose best friend is dealing with an unwanted pregnancy. Even though Ashley has never been in this situation, she can "feel her friend's pain" and this helps her know what to say. Judah, a community college student, writes about how he works with a number of people with severe cerebral palsy. Because some cannot communicate verbally, he finds it helps to "put his mind into theirs" and rely on physical cues. Ernestine, an older female student who has a household of daughters, explains how she struggles with their thinking about life. They have watched many of their friends die violently. As a result, her daughters prefer to focus on the present and not think about the future. Says Ernestine, "I try to imagine going to countless funerals of classmates and soulmates and babies, all because somebody dissed them or stepped on their shoes or looked at them the wrong way." These three students—Ashley, Judah, and Ernestine—are more effective communicators because they have the ability to step outside of themselves. They are not locked into their own way of thinking.

When people try to understand a variety of perspectives, it opens up lines of communication. People are more willing to share when they sense that others are really listening and not judging or comparing. Also, stepping outside of yourself can make you more aware of your own thoughts and feelings. In *I Know Why the Caged Bird Sings,* Maya Angelou talks about the development of this kind of self-awareness. "I had gone from being ignorant of being ignorant to being aware of being aware."[13] This revealing, empowering process is not easy. Yari, a college student, describes what it is like to really let herself go into the "inner world of another person." "It is one of the most active, difficult, and demanding things I do. And yet it is worth it because it is one of the most releasing, healing things that I have any occasion to do."

Gauging the Level of the Playing Field

On the surface, this area of development does not appear to relate to communication. What do concepts such as status and inequality have to do with language? Ask yourself whether you address your teacher differently than a fellow student, or your supervisor differently than a coworker. What if you are angry? Would you show that anger differently? The relationship between the speaker and the receiver influences communication. One aspect of this relationship is status and power. **Status** refers to one's position. **Power** is the ability to influence people. Our interaction with others takes the form of an equal or unequal status relationship. In the classroom, an unequal status relationship exists between teachers and their students. Simply put, teachers have more authority because of their position. In another setting, this relationship might change and so might the communication between teacher and student (see Diversity Box: Communication on the Court and in the Classroom).

Communication on the Court and in the Classroom

As a new young instructor teaching sociology at a predominantly Black college, I remember numerous times when I was the only White person. This often occurred when I walked into a classroom, ate in the cafeteria, or worked out at the gym. One day, I remember going over to the gym to play some basketball. There were pickup games at each of the six baskets. I was the only White person in the gym. No one knew me since I had only been teaching a few weeks and none of my students were present. When there was a break in the action, I started to take some shots at one of the baskets. Someone suggested that we pick sides. I got picked last. A few minutes into the game, I heard someone yell, "Hey, White boy!" Obviously, it was not difficult to figure who was being singled out by that comment. I tried to ignore it but he kept repeating. "Hey, White boy!" "Hey, White boy!"

I still remember that day as if it was yesterday. Even though I was 24 years old, it was the first time in my life I can remember my race being held against me. This experience also helped me understand the different dynamics on the basketball court and in the classroom. On the court, we were pretty much equals, especially since the other players assumed that I was just another student. Our age, class, and lifestyle did not matter. The student who called me "White boy" was treating me like he would any other White peer. Once in the classroom, however, the relationship as well as the communication changed. It was considerably more difficult to be open and honest because I was the teacher and they were the students. This was particularly evident when we talked about controversial and emotional issues such as race and social inequality. There was an unwritten script that each of us followed. Consequently, it was difficult for us to be spontaneous and communicate our true feelings.

Differences in power and status can be an obstacle to effective communication. With effective communication, the receiver interprets the message just as the sender intends. Those with less power are often ignored during the communication process. For example, we tend to listen and assign more importance to what an adult says than to what a child says. In the classroom, we want to know what the teacher thinks is important. What students say typically carries less weight. Those who sense they lack power may feel that their input is not as important. However, everybody has something important to offer.

> *Every opinion, every voice deserves to be heard. And it is a rare gift indeed to hear voices that are so very different from my own.*
>
> —Another perspective

One technique used in diversity training is to instruct people in a group to completely ignore each other's titles and degrees. The idea is to focus on the message rather than the messenger. Although this technique sounds promising, it is extremely difficult to put into practice in everyday life. Actually, young children are more effective communicators in this sense. Unlike adults, they do not get so caught up with the trappings of power.

THINKING THROUGH DIVERSITY

One of the challenges confronting doctors is to open up lines of communication with their patients. One doctor laments, "People put us on a pedestal. They see us as angels, and this makes communication difficult. They don't ask questions or express their concerns. But we make mistakes like anyone else." In communicating with their patients, what is one specific thing doctors might do to level the playing field and promote more open, honest communication?

Checking Up on Ourselves

Effective communication requires constant practice and self-examination. To improve our communication skills, we need to be open to *feedback*—people's responses to us. Otherwise, we do not know when we are relating well to others.

Despite our knowledge and sensitivity, misunderstandings will occur. Often, we are not even aware of a problem. Therefore, it is important to ask constantly for feedback from others. To illustrate, Michelle, a study group leader, uses several techniques to ensure that she is not simply "talking at" students in her group. As much as possible, she engages each student in a dialogue. She focuses on the students' body language as well as what they say. Furthermore, she is learning to provide more and more wait time. This encourages more thorough and thoughtful questions and answers from a larger number of people.

> *The problem with communication is the illusion that it has been accomplished.*
>
> —George Bernard Shaw

In any given situation, ask probing questions of yourself. This enables you to go deeper and examine what messages you send and receive. However, try not to get so caught up with analyzing yourself that it interferes with your ability to listen. Think through the following questions:

THINKING THROUGH DIVERSITY

What letter grade would you give yourself for your ability to communicate in a multicultural setting? Why?

1. *Am I considering my entire audience?* This includes people who will hear the message either directly or indirectly. At work, for example, your supervisor may eventually receive your message through someone else. Consider the personal and cultural characteristics of your entire audience, and how much they know and how they may feel about the subject matter.
2. *What is the situation?* What influences outside and within this particular setting might have an impact on communication? What cultural differences may exist? Is the setting formal or informal? Elijah Cummings, a U.S. congressman, describes how he communicates differently depending on the situation. When he is in the halls of Congress, he uses what some might refer to as "paycheck" or "edited" English. But when he is back home, he communicates more informally.
3. *What options are available to me?* In other words, what form or forms of communication might I use? Your message might be written, oral, visual, or a combination of these. A case in point is police work. In response to com-

plaints from the deaf and hard of hearing, police have increasingly reexamined the way they train officers. Some departments have started teaching sign language to selected officers; others have sensitized officers to the importance of using pen and paper to communicate with a deaf person when requested. To better deal with emergencies, departments have begun to recognize the need for having interpreters on call and TTY telephones for the deaf.

4. *What is the specific purpose of the communication?* Perhaps the purpose you have in mind is not shared by others. As an example, Westerners tend to emphasize the end product of communication, the message. In contrast, many Asians place more importance on the people themselves and getting to know each other.

5. *What feedback am I receiving regarding the messages being sent (content) and how they are sent (style)?* Tone of voice, volume, pauses, facial expressions, and gestures can be just as meaningful as words themselves.

6. *What might I do differently to communicate more effectively?* For example, what can I do to listen more actively? How can I make my verbal and nonverbal communication congruent? How can I communicate more inclusively? Toward the end of this chapter, some specific suggestions are offered.

7. *Am I using language that might be viewed as offensive?* Sometimes offensive terms or phrases, known as *hot buttons,* impair communication. Hot buttons are discussed in more detail later in this chapter.

> *A friend of mine at work told me a story about how she was home alone and two Black guys came to the door selling something. Later I started wondering why she felt she had to describe them as Black.*
>
> —Another perspective

Following Through

How did you do that? How did you make it look so easy? People may ask these questions of someone who has refined a skill by practicing it a countless number of times—perhaps a great athlete, a computer whiz, or an accomplished musician. What we tend to forget is the same thing applies to communication skills. Constant practice enables us to become excellent listeners as well as competent speakers in a wide variety of settings and circumstances. This is true for all of us.

Developing, expanding, and refining our communication styles and skills is a daily challenge. A teacher who is very task-oriented finds that her relationship with students improves if she makes a habit of engaging in a little chitchat before the start of class. An employee experiments with different ways of listening. He finds that nodding his head, using facial expressions, and making "listening noises" such as "hmmm" and "oh" allow him to show others that he does care. A father discovers that spending more time with his teenage daughter and approaching conversations with her a little differently opens up lines of communication on a variety of topics, including dating and other personal issues. Instead of trying to solve all of her problems and telling her what to do, he tries to simply listen much of the time and be more empathetic.

COMMUNICATION MATTERS

In job interviews, employers weed out prospective employees by evaluating their verbal and written communication skills. As the interview unfolds, the employer is getting a live demonstration of how well individuals get their points across to others. In *The Interview Kit*, author Richard Beatty provides numerous examples of questions employers often ask. One series of questions he cites is, "Give me an example of something complex that you needed to effectively communicate to others. What made it complex? Why was it difficult to communicate? What did you do to communicate effectively? What were the results? How might these results have been improved?"[14]

Regardless of the social arena, we can readily observe the value of good communication skills. In school, for instance, why do students like some teachers more than others? Most teachers are well liked because they "know their stuff" and they relate well to students. Relating well has to do with communication skills.

When people talk about the power of communication, what does that mean? Think of the last time you:

- *Heard a dynamic and charismatic speaker address a large audience.* The message conveyed by that person will probably remain with you for the rest of your life.
- *Had an extremely difficult time communicating with someone who is very close and important to you.* How did that make you feel? How did that affect your relationship?
- *Were part of a team whose members could not communicate very well.* How did this affect your ability to function as a team?
- *Felt hurt by what a teacher, relative, or supervisor said.* This kind of remark can poison your relationship with someone. At the very least, it can be difficult to forget. It can also make you view that person or even yourself in a different light.

> Words are powerful and have physical impact on the receiver. They assault and abuse if used offensively.
>
> —Another perspective

The Power of Language

Even one word can stick with us for a long time. Indeed, it can be the only thing that we remember about an event that took place a long time ago. In the following poem entitled "Incident," the lingering impact of a single word is described by Countee Cullen.

> Once riding in old Baltimore,
> heart-filled, head-filled with glee,

> I saw a Baltimorean keep
> looking straight at me.
> Now, I was eight and very small,
> and he was no whit bigger,
> and so I smiled, but he poked
> out his tongue, and called
> me "nigger."
> I saw the whole of Baltimore,
> from May until December,
> of all the things that happened
> there that's all that I
> remember.[15]

To a large degree, your success in all realms of life depends on your ability to communicate effectively. Whenever you encounter someone at school or work, you communicate something even if you say nothing. Each encounter poses a challenge. When communication is ineffective, mutual understanding and joint action are highly unlikely. However, when communication is effective, your chances for relating well are that much greater. Teaming, networking, and learning are easier and more rewarding if you can communicate effectively with different people in all kinds of situations. Consequently, many businesses report a great need for employees with cross-cultural communication skills (see Fig. 12.5).

FIGURE 12.5 Workplace Training Skills

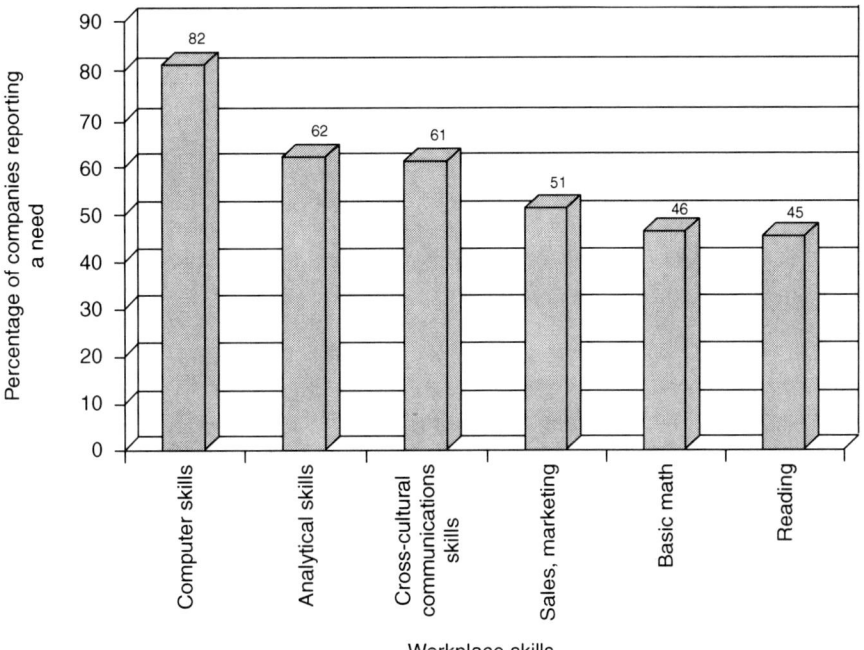

This information comes from a survey by the American Society for Training and Development. Companies were asked what kind of training their employees need. Although computer training is what companies cite as most needed, traning that targets communication skills ranks high as well.[16]

> *Once a human being has arrived on this earth, communication is the largest single factor determining what kinds of relationships she or he makes with others and what happens to each in the world.*
>
> —Virginia Satir

BARRIERS TO EFFECTIVE COMMUNICATION

There can be any number of barriers to effective communication, particularly when we communicate across cultures. These barriers include cultural biases, lack of awareness of cultural differences, language differences, ethnocentrism, and inactive listening.

   1. *Cultural biases.* In certain situations, we may make unwarranted assumptions about the person or persons with whom we are communicating. A person's dialect, for example, may trigger negative assumptions about a person's education, intelligence, or character. The term **dialect** refers to patterns in the way people use language. These patterns, which reflect people's cultural and regional backgrounds, include pronunciation or "accent" as well as vocabulary and grammar. Children learn dialect prejudice at an early age, as evidenced by comments like "You talk funny" or "Did you hear how she said that?" In the media and in the classroom, accents are described with adjectives such as *foreign, hick,* and *weird.* People who are very cautious about saying anything that might have racist or sexist overtones are much more open when it comes to belittling language differences.

   In a film on cross-cultural communication, two people are shown interviewing for a job. Both answer the questions in exactly the same way. However, one of the interviewees talks with a noticeable accent. After hearing both interviews, the narrator of the film poses the question, "Who would you hire?" Too often, a person with an accent is assumed to be less intelligent or less qualified. One study by researchers at the University of North Texas lends credence to the possibility that this kind of discrimination is commonplace. Fifty-six executives listened to a CD of ten men from different regions of the country recite the same 45-second passage. The jobs, and particularly high-prestige jobs, went to speakers with less identifiable regional accents. One of the researchers, Dianne Markley, says her research shows that companies need to monitor their job hirers more closely, perhaps by using tools like this CD.[17]

> *Personally, when I have had the occasion of speaking with students from other cultures I have found myself focusing on how they differed from what I felt normal for me. While focusing on differences, I was really missing the point of what was being said. I found myself making a judgment on the person speaking based solely on his culture.*

> *Having another language is treated like it's a disease. If you're in America, it is assumed that you ought to automatically speak THE language—that is, English.*
>
> —Other perspectives

2. *Lack of awareness of cultural differences.* If you are communicating with someone from a different culture, the two of you may interpret the same symbol differently. Several examples follow.

- What does holding your thumb up mean to you? If you are in the United States, most people would probably interpret this gesture to mean "okay." However, in another country, you might interpret this differently. In his book *Cultural Diversity in the Workplace,* George Henderson examines various meanings that people attach to this gesture in different parts of the world.[18] In Japan, it means money. In Ghana and Iran, it is a vulgar gesture, similar to raising the middle finger in the United States.

- When a teacher asks a question of the entire class and there is a long period of silence, what does this mean to you? Does it make you feel uncomfortable? In most classrooms in the United States, silence is viewed as something to fill up. This is a reflection of our cultural upbringing. According to George Henderson, many Native American cultures admire a person who has the ability to remain silent. Many Asian students learn to listen to what is not said as well as to what is said. Zen Buddhism, which is influential in many parts of Asia, reinforces this lesson. According to a Zen proverb, "He who knows does not speak and he who speaks does not know."

- During an argument, how do you feel when other students all try to talk at once? In *Aspects of Ethnicity: Understanding Differences in Pluralistic Classrooms,* Wilma Longstreet describes how different students react during a heated debate in a seminar.[19] When a number of Black students start talking at the same time, the rest of the class remains quiet. After a few minutes, the Black students appear angry. They want to know why the rest of the class is no longer talking. The White students explain that they are waiting for their turn in the discussion. Meanwhile, the Asian students express a need to think and reflect for a moment before talking.

3. *Language differences.* Communicating in an unfamiliar language can be challenging. For example, some businesses cater to customers who speak a variety of languages. When people try to communicate in a language other than their own, the results can be amusing. The following attempts to communicate in English did not come across as intended:

- "Our wines leave you nothing to hope for." (From a restaurant menu in Switzerland)
- "Ladies are requested not to have children at the bar." (From a bar in Norway)
- "Fur coats made for ladies from their own skins." (From a Swedish furrier)[20]

Even when people speak the same language, such as English speakers in the United States and other parts of the world, they may find it difficult to communicate. To lessen the confusion, the *Encarta World English Dictionary* was recently published. Linked by e-mail, more than 320 lexicographers (dictionary editors), linguists, and other specialists in 20 nations worked for more than two years to define words that can mean different things in different English-speaking countries. In South Africa, for instance, people refer to a stoplight as a "robot." The word *hotel*, in Australia, is an establishment that sells alcoholic beverages. And job seekers in Southeast Asia provide prospective employers with a "biodata" rather than a resume.[21]

4. *Ethnocentrism.* Ethnocentrism shows itself in the language we use. When we talk about the *culturally disadvantaged*, what does this mean? This once commonly used term implies more than just difference. According to this label, anyone who does not share a certain way of life is assumed to be at a disadvantage. Another example of ethnocentric language is the way we fail to differentiate between *arrival* and *discovery*. A number of years ago, many people celebrated the 500th anniversary of Columbus's *discovery* of the "New World." This touched off a heated public debate because Native Americans lived here long before Columbus *arrived* in 1492. Some history books still describe Euro-Americans as defending *their* homes against "Indian" attacks, rather than invading Native American lands. Words such as *primitive* and *backward* have been used to distort history and describe highly defined and complex Native American societies.

5. *Inactive listening.* Poor listening skills can make it much harder to communicate across cultural boundaries. Listening intently and actively helps to overcome misunderstandings and maximize effective communication. Later in this chapter, we examine specific skills that promote active listening.

HOT BUTTONS

> *I was grocery shopping one day when an elderly woman called me a "nigger." All of the hate and venom was there. I didn't know what to do. I thought of going to the manager and demanding that he do something. But what could he do? I wanted the world to stop and pay attention to me because I had just been assaulted! I did my shopping in stunned, confused, and angry silence. Now I am sorry I didn't tell management in the store this happened while I was buying their groceries. I may not have gotten validation, but I would not have kept it quiet.*
>
> —Another perspective

Hot buttons refer to language that triggers negative reactions from people who view it as insulting and derogatory. Hot buttons are not the same for everyone. What is insulting and derogatory to one student might be perfectly acceptable to another. Similarly, a supervisor might consider a sexist joke "just playing around" or "part of the territory." An employee might view that same joke as threatening, serious, and possibly grounds for a lawsuit.

For some, the issue of hot buttons is a game of *political correctness*. There are those in the workplace who complain that they feel like they are "walking on eggshells" all the time. They maintain that they cannot be themselves. Others make the point that we are simply talking about being respectful of others. Regardless of where you stand on this issue, it is important to understand just how powerful language can be. Saying something offensive can jeopardize communication, create mistrust and hostility, and damage a person's reputation.

Good intentions do not protect us from using hot buttons. A fellow teacher shared with me how his students became visibly upset in class when he referred to a few of them as "you people." He was completely taken aback by their reaction. After all, he did not mean anything negative by it. He explained "you people" was directed at certain students who did poorly on a test; it was meant to motivate them to do better. Only later did he find out the negative connotations of this hot button. Some students said it made them feel inferior and different. One student compared it to being called "you dog" or "you good-for-nothing."

Randall Kennedy, a professor of law at Harvard, examines the historical significance and political power of a single word in his book *Nigger: The Strange Career of a Troublesome Word*. "I have invested energy in this endeavor because *nigger* is a key word in the lexicon of race relations and thus an important term in American politics," Kennedy tells us. "To be ignorant of its meanings and effects is to make oneself vulnerable to all manner of perils, including the loss of a job, a reputation, a friend, even one's life."[22]

No matter how hard we try, periodically, each of us will use language that may take the form of a hot button. It is important to learn from our mistakes and accept responsibility for what we say and do.

Using appropriate language is not something we can easily turn on and off. It always helps to think things through before and after communicating. For instance, change a key word in a phrase and see if it still applies. Suppose that you read an article about "*the* gay lifestyle." Ask yourself, would it make sense to talk about "*the* heterosexual lifestyle?" Someone might consider the phrase "I don't think of you as Latino" a compliment. Change it. Would someone say "I don't think of you as White?"

Another point to consider is the history of a phrase or the context in which it is used. Comparing a hard-driving boss to a slave driver serves to trivialize a period of history that is very painful to some. This same kind of reasoning may apply to fans mimicking "tomahawk chops" and "war chants" at sports events. Whether these actions honor or slight Native Americans is currently the subject of much debate.

Another example is marketing. Sports teams have adopted names and mascots such as Redskins, Redmen, or Red Raiders (see Fig. 12.6). Because of efforts by Native American activists, many of these teams at the high school and college level have changed their names. Professional sports teams, such as the Washington Redskins, Atlanta Braves, and Cleveland Indians, insist on keeping their names. To support their position, they point to research that shows considerable disagreement among fans and Native Americans regarding the use of Indian nicknames, mascots, or symbols.[23]

The controversy over the volatile issue of culturally insensitive marketing is by no means limited to sports teams. A case in point is a company in New York that sells a malt liquor under the name Crazy Horse. The bottle features a Native American in headdress. Although the makers of this product argue they are simply capitalizing on a clientele that identifies with the "Old West," others feel that it is one more example of how Native Americans have been dishonored and dehumanized throughout American history. One state lawmaker, who tried to ban Crazy Horse malt liquor in Minnesota, suggests that this debate illustrates a double standard. "Everybody would understand how insulting it would be to have, say, a Martin Luther King Jr. dark ale or a Golda Meir dark stout. But when it comes to Native Americans, somehow it's a different thing."[24]

FIGURE 12.6 Hot button or not?
Source: Used with permission from Tribune Media Services.

THINKING THROUGH DIVERSITY

What are your personal hot buttons? How do you feel when someone triggers one of your hot buttons? Why? Do your encounters with hot buttons make it difficult for you to communicate effectively?

What Not to Say

In the early 1970s, Sheila Rush and Chris Clark authored the book *How to Get Along with Black People*. The authors cited a number of clichés that were extremely objectionable to Blacks. Interestingly, many of these clichés are still commonplace today.

- "What do you people want? . . . ."
  Rush and Clark: "It assumes that Blacks must want something different from what White people want." When used in this context, the word *you* can be seen as degrading and dehumanizing."
- "A credit to his race . . . ."
  Rush and Clark: "The phrase assumes that Blacks need crediting or something to balance their dark doom. To become a 'credit,' one must be compliant." It is also interesting to note when this phrase is or is not used. Have you ever heard a White male referred to as a credit to his race?"
- "But the Irish (Jews, Italians, Cubans) did it, why can't you? . . . ."
  Rush and Clark: "The implication, of course, is that if Blacks had worked harder, their fate would have been different. . . . No group ever worked harder in the service of building America. (Remember slavery?) So why are Blacks still 'last'? For all but the fairest Blacks, the possibility of melting in the great American pot did not exist. Blacks could never get lost in the crowd. . . ."[25]

DIFFICULT DIALOGUES

One day, I called a local radio station. A conservative talk show was on. The only thing I wanted to say was that until Black people and White people, or just people in general, start talking there will always be racism. I was really upset and the talk show host made a fool out of me on the radio. For days after that, he made comments about me . . . like "her name's Utopia (he didn't think that was my real name); she must live in a utopia."

I cried that whole weekend. On Monday I went to school. I attended a predominantly White school. In most of my classes, I was the only Black. I remember walking into class and sharing with them what happened to me. I then said, "I don't know if White people don't understand or they don't want to understand." I was just sitting there crying and that was the first time they all paid attention to me and listened to everything I had to say. That was the first day I felt I made a breakthrough with White people. I realized that it's possible that we can communicate, we can talk, and we can listen. Maybe not necessarily always agree but respect what each other has to say. That was the first year I even allowed myself to have White friends.

—Another perspective

Difficult dialogues are sometimes necessary. If we handle them well, these kinds of discussions can bring diversity issues out into the open and "clear the air." In one study, college students praised professors who know how to create a "comfort zone," and understand the importance of letting discussions continue even if they become heated. At the same time, these professors establish ground rules in advance, emphasize respect, and encourage students not to personalize issues.[26]

Another study cited earlier illustrates the importance of dealing with student concerns about intolerance, especially when it touches them personally. Of those minority students surveyed at five colleges in the eastern United States, one-fourth said that acts motivated by prejudice interfere with their ability to study.[27] If one considers co-victimization, the numbers are apt to be much higher. **Co-victimization** means that you can feel the pain of victimization even if people do not attack or victimize you directly.

Despite the importance of opening up and engaging in difficult dialogues, people rarely do it. This is the case in classrooms, offices, communities, and even on a national level. According to Cornel West, author of *Race Matters,* our society has never had an open and honest discussion about race.[28] The same can be said about many other diversity issues.

Some of the reasons for the lack of dialogue may have more to do with the social setting than with the person. According to a report entitled *Racial Issues on Campus: How Students View Them,* many college students cite a lack of opportunity to voice their concerns. Many of these students, who attended 20 predominantly White and 20 predominantly Black campuses, felt a sense of alienation and isolation. They had concerns about campus climate and personal experiences but few formal opportunities to address them.[29]

Often we reserve difficult dialogues for friends and family. This is because we feel that we know and trust them. In all likelihood, we will not risk opening up elsewhere unless we also feel a certain level of trust or a high degree of anonymity. "Y? The National Forum on People's Differences," one of the most innovative uses of technology in recent years, allows people to ask embarrassing, personal questions in a safe, anonymous setting on the Web. This low-tech site, www.yforum.com, relies on simple text with questions typed in by users worldwide. Interestingly, most of the questions revolve around small everyday issues. Typical inquiries include: "Is there a way to tell the difference in Asian nationalities?" "Is it true that the direction the eyes slant is an indicator?" "Why do Jewish people eat matzos?" "Why is it that Caucasians seem to spend so much time on lawn care?" "What would take place during a typical week night in a Black family?"[30] Questions like these illustrate just how much we don't know about each other, and the critical need for honest dialogue.

In my classes, my students and I work very hard to get to the point where we can talk about race, gender, social class, and other issues related to sociology. This process starts on the first day of class with each of us sharing some aspect of our personal background. Our comfort level with diversity increases as we discuss its relevance throughout the semester. Although students do not always agree, they learn to respect each other's opinions.

> *People don't get along because they fear each other. People fear each other because they don't know each other. They don't know each other because they have not properly communicated with each other.*
>
> —Martin Luther King, Jr.

Prior to difficult dialogues, it helps to discuss and agree on certain ground rules. Some examples follow:

Nine Ground Rules for Difficult Dialogues

1. If someone pushes a "hot button" of yours, it's okay to let the group know what it is and how it makes you feel.
2. Be as open and honest as you feel you can be. Try to move outside your comfort zone.
3. Respect each person's right to be heard.
4. Realize that we are all teachers and learners.
5. Be an active participant. Remember that we participate in different ways.
6. Listen even when you do not want to listen.
7. Do not judge another person's feelings.
8. Focus on the behavior rather than the person.
9. Do not ask people to be spokespersons for their groups.

COMMUNICATING INCLUSIVELY

There is a growing body of literature on multicultural or inclusive communication. As the world grows smaller and our society becomes more diverse, employers are more apt to view people who lack skills in this area as liabilities. Communicating in a way that makes people feel included rather than excluded is not a lesson that can be taught in a matter of minutes. It requires commitment and practice. The following 11 strategies provide a good starting point. Rather than focus on all of these at once, it might be helpful to prioritize.

1. *Address people the way they want to be addressed.* Many Native Americans identify with their tribal background. Consequently, they may prefer being called Navaho or Sioux rather than Native Americans. Do not judge a person's preference. Simply respect it. Also, keep in mind that different people within a group may want to be addressed differently.

Negative Messages Surround Adoption

Recently, a teacher e-mailed me regarding a "perspective" that appeared in an earlier edition of *Diversity Consciousness*. A student who is more light-skinned than the rest of her family had shared a perspective that caught the teacher's attention. Because of her skin color, the student explained how people constantly tease her and joke about how she must have been adopted. The teacher, a parent of an adopted child, reacted strongly to this perspective. "As a parent, I feel angry at the implied message—that being adopted is always second class to being 'born into' a family. Being adopted means you don't really belong. That being 'adopted' was very hurtful to this student is indicative of a prevalent social attitude that those of us who formed our families by adoption frequently encounter. My son has been asked who his 'real' parents are, and I have been asked if I have any kids 'of my own.' Upon finding out how our family was formed, some people express pity that we couldn't have children. Negative language around adoption abounds—we have been asked (within our son's hearing) why his 'real' mother didn't want him, or if we knew his 'father' (with my husband standing there)." By sharing her view of a significant but often disregarded dimension of diversity, the teacher made me more aware of gaps in my thinking.

2. *Keep an open mind.* People can view the same thing differently. Be open to the "different lens" through which people view the world (see Fig. 12.7). Also, be willing to question your own assumptions and learn from the feedback you receive from others.
3. *Listen actively.* Active listening skills require practice (see Diversity Box: Active Listening Skills Checklist). Often, we are so intent on getting our point across that we do not carefully listen to what people are saying and how they are saying it. For instance, we can learn something from inflections in a person's voice, and even from pauses. Remember to focus on body language.

FIGURE 12.7 After Hurricane Katrina: Different race, different description. Source: Courtesy of kchronicles.com.

According to research, most of what we communicate during a conversation is nonverbal.

In part, effective listening hinges on our ability to attune ourselves to other's feelings. *Mirroring,* commonly used in marital therapy, allows us to build rapport as we listen. When a person says something, we try to repeat or mirror what was said, attempting to capture the person's feelings and thoughts. Without being too obvious, we might start by aligning our body language and noticing the pace and tone of the individual's voice. As we do this, we check to make sure we are on target, and if not, we try again.

Active Listening Skills Checklist

- Do you listen intently even when you disagree with someone?
- Do you listen intently even when you have a difficult time understanding someone?
- Do you listen intently when someone talks very slowly and deliberately?
- Do you listen carefully, even when you don't want to?
- Are you aware of verbal and nonverbal messages?
- Do you restate, summarize, and question to promote understanding?
- Do you provide positive feedback through body language and "listening noises"?
- Do you give people enough time to respond?
- How do you make sure your biases do not interfere with your ability to listen?

4. *Check understanding.* Instead of assuming that someone understands you, assume just the opposite. Ask questions that might pinpoint possible problems. "Is this clear?" "Do I need to explain further?" "What do you think I have been saying up to this point?" Repeat these questions continuously. When you are the receiver of information, ask questions, too. "Is that idea like . . .?" "Are you suggesting that . . .?" "Can you give me an example of . . .?"
5. *Do some research.* Businesspersons who travel abroad or venture into unfamiliar markets at home often ignore this sort of preparation. The Internet can provide a wealth of current information. College libraries or ethnic organizations in your community may be other valuable resources. Perdue Farms is one company that did not do its homework. When its slogan, "It takes a tough man to make a tender chicken" was carelessly translated into Spanish, it read, "It takes a sexually excited man to make a chick affectionate." Another big company, Adolph Coors, discovered too late that its slogan "Turn It Loose," when translated into Spanish, meant the beer that would make you "Get the Runs."
6. *Think through what you are going to say before you say it.* When you talk about others, do you refer to them by their race, ethnic background, social class, gender, or some other distinguishing characteristic? If so, ask yourself why.
7. *Avoid slang.* Telling someone she has "sick" clothing can lead to misunderstanding. To some teens, it can mean awesome or good. To an older colleague at work, it might mean something quite different.
8. *Do not share ethnic jokes.* This is a serious matter, especially in the workplace and at school. To some, ethnic jokes or ethnic humor in general may be acceptable. This is particularly true of self-directed ethnic humor. However, you cannot assume or predict that people will interpret something the same way you do. Jokes are usually made at the expense of others. Think through how you should react if someone decides to tell an ethnic joke in your presence.
9. *Use as many different styles of communication as possible.* Visual aids can help. You might want to write something down or spell difficult words if simply saying

something does not seem to be working. Constantly question your assumptions about the right or preferred way to communicate. Be open to the existence of different cultural norms and their impact on communication styles. At the same time, remember that cultural norms may not apply to the behavior of any particular individual. Numerous factors, such as family background, schooling, and personalities, shape and alter the modes of communication we use and prefer.

THINKING THROUGH DIVERSITY

If a fellow employee tells you a joke about gays during your lunch break, how would you react? Why?

10. *Do not assume that you can or should ignore differences.* The problem lies in the value judgments we attach to individual or cultural differences, not in the differences themselves. For example, noticing someone's accent does not make you prejudiced. Having negative thoughts about the accent does.

The poem "For the White Person Who Wants to Know How to Be My Friend" suggests how we should and should not respond to cultural differences.

> *The first thing you do is to forget that I'm black.*
> *Second, you must never forget that I'm black.*
> *You should be able to dig Aretha,*
> *but don't play her every time I come over.*
> *And if you decide to play Beethoven—don't tell me*
> *his life story. They make us take music appreciation too.*
>
> —Pat Parker[31]

11. *Be conscious of how fast you are talking.* If you were raised in one region of the United States and now live in another, you may know how difficult it is to adjust to differences in pronunciation and terminology. Generally, it helps to slow down a little. Repeat yourself if necessary.

In this chapter we have addressed the importance of effective communication. Moreover, we have examined the interrelationship of diversity consciousness and communication. Communication is a diversity skill that we learn, develop, and refine throughout the course of our lives. As we become more conscious of diversity, our communication skills will improve. And as our communication skills improve, we become more diversity conscious.

> *Acknowledge each other's differences and move past them; just don't move too fast.*
>
> —Another perspective

CASE STUDIES

Case Study One

The student population at Ligua's college is predominantly white. In spite of her desire to be as inconspicuous as possible, Ligua often feels the urge to educate other students and even the teachers in her classes. These difficult dialogues often revolve around issues of social inequality. In her history class, for instance, students were talking about the legal, economic, and political changes in the United States that have opened up all kinds of opportunities for minorities. Ligua interjected, "I hope no one here thinks that by earning a degree, and getting an education, that you're going to level the playing field." A heated discussion took place, and the class ended before there was any closure on this subject.

Because of her complexion and Spanish-sounding name, assumptions are made. Born in the United States, Ligua speaks English fluently but finds it difficult to communicate in Spanish. Last semester, in Intermediate Spanish, Ligua's teacher would make references about her knowledge of the language, assuming that the class was easy for her. In reality, Ligua had to work harder just so she wouldn't embarrass herself.

Ligua does not know how to handle these difficult dialogues. She doesn't want to bring attention to herself or alienate the teachers or students, but she feels she must say something.

Questions:

1. What advice might you offer Ligua to help her deal with the difficult dialogues she encounters in her classes?
2. If you were one of Ligua's classmates in Intermediate Spanish, what would you do, if anything? Why?

Case Study Two

Mary is currently doing a practicum at a children's mental hospital. In her role as a social worker, Mary often speaks to a family several times over the phone prior to meeting with them. With the background information she receives on each case, Mary is aware of the family's racial background before the family is aware of hers. In one instance, Mary had really connected with the mother of one of her patients. She and the patient's mother, Mrs. K, had talked on the phone several times. Mrs. K made a point of acknowledging Mary's competence and thanked her for how much help she had been.

When Mrs. K and Mary finally met, Mrs. K had a surprised look on her face. From the sound of Mary's voice over the phone and her ability to empathize and understand what the family was going through, Mrs. K had assumed that Mary was African American. She was shocked to see that Mary was White. The meeting was very uncomfortable. Mary could tell that Mrs. K was hesitant to share information, and the working relationship they had formed seemed to disappear. When Mary came to work the next day, there was a message from Mrs. K stating that she wanted to work with a different social worker, someone who was not White. Mary was taken aback and did not know what she should do. All of the social workers at the hospital were White, and she knew something had to be done so that the patient would continue to receive the best care possible.

Questions:

1. If you were Mary, how would you feel in this situation? Why do you think Mrs. K reacted the way she did to Mary?
2. If you were Mary, what would you do? Specifically, would you call Mrs. K and talk with her, or would you handle it some other way? Explain.

Case Study Three

Michael is constantly reminded that he is exceptional and deserving, unlike so many others. This can be uncomfortable, because the word *others* seems to apply to people who supposedly share his racial or cultural background.

A whole lot of stress in his life comes from his job as a consultant. For instance, there are people who are comfortable talking to him on the phone but are suddenly uncomfortable when they meet him. They might complain or question his competence by saying, "I don't feel comfortable working with Michael," or "I don't think Michael is the right person for this job." At times like this, he is left wondering, and angry.

Questions:

1. Michael is being confronted with a number of barriers to effective communication. Discuss two of these barriers.
2. What "hot buttons" does Michael encounter? If you were Michael, how would you respond to these hot buttons?

Key Terms

Communication	Linguistic diversity	Material culture
Symbol	Bilingual	Ethnographer
Kinesics	Multilingual	Status
Culturally specific	Linguicism	Power
Intercultural communication	Electronic communication	Dialect
	Impression management	Hot buttons
Sign language	Cultural diffusion	Co-victimization

EXERCISES

In-Class

Exercise 1: Active Listening

Directions for Instructor

Divide students into pairs. One student in each pair tells the other student about a problem at school or work that he or she is experiencing. The problem should not be too complex. The time limit is 1 minute. The listener may ask for clarification but cannot say anything else. In addition, the listener may use "listening noises" or body language. Notes may not be taken. After the speaker finishes, the listener gives feedback by "reflecting content," restating what was said without being judgmental. This reveals whether the listener heard and understood the speaker. Moreover, this type of feedback affirms the speaker and puts him or her at ease. When necessary, the speaker can correct and help the listener remember exactly what was said. Repeat this process with the listener and speaker exchanging parts.

Analysis. What did you learn from this experience? Were you more comfortable taking on the role of the speaker or the listener? Why? Did you have a difficult time tuning in and remembering what your partner said? If you did this again, what might you do differently to be a better listener?

Exercise 2: Responding to Hot Buttons

Directions for Instructor

Form groups of three to four students. Ask students to read the following four scenarios. Each group member should then pick one scenario and act out how he or she would respond. Afterward, the group discusses the appropriateness and effectiveness of each student's response, using the "Nine Ground Rules for Difficult Dialogues".

- You are at work. Your boss calls you "honey," but you prefer that he call you by your first name or as Ms. _____ (last name). You explain this to your boss as tactfully as possible, but he laughs it off. You don't want to offend your boss, but you don't feel that he understands how strongly you feel about this. How do you respond?
- You are a middle-aged man who works in an office. A coworker whose desk is next to yours makes a habit of cornering you one-on-one and sharing his latest joke. Most of the jokes are aimed at women and have sexual overtones. Initially, you try to humor him but you are growing increasingly uncomfortable with this situation. You try to avoid this person, but it is not working. You feel that you must say something to him or your supervisor. How do you respond?
- You are at a party with a group of students that you do not know really well. You are watching a professional football game and one of the students makes a racist remark about one of the players. A number of people laugh, but nothing is said. How do you respond?
- You and your friend are using the photocopying machine in the library. You accidentally copy the wrong material. Your friend, realizing the mistake that you just made, says: "You're such a retard." How do you respond?

Out-of-Class

Exercise 1: Ethnic Jokes

Imagine that you and other employees at work correspond by e-mail. You have just received the following message on your computer:

> "Just keeping you informed so that you won't embarrass yourself.
> Due to the climate of political correctness now found throughout America, those of us in Tennessee, West Virginia, and Kentucky will no longer be 'HILLBILLIES.' Now, you must use the term, 'APPALACHIAN-AMERICANS.' Thank you.
> Now, if you don't mind, I've got possums to fry."

After reading this, you decide to respond by sending an e-mail message to the sender of this joke. Type your response.

Exercise 2: Creating an Action Plan

Imagine that you are the director of student affairs at a small liberal arts college in the Midwest. During a staff meeting, the president of the college shares a number of complaints from gay students. The complaints allege that many gay students encounter prejudice and discrimination both on campus and among townspeople. The students feel that these problems are college-wide and need to be addressed by the president and her staff as well as by community leaders.

The president asks you to create an action plan. She feels that the college needs to open the lines of communication and encourage inclusive, honest dialogue on this issue. Develop a two-page typewritten summary of what you propose. Include the rationale behind your action plan.

INTERNET ASSIGNMENT

Google the phrase "diversity blog." Join the conversation in one of the links that is displayed.

Print at least one page that includes your post.

How do you think your comment impacted the conversation? Do you see blogging as an effective way to develop *your* diversity consciousness? Explain.

NOTES

[1] Roger E. Axtell, *Gestures: The Do's and Taboos of Body Language Around the World* (New York: Wiley, 1991), 10.

[2] Alice Reid, "Mosque's Children Await Playground," *The Washington Post,* Nov. 22, 1998, B4.

[3] Deborah Tannen, *You Just Don't Understand: Men and Women in Conversation* (New York: William Morrow, 1990); *Talking from 9 to 5: How Women's and Men's Conversational Styles Affect Who Gets Heard, Who Gets Credit, and What Gets Done at Work* (New York: William Morrow, 1994); *That's Not What I Meant* (New York: Ballantine Books, 1992).

[4] Oliver Sacks, *Seeing Voices: A Journey into the World of the Deaf* (Berkeley: University of California Press, 1989), 127.

[5] E. Goffman, *Interaction Ritual: Essays on Face to Face Interaction* (Garden City, NY: Doubleday/Anchor, 1967).

[6] Glenn McNatt, "Instant Communication Is Changing Our Very Form of Government," *The Sun,* Feb. 9, 1997, 5E.

[7] L. Sproull and S. Kiesler, *Connections: New Ways of Working in the Networked Organization* (Cambridge, MA: MIT Press, 1991), 61.

[8] Jennifer Rudick Zunikoff, conversation with the author, June 4, 2002.

[9] Emily Wax, "The Fabric of Their Faith," *The Washington Post,* May 19, 2002, C1.

[10] Shirley Brice Heath, *Ways with Words* (Cambridge: Cambridge University Press, 1983).

[11] Raymond Bingham, "Leaving Prejudice Behind," *The Washington Post Health Section,* Sept. 6, 1994, 9.

[12] "Preserving A Language and Tribal History," *AARP Bulletin,* November, 2006, p. 8.

[13] Maya Angelou, *I Know Why the Caged Bird Sings* (New York: Bantam Books, 1993).

[14] Richard Beatty, *The Interview Kit* (New York: John Wiley & Sons, 2000).

[15] Countee Cullen (ed.), *Caroling Dusk* (Secaucus, NJ: Carol Publishing Group, 1993), 187.

[16] Kristin Downey Grimsley, "Training in the Theater of the Real," *The Washington Post Business Section,* Mar. 24, 1997, 12.

[17] Nancy Kolsti, "Accents Speak Louder Than Words," *North Texan Online,* Winter 2000. Available: http://www.unt.edu/northtexan/archives/w00/accents.htmrl.

[18] George Henderson, *Cultural Diversity in the Workplace: Issues and Strategies* (Westport, CT: Praeger Publishers, 1994).

[19] Wilma Longstreet, *Aspects of Ethnicity: Understanding Differences in Pluralistic Classrooms* (Williston, VT: Teachers College Press, 1978).

[20] Charles Goldsmith, "Look See! Anyone Do Read This and It Will Make You Laughable," *The Wall Street Journal,* Nov. 19, 1992, B1.

[21] Anne Soukhanov, *Encarta World English Dictionary* (New York: St. Martin's Press, 1999).

[22] Randall Kennedy, *Nigger: The Strange Career of a Troublesome Word* (New York: Pantheon, 2002), 4.

[23] S. L. Price, "The Indian Wars," *Sports Illustrated,* March 4, 2002, 67–72.

[24] Michael Fletcher, "Crazy Horse Again Sounds Battle Cry," *The Washington Post,* Feb. 18, 1997, A03.

[25] Sheila Rush and Chris Clark, *How to Get Along with Black People,* copyright © 1972, Third Press, Joseph Okpaku Publishing Co., Inc., reprinted by permission of Okpaku Communications Corporation, New Rochelle, NY.

[26] Barbara Gold, "Diversifying the Curriculum: What Do Students Think?," *Diversity Digest,* Winter 2001, 12–14.

[27] Howard Ehrlich, *Campus Ethnoviolence: A Research Review,* Institute Report 5 (Baltimore: National Institute Against Prejudice and Violence, 1992), 8.

[28] Cornel West, *Race Matters* (New York: Vintage Books, 1993).

[29] Ansley Abraham, *Racial Issues on Campus: How Students View Them* (Atlanta, GA: Southern Regional Education Board, 1990).

[30] Philip Milano and Larry Lane, *Why Do White People Smell Like Wet Dogs When They Come Out of the Rain?* (Orlando Park, FL: Y Forum, 1999), 2, 3.

[31] Pat Parker, *Movement in Black* (Ithaca, NY: Firebrand Books, 1978), 68.

TOPIC 8

HR PRACTICES AND CULTURAL DIMENSIONS PART 1 AND 2

Chapter 13

Cultural Diversity in Organisations

The word 'diversity' is ambiguous, especially when associated with the term 'organization'. An organization can be a domestic one, with many of its employees who have their roots abroad – reflecting the social diversity of the country in question. It can also be an international organization whose cultural diversity is reflected in its foreign subsidiaries. At the same time, diversity can refer to the collection of groups who form the organization: groups differentiated in terms of gender, mother tongue, education, as well as their position or salary.

Moore (1999: 212) analysed the attitudes of organizations towards diversity generally and identified four different perspectives:

1. Diversity blindness: no provision is made within the organization for addressing the problems and/or opportunities relating to diversity.
2. Diversity hostility: the organization attempts to 'homogenize' its employees and actively suppresses expressions of diversity.
3. Diversity naïveté: the organization views diversity positively and encourages diversity awareness, but is probably unable to cope with any problems which diversity may cause.
4. Diversity integration: the organization addresses diversity in a pragmatic way. It helps its employees to develop skills in diversity management and creates the preconditions needed for effective communication between the different groups in the workforce.

The concepts in this chapter will focus specifically on the management of cultural diversity in multinational operations. Concept 13.1 examines how managers can deal with cultural diversity and how they can turn this diversity to their advantage. Concept 13.2 takes an initial look at the notion of transcultural competence, the term used to describe the attitudes and behaviour needed to manage cultural diversity effectively. These elements will be developed further throughout Part Three.

Learning outcomes

After reading this chapter, you will gain insight into:

- The features of management culture required in multinational companies.
- The skills managers need to manage cultural differences in a global environment.

Concept 13.1 Managing diversity in a global environment

Globalization is one of the most discussed topics in business. International business research is directly affected by a globalization process that does not seem to end. Furthermore, researchers of other disciplines are also being urged to reflect on this process, which concerns all institutions of human society.

Compared with political, social and educational institutions, however, businesses appear to be the most suitable candidates for globalization, particularly those in the industrial, financial and service sectors. According to de Woot (2000), companies in these sectors have cleared most obstacles in the globalization process: that of size (with multinationals), that of time (with long-term strategies), that of complexity, and finally that of information and communication. The globalization of companies seems to be linked to the cultural diversity of organizations, which in turn is connected to the internationalization of organizations.

Management culture and multinationals

As many writers on the subject indicate, one fundamental problem which the globalization of the economy causes organizations is the management of cultural differences. Steinmann and Scherer (2000) raise some fundamental issues with regard to the effects of the globalization process on managerial functions. These include the way the executives of a company conceive the interaction between the different cultures present. If, for example, a multinational embraces operating companies in Asia, should it advocate Western values (what Steinmann and Scherer call a 'strategy of proclamation'), or should it embark on the new process of intercultural learning, based on the application of reasoning (a 'strategy of learning')? This last option seems to them the best way of settling the intercultural conflicts in multinational companies.

What sort of management culture is to be found in multinationals? Théry (2002) distinguishes three types:

- A dominant management culture that is a copy of the multinational's home country (e.g. American management in a US multinational).
- A dominant transnational management culture created by the mother-company's founders using clearly defined specific values, a culture present in all the multinational's operating companies.
- A minimum management culture, leaving considerable room for national cultures in all their diversity.

In all three cases, the multinational must perform two roles at once: an integrating role and an adapting role. It not only has to ensure that the companies forming the group remain integrated and thus able to continue as a multinational; it also has to ensure that it respects the different national groups of clients and employees by making the necessary adaptations.

> **SPOTLIGHT 13.1**
>
> **Talent retention is vital**
>
> The Business Times Singapore asked a number of executives from multinationals operating in Asia to pinpoint the key workforce-related issues that affect Asia-focused organisations today. They were also asked to describe some of their key 'people-strategies' for Asia. Here is the response from Charles M. Ormiston, Director Bain & Company, a global management consulting firm.
>
> 'I think it would be difficult to exaggerate the enormous people-development challenges facing Asia. The gap between organisations who "get it" and those who don't is tremendous. There are MNCs where the bulk of their Asian senior management is of Asian origin, many "Asian expatriates" who have spent years of their life working in different markets and who are fully comfortable with working in either the "East" or the "West". Citibank, Standard Chartered, Hewlett-Packard, Schlumberger and Unilever are examples of great companies that attract and develop talent in the local markets they work in, and then deploy the best talent globally. And yet there are still MNCs dominated by foreign expatriates on three-year rotations from head office, who seem to begin thinking about how to return to New York or Chicago within weeks of arriving in Singapore.
>
> There are "local firms" who have also mastered the art of working with talent from a range of sources – SingTel is doing an impressive job with diverse assets in Australia, India and the Philippines as well as in their home market; Temasek is one of the most innovative institutions I have come across in terms of flexible work practices and creating opportunities for employee development. And yet there are local firms who have visibly failed with virtually all attempts to diversify their talent base.'
>
> Mr Ormiston then outlines fundamental shifts which he believes most 'Asia-focused' corporations will need to undertake in their thinking. These include the following:
> 'Create diversity in your senior ranks. If your senior ranks are primarily people from one nationality or ethnic group, you will never be an attractive workplace for people who are from other backgrounds – no matter what platitudes you convey. You have to take visible risks with non-traditional employees to be credible.
>
> Employers need to actively coach their employees on their careers. When I talk to employees of the best employers in Asia, they focus on the fairness and objectivity of their performance appraisal systems and the "good advice" they receive from key mentors over the years. With the firms that "don't get it" in Asia, this type of system is often non-existent – the rotating expatriates in MNCs simply don't take the time to bond with the local employee base in a productive way and the poorly run local firms have a tremendous wall between the "top team" and the up-and-coming generation.'
>
> Source: *Business Times Singapore*, 5 October 2009.

Transnational organization

That globalization has become a reality and that it is still progressing at high speed is not in doubt. The same holds true for the increase in cultural diversity in domestic and international companies where people from different cultural backgrounds are working together more and more. In view of these changes, Bartlett and Ghoshal (1989) propose a model for the organization of the future: the transnational company (see Concept 7.1). The 'transnational' is a management mentality combining the abilities of the multinational, global or international firm: flexibility, efficiency and the transfer of expertise. The managers at the headquarters and in the subsidiaries abroad are responsible for co-ordinating these capacities throughout the different units of the organization. Trompenaars and Hampden-Turner (1997: 188) state 'the transnational corporation is polycentric rather than co-ordinated from the centre'.

Bartlett et al. (2003) go further. They believe that top management must bring added value to the transnational company in the same way as the executives operating at all levels of the organization. This means that the top managers are not just content to create an operational framework in which the responsibilities of the functional and geographic groups are clearly defined. They also have a federating role by integrating the different influences of these groups in the management process. While recognizing that diversity and internal tensions can be the source of new ideas, it seems that the role of top management is rather to create a common vision for the future, a shared set of values to reflect managers' goals.

Concept 13.2 Diversity and transcultural competence in organizations

What is diversity? Gómez-Mejìa et al. (2001) see in the notion of diversity a human characteristic that allows a differentiation to be made between people. On the one hand there are individual characteristics, such as race, age or gender, over which the individual has no or little control. On the other hand there are characteristics an individual can act on during his life, such as work background, geographical situation and education. In everyday business life, managers may well see their employees as individuals. However, they should also be aware of the diversity and the characteristics inherent in each specific group. In fact, diversity among employees may well not only cause misunderstandings but also obstruct team work and productivity. Good management is therefore crucial to prevent this happening.

How do the managers in a transnational organization perceive cultural diversity? Adler (2002: 157) refers to a survey (Adler and Ghadar, 1990) to show that it can be a source of both problems and advantages.

Problems caused by cultural diversity are to do with communication and integration, particularly when the organization requires its employees to think and act in the same way. The more an organization demands transparency and convergent opinions, the greater the ambiguity, complexity and confusion. Problems with diversity also arise when certain practices and procedures are adopted by the organization across the board. Export managers may use the same marketing campaign across countries without taking account of the different cultures involved.

As for the possible advantages of cultural diversity, Adler (2002) notes that some managers describe multicultural organizations as being more flexible and open to new ideas. Other managers find such organizations to be more aware of consumer needs. Diversity is also considered an advantage when the concern needs to reposition itself, to generate ideas, to develop projects, to open itself up to fresh perspectives.

Within organizations operating in an international environment, partners, collaborators and co-workers will be brought into intercultural situations that need to be turned to their advantage to prevent failure of the strategy of internationalization. This means that knowledge, tools and working methods need to be acquired to help develop the attitude and behaviour desirable in a specific cross-cultural context. Managing diversity in this kind of organization and its environment demands, at all management levels, a competence that is often referred to as 'transcultural'.

SPOTLIGHT 13.2

Year of the accountant?

Below is an extract from an article by Victor Smart which examines the changing corporate environment in China, with particular reference to the adoption of international accoounting standards.

Jennifer Zhao ACMA, a finance manager at Shell Bitumen, recently moved into [the company's] new offices in the Chao Yang district of Beijing. The previous tenant was a Chinese firm and the layout is a warren of small offices. 'Typically in China people meet in small offices and sometimes only the boss talks,' she says. 'Shell, like most multinationals, has a much more managerial approach where everybody gives their views.'

A bulldozer-style of management is valuable if you are trying to force a way through China's undergrowth of bureaucracy, according to one independent consultant. 'You need a big, robust personality to get anything done,' he says.

But in this kind of top-down management culture you aren't expected to tell your bosses anything they don't want to hear – which can severely compromise the integrity of management information. For companies such as Unilever China, which is based in Shanghai, this is a serious problem. It runs its business not only by the book, but by the 'bulletin' – a thick internal report updated monthly with facts and figures showing how each product line, from shampoos to a new range of deodorants, is faring with the PRC's 1.3 billion consumers. James Bruce, vice-president of finance for Unilever's China Group, explains how the firm clearly sets out what it expects of its recruits: 'We tell them that there is a professional way of behaving. You don't supply wrong information simply to please your boss.'

Source: *Financial Management*, 1 February 2009: 21 (extract) Retrieved from Activa.com database.

Transcultural competence

To develop the capacity to act effectively at international level, companies must opt for intercultural management, in other words management that adapts its way of communicating, negotiating and leading to the cultural context of the country in question. According to Théry (2002) imparting recipes or dos and don'ts is not the answer: such quick fixes are too anecdotal and offer no insight into the situation at hand. Nor is providing instruments for 'cracking' cultural codes the answer on its own. What is needed is the application of a global approach across the board, or a country-by-country approach. Moreover, the managers involved must become aware of their own cultural preferences and, case by case, look for ways of working that are adapted to those of another culture.

Trompenaars and Woolliams (2000) argue that cross-cultural comparisons are helpful to demonstrate the different ways in which dilemmas are approached. In particular, they have observed that some cultures begin from their own orientation and accommodate the opposing dimension in a process of reconciliation. In contrast, some cultures (managers) are quick to abandon their own orientation and to start from the opposing viewpoint before returning to their initial orientation to ensure it is accommodated in the reconciliation process (see Concept 5.1).

> **SPOTLIGHT 13.3**
>
> **Gender and reconciliation**
>
> Trompenaars and Woolliams (2000) found that women in American/Anglo-Saxon middle management tend to have a higher propensity to reconcile than their male counterparts. Women also appear to be more synchronic than men. However, when severely challenged and unable to reconcile a dilemma, women also show a certain readiness to adopt a compromise whereas men – in this case Americans/Anglo-Saxons – tend to fall back on their own comfort zone, which may be dogmatic in nature.

In an article, Trompenaars and Woolliams (2000: 20–21) explain their viewpoint on transcultural competence:

> Over the last ten years, many business school researchers, consultancies and organizational psychologist groups have developed a range of competency frameworks that claim to delineate effective behaviours of high performing managers. They often form a reference for job design, person specification, organization structuring and training needs analysis. These models often seek the same end but often differ considerably as they each try to encapsulate the existing and traditional body of knowledge. Often, these are only prescriptive lists, like a series of ingredients for a recipe.
>
> Many of the derived underlying behaviours owe their origin to observations of business practice or research in American/Anglo-Saxon studies. Their often ethnocentric nature can cause managers operating internationally additional problems. These prescriptions for behaviour, we increasingly find, do not transfer to other countries or other types of organization from where they were originally developed and tested. At first sight they seem to prescribe a change of behaviour in new destinations as in 'When in Rome, do as the Romans do'. A different set of competencies or framework seems, therefore, to be required for a different destination culture – and even for working with a diverse workforce or in a transcultural team. As a consequence, it becomes like trying to impress on your first date. Our approach is completely different.

The approach used by Trompenaars and Woolliams (2000) is what they call 'the new framework of transcultural competence'. This framework, described in Chapter 5, entails the ability to bridge the differences between the native and destination culture through developing the propensity to reconcile seemingly opposing values. This principle of reconciliation is what lies at the heart of transcultural competence. The extent to which managers display this competence is, on the basis of feedback received by peers on their business performance, closely correlated to the degree of success these managers achieve in business abroad. The amount of experience working on international assignments and with a diverse workforce is also closely correlated to their degree of success.

Hyper-cultural competence

When putting forward a general framework of competence for what they call 'today's global village', Trompenaars and Woolliams (2009) consider transcultural competence to be one of a number of sublevels of competence which together form hypercultural competence. Preceding transcultural competence are:

- Cross-cultural competence – the ability to function according to the rules of more than one cultural system and to respond in a culturally sensitive and appropriate manner;

- Intercultural competence – the ability to communicate and collaborate successfully and effectively with those from other cultures by recognizing and respecting differences as well as other points of view.

Following on from transcultural competence is intracultural competence which Trompenaars and Woolliams (2009: 443) define as 'the capability to leverage cultural and/or ethnic diversity within teams'.

Contrary to what would have been expected, internationalization has reinforced the importance of cultural diversity, rather than reducing it. It is therefore a question of a company having a management that can actually manage this diversity in some way. This means having managers who are able to adapt and who can use the intercultural situations present both within and outside the company to the company's advantage. Managers need to acquire tools and working methods to allow them to develop sufficient competence in the cross-cultural context to turn diversity into a competitive advantage.

Intercultural competence is everyone's business. It is not just a requirement for expatriates, but also for managers who work in multicultural teams. The question as to how this competence can be acquired, or at least developed, is partially addressed in the introduction to Part Two.

Conclusion

This chapter has examined how managers in multinationals can best deal with cultural diversity and do so to the company's advantage. One problem was addressed: how can managers embrace the values of the country in which each subsidiary is operating while ensuring that the subsidiary remains an integral part of the multinational? Bartlett and Ghoshal's concept of the transnational organization, with its flexibility, efficiency and transfer of expertise, was put forward as a way of resolving the local/global issues because it allows the integration into the management process of the influences of the diverse culture groups within the organization.

The chapter finally put forward the notion of transcultural competence as exemplified in the process of reconciliation (referred to earlier in Chapter 5). Using the reconciliation approach can turn cultural diversity into a competitive advantage.

Points for reflection

1. Certain companies regard the management of cultural diversity as a way of developing new competencies that give them certain advantages. They are, for example, able to recruit and hold on to good employees, to diversify their markets and to promote creativity and innovation. For most of the time, however, it is just a question of managing differences between genders and ethnic minorities.

    What, in your opinion, are the reasons for companies adapting their recruiting, training and communication policies to the cultural diversity of their personnel?

2. Managers in international companies increasingly find themselves in situations where they encounter representatives of many different cultures with which they are totally unfamiliar or of which they have only superficial acquaintance. Rather than using a country-by-country approach in such encounters, they are compelled by circumstances to adopt a global stance, as Théry points out in Concept 13.2.

   What do you consider to be one key element in this global approach?

3. Transcultural competence is considered to be an essential element when managing diversity of whatever kind.

   To what extent do you believe this competence can be developed, one which a number of observers claim is essentially innate?

Further reading

Adler, N.J. (2002) *International Dimensions of Organizational Behaviour*, 4th edn, Cincinnati, OH: South-Western Thomson Learning. This book, devoted to cross-cultural management, examines what Nancy Adler calls 'the international dimensions of people's behaviour in organizations' and which she defines as 'a new field relative to the traditional study of management'. This work is particularly interesting because it deals with studies of human behaviour carried out in essentially North American organizations while, at the same time, adopting an approach to take account of the diversity and complexity involved in the globalization of present-day organizations.

References

Adler, N.J. (2002) *International Dimensions of Organizational Behaviour*, 4th edn, Cincinnati, OH: South-Western Thomson Learning.

Adler, N.J. and Ghadar, F. (1990) 'International strategy from the perspective of people and culture: the North American context,' in Rugman, A.M. (ed.), *Research in Global Strategic Management: International Business Research for the Twenty-first Century; Canada's New Research Agenda*, Vol. 1, Greenwich, CT: JAI Press: 179–205.

Bartlett, C.A. and Ghoshal, S. (1989) *Managing Across Borders*, Boston, MA: Harvard Business School Press.

Bartlett, C.A., Ghoshal, S. and Birkinshaw, J. (2003) *Transnational Management*, 4th edn, New York, NY: McGraw-Hill Education.

Gómez-Mejía, L.R., Balkin, D.B. and Cardy, R.L. (2001) *Managing Human Resources*, 3rd edn, Upper Saddle River, NJ: Prentice Hall.

Moore, S. (1999) 'Understanding and managing diversity among groups at work: key issues for organizational training and development', *Journal of European Industrial Training*, 23/4/5: 208–217.

Steinmann, H. and Scherer, A.G. (2000) 'Considérations philosophiques sur le pluralisme culturel et le management', in Ricciardelli, M., Urban, S. and Nanopoulos, K. (eds), *Mondialisation des sociétés multiculturelles*, Paris: PUF: 99–130.

Théry, B. (2002) *Manager dans la diversité culturelle*, Paris: Éditions d'Organisation.

Trompenaars, F. and Hampden-Turner, C. (1997) *Ridings the Waves of Culture*, 2nd edn, London: Nicholas Brealey.

Trompenaars, F. and Woolliams, P. (2000) 'A new unified competency framework for the millennium manager', in Browaeys, M.-J. and Trompenaars, F. (eds), *Case Studies on Cultural Dilemmas*, Breukelen, Netherlands: Nyenrode University Press: 21–28.

Trompenaars, F. and Woolliams, P. (2009) 'Towards a general framework of competence for today's global village', in Deardorff, D.K. (ed.), *The Sage Handbook of Intercultural Competence*, Thousand Oaks, CA: Sage: 438-455.

Woot, Ph. de (2000) 'Ambiguïtés de la globalisation', in Ricciardelli, M., Urban, S. and Nanopoulos, K. (eds), *Mondialisation des sociétés multiculturelles*, Paris: PUF: 155-170.

Chapter 13 Activities

ACTIVITY 13.1

Diversity versus localization within a telecommunications company in Latin America*

Read the case study below and answer the questions that follow it.

INTRODUCTION

This case study is related to the field of cultural management and focuses on a large international telecommunications company, which has operations in Latin America. It is specifically related to the networks division of this company.

The telecommunications industry has seen huge growth during the last couple of years in this part of the world. One important factor is that the GSM technology has been adapted as the standard in most Latin American countries and the local operators have adapted their mobile networks to this technology. The operations of the company in question consist of providing equipment and services for the local operators so they can build, operate and maintain a GSM mobile network. During the last few years there has been important growth in terms of revenues, personnel and offices. The company is present in most Latin American countries (Figure 13.1).

Figure 13.1 **Company's presence in Latin America (2005)**

*Case study adapted from a case written by Roberto Danker (2006), Nyenrode Business University.

To manage the growth of the personnel in this region efficiently and effectively, the company is using two approaches. First, existing employees of the company are moved to Latin America and offered positions for a fixed period ('expatriates', often abbreviated to 'expats'). Second, employees are being hired from the country itself ('locals'). With regard to this second approach, the network division of this company is facing a cultural dilemma: should it maintain a diversified organization in the specific country or should it 'localize' the organization?

Diversity can be defined as a mixture of people with different groups of identities, such as gender, age, education, ethnicity, language or marital status. Diversity can also be related to work, such as seniority, management status, income or functional level of an employee. The advantages of diversity might be that it increases creativity, generates different opinions and opens the mindset. This element of diversity plays an important role in the company. In fact, it sees itself as a multicultural company in which diversity is an important asset that enables the company to achieve extraordinary results. On the other hand, 'localization' of personnel is also an important driver as it can, for instance, bring down costs and so make the company more competitive in the market. Another advantage of localization can be that it increases cultural awareness within the company of the country within which it is operating. Locals naturally understand their customs, behaviours and language better than outsiders do.

COMPANY VALUES AND DIVERSITY

The corporate culture of the company is embedded in its culture and values. Despite the company's rapid growth, including that of the network division, it has continued to stress a corporate culture more typical of an independent, innovative and creative start-up. The objective has always been to maintain this culture, no matter how large the company might become. The company believes the best way to achieve this goal is through leadership rather than traditional management. This first entails the leaders disseminating the company's four values, defined in the 1990s, to everyone in the organization. These values are: customer satisfaction, respect, achievement and renewal. They are applied worldwide and form the core element of the company culture as well as the basis for operations.

Furthermore, the company has defined goals with respect to diversity, a concept it defines as: 'Any demographic and individual attribute that defines each person as a unique individual. It means all the ways we are different from each other.' First of all, the company wants to encourage innovation which, it believes, can best be achieved by well-managed teams whose members come from diverse cultures. These teams are usually more creative and find better solutions than homogeneous teams. The company also aims to improve its understanding of customers. This can be best achieved through it mirroring a diverse marketplace to meet customer needs and so anticipate future opportunities. Finally, the company wants to maximize the pool of talent available. This entails attracting and retaining the best people within a competitive environment.

QUALITATIVE RESEARCH

To identify the corporate culture embedded in the company's values, qualitative research was conducted among forty middle managers of the company in Latin America. An investigation was also carried out to identify the company's corporate diversity policy and the attitude of the employees in this particular region towards it. Topics were analysed such as 'the (dis)advantages of diversity' versus 'the (dis)advantages of localization' in Latin America and the extent to which the company should 'localize' different functions. The total group was further split into three subgroups to identify any differences in views between certain types of employees. The following subgroups were made (Figure 13.2):

- Latin and Europeans;
- Locals and Expats; and
- Females and Males.

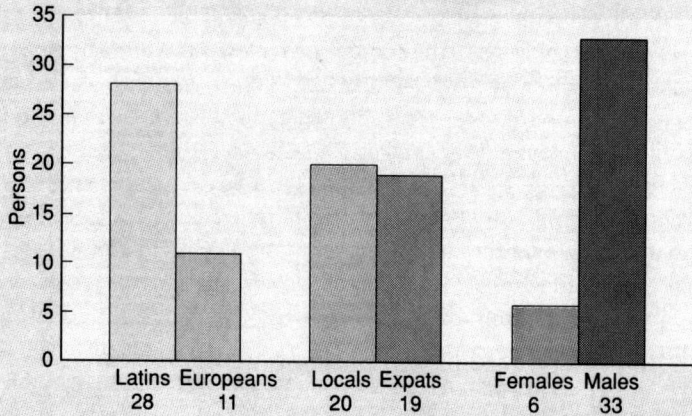

Figure 13.2 Subgroups of respondents to the questionnaire in the Latin American region

RESULTS OF THE RESEARCH

Cultural dimensions of the company in Latin America

From the research comes the identification of the characteristics of the corporate culture and the cultural dimensions of the company in Latin America. Figure 13.3 shows the characteristics of the corporate culture (using Trompenaars' model; each shade represents a different type of corporate culture). The three most

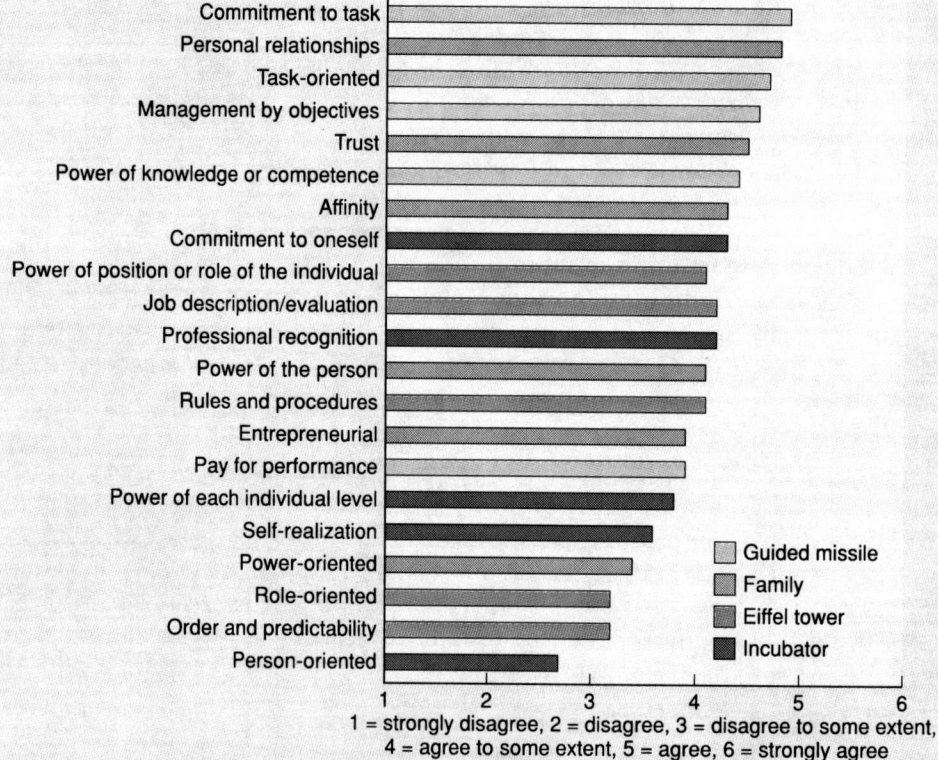

Figure 13.3 Corporate culture of one of the company's divisions in Latin America

dominant characteristics of the company culture in Latin America are 'commitment to tasks', 'personal relationships' and 'task-oriented'. On the other hand, a characteristic such as 'person-oriented', which basically means that a company exists only to serve its employees, is a characteristic with which the respondents of the company are not identified.

The results were based on the entire group: no distinction was made between different subgroups. It is interesting to look at each subgroup and analyse how people in it identify themselves with, for instance, cultural dimensions. Figure 13.4 shows the trends among the three subgroups in Latin America in terms of cultural dimensions. The 'diffuse' dimension, for example, which is the degree of involvement in personal relationship among colleagues, is a cultural dimension valued much more highly by Europeans and Expats than by Latins and Locals. This might seem to be atypical since Latins naturally value this dimension more highly than Europeans. An explanation for this result might be that all the Europeans are also Expats in Latin America and therefore are much more open to having close personal contact among their colleagues. The results might have looked different for Europeans when based in their own country in Europe. Another example is that the females do not see the company as 'diffuse', which means that the females do not tend to share many personal issues among their colleagues. Their male colleagues, on the other hand, see 'diffuse' as a dominant cultural dimension of the company in Latin America. Males tend to share their personal life and issues much more easily among colleagues.

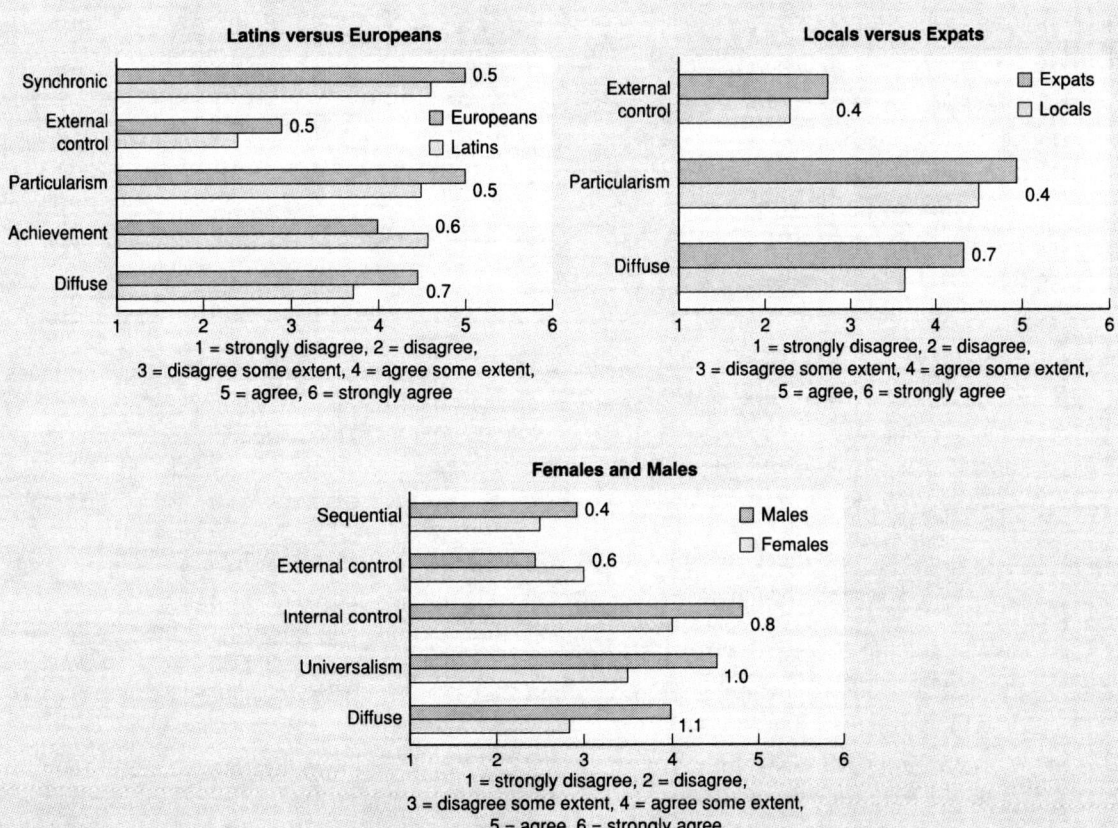

Figure 13.4 **Largest differences among the three subgroups regarding cultural dimensions**

Advantages and disadvantages of localization versus diversity

The research also consisted of open questions by which those interviewed were asked to identify advantages and disadvantages of localization and diversity. Table 13.1 summarizes the responses.

Table 13.1 **Localization versus diversity: advantages and disadvantages**

Localization	
Advantages	**Disadvantages**
• Cost reduction and cost efficiency • Knowing the local culture, better insight, understanding of the local reality, local way of thinking • Customer intimacy and understanding customer needs • Language • Locals are able to solve things faster • Everybody understands each other's position when discrepancies arise • More realistic approach to solving problems	• Lower awareness of company culture or company way of working. Local culture cannot be appropriate for company culture • Limited experience, lower exchange of experience • Lack of global connections and global guidance • Less control • Certain local habits may not be supportive to business • Local people tend to create their own rules • Creation of small political groups • It creates too narrow a mindset

Diversity	
Advantages	**Disadvantages**
• Different opinions, mindsets, points of view • Stimulates more creativity • Brings in more experience • Puts flavour in work environment	• Cultural barriers and distance might lead to misunderstandings • Language (difficult to understand and communicate) • Higher costs • More difficult to manage • Adaptation of foreigners to local culture might be a risk • Locals are not as well respected as they should be

It is also interesting to see the differences in opinion within each subgroup regarding the (dis)advantages of localization and diversity. A Latin might have a different perception or preference from a European. The same can be said about a Local compared to an Expatriate (who may be either a Latin or a European). Some typical 'quotes' show the different perspectives within each subgroup:

Advantages of localization:

Local: 'Knowledge of the local situation can be very important in particular places like Latin America.'
'The cost of these resources is significantly lower.'
'The deep knowledge, contacts, behaviour, networking and cultural aspects bring potentially better positions for dealing with the local culture of the customers and suppliers. Also the roles that do not add value to the overall business are better contracted locally to reduce the cost of the operation.'

Expat: 'Apart from minimizing the disadvantages of diversity, localization in general matches the cost levels our customers can accept. Also, certain jobs, especially in the field and customer support functions, would prefer local personnel for language and cultural reasons. The company will additionally have access to the local ways of doing things, which are most often the most efficient.'

Disadvantages of localization:

Latin: 'The company culture is still based on its European background (transparency, respect, flat organizations, etc.). If key positions are localized without there being a good understanding of the person's background, there is a high risk of basic principles being lost.'

European: 'Less possibility of ensuring that the local organization stays in line with the way the company works.'

Advantages of diversity:

Local: 'People with different experiences in other projects in which our company participated enriched others with a broader knowledge of the mobile business around the globe. Diversity itself motivates tolerance. This means that people of different nationalities, education and language working together is itself a challenge that creates an environment of co-operation and flexibility to work under potentially difficult circumstances.'

Expat: 'Having foreigners keeps the company's way of working alive, and ensures that our company does not become too "localized" in terms of behaviour. A diverse organization also impresses our customers: they have the feeling that they are getting the best of the company's global reach.'

CONCLUSIONS

On the basis of the research findings, conclusions can be made with respect to the cultural dilemma: why should the company have a diversified organization and what are the main reasons for having localization? The main incentives for having a diversified organization in Latin America can be summarized as follows.

a) Having cultural differences and multicultural teams in the organization in Latin America can lead to more creativity and better solutions.

b) Diversity is necessary for remaining in business. This is because the organization in Latin America has been growing fast during the last two years with a lot of new local employees, so experienced employees (mostly foreigners) must be kept inside the organization for it to remain successful and competitive. With regard to its customers, the company feels that it needs strong international back-up support in Latin America to ensure that its customers get the best possible attention.

c) Diversity keeps the company way of working alive.

As for localizing resources in the region, this is needed to reduce costs to stay competitive in the market. Furthermore, the company should have local knowledge in Latin America to gain a deep understanding of the market and to be close to the customer. Localization also helps to remove possible language barriers and to gain a closer cultural match with local circumstances (customers, suppliers, customs, etc.).

Questions

1. Look at Chapter 5 for a description of Trompenaar's seven dimensions, and then examine how the author in his case study describes the results for the 'Diffuse' dimension with regard to the three sub-groups (Figure 13.4).
2. Do the same analysis for the two dimensions 'External control' and 'Particularism', using the information given in Figure 13.4 and Trompenaar's definitions of these dimensions.
3. Read the quotes from the different sub-groups and then decide which (dis)advantages of Localization and Diversity are most referred to.
4. Discuss the conclusions given by the author at the end of the case study.

5. Below is the author's answer with respect to the cultural dilemma: 'Which positions should be localized, and which not?'

Author's analysis
The cultural dilemma comes down basically to the following question: which positions should be localized in Latin America and which not? The results of the survey show that the organization does not have a clear answer to this question. All respondents, whatever subgroup they belonged to, replied that the localization 'policy' was not clear. However, if we look at the issue of localization in terms of different job grades, and the percentages involved, the survey findings show that for positions such as assistants and engineers the localization is around 90 per cent. Furthermore, the survey shows a tendency whereby the higher the position inside the company, the less localized it should be. For higher management positions the localization is at least 75 per cent or more. Considering the 'Latin – European subgroup', the Latins believe there should be higher localization for high management positions (around 75-80 per cent). The Europeans would like to see a lower localization percentage (50-75 per cent). The reason for this might be that Latins believe that higher management also has to deal with political issues in the country, in which case a local person is more suitable. The Europeans believe that the company headquarters needs to keep control of local subsidiaries such as the one in Latin America, and that the localization should therefore be less.

a) Discuss the author's analysis with your peers.

b) Using the information given in the case and/or your knowledge of the area in question, what other alternative(s), if any, could you put forward?

ACTIVITY 13.2

Read the article below and answer the questions that follow.

Why multinationals struggle to manage talent

By Matthew Guthridge and Asmus B. Komm

Managing talent in a global organization is more complex and demanding than it is in a national business – and few major worldwide corporations have risen to the challenge.

A McKinsey survey of managers at some of the world's best-known multinationals covered a range of sectors and all the main geographies. Our findings suggest that the movement of employees between countries is still surprisingly limited and that many people tempted to relocate fear that doing so will damage their career prospects.

Yet companies that can satisfy their global talent needs and overcome cultural and other silo-based barriers tend to outperform those that don't.

We've long observed that global corporations grapple with a more difficult talent agenda than their domestic counterparts – partly because they need to share resources and knowledge across a number of business units and countries, partly because of the especially demanding nature of global leadership. To find out more, we undertook in-depth interviews with executives at 11 major global corporations and separately invited senior managers at 22 global companies to participate in an online survey investigating how effectively they manage their talent. More than 450 people, ranging from CEOs and other directors to senior managers, including HR professionals, took part in the survey.

The responses confirmed impressions from the interviews that companies now struggle on a number of talent-management fronts, such as achieving greater cultural diversity, overcoming barriers to international mobility, and establishing consistent HR processes in different geographical units.

Despite the value companies claim to place on international management experience, the senior managers who took the survey had made, on average, only 1.5 cross-border moves during their careers, as against an average of 2 for managers at the top-performing companies. Interestingly, we found that the respondents had also moved, on average, 1.7 times between different divisions within the same geography but only 1.3 times between different functions – another sign that movement from silo to silo is still limited.

Participants cited several personal disincentives to global mobility, but one of the most significant was the expectation that employees would be demoted after repatriation to their home location. 'Overseas experience is not taken seriously and not taken advantage of,' commented one senior manager. 'Much valuable experience dissipates' because companies have a habit of 'ignoring input from returnees, and many leave.' The quality of the support for mobility a company provides (for instance, assistance with housing and the logistical aspects of a move) also plays a decisive role in determining how positive or challenging an overseas assignment is for expatriates.

Perhaps the most provocative finding from the research was the relationship between financial performance, as measured by profit per employee,[1] and ten dimensions of global talent management. Companies scoring in the top third of the survey (when all ten dimensions were combined) earned significantly higher profit per employee than those in the bottom third. The correlations were particularly striking in three areas: the creation of globally consistent talent evaluation processes, the management of cultural diversity, and the mobility of global leaders. Companies achieving scores in the top third in any of these three areas had a 70 per cent chance of achieving top-third financial performance. Companies scoring in the bottom third of the survey in these three areas had a significantly lower probability of being top performers, particularly if the company had inconsistent global talent processes. Although providing no evidence of true causality and lacking a longitudinal perspective, the strong associations between company financial performance and these global-talent-management practices strengthen our belief that these are important areas on which businesses and HR leaders should focus their attention.

Global consistency in a company's talent evaluation processes is important, because for mobility to succeed, line managers need to feel confident that employees transferring into their units from other parts of the organization meet the same standards that their own people do. Moreover, company support and training is vital to the promotion of diversity. HR managers stressed the need for expatriates to learn more about the culture of the countries they transfer to than just the local language. 'If you have to choose,' explained one HR director, 'it's more important to have an open-minded leader than to have someone with the right language skills.'

In our view the key implication of the research is that companies should focus hard on rotating talent globally across divisions and geographies. Not only will this rotation support the development of company talent, it will also promote greater cultural awareness and diversity. The research further examined why some companies are better than others at developing global talent in this way. It found that those with top managers and promotion systems that actively encourage their people to gain international experience – and provide managers with incentives to share their talent with other units – were roughly twice as likely to have effective global mobility practices than those that don't.

Global companies should consider devoting more resources and senior-management time to liberating talent 'trapped' in national silos and more wholeheartedly supporting global-mobility programs. Instilling a common set of talent evaluation processes throughout the world – especially standardized individual performance evaluations – will underpin this effort and build the confidence of line managers.

More and more companies are stepping up their international revenues, their overseas customer base, and their non-domestic workforce. What our research suggests is that many of them need to match these achievements with truly global talent-management attitudes and practices.

[1] See Lowell L. Bryan, 'The new metrics of corporate performance: Profit per employee', *McKinsey Quarterly*, 2007 Number 1, pp. 56-65.

Source: Guthridge, M. & Komm, A. (2008), 'Why multinationals struggle to manage talent', *McKinsey Quarterly*, (4), 10-13. Retrieved from Business Source Complete database.

Questions

1. Summarize the cultural factors that according to the survey, correlate strongly with strong financial performance. Which do you consider to be the key factor? Explain your reasons.
2. On the basis of the survey's findings, how can the cultural experiences of managers returning from working abroad best be used for the company's benefit?
3. What, in your opinion should be the shared 'talent evaluation processes' which could liberate 'talent trapped in national silos'?

CHAPTER FOURTEEN

Culture and Human Resource Management

> The role of the Human Resource Manager, the 'priest' in whose hands the company's 'Ten Commandments' lie, is to ensure the survival of its soul. Far from merely providing a functional service determining salary rises and fringe benefits, the human resource management function forms the very heart of a company, and its manager exists to confirm the company's particular values and try to apply them in practice.
>
> **Michel Perez, Apple Computer, Europe**[1]

Any international company hoping to implement a global strategy must choose the human resource policies and practices that will best support that strategy. This is, in essence, the meaning of *strategic international human resource management*. Or, as the HR Director of Honeywell Europe put it, 'HRM is the local implementation of strategy'. However,

> 'If we accept the view that HRM approaches are cultural artifacts reflecting the basic assumptions and values of the national culture in which organizations are embedded, international HRM becomes one of the most challenging corporate tasks in multinational organizations.[2]'

Unfortunately, the same policies will not produce the same effects in different cultural contexts. A major challenge facing companies with international or global aspirations is how to internationalize HRM, the policies, and the function. In keeping with the spirit of 'war is too important to leave to the military', the task of internationalizing HRM may be, in the words of one Honda executive, too important to leave to the HR department.

This chapter discusses the influence of national culture on the development and transfer of HRM practices: selection, socialization, training, performance appraisal, compensation, and career development. Here we surface the basic assumptions underpinning the very notion of HRM, as well as the various HR practices (or artifacts such as socialization rituals), and beliefs (such as who is the right person for the job). This allows us to consider how HRM may be viewed differently through other cultural lenses and may thus have unintended consequences when transferred abroad.

Questioning these HRM practices can serve as a basis for dialogue between headquarters and subsidiaries, or between partners in strategic alliances, in their efforts to achieve a balance between global integration and local adaptation of HRM. The challenge is to determine where policies need to converge, where variety may prove more beneficial, and what local practices might be well-suited for global diffusion. Finally we consider the extent to which the HR function is equipped and prepared to handle these difficult international challenges.

The cultural meaning of HRM

The extent to which HRM can be considered *strategic* or *global* depends to a great extent on national context and culture. For example, in Europe, government, unions, and works councils have a greater impact on the strategic use of HRM practices than in the United States.[3] Different cultural assumptions regarding, for example, organizations as systems of tasks versus relationships, the role of the individual and the collective, and the importance of being versus doing (achievement versus ascription) make HRM practices culture-bound. Indeed many question whether the very notion of HRM is appropriate to other national contexts: 'HRM can be seen as a contemporary manifestation of the American Dream'.[4]

The idea of humans as resources assumes that people can be utilized like capital or raw materials, another factor of production which can easily be bought or sold, and whose value must be maximized and exploited. This difference has been referred to as the 'hard' or calculative approach versus the 'soft' or collaborative approach.[5] This view of human resource management (which some consider to be 'very American'[6]) may cause genuine offense in cultures which take a less instrumental (task-oriented) and more social view of organizations.

The approach to human resource management in the United States and Europe has evolved from different disciplines, psychology and sociology, which have different assumptions regarding the nature of the relationship between people and organizations.[7] In the United States, HRM has its roots in psychology, its prime concern being the improvement of worker motivation. This leads to focusing on the individual, analyzing employee needs, reward systems, and job enrichment. This approach is evident in the current interest in 'performance management'.

In Europe, HRM has evolved more from a sociological perspective, which pays more attention to the social system, the economic and political context, and the nature of the relationship between key actors, such as government, unions, and management. Here the primary concern is who has the power to decide, leading to efforts to promote industrial democracy (the workers decide) and industrial policy (the government decides). This results in legislation for worker representation on the board of directors, as in Germany and The Netherlands, quality of work-life councils in Sweden, and the *Code du Travail* in France. These issues are still being hotly debated at the European level in the EU, with differing concerns and opinions regarding the role of government and the welfare of workers.

As a result, the nature of the employment contract, which defines the relationship between the employer and employee both legally and psychologically, differs. Whether or not explicit, the psychological contract between the individual and the company establishes mutual expectations. The legal contract determines what is regulated and to what degree.

In the United States, this relationship is considered 'contractual', based on notions of fair exchange, such that both parties, for example, guard their rights, preserving autonomy and independence (self-determination). Many HR practices, such as performance appraisals, equal opportunity recruitment and promotion, and training programs addressing ethics or diversity issues, are in fact designed to avoid lawsuits.

In Europe, many aspects of the employment contract such as how to recruit, what salaries to pay, and how to terminate are decided outside the company walls. In The Netherlands, where legislation makes it extremely difficult to fire employees, court procedures and severance payments make the approval of lay-offs lengthy, costly, and traumatic. Employee rights are not only safeguarded by legislation, but are also vigorously protected by strong unions, as in Germany. Here, employment is seen more as a 'social contract' based on a moral commitment: long-term employment promised by the company in exchange for loyalty or social welfare provided by the state. The European approach to HRM as such reveals a more social rather than instrumental view.

Indeed a recent study conducted by Watson Wyatt of 200 European and 20 Swiss companies found that HR practices such as merit pay (instrumental) was most likely to create shareholder value whereas 'paternalism' (social) did not. Not surprisingly, when comparing US and European HR practices, European firms were found to be more paternalist, while US firms which were more instrumental in their approach had higher turnover. However, no differences were found with regard to employee focus. The companies which strategically and professionally managed their human resources were found to increase shareholder value by a factor of eight.

Another study showed British firms were the most likely to adopt both calculative and collaborative HR practices. In contrast, Denmark and Norway were the least likely to adopt calculative practices but the most likely to adopt collaborative practices. These differences were thought to be a function of the institutional, in this case regulatory, environment and power structures.[8] Cultural differences may also help to explain these findings, as Denmark and Norway are more concerned with promoting well-being (femininity versus masculinity). Thus different approaches exist within Europe as well, for both institutional and cultural reasons.

More recently many European companies have been faced with downsizing and restructuring activities, which has meant renegotiating these social contracts. Nevertheless, the underlying cultural assumptions remain firmly embedded, creating a demanding challenge as companies within Europe, America (North and South), and Asia are forced to deal with changing economic and political realities. The challenge remains: how to meet competitive demands without alienating their workforce or making matters worse, as in the case of France, provoking massive strikes (of transportation workers, airline employees, even doctors).

Given these cultural differences in the perceived relationship between employee and employer, it is easy to appreciate that certain subsidiaries or partners will be more or less receptive to particular HR initiatives or policies. The responsibility of the HR function is to navigate through the cultural differences in designing practices which will support specific strategies and develop the corporate culture.

Choosing from the HR menu

Companies can choose from a menu of HRM practices that concern selection and socialization, management training and development, appraisal and compensation, and career development. However, it is important to decipher the cultural assumptions underlying these choices in order to consider how these practices may need to be modified, or how their implementation needs to be managed.

Table 14.1 provides a set of questions that enables us to surface these cultural differences. The divergence of responses provides a basis for discussing the appropriate HRM strategy.

Selection

Finding the right people is often one of the most important challenges, particularly when unfamiliar with the nature of the local labor market or the available human resources. This makes difficult the task of finding those candidates who have the competence to get the job done and who seem likely to fit in with the existing corporate culture. This may mean that a company has to look in very different places to find the same kind of people in terms of abilities as well as behavior, beliefs, and values. What represents a standard profile in one country may be quite exceptional in another. For example,

> When K-mart bought the staid, state-owned *Maj* department store in Prague, some employees found the notion of service with a smile so repellent that they quit. "They felt that they had to be too nice to customers." ... Czechs are notorious for what some call moodiness and others call cynicism. "This won't work with Czechs. We don't smile at people on the street."[9]

IKEA, the Swedish home furnishings company, uses extensive screening and hiring procedures to select people whose values are similar to those of the organization. An executive listed the characteristics of the successful new applicants to IKEA:

> They are people who accept our values and are willing to act on our ideas. They tend to be straightforward rather than flashy, and not too status-conscious. They must be hardworking and comfortable dealing with everyone from the customer to the owner to the cashier. But perhaps the most important quality for an Ikean is *ödmjukhet* – a Swedish word that implies humility, modesty and respect for one's

Table 14.1 HRM menu: cultural determinants

HRM issues	Cultural determinants
Selection	
Who to hire? How to hire?	
• Desired behaviors – focus on skills/personality?	Doing versus being
• Specialists versus generalists?	Uncertainty avoidance
• Necessary qualifications?	Power/hierarchy
Level, discipline, or preferred institutions?	Individual versus collective
• How important is 'what you know' versus 'who you know'?	Task versus relationship
Socialization	
• What kind of 'initiation rites' are acceptable? Team building?	Task versus relationship
• What are the messages being sent? Competition versus cooperation? Individual versus team effort?	Individual versus collective Private versus professional life
• To what extent will people engage in/reject social events?	High versus low context
• To what extent should efforts be made to ensure 'corporate culture' is shared?	
• To what extent should the corporate culture be made explicit (pins, posters, slogans, etc.)?	
Training	
For what purpose?	
• Develop generalist versus specialist perspective?	Uncertainty avoidance
• Acquire company versus skill specific (technical) knowledge?	Individual versus collective
• Extent of job rotation?	Hierarchy
• Role of mentorship?	Task versus relationship
• Competences versus networking?	
How are training needs determined?	
• By company? By individual?	
• Who is sent for training? 'High-flyers' versus 'rank and file'?	
What training methods are most effective?	
• Case approach?	
• Reading and lecture?	
• Experiential exercise?	
• Professor versus student driven?	
• Groupwork?	
Performance appraisal	
• To what extent is individual versus team effort evaluated?	Individual versus collective
• To what extent is goal setting (MBO) useful?	Hierarchy
• To what extent do people expect feedback? And from whom?	Being versus doing Time monochronic versus polychronic
• To what extent will criticism be accepted?	High versus low context

Table 14.1 (cont.)

HRM issues	Cultural determinants
Compensation and rewards • Who gets what? • To what extent should pay be linked to performance? • What degree of pay differential is acceptable? • To what extent are bonuses effective? • To what extent should team versus individuals be rewarded? • How much of salary should be fixed versus variable? • To what extent are financial versus non-financial rewards preferred?	Equity versus equality Doing versus being Hierarchy Control over nature Individual versus collective Uncertainty avoidance Masculinity versus femininity

Career development
• Who gets promoted?
• What determines career success?
• What type of career paths are desirable?
  Internal versus external hiring?
  Within functions/across functions?
  Within company/industry?
  Across companies/industries?
  Between government and business?
• To what extent are people mobile? Willing to move?
• At what stage are 'high potentials' identified? At entry? After 5 years?
	Being versus doing
	Individual versus collective
	Task versus relationship
	Uncertainty avoidance

fellow man. It may be hard to translate, but we know it when we see it. It's reflected in things like personal simplicity and self-criticism.[10]'

This caused some difficulty for IKEA when it expanded into southern parts of Europe.

A study of 18 Western companies in Russia found that personality and previous work experience were the most important criteria for selection.[11] According to one HR manager at Coca-Cola in Russia:

'A company can teach or train any person to do some specific job, but if the attitude is wrong that person wouldn't be a good employee. So, at times, we prefer to hire someone who is underqualified but has the right work attitude.[12]'

Grades and diplomas were considered to be less important than qualities such as being seen as honest, ambitious, hardworking, a team player, but above all, willing and able to learn.

When recruiting internationally, companies need to understand how to access 'equivalent' labor pools. Differences in education systems make it difficult to figure out who has the right profile. For example, the age of college graduates may differ due to the length of study. College graduates in Germany, due to the combination of long university courses (six years for economics students), apprenticeship, and national service, might not reach the job market until 28 years of age, compared to 22 years old for their British and Japanese counterparts. This can create problems when someone younger with more experience is assigned to manage older employees with more education, as in the case of a 28-year-old American manager sent to work in Germany.

Local 'talent' may also have very different types of skills and abilities owing to different national values placed on education: the amount and the subject. For example, in Spain, many top managers have university degrees in law and/or economics, while their German counterparts may have advanced engineering degrees or doctorates in science.[13] In Italy, the title of *Dottore* does not necessarily reflect the same level of education as in Germany, and a degree in philosophy earns more respect than it would in France. In contrast, British recruiters pay very little attention to the actual subjects studied, with about half of all opportunities being open to graduates of any discipline. In the United States, job candidates might hide their doctoral degree for fear of being rejected as overqualified for the position.

A recent study based on scenarios with 300 managers in 25 firms from France, Germany, Italy, Spain and the UK found considerable differences in attitudes towards hiring practices within Europe. For example, the English, French and Italians chose foreign multilingual employees with a generalist background, while the Germans and Spanish preferred to hire local employees with a more technical background. The Spanish were more likely to avoid recruiting graduates from elite business schools; age (being young) and nationality (being a Spaniard) were found to be important.[14]

Not understanding the different educational systems can create obstacles to recruitment in that candidates with similar educational credentials may be neither able nor willing to do the same jobs. For example, in The Netherlands and Germany, having a vocational or technical education does not mean the same thing as it does in the United States. This created ill-will with a Dutch subsidiary of an American multinational when it tried to implement a program to 'upgrade the workforce' using a college degree as the referent criterion. In Germany, the status accorded to *Technik* means that the applied sciences criterion taught in polytechnics is valued as highly as the 'pure' sciences taught in the university.

In France, graduates of engineering schools, such as the *Ecole Polytechnique* or the *Ecole Centrale*, or the school of public administration *Ecole National d'Administration* (ENA) are considered to be the elite. These graduates, however, may not be particularly interested in working for a foreign company, having loftier aspirations.

> '[The] alumni of France's *grandes écoles* – of which the military-style Polytechnique views itself as the grandest – take leadership as a natural right. Whatever their subsequent performance, their diplomas guarantee them a lifelong career in government or at the head of large corporations.[15]
>
> More than in any other western democracy, power in France is concentrated in the hands of a tiny elite. Every year, ENA takes in fewer than 100 graduates ... They spend 27 months there and, on graduation take up life-long employment in one of the grands corps (such as the Inspection de Finances, ...). From these institutions – the inner sanctum of the French state, the *énarques* fan out to run the civil service, state-owned industries, banks, the arts, and of course, politics.[16]'

As French companies are primarily interested in products of the foremost business or engineering *grandes écoles*, university graduates are often considered 'second best' by many French corporate recruiters. For this reason, IBM-France has established a department called *Relations Grandes Ecoles*. So when French companies deliberately recruit university graduates instead, they are clearly distinguishing themselves from the norms of French industry and making a statement about the corporate culture. Michelin deliberately does not recruit from the *grandes écoles*. L'Oréal makes a point of hiring *personnes atypiques* (unusual people), reasoning that as a marketing company they need to encourage different perspectives.

Foreign multinationals may also have difficulty accessing the most exclusive labor pools, as competition from local companies may be quite intense. For instance, Japanese companies aggressively outbid each other to try to secure graduates from the most prestigious institutions. The rush to grab top students from Tokyo University has led to complaints about the 'strong-arm tactics' used by prospective employers to prevent graduates from seeing competitors during the annual recruiting season.[17]

These local practices may in effect provide a source of potential competitive advantage by creating important pools of labor which are relatively neglected. For example, although women are well represented among university graduates in Japan, they are not always well accepted in the Japanese corporate environment. This presents an opportunity for foreign firms. Some experts, in fact, advise that 'Foreign firms should employ more Japanese female managers; they are more motivated than their male colleagues.'[18] For example, Japanese women bankers have proved particularly successful in selling financial products to customers in Japan, as it was more often the housewives who handled the family finances.

Citibank in Taiwan, having been frustrated in its attempts to hire talented locals, began to recruit more local women to become private bankers. The bank was surprised at how successful these women were, having failed to recognize the importance of their being well-connected through family ties to high-income clients. Because of the assumed negative attitudes towards women, US multinationals have been reluctant to send women abroad as expatriates to countries like Japan. However, women expatriates are seen more as *gaijin* (foreigners) than as women, and they do not necessarily encounter the same barriers as their local counterparts.[19]

Indeed, this is not just the case in Japan. When Marjorie Scardino, in 1997, became the first woman to head a FTSE 100 company, her success in breaking through the glass ceiling was attributed to her foreign-ness: 'Experts on sex discrimination have said that the British establishment is likely to define her first as an American and then as a woman. Americans, even those with the vestiges of a drawling southern accent like Scardino's, enjoy a gutsy, go-getting reputation. "Feisty" is an adjective that crops up often. It is usually closely followed by "extremely competent"'.[20]

Cultural differences do not just influence *where* companies need to recruit, but also *how* they go about it. For example, hiring in China may require going through government agencies, such as the Foreign Enterprise Service Corporation Offices (FESCO) and local labor bureaus, and personal connections *(guanxi)*. This may make some managers, especially Americans, uncomfortable, as it is seen as nepotism. In the United

States such practices would be avoided (or not openly admitted). What is considered to be important is the match between the person and the job description (task versus relationship orientation).

However, in more collectivist countries, nepotism is a natural outcome of the logic of interdependence. When an employer takes on a person, a moral commitment is established. There is an implicit understanding that the employer will look after the employee and quite possibly his or her family too. Family ties in turn provide social controls that are often more powerful than the organization hierarchy.

Interviews conducted in 65 Chinese–Western joint ventures implemented in China regarding HRM practices, revealed selection and retention to be the major concern and that nepotism was the biggest problem. Expatriates had learned to play active roles in selection to make sure that key selection criterion remained professional qualifications rather than just personal relationships.[21]

In summary, MNCs must discover and pick their way through these national differences in recruitment norms. They must find out what disciplines or schools are favored by would-be managers in those countries. They must consider whether the skills, experience, and values fostered by these institutions are compatible with the corporate values and job requirements. For example, hiring elite *grandes écoles* graduates may be at odds with a company's egalitarian culture, but may be the most effective choice for operating in France, especially if the company needs to rely on the strong personal network which cuts across French industry and government.

MNCs must also assess whether the national companies have a 'blind spot' which means they are missing a potential source of talent (such as women in Japan, university graduates in France, or language majors in the United States). In other words, the MNC has to find a balance between imitating local firms and making its own path. It must learn about the local norms, values, and assumptions, in order to decide which ones must be respected and which, if ignored, may actually provide a competitive edge vis-à-vis local rivals.

Looking for a job?

Looking for a job can also vary across cultures. One survey found that Greeks, Spanish and French were most likely to look for work through the Internet while Italians were the least likely to do so. The Italians preferred the most to send résumés (43 percent), the Germans the least (15 percent). Responding to job advertisements was most popular in Spain but not in Italy. Italians, Germans and French were the least inclined to use search companies, while Belgians use headhunters the most. Greeks and Swiss were the most inclined to start their own business, the Spanish were the least. And the British took the shortest time to find new jobs (3 months) (77 percent within 6 months) while the Spanish took the longest (on average more than 6 months).[22]

Socialization

Once selected, employees have to learn the 'company ropes'. Socialization is the process by which new members absorb the corporate culture and become acquainted with the values and behavior expected of them. These are transmitted in a variety of ways: they may be learned through arduous training programs designed to foster an *ésprit de corps*; or they may be absorbed informally by observing other members, and learning the company language and folklore.

Socialization practices, however, may not be eagerly embraced abroad. Embedded in these practices are cultural assumptions regarding, for example, the nature of peer and hierarchical relationships. Furthermore, how they are transmitted, to what degree they are made explicit, is closely tied to use of language, high-context/low-context. These differences can become a source of friction.

As with initiation rites in the army or academic institutions (fraternity hazing or its French equivalent *bizutage*), socialization techniques aim to strengthen the identification of the individual with the group or organization. In Japan, newly recruited bankers are often given menial tasks, ringing doorbells to provide community service, or may undergo Zen training to teach them humility.[23] These initiation rites or tests of endurance are designed to make group membership more valuable. Once you have passed the test you are in. Thus they reinforce the importance of the group over the individual.

Socialization practices also transmit the importance accorded to the hierarchy. At Avis, for example, a tradition established by Bud Morrow in the 1960s required every executive in the company to spend time working on the front line, meaning behind the rental counters and underneath the automobile hoods. Or again, at Disney, every 'cast member', including the sweepers, plays an important role in the show; even senior managers are expected to spend time in the park flipping hamburgers (including CEO Michael Eisner). One senior executive assigned to sweeping, irritated by the lack of respect shown to him, turned to his counterpart (the real sweeper) demanding, 'Do you know who I am?'. His counterpart replied, 'Yes, you are a sweeper'.[24] This reminds members, both senior and junior, that the hierarchy does not provide special privileges.

Not all initiation rituals are intended to foster mutual respect, comradery, and cohesiveness. Instead they may reinforce a corporate culture which is highly individualist ('every man for himself'), aggressive, and intensely competitive. For example, trainees at Salomon Brothers, the New York investment bank, were told they were 'lower than whale [manure]' and had telephones thrown at them for asking too many questions. Company heroes were macho and aggressive, sporting nicknames such as 'BSD' (referring to alleged sexual prowess) and the 'Piranha'.

The spirit of competitiveness was embodied in the story of two very senior executives betting millions of dollars playing 'liar's poker'.[25] Recruits had to prove their nerve and competitiveness before being taken seriously. At Salomon Brothers, the underlying assumptions being reinforced were individual achievement, control over nature (or financial markets, regulators, and customers), masculinity, and the pre-eminence of task over relationships.

Even within the same industry (investment banking) and country (United States), socialization rituals can reveal a different set of cultural assumptions. At Goldman Sachs, another American investment bank, recruits were severely reprimanded for taking personal credit for achievements rather than acknowledging the contribution of others, reinforcing the importance of teamwork and cooperation. Junior members often spend weekends at retreats with senior mentors, called 'rabbis'.[26] This collective spirit might make it easier for Goldman Sachs to expand into certain parts of Asia, though perhaps not Hong Kong.

'Home' visits and seminars also present opportunities for socialization. 'IKEA Way' seminars, a must for all employees, explain the company's roots and values, and how the name IKEA was derived (from the initials of the founder and of the farm and parish where he grew up). Included are trips to Sweden to visit the shed where the founder started the business and to witness at first hand the difficult farm land in order to get across the important values of frugality, hard work, and simplicity.[27]

Social events are also used to strengthen the ties between workers and the company. In Japan, young managers quickly learn that working long hours, drinking with the boss at karaoke bars, and playing golf on weekends with customers are not entirely voluntary activities. Japanese companies in France have been frustrated when trying to introduce the *'Bonenkai* party' (around Christmas) to create a sense of corporate community. The French employees preferred to have the money spent on the party put in their paychecks and they would rather party at home with friends and family, not colleagues.[28] While Japanese managers tend to derive their identity from the company (group), this is not true for the French, who are far more individualistic.

Similarly, company rituals such as weekend company picnics, Friday night 'beer busts' or the 7 a.m. 'power breakfasts' which seem perfectly natural in America might be resented in countries such as France or Germany, where the line is more clearly drawn between work and private life. And the prospect of taking on the boss in a game of tennis at a company weekend retreat can be daunting, as it may not really be considered equal competition. The idea of mingling with colleagues from work (and from different company ranks) wearing shorts and swimsuits can be a source of further discomfort. Assumptions regarding the hierarchy and formality remain firmly in place.

Other artifacts, such as booklets, posters, cards, and pins, are also supposed to remind employees of the visions, values, goals, and corporate identity. For example, many Disney executives are reminded of the company whenever they check the time, thanks to Mickey Mouse wrist watches or wall clocks. The SAS little red book or the blue book at Hafnia (a Danish insurance company) has important symbolic value apart from the actual content. Many managers, mainly in the United States but increasingly in Europe too, carry mission cards in their breast pockets (close to their hearts or wallets). Being a card-carrying member further strengthens identification and a sense of belonging.

European managers tend to view the use of these artifacts cynically as 'terribly American' in their naivety, enthusiasm, and lack of subtlety. As one British HR manager of a US MNC, visibly embarrassed, stated, 'Imagine having to put such things in writing!'. Although agreeing with the principles, this British HR manager felt that it was 'pretty pathetic to have them posted on the wall in every office'. From a European perspective, their very explicitness may be considered condescending.

The need to spell things out, clearly and directly, reflects the low-context culture in the United States. In many European countries, where populations tend to be more homogeneous, there is more of a shared understanding and therefore less need to state the obvious. In the United States, the greater heterogeneity is managed through explicit pressures to fit in, to be American. Within European countries, given the homogeneity, the pressures to conform have already been internalized. Thus the use of socialization techniques to transmit the corporate culture is often regarded as manipulative and as an intrusion into the private or personal realm of the individual.

MNCs have to consider carefully the type of socialization practices used to diffuse or modify the corporate culture. Certain values are clearly core to the quality of internal communication or the company's global reputation. These should be upheld, at least in spirit, even if it means breaking local rules; indeed, breaking local rules may usefully distinguish the company and help it position itself against rival local firms. For example, efforts undertaken in Japanese greenfield operations in the United Kingdom to reduce the class distinction between workers and managers by wearing similar corporate uniforms and eliminating the trappings of managerial status, such as executive dining rooms, have been appreciated by the local workforce.

On the other hand, the company should be prepared to give way to local norms where corporate norms either cannot be justified or where they cause excessive disruption. There is no sense in pursuing a strong culture for the sake of it. If individuals are forced to comply with norms which seem arbitrary or out-of-touch with local ones, they may feel that these infringe on their integrity or freedom, leading to alienation rather than cohesion.

Training

Besides teaching the 'rules of the game', companies have to train and develop technical and managerial competencies. Again, organizations develop their own specific programs in view of the perceived needs of their business and their managers. But cultural views differ on how training is provided, by whom, and for what purpose.

For what purpose?

Training is provided to develop the 'know-how' thought necessary for success on the job and within the company. The type of know-how thought necessary, for example generalist or specialist knowledge, differs across companies as well as countries. The value placed on generalist or specialist know-how, as well as on the building relationships versus task competencies, will be reflected in the nature of job rotations and the extent to which training is conducted through in-house or external seminars.

To develop generalists, university recruits may be rotated between jobs for several months, even years, before finding a 'home'. This approach serves to acquaint trainees not only with a broad range of business activities but also helps to build an informal network by providing opportunities to establish personal connections. Seminars are then provided on more specific technical or managerial subjects. Developing specialists may involve recruiting those with previous business experience, and immediately assigning them to particular homes, so that they learn by doing, on the job.

For example, in the United Kingdom, job mobility across several functions and businesses is encouraged, as is attending external seminars.[29] Acquiring a broad range of skills and experience is considered to encourage versatility. (Unfortunately, the French connotation of 'versatile' is fickle, inconsistent, and unpredictable.)

German managers tend to identify more closely with their technical background and to describe themselves as specialists – *Kaufmann* or *Techniker*. Career moves are carefully integrated with relevant technical training, and management training is almost exclusively conducted internally. This promotes more in-depth, company-specific knowledge. Technical training also prevails in China which fits well with their strong analytic skills and an engineering approach to management.[30]

The Japanese approach is designed to produce company generalists. Management, as the Japanese see it, is like a craft which can only be learned by watching, listening to and practicing under more experienced colleagues. Knowledge acquisition is considered to be more tacit than explicit[31] (in keeping with high- and low-context language). Thus training is achieved on-the-job through a combination of mentorship and job rotation.

In many Japanese companies the role of mentor has actually been made into a formal requirement of every manager. It is a role which Japanese managers seem particularly inclined to take on, given the high esteem in which teachers are held in Japan, a legacy of Confucian respect for learning and wisdom. Recent efforts by US companies to assign mentors have met with mixed success, as achieving tasks often takes priority over developing relationships. However, managers in these companies are now being assigned coaches that are often outside corporate walls as the importance of developing interpersonal skills is more and more acknowledged.

Who decides?

Cultural differences will also influence *who* decides on training needs – the firm or the individual. For example, at Apple Computer there is a strong commitment to the quality and availability of training. However, it is up to the individual to decide which courses to take. One French employee of Apple Europe was clearly overwhelmed by the choice:

> 'It's help yourself time. It's self-help taken to the ultimate. But unless someone tells me that I'm going to be a good marketeer or sales guy or finance man by going on this or that course, I don't know which ones to go on.[32]'

Apple helps those who help themselves. That philosophy is perfectly in tune with American belief in self-improvement; nothing is predetermined at birth and it is never too late to change. In addition, the American workforce is now being exhorted to develop a portfolio of skills that will guarantee employability, as they cannot expect to stay within the same company. Thus individuals are expected to take responsibility for their training needs and encouraged to proactively seek training opportunities. Employees at HP Europe's Discovery Center are given 'checks' to pay for training that they choose themselves. Managing your own career has also become the fashion in European companies as well.

This attitude may not be so eagerly received in cultures where people are less accustomed to taking responsibility for their own development, as shown by the above quote. In France, the top-down system is more prevalent. Here it is the company (line or HR manager) which nominates people to go on courses. Being sent on seminars often serves more to confirm managerial potential than to develop it. Being identified as having high potential is considered by French managers to be the most important criterion for company success.[33]

How to learn and from whom?

Cultural differences also assert themselves when it comes to how and what managers should learn and from whom. Different cultural responses to management education are particularly revealing.[34] For example, German and Swiss managers tend to favor structured learning environments with clear pedagogical objectives, course outline and schedule, and the 'right answer' or superior solution. This is very much in contrast with the view typically held by Anglo-Saxons: 'Most British participants despise too much structure. They like open ended learning situations with vague objectives, broad assignments and no timetables at all. The suggestion that there could be only one correct answer is taboo with them'.[35]

The idea of working in groups may come more naturally to Asian managers than to the more individualistic Anglo-Saxons. On the other hand, Asian participants experience more difficulty having to 'sell' their ideas in a group, with the potential for open disagreement and conflict, and therefore possible loss of face. Nor do they quite see the point of learning from other students who are no more knowledgeable than themselves. Wisdom resides in the hierarchy.

Class discussion may seem perfectly natural to American students who have been encouraged to express their own ideas and opinions, and are ready to jump in to add their two cents' worth. British students have been educated to challenge and debate the ideas put forth by each other, including the professor. British culture values the ability to prove one's case, eloquently, even at the expense of others. Anglo-Saxon culture is more tolerant of confrontation and uncertainty, and is less concerned with status differences, either among participants or between themselves and the teacher. This is quite shocking to French and Asian students who are not used to either voicing their opinions in class, disagreeing with each other, or actively debating with the professor.

The extensive use of case studies, business games, and management exercises (role plays) favors learning by doing rather than learning by lecture and reading. It indicates a preference for experiential (active) rather than cognitive (more passive or reflective) learning.³⁶ It also reflects an inductive rather than a deductive approach, as cases or exercises are used to arrive at general principles or theories (the American approach) rather than starting with a theory or framework which is then applied to a given situation (the European approach). As a result, European managers often do not see the point of these exercises, and complain that seminars conducted by American trainers are not sufficiently abstract nor theoretical. American managers, on the other hand, want training to be more concrete and practical.

Computer based training, or distance learning, has become quite fashionable recently. However, in Russia, this is reminiscent of education by correspondence (or getting degrees by mail) which is considered to be third tier. Serious education is considered to happen in school by day, or by night but only with proof of having a full time job.³⁷

With each culture favoring different training and development practices, it may be difficult to integrate these into a coherent or consistent policy. Standardizing training methods may be important if the company needs to communicate specialized knowledge quickly across different units, or if the uniqueness of the company training programs is regarded as a major source of attracting new recruits.

On the other hand, MNCs may have a lot to gain from cross-fertilizing different approaches, and providing opportunities for training and development that appeal to people with different abilities, learning styles, educational backgrounds, and, of course, cultures. Working with groups of managers from different countries often requires a mixed pedagogical approach, and using trainers of different nationalities.

Companies are increasingly using management training to create a 'one-company' mentality, as well as to enhance specific technical or conceptual skills among managers from different parts of the world. Very often these managers learn as much from each other as from the course material or professor. Often this training serves as an excuse for socialization and establishing relationships rather than the acquisition of formal knowledge. This intention may be more or less explicit. The British CEO of one Hong Kong-based company opened a management seminar in France by explicitly stating that the purpose of being there was for the participants to get to know one another and to establish working relationships; the course content was of secondary value.

Performance appraisal

Performance management involves setting goals, measuring outcomes, and providing feedback to improve future performance. In theory, it is supposed to shape behavior in the desired directions and to motivate people, like ten-pin bowling, by having clear targets, and the possibility to correct behavior based on the feedback of results. Some even argue that goal setting and feedback are *the* most important contributions made by psychologists to management: 'One of the clearest findings from 50 years of applied behavioral science research is that goal-setting procedures are the most powerful tool for performance management'.³⁸ Yet the notion of managing performance is heavily embedded in an instrumental view of organizations which might have little appeal to those cultures that see organizations in terms of social relationships where what counts is managing people, not tasks.

Other cultural assumptions underlying performance management systems can also be recognized: that goals can be set and reached (control over the environment), that objectives may be given 6- to 18-month time frames (time can be managed), and that the attainment of goals can be measured (reality is objective). Bosses and subordinates are expected to engage in a two-way dialogue to agree on what has to be done, by when, and how. This assumes that power differences are not an issue, and that employees have the right of input in determining their goals, and are willing to take responsibility.[39] These assumptions were well-suited to the Germans who readily embraced management by objective (MBO) as it helped to reduce uncertainty by clarifying targets, roles, and responsibilities, and to reduce status differences between boss and subordinate.[40]

In contrast, the idea of concrete, mutually established annual objectives may prove uncomfortable for many French managers, many of whom refuse to put these objectives in writing.[41] MBO largely failed in France because French managers felt that they had no control over the objectives they were being asked to achieve. Rather than empowerment, it was seen as entrapment – experienced by employees as signing their own punishment. Furthermore, the idea of having a two-way conversation ('between equals') with the boss seemed untenable.[42]

Russian managers may also balk at formally setting objectives as it is reminiscent of their 'comprehensive personal plan' which was part of the Lenin exams imposed by the Young Communist League (*Komsomol*). Objectives such as academic achievements, community service (cleaning streets), and the number of papers by Lenin to be mastered were expected to be put in writing and reported on by the end of the year. Therefore, trying to implement goal setting may be met with a skeptical 'been there done that' attitude.[43]

Cultural assumptions are also evident in the term 'performance appraisal' which implies that 'performance', what is done or achieved, is important, and can be measured objectively, that is, 'appraised'. In other words, what counts is results, not personality. This is even upheld in US law courts to protect employees from being evaluated based on who they are rather than what they do, unless it can be empirically demonstrated that personality is directly linked to performance. What is appraised is behavior and not traits; thus doing is more important than being.

In Asian firms, people are more likely to be judged on their integrity, loyalty, and cooperative spirit, not just on their ability to achieve high sales volume. Thus the very notion of performance appraisal may be at odds with the values of many cultures where 'character appraisal' is considered to be more important. Indeed, the appraisal process itself may be interpreted as a sign of distrust or even an insult.[44] According to one French manager, 'The French get offended by positive or negative feedback. If you question my job, you are questioning my honor, my value, and my very being'.[45] For Americans, feedback serves to give them information on how they are *doing*. For the French, feedback serves as an unwelcome commentary on who they *are*.

Giving feedback can thus present a cultural minefield. While giving and receiving feedback is not a particularly comfortable experience for any manager, different norms for being critical and being direct make it even more difficult. In one acquisition of a US firm by a Swedish company, American managers complained that the Swedes were far too critical, and never gave any positive feedback. Europeans, in turn, complain about the American 'hamburger' approach to feedback: surrounding the criticism (the meat) with the soft stuff or empty praise (the bun).[46]

In Asia, the process of giving feedback often clashes with the need to 'save face' (that is, guarding an individual's public reputation) which protects the person's 'social capital' and preserves harmony. Thus confronting an employee with 'failure' is considered to be very tactless and even dangerous. Western multinationals operating in certain Asian countries have had to adapt other approaches such as using a third party as a go-between. For example, in the Indonesian subsidiary of a large US multinational, negative feedback in performance appraisals was avoided as it was considered to bring about 'an unhealthy pollution of harmonious hierarchical relationships'.[47] A more dramatic example is that of a Dutch medical doctor who was killed after giving critical feedback to an Indonesian colleague.[48]

In China there is also a tendency to avoid performance appraisal so as not to create bad feelings. In one Chinese–Western joint ventures study,[49] all of the Chinese managers reported being unwilling to give their subordinates poor ratings as it would interfere with their personal relationships. Nevertheless, despite resistance, almost 50 percent of these joint ventures had introduced such appraisal systems. According to one expatriate,

> 'Because they are not used to direct criticism at all, you have to be very sensitive. You cannot tell them that they are doing a lousy job. You have to focus on the positive. If you're sensitive enough they accept it, and use it themselves later on when dealing with their own people ... One should be very sensitive, and you can do a lot of damage if not.... (p. 318).'

However, concern for 'face' and 'harmony' did not stop the Chinese-owned Haier group from publicly displaying performance rankings and requiring poor performers to publicly confess and state how they expected to improve.[50]

Appraisal systems typically emphasize individual responsibility for assigned work. Yet this focus on the individual may seem inappropriate in collectivist cultures. In Japan, for example, there are festivals where dozens of people carry a heavy portable shrine known as a *mikoshi* through the streets. Because it is impossible to tell who is actually doing the lifting, some end up doing more carrying than others. This has given rise to the expression '*mikoshi* management' in Japanese companies. People work as a group, with the achievers often carrying the laggards along. This is considered normal, not free-riding.

The implications for managing performance and appraisal are twofold. It is crucial to recognize that the very notion of performance management is loaded with cultural assumptions that are not necessarily shared by others. Managers in different cultures will react differently to looking at objective performance data (the facts) and to having an open, honest dialogue. Insensitivity to these issues may alienate or demotivate local employees. MNCs also have to beware of relying strictly on the same criteria used for evaluation back home. Being assertive, showing initiative, and achieving results may count more in some cultures than others. These cultural biases may be responsible for the 'glass ceilings' experienced by foreigners in many international companies.

Take the case of American executive Barbara Cassani. She recalls her initial exposure to the British business culture, working in the City. 'The City was much more constrained – it was "you must be like this, you must be like that, or you won't make it"'. At one of her appraisals she was told she was doing well, apart from being 'too enthusiastic'. What in her home culture would have been viewed as a tremendous plus, was not particularly valued by Coopers & Lybrand in London. In fact, Cassani came to realize that it was a potential career-stopper: 'I was too keen, too challenging, I was a little irreverent and I didn't respect the hierarchy enough'.[51] To have a better chance of success, she did not leave Britain, but instead changed sectors. Joining British Airways, she ended up in charge of BA's own low-cost venture, Go, flying out of Stansted – which became fully independent in 2001.

Given the fairly universal discomfort (more or less intense) which surrounds feedback sessions, companies should probably encourage some local interpretation. What is more, companies may actually find that far-flung operations actually have novel ways of delivering or depersonalizing negative (or even positive) feedback, so that it does not demotivate. Nor should it be assumed that judging on merit will necessarily be rejected. In fact, as P&G found out in India, many local managers working for foreign multinationals which strongly believe in meritocracy are pleased that good performance is finally being recognized.

Compensation and rewards

Cultural differences also play a role in determining who gets rewarded and how. The belief that 'money talks' in every language turns out to be far too simplistic to provide a basis for determining salary policy. The very notion of working for a bonus, of being motivated by money, might cause offense and be taken as demeaning ('After all, we're not trained seals'). Different cultures attach value to different types of reward, and vary in the extent to which they believe reward should be individual or collective.

The current trend of linking pay to performance is particularly culturally suspect. As one American expatriate in Paris discovered, 'Quantifiable objectives freak out [French] executives. They don't want clearly defined objectives. Relating increased performance to increased bonus doesn't work. They're really turned off to discussions about finance and money'.[52] Pay for performance assumes that rewards should be based on contribution to the bottom line, or *equity*, rather than based on belonging to the group, or *equality*.[53] Notions of equity are embedded in the contractual view of employment – 'you get what you deserve';[54] notions of equality correspond to the social view – 'you deserve what you get'.

While it would be unthinkable for most American managers to consider implementing a system at home where the amount that family members are given to eat is related to their contribution to the family income, at work the notion of pay for performance seems quite logical. In contrast, in many African societies a collective logic prevails; the principles applied to family members also apply to employees. One multinational, in an effort to improve the productivity of the workforce by providing nutritious lunches, met with resistance and the demand that the cost of the meal be paid directly to the workers so that they could feed their families. The attitude was one of 'How can we eat while our families go hungry?'.

The dominant influence in American managerial thinking is the principle of equity, that individuals are rewarded according to their individual contribution and if not, are prepared to move on. This reveals cultural assumptions of individualism, control over nature, and achievement. Like the American hero, Horatio Alger, anyone can succeed if he or she just keeps trying. And the sky is the limit! In fact, there may be no upper limit on salary, which means that star performers could be earning up to 200 percent of their core wage. Indeed, at one investment bank, some stars were making more money than the chairman.

The idea of special rewards for special efforts may not be so readily accepted elsewhere. In the Danish subsidiary of one American MNC, a proposal for incentives for salespeople was turned down because it favored one group over the others. In addition the Danish employees argued that everyone should get the same amount of bonus, not 5 percent of salary, and some even insisted that there should be no differences in pay between bosses and secretaries.[55] This reflects strong assumptions of egalitarianism. This assumption may underlie IKEA's decision to throw a one-day promotion to lure shoppers and then distribute proceeds to employees. That day 43,000 IKEA employees sold $80 million worth of merchandise in 152 stores worldwide which translated into a bonus for each employee of $1,800.[56]

Recently shareholders of Swiss companies such as ABB, Swissair, Kuoni, and Zürich Financial Services have been challenging their CEO's compensation (and severance) packages which were seen to be excessive, particularly given falling share prices.

> 'Americans may be accustomed to stratospheric executive pay, but in Western Europe, such figures can be near scandalous. "In Europe, especially in Protestant countries, if you make big money, you'd better hide it.... This is especially true in a Calvinist country like Switzerland." By custom and law, Swiss companies are permitted to keep executive pay a secret, and nearly all do so.[57]'

When Peter Brabeck, CEO of the Swiss company Nestlé, was asked why he did not want to reveal his salary he answered that as a foreigner (he is Austrian) one should always respect the local countries' sensitivities: in Switzerland, salaries are not discussed and private life is protected. When answering what would be the problem if his salary were known, he responded that his American colleagues would die laughing.[58]

Pay for performance is also largely assumed to mean *individual* performance. This assumption was not shared in Indonesia, obliging ARCO Oil and Gas Company to adapt its reward system. According to the Human Resources Manager:

'Indonesians manage their culture by a group process, and everybody is linked together as a team. Distributing money differently amongst the team did not go over all that well; so, we've come to the conclusion that pay for performance is not suitable for Indonesia.[59]'

Attempts to introduce merit pay have also provoked outcries in Japan for fear that this could ruin the harmony (*wa*) of the group and encourage short-term thinking, something that Japanese executives have long criticized in American companies. Some Japanese companies which have experimented with merit pay have found that rather than reducing labor costs, it has actually increased them, finding themselves unable to cut salaries since this would be a blow to employee self-esteem (loss of face). Thus they simply had to pay more to good performers without penalizing the others.[60]

In the Chinese–Western joint ventures, most had experienced significant problems when introducing a performance-based compensation system. These systems were based on individual and then a combination of individual and collective performance. A majority of the companies that had implemented the individually-based system considered it a success: 'It has to be fair and just. You have to be careful that it's distributed in the right way, that everybody understands the rationales. Therefore, there is always lots of explanations going with it'.[61]

In the United States, merit-based pay is now being challenged as demotivating, particularly in view of the movement towards team management which requires cooperation rather than competition among individuals. As companies are trying to create 'high involvement'[62] or strong commitment to the company, rewarding individual achievement is seen as a potential handicap.

Assumptions regarding uncertainty, risk-taking, and control influence the preference for *variable* rather than *fixed* compensation. In one study American managers claimed to be prepared to increase the proportion of variable compensation to nearly 100 percent.[63] In cultures which tend to avoid uncertainty and perceive less control, efforts to introduce discretionary incentives may be met with suspicion and fail to produce the desired effect. Foreign firms expanding into Russia have found that 'most Russians don't like a bonus to be more than about 25 percent of their fixed salary because on average Russians have high uncertainty avoidance'.[64]

Preference for *financial* or *non-financial incentives* is also culturally related. The relative importance of money, status, or vacation time varies across countries and affects their motivating potential. In Sweden, given a choice between a bonus and time off, the latter is likely to be chosen. Monetary rewards are less motivating, because the egalitarian ethos breeds a reluctance to stand out financially (as do the high tax rates). Swedes are also more concerned with quality of life, with Sweden ranking highest on Hofstede's femininity dimension.

In Japan, on the other hand, there would seem little point in offering more time off when employees only take half of their 16-day holiday entitlement as it is (as compared to 35 days in France and in Germany). *Karoshi* (or death through overwork) is regarded as an occupational hazard by many white-collar workers in Japan; surveys show that a third of Japan's managers are seriously worried about falling victim to it.[65]

Workers who take full vacation or avoid working overtime are labeled *wagamama* (selfish), a harsh criticism aimed at those who let down their peers. Concern for the company is supposed to override concern for oneself and even one's family.

For example, in Russia, while good salaries are important other characteristics such as a nice atmosphere, the presence of friends, free meals and social activities, and the promise of a stable future with the firm are often deciding factors in retaining employees. As one HR director reports, 'Baxter may not be offering the highest salaries, but we offer quality, stability and fair treatment to all. Employees understand and value that'. Russian managers were also found to be willing to forgo a bonus of $2000 (representing one to two months' salary) to receive one week's training abroad.[66]

Companies which operate internationally clearly have to appreciate the different values and evaluate their potential impact. The remuneration package is a very strong indicator of the culture and the behavior expected and can be used to encourage cooperation or competition, information sharing or information hoarding, and risk-taking or conservatism. For aspiring recruits, the remuneration package is a very important signal. The company can choose to align itself with local norms if it wants to attract the local elite or it can offer an 'alien' package if it seeks to attract the more adventurous or less mainstream. In addition, it may attract those who are frustrated with local practices, and are looking to be rewarded for their efforts and success.

Career development

National culture also has an impact on career development. The preferred paths for advancement, the traits and behavior required for promotion are different. Young managers quickly learn what they can aspire to and what they have to do to get promoted. What it takes to get ahead, however, varies according to assumptions regarding *being* versus *doing* (who you are versus what you do), and beliefs regarding the nature of the managerial task, or what managers are supposed to do or be.

An interesting cross-national study, conducted by André Laurent, provides insight into what managers in different countries perceive to be necessary for career success.[67] For example, 'drive and ability' are considered by American managers to be the most important determinants. This reflects a pragmatic, individualistic, achievement-oriented, and instrumental world-view.

While 'achieving results' was considered important by 88 percent of American respondents, only 52 percent of the French managers agreed. It therefore comes as something of a surprise to American managers when they find out that the same criteria do not apply in countries where people may be promoted because of the schools they went to and their personal connections. As one disillusioned HR director in the American subsidiary of a French group observed, 'Becoming a *cadre* through hard work alone does not seem to be part of the system – or if it is, it is highly unusual'.[68] For the most part, becoming a manager (achieving *cadre* status) is determined by having attended an elite *grande école*.

For this reason, 88 percent of the French managers perceived being labeled as having 'high potential' as the most important determinant of career success as compared with 54 percent of the German managers. In Germany, technical competence and functional expertise, or *Leistung* (achievement), are considered necessary for advancement.

In the same study, 89 percent of the British respondents selected 'skills in interpersonal relations and communication' as the most important determinant of career success. The British score reflects the traditional belief that management is essentially an interpersonal, rather than a technical (German) or a conceptual (French) challenge. British firms tended to favor those with a more classical education and a broader, generalist approach to management. 'Generally, it remains true to say that the promotion to top level posts of 'gifted amateurs' remains a uniquely British phenomenon.'[69]

Favored career paths – staying within the same function, company, or industry – also differ. The possibility of switching in and out of companies or industries and the potential career leverage in doing so varies between countries. This is bound up with cultural assumptions regarding the importance of the individual versus loyalty to the group, doing versus being, and tolerance for uncertainty.

In large Japanese companies moving between companies, much less business sectors, was virtually unknown up until recently. Nissan's Carlos Ghosn caused quite a stir, in 1999, when he poached 25-year veteran design chief, Shiro Nakamura, from rival automaker Isuzu.[70] In Japan, graduates have traditionally been the raw material from which companies fashioned their senior managers; hence the importance for companies of attracting university recruits of the highest caliber. Job rotation reinforces company-specific knowledge. Mid-career moves were therefore difficult or tantamount to treason and cause for family shame. Many Japanese sent by their companies to obtain MBA degrees in the United States or Europe found themselves emotionally torn between returning to their employer and taking a job (often with a foreign multinational) where they may be offered not only more money but also more responsibility and better career opportunities.

Career mobility is not particularly valued by German companies either. But the reason is not so much to do with loyalty, as with the preference for specialized know-how. Titles are job-specific and skills or experience acquired in one job are not perceived as transferable to another function or company. Senior managers are expected to have not only the technical skills, but also an in-depth understanding of the business and the company which comes from a long-term career therein.

Managers in the United States and Britain, having a more generalist view, are less worried about being in charge of functions or businesses which they do not technically master. Therefore moving into jobs with which they are unfamiliar is not considered to pose a problem.[71] In France, top managers also move in and out of companies from different industries and even from public service positions. This type of career path was held responsible for the financial problems of the French bank, Crédit Lyonnais, which was blamed on the former CEO's lack of understanding of how to run a bank rather than a government agency.[72]

Thus different patterns of career development are found in different countries. These patterns differ in terms of whether managers are developed internally or recruited externally, the stage at which those with high potential are identified (entry or later on), the type of work experiences acquired within or outside the company or industry (specialist versus generalist), and the criteria for selection and promotion. Distinct cultural patterns of career development labeled as the Latin, Germanic, Anglo and Japanese approach, have been proposed by Paul Evans as shown in Figure 14.1.[73]

These different career systems may affect the strategies for internationalization for companies as well as for their managers. For example, the German functional specialist model is considered more suited to an export-based international strategy than one involving international production.[74] The French promotion system of 'political tournament' may discourage overseas assignments because of the fear of 'out of sight out of mind' and the difficulty in developing and maintaining the necessary personal networks.

These different career patterns can also cause problems for multinational companies in implementing their plans for management development. For example, Japanese Nissan Motor Company was frustrated in Italy and Spain where local managers, after extensive (and costly) training and development, readily accepted the offers of rival companies. For the Japanese, this job mobility prevents the accumulation of company expertise and inhibits their planning for human resource management. On the other hand, non-Japanese managers have little reason for loyalty when they discover the glass ceiling, or limited career opportunities, for foreigners.

MNCs have to ensure that the perceptions of what it takes to reach the top, and the patterns of career development, do not exclude people with different skills, abilities, and perspectives. This could be done by reflecting on the composition of the top two or three layers of their company, and considering whether the over-representation of particular groups may be due to implicit biases in the identification and development of high potentials. Otherwise, there is the danger of exclusively promoting managers with the same profile and characteristics. While this like-mindedness may create cohesiveness, there is the risk of serious blindspots.

What it means to have high potential and to be successful is highly context- and culture-specific. Many executives with excellent track records at home have learned this the hard way. MNCs should therefore take advantage of these differences in promoting and developing managers to be effective in different time zones.

Making HRM meaningful across cultures

Faced with pressures for globalization and competition for top talent, many MNCs are looking to learn from 'best practices'. Clearly there are signs of convergence in HR practices, for example in adopting performance management systems (including 360-degree feedback appraisals) and in defining and developing 'global competencies'. The question remains: to what extent do HR practices reflect the country of origin, the country of operation (host country), or some sort of hybrid? A study of 36 German MNCs involved conducting interviews between 1996 and 1998 with 46 subsidiaries (40 in the UK; 6 in Spain). German MNCs were indeed found to be adopting 'Anglo-

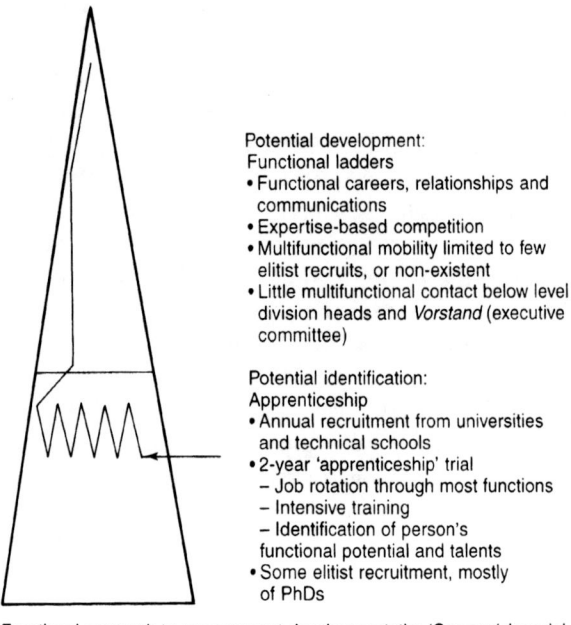

Functional approach to management development: the 'Germanic' model

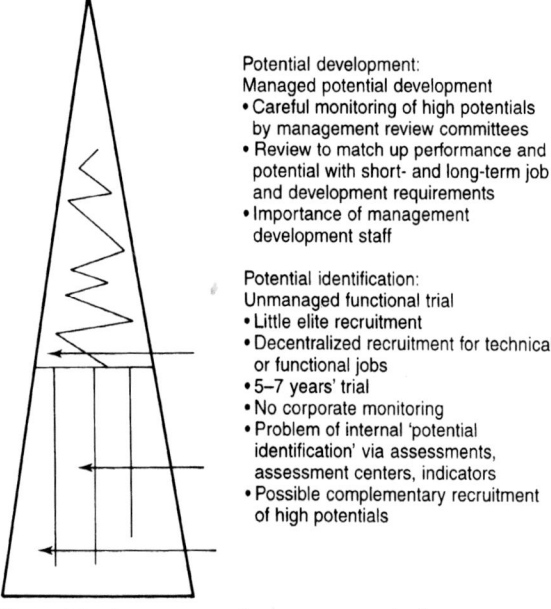

Managed development approach to management development: 'Anglo–Dutch' model

Figure 14.1 Country patterns for career development. (Continued overleaf)
Source: P. Evans, Y. Doz and A. Laurent (eds) (1989) *Human Resource Management in International Firms*, Macmillan, London.

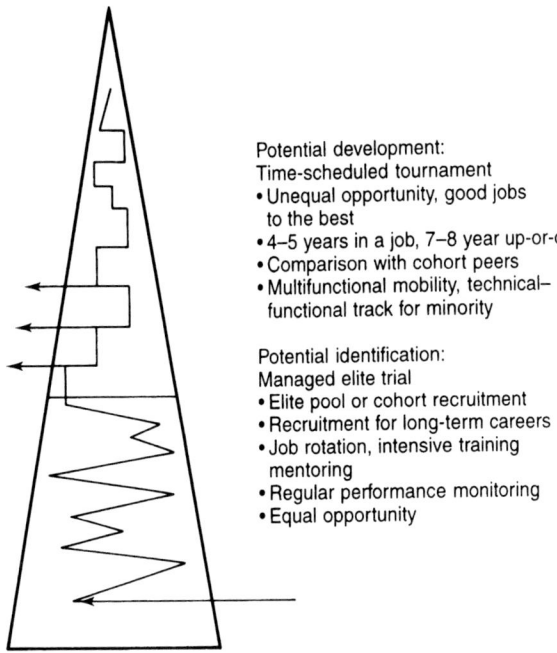

Elite cohort approach to management development: the 'Japanese' model

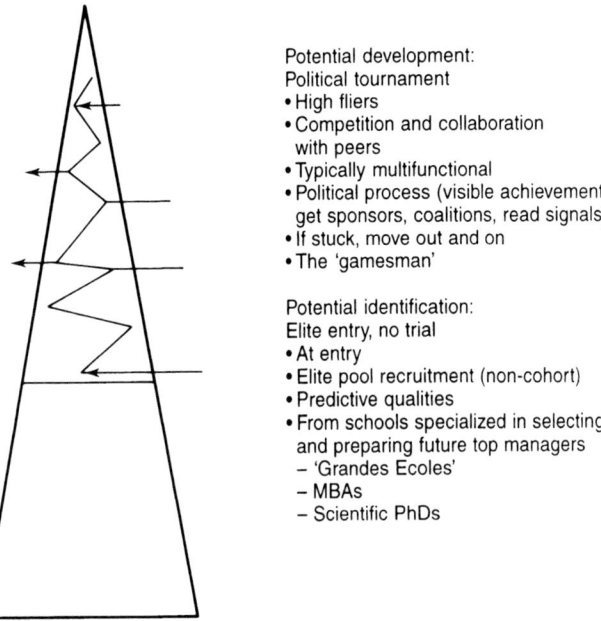

Elite political approach to management development: the 'Latin' model

Figure 14.1 (cont.)

Saxon style' HR practices: international management development; global performance management systems (linking pay to performance; increasing proportion of variable pay and formalizing performance evaluation systems); and using culture as a formal tool (developing mission statements, defining quantitative strategic business objectives).[75]

Despite these signs of convergence, they found that the HR practices remain distinctively German. For example, policies were developed systematically in great detail. Also, creating an international cadre of managers remains head-office driven and dominated by Germans. This supports the findings of Harzing[76] that German companies tend to use expatriates as control mechanisms: using more personal rather than formal controls (as in the US). In terms of performance management, there remains a rather limited percentage of variable pay, and performance appraisals are not considered to be very 'tough'. And the corporate culture still emphasizes employees as stakeholders, collective interests, partnership, cooperative style, responsibility to employees, and to protect jobs. German companies seek to cooperate with unions, whereas UK companies cooperate to avoid unions. Shareholder value is considered to be a long-term affair – involving family or banks.

Nevertheless, the impact of the local environment and more global pressures for convergence cannot be ignored. And the resulting HR practices can be considered to reflect the dynamic interaction of the MNC home, host and institutional environments. For example, although the Spanish labor market is highly regulated (in terms of layoffs and employment contracts for some workers but not for all), the German MNCs used standard contracts for 97 percent of their local workforce to gain commitment. In addition, more Anglo-style HR practices may exist already in Spain due to the development of MBA programs, and the number of local managers who have experience in Anglo MNCs. The Spanish are eager to develop quickly and may more readily accept corporate directives which their UK counterparts might tend to ignore. But the Spanish subsidiaries may adapt them for more locally specific needs, for example using training programs as a selection mechanism. The resulting set of HR practices is a sort of hybrid that emerges from the home country and host country practices, as well as other 'global' forces or institutional actors that encourage the convergence of practice, such as MBA programs and management consultants.[77]

When developing international HRM policies, there needs to be discussion about how much similarity or variation is necessary. Which practices should be designed centrally by an international team, and which ones need to be adapted locally? For example, German-based Bertelsmann introduced what it called its 'January discussion' – an opportunity for bosses throughout the company to receive collective feedback from their subordinates. The practice was intended to encourage more open communications and to relax the rather formal boss–subordinate relations that still characterize many German firms. Significantly though, this feedback mechanism was not imposed on its US operations. Why? Because, in the US, the relationship between executives and other employees is considered more open and less complicated, with 'day-to-day business carried on in a critical and even adversarial spirit'.[78]

Decisions regarding which HR policies can be globally exported and which need to be locally adapted can be effective only if the cultural assumptions embedded in these policies are brought to light and the differences evaluated in terms of their likely impact. This first step is vital in avoiding the possible alienation or low morale which comes from imposing HR policies that are ill-suited to the local culture, or the risks of confusion and lack of coherence which can arise when each local unit determines its own policies.

The discussion, however, often hides a political subtext, as each party wants to reserve the power and autonomy to do things as they see fit. For this reason, cultural differences may be invoked as a pretext for retaining local control, or ignored as a pretext for preserving head-office prerogative. Comments such as '... but that will never work in Italy', or '... but this is the way we do business' need to become subjects for debate rather than accepted as given.

On one hand, increasing the breadth of the discretionary zone regarding implementation of HR policies increases the opportunities for creative interpretation locally. Too much explicitness or imposition may provide a focus for resistance, whereas a certain vagueness may enhance local buy-in and receptiveness. For example, Pepsi-Cola International has accepted that one local unit might develop an individual incentive plan for the general manager, tied to the sales of the local operation, while another unit might develop a group incentive plan for the entire top management team tied to the sales of the local operation.[79]

On the other hand, it is also worth remembering that there are different ways to ignore local norms. One extreme is to impose HR policies direct from HQ, out of ignorance of cultural differences or insistence on 'one best way'. Another possibility is to exploit the differences to make use of local blindspots, for example by recruiting from undervalued labor pools, as previously discussed.

At Nissan, striking a balance between adapting and imposing HR policies has been resolved by adopting a position of 'clear ends and loose means'. This means that as long as the means are in line with the realization of Nissan's company objectives, no standardized way is enforced. So while the Mexican plant is run in a typical Japanese style, the American one in Tennessee is run in an American way with American top management. The British plant in Sunderland is half British and half Japanese in style. The factors which determine how to operate include the location, ownership (greenfield investment or joint venture), past history, level of technology, the nature of the product, and the human resources available.[80]

However, HR policies which ignore or aim to segregate cultural differences are missing out on the potential benefits of utilizing them. A more ambitious approach would be to try to seize the opportunity of mutual dialogue to experiment with creative variations. The pursuit of divergent initiatives around an agreed-upon theme may be the key to strategic flexibility and learning.[81] These deviations should not be killed off but allowed to run their course, then assessed for viability. Those retained can then be considered as candidates for global diffusion.

For example, different interpretations of what is meant by 'high potential' encourages managers with different profiles to be selected and promoted in different locations. This can significantly enrich the company's understanding of the meaning of 'effectiveness', particularly in an international context. Having highlighted the challenges and trade-offs that face companies in creating effective international HR practices, we now consider the extent to which the HR function is prepared to take on this effort.

Internationalizing HRM

Internationalizing a company makes heavy demands on the HR function. First, it requires a sound understanding of the corporate strategy to make sure that the HRM policies are aligned. Second, it demands a thorough awareness of the cultural assumptions embedded in HR practices themselves, as well as those which prevail in local subsidiaries. And third, it requires the judgement to assess political concerns such that local resistance to HQ policies is really driven by cultural differences, or desire for local autonomy, or that HQ just wants to have its own way. Headquarters' HR personnel also have to be ready and willing to accept that they may have something to learn from their foreign subsidiaries and partners.

Unfortunately, the level of strategic, political, and cultural awareness required of the HR function to make it effective internationally is rarely achieved. A study of 1500 European HR executives reveals widely different levels of specialized HR training and of business experience.[82] Furthermore, it was found that HR managers rarely attain high levels in organizations (except in Scandinavia) and tend to be poorly integrated, if not isolated, from both operations and strategic planning. And while gaining competence in cross-cultural management was considered crucial by senior executives, very few HR directors considered this a priority. This creates an overwhelming challenge for HR managers, with the added headache of having to worry about internationalization.

One of the barriers preventing the HR function from fulfilling its role is its own lack of international experience. HR professionals, having very few transfer opportunities outside their home country, do not get the international exposure they need. HR jobs are thought of as fundamentally local, so HR positions are filled from outside only when a local solution is unavailable. The results of one survey indicate that only 30 percent of HR respondents considered international experience to be very important for promotion at corporate HR level; a mere 16 percent considered it to be very important for promotion to the regional HR group level.[83]

The lack of international perspective was revealed by a study conducted by Adler and Bartholomew[84] who found that a large number of American firms were *not* benchmarking excellence in global human resource management. Of the fifty HRM directors contacted, almost one-fifth could not name a single leading North American firm, more than one-third could not name a single excellent European firm, and one-half were ignorant of Asian examples. Paradoxically, then, the function in charge of implementing internationalization is itself rather parochial. This lack of international experience and understanding no doubt helps to explain why devising the appropriate international human resource strategies remains problematic for MNCs.

Companies also seem to make little effort to leverage the knowledge gained from operating in different cultural environments. Too often HR departments miss the opportunity to learn from the experiences of returning expatriates. In fact, it seems as if they pay little attention to these resources rich in cultural knowledge and do little to integrate this knowledge companywide. Apparently, only 20 percent of firms actively plan expatriates' return to specific, identified home positions.[85]

This means that returning executives often find that their new job does not encourage bringing home the international perspective developed abroad. With their experience so little valued, it comes as no surprise that among US firms 20 percent of repatriated managers leave their company within one year, and rates as high as 40–50 percent within three years have been reported.[86] Thus the company loses the very seeds needed for developing the international competence of the firm as a whole.

It is time to take stock of the lessons to be learned from the difficulties experienced by companies and indeed managers who have ventured abroad. It is also time to face the need for greater international experience overall, and the reality of the increasing international interactions in doing business anywhere. This means that individuals, teams, and organizations have to learn how to manage cultural differences which they will be confronting more and more on a daily basis, at home as well as abroad. Part III addresses these issues.

QUESTIONS TO ASK

Selection

How does local recruitment differ from home country policy?

How to interact with local networks?

Who is valued and why?

Socialization

How do local norms/expectations regarding socialization differ from home country policy?

Should managers at the local operation blend in with the local environment or do we want to differentiate ourselves?

Would a difference in values or attitudes inhibit internal dialogue?

To what extent should we articulate 'the company way' in manuals?

To what extent should we organize exchanges of personnel?

Training

What sort of knowledge-acquisition is valued by the local organization?

Is this knowledge-acquisition complementary to that at HQ? To what extent will it inhibit communication and learning?

How important is it for the company to leverage knowledge across borders?

What does this mean for the nature and content of training sessions and who attends?

What is the possible reaction to computer-based training?

Performance appraisal

Is there a marked difference between the evaluation of performance from home country policy?

Is there a danger of alienating or demotivating the local team by imposing home rules?

Does the local operation have novel ways of delivering or depersonalizing negative feedback without demotivating?

Compensation and rewards

Do local preferences differ significantly from 'home' ones?

Is the aim to instill competition or cooperation, information sharing or individual initiative?

Can these be encouraged by other than financial rewards?

Might an 'alien' compensation package attract younger, more adaptable, or less typical managers disillusioned with local practices?

Career development

Do local mobility and poaching norms differ much from 'home' ones?

What is the proportion of 'foreigners' at HQ?

To what extent do company career paths favor some cultures over others?

Are there unintended biases in the identification of high potentials?

NOTES

1. Evans, P. (1986) Apple Computer, Europe, INSEAD case.
2. Laurent, A. (1986) 'The cross-cultural puzzle of international human resource management', *Human Resource Management*, 25(1), pp. 91–102, p. 97.
3. Brewster, C. (1993) 'Developing a 'European' model of human resource management', *The International Journal of Human Resource Management*, 4(4), pp. 765–84.
4. Guest, D. (1990) 'Human resource management and the American Dream', *Journal of Management Studies*, 27(4), pp. 377–97.
5. Legge, K. (1995) *Human Resource Management: Rhetorics and Realities*, London: Macmillan.
6. Brewster, C. and Bournois, F. (1991) 'Human resource management: A European perspective', *Personnel Review*, 20(6), pp. 4–13.
7. Evans, P.A.L. (1984) 'On the importance of a generalist conception of human resource management: A cross-national look', *Human Resource Management*, 23(4), pp. 347–64.
8. Gooderham, P.N., Nordhaug, O., and Ringdal, K. (1999) 'Institutional and rational determinants of organizational practices. Human resource management in European firms', *Administrative Science Quarterly*, 44, pp. 507–31.
9. 'Selling is tough if you hate to smile', *Business Week*, August 1, 1994, p. 4.
10. Bartlett, C.A. and Nanda, A. (1990) Ingvar Kamprad and IKEA, Cambridge, MA, Harvard Business School case 9–390–132, 6.
11. Fey, C., Engstrom, P. and Bjorkman, I. (1999) 'Doing business in Russia: Effective human resource management practices for foreign firms in Russia', *Organizational Dynamics*, Autumn, pp. 69–80.
12. Ibid., p. 73.
13. Handy, C., Gordon, C., Gow, I. and Randlesome, C. (1988) *Making Managers*, London: Pitman, p. 2.
14. Segalla, M., Sauquet, A. and Turati, C. (2001) 'Symbolic vs. functional recruitment: Cultural influences on employee recruitment policy', *European Management Journal*, 19(1), pp. 32–43.
15. James, B. (1992) 'New skills are knocking on French firms' doors', *International Herald Tribune*, February 6.
16. 'Enarchy', *The Economist*, April 15, 1995, p. 27.
17. 'Get 'em young, boss!', *Far Eastern Economic Review*, September 22, 1988.
18. Lasserre, P. and Probert, J. (1994) 'Human resource management in the Asia Pacific region', INSEAD Euro–Asia Centre Research Series, 18.
19. Adler, N.J. (1987) 'Pacific basin managers: A Gaijin not a woman', *Human Resource Management*, 26(2), pp. 169–92.
20. Ryle, S. (1997) 'Texas arranger', *The Guardian*, August 11, p. 4.
21. Bjorkman, I. and Lu, Yuan (1999) 'The management of human resources in Chinese–Western joint ventures', *Journal of World Business*, 34(3), pp. 306–24.
22. Jampol, J. (2001) 'Looking for a job? Networking is best bet', *International Herald Tribune*, June 29, p. 18.
23. Rohlen, T. (1978) 'The education of the Japanese banker', *Human Nature*, January, pp. 22–30.
24. Van Maanen, J. and Laurent, A. (1993) 'The flow of culture: Some notes on globalization and the multinational corporation', in S. Ghoshal and D.E. Westney (eds)

Organization Theory and the Multinational Corporation, New York: St Martin's Press, pp. 275–312.
25. Lewis, M. (1989) *Liar's Poker*, New York: W.W. Norton.
26. Lee, P. (1993) 'Which is the real Goldman Sachs?', *Euromoney*, October, pp. 50–7.
27. Adent Hoecklin, L. (1993) *Managing Cultural Differences for Competitive Advantage*, London: The Economist Intelligence Unit.
28. Schneider, S. and Inoue, R. (1988) Mitsuhoshi France, INSEAD case.
29. Stewart, R., Barsoux, J.-L., Kieser, A., Ganter, D. and Walgenbach, P. (1994) *Managing in Britain and Germany*, London: Macmillan.
30. Bjorkman and Lu, *Op. cit.*
31. Nonaka, I. (1991) 'The knowledge-creating company', *Harvard Business Review*, November–December, pp. 96–104.
32. Evans, P. (1986) Apple Computer, INSEAD case, 24.
33. Laurent, *Op. cit.*
34. Saner, R. and Yiu, L. (1994) 'European and Asian resistance to the use of the American case method in management training', *The International Journal of Human Resource Management*, 5(4), pp. 955–76.
35. Ibid., p. 962.
36. Kolb, D.A. (1974) 'Four styles of managerial learning', in D.A. Kolb, I.M. Rubin and J.M. McIntyre (eds) *Organizational Psychology: A Book of Readings*, 2nd edn, Englewood Cliffs, NJ: Prentice Hall, pp. 27–34.
37. Konstantin Korotov, former director of professional development, CIS Ernst & Young.
38. Evans, P.A.L. (1992) 'Developing leaders and managing development', *European Management Journal*, 10(1), pp. 1–9, 4.
39. Schneider, S.C. (1988) 'National vs corporate culture: Implications for human resource management', *Human Resource Management*, 27(2), pp. 231–46.
40. Hofstede, G. (1980) *Culture's Consequences*, Beverly Hills, CA Sage.
41. Orleman, P. (1992) 'The global corporation: Managing across cultures', Masters Thesis, University of Pennsylvania.
42. Trepo, G. (1973) 'Management style à la Française', *European Business*, Autumn, pp. 71–9.
43. Korotov, *Op. cit.*
44. Dowling, P.J. and Schuler, R.S. (1990) *International Dimensions of Human Resource Management*, Boston, MA: PWS-Kent.
45. Orleman, *Op. cit.*
46. Kanter, R.M. and Corn, R.I. (1994) 'Do cultural differences make a business difference?', *Journal of Management Development*, 13(2), pp. 5–23.
47. Laurent, *Op. cit.*, p. 99.
48. Trompenaars, F. (1993) *Riding the Waves of Culture*, London: Nicholas Brealey.
49. Bjorkman and Lu, *Op. cit.*
50. Zeng, M. (2000) China's Haier Group: Growth through acquisitions, INSEAD–EAC case.
51. Hall, A. (1998) 'Go's go-getter', *Sunday Telegraph*, October 4, p. 7.
52. Orleman, *Op. cit.*
53. Eretz, M. and Early, P.C. (1993) *Culture, Self-identity, and Work*, New York: Oxford University Press.
54. Pennings, J.M. (1993) 'Executive reward systems: A cross-national comparison', *Journal of Management Studies*, 30(2), pp. 261–80, p. 264.
55. Schneider, S.C., Wittenberg-Cox, A. and Hansen, L. (1991) Honeywell Europe, INSEAD case.

56. 'Ikea booms in bonus sale', *International Herald Tribune*, October 13, 1999.
57. Olson, E. (2001) 'A spotlight on Swiss executives: Companies under fire over chiefs' salaries', *International Herald Tribune*, May, pp. 19–20.
58. 'Interview with Peter Brabeck' *L'Hebdo*, March 23, 2000, pp. 48–50.
59. Vance, C.M., McClaine, S.R., Boje, D.M. and Stage, H.D. (1992) 'An examination of the transferability of traditional performance appraisal principles across cultural boundaries', *Management International Review*, 32(4), pp. 313–26, p. 323.
60. Sanger, D.E. (1993) 'Performance related pay in Japan', *International Herald Tribune*, October 5, p. 20.
61. Bjorkman and Lu, *Op. cit.*
62. Lawler, E.E. and Mohrman, S. (1989) 'High-involvement management', *Organization Dynamics*, April, pp. 27–31.
63. Pennings, *Op. cit.*
64. Fey, C., Engstrom, P. and Bjorkman, I. (1999) 'Doing business in Russia: Effective human resource management practices for foreign firms in Russia', *Organizational Dynamics*, 28(2): pp. 69–80, p. 76.
65. 'Wages of death delight Japanese', *Sunday Times*, December 11, 1993, pp. 1, 21.
66. Fey, *et al.*, *Op. cit.*
67. Derr, C.B. and Laurent, A. (1989) 'Internal and external careers: A theoretical and cross cultural perspective', in M.B. Arthur, D.T. Hall and B.S. Lawrence (eds) *Handbook of Career Theory*, Cambridge: Cambridge University Press, pp. 454–71; see also Derr, C. (1987) 'Managing high potentials in Europe', *European Management Journal*, 5(2), pp. 72–80.
68. Coale, D.J. (1994) 'International barriers to progress', *Journal of Management Development*, 13(2), pp. 55–8, p. 57.
69. Lane, C. (1989) *Management and Labour in Europe*, Aldershot: Edward Elgar, p. 92.
70. Raskin, A. (2001) 'It's not easy being "Z"', *Business 2.0*, October, pp. 57–9.
71. Stewart *et al.*, *Op. cit.*
72. 'The old pals act', *The Banker*, May, 18, 1994.
73. Evans, *Op. cit.*
74. Hendry, C. (1994) *Human Resource Strategies for International Growth*, London: Routledge.
75. Ferner, A., Quintanilla, J. and Varul, M.Z. (2001) 'Country-of-origin effects, host-country effects, and the management of HR in multinationals: German companies in Britain and Spain', *Journal of World Business*, 36(2), pp. 107–27.
76. Harzing, A.-W. (1999) *Managing the Multinationals: An International Study of Control Mechanisms*, Cheltenham: Edward Elgar.
77. Ferner *et al.*, *Op. cit.*
78. von Keller, E. and von Courbière, V. (1996) *In Search of Homo Bertelsmannensis: A Collection of Essays in Honor of Reinhard Mohn*, Gütersloh: Bertelsmann Publications.
79. Fulkerson, J.R. and Schuler, R.S. (1992) 'Managing worldwide diversity at Pepsi-Cola International', in S.E. Jackson (ed.) *Diversity in the Workplace*, New York: Guilford Press.
80. Schneider, S.C. and Asakura, A. (1993) Nissan Motor Co., Europe, INSEAD case.
81. Burgelman, R.A. (1991) 'Intraorganizational ecology of strategy making and organizational adaptation: Theory and field research', *Organization Science*, 2(3), August, pp. 239–62.
82. Hiltrop, J.-M., Despres, C. and Sparrow, P. (1995) 'The changing role of HR managers in Europe', *European Management Journal*, March, 91–8.

83. Gates, S. (1994) 'The changing global role of the human resources function', New York: The Conference Board, Report No. 1062-94-RR, 22.
84. Adler, N. and Bartholomew, S. (1992) 'Managing globally competent people', *Academy of Management Executive*, 6(3), pp. 52–65.
85. Gates, *Op. cit.*
86. Black, J.S., Gregersen, H. and Mendenhall, M. (1992) *Global Assignments: Successfully Expatriating and Repatriating International Managers*, San Francisco: Jossey-Bass.

CHAPTER FIFTEEN

The 'International' Manager

> Let my house not be walled on four sides, let all the windows be open, let all the cultures blow in, but let no culture blow me off my feet.
>
> Mahatma Gandhi

Traditionally, the *international manager* was synonymous with the expatriate manager. But as companies devise more sophisticated cross-border strategies, they increasingly search for executives who can leap borders in a single bound to do the implementing. This has prompted the call for a new type of cosmopolitan, multilingual, multifaceted executive who is operational across national borders (somewhat like James Bond). This search is especially frenetic in Europe where the global manager has spawned a subspecies, the Euromanager.[2]

The 'international manager' has also come to mean an international elite of executives, drawn from the company's operations worldwide, portrayed as members of a global commando or SWAT team, living out of airplanes and recognizable by their constant jetlag. One story has it that a French IBM executive arriving at JFK airport in New York while searching for his entry visa pulled out his IBM identification card. The customs official, seeing it said, 'Oh, it's OK, you're IBM, you can go ahead'.

Companies having developed an international corps of executives, developed through frequent and multiple transfers, have often found that such an elite is difficult to integrate into the corporate mainstream; nor are those with 'helicopter views' necessarily capable of doing the work of more down to earth experts.[3] Thus rumors of the existence of a 'global' manager as someone who pursues a 'borderless career', and whose corporate identity overrides that of country and even family,[4] may be somewhat exaggerated.

In any case, the mere fact of operating across national boundaries does not mean that the minds of international managers are also traveling across boundaries. It is sometimes questionable whether English-speaking, Hilton-based executives, with little local interaction, even warrant the international tag. This is internationalism on the 'accidental tourist'[5] model (where the key character traveling to Europe is greatly relieved to find McDonald's), making sure that nothing encountered abroad will differ too much from back home and bringing along all the supplies necessary for survival. International mobility does not necessarily enhance the ability to think internationally.[6]

Changes over the last decade or so have made business not just more international but also more interdependent. Global expansion is increasingly achieved through alliances and joint ventures, as well as cross-border mergers and acquisitions. Companies expect their employees to operate across borders, perhaps for short periods or as part of multidisciplinary, multicultural teams. Furthermore, thanks to advances in communication and information technology, contact by fax, e-mail, and teleconferencing has become commonplace. So even those who rarely leave their home base may find themselves interacting with foreigners.

One of the most striking findings of a survey undertaken by Fiat was that 40 percent of managerial positions dealt with international work matters.[7] This survey suggests the extent to which even MNCs are underestimating the amount of international management being done by their employees, and that the notion of international responsibility is being interpreted too narrowly.

What is more, cultural sensitivity is now demanded at all levels of the organization. Front-line employees (such as security guards, chauffeurs, and receptionists) are the first to greet foreign visitors and a company's global pretensions are easily shattered when foreign clients or employees cannot get past the front door or beyond the receptionist. The international content of jobs clearly varies depending on the nature of the business, the company, the function, and the level of experience, but being able to handle cultural differences is becoming more and more a part of everybody's job.

While the image of the global manager may be more myth than reality, the conventional distinction between international and domestic managers is fading, given the much broader distribution of international responsibilities. Increasingly, people from all over the world must work with each other and consciously manage their cultural differences. So, as Barham and Antal observe, companies need to focus less on *who* is an international manager, and consider instead *what* international tasks and responsibilities employees really do fulfill and use this as a basis for reviewing the actual competencies required for each job.[8]

Before looking specifically at the competencies needed by international managers, it may be worth considering what has been learned from expatriates who have been roaming the world for the past several decades. We will then consider the evolving portrait of the international manager, which now includes those who deal with cultural differences at home, not just abroad. This leads to a far wider definition of international manager and to reconsidering which skills and competencies are necessary. What personal histories, characteristics, or work experience predispose managers to work well with diversity? And finally, what can be done to manage cultural differences so that managers can navigate more effectively (whether abroad or at home) in international business.

Lessons from abroad

Much of what we know about managing cultural differences at an individual level comes from the experience of expatriates (missionaries sent out by companies as well as the Peace Corps). Unfortunately, companies have not been particularly attentive when listening to feedback from expatriates and to learning from their experiences. So what can we learn from the expatriate experience about the trials and satisfactions of working abroad?

For many expatriates, international assignments turn out to be the most memorable career experience, but not always for the right reasons. Of course, there is the opportunity for greater challenge and responsibility, and for personal as well as professional development. Yet failure rates of up to 30 percent within US multinationals reveal the difficulties of adapting to a new culture, although some question the accuracy of these rates and their current validity.[9] Expatriate failure is estimated to cost US business $2 billion a year.[10] What are some of the potential reasons for these difficulties in adjusting?

Consider the experience of these two expatriates. First, the reaction of a German manager with IBM on arriving in England:

> 'Dieter Shultz took up his post as a product manager and found that most lunchtimes and particularly on Fridays the vast majority of his management team decamped to the pub. "I stopped that right away', he says. 'Now they are not allowed off the premises. It didn't make me very popular at the time but it is not good for efficiency. There is no way we would do that in Germany. No way."[11]'

And the poignant testimony of an American manager sent out to head up a newly acquired operation in France:

> 'After months of trying my best to break down the barriers, I pretty much abandoned all hope of establishing trust with my staff. I had used up all my tricks within a year or so – setting clear goals, working longer hours than anyone, joining in the actual nuts-and-bolts work of each project, maintaining an open-door policy, roaming through the editorial offices (management by walking about like mad), and that ultimate seducer I had been advised would always work in France: taking them out to a good lunch one by one. They could never overcome the deep-seated belief that management was out to exploit them.[12]'

Had Herr Schultz been assigned to a more distant country he might have better anticipated the cultural differences. That he reacted so strongly indicates that these differences were unexpected. His reaction, nevertheless, tells us as much about his home culture (and perhaps that of the company, IBM) as the host culture: concerns for efficiency and for universal policies and procedures. IBM had a very explicit rule regarding alcohol consumption during the work day: none. As he saw it, the difference, or problem, lay in 'the others'. A critical step for managers working internationally is when they realize that the cultural difference also resides in them, and in the company.

The exasperated American manager, having tried everything possible from his own repertoire of behaviors (or bag of tricks) to break down the barriers, finally tries the prescribed 'French' way. His own approach is highly *instrumental* and task-oriented, setting clear goals, joining in the nuts-and-bolts. Even the lunch option is used as a last resort. This approach only serves to reinforce the feeling of exploitation and manipulation, that getting the job done is more important than the personal relationships. 'Management by walking about' signals surveillance, not supportiveness. He has thus unwittingly fulfilled the prophecy of 'the deep-seated belief that management was out to exploit them'.

For expatriate managers, then, living in a foreign country produces constant and unexpected challenges to their ways of perceiving, acting, and valuing things, making it difficult to correctly process and act on information. Inevitably, this leads to committing cultural gaffes or *faux pas* that leave the expatriate feeling confused and uncomfortable. They may find it difficult to make sense of other people's behavior. Worse still, their own behavior does not have the expected impact. The techniques which worked back home simply fail to get results.

Indeed, the most often cited reason for failed assignments is the inability of expatriates and their families to adapt to the local culture. The strain is perhaps even greater on families, as the manager is often buffered by work from the more mundane cultural encounters. Thus, it is often the family that takes the shock full force. Therefore, it is important to understand the processes of adjustment and to recognize the warning signs of culture malaise.

The process of cultural adjustment

The process of adjusting to a foreign culture is said to follow a U-curve[13] comprising three main phases: an initial stage of elation and optimism (the honeymoon), soon followed by a period of irritability, frustration, and confusion (the morning after), and then a gradual adjustment to the new environment (happily ever after). Although the inevitability of these stages has been challenged, these emotional experiences are not uncommon. The intensity of these reactions often depends upon the motivation and prior expectations of the expatriates and their family to go abroad, the amount of cultural distance between the home and host countries, and the degree of uncertainty in job and/or daily living activities.[14]

Attention has been drawn particularly to the phase following the 'honeymoon', when cultural differences are no longer experienced as charming but rather annoying. This phase is when most assignments are at risk of failure. The increased involvement with the new culture brings the realization that there are unsettling differences in interpersonal behavior as well as work behavior. These can come as quite a surprise, especially in culturally or economically neighboring countries. The same emotions may be experienced for the return journey. Indeed the shock of returning home can be more severe because it is less expected. Where expatriates may have a sense of *déjà vu* when going abroad, coming home can feel as if never having been there before; a sort of *jamais vu*. The returning manager is more often treated like the prodigal son than the conquering hero.

The term 'culture shock', often used to describe this sense of frustration, is actually rather misleading. It tends to suggest a sudden impact with a single cause. More likely, it will result from a simmering reaction to a succession of minor events which are difficult to identify. It is more like tennis elbow than a dislocated shoulder. The symptoms of cultural malaise go from simple embarrassment, through homesickness and identity confusion, and can culminate in a full-fledged depression.

Given that culture shock or malaise is a kind of 'rite of passage' in international assignments, there are reasons for welcoming its arrival. First, it signals that the expatriate manager is becoming involved in the new culture, not hiding out in an expatriate ghetto. Second, it provides the motivation, which may not have been there at earlier stages, to try to understand and come to grips with the cultural differences. However, if the anxiety of culture shock is too high, it may prevent people from learning.[15]

Over time, it is thought that adjustment evolves through acquiring greater knowledge of the local culture and language and working together with others to achieve shared goals. When all goes well, greater cross-cultural interaction can foster greater perceived cultural similarity, reducing 'we–they' stereotypes. More interaction also increases the likelihood of shared understandings, providing a greater sense of predictability and control.[16] This in turn facilitates adjustment. However, when cross-cultural interaction is marked by friction and frustration, stereotypes may indeed be reinforced, and conflicts can become entrenched, thus impeding adjustment. Being sociable and 'open' are additional necessary ingredients; increased contact alone is not enough.[17]

Research has found that European managers based in other European countries than their own reported less cultural interaction than those based in the United States or Asia. This was attributed to less perceived cultural distance, and that Europeans were less likely 'to mix' socially, having more support from 'back home'.[18] Paradoxically, it seems that being closer to home, both in terms of culture and geography, may limit the needed cultural interaction and potentially impair adjustment. Assumptions of similarity as well as assumptions of differences therefore need to be challenged.

In addition to resolving the challenges posed when confronting a new culture, the expatriate manager must come to terms with a number of inevitable dilemmas.[19] These tensions derive from the manager's position as mediator between the two cultures and the two parts of the same organization. For instance, a basic dilemma for expatriates is how much of their own way of doing things they are prepared to relinquish, and how much of the new ways they are willing to embrace. Remaining behind the closed doors of the expatriate community or 'going native' may not be the most effective solutions.

Expatriate managers are also caught in the dilemma of reconciling responsibility and power, invested with a great deal of responsibility but having to depend on local management and employees to achieve their objectives. Furthermore, they have to manage their allegiances between parent firm and local operation.[20] Where head-office directives conflict with local values, expatriate managers gradually learn to pick those battles they can win and avoid those they cannot.

Being faced with conflicting demands or contradictory truths requires the ability to see situations from both angles and to assess the strengths and weaknesses from each perspective (a bicultural perspective). This means that dogmatic thinking, assuming there is one best way (my way), is doomed. What is needed is well-captured by American author, F. Scott Fitzgerald's remark, 'Intelligence is the ability to hold two conflicting ideas in mind and retain the ability to function.'

Competencies for managing internationally

Having highlighted some of the challenges of working abroad, we can now consider what skills and abilities are needed in order to be effective, as shown in Table 15.1. Individuals clearly have different aptitudes for managing in new cultural surroundings.

Managing differences abroad

Interpersonal skills

'Interpersonal skills' are often identified as crucial, if not *the* most important. The ability to form relationships helps the manager integrate into the social fabric of the host culture. Not only does this satisfy the needs for friendship and intimacy, but also facilitates the transfer of knowledge, and improves coordination and control. Establishing relationships and building trust allows the expatriate manager to tap into critical information, thus reducing the stressful uncertainties surrounding both work and personal life.

While many companies acknowledge the importance of interpersonal skills, it is rarely seen as a critical criterion for selection. In practice, expatriate managers are primarily selected on their strong track record at home, that is, their reputation for getting the job done. Companies also send abroad those who have been identified as 'high fliers' for the purpose of career development. Either way, expatriates are most often chosen based on technical or conceptual abilities rather than interpersonal skills.

Those having been placed on the fast track often arrive on assignment ready to prove themselves, to make their mark. Thus they tend to be quite focused on the task, and on achieving the objectives set by corporate headquarters. As assignments may last only 18 months, they have to move quickly to make things happen. This can create tension with the local staff, who refer to them as 'birds of passage',[21] laying low waiting for this latest arrival to fly off again, until the next one arrives, with yet another personal agenda.

Time pressures and a strong task orientation can interfere with the need to build relationships and to establish trust. Often local staff feel exploited, as instruments to achieve goals that are not their own. This exacerbates feelings of mistrust and resent-

Table 15.1 What it takes

Competencies for managing differences abroad
Interpersonal (relationship) skills
Linguistic ability
Motivation to live abroad (cultural curiosity)
Tolerance for uncertainty and ambiguity
Flexibility
Patience and respect
Cultural empathy
Strong sense of self (or ego strength)
Sense of humor

ment towards head office. In fact, some experts argue that successful expatriates actually need to have *low task orientation*![22]

The need for more *people-oriented* managers is confirmed by the personnel director for the European division of ICI, a British chemical company, who looks for people who are 'good at getting along with colleagues at home'. This is deemed essential for the simple reason that any problems a manager has in dealing with colleagues will be magnified in a foreign setting, where much more effort is needed to build understanding and trust. The former co-chairman of Unilever, Floris Maljers, agrees by stating, 'We tend to look for people who can work in teams and understand the value of cooperation and consensus'.[23] Thus the ability to get along with others is considered to be an important passport to international business.

Nevertheless, a survey conducted of US companies that post staff internationally found that the most important employee selection criteria remain technical expertise (95 per cent of respondents), employee interest in the assignment (88 per cent) and personal flexibility (84 per cent).[24] Interpersonal skills do not seem to be high on the list.

Linguistic ability

Linguistic ability is also important as it helps to establish contact. However, having total command of the other language may not be feasible and may be less important than trying to develop a feel for what matters to others, picking up bits of 'conversational currency': local expressions, information, and interests.²⁵ For example, Rajat Gupta, the Indian CEO of McKinsey recalls:

'I was also quick to adopt many of the things that get you into the mainstream. I followed football and basketball, went to games, and did all of those things which somebody living in this country typically does and are part of the cultural experience. But at the same time, I was different. If you can become the same in many respects and at the same time stay visibly different, I think you can have the best of both worlds.²⁶'

On short overseas assignments in particular, efforts to speak the local language may have more symbolic than practical value, but the impact is highly significant. It indicates an eagerness to communicate and to connect with host nationals. A resolute unwillingness to speak the other's language can be very damaging in that it may be taken as a sign of disdain, or an unwarranted display of power.

'Originally, billed as a "merger of equals" the real intentions of Daimler vis-à-vis Chrysler showed through in the earliest stages of the deal: some Daimler-Benz officials held meetings with Chrysler staffers and spoke only in German, knowing full well the provincials couldn't understand.²⁷'

Motivation to work and live abroad

Motivation to work and live abroad has been shown to be a key ingredient to the successful adaptation of the expatriates and their families. This is manifested as 'cultural curiosity'. Expatriates and their families should be selected based on a genuine interest in other cultures and new experiences. For Swedish managers, *Wanderlust* was rated as their top motive for going abroad.²⁸

Ability to tolerate and cope with uncertainty

Ability to tolerate and cope with uncertainty and ambiguity is also needed. Action often has to be taken on the basis of insufficient, unreliable and/or conflicting information.²⁹ Circumstances change unexpectedly, the behavior and reactions of local employees may be unpredictable, so that the international manager has to be able to adapt almost instinctively. This requires, first of all, acknowledging that uncertainty and ambiguity exist, that everything is not as straightforward as it seems, and that multiple perspectives are possible. The inability to do so encourages dogmatic thinking and rigid behavior, which interfere with the flexibility and resourcefulness necessary for responding effectively.³⁰ Top executives at Colgate asked to identify the kind of executive who worked best in an international setting cited the main attribute to be flexibility. The consensus was, 'You don't always go by the book'.³¹

Faced with the threat of greater uncertainty and ambiguity of international assignments, managers often feel a strong need to reassert control. This response, in effect, interferes with remaining flexible. Research has shown that under conditions of threat, managers tend to engage in efforts to impose greater controls, restrict information flows, and revert to well-known behavior.[32] This can result in stereotypical responses, not necessarily well-adapted to the situation at hand. In these circumstances, expatriates may more often need to let go of control, to 'go with the flow'.

This is quite difficult especially when managers are used to being rewarded for being in charge and staying on top of things. This is particularly evident in cultures where control over the environment is an underlying assumption. Indeed, the success of Japanese company strategies (as in the case of Honda) was often attributed to their flexibility which enabled them to capitalize on unexpected opportunities. This flexibility comes from their readiness to adapt rather than to impose controls over changing circumstances.

Patience and respect

Perhaps even more crucial for the international executive are patience and respect. Patience is necessary, not only because different cultures have different rhythms, but also because it takes time to 'learn the ropes'.[33] Expatriates have to avoid the temptation constantly to benchmark the new culture against the home culture, but must instead try to understand the local reasons for the way things happen. While having patience and respect may be the golden rule of international business, it seems to be the one most often broken.

Cultural empathy

Respecting the behavior and ideas of others requires empathy. Some individuals find it easier to appreciate the thoughts, feelings, and experiences of others. Focused listening and a non-judgemental approach help managers to understand the other person's viewpoint. But one's capacity for empathy is deeply rooted in one's character and may not be a skill easily acquired.

Narcissism, which evolves from one's psychological development, interferes with the capacity for empathy.[34] Narcissistic managers often treat others as mere extensions of themselves making it difficult to recognize, let alone appreciate, the attitudes and behavior of others, especially those who are different. These managers see others as objects or instruments to satisfy their own needs, or as mirrors to reflect their own glory. In their efforts to prove their worth, they fail to take into consideration the needs and the *value* of others.

Strong sense of self

On the other hand, expatriates do need a strong sense of self, or ego (healthy narcissism). This allows interaction with another person or culture without fear of losing one's own identity. This also enables the expatriate to be self-critical and open to feedback. It permits expatriates to respond appropriately to failure, treating it as a learning experience rather than as a narcissistic injury, a blow to their self-image which can undermine their self-confidence.

A strong ego also reinforces the ability to handle stress. This is particularly critical in an environment where the manager is deprived of familiar surroundings and social support. The anxiety created by the uncertainties and frustrations of international experiences needs to be appropriately handled, rather than triggering dysfunctional coping devices, such as alcohol abuse.

Creating 'stability zones'[35] – hobbies, diaries, favorite pastimes, meditation, or religious worship – can provide refuge into which the expatriate can temporarily withdraw and get refueled. Taking time-out is vital because it reintroduces the element of choice and control over the rhythm of involvement with the new culture and enables the manager to regain a sense of perspective, 'observing ego'.

Sense of humor

Finally, a sense of humor is one quality which is often cited but only in passing. Humor is actually important on two levels: as a coping mechanism and for relationship building. Retaining a sense of humor is seen as a way for managers to buffer the frustration, uncertainty, and confusion they are bound to encounter in an unfamiliar environment. Humor provides a way of distancing oneself from the situation, to regain a sense of perspective. Also, 'the ability to laugh at one's mistakes may be the ultimate defense against despair'.[36] Or in the words of one oil industry veteran, 'The first few months in an international posting can seem like one long round of social gaffes and management blunders. If you didn't laugh, you'd cry'.

Humor can also be used proactively to break the ice, to establish a link with others, and to deal with sensitive issues. A well-timed bit of humor can put people at ease, break the tension in an interaction, allowing a more open and constructive discussion to follow, and to say what might not be said otherwise.

For example, in 2000, when Dieter Zetsche was sent in by headquarters in Stuttgart to repair the ailing Chrysler, tensions were running very high. At one of the early press conferences, a reporter asked the question that was on everybody's mind: 'How many more Germans are you going to bring over?'. Unflustered, Zetsche leaned into the microphone and answered: 'Four.' A wry smile appeared through his enormous moustache: 'My wife and three kids'.[37] Though greeted with suspicion and resentment on arriving, within three months Zetsche was enjoying 'remarkable support', among both employees and dealers.[38]

Besides connecting with people, humor can serve to create the space for an 'emotional time-out', to let off steam and alleviate tension.[39] One person noted for his humor in international relations was Henry Kissinger. He made humor a tool of diplomacy. His banter inspired banter in others and usually led to a more relaxed atmosphere in the private, formal discussions or negotiations with world leaders. The humor opened the door to more frankness and less ritualized recitations as well. In that regard, Kissinger lightened the whole heavy international diplomatic scene.[40]

But it must be remembered that what is considered funny in one culture does not necessarily translate to another. British humor often involves poking fun at oneself and others, dosed with a bit of sarcasm and wit (sometimes biting). In France, *se moquer* (or 'to mock' self or others) has a different, more pejorative, connotation. Thus teasing or making fun of someone may be experienced as humiliation. For Asians this type of humor does not adequately 'save face', or protect self-esteem.

In Latin America, teasing and joking at work are pervasive. Not only does humor 'grease the wheels' of the organization, but can be used to keep people in line – an acceptable way to convey feedback. It can also serve as a safety valve: the more powerless, the more joking.[41]

Humor can also be used to reinforce the power distance, in the form of 'put downs', or one-upmanship. French comedy, for example, often depicts situations where different social classes are forced to interact. In the UK as well as in France, humor is often based on intellectual or linguistic prowess – witticisms or *jeux de mots*, that is, plays on words or double meanings. This demands a high level of language sensitivity which excludes most foreigners, even the most fluent. Humor, such as 'inside jokes', can also reinforce notions of who's in and who's out. Thus the use of humor has great potential for facilitating or destroying cross-cultural interactions.

Most of the above skills and competencies, traditionally considered crucial for expatriate effectiveness, are equally valid for those who deal with foreigners at home. The experiences of expatriates provide important lessons for handling this diversity. However, international management is no longer the exclusive domain of expatriates.

Managing differences at home

With more and more managers having international responsibilities, what are the new challenges, and how do the skills needed differ from those expected of expatriate managers? While there is much overlap between the demands made of expatriate managers and of those managing internationally, contrasting the two roles is instructive.

Understand interdependencies

To start with, managing internationally demands a more complete understanding of the interdependencies between different parts of the organization worldwide, and a wider appreciation of the impact that a course of action in one area will have on another. International managers do not just deal with straight up and down relationships between a subsidiary and head office, but engage in much more complex interactions across country and functional boundaries. They play multiple roles participating in multiple teams, as leaders in some, and as members in others.

Respond to different cultures simultaneously

The cultural awareness of the international manager therefore has to extend beyond expertise in a single culture. Dealing with people from many different cultures makes learning all their diverse customs, attitudes, tastes, and approaches to business a difficult, if not impossible, task. What is more, contact with other cultures is not sequential, as in the case of the expatriate manager, but *simultaneous*. In other words, 'international' managers have to be able to deal with a mixed group of individuals all at the same time.[42] The conventional wisdom that expatriate managers are people who can get results from people who are very different from themselves is given an added twist: the international manager is actually someone who can get results from people who are very different from each other as well.

Recognize cultural differences at home

This task is rendered even more difficult by the tendency to overlook cultural differences 'at home'. Cultural differences are expected abroad, but at home it is often assumed that the foreigner will make the effort to adapt to 'our ways' or to fit in with the dominant culture. Taking this view can alienate others, but more importantly fails to capitalize on the potential benefits of recognizing diversity and the unsuspected value added which outsiders can contribute from their different experience, skills, and perspective. Beyond that, it also ignores the shift in the balance of power between managers from various parts of the globe. Foreign managers are beginning to be seen at the top!

Be willing to share power

Relations between home country and foreign nations are no longer those of boss and subordinate. Companies with global aspirations can no longer assume, as in the past, that the most sophisticated customers, the most important market, and the leading suppliers are home-based.[43] The dispersal of key resources and markets means that head office is no longer all-powerful. And more and more shareholders are no longer necessarily compatriots.

Increases in economic power, wider access to business education, and the decentralization of organizations have put these relationships on a much more equal footing. This means that head-office representatives can no longer 'tell' sophisticated foreign counterparts what to do, but have to 'sell', just as they would with colleagues at head office. Furthermore, they may just find that the foreigner is their boss. By the mid-1990s it was estimated that there were more than two million Americans working for foreign employers in the United States.[44]

Thus, the role of the international manager has evolved in two important ways. First, the pattern of cultural contact has changed; it is more varied and fragmented than it was, it is simultaneous rather than sequential, and it is not always recognized as such, since much of it happens on home turf. Second, the nature of the relationships has changed. The relations of power and dominance between HQ and subsidiaries are no longer what they were; and with competitive advantages harder to come by, MNCs can no longer afford to ignore learning opportunities from their foreign counterparts. Head-office managers therefore have to engage in a dialogue with subsidiary managers, and listen. They also have to search for new ideas around the world. So what additional skills are required to manage across cultures at home?

The changing demands on international managers described above mean that additional skills and competencies are required and may even differ from those required of the expatriate. Managers need cross-cultural skills on a daily basis, throughout their careers, not just during foreign assignments, but also on regular multi-country business trips and in daily interaction with clients or colleagues worldwide.[45]

Demonstrate cognitive complexity

For managers to be effective across cultures requires the ability to simultaneously recognize the need for differentiation while understanding the need for integration, at multiple levels and at multiple sites within and outside the organization. The ability to respond to the concurrent needs for local responsiveness and the demands for global integration means creating a 'matrix of the mind'.[46] The ability to think along multiple dimensions while seeing the ways that these dimensions are interrelated has been labeled 'cognitive complexity'.[47] According to Jacques,[48] this ability is the determining factor of a manager's position in the hierarchy, and their degree of freedom in decision-making. Cognitive complexity is also considered to be a fundamental component of a 'global mindset' as will be described later on.

However, in international settings, this ability cannot be considered to be the preserve of an elite. This, in effect, is a key challenge for training and development. Job rotation, brief assignments, and joint seminars can facilitate the development of a better appreciation of the different pieces of the organization puzzle, and foster a better understanding of the potential synergies in their interrelationships.

Adopt a 'cultural-general' approach

Furthermore, in dealing simultaneously with multiple cultures, managers need to develop a 'cultural-general' approach. Rather than a thorough knowledge of one particular culture, international managers need to be aware of the cues signaling culture differences be they national, corporate, or functional. According to this approach (which is indeed the one favored by the authors), it is important to identify which dimensions of culture may be relevant, rather than knowing the central tendencies of each particular country represented in meetings, or encounters in the course of a day's work. This approach contrasts with the 'cultural-specific' approach typically offered in training expatriates in the past.

While programs preparing expatriates for international assignments sometimes included language training, international managers cannot hope to master all the languages they need. But it is important, as one Dutch banker observed, 'to learn a language – any language – simply to give yourself another perspective on the world'. International managers must also learn to communicate more effectively, avoiding slang, pausing frequently, and speaking slowly and clearly (not loudly – it is not a problem of deafness). Although English may be the lingua franca of international business, strong regional accents (such as those in the deep South in the United States or Scotland in the United Kingdom) can leave even native English-speakers at a loss. Training anglophone managers with international responsibilities to speak 'middle English' may not be such a bad idea.[49]

Rapidly learn and unlearn

Finally, faced with the need to simultaneously manage multiple cultures, there is the need to *rapidly learn* and *unlearn*. This means constantly challenging basic assumptions and not falling into the comfortable trap of assuming that 'since we have a common corporate or professional culture we see things the same way'. It means being constantly ready to take on new perspectives and try new approaches. This can prove to be a highly demanding, if not exhausting, exercise. However, the energy derived from discovering exciting new possibilities and pursuing new horizons beyond those given, serves to replenish and reinvigorate. Thus faced with the challenges of managing cultural differences at home, additional skills are required, as shown in Table 15.2.

Table 15.2 ... And more

Additional competencies for managing differences at home
Understand business interdependencies
Respond to multiple cultures simultaneously
Recognize the influence of culture 'at home'
Be willing to share power
Demonstrate cognitive complexity
Adopt a 'cultural-general' approach
Rapidly learn and unlearn

Having a Global mindset

What is necessary for managing cultural differences, whether at home or abroad, is now often referred to as a 'global mindset'.

> 'The concept of global mindset helps to differentiate between expatriate and global managers. Expatriates are defined by location, as managers who are working in a different country from their own. In contrast, global managers are defined by their *state of mind*. They are people who can work effectively across organizational, functional, and cross-cultural boundaries.[50]'

A global mindset can be described in terms of cognitive structures and processes: not only what one thinks but also how.[51] *Cognitive structures* refer to the maps and scripts that managers use to navigate globally. Much like Christopher Columbus, these may include beliefs that the world is not flat, nor that corporate head office is the center of the universe. It may also involve beliefs about people, for example, that passports are not the most important indicator of competencies. Scripts provide guidance on what to do in various situations, such as the familiar adage 'When in Rome...'. Or how to recruit in the local labor markets.

These cognitive structures need to be well differentiated, to comprehend differences, while at the same time be well integrated, to find similarities. This means being able to see the pieces of the puzzle and how they fit together – cognitive complexity, as described above. But like a kaleidoscope, these pieces are likely to be changing and reconfiguring over time. Therefore,

> 'A global mindset incorporates an assumption that such knowledge and scripts are dynamic, and the cognitive structure organizing them must evolve to maintain and improve global business effectiveness.[52]'

Thus a global mindset refers to the ability to look for and learn from relevant differences while at the same time looking for commonality. On one hand this requires,

> '... the capacity to appreciate, value, and act on the factors that influence the beliefs, values, behaviors, and business practices of individuals and organizations from a variety of regions and cultures around the world.[53]'

On the other hand it involves finding commonalities across places – what Rosabeth Moss Kanter[54] refers to as *cosmopolitanism*. This ability to be ambidextrous enables managers to 'use the knowledge gained from this worldwide search to design and execute strategies that will maximize the benefits to all (local and global) stakeholders'.[55]

Cognitive processes refer to the way information is gathered and interpreted. Information may be 'assimilated' into pre-existing cognitive structures, reinforcing certain beliefs, such as stereotypes. Or new information can be 'accommodated', thus allowing for changes in what we know (beliefs) and how we go about doing things (scripts). These processes determine the way in which cognitive structures evolve and develop over time, reflecting learning capability.

Having a global mindset requires broad scanning, peripheral vision, and keeping in mind that multiple interpretations are likely. This represents a 'way of thinking' – being 'open-minded' rather than dogmatic and insisting on 'one best way – my way', or overly relying on stereotypes. It also means being able to see both ways, my way and your way. According to Ghoshal and Bartlett,

> 'Diverse roles and dispersed operations must be held together by a management mindset that understands the need for multiple strategic capabilities, views problems and opportunities from both local and global perspectives, and is willing to interact with others openly and flexibly. The task is not to build a sophisticated structure, but to create a matrix in the mind of managers.[56]'

What kinds of individuals are more likely to have these qualities, or to be able to develop them? And just how can this global mindset be developed?

Austrian-born Peter Brabeck became CEO of Swiss company Nestlé in 1997 after having spent many years with Nestlé in Latin America, and as EVP of international marketing. He claims that this background gives him his 'Germanic rigor' and his love of communicating with people: 'I meet each year 3000–4000 of our employees in every category'. Tolerance, *'ouverture d'esprit'* (open-mindedness), and interest in people are for him the most important factors for managing a multicultural company like Nestlé.[57]

We will now consider, in turn, individual background and work experience.

Developing cultural competencies

Individual background

The invention of the bicycle is said to have led to a dramatic increase in the average distance separating the home towns of people getting married. Today, international travel means that more and more children have parents of different nationalities. This may mean that the children change countries several times when young, as well as growing up with two, if not more, languages in the home, neither of which may be the local language. Again this helps individuals acquire a certain receptiveness to cultural differences from an early age. According to Catherine Bateson, having grown up in different cultures as the daughter of the famous anthropologists Margaret Mead and Gregory Bateson, this early experience of other cultures develops better 'peripheral vision', or other ways of seeing things.[58]

Such exposure to cultural differences is obviously more likely in some regions of the world than others. Europe, when compared with Japan, packs big cultural differences into small spaces, and would thus seem a useful training ground for would-be international managers. And within Europe, it could be argued that certain countries such as Belgium and Switzerland provide their inhabitants with a special head start, due to the cultural and language differences that exist within these countries. Unfortunately, this familiarity can breed contempt. Cultural differences in Belgium and Switzerland may be acknowledged but they are not necessarily valued.

Nevertheless, in these countries, television programs and cinema are available in several languages and subtitled in others, such as German and French. Living in international cities such as Brussels or Geneva, schoolchildren are quite likely to find classmates from the rest of the European or international community. Growing up in places such as New York, London, or Paris, one is likely to take cultural differences for granted, as part of everyday life.

In terms of further education, there are increasing numbers of exchange programs on business courses at university level. European universities are becoming more involved in these initiatives because of the geographical proximity of distinctive cultures and EU-sponsored efforts to encourage exchanges for both students and staff. American universities have also planted stakes in Europe through alliances such as that of Northwestern University's Kellogg School of Business and IESE in Barcelona.

European business schools emphasize the international background of both their students and faculty as a competitive advantage over their US or UK counterparts.[59] For example, the distinctive competence of INSEAD is considered to be its genuine multiculturalism among both students and faculty. This multiculturalism is enforced by a policy which limits the proportion of students of any one nationality to less than 25 percent. This means that students confront cultural differences on a routine basis. Much of the work involves group assignments designed to maximize diversity by putting together individuals of different nationality, work experience, age, and gender. Indeed the *content* of the coursework may be secondary to the *process* of learning how to work across cultures.

Graduates from these international business schools are particularly attractive to multinational companies and large consulting firms. As employers see it, students from international business schools are well prepared to work globally due to their linguistic ability, their willingness to study abroad, and their experience in working in multicultural teams. As one human resource specialist with a large multinational saw it, 'The most valuable service performed by [these schools] is not just training, but selection and socialization'.

Work experience

While the background and education of individuals may help them to operate in an international context, those skills can be enhanced within companies. As Rajat Gupta, the managing director of McKinsey, once put it:

'I also found that, because of the background you come from, because of the global exposure you have, of where you grew up and so on, I would say fundamentally you're a more interesting person. I look at my colleagues, and I've been to more places and had more diverse exposure than many of our American colleagues. They're no less smart, but I have had more interesting experiences.'[60]

Early challenges and diversified experience are considered important in developing international managers. The idea behind sending people abroad is that they will learn to understand and appreciate cultural differences in management style and perspective. Consider the testimony of one Shell manager.

'I was trained as a geologist and spent the first seven years of my career trying to discover oil. One day when I was heading an exploration assignment, they called me to London and told me that they wanted me to take over the responsibility for a troubled department of 80 maintenance engineers on the other side of the world. Geology is the noble elite, and maintenance engineering is somewhere between here-and-hell in the value system. I didn't want the job, and I told them that I knew nothing about maintenance engineering. "We're not sending you there to learn about engineering" they said, "We are sending you there to learn about management."'[61]

The implicit assumption is that if managers are moved around enough, they will develop cultural sensitivity. Mobility is indeed considered the key to the internationalization of both managers and companies.[62]

While essential, it becomes clear that exposure to other cultures is not a sufficient condition to develop the skills needed to manage across cultures. It may happen that executives sent abroad can become more rigid in their thinking rather than less so. A colonial mentality can result when these executives are charged with implementing standardized policies and procedures dictated by the home office.

Furthermore, pressures created by performance expectations and time constraints inhibit experimenting with new approaches that may be more locally (and perhaps even more globally) effective. Companies provide too few chances for their executives to reflect on their experiences, to draw out the learning and assimilate it in new behavior in discussions with peers, coaches, or mentors. Also lost is the opportunity for the company to learn and develop through these experiences and discussions.[63]

A further problem with international development through mobility is that companies can spend a great deal of time and money identifying people who can work internationally, only to find that those individuals are actually unwilling to relocate. Perhaps more pertinent than whether they *can* be international managers is the question of whether they *want* to be. This is confirmed by one IBM executive who claims that, 'Personal and family reasons, often genuine though sometimes as an excuse, are certainly the greatest inhibitor to moving people. And it is increasingly so with the dual career situation.'[64]

The problem of mobility itself differs across cultures. For example, the proportion of managers with working partners is particularly high in Sweden. For this reason, Swedish companies often make it their business to assist spouses in finding jobs in the local community. Spaniards are less inclined to live abroad, preferring to remain in close contact with their extended family, while British managers may be more mobile, as they may be more accustomed to leaving their children in distant boarding schools.

Companies have found two ways of getting round this increased resistance to mobility. The first is to push managers out of the nest as early as possible, before family responsibilities enter into the picture. This approach is favored by Schlumberger, the French engineering company, which sends young (male) recently graduated engineers off to exotic places. One British company, ICI, does not wait for them to graduate, offering twenty university students two-month internships at an ICI site outside their home country. Trainees therefore can combine their operational apprenticeship with a cross-cultural experience, rather than making the two phases sequential.[65]

Procter and Gamble is another company which believes that exposing new graduates to cultural differences from the start is the best way to learn about them.[66] The head of recruitment for P&G in Brussels claims that the idea of a first job outside their country of origin appeals to more and more graduates. It is also believed that early experiences help these aspiring international managers to better manage cultural differences.

Of course, the mobility norms within the national culture also interact with the prevailing company norms. For example, when Daimler and Chrysler merged in 1998, one of the first integration initiatives was to exchange 60 employees between Germany and the US on merger-related assignments lasting between two and five years. But finding American volunteers proved exceedingly difficult owing to organizational differences. Chrysler had never placed much value on international assignments – and only 300 of its employees were living outside the US, compared with about 1500 of Daimler's employees living outside Germany.[67] This may explain the sense of a 'German invasion' and perhaps the (im)balance of power in this so-called 'merger of equals'.

Besides foreign postings, managers can acquire a global perspective through working in mixed-nationality teams. Improvements in communications and transportation mean that it is increasingly feasible (and strategically important) to assemble geographically dispersed teams in project groups and ad hoc task forces. This exposes local managers to more global concerns without requiring extensive relocation of personnel.

For example, when 3M radically restructured its European operations, involving 21,000 people, it managed to limit relocation to only 40 managers. On the other hand, about 1000 of their managers were given permanent and/or project responsibilities across national borders; this involved them spending about one-third of their time outside their home country.[68]

Figure 15.1 provides a summary of the background and career factors which influence cross-cultural competence.

Personal strategies for managing across cultures

The traditional approach to preparing expatriates for international assignments focused on cultural briefings, language training, and 'suggested' readings (How to do business in …). The implicit advice was 'when in Rome do as the Romans do'. That strategy is far less applicable today, since much of the cross-cultural contacts take place in yet another country or else on virtual territory (via satellites and video screens). Under these circumstances, the principle of 'when in Rome …' becomes less meaningful.

Furthermore, with increasing exposure to other cultures, through media, travel, training and education, and through experience with international business ventures, familiarity with other cultures is growing. Thus it is not unlikely that each side has been prepared to adapt to the other.

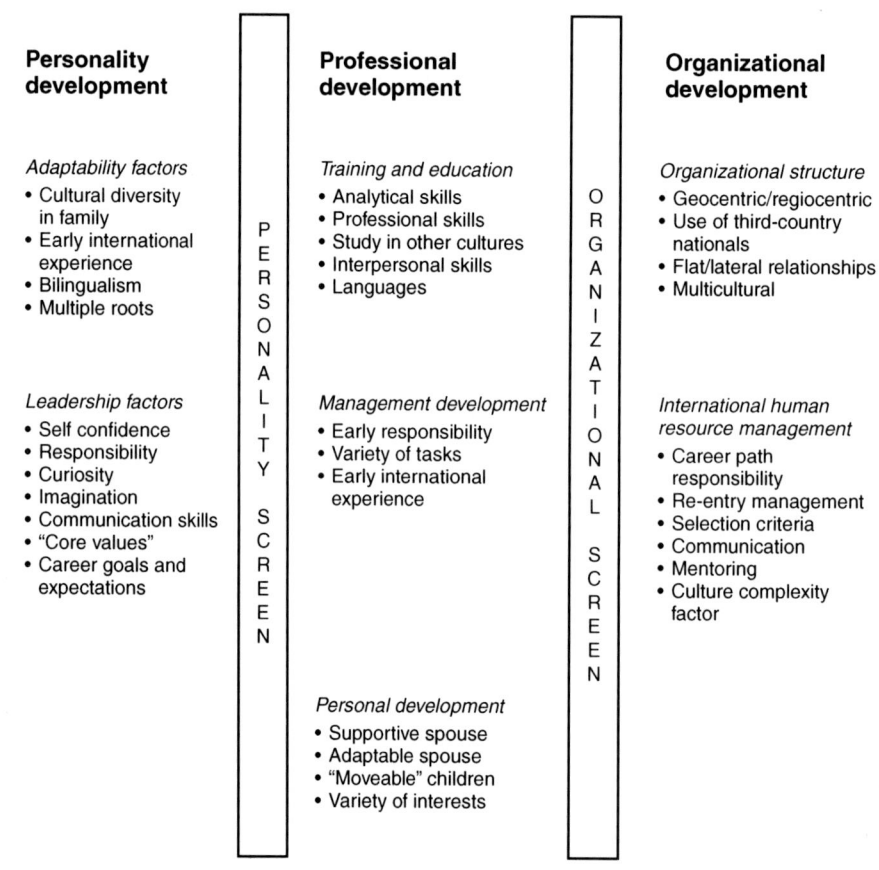

Figure 15.1 Creating cultural competence.
Source: K. de Vries and C. Mead (1991) 'Identifying management talent for a pan-European environment', in S.G. Makridakis and associates, *Single Market Europe: Opportunities and challenges for business*, Jossey-Bass, New York.

Yet the degree of cultural familiarity may be asymmetrical. For example, a Malaysian may be more familiar with American culture than the American with Malaysian culture. Based on differences in the degree of familiarity with the other's culture, according to Steven Weiss, different strategies may be appropriate.[69] In cross-cultural negotiations, for example, using a go-between or third party is suggested when each party is unfamiliar with the other culture. On the other hand, it may be possible to induce others to follow your 'negotiating script' when they are more familiar with your culture than you are with theirs. Nevertheless when undertaking this strategy care should be taken to demonstrate that this approach is not taken out of ignorance of cultural differences (assuming that your way is universal) or from lack of respect for the other culture.

Another strategy is to embrace the other culture's way of doing things. This, however, requires high levels of familiarity, marked by language fluency and extensive experience with the other culture: being bilingual and bicultural. Finally, when both cultures are quite familiar with each other, there is more opportunity to create something better, beyond adapting to one or the other.[70]

This allows something akin to jazz improvisation[71] wherein one musician picks up from where the other leaves off, leaving room for each party to display their virtuosity and even to go off in unexpected directions, based on personal interpretation. This requires that both parties know the score, the underlying structure of the music and key themes, and listen intently to be able to pick up from and build upon the contribution of the other.

Weiss also proposes criteria for selecting a culturally responsive strategy including its *feasibility* and *acceptability* in light of the manager's repertoire of behaviors and values, its *appropriateness* given the prevailing relationship and circumstances, and the need to insure *coherent interaction*.[72] For example, it may simply not be possible to behave as the other (kissing *à la russe* – on the lips of your counterpart) or to expect them to behave as you would (confronting conflict). Even if it were possible, behavior such as use of facilitating payments (bribes) may conflict with one's own value systems.

What is *appropriate* is determined by the nature of the relationship, notably the history of previous interactions and the balance of power. Appropriateness is also determined by the nature of the circumstances, such as timing constraints and the audience present. Highly public events and media attention may constrain the flexibility of those involved. In any event, the goal is to provide coherent interaction and to develop a viable relationship.

Familiarity can be increased by preparing cultural profiles, not only of the other culture, but also of one's own culture. In this way similarities can be identified which can serve as bridges to establish a common ground. Potential clashes due to differences can also be better anticipated and negotiated. While this can be done in advance, based on country-specific information and training, it needs to be modified in real-time when faced with the actual people involved.

With the increasing international experience of individuals worldwide, managers can no longer assume that the person facing them will act in accordance with national norms. Many managers from around the world have been educated, or have spent a large amount of time, outside their home countries. Furthermore, they may be second- or third-generation immigrants, as in the case of the Chinese or Indian migration. Therefore, it is quite misleading to assume nationality based on name, physical appearance, or accent.

In addition, it is also risky to assume, for example, that American-born Chinese or UK-born Indians are the best suited to take on missions 'back home'. Although familiar with the culture and perhaps fluent in the language, the cultural identification of those managers born or educated abroad is not necessarily with the 'homeland'. Furthermore, the experiences and memories of their parents, or grandparents, may be far removed from the current realities. Nor are they immediately accepted by the local staff as there may be feelings of resentment for having had opportunities not available to the others (not to mention salaries that are often beyond their imagination).

It is also important to recognize that people belong to several cultures – professional or functional, corporate, or industry – as shown in the multiple identities exercise below. Thus, creating a cultural profile of the other means focusing on the relevant dimensions of culture, not the specific national norms. This involves recognizing the visible cues of the relevant cultural dimensions, asking questions to discover core values and beliefs, and developing hypotheses regarding underlying assumptions. Focusing on the cultural dimension relevant to the situation or issue at hand, rather than specific country norms, avoids the trap of stereotypes, encourages recognition of the individual apart from his or her national culture, and enhances the possibility of creating a shared culture for working together.

While creating cultural (not necessarily national) profiles provides an initial starting point, it must be recognized that the individuals involved, including oneself, may fall outside cultural norms (whether national or corporate). To further complicate matters, individuals may strongly adhere to certain cultural norms while being less wedded to others, as discussed by Mary-Yoko Brannen.[73] Which norms are relevant is a function of the situation or issue at hand. Thus according to the issue, different constellations of norms, and degrees of 'normality' and 'marginality' can be found.

Nevertheless, although you may consider yourself culturally marginal, for example less outgoing than your compatriots, the other may still see you as quite outgoing in comparison with their own behavior. The Johari window technique can be useful as a tool for bringing to the surface and discussing these perceptions of cultural differences, and degrees of normality. It provides the opportunity for each party involved to come to grips with differences in perception of how we see us and how they see us, and to reduce the blindspots that can lead to cultural misunderstandings.

This technique can be revisited when confronted with key issues and situations. For example, in creating a new organization structure, it may be apparent that greater decentralization will require more delegation. While you may perceive your style to be highly participative, others may experience it to be fairly autocratic, particularly under pressure. Thus this technique can be used in an ongoing manner to provide feedback regarding your personal behavior, espoused values and beliefs, and underlying assumptions. In fact it was for this purpose that the Johari window was originally designed.

Furthermore, cultural interactions must not be regarded as static, but as evolving in a dynamic process. Borrowing Brannen's analogy,[74] rather than imagining this interaction as two billiard balls bouncing off of each other, one with the power to push aside the other, cultures interact and rub off on one another. Mutual adjustment evolves over time as the relationship develops.

As mentioned earlier, cultural interactions are no longer sequential, but simultaneous. This makes the above suggestions even more complicated to implement. It may be useful to consider how different people involved are likely to respond to the situation at hand, such as a corporate change effort or developing a new market strategy. For example, faced with a multicultural team, cultural differences regarding the task and process issues can be mapped.

Take a simple cultural artifact such as forms of address. If some members of the team prefer to be called 'Herr Doktor' while others prefer 'Joe', then it should be possible to use these forms of address, without assuming that one is trying to pull rank or that the other is behaving in an unprofessional manner. It is not that the behavior has to conform. Differentiated responses may even be more desirable as it encourages flexibility and learning.

What is necessary is that the other's behavior is no longer evaluated as good or bad as viewed through our own cultural filters. What is good or bad needs to be defined through discussion of the behavior, values and beliefs, and underlying assumptions considered necessary given the task at hand. It requires discussion and negotiation to arrive at an agreed-upon way of working together, even if that means doing things differently (agreeing to disagree).

So where the conventional approach focuses on national culture, and the corresponding 'do's and don'ts', the approach recommended here recognizes people as cultural composites. Here the focus becomes more personal, with different approaches to different people, and perhaps different approaches with the same person depending on the circumstances. As relationships evolve over time, international managers should be guided less by role and stereotype, and should become more attentive to the individual and the circumstance.

Triandis et al.[75] propose a model of managing workplace diversity that is useful, particularly given that cultural differences exist at home as well as abroad. They argue that perceived similarity creates greater interaction which, in turn, encourages greater perceived similarity. Several methods can be used to increase perceived similarity. For one, past history of conflict should be minimized (in Europe, for example, between the French and the English, and between the Germans and the Dutch). Secondly, perceived cultural distance can be reduced through learning about the other's culture and language. Perceived similarity is also greater when working with people from other cultures with whom one has common friends or colleagues (network overlap) and with whom one shares equal status. Furthermore, opportunities must be created for cross-cultural interactions that provide rewarding experiences such as achieving a shared goal. Of course, the relationship between perceived cultural similarity and interaction is further enhanced by non-ethnocentric attitudes, high task structure, and a broader social context which encourages pluralism rather than homogeneity.

Easier said than done

Many of the recommendations regarding the handling of cultural diversity often sound like common sense: more recognition, more trust, more respect, more communication, more patience, more confrontation of differences. But the fact that the prescriptions are simple does not imply that they are easy. Recognizing and valuing cultural differences is fine in theory, but in practice remains elusive. For one, it means questioning our own ways of being and doing which can be perceived as a threat to our identity and autonomy. Many managers are concerned that managing cultural differences means adapting to the other culture and finding themselves lost at sea, without a point of reference.

That anxiety stems in part from a misconception about what it means to be an effective international manager. While recognition of cultural differences is vital, the cross-cultural message is not that managers need to accept everything about other cultures in order to be effective across borders. The idea is not to become some sort of cultural chameleon, receptive to every new view that comes along, and changing accordingly. As Evans puts it, 'It is not a question of making some composite person. That would be the quickest way of making an individual into a schizophrenic'.[76] At best, this would lead to 'feeling at ease anywhere but belonging nowhere'.[77]

Receptiveness to other cultures does not mean losing one's own values, as these provide the solid ground from which managers move forward. As Kets de Vries points out, 'Truly global leaders need a set of core values that will guide them and provide support in whatever environment they may find themselves'.[78] To be effective in a cross-cultural setting demands an ability to tap into one's roots when one is unsure. This provides a sense of who we are, a vital landmark when cultural differences seem overwhelming.

International managers have to consciously manage concerns regarding personal boundaries and control. They have to be sure of their own identity, to let others know where they stand. Having a strong sense of self is required to be able to acknowledge the identity of others. Having secure personal boundaries enables us to interact comfortably with others. Therefore, international managers need to have a strong sense of autonomy and control over their lives, to feel that they have freedom of choice in their actions and do not feel coerced. When this is the case, there is less sense of threat in allowing others autonomy and self-control, in other words, empowerment. With less fear of letting go, there is more opportunity for exposure to new experiences and new ideas, and a greater potential for learning.

The value of cross-cultural interactions, then, lies in learning new possibilities, new ways of thinking, new ways of behaving. While this experience is unlikely to change people's deep-seated assumptions, it can make them aware of what these might be and how they influence behavior. Far from leading to a loss of identity or individuality, contact with other cultures tends to make people more aware of themselves and their cultural heritage. To quote Kipling, 'What know they of England, who only England know?'.[79] Experience with other cultures leads to a better understanding of one's own culture. This in turn leads back to a better understanding of the other.

The challenge is to have the willingness to confront our own assumptions, to question them, and to hold on to the essential ones out of a sense of conviction rather than fear of something different. With that as an anchor, it becomes possible to share differences by creating openness and encouraging empathy, as well as to test them and disagree without destroying one's sense of self.[80] Cross-cultural recommendations may sound like little more than common sense but it takes considerable robustness, openness, and effort to see to it that common sense prevails.

Multiple identities

Not only do international managers have to manage different cultures at home and abroad, but within themselves as well. Many international managers have been born and raised in different cultures, have lived with parents and partners of different cultures, and have gone to school and to work in different places. As a result, they often find it difficult to respond to the question, 'What am I?'. Indeed, most of us have several identities that are rooted in different cultures, for example, being American from California, born to Mexican parents, married with children, age 30, male, a software engineer, etc. These different identities may become more or less salient depending on the situation and issues at hand – being sent as an expatriate to Spain or to Germany, or being assigned to a task force to increase the number of women and minorities in the workforce. And these different identities can provide a sense of power and effectiveness. Some identities may give more 'voice' than others. Therefore, being an effective 'international' manager may depend upon different identities, which become more or less salient, and which can contribute to seeing oneself and being seen by others as effective.

The following exercise may help to illustrate this.

Exercise

Which of the following identities are important to you, in general? For you at work? As seen by others? To what extent are these identities considered to be positive or negative, that is, providing a sense of power and efficacy? To what extent do they influence your effectiveness (as perceived by you and others) as an international leader?

As an international manager, how do these identities influence your effectiveness ...?

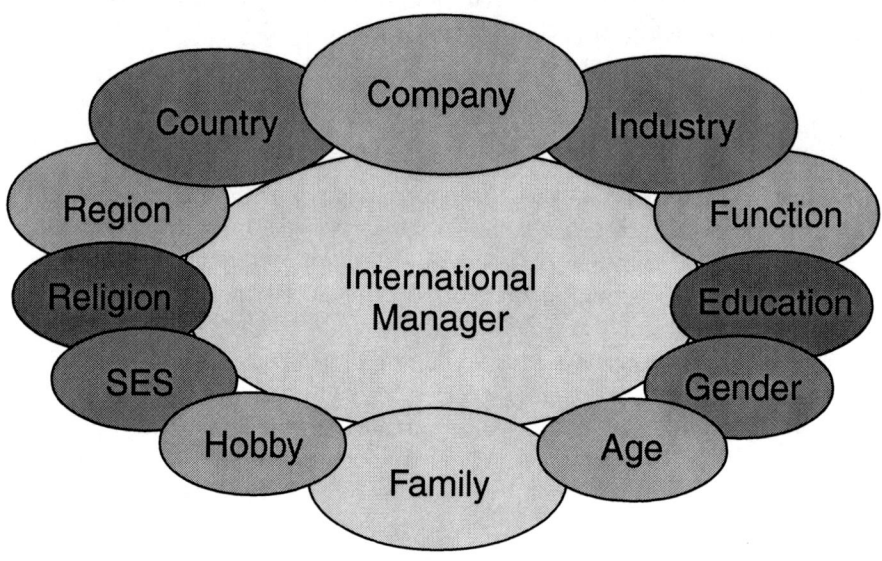

Identities

Multiple identities

To what extent is the following identity important to you ... ?

1 (not at all) – 7 (very much)

IDENTITIES	Important to me in general	Feel to be positive in general (a)	Important to me at work (b)	Feel to be positive at work (c)
Nationality (e.g. Swiss)				
Regional (e.g. Swiss Romand)				
Company (e.g. IBM, ABB)				
Industry (e.g. computers, pharmaceuticals)				
Function (e.g. finance, marketing)				
Education level (e.g. postgraduate)				
Education by subject (e.g. economics, engineering)				
Gender				
Age				
Family				
Race/ethnicity				
Religion				
Socio-economic status				
Political orientation				
Hobbies (e.g. sports, art, travel)				

a. To what extent do you feel this identity as something *positive*?
b. To what extent do you feel this identity is important to you at work, in your company?
c. To what extent do you feel this identity is considered as something positive at work? Gives you a source of power? Or voice?

SUGGESTIONS FOR MANAGING DIFFERENCES

- Use a cultural-general approach – diagnose cultural dimensions, not countries.
- Avoid assuming differences or similarities where there are none. Seek similarities as well as differences.
- Analyze different levels of culture: use multiple approaches of observation, questioning, and interpretation.
- Recognize your own cultural profile. Anticipate clashes with others.
- Recognize individual variance within your own culture as well as the other in terms of specific dimensions. You/they may be more or less 'normal' on different dimensions.
- Recognize that cultural interaction is not a static, but a dynamic process; look for rub-off effects and enjoy.
- Depending on the degree of familiarity of each culture, use different strategies for interaction.
- Confront concerns regarding identity and autonomy, both yours and theirs. People need to feel valued and not coerced.

NOTES

1. Thubron, C. (1987) *Behind the Wall*, London: Penguin, p. 158 (as cited by Weiss, 1994).
2. 'The elusive Euro-manager', *The Economist*, November 7, 1992, p. 81.
3. Bartlett, C.A. and Ghoshal, S. (1992) 'What is a global manager?', *Harvard Business Review*, September–October, pp. 124–32.
4. Ouchi, W.G. and Jaeger, A.M. (1978) 'Type Z organization: Stability in the midst of mobility', *Academy of Management Review*, 3(2), pp. 305–41.
5. Tyler, A. (1985) *The Accidental Tourist*, New York: Knopf.
6. Barham, K. and Oates, D. (1991) *The International Manager*, London: The Economist Books.
7. Auteri, E. and Tesio, V. (1990) 'The internationalization of management at FIAT', *Journal of Management Development*, 9(6), pp. 6–16.
8. Barham, K. and Antal, A. (1994) 'Competences for the pan-European manager', in P.S. Kirkbride (ed.) *Human Resource Management in Europe*, London: Routledge, Ch. 14, pp. 222–41.
9. Harzing, A.W. (1995) 'The persistent myth of high expatriate failure rates', *International Journal of Human Resource Management*, 6(2), pp. 457–74.
10. Black, J.S., Gregersen, H. and Mendenhall, M. (1992) *Global Assignments: Successfully Expatriating and Repatriating International Managers*, San Francisco: Jossey-Bass; Tung, R. (1988) *The New Expatriates: Managing Human Resources Abroad*, Cambridge, MA: Ballinger.
11. Cope, N. (1992) 'In search of Euroman', *Management Today*, June, 50–3.
12. Johnson, M. (1993) 'Doing le business', *Management Today*, February, pp. 62–5.
13. Lysgaard, S. (1955) 'Adjustment in a foreign society: Norwegian Fulbright grantees visiting the United States', *International Social Sciences Bulletin*, 7, pp. 45–51.
14. Brett, J.M., Stroh, L.K. and Reilly, A.H. (1992) 'Job transfer', in C.L. Cooper and I.T.

Robinson (eds) *International Review of Industrial and Organizational Psychology*, Chichester: Wiley, pp. 93–138; Black *et al.*, *Op. cit.*
15. Brislin, R.W. (1981) *Cross-Cultural Encounters: Face-to-Face Interaction*, New York: Pergamon Press.
16. Triandis, H.C., Kurowski, L.L. and Gelfand, M.J. (1994) 'Workplace diversity', in H.C. Triandis, M.D. Dunnette and L.M. Hough (eds) *Handbook of Industrial and Organizational Psychology*, Vol. 4, Palo Alto: Consulting Psychologists Press, Ch. 16, pp. 769–827.
17. Caligiuri, P.M. (2000) 'Selecting expatriates for personality characteristics: A moderating effect of personality on the relationship between host national contact and cross-cultural adjustment', *Management International Review*, 40, pp. 61–80.
18. Janssens, M. (1995) 'Intercultural interaction: a burden on international managers?', *Journal of Organizational Behavior*, 16, pp. 155–67.
19. Osland, J.S. (1995) *The Adventure of Working Abroad: Hero Tales from the Global Frontier*, San Francisco: Jossey-Bass.
20. Black, J.S. and Gregersen, H. (1992) 'Serving two masters: Managing dual allegiances', *Sloan Management Review*, Summer, pp. 66–71.
21. La Palombara, J. and Blank, S. (1977) *Multinational Corporations in Comparative Perspective*, New York: The Conference Board, Report 725.
22. Kohls, L.R. (1979) *Survival Kit for Overseas Living*, Yarmouth, ME: Intercultural Press.
23. Hagerty, B. (1991) 'Companies in Europe seeking executives who can cross borders in a single bound', *The Wall Street Journal*, January 25, p. B1.
24. Clerk, J. (2001) 'How to become an expatriate', *International Herald Tribune*, June 29.
25. Brein, M. and David, K.H. (1973) *Improving Cross-Cultural Training and Measurement of Cross-Cultural Learning*, Vol. 1, Denver: Center for Research and Education.
26. Singh, J. V. (2001) 'McKinsey's Managing Director Rajat Gupta on leading a knowledge-based global consulting organization', *Academy of Management Executive*, May, pp. 34–44.
27. Yates, B. (2000) 'Daimler drives Chrysler into a ditch', *Wall Street Journal*, November 8, p. A26.
28. Borg, M. (1988) *International Transfers of Managers in Multinational Corporations*, Uppsala: Studia Oeconomiae Negotorum.
29. Lobel, S. (1990) 'Global leadership competencies: Managing to a different drumbeat', *Human Resource Management*, 29(1), pp. 39–47.
30. Frenkel-Brunswik, E. (1949) 'Intolerance of ambiguity as an emotional and perceptual personality variable', *Journal of Personality*, 18, pp. 108–43.
31. Hagerty, *Op. cit.*
32. Staw, B.M., Sandelands, L. and Dutton, J.E. (1981) 'Threat rigidity cycles in organizational behavior', *Administrative Science Quarterly*, 26, pp. 501–24.
33. Ferraro, G.P. (1990) *The Cultural Dimension of International Business*, Englewood Cliffs, NJ: Prentice Hall.
34. Kets de Vries, M. and Mead, C. (1992) 'Development of the global leader', in V. Pucik, N. Tichy and C. Barnett (eds) *Globalizing Management*, New York: John Wiley, pp. 194–205.
35. Ratui, I. (1983) 'Thinking internationally: A comparison of how international executives learn', *International Studies of Management and Organization*, XIII (1–2), pp. 139–50, p. 144.

36. Ferrano, *Op. cit.*, p. 151.
37. Muller, J. and Tierney, C. (2001) 'Can this man save Chrysler?', *Business Week*, September 17, pp. 86–93.
38. Meredith, R. (2001) 'Batman and Robin', *Forbes*, March 5, pp. 66–9.
39. Van Maanen, J. and Kunda, G. (1989) 'Real feelings: Emotional expression and organizational culture', *Research in Organizational Behavior*, Vol. II, Greenwich, CT: JAI Press, pp. 43–103.
40. Valeriani, R. (1979) *Travels With Henry*, Boston: Houghton Mifflin, p. 9.
41. Osland, J.S., DeFranco, S., and Osland, A. (1999) 'Organizational implications of Latin American culture. Lessons for the expatriate manager', *Journal of Management Inquiry*, 8(2), pp. 219–34.
42. Adler, N. and Bartholomew, S. (1992) 'Managing globally competent people', *Academy of Management Executive*, 6(3), pp. 52–65.
43. Reich, R. (1990) 'Who is us?', *Harvard Business Review*, January–February, pp. 53–64.
44. Rosenzweig, P.M. (1994) 'The new 'American Challenge': Foreign multinationals in the United States', *California Management Review*, 36(3), pp. 107–23.
45. Adler and Bartholomew, *Op. cit.*
46. Ghoshal, S. and Bartlett, C.A. (1990) 'Matrix management: Not a structure, a frame of mind', *Harvard Business Review*, July–August, pp. 138–45.
47. Barham and Antal, *Op. cit.*
48. Jacques, E. (1990) 'In praise of hierarchy', *Harvard Business Review*, January–February, pp. 127–33.
49. Kiyoi, M. (1995) 'Dear English speakers: Please drop the dialects', *International Herald Tribune*, November 3, p. 9.
50. Evans, P., Pucik, V., and Barsoux, J.-L. (2001) *The Global Challenge: Frameworks for International Human Resource Management*, New York: McGraw-Hill Irwin, p. 385.
51. See Schneider, S. and Angelmar, R. (1993) 'Cognition in organization analysis: Who's minding the store?', *Organization Studies*, 14(3).
52. Maznevski, M.L. (1999) Developing the ultimate international management tool: The global mindset. Working paper.
53. Don't be an 'ugly American', *Fortune*, October 16, 1995, p. 99, citing D. Ready.
54. Kanter, R.M. (1995) *World Class: Thriving locally in the global economy*, New York: Simon and Schuster.
55. Kefalas, A.G. (1998) 'Think globally, act locally', *Thunderbird International Business Review*, 40(6), pp. 547–62, p. 556.
56. Ghoshal and Bartlett, *Op. cit.*
57. Interview with Peter Brabeck. *L'Hebdo*, March 23, 2000, pp. 48–50.
58. Bateson, M.C. (1994) *Peripheral Vision*, New York: Harper Collins.
59. 'Les MBA font un retour en force', *Le Nouvel Economiste*, March 30, 1995, pp. 66–7.
60. Singh, *Op. cit.*
61. Evans, P.A.L. (1992) 'Developing leaders and management development', *European Management Journal*, 10(1), pp. 1–9.
62. Evans, P., Doz, Y., and Laurent, A. (eds) (1989) *Human Resource Management in International Firms*, London: Macmillan.
63. Barham and Antal, *Op. cit.*
64. Evans *et al.*, *Op. cit.*
65. Hagerty, *Op. cit.*

66. Beslu, E.-X. and de Vendeuil, R. (1991) 'Cadres: Manager les différences', *L'Express*, December 19, pp. 160–64.
67. Ball, J. (1999) 'DaimlerChrysler's transfer woes', *Wall Street Journal*, August 24, p. B1.
68. Lorenz, C. (1993) 'Here, there and everywhere', *Financial Times*, November 10, p. 11.
69. Weiss, S.E. (1994) 'Negotiating with "Romans" – Part 1', *Sloan Management Review*, Winter, pp. 51–61.
70. Ibid.
71. Weick, K.E. (1995) 'Improvisation as a mindset for organizing', Academy of Management Meetings, Vancouver, BC.
72. Weiss, S.E. (1994) 'Negotiating with "Romans" – Part 2', *Sloan Management Review*, Spring, pp. 85–99.
73. Brannen, M.-Y. *Negotiating Cultural Change: Dynamics of Work Culture Formation in a Japanese Takeover*, Oxford: Oxford University Press, forthcoming.
74. Ibid.
75. Triandis *et al.*, *Op. cit.*
76. Wood, L. (1990) 'The Euromanager: Is it a myth or a real Superman?', *Financial Times*, February 14, p. 16.
77. Osland, *Op. cit.*, p. 5.
78. Kets de Vries and Mead, *Op. cit.*, p. 193.
79. Kipling, R. (1987) 'The English flag', quoted in *The Everyman Dictionary of Quotations and Proverbs*, London: Cathay Books.
80. Irene Rodgers, Personal communication.

CHAPTER SIXTEEN

The 'Global' Organisation

> A company is made of [people] with different backgrounds, different cultures, different inclinations, different aspirations ... different jobs ... All of these [people] ... of different ages and cultures, with different jobs, have to produce the miracle of their own striving together so that the company's balance sheet can be good. Today and tomorrow.
>
> **Giovanni Agnelli, retired CEO, Fiat**

So far in Part III of this book we have looked at how individuals and teams manage cultural differences. In Chapter 15 we asked: How do individual managers react to cultural differences? What does it take to be an effective international manager, whether at home or abroad? Where can those competencies be found and how can they be developed?

We now address the question of how organizations manage cultural differences. What are the best strategies? What does it take to become an international, or truly global, company, and how can organizations actually go about doing it?

We start by considering three basic organizational strategies for managing cultural differences: ignore, minimize, or utilize. These strategies, discussed more or less explicitly by international management scholars, are embedded in the nature of relationships between headquarters and subsidiaries, which often correspond to different stages of internationalization. These strategies also drive the way in which multinational companies manage the often conflicting needs for global integration and local responsiveness.

For example, relationships between headquarters and subsidiaries have been classified by Heenan and Perlmutter according to the degree to which they are ethnocentric, polycentric, regiocentric, or geocentric.[1] Where the relationship between HQ and subsidiaries is *ethnocentric*, all policies and procedures come from the top (HQ decides what and how). Where the relationship is *polycentric*, how policies and procedures are implemented is determined locally (HQ decides what, locals decide how). In the case of *regiocentric* relationships, regional HQ serves as a buffer, negotiating between home country HQ and host country subsidiaries in a particular region, for example northeast Asia, Latin America, or central and eastern Europe. Where a *geocentric* relationship prevails, policies and procedures, the *whats* and the *hows*, are developed with input from both HQ and subsidiaries, as well as across subsidiaries.

These different approaches tend to evolve over time as multinationals develop their activities abroad. Many companies start with an ethnocentric approach, and move to a polycentric one when they realize that the local product standards, markets, or rules of the game are very different. The *regiocentric* approach evolves in response to needs to rationalize or to better coordinate business activities among countries in a particular region. Many companies today are moving to a *geocentric* approach, such as worldwide product divisions or business units, in efforts to become more global. Paradoxically, creating global business or product divisions may appear to be a return to an ethnocentric approach, as was the case when one American multinational moved its European regional headquarters from London to New Jersey (USA).

Different approaches and their development can indeed be found in the 'mindsets' of managers as well as companies. A survey of 65 US Fortune 500 firms demonstrated a company's geocentric 'mind-set', as revealed in HRM policies (for example, the percentage of third country nationals (TCNs), of non-US directors), and in its geographic scope (percent of sales abroad and per cent of employees abroad). Geocentric companies placed greater importance on cultural adaptability and ability to deal with diversity as criteria for selection. These companies were more likely to be involved in information-intensive industries and activities, for example R&D and advertising. Neither size, strategy, structure nor international experience seemed to matter.[2] Another survey conducted in 1992 and 1995, with 370 managers in 13 country affiliates of a US-based diversified MNC, was able to demonstrate the extent to which managers had a geocentric 'mindset', its development over time, and their understanding of the relationship of this global mindset with company policies, individual performance, and career opportunities.[3]

According to management scholars Prahalad and Doz[4] and Bartlett and Ghoshal,[5] multinationals have to manage between the often conflicting demands to develop standardized products and policies (global integration) and to respond to local tastes and requirements (local responsiveness), as well as searching for ways to stimulate innovation and learning. Innovations, for example, can be developed by HQ and then diffused to local subsidiaries (global for local), developed by subsidiaries for the local market (local for local), or diffused to the wider organization (local for global). Given these options, relationships between headquarters and subsidiaries can be better differentiated in order to satisfy these demands. Indeed, the very notions of headquarters and subsidiaries can be questioned.

Strategies for managing cultural differences

Underlying these different approaches to managing multinational companies are different strategies for managing cultural differences. Embedded in them are assumptions of culture as irrelevant, as a problem or threat, or as an opportunity for learning and innovation, and even a source of competitive advantage as shown in Table 16.1.

These strategies – ignore, minimize, utilize – have implications for relationships between headquarters and subsidiaries, as well as for managing the conflicting demands for global integration, local responsiveness, and organizational innovation and learning as discussed above. We recognize that many companies use several strategies simultaneously, and that the examples are not entirely pure. Nevertheless, we do think it is important for companies to question the extent to which they are achieving their aspirations to become more international or truly global. We encourage companies with global aspirations to recognize their implicit strategies for managing cultural differences and to challenge themselves as to whether they are not missing opportunities for creating competitive advantage. Although today many companies 'talk global' and espouse 'the value of diversity', utilizing cultural differences remains more rhetoric than reality.

Table 16.1 Strategies for managing cultural differences

	Ignore	Minimize	Utilize
Assumptions: culture as	Irrelevant	A problem/threat	An opportunity A source of competitive advantage
Headquarter/subsidiary relationships:	Ethnocentric	Polycentric/regiocentric	Geocentric
Expected benefit:	Standardization Global integration	Localization Responsiveness	Innovation and learning
Performance criteria:	Efficiency	Adaptability	Synergy
Communication:	Top-down	Top-down Bottom-up reporting	All channels
Major challenge:	Gaining acceptance	Achieving coherence	Leveraging differences
Major concern:	Inflexibility Missed opportunities	Fragmentation Duplication of effort and loss of potential synergy	Confusion Friction

Ignoring cultural differences: business is business

When companies choose to *ignore* cultural differences, they are operating on the assumption that business is business, and that managers, engineers, or bankers are the same throughout the world. They assume convergence in management practice due to economic and technological development, a universal desire for modernization, and the diffusion of professionalism through management education and management consultancy.

For these companies, policies and practices developed in the home country are considered to be readily transferable. And host country subsidiaries are expected to apply them to the letter. This, they argue, is necessary in order to maintain product quality, to uphold customer service and technological standards, and ensure that the corporate culture is shared by all employees. Such companies may even create their own training centers or universities to inculcate the necessary management practices and behavior, core beliefs and values. While compliance may be achieved at the surface level of behavior and espoused values and beliefs,[6] it is not evident that underlying assumptions are truly shared.

American companies, such as Disney, provide the best examples of this approach. At the level of artifacts and behavior, this can be seen in insistence on uniform dress codes and standardized procedures. For example, Disney executives, when they landed in France, insisted on the same dress codes for employees as in the United States and Japan: minimal make-up, short nails with no colored polish, earrings no larger than the size of a franc (none for the men), no more than one ring per hand, no dark stockings for women, and neither long hair nor beards for men, all spelled out in a nine-page document. Disney even put a shower scene in a video shown to potential recruits to get across the message that Disneyland Paris cast members must show up 'fresh and clean every day' upholding the 'squeaky clean' image of Disney.[7] This created quite an uproar among French employees who brought their displeasure to court.

While personal appearance and dress codes are understandable for cast members 'on stage' (in the park), these policies also apply to office workers, managers included. One Irish MBA stated that she did not mind the dress code as it coincided with her own style (not surprisingly), but she did resent being told what she had to wear. Another manager was reprimanded by the CEO because her earrings were too large.

Even customers ('guests') are expected to behave properly. They are reminded that they cannot eat while waiting in line for attractions, that they cannot bring food into the park, and that they must keep their shirts on even when temperatures reach 40°C (105°F). The responsibility for crowd control lies not only with the unobtrusive security force but also with the sweepers. While Disney controls the entire 'cast', the cast in turn control the 'guests'.[8] The painstaking attention to and use of language ('cast', 'on stage', 'guests') is another indication of the extent to which shared artifacts and conformity in behavior are expected. And intensive training closely follows the script, at Disney University, located below the park.

Standardized procedures are also sacrosanct. McDonald's Hamburger University insists on split-second timing of hamburger flipping and service delivery, and holds contests to encourage this spirit. Standards of cleanliness are scrupulously upheld. Potatoes for french fries have to meet certain taste and size requirements to ensure product standards. This meant shipping in potatoes from the United States to Russia where the local potatoes were too small – at least until they were able to source them from 'nearby' Holland.[9]

While many customers appreciate the consistency in quality, service, and cleanliness of McDonald's worldwide, local adaptation is not totally ruled out. While the golden arches remain clearly visible, McDonald's now serves beer and wine in Europe as well as adapting the menu to local tastes. Even Disneyland Paris has now allowed alcoholic beverages to be served within the park, at sit-down restaurants.

Although these companies may make concessions to satisfy customers, they are often less willing to adapt to satisfy employees. Local adaptation is only made under duress. The prevailing attitude of headquarters to subsidiaries is one of 'universalism', the idea being that there is one best way; and 'ethnocentrism', that what has been tried and tested at home will work best in the local country. Paradoxically, according to Nancy Adler, this universalist view of business is actually quite 'parochial'.[10]

There are, perhaps, other examples of successful MNCs which have not paid much attention to cultural differences. Here managers do not see much evidence that culture makes a difference, or at least not one worth worrying about. In fact competitive advantage may be perceived as derived from standardized ways of operating worldwide. This may be particularly true in industries which are engineering-driven, such as oil or construction, or rely on high technology, such as telecommunications. Or where doing business is dependent on compliance with international standards, such as ISO 9000. Indeed, many multinational companies may seek to hire accounting firms which promise to use the same standards and procedures worldwide. And consultants from firms such as McKinsey or Andersen Consulting (now Accenture) carry a strong imprint of their corporate, if not national, culture around the world.

Competitive advantage may also be derived from providing an alternative to local offerings. Take, for example, the case of Citibank in Japan.

> 'In Japan, where more than half of the money is in savings accounts that earn almost no interest (representing $10.5 trillion personal savings), Citibank distinguished itself with an entirely un-Japanese feature: its sales pitch. In a country where nine out of 10 people consider themselves middle-class, banks often move in lockstep offering "one-size-fits-all" financial products. Comparative advertising is shunned as crass in Japan where companies try to project a friend next door image of reliability and plainness.
>
> When Koichiro Kitade took over private banking operations in 1997 and ran advertisement asking only the wealthy to apply, Japanese banks accused him of discrimination. Nevertheless this approach was an instant hit: 20 per cent of respondents signed on as clients. Citibank is private and global so as a customer you become part of a self selected elite.[11]'

Protecting brand image and meeting customer expectations and demands may be another reason for ignoring cultural differences. Even Disney was surprised to find out that its Japanese partner wanted Disneyland Tokyo to be 'just like America'.[12] And that the European 'guests' wanted Disneyland Paris to be identical with those in the US, hence the change in name from Euro Disney to Disneyland Paris.[13]

The assumption of 'one best way' means that management practices just require fine-tuning for optimal effectiveness. A study of eight foreign acquisitions of US firms found that while cultural differences were easy to identify, they did not seem to have important operational consequences. Problems were more readily attributed to contextual, structural, and political factors. Sensitivity to cultural differences and willingness to deal with related problems were considered important only insofar as they improved mutual respect and communication. This finding led to recommendations to follow the golden (universal) rules: finding the right strategy and structure, the right amount of interpersonal sensitivity and communications, limiting politics, and preserving managerial autonomy.[14]

But although the debate continues as to whether Disneyland Paris's initial problems were cultural, strategic, or financial, one Disney executive reckoned that the company could have saved millions of dollars had they taken cultural differences into consideration *before* rather than *after* the set-up. This is a familiar lament among managers who have been sent to set up operations abroad.

Cultural differences may indeed represent convenient excuses for failure to make an effort on other fronts. For example, cultural problems are typically invoked to explain failed mergers, when the business merits of the merger may have been doubtful in the first place. Invoking culture as the reason for failed mergers is like invoking communication problems for failed marriages. There is a need to dig more deeply to understand what are the underlying problems and how culture may play an important part. Failure to consider the potential consequences of cultural differences when implementing policies and procedures abroad can prove costly.

For example, although McDonald's had the sensitivity to offer beef-less burgers in India, it saw its outlet in Bombay vandalized following the results of a lawsuit brought by Hindus in Seattle (USA). The company had announced in 1990 that it was no longer using beef fat in cooking french fries, but it failed to mention that the french fries were seasoned with beef flavoring in the factories before being sent to restaurants.[15] McDonald's protested that it had never been said that the french fries in the US were vegetarian, and that beef extract is considered as a natural flavor according to FDA guidelines. Furthermore it asserted that it had *no plans to change the recipe*, which would have been secret had it not been for the lawsuit.[16]

The company also fell foul of French activists defending their cheese heritage. They protested that McDonald's 'cheese of the day' burgers did not respect the percentage of cheese required to earn the label "Beaufort", and even went as far as mixing Savoyard cheese with cheddar! Accused of trying to trick consumers, McDonald's *refused to renege* on its recipe, claiming that the cheese represented a sauce and not a slice.[17] These examples demonstrate the dangers of backlash when culture is disregarded. Most recently, McDonald's has been the victim of bombing attacks in France, Pakistan, and China.

Although one could question the cultural sensitivity of the practices discussed above, the very 'American' culture of both Disney and McDonald's makes them targets for anti-American and anti-globalization boycotts and attacks:

> 'McDonald's, which has planted its trademark golden arches outside more than 29,000 outlets in 120 countries, stands as one of the most visible and ubiquitous symbols of America in the world – and one of the most American of American companies, at least in the minds of many around the world.[18]'

Globalization in the minds of many means Americanization and the fear that the global village foreseen by Marshall McLuhan[19] will look like 'McWorld':

> 'McDonald's restaurants have become a dominant symbol of the globalization of the economy and target of the wrath of globalization's many opponents. But local values still wield great influence on culture, so don't look for McWorld to emerge anytime soon.[20]'

Thus despite globalization, national differences are expected to remain as 'shared experience and educational and cultural institutions shape the values of almost everyone in that society'.[21] Therefore the decision to ignore cultural differences or to impose 'our way of doing things' needs careful consideration of the strategic consequences.

Minimizing cultural differences

Another strategy for managing cultural differences is to try to *minimize* its impact. This approach recognizes cultural differences as important, but mainly as a source of problems or threats to efficient and effective operations. Trying to minimize cultural differences means finding ways of homogenizing them, creating sameness, or of isolating them, creating segregation, in order to reduce potential conflict. This can be done by developing a 'global' corporate culture or allowing autonomy while relying on rigorous systems of reporting and financial control.

These companies assume that a strong corporate culture can be created to serve as a melting pot to reduce the impact of the different national cultures. Or they assume that they can allow subsidiaries to 'do their own thing' (polycentric approach) as long as they deliver results. However, it is difficult to implement standardized systems and procedures or to create a global corporate culture that does not reflect the head-office national practices and culture, and thus may resemble an ethnocentric approach. For this reason, these efforts to standardize corporate practices, systems, and values are often resisted.

Creating a global corporate culture – the melting pot

GE is one company which is trying to develop a global culture to assure its success worldwide.

‘GE "... is working hard to create a truly global corporation. GE's formula: take a universal corporate culture, transplant it into a multitude of native soils, and then, by nurturing local talent, let it grow to suit local conditions." Nevertheless, the firm is highly centralized when it comes to a handful of issues: core values; financial targets; one of the most rigorous and exhaustive procedures anywhere for selecting and developing personnel; and certain initiatives, such as "Six Sigma" quality programs.

GE works hard to mesh this global set of standards, tools, and principles with local conditions. It does this through vast training programs, integrity guidelines that are put online for all to read, and constant conversations about environmental and safety issues. Each local manager is expected to run his or her business within these global standards. Those core values aren't negotiable. When asked "How do you transfer GE values somewhere?", Jack Welch responded that the answer lay in "really [the] most simple values of all: human dignity and voice. What our managers try to do is let everybody raise their hand and say what they think".

One of GE's most powerful global weapons is something it calls cross-border leveraging – using people, processes, and products more effectively to enhance businesses in other countries. In the last 2 years, GE has sent half the Americans it had overseas home. This was considered to have been an enormous benefit for globalization. Welch believes that the next step is the globalization of intellect. "The real challenge is to globalize the mind of the organization. Until you globalize intellect, you haven't really globalized."[22]’

Other companies choose to assign senior management from the parent company culture to head up the local subsidiary, someone that has been sufficiently 'socialized' to serve as a *cultural transfer agent*, the official bearer and custodian of the head-office culture.[23] This is often the European approach, which relies more on behavioral control that is normative (based on shared norms and values) rather than on reporting control, which is considered more calculative and coercive.[24]

Parent company executives may frequently visit subsidiaries and meet with local managers to discuss how things are going, using personal contact to resolve problems and to help get things online. This type of headquarter–subsidiary relationship, often found in Swedish multinationals, is referred to as 'mother–daughter' – built on trust and information sharing, visits and involvement, and ultimately partnership.[25] Local managers may also be invited to spend some time at 'home', headquarters, to become familiar with the parent's policies and procedures as well as to immerse themselves in the preferred behavior and values.

When 3M started international operations in 1929, its philosophy for developing new ventures was one of minimal investment in order to create a strong sense of personal ownership at the local level, while providing a lot of top management attention and time. 'Our management since the beginning has traveled around quite a bit getting into these overseas 3M companies so that we can work with, talk with and know the local people.'

Within each country subsidiary the local language and culture prevailed while finding its own way to import the 3M corporate culture with national culture. This created a very local image for 3M:

> 'For instance, if someone talks about 3M France, they do not talk about it as an American company. Even when they put up these laws against foreign companies, 3M is never included as a foreigner. It is a local company with foreign shareholders.[26]'

However, while country subsidiaries had a great deal of autonomy, country heads were never country nationals:

> 'One of the advantages of not having a national as the head of the country is that you reduce the departure from the 3M culture that you might get otherwise. The American or third country national is the representative of St. Paul and provides the glue that connects the country subsidiaries to 3M in the US.[27]'

By 1992, 3M products were sold worldwide, with 50 per cent of its revenues coming from markets outside the US. In addition, 3M had research labs in 22 different countries and manufacturing plants all over the globe.

Many Japanese companies try to minimize the influence of local cultural differences by combining frequent personal interaction between head office and expatriate Japanese with strong socialization practices for locals. Subsidiary heads, mostly Japanese nationals, remain in close contact with headquarters, making frequent trips back (sometimes monthly), as it is vital to keep informed and to maintain the network of contacts in order to get things done. Local nationals are carefully screened to match desired company values and behavior. Local workers receive intensive training not only in work techniques but also in philosophy, and are then often sent to Japan to observe and experience the Japanese way of doing things.

However, non-Japanese managers, even those who speak fluent Japanese, are not able to develop the necessary personal network and, according to their Japanese counterparts, would never really be able to understand the Japanese way of doing things. This was the justification given by Matsushita for sending over 700 Japanese expatriates on four- to eight-year assignments. According to one Matsushita expatriate, 'This communication role ... almost always requires a manager from the parent company. Even if a local manager speaks Japanese, he would not have the long experience that is needed to build relationships and understand our management processes'.[28]

Consider the more recent case of Toyota. Toyota has set up its most modern and efficient factory in the north of France, its first in Europe. The factory is located in a former coal and steel region which now has an unemployment rate of 16 percent. Around 30,000 people applied for the 2000 jobs. This includes 200 Japanese, of which 150 were temporary 'trainers'; 24 Japanese executives were expected to remain. Toyota hired mostly young (average age 27), unskilled workers with little or no auto industry experience.

Employees gather for morning exercises at 8am, before the first shift. No alcohol is served in the company cafeteria, and there is no executive dining-room. Everyone wears the same blue and gray windbreakers with Toyota's name in red on the back and the employee's name on the front. However, as French employees value individuality and privacy they did not appreciate having 'to wear' their names, and have refused to accept free company work clothes. Lack of private office space was also considered intrusive.[29]

While these approaches may take into account national cultural differences, they aim to assimilate these differences into an overriding corporate culture. Efforts to create a strong corporate culture in order to reduce cultural differences often meet with resistance because the parent company culture (which is often embedded in the national culture) remains dominant. This results in local managers feeling like minorities in their own countries. Even when the company culture is concocted in a melting pot, national cultural differences tend to be absorbed, not utilized. Thus differences may add some spice, but risk losing their distinctive flavor.

Separate but equal – cultural segregation

Another way of minimizing the impact of culture is to isolate the different cultures, thus avoiding clashes. This approach reflects a polycentric approach to headquarter–subsidiary relations; each local company has the autonomy to make operating decisions, to do as it sees fit, provided targets are met. In other words, the parent company determines what has to be done, and the local subsidiary is free to figure out how. Thus, strategy formulation is centralized, while strategy implementation is a local decision. This is particularly the case when local business is considered to be important due to historical or strategic reasons. For example, being close to the customer can provide the flexibility to adapt while being close to the local government can provide stability.

Consider the case of Nestlé in China. After 13 years of talks, Nestlé was finally invited into China in 1987 to help boost milk production. It opened a powdered milk and baby cereal plant in 1990 where it had to create its own infrastructure of 'milk roads' between 27 villages and points of collection. It hired local retired teachers to serve as farm agents and as cultural brokers. Swiss experts were sent in to train in animal health and hygiene. Nestlé believes that such major investment demonstrates long-term commitment and creates goodwill with governments which will protect it from instability.[30]

In addition, Nestlé wants to remain close to the customer. CEO Peter Brabeck strongly believes that there is no such thing as a global consumer. He argues that since people have local tastes based on unique cultures and traditions, decision-making needs to be pushed down: 'We can't establish emotional links with consumers in Vietnam from our offices in Vevey'. For this reason he insists that decentralization remains a core value at Nestlé.[31]

Thus some consider 'Nestlé [to be] a global company living mostly on local brands. ... The company prefers brands to be local and people regional; only technology goes global. Call it the Roman Empire school of marketing.' Although Nestlé owns 8000 different brands worldwide, only 750 are registered in more than one country. Managers make their career away from head office, spending 4–5 years in different regions, and regional managers circulate constantly between developed and developing worlds. According to Helmut Maucher, Nestlé's former CEO, 'developing a pool of cross-border Asian managers is far more important than sending Americans or Europeans ... They can never know the culture as well as a local'.[32]

European MNCs often provide the best examples of a 'multidomestic' (or polycentric) business approach for historical reasons (notably two world wars and several economic recessions), and because of different national technical standards and market requirements. Michael Porter[33] argues that most European business, German pharmaceuticals being an exception, is still very local and is therefore more sensitive to local needs and better at delegating decisions to local management. As a result, European companies tend to do well in businesses that are not very global but depend on local responsiveness.

While allowing for local autonomy, standardized and sophisticated reporting procedures and systems are often used to keep control. This is common among American multinational companies. Their European managers often complain that they spend most of their time gathering information for head office and that they are judged solely on results without concern for local conditions. They also complain that this leads to an obsession with numbers and to short-term thinking. However, too much local autonomy can interfere with global strategy.

Bertelsmann is a case in point. Although it is Europe's largest media company, the company's name sparks off little public recognition outside its native Germany. In fact, when CEO Thomas Middelhoff told people in the US that Bertelsmann was the third biggest media group in the world, 'they looked at me as if I was crazy'.[34]

The company's European subsidiaries, such as Gruner & Jahr in Germany, France Loisirs in France, Plaza y Janés in Spain or RTL in European broadcasting, are far better known than the parent company. Several of its magazine titles, such as *Fast Company*, *Family Circle* and *McCall's*, are specific to the US market. And even magazine concepts such as *Geo* or *Prima*, which have been rolled out across several European countries, do not carry the same content. Similarly in music, it has accumulated 200 record labels in 53 countries, and most of its revenues come from local artists, rather than international artists. The company has grown big on the principles of decentralization and entrepreneurship – and on the idea that products should cater to the requirements of each particular market.

This strategic posture enabled the company to be highly responsive to local opportunities. For example, when central and eastern Europe opened up to foreign companies following the fall of Communism, Bertelsmann quickly carved out strong positions in these new markets by entering the daily newspaper business. On the other hand, Bertelsmann ran into serious difficulties in the late 1990s when it had to respond *as a group* to the threat of electronic commerce.

In 1996, Amazon launched its online book store which quickly spelt trouble for Bertelsmann's book and music clubs. It took Bertelsmann two years to respond to the threat. By that time, Amazon had established itself as a powerhouse in online book retailing. Bertelsmann therefore had to pay a high price to close the gap, forking out $200m for 50 percent of the website business of Barnes & Noble, a leading US bookstore.

Bertelsmann's initially sluggish response was largely attributable to its decentralized structure. Some blamed the gap between New York and provincial Gütersloh for Bertelsmann's failure to perceive how the Internet would affect its business. According to employees in New York, the American subsidiary had been warning Gütersloh about the dangers of Amazon for eighteen months before anybody paid attention. In other words, the threat had been identified by the subsidiary but the local managers did not have sufficient voice back at headquarters.

Another problem, given Bertelsmann's heavily decentralized structure, was that no one could decide which unit should lead the charge since the response necessarily involved collaboration between entrenched divisions: the publishing houses, the book and music clubs, the distribution and multimedia divisions. As the CEO himself put it: 'For too long we sat in endless coordination sessions and asked: Who should respond? To whom does this business "belong"?'[35]

This example gives some indication of the limits of a locally responsive strategy. When it goes unchecked, sensitivity to local conditions can inhibit collaboration and cause communication difficulties. It can also generate other inefficiencies such as duplication of effort (reinventing the wheel), needless differentiation, and resistance to external recommendations or ideas.

Furthermore, being seen as too close to the local authorities can also create problems:

'For example, in the regulated world of petroleum exploration and marketing, being close to local authorities is important, as Royal Dutch Shell recognizes. Deutsche Shell is expected to be a German company, and Shell Malaysia is expected to present a Malaysian face to the government and consumers ... [But] being too close to the authorities can spill over negatively onto public image.[36]'

Shell's image suffered when it was perceived to be colluding with corrupt government practices in Nigeria and apartheid practices in South Africa.

While the polycentric approach acknowledges cultural differences and allows local firms to do it their way, encouraging pluralism, many firms are finding this approach costly and are discovering a greater need for regional integration and rationalization. This is particularly evident now within Europe where the single market and currency allows for a greater flow of goods, capital, and people across borders. This has stimulated a search for a pan-European approach. For example, with the aim of improving pan-European logistics, companies such as Philips, and Jacobs Suchard, the Swiss chocolate company, have rationalized factories. Indeed, more and more independent local (national) units have been drawn into the web of integration.

Creating a buffer

In order to balance the need for global integration while remaining sensitive to local conditions, many MNCs have created regional headquarters (regiocentric approach). Regional headquarters help to improve coordination between national organizations and to seek out potential synergies between them. Regional headquarters also help to reconcile local responsiveness and global integration by mediating between local conditions and global strategic directives from headquarters. The idea is to provide a 'buffer' between national units and head-office cultures. Functions such as marketing and HRM, where local sensitivity is often considered more important, may be delegated to the regional level, while finance and R&D may remain centralized at headquarters.

Honeywell, as early as the 1970s, created a regional headquarters for Europe when previous efforts to coordinate national organizations had failed. In addition, it created vice-president positions for different regions within Europe, Centers of Excellence responsible for pan-European business, and the European Policy Committee. Another committee, the HR Advisory Board, took up the challenge of developing a corporate culture campaign to find the *ONE* in *HONEYWELL*. Starting with the one-page list of 'Honeywell Principles', they turned it into a colorful booklet which was translated into several languages.

Despite these efforts, many European senior managers complained that the regional headquarters was 'too American'. In particular the marketing and HRM functions which were being run by Americans were not considered sufficiently sensitive to the different local market and labor conditions. By 1986 European headquarters had its first non-American President replacing Mike Bonsignore who went on to become CEO of Honeywell.[37]

While models with a regional headquarters may provide a balance of local responsiveness and global integration, this proves a difficult juggling act, creating tensions and dilemmas. Often regional headquarters are set up as a step towards a geocentric, or global organization, for example, on the way to establishing global products or business groups.

But even global products can have different consumer perceptions. While consumer tastes may be converging, many companies deny that convergence means homogenization. While the Germans and British may be drinking more wine, and the French and Italians more beer, the Germans consume six times as much beer per capita as the Italians, and the French six times as much wine per capita as the British. 'Going global does not make things simpler by reducing everything ... to one standardized reality. ... If anything it makes them more complex.'[38] This means having to create a complex menu of options and possibilities, and deciding which elements to standardize and leaving local managers an important strategic role, as well as space for autonomy and creativity.

Whether using regional headquarters as buffers or creating complex matrices to resolve balancing demands for global integration and local responsiveness, the logic remains one of reducing the impact of national cultural differences. This tends to ignore the potential value-added of the local units in terms of innovation, not just in products and technology, but also in management practices. Strategic thrust, transfer of technology, and learning are still seen as a top–down affair, but not without consequence as Coca-Cola learned the hard way.

> Although former CEO Goizueta maintained that the company could create cravings for Coke and Sprite around the world, many consumers are becoming "pickier, more penny-wise, or more nationalistic", spending more on local drinks. Believing that they had the world's greatest brand made them arrogant, ignoring local flavors.

Coke's failure to respond quickly to reports of Belgian children becoming ill after drinking Coke was attributed to the new CEO Douglas Ivester not understanding or listening to the environment – and at a more strategic level, Coke's failure to acquire the French soda company Orangina and the overseas business of Cadbury Schweppes was also put down to Coke's arrogance and Ivester's tin ear to political and cultural realities.[39]

When Ivester was removed, there was a clear change of philosophy. In what amounts to a rare admission of failure, Coca-Cola is trying to make itself into a friendlier company more adapted to local markets around the world.... A recurring theme since Mr. Daft's appointment has been decentralization, first signaled by an announcement this month that executives in charge of Asian and European operations would live not in Atlanta but in their territories. Decentralization will also be a key in marketing, where local tastes and local brands are expected to play a larger role than they have in the past.[40] Coke has now begun to recognize local preferences and tastes. In Japan, Coke's most popular product is canned coffee and canned tea.[41]'

Utilizing differences: going global?

Whether the corporate mantra be 'Think global, act local' (as in the famous last words of Percy Barnevik), or 'Act global and think local', companies have to manage the need for both global integration and local responsiveness. Many MNCs are trying to improve integration between national companies by developing global business areas or product lines. National organizations are matrixed with these global business or product lines, creating a dual reporting structure, to a country manager and a business/product manager. While country heads are seen to be very important to preserve local responsiveness, business or product heads are responsible for optimizing global integration. Local resistance is high as formerly powerful country heads see their power and autonomy being diminished.

Efforts to achieve greater integration may be sabotaged unless local managers are committed to a regional or global perspective. It is therefore necessary to involve country heads in developing global plans and enlarging their sphere of influence. This may include giving them responsibility for coordination, as well as career opportunities outside their local operations, not waiting until they reach 45 years old to do this, but exposing them much earlier in their careers to international management experience. In this way, cultural differences are brought into the mainstream.

However, local managers cannot be expected to work successfully with other nationalities if they are not provided with appropriate language and cultural training. Nor can they be expected to cooperate with people in other units if there is no mechanism nor incentive to do so. For example, IBM introduced explicit performance measures to reward managers for cooperating with colleagues around the world.[42] And Unilever has 25,000 employees using Lotus Notes to share their globally acquired expertise with others.[43]

Cross-border cooperation can also be encouraged by structural mechanisms. Companies can build interdependencies into their structures. For example, Nestlé has a network of some twenty research and technology centers dotted around the world.[44] When a new research center was established in Singapore, it was given responsibility for quality assurance for the whole of the Far East region in order to accelerate the center's integration into its network of research units. This structural interdependence forced intensive communication between the existing units and the new operations. Had the Singaporean operation been given strictly an R&D role, it would have taken far longer for the informal connections to build up in that area and for the center to contribute actively to the organization. Furthermore, Nestlé benefited from Singapore's culture. The emphasis on the accrual of factual knowledge, and the pursuit of detail fitted well with the mandate for quality assurance.

To ensure that such cultural advantages can be utilized, managers from different countries need the skills to operate across country boundaries, such as cultural and language skills, and an infrastructure (such as information and accounting systems, structures, and incentives) to make that happen. They also need to understand and even *create* interdependencies among units, for example to respond to global clients, as well as having an important role in the broader organization.[45]

Finding the proper balance between responsiveness to local needs and central control is an ongoing dilemma for most multinational companies today. For historical as well as cultural reasons, the balance is different between Europe, the United States, and Japan. Typically, European MNCs, the first to enter the international arena, have been more aware of and responsive to local needs and are now trying to get more global. Meanwhile, Japanese firms have run into difficulties in internationalizing. Having used a highly centralized export model, they are now striving to allow more autonomy and local decision making.[46] American MNCs who have tended to treat the world as one, relying on formalization and standardization, have also tended to under-adapt to local differences.

Strategies for 'going global' becomes the key challenge as 'foreign' markets become more and more important in contributing to the bottom line. But even the meaning and models of globalization are different in different countries. Globalization for Americans means economies of scale and the assumption that technology permits the normalization of production. The logic of Henry Ford (you can have any color car as long as it's black) is evident in the 'world' car, 'Mondeo'. In contrast, Toyota abandoned the idea of a 'world' car, choosing instead to reproduce its own organization, or process. Japanese companies have subscribed to the model of globalization as an activities chain wherein segments of the chain can be de-localized.[47]

These differences may be in part culturally driven. American expansion overseas, particularly in Europe, has tended to be regiocentric, in part due to the lack of understanding of the different cultures within Europe. Many American companies have in some ways treated Europe as one country, a mistake which some say may now serve as a competitive advantage. In addition, the American penchant for standardization may come from a history of accepting foreigners (that is, cultural differences) but expecting them to conform to local practice, to become Americans. This means that the rules and procedures apply to everyone, such is the American desire for universalism.[48] This may explain their somewhat 'ethnocentric' approach.

The same can be said for Japan, where everyone is expected to fit into the group, to succumb to social pressures for conformity. Being different is considered a stigma, and outsiders can never hope to be fully integrated. This does not help Japanese to recruit and retain highly talented locals. While creating greenfield sites provides the control that Japanese firms are accustomed to, acquiring local firms creates more problems, as Nissan learned painfully in Spain.[49] Thus Japanese companies are trying to become more international and to be more receptive to other cultures.

In the wake of the Asian financial crisis and the souring of the Japanese economy, Japanese businesses have become more open to foreigners, partly out of necessity as foreign companies bought up those struggling for survival. Certainly the most spectacular example has been Carlos Ghosn. He joined Nissan from its alliance partner, Renault, in mid-1999, having held major jobs on four continents. Very few observers gave him a chance, particularly when he announced his intention to cut 21,000 jobs, close five plants and reduce by 50 percent the number of Nissan's suppliers – all running contradictory to Japanese traditions of lifetime employment and time-honored links with suppliers. One senior Nissan executive, speaking anonymously, commented that this basically sound strategy was likely to 'step on a lot of toes', including those of Nissan's still-influential past presidents and top executives. Of course, he added, 'Mr. Ghosn is a *gaijin* (foreigner), so it may be easier, but he is brushing with the danger of opening up a valve of bad feelings inside Nissan, as well as outside'.[50] Nonetheless, Ghosn succeeded beyond all expectations, helping the company return to profitability within six months. He not only became a respected figure in Japan – he even became the hero of a comic book series targeted at young professionals.[51]

Many Europeans consider themselves in the best position for going global and incorporating cultural differences, as they are more accustomed to living closely with neighbors of different cultures.

> 'More than many Americans or Japanese, Europeans are often very comfortable in international situations. The better run companies – like Nestlé – have corporate boards that closely resemble the UN Security Council ... Our diversity is a huge asset ... Europeans are better equipped for globalization.[52]'

The consequences of these different approaches can be seen in a study of Hungarian firms involved in joint ventures with American, German, and Japanese companies. Hungarian managers resented the imposition of American systems and procedures, as well as the heavy-handed socialization tactics of Japanese partners. They preferred the German partner's transfer of technology and techniques without the accompanying pressures to comply, in terms of either systems or behavior.[53]

While trying to manage the tensions created by balancing demands from headquarters and subsidiaries, there is the need to step back and to consider how to be most effective on a worldwide basis (geocentric approach). This means searching for new constellations of business activities, redefining the role and meaning of headquarters and subsidiaries, and discovering opportunities for organizational innovation and learning.

‘The "multicultural multinational", as some are calling this new animal, is based on [the idea] that innovation is the key to success. An organization that relies on one culture for its ideas and treats foreign subsidiaries as dumb production-colonies might as well hire subcontractors.[54]’

Creating added value

Although international competitive advantage may depend on national conditions which stimulate innovation, it is increasingly evident that competitive advantage is also a matter of creating assets across borders, such as human capital or R&D.[55] Companies are having to search outside national boundaries to develop their capacity fully.

One such example is Otis Elevator, a subsidiary of United Technologies.

‘Being deployed globally helped Otis Elevator Inc ... to develop the customized Elecvonic 411 at the lowest possible cost. The elevator ... was developed by six research centers in five countries. Otis' group in Connecticut [USA] handled the systems integration, Japan designed the special motor drives that make the elevators ride smoothly. France perfected the door systems, Germany handled the electronics, and Spain took care of the small-geared components. Otis says the international shuttling saved more than $10 million in design costs and cut the development cycle from four years to two.[56]’

Other examples include placing functional, product, and business unit headquarters in countries where the best resources are available. Thus, software development might be located in Bangalore (India) which has one of the highest number of well-trained software engineers per capita.[57] Swatch has placed its design units in Italy and production engineering in Switzerland (ETA).[58] R&D laboratories could be situated wherever conditions such as university facilities or government grants were likely to encourage technological innovation.

Several MNCs have in fact taken steps in this direction. For example, when SKF downsized its headquarters in Gothenburg, Sweden, it decided to move its R&D facilities to Holland and its worldwide logistics center to Brussels. Nestlé put its confectionary business headquarters in the United Kingdom (following the takeover of Rowntree) and its pasta business (Buitoni) in Italy.[59] Philips transferred its digital audiotape business to Japan and its medical equipment business to the United States because of the high levels of market and technological development.[60] The eventual spin-off of some of these businesses may indicate that they were not considered to be 'core businesses' and thus were allowed some autonomy from home. Another possible explanation is that leaving home encourages independence and 'foreign marriages'.

Some of the more innovative Japanese companies have also taken this route. For example, one pharmaceutical company, Eisai, realized that to maximize its chances of finding a 'blockbuster' drug it needed to locate in Europe, which is at the forefront of pharmaceutical research. As a result it has set up research labs (headed by locals in order to tap into the local research networks) notably in Britain, which enjoys world leadership in molecular and cellular biochemical research.[61]

Similarly, Shiseido, the cosmetics company, realized that the only way to become a leader in the perfume business was to relocate its R&D in France, which represents both the most competitive market and the center of expertise in the field. France boasts the best glass bottle manufacturers, the leading perfume specialists, and the top source of skilled labor in the cosmetics industry. By short-cutting the traditional sequence of international expansion and decentralizing R&D early on (rather than later, following sales and production) Shiseido has stolen market share from its bigger and more established rival, Kao.

The rationale behind such moves is that product or business groups should have a home base wherever world strategy is set, core R&D takes place, and a critical mass of sophisticated production occurs.[62] The idea is to benefit from the competitiveness of the most advantageous country, rather than being tied unnecessarily to the country of origin.

Nevertheless, this characterizes a new model of the multinational firm – or transnational – where specialized units are coordinated into integrated networks.[63] Rather than being an assemblage of semi-independent units which contribute individually to HQ coffers, the MNC becomes a *heterarchy* with many centers playing a strategic role in formulating as well as implementing strategy. This fosters a broader range of strategic thinking, and encourages a global mentality among all employees. The company comes to resemble a hologram, as information regarding the whole is contained in each part.[64]

These approaches provide opportunities for organizational innovation and learning from any direction. They encourage reflecting on which local innovations may have applications in other national units or might even warrant global diffusion. They force companies to consider what is the opportunity or incentive for 'local for global' organizational learning, or transfer of 'best practice' from the subsidiaries to headquarters.[65]

The ability to benefit from local thinking and to tap into the roots of pluralism and diversity for innovation, was seen in the case of P&G in India. By positioning products to take advantage of the preference (and legislation) for using natural herbal products (based on the ancient Ayurvedic system of medicine) P&G was able to gain an important share of the market. According to Gucharan Das, a global manager for P&G, strongly tied to his local (Indian) roots,

> 'Globalization does not mean imposing homogeneous solutions in a pluralistic world. It means having a global vision and strategy, but it also means cultivating roots and individual identities. It means nourishing local insights, but it also means reemploying communicable ideas in new geographies around the world.[66]'

While he believes that the key to success is local passion, pride, and ownership of brands, Das reminds local managers to 'think global'. Taking ideas from elsewhere and adapting them to new circumstances requires humility, flexibility, and open-mindedness. But local managers also must seek to develop local insights which have potentially universal appeal. After all, the benefit of being a multinational company is to have talented people in different parts of the world seeking opportunities and solving problems for common products and brands.

Most multinational companies have headquarters in their country of origin and have subsidiaries scattered throughout the world. Some multinationals are better at capturing the knowledge that exists in their different subsidiaries and have been able to diffuse innovation practices in all directions: from the top, from the bottom, and laterally. However, few companies are actually born or develop by bringing together pockets of expertise from around the world. This is the case of the 'metanational':

> 'The metanational companies do not draw their competitive advantage from their home country, nor even from a set of national subsidiaries. Metanational companies view the world as a global canvas dotted with pockets of technology, market intelligence, and capabilities. . . . By sensing and mobilizing this scattered knowledge, they are able to innovate more effectively than their rivals. . . .
>
> . . . Metanationals will thrive on seeking out and exploiting uniqueness. They value geographic and cultural differences. And because they fish for knowledge in a global pond, they can potentially create new and better competencies than any multinational player's headquarters, national subsidiary, or center of excellence.[67]'

Thus the challenge for multinational companies is one of how to capture the benefits of cultural differences rather than trying to minimize their effects. But in order to capitalize on it, companies have to honestly assess their level of internationalism, because few companies are as international as their managers would like to believe.

Less global than we thought

Given all the talk about going global, it may be worth considering to what extent business is truly international.

> 'We are living in a world which is about as integrated as the world of the 19th century. Trade in goods and services is only slightly larger now as a fraction of gross world product than it was before 1914. Measured against GDP, US imports are only slightly bigger now (11 percent) than they were in 1880 (8 percent). The world of 1913 had many of today's earmarks of globalism, including multinational companies whose linkages spanned the world [e.g. German pharmaceuticals company brought Bayer aspirin to America]. Fewer than 10 percent of the businesses that inquire about going global actually try it.[68]'

Answering the question, 'Just how international are we?' may therefore require some pretty painful self-examination. In this respect, the process undertaken by Fiat, the Italian automaker, is instructive.

Fiat, with a $34 billion turnover, operates in 52 countries, and has 290,000 employees, one-fifth of whom are abroad. Given the extent of operations and people outside Italy, Fiat management wanted to define what internationalization really meant, to know how they measured up, and how to become more international.[69] Working groups were set up to address issues such as the nature of international positions, the profile of the international manager, and the appropriate HRM systems.

In analyzing the international nature of jobs, they found four types of managers: transnationals (300) who lived abroad mostly on airplanes, multinationals (1700) who traveled extensively but lived in Turin, 'open locals' who received foreigners, and locals, who had little international contact. They also realized that more than 40 percent of managerial positions dealt with international work matters and that three-quarters of these jobs were in Europe. On the basis of these findings, Fiat management began developing ways to recruit, train, and develop international managers, both within Italy as well as abroad. They also planned to create a 'company culture that is increasingly sensitive to the international context . . . [which required] greater participation and integration of managers in various national contexts within the culture and values of the Fiat group'.

A closer look at so-called global companies raises similar concerns. 'Going global' means more than operating in markets in many countries or having products that sell around the world. Having global products, like Levi jeans and McDonald's hamburgers, or having sales offices and bank branches in the far reaches of the world, or having done business internationally for over 200 years, is no indication of an international mind-set. Head offices and most of the functional and product/business unit heads often remain firmly planted in the home country. Even the international division is often housed in the same building, or just next door.

This was confirmed by a leadership study of 1500 executives from 12 large companies around the world which described themselves as 'global'. Out of 34 dimensions considered vital to competitiveness, they rated last their ability to cultivate a global mind-set in their organization. A *global mind-set* was defined as 'the capacity to appreciate the beliefs, values, behaviors, and business practices of individuals and organizations from a variety of regions and cultures'.[70]

It is therefore important to take a good look in the mirror.

> 'Don't believe in your own press releases. It's too easy to think that you're a global company because you keep saying you're a global company. Search for measurable indicators that your organization is behaving more globally than it was last year and the year before. Believe in behaviors not rhetoric. Celebrate your progress, but never allow yourself to become fully satisfied that you have made it. Holding on to that nagging anxiety is what being globally minded is all about.[76]'

The real test of a global company is the extent to which strategic thinking actually benefits from cultural diversity. How many members of the managing board are not from the same country? How many of the top 200 managers? Can a company really be considered global if the top 200 are all Americans, French or Japanese? Even in

> **Global Mind-set[71]**
>
> - Top managers in our organization have a global outlook.
> - Top management has comprehensive awareness and knowledge of changes in the nature of global competition and global markets.
> - Top management spends a significant portion of its time on internal meetings and running in-house committees.[72]
>
> - Top management supports cross-national knowledge-sharing and collaboration.
> - Top management promotes collaboration with strategically important customers and suppliers.[73]
>
> - In the next decade I expect to see a non-[American] CEO of the company.
> - In my company, nationality is unimportant in selecting individuals for managerial positions.[74]
>
> *As the company globalizes, it is important for (I believe that) the country operations most familiar to me to (will)*
>
> - Have global marketing responsibility for one or more products
> - Produce one or more products for global markets
> - Go global with locally developed products
> - Lead global product development processes
> - Influence global product development processes.
> - Demonstrate clear benefits to the local economy
> - Have flexibility to respond to local conditions
> - Harmonize the company's activities and products with national government policies
> - Adapt existing products to local markets.[75]

companies such as ABB, heralded as the truly global company, the board of directors remains largely Scandinavian and Anglo-Saxon. And the CEOs have all been Swedes. Likewise Bertelsmann which ranks as *the* most international of the large media companies, with 70 percent of its revenues generated outside its domestic market, still only has one non-German board member.

Other oft-cited exemplars like Royal-Dutch Shell or Unilever turn out to be closer to bi-national than global companies, if we focus on those at the top. And several companies which started out as bi-national have actually drifted towards one dominant culture, rather than multiple cultures. For example, several British–French joint ventures – notably Alstom, Eurotunnel, and Messier-Dowty – are now dominated by French executives, with the British executives playing a junior role.[77] Similarly, the combination of Daimler and Chrysler in 1998, billed as a merger of equals, has seen many of Chrysler's most senior executives leave or get forced out – with German executives taking control of the US operation to stem its losses. Clearly, global aspirations are easier pronounced than executed.

For all the talk about globalization, top management teams tend to be comprised of parent country nationals who have little international experience. A study conducted in 1996 by German management journal, *Managermagazin,* found that of the top management teams (managing board) of the top 50 German companies very few had foreigners, and that most board members had little or no international experience.[78]

The composition of the management board is thus revealing. The boards of directors in both US and foreign-owned global corporations remain almost exclusively a native affair. In Asian corporations, 'foreign board members are as rare as British sumo wrestlers'. Similarly, stock ownership is almost always concentrated in the home country.[79] For example, Nestlé, although considered to be a very global company, has decided not to be quoted on the US stock exchange and continues to report in Swiss francs, arguing that it is a Swiss company with mostly Swiss shareholders even though a large majority of shareholders are American.[80]

Even within MNCs which do include a vice-president or board member who is French, Brazilian, Chinese, or female, the undertow of the dominant culture is often strong enough to silence them. Despite representation of foreign managers in top management, at the board level, or across the board in any function (structural integration), what is often more revealing is the extent to which foreign managers are involved in informal networks and social activities, or informal integration.[81]

And even then, non-Japanese managers may go out drinking with the boys after work but will never be considered one of the boys. In Switzerland, as in Israel, top management is connected through continuing military service, although less so than in the past. And in France, half of the CEOs of the top 200 companies come from the top six *grandes écoles*, making it very difficult for outsiders to break into senior management. Furthermore, out of the 144 CEOs of the top French MNCs, only 16 had foreign managerial experience. Even now, 'The typical top management team remains remarkably like those of the past: very French, very male, and very elite'.[82] So, there remains quite a gap between the global representation within many MNCs and their global pretensions.

The mark of a truly global company is not the tradition of operating abroad, nor a product that appeals around the world, but the multiple nationalities of the top and senior management ranks involved in formulating strategy, not just in implementing it. The central question is to what extent national strengths and cultural differences are drawn upon to create global synergies. It may just be true that, 'The fittest – those who survive – are those who cooperate best with other living things'.[83]

Creating culturally strategic alliances

Perhaps the best model for managing diversity can be found in strategic alliances and joint ventures. Given the competing interests of nationalism and globalism, companies may operate more like political federations, in which each company retains local ownership and governance but seeks an alliance to accomplish difficult or expensive missions. Thus companies retain independence, avoiding antitrust regulations, and retain local identity, keeping political ties and the facility to raise capital.

For example, in March 1992 a consortium of insurance companies agreed to form a pan-European insurance group. This consortium included insurance companies from The Netherlands, the United Kingdom, Sweden, and Denmark. Each national company was responsible for and had full autonomy in its home market. In a joint effort to take on Europe, they took significant cross-holdings, creating a headquarters 'shell' of ten people with a rotating chairman. In their vision to create a pan-European financial services company, they extended their reach to include a Portuguese bank. In creating this alliance, one of the most important tasks to be accomplished was to make clear to each partner the benefits of cooperating, and to encourage the sharing of best practice. One of the key concerns that had to be addressed was preserving the autonomy of each partner. Now the alliance has given birth to new businesses, for example in Ireland, and has grown to include new partners from Germany and France. Some partners, the Portuguese and the Dutch, have even decided to get married and merge their respective households!

Take also the example of Airbus, a European consortium supported by the French, German, British, and Spanish governments. Many thought that the idea of bringing together experts from four separate, and sometimes hostile, cultures to build and market a complex piece of machinery was sheer folly. As the director of strategic planning recalls, 'To be frank, none of us really thought this project had much chance of taking off'. Though heavily subsidized, the Airbus venture has proved successful and is regarded by many as the model of high-tech multinational cooperation. According to its French CEO, 'Aeronautical engineers tend to think beyond national boundaries. ... We are an international fraternity. We have invented our own system'.[84]

Clearly, boundaries between sectors and nations are becoming less and less distinct. Companies can engage in joint ventures or strategic alliances with companies worldwide, sometimes even with rival companies. Firms might have very different relationships in different markets or businesses; they could be partners in one, competitors in another, and suppliers and customers of one another in a third. Marriage, divorce, and remarriage are not unlikely.

For example, Rover, the British car group, linked up with Honda in order to acquire technology and management skills, while Honda gained market access in Europe. Ten years later BMW came along with a better offer, facilitating Rover's entry into the long-abandoned US market while enabling BMW to move into the small car market.[85] But since then, they too have split up.

In 1990, a joint venture was created between a large, state-owned, bureaucratic French conglomerate and a mid-sized, entrepreneurial, publicly traded American pharmaceutical company with the vision of becoming a global corporation.[86] According to the British Chairman and CEO,

> 'We've abolished the idea of a domestic and international business. We're not French – we're not American – we're global. The fact that neither of the two cultures is fully dominant can be an advantage. The different backgrounds and different ways of looking at things can cause innovation. Not just in France and the US, but everywhere around the world. From two "OK" companies in the pharmaceutical business, we've been given the opportunity to create something great.'

Initially, however, each company felt taken over by the other. This reaction was countered by publicly stating that RPR would be a global company, respecting all cultures. An executive council was created consisting of French, American, British, Austrian, and Australian members. Dual HQs were established, one in Philadelphia and one in Paris. Key functions were globalized, such as R&D, finance, and HR, while sales and marketing were regionalized. Heavy investments were made in technology – global e-mail, videoconferences – and travel to encourage face-to-face relationships. Short-term exchanges (one week to three months) were organized, even among secretaries.

Top management openly talked about cultural issues and each team was encouraged to define its own culture. The 150 expatriates were chosen based not solely on job competence but on being adaptable, having a sense of adventure, being a detective or investigator in order to be able to 'get at what's really going on'. Good support was provided before and after expatriation by outside consulting firms (e.g. relocation). Training was provided, depending on the needs of the expatriates and others throughout the organizations. And training itself was globalized, using methods, materials, and trainers from different cultures. Nevertheless, three years later the rank and file still closely watched who would get the next available senior management position, French or American? Unfortunately, that marriage ended up in divorce with the French partner now re-married to a German company.

Whether seeking to leverage local innovations globally, or to collaborate with foreign competitors, the lessons are the same. Companies need to be able to spot the value-added that is embedded in each culture while focusing on shared interests both within and outside the organizational boundaries. Or, in the words of the Director of Human Resources of Sony France, 'The cultural split between the intellectual flexibility of the French and the team spirit of the Japanese is an obvious enrichment for each party'.[87] And with collaboration being in constant flux, the need to develop routines to manage this process is absolute: 'Managers thus need to acquire skills important to the diplomat and politician such as cultural sensitivity and a talent for discerning shared interests'.[88]

While many of the above examples proclaim the benefits of capturing strategic or structural differences in creating global companies, they also demonstrate the difficulties. The question remains as to how to utilize cultural differences in order to provide competitive advantage.

Gaining competitive advantage from cultural differences

A truly multicultural organization can be defined as one wherein diversity is *valued* and *utilized* rather than just contained.[89] The strategy of *utilizing* cultural differences can create competitive advantage. Thus, rather than one culture overriding another, or compromising to find 'safe' solutions that will antagonize neither, the challenge is to discover solutions that capture the differences in creative ways so that the sum of the parts is greater than the whole.[90]

> 'Diversity is taking people from different backgrounds, with different expectations and at different stages of life and melding them into a force that will drive the company's profitability and competitiveness.[91]'

Unfortunately most companies do not think about cultural differences as a source of competitive advantage. And efforts to address the issue of diversity get dismissed as 'too American' and not relevant 'here'. However, in many cases, being a minority may mean being the only French-speaking manager in a team of Swiss-Germans, or a British senior executive in a Japanese firm in London.

While much of the literature on managing diversity comes from American companies' efforts to integrate women and minorities in the workforce, some lessons can be taken for managing national diversity. Consider the example of Hewlett Packard.

Hewlett Packard (now HP) is a US company, based in Palo Alto, California, known for its strong people-oriented corporate culture, 'The HP Way'. The company is often taken as a benchmark for human resource practices. Lew Platt, former CEO and chairman, defined diversity as follows: 'I believe the word 'diverse' includes not only different genders and races, but also different cultures, lifestyles and ways of thinking'. In a letter to shareholders (HP Annual report 1994), Platt explains why diversity is a strategic priority.

> 'Our diversity efforts are focused on creating a work environment where all people can contribute to the company and have an opportunity to reach their personal goals. Diversity is much more than a program or legal requirement at HP; it's a business priority for several compelling reasons. We sell to a diverse, global customer base. We operate in many different countries and cultures, where we need to attract and retain outstanding employees and partners. In addition, a culture that fosters respect for and appreciation of differences among people clearly helps teamwork, productivity, and morale.'

Following CEO Lew Platt's initiative, HP formed in 1995 a diversity leadership council consisting of 13 senior managers which sponsored a worldwide dialogue on diversity. In Europe, a position of diversity manager was created reporting to the corporate head of diversity in Palo Alto, and the head of HR Europe. A European task force on diversity was set up to coordinate a Europe-wide policy. Various initiatives, seminars, and training programs had already taken place in different European sites.

However, gaining legitimacy, getting 'buy-in', and ensuring accountability would not be easy. It was important that diversity was considered to be a strategic necessity and not just another 'American gimmick'. This would be difficult in an environment where, according to one European manager, 'HP senior managers had, traditionally, been tall, white, married men with engineering degrees who speak fluent English'.

The challenge was to develop more systematic diversity policies and practices that made sense in the local environment. For example, a customer survey in Belgium revealed that women, French-speakers and non-technical people were minorities at HP. Therefore an FFU (French, Female, University) program was set up to focus on recruitment. This led to an advertising campaign encouraging women as well as men to apply, which was subsequently adopted in Spain and Switzerland.[92]

This points out the need to make diversity initiatives locally meaningful. While it may be quite apparent that there are no women or non-nationals on the board, what may be more relevant is that there are too many engineers. This could become a handicap when a company tries to become more market-oriented. Thus the diversity argument is better understood and accepted when presented in a broader fashion. It is important that a Swiss bank based in Zürich (German-speaking), for example, realizes that it may be losing talented French-speaking Swiss who feel like a minority in their own country.

Deutsche Bank posted this message on the Internet:

> **Diversity as a success factor** (*Diversity als Erfolgsfaktor*)
> More than any other company, Deutsche Bank is an extremely international, intercultural, inter-religious, and inter-social company. We appreciate the diversity with which men and women approach new tasks. We use the synergies when bringing together younger and older employees working in a team. Diversity concerning professional knowledge, perspectives, and experiences allows us to develop better ideas which is a competitive advantage fostering and strengthening our competitiveness. We see diversity as a success factor to position a company like DB successfully worldwide.

This personal vision of Dr Heinz Fischer, Head of Human Resources and member of the managing board (*Vorstand*) of Deutsche Bank, is perhaps not surprising given his prior position as HR director for Hewlett Packard Europe.

Cox and Blake[93] argue that competitive advantage derives from cultural diversity, in the ways shown in Table 16.2. The most obvious reason given for utilizing cultural differences is greater sensitivity to different markets. Product development teams composed of people from differing cultures are more likely to develop products that appeal to the different tastes of customers. Diversity also can enhance problem-solving capability, innovation, and creativity. Top management teams designing strategy require different perspectives to reflect the complexity of operating in an international arena, emphasizing national differences, while providing the forum for integrating those perspectives.

Research on top management teams does in fact demonstrate that different types of diversity result in different types of strategies and have different performance out-

Table 16.2 Advantages of cultural diversity

1. Marketing argument: increases the ability to respond to cultural preferences of local markets
2. Resource acquisition: increases ability to recruit employees of different national backgrounds, and host country elites
3. Cost argument: reduces cost incurred by turnover of non-home country managers
4. Problem-solving argument: improves decision-making through wider range of perspectives and more thorough critical analysis
5. Creativity argument: enhances creativity through diversity of perspectives and less emphasis on conformity
6. Systems flexibility argument: enhances organizational flexibility and responsiveness to multiple demands and changing environments

Source: Adapted from T.H. Cox and S. Blake (1991) 'Managing cultural diversity: Implications for organizational competitiveness', *Academy of Management Executive*, 5(3), 45–56.

comes.[94] Not surprisingly, research has demonstrated that top management teams that had members with international experience were more likely to develop strategies to internationalize.[95]

Ernie Drew, CEO of Hoechst Celanese, quickly embraced the idea of diversity as a source of strength in problem-solving when, at a management meeting composed of 150 top (mostly white male) managers and 50 women and minorities drawn from the ranks, he saw that diverse teams came up with broader solutions. In addition, he discovered that productivity had surged at plants where the workforce was more diverse. Thus he made diversity a top priority in the following ways.

First he made diversity a business objective: creating a target of 34 percent at *all levels* of the organization by the year 2001. Then he required 26 top executives to join in two groups where they were a minority. The company favored sources supplying recruits of diverse backgrounds (universities), and took care in the event of downsizing to ensure that minorities were not the primary casualties.[96]

This points to another reason for creating diversity, which is the cost of not being able to attract or retain top local talent. In fact the most common complaint heard among managers working for foreign MNCs is a sense of always being an outsider, not eligible to join the inner circle. Meanwhile, these companies complain that they cannot tap into the local elite, or lose valuable local managers after much investment, for example, in training and development. As mentioned before, senior management remains reserved for home-country nationals, whether in Europe, Japan, or the United States. Thus limited career opportunities is one reason that many qualified managers jump ship.

The best and brightest locals tend to prefer to join and stay within national firms, albeit for different reasons. For some, such as the Japanese, it may be a sense of national duty or pride. For others, such as the French, it may represent a source of social prestige or sensitivity to foreign control. And for others still, particularly for Americans, it is attributed to strong cultural needs for autonomy and independence. It is difficult for people from dominant cultures to realize that the other culture is calling the shots. 'Americans are used to seeing the dog, not the tail of the dog',[97] in other words, the Americans are used to being in charge.

Another interesting argument for the benefit of using cultural diversity is that it creates systems flexibility. Given the complexity of the current business environment, there is a need for organizations to match that variety internally, to have what is known as 'requisite variety'.[98] In addition to the complexity, the pace of environmental change requires the ability to live with, even thrive on, ambiguity and chaos in order to achieve maximum organizational flexibility and adaptability. Multicultural organizations foster both the variety of perspectives and the practice of managing ambiguity. Less is taken for granted, and there is not the assumption of one best way of doing things.

Furthermore, there is evidence that non-Western, non-white, and non-males (Asians, Africans, women) have different cognitive styles: issues tend to be seen as 'both–and' rather than as 'either–or', the links between things are viewed more in relational than hierarchical patterns (collaborate versus control), and there is greater sensitivity towards the more emotional side of the argument.[99] Furthermore, bilinguals have been found to have higher levels of divergent thinking and cognitive flexibility.[100] Thus other ways of seeing and thinking may be particularly useful, as business paradigms need to be constantly questioned. As André Laurent puts it, 'It is the very richness in the diversity of cultures that makes them an asset to international companies. Each culture has some specific and unique insights and some specific and unique blind spots'.[101]

These reasons are supported in a survey of HR executives from Fortune 100 companies. When asked their primary business reasons for engaging in diversity management they found the following: better utilization of talent (93 percent), better market place understanding (80 percent), developing broader understanding in leaders (60 percent), enhanced creativity (53 percent), and increased quality of team problem solving (40 percent).[102]

European companies, such as Fiat, are making efforts to actively recruit and train non-nationals, and to track their careers more closely, 'Europeanizing' their personnel strategies. The European round table, an association of forty of Europe's biggest companies, has even arranged for members to swap managers for short periods.[103]

The argument in favor of embracing cultural diversity clearly has moral undertones. It is an argument which upholds equal opportunities and which condemns cultural imperialism. It can therefore seem somewhat utopian. But this should not overshadow its firm practical foundations. In any case, the reality of demographics indicates that most of the workforce in the 21st century will not be white males, from the northern and Western parts of the world map, who presently dominate the top management teams of many multinational companies. Thus the ability to utilize cultural differences can provide companies with competitive advantage.

Prescriptions regarding managing cultural differences are inevitably culturally biased. Even our tendency to stress the need to raise differences, confront them, and utilize them points to our own cultural programming – explicit (low-context), egalitarian (low power distance), and instrumental (doing, not being). Nevertheless, we need to begin to take actions such that competitive advantage can indeed be derived from cultural differences.

Start at the top

What is the nationality of the corporate leader? The head of McKinsey is Indian, the head of GlaxoSmithKline is French, Australians head up British Airways and Coca-Cola, at JP Morgan and L'Oréal the top managers are British and, until recently, the head of Ford was Lebanese. As Geoff Unwin, the British chief executive of Cap Gemini, the French information technology consultancy, explains:

> ‘People ask why this very French company put a Brit in charge. My answer is that it was because I was different. I thought differently. Not better, just differently. When people think differently, it puts a different perspective on problems. We exploit that. . . . It is a very, very multi-cultural organization. This diversity brings a lot to the company.[104]’

The representation among the top ranks of non-national managers sends the signal that capability not passport is what counts. Involvement of top management in selection and promotion, even mentoring, of other nationalities is crucial.

Even Disney is getting the message. According to a recent interview with CEO Michael Eisner, '. . . 'non-American born' executives will play a much more important role in the management of the company. I think you will see names in our top management that are hard to pronounce as time goes on'.[105]

Create opportunities for learning

Learning across cultures means learning to be open to self-awareness and to be willing to analyze one's own cultural baggage. It means being able to assess views of own and others' culture, to evaluate the effectiveness of interaction, and to develop strategies for dealing with differences. Above all, learning across cultures means continuously learning how to learn about cultures. Training seminars provide the opportunity for face-to-face interaction among different nationalities, and for developing problem-solving skills in multicultural teams.

The program goals for cross-cultural training, more specifically, include developing observation and interview skills, being able to recognize the role of emotions and values in cross-cultural interactions and the avoidance of sensitive issues, and being able to define problems and gather information in real time.[106]

Check the pulse

Employee surveys need to be conducted to check on attitudes and perceptions regarding how the company is dealing with diversity, the representation of foreign nationals at various levels, as well as their career experiences. Auditing HR systems is needed to ensure that recruitment, performance appraisal, compensation, and career tracks do not undermine attempts to attract and retain talented foreigners. For example, in certain cultures, as in the US, you are encouraged to 'promote' or sell yourself, whereas in other cultures, Nordic and Northern European cultures, you are expected to be more circumspect. This could lead to what some might consider over-inflated self-appraisal in job applications, as well as in discussions evaluating performance or career opportunities. In conducting job interviews in China, expatriates have learned not to rely on first impressions as candidates are usually so nervous that they can hardly talk in the beginning.[107]

When Helen Wellian, director of diversity at HP Europe, was trying to recruit more women engineers in Europe, she was told that there just were not enough women engineers around. Digging deeper, research revealed that when women engineers read the qualifications specified in the job advertisements, they applied only if they possessed 7 out of 10 of those qualifications. Men applied if they fulfilled only 3 out of the 10 criteria listed. This led them to changing the job announcements and resulted in many more women candidates.

The problem is to recognize how deeply embedded these biases are. For example, in order to encourage more women to join the managerial ranks, the Ms. Foundation organized a 'Take our daughters to work' national day, where adolescent girls could engage in 'realistic' management activities and become more familiar with the corporate environment. After nine years, this has become a popular event sponsored by 3 out of 10 US companies such as Microsoft, Merrill Lynch, and IBM among others. However, as Figure 16.1 shows, these girls may learn more about the biases than about the opportunities. After a day immersed in the world of work, when asked whether she enjoyed the 'initiation to work' day and what she wanted to be when she grew up, the answer was 'a boy'!

And the corporate culture has to be checked for biases. In corporate cultures where it is important to put in 'face time', to stay long hours at the office and be available on weekends to entertain clients, people from cultures which are more family-oriented and which place a strong value on separating work and family life would be placed at a disadvantage. Furthermore, given these demands, they may prefer not to apply for the job or accept a job offer.

The degree to which an organization is truly multicultural can be evaluated by the degree of prejudice and discrimination that exists, using survey feedback (as do Xerox and P&G) and the degree of intergroup conflict which is based on national or cultural differences.[108] A greater mix of nationalities enhances identification with the company by erasing the distinction between insiders and outsiders, and reduces the 'them and us' mentality based on nationality.

Consider the following 'modest proposal'.[109] Imagine a world where everyone measures 1.50 m. When recruiting tall people (1.80 m) in the land of the short, we have several options: 1) teach them how to live like us; 2) create positions that are not too demanding for those who can't adjust (put them in jobs where they don't have to move around too much so that they don't hit their heads in the doorways); 3) create a more friendly environment (higher ceilings, bigger chairs). Perhaps a more enlight-

Figure 16.1 Growing up to be a boy!
Source: The artist, Wazem.

ened approach would be to give them jobs where height is an advantage: assignment to the warehouse (inventory control), developing a new product line for tall people, or sending them to countries like Holland where people are also tall.

While this example seems silly, this is indeed the experience of those who are 'different' for whatever reason. Thus we need to create a detailed scenario to describe what this company would look like if it were truly to integrate differences in a meaningful way.

Le défi: the global challenge

The challenge, then, is to find ways to capitalize on differences, to utilize cultural differences in order to gain competitive advantage. But to do this, differences have to be acknowledged and accepted as legitimate. This means they have to be discussed. They must also be seen as an opportunity and not as a threat to efficiency, to existing power bases, nor to harmony. It is easier to try to dominate, to assert that our way of doing things is better, more efficient, more effective, and so on. After all, it has always worked in the past.

It is difficult to acknowledge that there may be a better way, one which involves many people of different nationalities, races, religions and gender trying to figure it out together. Acknowledging differences may threaten individual identity (how are we different?) or threaten the cohesiveness of the group (one big happy family). Acknowledging differences raises the possibility of conflict, which may upset the harmony. Ignoring or denying differences, however, means losing the richness of diversity.

MNCs have understood the changes that need to take place in order to become global companies. Many are in the process of adapting their strategies, structures, and systems accordingly. But globalization has to happen in people's minds too. Ethnocentric thinking, 'our way is best', has to change. Multiparadigm thinking is necessary. To derive the potential benefits from cross-cultural interactions, we need to open our minds to alternative perspectives, and be willing to go towards others, rather than hide behind sameness. Cultural mosaics, where each culture preserves its uniqueness, not melting pots where cultures are merged losing their distinctiveness, can create multiple patterns that better reflect and respond to the complexity of operating in a global arena.

This is the challenge for managers, organizations and nation states. There is no other way to move forward than to take on this challenge, quickly. Otherwise, we will stay mired in the mess we see around us today, where one culture tries to impose its ways on the other, where turf battles continually multiply, and where the hope for economic and political integration, not least for a global civilization, is shattered.

SUGGESTIONS FOR MANAGING CULTURAL DIVERSITY

- Build face-to-face relationships.
- Create international project groups.
- Develop international management training and development.
- Build shared values, while encouraging local interpretation.
- Promote divergent values to provide seeds for flexibility.

QUESTIONS TO ASK

To what extent are cultural differences open to discussion and negotiation?

To what extent do different interpretations of company culture, values, and behavior exist in the organization?

To what extent are ideas from outside HQ listened to and implemented?

To what extent do HR initiatives, selection and recruitment, training programs, performance appraisal and compensation, and career systems, reflect cultural bias?

What opportunities exist for learning from other cultures?

To what extent does top management 'walk the talk' of valuing and utilizing cultural differences?

To what extent are different nationalities present in top management? Top 200?

NOTES

1. Heenan, D.A. and Perlmutter, H.V. (1979) *Multinational Organizational Development*, Reading, MA: Addison-Wesley.
2. Kobrin, S.J. (1994) 'Is there a relationship between a geocentric mind-set and multinational strategy?', *Journal of International Business Studies*, 25(3), pp. 494–512.
3. Murtha, T.P, Lenway, S.A. and Bagozzi, R.P. (1998) 'Global mind-sets and cognitive shift in a complex multinational corporation', *Strategic Management Journal*, 19, pp. 97–114.
4. Prahalad, C.K. and Doz, Y. (1987) *The Multinational Mission: Balancing Local Demands and Global Vision*, New York: Free Press.
5. Bartlett, C.A. and Ghoshal, S. (1989) *Managing Across Borders: the Transnational Solution*, Boston, MA: Harvard Business School Press.
6. Sathe, V. (1983) 'Implications of corporate culture: A manager's guide to action', *Organizational Dynamics*, Autumn, pp. 5–23.
7. Nehrer, J. (1991) 'France amazed, amused by Disney dress code', *International Herald Tribune*, December 26.
8. See Van Maanen, J. (1991) 'The smile factory: Work at Disneyland', in P.J. Frost, L.F. Moore, M.R. Louis, C.C. Lundberg and J. Martin (eds) *Reframing Organizational Culture*, Newbury Park, CA: Sage, pp. 58–76; also Van Maanen, J. and Laurent, A. (1993) 'The flow of culture: Some notes on globalization and the multinational corporation', in S. Ghoshal and D.E. Westney (eds) *Organization Theory and the Multinational Corporation*, New York: St Martin's Press, pp. 275–312.
9. Presentation at INSEAD by George Cohn, CEO McDonald's Canada, with Video of McDonald's in Russia.
10. Adler, N.J. (1983) 'Organizational development in a multicultural environment', *Journal of Applied Behavioral Science*, 19(3), pp. 349–65.
11. Belson, K. (2002) 'Citigroup wins favor with Japan's cautious rich,' *International Herald Tribune*, March 5, p. 10.
12. Brannen, M.Y. (1992) ' 'Bwana Mickey': Constructing cultural consumption at Tokyo Disneyland', in J.J. Tobin (ed.) *Remade in Japan: Everyday Life and Consumer Taste in a Changing Society*, New Haven, CT: Yale University Press, pp. 216–34.

13. 'Disneyland Paris: le plan marketing qui a sauvé le parc', *L'Essentiel du Management*, February, 1996, pp. 42–8.
14. Kanter, R.M. and Corn, R.I. (1994) 'Do cultural differences make a business difference?', *Journal of Management Development*, 13(2), pp. 5–23.
15. 'McDonald's apologizes for confusion over french fries', *International Herald Tribune*, May 26–27, 2001.
16. Goodstein, L. (2001) 'McDonald's being sued over fries', *International Herald Tribune*, May 21.
17. Merckling, N. (2000) 'Tout un fromage pour un McDo', *Tribune de Genève*, February 24.
18. Barboza, D. (2001) 'From Golden arches to lightning rod', *International Herald Tribune*, October 15, pp. 1, 4.
19. McLuhan, M. (1968) *War and Peace in the Global Village*, New York: Bantam Books.
20. Inglehart, R. and Baker, W.E. (2001) Modernization's challenge to traditional values: Who's afraid of Ronald McDonald?', *The Futurist*, March–April, p. 21; see also http://wvs.isr.umich.edu and Watson, J. (ed.) (1998) *Golden Arches East: McDonald's in East Asia*, Stanford: Stanford University Press.
21. Inglehart and Baker, *Op. cit.*, p. 20.
22. Rohwer, J. (2000) 'GE Asia', *Fortune*, October 2, pp. 51–60.
23. Edstrom, A. and Galbraith, J. (1977) 'Transfer of managers as a coordination and control strategy in multinational organizations', *Administrative Science Quarterly*, 22, pp. 248–63.
24. Doz, Y. and Prahalad, C.K. (1984) 'Patterns of strategic control within multinational corporations', *Journal of International Business Studies*, 15(2), pp. 55–72; Baliga, B.R. and Jaeger, A.M. (1984) 'Multinational corporations: Control systems and delegation issues', *Journal of International Business Studies*, 15(2), pp. 25–40; Etzioni, A. (1988) *The Moral Dimension*, New York: Free Press.
25. Hedlund, G. (1980) 'The role of foreign subsidiaries in strategic decision-making in Swedish multinational corporations', *Strategic Management Journal*, 9, pp. 23–6.
26. 'The 3M Company: Integrating Europe', INSEAD case, 1994, p. 8.
27. Ibid.
28. Lightfoot, R.W. (1992) 'Philips and Matsushita: A portrait of two evolving companies', Harvard Business School.
29. Tagliabue, J. (2001) 'French workers do it Toyota's way', *International Herald Tribune*, February 2, pp. 13–14.
30. Rapoport, C. (1994) 'Nestlé's brand building machine', *Fortune*, September 19, pp. 129–33.
31. Wetlaufer, S. (2001) 'The business case against revolution: An interview with Nestlé's Peter Brabeck', *Harvard Business Review*, February, pp. 113–19.
32. Rapoport, *Op. cit.*
33. 'A conversation with Michael Porter', *European Management Journal*, 1991, 9(4), pp. 355–9.
34. F. Studemann (1998) 'Publisher with his eye on cyberspace', *Financial Times*, December 7, p. 15.
35. Middelhoff, T. (1998) 'Bertelsmann in Transition', published version of speech delivered at the 5th Bertelsmann Management Congress, Gütersloh, October 28–30.
36. Evans, P., Pucik, V. and Barsoux, J.-L. (2002) *The Global Challenge: Frameworks for International Human Resource Management*, Chicago: McGraw-Hill.
37. Schneider, S.C., Wittenberg, A. and Hansen, L. (1990) Honeywell Europe, INSEAD case.

38. Riesenbeck, H. and Freeling, A. (1993) 'How global are global brands?', *European Business Report*, 2Q, Summer, pp. 12–17.
39. McKay, B., Deogun, N. and Lublin, J. (1999) 'Tone deaf: Ivester had all skills of a CEO but one – ear for political nuance', *The Wall Street Journal*, December 17: A, 1:6.
40. Hays, C.L. (2000) 'Coke's plan: Fitting in overseas', *International Herald Tribune*, January 20.
41. Hays, C.L. (2000) 'Daft shakes up Coke, pushing local decisions', *International Herald Tribune*, February 7, pp. 13, 15; 'Coke to pay $192.5 million to settle suit', *International Herald Tribune*, November 17, 2000.
42. 'The discreet charm of the multicultural multinational', *The Economist*, July 30, 1994, pp. 59–60.
43. 'Don't be an ugly American manager', *Fortune*, October 16, 1995, p. 99.
44. DeMeyer, A. (1993) Nestlé, S.A., INSEAD case.
45. Blackwell, N., Bizet, J.P., Child, P. and Hensely, D. (1992) 'Creating European organizations that work', *The McKinsey Quarterly*, No. 2, pp. 31–43.
46. Kriger, M. and Solomon, E.E. (1992) 'Strategic mindsets and decision-making autonomy in US and Japanese MNCs', *Management International Review*, 32(4), pp. 327–43.
47. Ruigrok, W. and van Tulder, R. (1995) *The Logic on International Restructuring*, London and New York: Routledge.
48. Hampden-Turner, C. and Trompenaars, F. (1994) *The Seven Cultures of Capitalism*, London: Piatkus.
49. Asakura, A.E. (1989) Schneider, S.C., Nissan Europe, INSEAD case.
50. Shirouzu, N. (1999) 'Nissan's plan for jump-start faces challenge', *Asian Wall Street Journal*, October 18, p. 3.
51. Grist, L. (2001) 'Nissan puts merit before service', *The Irish Times*, 27 July, p. 6.
52. Hofheinz, P. (1993) 'Europe's tough new managers', *Fortune*, September 6, pp. 20–3.
53. Child, J., Markoczy, L. and Cheung, T. (1992) 'Managerial adaptation in Chinese and Hungarian strategic alliances with culturally foreign partners', Paper presented at the British Academy of Management Annual Conference, Bradford, September.
54. *The Economist*, July 30, 1994, *Op. cit.*, pp. 59–60.
55. Dunning, J.H. (1993) 'Internationalizing Porter's diamond', *Management International Review*, 33(2), pp. 7–15.
56. 'The stateless corporation', *Business Week*, May 14, 1990, pp. 52–9, p. 55.
57. Gargan, E.A. (1993) 'India's Silicon Valley moves to state of the art', *International Herald Tribune*, December 31.
58. Taylor, W. (1993) 'Message and muscle: An interview with Swatch titan Nicolas Hayek', *Harvard Business Review*, March–April, pp. 99–110.
59. *European Management Journal* (1991), *Op. cit.*
60. Lightfoot, *Op. cit.*
61. K. Asakawa, Professor Keio Business School, Japan.
62. *European Management Journal* (1991), *Op. cit.*
63. Ghoshal, S. and Bartlett, C.A. (1990) 'The multinational corporation as an interorganizational network', *Academy of Management Review*, 15(4), pp. 603–25.
64. Hedlund, G. (1986) 'The hypermodern MNC: A heterarchy?', *Human Resource Management*, 25, pp. 9–35.
65. Bartlett and Ghoshal (1989), *Op. cit.*
66. Das, G. (1993) 'Local memoirs of a global manager', *Harvard Business Review*, March–April, pp. 38–47, p. 38.

67. Doz, Y., Santos, J. and Williamson, P. (2001) *From Global to Metanational*, Boston, MA: Harvard Business School Press, p. 5.
68. Farnham, A. (1994) 'Global – or just Globaloney', *Fortune*, June 27, pp. 49–51.
69. Auteri, E. and Tesio, V. (1990) 'The internationalization of management at FIAT', *Journal of Management Development*, 9(6), pp. 6–16.
70. *Fortune*, October 16, 1995, *Op. cit.*
71. Excerpts taken from questionnaires by Taylor, S., Boyacigiller, N., Levy, O. and Beechler, S. (2001) 'The darker side of MNCs: Is it globalization or poor management?', Presented at the Academy of Management Meetings, Washington, DC; Murtha, T.P., Lenway, S.A. and Kimmel, S.K. (1994) 'Mind over matrix: Measuring individual potential for transnational thought', *Proceedings of Annual Academy of Management Meetings*, pp. 148–52.
72. Askenas, R., Ulrich, D., Jick, J. and Kerr, S. (1995) *The Boundaryless Organization*, San Francisco: Jossey-Bass, pp. 290–2.
73. Ibid.
74. Kobrin, S.J. (1994) 'Is there a relationship between a geocentric mind-set and multinational strategy?', *Journal of International Business Studies*, 25(3), pp. 494–512.
75. Murtha *et al.*, *Op. cit.*
76. *Fortune*, October 16, 1995, *Op. cit.*
77. Skapinker, M. (2001) 'Worlds apart', *Financial Times*, March 1, p. 18.
78. 'Multikulturelle Gesellschaft?', *Managermagazin*, April 1996, p. 246.
79. Farnham, *Op. cit.*
80. 'Interview with Peter Brabeck', *L'Hebdo*, March 23, 2000, pp. 48–50.
81. Cox, T. (1991) 'The multinational organization', *Academy of Management Executive*, 5(2), pp. 34–47.
82. Schmidt, V.A. (1993) 'An end to French economic exceptionalism: The transformation of business under Mitterand', *California Management Review*, Fall, pp. 75–98, p. 94.
83. Perlmutter, H.V. and Heenan, D.A. (1986) 'Cooperate to compete globally', *Harvard Business Review*, March–April, pp. 3–8.
84. Labich, K. (1992) 'Airbus takes off', *Fortune*, June 1, pp. 26–30.
85. Done, K. (1994) 'Don't cry over Rover', *Financial Times*, February 1, p. 19.
86. Farnham, *Op. cit.*
87. *L'Express*, December 19, 1991, p. 8.
88. Orleman, P.A. (1992) The global corporation: Managing across cultures, Masters thesis, University of Pennsylvania.
89. Cox, *Op. cit.*
90. Adler, N.J. (1980) 'Cultural synergy: The management of cross-cultural organizations', in W.W. Burke and L.D. Goodstein (eds) *Trends and Issues in OD: Current Theory and Practice*, San Diego: University Associates, pp. 163–84.
91. Noble, B.P. (1994) '"Diversity" fails to catch on', *International Herald Tribune*, November 10, p. 9.
92. Brimm, L. and Arora, M. (1996) Diversity Management at Hewlett-Packard, Europe. INSEAD Case 4651.
93. Cox, T.H. and Blake, S. (1991) 'Managing cultural diversity: Implications for organizational competitiveness', *Academy of Management Executive*, 5(3), pp. 45–56.
94. See Hambrick, D.C., Cho, T.S. and Chen, M.-J. (1996) 'The influence of top management team heterogeneity on firms' competitive moves', *Administrative Science Quarterly*, 41, pp. 659–84.

95. Elron, E. (1997) 'Top management teams within multinational corporations: Effects of cultural heterogeneity', *Leadership Quarterly*, 8, pp. 393–412.
96. Rice, F. (1994) 'How to make diversity pay', *Fortune*, August 8, pp. 44–9.
97. Rosenzweig, P.M. (1994) 'The new 'American Challenge': Foreign multinationals in the United States', *California Management Review*, Spring, pp. 107–23, p. 115.
98. Ashby, W.R. (1956) *Introduction to Cybernetics*, London: Chapman & Hall.
99. Noble, B.P. (1993) 'On women's 'difference': Companies are listening', *International Herald Tribune*, August 18, pp. 9, 11; see also Tannen, D. (1994) *Talking From 9 to 5*, New York: William Morrow.
100. Cox and Blake, *Op. cit.*
101. Laurent, A. (1987) 'Vive la différence!', *Strategic Direction*, March, 18.
102. Dechant (1995), *Fortune*.
103. 'The elusive Euro-manager', *The Economist*, November 7, 1992, p. 81.
104. Houlder, V. (1998) 'A language to unite our multicultural team: My secret weapon', *Financial Times*, April 4, p. 24.
105. Sims, C. (1994) 'Disney wants to learn languages', *International Herald Tribune*, April 28, pp. 9, 11.
106. Lobel, S.A. (1990) 'Global leadership competencies: Managing to a different drumbeat', *Human Resource Management*, 29(1), pp. 39–47.
107. Bjorkman, I. and Lu, Y. (1999) 'The management of human resources in Chinese–Western joint ventures', *Journal of World Business*, 34(3), pp. 306–24.
108. Cox, *Op. cit.*
109. Meyerson, D.E. and Fletcher, J.K. (2000) 'A modest manifesto for shattering the glass ceiling', *Harvard Business Review*, January–February, pp. 126–36.

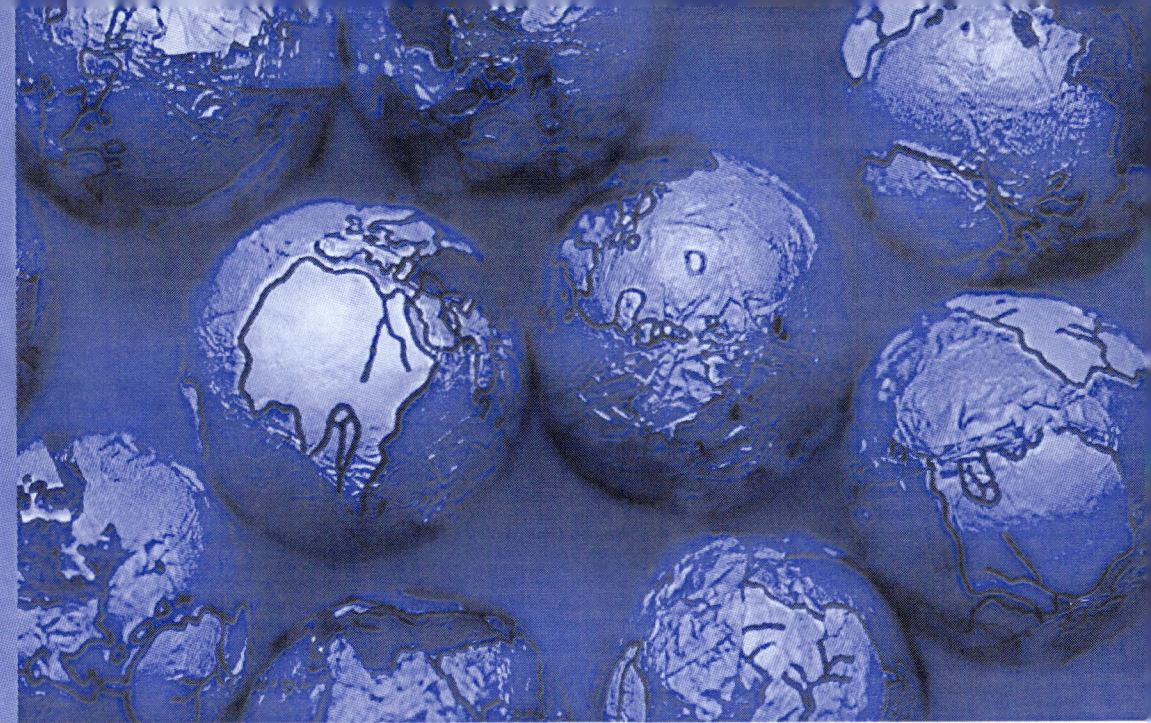

TOPIC 9

DIVERSITY IN A CULTURALLY CONTESTED ENVIRONMENT

IMPROVING INTERPERSONAL COMMUNICATION IN TODAY'S DIVERSE WORKPLACE

Gina Colavecchio
Children's Hospital Boston

Carol P. Harvey
Assumption College

GOALS

- To understand how the elements of the communication process can be affected by cultural differences
- To develop a culture general approach to mindful interpersonal communication that recognizes communication patterns in the major cultural subgroups in the United States
- To identify the preferred communication tendencies of coworkers, customers, vendors, and supervisors in today's diverse workplace
- To understand and identify elements of communication styles such as differences in power distances, degree of tolerance of uncertainty, non-verbal communication, tendencies towards directness, and differences in time orientation

When dealing with intercultural communication on a global basis, people are more apt to anticipate having some communication issues. However, it is no longer realistic to ignore cultural communication differences *within* the U. S. workplace. Research indicates that communication between culturally diverse sub-group members are increasingly dissimilar rather than homogeneous (Searight and Gafford, 2005). With the workforce being more diverse, immigration increasing and technology rapidly advancing in terms of e-commerce, Skype, video conferencing, global call centers, and webcasting, nearly everyone participates in intercultural communication even if they never leave the United States. However, we tend to be less mindful of the differences in styles when communicating with coworkers, supervisor, suppliers and customers whose communication styles may differ considerably from our own.

THE COMMUNICATION MODEL

While all communication follows a basic model, cultural differences can complicate the process and contribute to misunderstandings in the workplace. All communication, verbal and non-verbal, involves a sender who encodes a message that he transmits over some channel to a receiver who decodes the message and provides feedback. This transmission happens within a context of "noise," i.e., all of the factors that can reduce the clarity of understanding the message (See Figure 1).

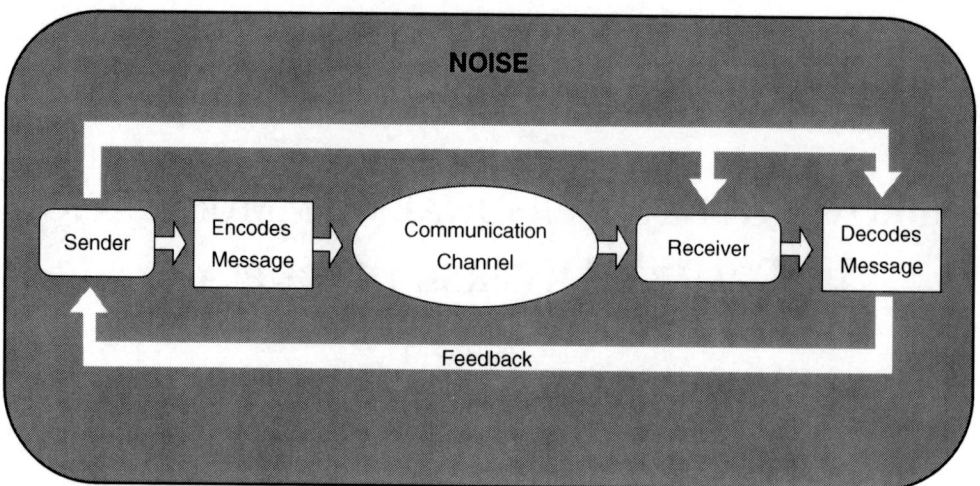

FIGURE 17-1 The Basic Communication Process

Certainly, when individuals exhibit communication styles that are based on different norms and values, i.e., create noise, the possibility of miscommunication increases significantly.

GROWTH AND FLEXIBILITY

Effective communication in the workplace can be both confusing and challenging. It requires not only significant knowledge of many different cultural frameworks, but also the willingness to attain personal growth and flexibility throughout the process. First, one needs to accept that the communication style that we are most familiar with often becomes the unconscious norm against which we judge others' communication styles.

For example, if you were socialized to believe that making eye contact indicates that a person is telling the truth, you may have an unconscious tendency to judge people who consider *not* making eye contact as a sign of respect as untrustworthy.

Second, in communication exchanges, there is a tendency to "categorize" individuals as being representative of their entire culture. So, when you start to communicate with a person, his appearance, clothing, accent or name may lead you to inaccurate interpretations conclusions and judgments about his message. However, such generalizations do not leave one open to an individual's life experiences and socialization.

> While generalizations may be accurate about groups, they're never going to be wholly true of individuals . . . This doesn't mean that we have gotten the facts wrong but only that in any culture you will always find a broad range of behaviors vis-à-vis particular characteristics (Storti, 1994, pp. 7–8).

So, in dealing with a customer from a Hispanic culture, or with a Hispanic name, it is easy to assume that he will typify all Hispanics when in fact his life experiences, could include many non-Hispanic influences.

Third, people have many social identities and some more salient or important influences on their patterns of communication than others. So, an African American woman may develop a communication style more influenced by her status as a woman, i.e. gender, or her generational cohort, i.e., as a baby boomer than her race.

Flexible communicators avoid using a **culture specific** approach which assumes that all members of a subgroup communicate in the same way. For example, if a person is working with a client from a group that tends to be sensitive to time, direct and not emotional, it does not mean that this particular person will respond well to communications that stress those elements. For many reasons, these parameters may not be strong in her personal communication framework. A better approach is to be *mindful*, i.e., more observant and tuned into her communication style, and listening for cues to determine if she seems to value this communication approach or not. Jandt (2004) proposes that by nature, people of all cultural backgrounds are inherently the same, and it is their exposure over time to their society and its values (i.e., socialization) that shapes the communication style of the culture and each individual has a unique life experience.

Being able to communicate effectively with people of diverse cultural backgrounds is a skill that can provide a competitive advantage in the marketplace and capitalizes on one of the positive aspects of having diversity in an organization. Employees who understand and appreciate differences, such as greetings, meeting formalities, scheduling, negotiations, and presentation skills will have a better chance of doing business effectively than those who continue to overlook the importance of developing more mindful and flexible intercultural communication skills or who assume that all members of a particular culture communicate with the same style. The key is to develop one's self-awareness to improve understanding.

THE NEW WORKFORCE: FACTS, FIGURES, EDUCATION AND LANGUAGE

Based on current trend analysis in the United States, by 2050 white Euro-Americans will compose 46% of the population, a decline of 20%, with approximately half of the country made up of ethnic minorities (Berry, 2009). The implications for the American workplace are remarkably similar: 1 out of 2 new workers in the US will be an ethnic minority (Morse, 2004). In contrast, as recently as 1999, white Americans made up approximately 72% of the United States population. As of 2006, according to the U.S. Census Bureau, the minority population in the U.S. reached 100.7 million of the 300 million people in the country. The 44.3 million Hispanics are the largest minority group (14.8% of the population), Blacks comprise 40.2 million, Asians 14.9 million and American Indian and Alaska Natives 4.5 million.

A recent CareerBuilder.com and America Online survey found that at least 50 percent of new hires in 2006 were Hispanics and one-third of hiring managers expect diverse candidates to make up a quarter of their new hires in the coming years (Barger, 2006). California has a minority population of 20.7 million—22% of the nation's total and Texas 12.2 million or 12% of the U.S. total. Over the past 40 years, 65% of the immigrant population has located in one of six states; New York, California, Texas, Florida, New Jersey and Illinoi (Shrestha, 2006).

EXHIBIT 1 Changing Composition of the U.S. Work Force

Race/Ethnicity	1999	2050
Whites	72%	24.4%
Blacks	12%	15%
Hispanics	11%	50.1%
Asians	5%	8%
Other	0%	14.6%

EDUCATION AND SOCIO-ECONOMIC CONSIDERATIONS IN COMMUNICATION IN STYLES

Differences in education and socio-economic levels may also account for some of the communication differences that are often attributed to one's culture. A 2000 U.S. Census identified that there were more than 1.5 million Asians enrolled in colleges and universities in the United States. So, as might be expected, Asian Americans as a group earn more money than any other ethnic group and almost half are employed in managerial or professional careers. Comparatively, about 10% of Hispanics work in white collar or professional careers and Hispanic women attain higher educational levels than Hispanic men.

EXHIBIT 2 Employment Levels of Asians & Hispanics

Race/Ethnicity	White Collar	Blue Collar
Asian	48%	52%
Hispanic	10%	90%

Although, the unemployment rate among Hispanics is still high and their earnings are lower compared to Euro-Americans, as the percentage of Hispanics in the population grows, the group as a whole will experience increased political and economic power.

This growing talent pool of workers includes 80% of Black Americans who have completed high school, 44% who have some college education and 25% who have a college degree (compared to 90%, 56%, and 38% respectively for white Americans). The difference in attainment percentages between White and Black Americans may relate to socioeconomic, access issues as a significantly larger percentage of Black Americans are living below the poverty level in the United States.

EXHIBIT 3 Educational Levels of the U.S. Workforce

Educational Level	Black Americans	White Americans
High School	80%	90%
Some College	44%	56%
College Degree	25%	38%

LANGUAGES

Of 132 million workers in the United States, 77 percent speak fluent English, indicating that almost one-fourth of the U.S. workforce does not communicate in English very well (Peden, Mandell, & Moore, 2007). In a recent Gallup survey, 96% of Americans believed it was either crucial or very important for members of the U.S. workforce to speak English. However, approximately a quarter of the U.S. workforce can hold a conversation in a language other than their primary language, 55% of which is in Spanish (Fry, 2005). In the Hispanic community, 47% of Spanish youth are bilingual in Spanish and English. However, younger Hispanics often speak English as their primary language. With the median age of Hispanics in the United States at 27.4 years of age, compared to the median age of Euro-Americans at 36.4 years of age, the opportunity for this cultural group to utilize their English and bilingual communication skills to advance in business organizations is unprecedented.

Language is inherently problematic because it can be indefinite, vague, and unclear. As communicators, we are constantly subjectively interpreting everything we observe and hear, a concept described by Shramm and Osgood's circular theory that defines communication as an endless process with information constantly being received and redirected between sender and receiver. It is an art that is based on personal life experiences, cultures, stereotypes, and assumptions that leads differing degrees of ambiguity, difference, and inferences.

COMMUNICATION STYLES AND AMERICAN SUB-CULTURES

In communicating, each person participating in the conversation must understand their own experiences, culture, stereotypes, and assumptions, as well as put forth an effort to understand the experiences, culture, stereotypes, and realized and unrealized assumptions of the other participants. Stereotypes can be based on a variety of different experiences, including family beliefs, religion, previous interactions with people of that cultural background, travel, education, or having done business with someone from a particular country. These stereotypes are primarily subjective generalizations and are not necessarily an accurate way to describe the communication styles of each member of an entire culture. To think that everybody will communicate the same is of course a generalization and referred to as a culture specific approach. However, this often happens as an unconscious process. So, rather than assuming that *all* Asians will value and need time to establish a relationship before reaching an business agreement, it is preferable to observe the communication cues and behaviors of your Asian American client to determine *if* this seems to be important for him.

In Asian cultures, indirectness is often considered polite, but a common stereotype is that Asians are sneaky or hard to figure out, undoubtedly a result of their indirect communication style. This has led many to distrust Asians in the workplace. Some people may even feel that Asians are deceptive or hiding pertinent information while in fact they may have been socialized to communicate in a less directive style to demonstrate respect.

Another example is the stereotype that Black Americans are more violent and aggressive than whites. Black Americans as a group tend to have a more direct communication style than many White Americans or Asians. Black Americans consider it admirable to express feelings, and emotions and value members of society who do so. Early communications research by Foeman and Pressley (1987) identified five Black-American cultural values that, if leveraged appropriately, can be beneficial in an organizational environment and communication: assertiveness, directness, morality, receptiveness, and cohesion.

COMMUNICATION STYLES

Different styles of speech and language can cause anxiety in interpreting directions and verbal and non-verbal cues, especially when there are differences in the way words are articulated. It is assumed that people will contribute to an interaction in a greater capacity when they are comfortable and have similarities with their counterparts, including common economic, social, and cultural backgrounds (McComb, 2001).

While sociologists view different dialects as all being correct ways of speaking, others perceive some dialects, such as British English, as more prestigious (Langmia & Durham, 2007). In contrast, in Black American culture, language is individualistic and complicated, as described by Gudykunst and Ting-Toomey and uses vivid descriptive words, images and metaphors (Taylor, 1990). The language is a combination of the English vocabulary and complex Black structure that sometimes results in differences in the way that Black Americans use verb tenses. Black Americans sometimes talk in a more rhythmic speech than white Americans. So, conversations and presentations may appear more boastful and animated. Because of the percentage of Black Americans who live in poverty and their historically lower levels of academic achievement as a group, this speech style is sometimes unconsciously less respected than other styles.

Asian influenced communication styles tend to differ from Euro-American communication patterns in that Asians can be more indirect in providing information and data prior to making their main point. So, some may view this as a way to provide a complete rationale for the ultimate decision or strategy. However, this can leave other people searching for the substance at the beginning of a communication, lead to difficulty in identifying the main points and result in poor listening and a loss of interest. In contrast, many Euro-Americans tend to lead with the main point or decision (i.e., have more direct style), and then follow-up with supporting data and rationale. Asians listening to a presentation or reading this in an email could view this style as aggressive or forward.

Differences in communication styles often are unrecognized or denied because people are unsure of how to cope with these differences. For example, Asians have a tendency to shield others from knowing negative information and expect others to do the same (Searight, 2005). In contrast, African Americans can come across as blunt or too-straightforward because of their tendency to use a more direct style of communication (Gudykunst &Ting-Toomey, 1996).

MAINTAINING HARMONY AND EMOTIONALISM

People from different cultures may deal with conflict quite differently. For valid reasons, African Americans sometimes distrust the established ways of doings things, and challenge the norms and expectations within an organization. While Asians are more apt to conform to established processes, roles and hierarchies within an organization, while repressing public feelings and emotions (Searight, 2005).

For example, in terms of negotiation, Asians are often more willing to apologize as a way to continue moving forward especially when things become awkward. Asians are typically expected to apologize whenever there is tension or awkwardness but Euro-Americans and Black Americans often are less willing to take any blame and only offer an apology as warranted, if at all. Americans are also more likely to provide an explanation with an apology, while Asians tend to internalize the blame, acting in a more submissive manner, without necessarily providing any rationale (Carr-Ruffino, 2006).

> Common stereotypes about Native Americans have led to generalizations that they have little education and tend to work in low-level jobs at casinos, or making and selling crafts. People sometimes even refer to Native Americans in the past tense, in a way that suggests the culture no longer exists, even though today there are more than 800,000 Native Americans living in the United States. Since some are soft spoken or quiet, this can create an expectation that they will not participate in conversations, or in contrast, the assumption that they are overly aggressive when they do speak up (Hernandez, 2007).
>
> In Native American cultures, oral tradition is important and this may result in a less talk and more listening than most Americans expect. Because it is considered shameful in Native American culture to make mistakes in public, this may be another reason why some Native Americans tend to participate verbally in the workplace.

DECISION MAKING AND LEADERSHIP

From the values of Asian cultures, it is often more acceptable and normal to have greater respect for people in authority, i.e., employees maintain significant power distances between themselves and management. Centralization of organizational structures is a direct result of this power distance, as is the ability to eliminate uncertainty and risks, through the rigidity of hierarchical roles. If you work a subsidiary of an Asian company or for an individual who is strongly influences by Asian culture, there may be an expectation that you will have great respect for those in authority and feel comfortable with decisions being made top down.

In Hispanic cultures, major decisions, such as choosing career paths and arranging living situations, are often made as a family or a group and it's not uncommon to consult with siblings, parents and even grandparents. Because this culture is typically masculine and highly authoritarian, leaders and managers are considered all-knowing and are greatly respected, but in return are expected to provide for employees.

INDIVIDUAL AND GROUP COMMUNICATION

America as a whole is considered to be low context, highly individualistic culture where directness is valued and people are responsible for their own success. However, much of the U.S. population growth both through immigration and birthrate is more in the high context collectivist subcultures such as Asians, Africans, Native Americans and Middle-Easterners where the group is more important and indirect communication is more common (Lingley, 2006). Since these cultures are less direct, listening is more important and silence indicates understanding. Many Euro-Americans prefer a more direct communication style and rush to fill silences (McDowell, 2003).

In some cultures, there is a strong emphasis on group cohesiveness and belonging, i.e., collectivism. The group, which can span from anything as narrow as immediate family, to as broad as colleagues and acquaintances, is of utmost importance to members of these cultures, and they value conformity and commitment to the group (i.e., relationships), as well as compliance to maintain harmony, above even honesty, within the group.

This is in sharp contrast to the United States, where individualism and independence are critical to one's self value. In American culture, maintaining self-respect and one's image is extremely important and people will act more aggressively to preserve their self image in negotiations and conflict. In other cultures, such as Asian cultures, it is the group that matters more than any one individual. So, people may avoid conflict to not upset the collective group's image (McDowell, 2003).

In American Indian and Asian cultures, the individual is expected to remain modest and humble. Advancing or promotion of oneself and accomplishments or taking oneself too seriously violates this value (LeBaron, 2003). For example, a very talented American Indian student may hide academic competence to avoid seeming superior, which is considered inappropriate arrogance in that culture. To ensure harmony, American Indians may be less aggressively competitive and work best cooperatively (Deyhle & Swisher, 1997).

Frequently, people from these collectivist societies belong to a small number of very intimate groups to which they are extremely loyal over the entire course of their lives and this tendency has implications for teamwork and management. Reward systems benefit the group as a whole rather than any one individual and hard work is rewarded intrinsically. In contrast, low context cultures like the U.S., are more assertive, talkative, and direct in communication and often devalue the attentive listening and silences so common in high context communication.

When low context communicators actively question a speaker, it can make people in high context cultures uneasy because it can produce tension or disrupt harmony (Berry, 2009).

In contrast, in the United States an individual's personal needs are often placed above the needs of the group with minimal commitment or loyalty to the group.

GROWTH AND FLEXIBILITY

Intercultural communication in the global workplace can be both confusing and challenging. It requires not only significant knowledge of many different cultural attributes, but also the willingness to cultivate self-awareness and to attain personal growth and flexibility throughout the process. Accepting that everyone has some biases in regards to different cultures is essential to beginning to improve intercultural communication. As an increasingly vital component to the American workforce, the ability to communicate with people of diverse backgrounds and cultures can provide competitive advantages to those who support and embrace the concept. Employees who understand and appreciate different expectations, such as greetings, meeting formalities, scheduling, negotiating, and presentation skills will have a better chance of doing business effectively than a company whose employees continue to deal with disconnects or miscommunications.

In low context cultures, communication between people of different cultures can create additional uncertainty, which can diminish with extended exposure. Often, people are able to adapt their communication styles, over time, to successfully interact with those from difference cultures. In high context cultures, exposure to people from different cultures does not diminish the level of uncertainty, and can instead increase tension over time. In Asian cultures, extreme formality is expected in business communications and transactions, regardless of the level of intimacy between those engaged with adherence to strict rules and guidelines to ensure ambiguity is avoided.

Risk-takers, frequently financially successful in individualistic cultures, are more comfortable with risk and use risk to their advantage because they are willing to accept the possibility of loss, if the opportunity for gains is significant. Other cultural groups may value risk-avoidance, strict rules and adherence to set principles to minimize risk.

UNCERTAINTY REDUCTION THEORY

The **Uncertainty Reduction Theory** proposed by Charles Berger and Richard Calabrese, predicts and explains relationship progress during an initial reaction. This theory holds that during an interaction, people take certain steps to minimize uncertainty and enhance the comfort level of the interaction (Neuliep, 2003). Employees who are empathetic, and those who can identify *similarities* between themselves and others, are more likely to overcome the uncertainty of engaging with people from different cultures. For example, a doctor often meets patients in a tense setting. By sharing a conversation, common interest about a sport, etc., the doctor may be able to establish a more comfortable relationship with the patient, who will in turn be more forthright, responsive, and trusting. Think about the complications that inter-cultural communication differences could bring to this conversation.

NON-VERBAL COMMUNICATION

Many people utilize nonverbal cues to better understand communication when they are not certain they understand what the other person is trying to convey. Most cultures use different non-verbal cues, based on their own assumptions and values, making the combination of interpreting verbal and non-verbal cues particularly complex. For example,

> In the United States, eye contact, pleasantness of vocal expressions, affirmative head nods, head and arm gestures per minute, and closer physical distance between interactants are considered affiliative. In other cultures, these same behaviors may instead increase uncertainty and anxiety (Neuliep, 2003).

In Black American cultures, listeners may avert their eyes to indicate respect and attention, while speakers are expected to look at listeners directly in the eye. If one member of the interaction is unaware of this culturally accepted communication style, it could unknowingly create tension.

In North America there is far less emphasis placed on nonverbal communication than in high context countries. Non-verbal communication can also be challenging in terms of electronic communications because with little to no opportunity to view mannerisms or hear tones, the communication can likely be judged as too direct and can seem harsh and impolite (Sanders & Wiseman, 1993).

TIME ORIENTATION AND DECISION MAKING

The way that members of a culture perceive time is an element that affects both home and work life. In North America and most of Northern Europe, there is a short-term, highly scheduled orientation. Other cultures have an entirely different perception of time. In some cultures time is cyclical with little to no need for agendas, calendars or timelines. Tasks are guided by interactions between people. For example, many Hispanics do not adhere strictly to set times and schedules (Neuliep, 2003). In contrast, Asian cultures have a tendency to have a long-term outlook and value decision making based on resolve and determination in overcoming long-term obstacles regardless of available opportunities in the short-term. These tendencies can create communication conflicts in a work environment, where Euro-Americans are driven by deadlines and meetings and expect appointments to be punctual and decisions to be made rapidly. Workers from highly scheduled cultures can view those with a looser sense of time orientation as being unmotivated and lazy.

There is an expectation that older members of the culture will be consulted before finalizing any plans, as they are respected for their years and wisdom. Traditions are extremely important and Asian cultures sometimes leave decisions to fate, following the natural progression, with any changes expected to be introduced slowly to allow adaptation (LeBaron, 2003) Without understanding the psychological underpinnings of each person's perception of time management and decision making, working together can be extremely difficult (Neuliep, 2003).

BENEFITS OF INTERCULTURAL COMMUNICATION

Frequently, even leaders who understand the need for intercultural communication and the complexities of diverse organizations become tentative about the extent that they should assert themselves to encourage intercultural communication within an organization, questioning exactly how much change should be expected and what metrics will best measure success. It can be disruptive to promote intercultural understanding and communication without first observing and analyzing the organizational culture, individual attitudes, and potential buy-in. Then there is a need to develop a strategy to gain acceptance.

While all cultures have some strong beliefs and assumptions, others seem to have sharp contrasts with a wide range of values, beliefs, and assumptions. As a whole, one tendency will typically dominate another tendency and therefore be more influential, but not necessarily apply to every member of the culture equally.

Competency in intercultural communication creates a healthier, more productive workplace with an increased number of contributing perspectives and a better opportunity for creativity. Businesses, both domestically and internationally, have begun to focus on the idea that capitalizing on intercultural communication knowledge and development can provide diverse perspectives and competitive advantages. In essence, the overall goal of successful communications in business is increased commerce, decreased conflict, better understanding, more personal growth through tolerance and less uncertainty, anxiety and fear of difference (Neuliep, 2003).

DISCUSSION QUESTIONS

1. What makes it difficult for people to understand how differences in communication styles can cause serious misunderstandings?

2. Why is it so important not to think that all members of a cultural group exhibit the same cultural values in their communication styles?

3. Conversely, why is it important to understand some general cultural tendencies?

4. Briefly describe an example of an intercultural miscommunication exchange that you have either participated in or observed in the workplace, at college, or in a public place. How did the communicators exhibit some of the dimensions described in this article? In retrospect what could have been done differently to improve the communication in terms of the sender and the receiver?

5. Develop an original example of an intercultural communication misinterpretation in a job interview situation that could cause incorrect assumptions to be made about an applicant's potential suitability for a position.

Writing Assignment

Go to http://www.gmi.org and search for "The Ten Commandments of American Culture." This list presents ten sayings that represent commonly accepted American cultural values. Think about how these "American" values may not be as relevant to African Americans, Hispanic Americans, or Asian Americans as they are to Euro-Americans. Write a two- to three-page essay that analyzes how these could lead to lack of motivation, poor productivity, and conflict in the workplace.

Bibliography

Altwaijri, A.O. (1998). *The Arab Culture and other Cultures*, Morocco: The Islamic Educational, Scientific and Cultural Organization (ISESCO).

Barger, T.S. (2006). *Hispanics in the Workplace: Building Meaningful Diversity*, New York: The Conference Board Executive action series.

Berry, John. (2009). *Federal Equal Opportunity Recruitment Program Annual Report to Congress*, Washington, DC: US Office of Personnel Management.

Carr-Ruffino, N., PhD. (2006). *Managing Diversity: People skills for a multicultural workplace; 7th edition*, Boston: Pearson Custom Publishing.

Deyhle, D., & Swisher, K. (1997). *Research in American Indian and Alaska Native education: From assimilation to self-determination*, Washington, DC: American Educational Research Association.

Foeman, A. K., and Pressley G. (1987). Ethnic culture and corporate culture: Using black styles in organizations. Communication Quarterly, 35 (4) 293–307. doi:10.1080/01463378709369695.

Fry, R. & Lowell-Pew, B.L. (2005). *The Characteristics of Bilingual and Monolingual U.S. Workers*, Somerville, MA: Cascadilla Publishing.

Gudykunst, W.B., & Ting-Toomey, S. (1996). *Communication in personal relationships*

across cultures, Thousand Oaks, CA: Sage Publications, Inc.
Hernandez, C. (2007). *Old and New Stereotypes of Hispanics*, Washington, DC: The Washington Post Company.
Jandt, F.E. (2004). *Intercultural Communication: A Global Reader*, Thousand Oaks, CA: Sage Publications, Inc.
Langmia, K., & Durham, E. (2007). *Bridging the Gap*, Bowie, MD: Sage Publication, Inc.
LeBaron, M. (2003). *Cross Cultural Communication*, Boulder, CO: University of Colorado, Boulder.
Lingley, D. (2006). *Apologies Across Cultures: An analysis of intercultural communication problems raised in the Ehime Maru incident*, Japan: Kochi University.
McComb. Chris. (2001). About One in Four Americans Can Hold a Conversation in a Second Language. *Gallup*. http://www.gallup.com/poll/1825/about-one-four-americans-can-hold-conversation-second-language.aspx.
McDowell, M.J. (2003). *Native American Literatures: High Context & Low Context*, Portland, OR: Portland Community College.
Morse, A. (2004). *A Quick Look at U.S. Immigrants: Demographics, Workforce, and Asset-Building*, Washington, DC: http://www.ncsl.org/programs/immig/National Conference of State Legislatures.
Neuliep, J.W. (2003). *Intercultural Communication: A Contextual Approach. 2nd Edition*, Boston: Houghton Mifflin Company.

Peden, J., Mandell, A., & Moore, D.R. (2007). *Council on Interracial Books for Children*, New York, NY: Department of Teaching and Learning Technologies at the University of Nevada, Reno.
Rojjanaprapayon, R., Chiemprapha, P., & Kanchanakul, A. (2004). *Conflict Management in Thai Organizations*, Thousand Oaks, CA: Sage Publications.
Sanders, J.A., & Wiseman, R.L. (1993) *Intercultural Communication Studies III: Uncertainty Reduction Among Ethnicities in the United States*, CA: California State Polytechnic University.
Scollon, R., & Scollon, S.W. (2001). *Intercultural Communication: A Discourse Approach. 2nd Edition*, Malden, MA: Blackwell Publishers, Inc.
Searight, H. Russell, PhD, MPH, & Gafford, J., PhD. (2005). *Cultural Diversity at the End of Life: Issues and Guidelines for Family Physicians*, St. Louis, MO: Forest Park Hospital Family Medicine Residency Program.
Shrestha, L.B. (2006). *CRS Report for Congress: The Changing Demographic Profile of the United States*, Washington, DC: The Library of Congress.
Storti, C. (1994). Cross-Cultural Dialogues. Yarmouth Maine: Intercultural Press.
Taylor, Orlando L., Ph.D. *Cross-Cultural Communication-Culture; Communication and Language*, Bethesda, MD: The Mid-Atlantic - Equity Consortium.

Diversity on the Web

Go to http://www.diversityinc.com and search for "Things Never to Say to American Indian Coworkers" (Article # 3621). After reading this list and the blog that follows it, what have you learned about communicating with Native Americans and about workplace communication? You will have to register to use this Web site, but if you use your ".edu" address. There is no charge and this is a very helpful workplace diversity Web site.

Gina Colavecchio is currently the Web Project Manager for Children's Hospital Boston, managing the hospital's external Web site, search engine marketing, and social media strategies and projects.

TOPIC 10
CULTURE CHANGE

Chapter 18

Cultural Change in Organisations

So far, this book has examined organizational culture in terms of the various models put forward by researchers, the concepts of leadership and the cultural contingencies and variables involved. Furthermore, it has looked at the question of company strategy and corporate culture. All these elements come together when it is a question of a company needing to adapt its culture to ensure its success or even survival.

Concept 18.1 examines the process of adaptation, the starting point for any real cultural change in an organization. Concept 18.2 tackles the issue of changing the underlying culture of global organizations.

Learning outcomes

After reading this chapter, you will gain an understanding of:

- Certain mechanisms for changing an organization's culture as well as an instrument for diagnosing the changes required.
- The tensions between national culture and organizational culture in the change process, particularly the emergence of a so-called international corporate culture.

Concept 18.1 Organizational change as a cultural process

Whether an organization thrives, survives – or otherwise – depends on numerous factors, both within the company and outside it. There are, of course, external factors to which a company needs to respond, or circumstances to anticipate in the way it organizes its operations. Rapid technological change, changes in industries and markets, new deregulation policies, increased competition and the development of the global economy can all be seen as potential threats to a company's survival, or potential opportunities.

But success has also to do with internal factors. How can an organization adapt? Is it able to change its behavioural practices and structures, to deal with external pressures? Admittedly, the culture of a company is dynamic. However, does it need to change its core values to survive or will changing cultural artefacts suffice? It is generally acknowledged that successful change has to do with maintaining both continuity and change, retaining the cultural foundation on which the company rests while changing its strategies and practices. In short, can essential elements of culture be brought in line with responses to the external forces pushing on the company?

The process of change

André Laurent (1989) addresses the difficulties involved in the process of change. The way workers view organizational change, and the management thereof, is inhibited by their own assumptions and conceptions. For a start, they may have fixed ideas as to how an organization should be structured. They may not, for example, consider any alternatives to the hierarchical pyramid, where movements up and down are clearly defined. The idea of unity of command may also be taken for granted. Such concepts, the products of classical (Western) management thought, may not be appropriate when the organization has to take on fresh tasks or technologies, or deal with new people or environments. Moreover, the whole idea of change may be naive, if well-intentioned. People focus too much on the benefits from change without giving consideration to the idea that change is not an organizational shift from A to B, but a transformation from A into B.

These two differing concepts of change, shift versus transformation, reflect the 'doing' orientation of Anglo-Saxon cultures and 'being' of many Eastern cultures mentioned in Part One. In 'doing' cultures, people and groups are mostly defined in terms of what they do, what they achieve. In 'being' cultures, people and groups are defined more in terms of affiliation, the relationships they have with others in the organization. In 'doing' cultures organizational change is perceived more in linear fashion, a question of putting the past state of affairs behind and pushing on with the new. In 'being' cultures, however, the past state of affairs undergoes gradual transformation so that it eventually becomes a new state of affairs.

Laurent (1989) advocates a dual approach to organizational change: both the instrumental and social nature of the organization must be considered. Managing change in the sense of ensuring the continuing running of the organization, re-assigning tasks and maintaining overall stability, may well be necessary in the process, but it is not enough. What is also needed is inspirational guidance, a leader who engages people's minds through vision. According to Laurent, our minds are the receptacles of culture, and as such give meaning and guidance to our experiences. Minds cannot be managed, but they can be transformed through inspiring leaders who spread visions that advocate new meanings and new lines of thinking.

Such concerns are shared by Deal and Kennedy (2000: 158). Many company managers, they maintain, are concerned about change, but do not pay attention to the cultural issues involved. They may go about dealing with tangible factors, such as changing job descriptions, replacing managers, changing the company structure even, but essentially, 'the business of change is cultural transformation'.

> **These actions ... are not the kind of long-term, all-encompassing behavioural and cultural changes we are talking about. When we speak of organizational or cultural change we mean real changes in the behaviour of people throughout the organization.**

In their view, the decision to become, for example, more marketing-oriented or to become cost-effective cannot be taken without subjecting the company to a fundamental cultural change that involves everyone. The change is not just a matter of changing routines but of identifying with role-models who embody a new purpose or goal. Such fundamental change does not occur overnight; it is often a gradual and sometimes painful transformation.

The mechanisms of change

Schein (2004) proposed ways which enable a leader to implant and maintain the corporate culture. Such means can be used to change the culture of an organization.

Schein (2004) also lists what he calls 'secondary' means. These are mechanisms for shaping and reinforcing the culture that are only effective if consistent with the primary means:

- The design and structure of the organization.
- The systems and procedures used.
- The 'rites and rituals' used in an organization.
- The design and layout of the organization's physical space.
- Stories of important events and people.
- Formal statements of the organization's philosophy.

When a manager is intent on getting employees to perceive things differently, all the primary mechanisms must be used. Moreover, according to Schein, they must all be consistent with each other.

Schein's model refers to the group-learning process when responding to problems externally and internally. External problems are concerned with responding to the environment. Internal problems arise from managing the internal development of the organization. For Schein, culture plays an important role in determining not only how environmental developments are perceived by members of organizations, but also how members of the organization react to the strategies designed to respond to those environmental developments.

In his article 'Organizational culture: what it is and how to change it', Schein (1989) presents what he believes to be the culture issues predominating at each phase of a company's growth. In addition, he discusses the change mechanisms that could be operating during each phase of growth. These phases only apply to private organizations and the kind of change possible depends on the extent to which the organization is ready for change as a result of either an external crisis or an internal push for change. Table 18.1 summarizes Schein's insights and Table 18.2 outlines how he believes the cultural change mechanisms work.

Can organizational culture really be changed?

Table 18.2 triggers an important question: is it possible to bring about fundamental transformations? An analysis by Deal and Kennedy (2000) reflects the belief that the culture of an organization is deep-rooted, particularly if, in Schein's terms, it is in a mid-life or maturity stage. A culture that has developed along with the organization and been passed on from generation to generation will be difficult to change and involves all kinds of relations between individuals and subgroups.

If the external factors are believed to have a strong influence on the organizational culture, the values, beliefs and behaviours that employees bring to the organization, then there is little conviction that an organization can be changed unless the external environment changes in line with the desired changes. If organizational culture is seen as

Table 18.1 Growth states, functions of culture and mechanisms of change

Growth stage	Function of culture/issue
I. Birth and early growth Founder domination, possible family domination	• Culture is a distinctive competence and source of identity • Culture is the 'glue' that holds organization together • Organization strives towards more integration and clarity • Heavy emphasis on socialization as evidence of commitment
Succession phase	• Culture becomes battleground between conservatives and liberals • Potential successors are judged on whether they will preserve or change cultural elements
Change mechanisms 1. Natural evolution 2. Self-guided evolution through organizational therapy 3. Managed evolution through hybrids 4. Managed 'revolution' through outsiders	
II. Organizational mid-life • Expansion of products/markets • Vertical integration • Geographical expansion • Acquisitions, mergers	• Cultural integration declines as subcultures are spawned • Loss of goals, values and assumptions creates crisis identity • Opportunity to manage direction of cultural change is provided
Change mechanisms 5. Planned change and organization development 6. Technological seduction 7. Change through scandal, explosion of myths 8. Incrementalism	
III. Organizational maturity • Maturity or decline of markets • Increasing internal stability and/or stagnation • Lack of motivation to change	• Culture becomes a constraint on innovation • Culture preserves the glories of the past, hence is valued as a source of self-esteem, defence
Transformation option	• Culture change is necessary and inevitable, but not all elements of culture can or must change • Essential elements of culture must be identified, preserved • Culture change can be managed or simply allowed to evolve
Destruction option • Bankruptcy and reorganization • Takeover and reorganization • Merger and assimilation	• Culture changes at fundamental levels • Culture changes through massive replacement of people
Change mechanisms 9. Coercive persuasion 10. Turnaround 11. Reorganization, destruction, rebirth	

Source: Schein (1989): 66.

Table 18.2 Mechanisms of cultural change

Natural evolution	The culture will evolve a culture of what works best if the organization is not undergoing too much stress from the environment. This may also involve what Schein calls a 'general evolution' to the next stage of the organization's development through diversification and growing complexity. It may also involve 'specific evolution' where subcultures may emerge around the increasing number of subunits in the organization
Self-guided evolution through organizational therapy	The organization gains insight into own strengths and weaknesses, e.g. by using an outside consultant to 'unfreeze' the organizational culture and so allowing dramatic changes to occur
Managed evolution through hybrids	This approach is useful where the culture needs to change, but the organization may lose its identity as a result. People from inside the company are used in key positions, people who realize there is a need for change but may meet less resistance than outsiders
Planned change and organizational development	Differentiation through growth and increasing complexity may lead to increasing sub-cultures coming into conflict. A consultant initiates a change programme to reduce conflict, one that involves some sort of culture change
Technological seduction	Technological changes may bring about cultural change because they change behaviour patterns and compel the organization to examine the way it carries out business
Change through scandal, explosion and myth	Change may occur through discrepancies between the values that are espoused by the organization and the practices that it actually performs. 'Whistleblowers' may reveal, for example, how ethical standards are being bypassed in certain operations, safety procedures ignored, promotion policies undermined. Such exposures often lead to assumptions being reconsidered and cultural changes being made
Incrementalism	Cultural change is implemented gradually over several years and is hardly noticed. Recruitment and selection policies, for example, may result in all key positions in a company being filled by people who act according to assumptions that are different to those of the old culture
Coercive persuasion	A culture turnaround, usually in a mature culture, where change agents - possibly senior managers - challenge old assumptions, put forward new ones and give key managers psychological safety by rewarding them for embracing the new assumptions
Turnaround	A turnaround individual or team has a clear idea of where the organization must go and how it is to get there. Some or all of the above mechanisms may be used while the present culture is unfrozen and psychological safety offered to reduce resistance
Reorganization and rebirth	An unusual occurrence, whereby the group that bears the old culture is removed and replaced by a new group and a fresh culture

dependent on internal factors, then there is a belief that culture can be directed and changed. Ideas as to how these changes are brought about vary: some concentrate on the role of the leader as instigator of changes or as facilitator, others focus more on how to initiate change at the three levels of corporate culture as defined by Schein (norms, values and beliefs; then behaviours and norms; then symbols and artefacts).

The notion that cultural change is easier to implement in an organization with a 'weak' culture rather than a 'strong' culture is contested by Laurent (1989). In a way, both are doomed to extinction. The organization with a weak culture may eventually crash, even if there is an initial burst of creativity from its disparate body of workers. With employees who each give the organization a different meaning and who each have a different view of what needs to be done, an organization with a weak culture is poorly co-ordinated, lacking direction and consistency. An organization with a strong culture, however, may be throttled by rigid norms and behaviour and the resulting dearth of innovation.

Rather than the strong–weak paradigm, Laurent advocates a more conceptual differentiation, which takes account of the extent to which an organization knows itself and the environment in which it operates. The higher the degree of awareness, both internally and externally, the better an organization can interpret its environment and deal with it.

Schein (2004) takes this awareness-raising issue further. He suggests that one way of trying to 'grasp' the corporate culture is for members of the organization to examine their culture together and assess some of the main assumptions. One or more of these may need to be abandoned or re-defined so that those involved can help decide the way the organization needs to evolve. The leader can play a key role here in getting the 'self-guided' evolution under way and by managing the process.

SPOTLIGHT 18.1

Steadfastness in turbulent times

By Rob Goffee and Gareth Jones

In turbulent times steadfastness is a leadership virtue. Not in the sense of having a fixed view of what will happen next, but by being true to a set of core values. A naïve reading of this point would suggest that all the leader has to do is be their authentic self. But that is not enough. Change will require that leaders play different roles in different contexts. In our previous book, *Why Should Anyone Be Led By You?*, we noted that effective leadership involves a complex balancing act between using your authentic differences and adapting your behaviours to context. Being authentic is not about being the same all the time. The most effective leaders are authentic chameleons. The chameleon always adapts to context but remains a chameleon.

Source: 'The challenges facing leadership', *Financial Times* (FT.com), 12 February 2009 (extract).

A degree of culture change will almost always be necessary, Schein maintains, because what has been learned has become routine. Bringing unconscious values and norms to the surface, then questioning and redefining them, may lead to a considerable anxiety: the subjects involved may feel that their sense of identity or integrity is threatened. Everything must be done to reassure those involved, to show them that changes are possible and that they will not be humiliated in the process.

This brings us back to the role of transformational leaders. Their role is to provide that reassurance through communicating a vision of how things should be, of convincing those who feel under threat that there is a brighter, happier future for the organization.

An inquiry into secret accounts held by the European Commission is an example of the sort of crisis that can trigger organizational change. Consider Mini-case 18.1.

Change in an organizational culture does seem possible, but the effort involved may be considerable and time-consuming. Apart from needing to be motivated to undergo change, those involved need to go through a process whereby they can gain clear insight into important cultural assumptions and then work out which of these help or hinder the organization's future. A 'transformational' leader can be critical to such a process.

MINI-CASE 18.1

Irregular practices at the European Commission

Brussels launches probe into secret accounts

A widespread inquiry into secret bank accounts and fictitious contracts across the European Commission has been launched.

There is fear that the 'vast enterprise of looting' that fraud investigators found at Eurostat, the Commission's statistical arm, may exist elsewhere in the European Union's executive. Although problems were identified at Eurostat by trade unions in 1997, by internal Commission audits in 1999 and 2000 and by Paul van Buitenen, a whistleblower, in 2001, they were not taken seriously until newspaper reports surfaced in May 2003.

Neil Kinnock, EU administration commissioner, has since revealed the 'relatively extensive practice' at Eurostat until 1999 of setting up secret and illegal accounts, into which millions of euros are thought to have disappeared. The secret bank accounts at Eurostat were set up by Commission officials to hold money paid through inflated contracts to sub-contractors.

The commission has responded by initiating three disciplinary proceedings, suspending all directors and ordering an investigation into the work of some thirty heads of unit.

Source: from Brussels launches probe into secret accounts, *The Financial Times*, 16/07/2003, Copyright © The Financial Times Ltd.

Progress in the implementation of the Reform within the Commission

Extract from the 2003 annual report dealing with protection of the European Community's financial interests and the fight against fraud:

The modernization of the European public service continued to progress during 2003, in parallel to the work relating to the deepening of the antifraud reform of May 1999. In particular, the financial and administrative reform conceived in the White Paper of March 2000 on the internal reform of the Commission is being completed with the entry into force of the new Financial Regulation on 1 January 2003 which changes in particular the internal control system, and the decision of July 2003 on the Specialised Financial Irregularities Panel. As a result of the political agreement reached on 19 May 2003 in the Council and the opinion of the European Parliament of 19 June 2003, the Commission adopted an amended Proposal for the Staff Regulation. As from its entry into force on 1 May 2004, this Staff reform will have a major impact on the managing practices of departments and will contribute in particular to the prevention of irregularities. . . .

In response to the irregular practices detected at Eurostat, the Commission adopted complementary horizontal reinforcement measures: the September 1999 Code of conduct on the relations between the Commissioners and their services was revised in order to improve the information transmitted to Commissioners and to enable them to assume their political responsibility. To this end, a group of Commissioners including the President ensured that all the relevant information and/or allegations of fraud, irregularity and other reprehensible acts coming in particular from OLAF, IDOC and the Internal Audit Service are the subject of a rigorous follow-up. The group of commissioners is assisted by a high-level interdepartmental group.

Source: Report from the Commission Protection of the European Communities' financial interests and the fight against fraud, Annual report 2003, accessed 1 September 2010, (http://eur-lex.europa.eu/LexUriServ/LexUriServ.do?uri=CELEX:52004DC0573:EN:NOT).

Questions

1. How would you describe the effect that the whistleblower's actions had on the European Commission?
2. In what way do you think the 'culture' of Eurostat might have been changed as a result of the actions?

Concept 18.2 Organizational change in a global environment

So, organizational change in companies operating across a number of cultures is not just instrumental (becoming more cost-effective or market-oriented) but also transformational (giving new ways of thinking). How, therefore, does a multinational deal with change if it not only has to deal with policy changes, but also internal factors that may vary considerably from one part of the company to another? Equally important is how the multinational can handle the external factors that are said to have such an influence on the culture of the organization (Laurent, 1989).

The tension between organizational and national cultures

The first issue to be addressed is the one briefly described in Part One: the tension between organizational culture and national culture. Adler (2002) wondered whether organizational values in some way pushed aside or diluted the national culture of the organization's environment. She refers to the seminal research carried out by Laurent in the 1980s. The conclusions of this research were that cultural differences among managers working for a multinational company were significantly greater than those cultural differences among managers working for companies in their own (native) country. Although restricted to Western managers, Laurent's investigations showed that 'nationally bounded' collective perceptions of organizations did not appear to be diminished in any way through international business. On the contrary, as Adler indicates, these appear to be reinforced through the international exposure.

The conclusion is that the national companies of multinationals are likely to prefer different ways of bringing about the organizational changes that headquarters wish to implement. To use the terms adopted in Concept 18.1, the transformation of an organization from A to B may involve following a different path in one part of the multinational than in another, even if the end-result (B) is the same. The means used to reach the desired change will also depend on how the national organization determines what the starting-point should be. In other words, the outset of the transformation to B will depend on how the national organization interprets its own present situation (A).

Does an international corporate culture exist?

Despite the all-important influence of national cultures, the opinion is often expressed that there is a growing class of transnational business people who share a similar education, similar work experience and who are developing their own global business culture. Moreover, it is argued that the companies for which these people work are themselves developing commonalities in terms of efficient production processes, quality control, workers' rights and environment issues. More and more international norms concerning business are being established through various agencies and these are being followed by an increasing number of globally active companies. So, the argument runs, both the increasing homogeneity among international managers and the increasing convergence of business practices is leading to the establishment of a common management culture among more and more international companies and their national constituents, a common culture which has no roots in any particular national culture.

These arguments appear to be supported by investigations done by Despharde et al. (1997). They investigated whether there were any commonalties when comparing the organizational performance of multinationals based in Japan, the US, England, France and Germany. They found that, although the companies operated very differently, the most successful businesses surveyed used a similar organizational strategy. Whatever the country of origin, each successful multinational was most likely to foster competitive, entrepreneurial values. In particular, they found that those companies where innovation was most valued were the most successful.

Their findings may indeed highlight values that account for the success of the companies investigated, but to suggest that these companies have adopted an organizational culture at the expense of national cultures is considered by many in the field to be wishful thinking. There may indeed be a growing consensus among multinationals as to what best practice is for international business. However, the idea that a shared organizational culture of many multinationals is pushing aside national cultures not only downplays the deep-seated nature of national cultures, but also discourages the transfer of know-how between the culturally different subsidiaries of the company, particularly when it comes to organizational change. Moreover, there is always the risk that multinational constituents become estranged from their national roots and that local relationships of all kinds are put under strain.

In short, a true multinational does not subordinate national cultures, but regards them as a source of learning and increased synergy within the company. To return to the analysis made by Laurent (1989: 93) and summarized at the start of this concept, this increased learning and synergy:

> ...cannot be the result of a rational management decision. It requires an evolution in ways of thinking – from a parochial and ethnocentric conception of management and organization to a world view.

Mapping corporate culture change

At this stage it is worthwhile looking at the framework of reference used in the survey carried out by Despharde et al. (1997) to allow the issue of corporate culture change to be taken further. Cameron and Quinn (1999) categorize organizational effectiveness perspectives and associated types of organization (Figure 18.1). They emphasize that this categorization should not be seen in any way as comprehensive. It is, however, based on many scholarly analyses of corporate culture and has, they claim, proved its value in many subsequent investigations into corporate culture change.

As can be seen in Table 18.3, two dimensions are used to differentiate effectiveness criteria: one emphasizes either flexibility and discretion or stability and control; another emphasizes either internal orientation (integration and unity) or external orientation (differentiation and rivalry). These two dimensions produce four quadrants, which each represents a set of values that are at the base of judgements about organizations. The quadrants are contradictory or competing on the diagonal. Hence the name of the model, the competing values (CV) framework.

The characteristics of these quadrants, as described by Cameron and Quinn (1999), are summarized in Table 18.3.

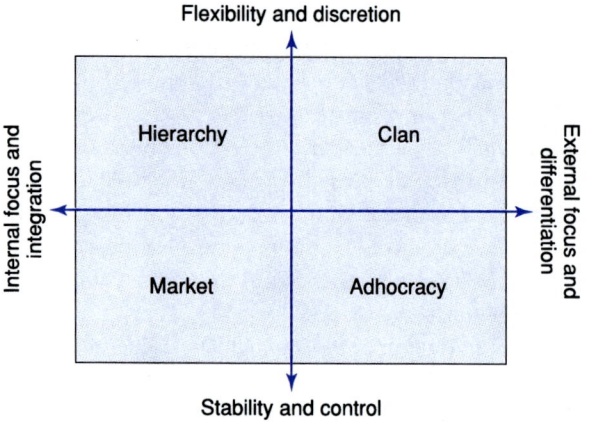

Figure 18.1 The competing values framework
Source: Cameron and Quinn (1999): 32.

Table 18.3 The characteristics of the CV framework quadrants

Hierarchy culture	Values tradition, continuity, rationalization and regulation. It focuses more on internal than external (market) issues, and values stability and control over flexibility and discretion. This is the traditional 'command and control' model of organizations, which can work effectively if the goal is efficiency and the organizational environment is stable and simple
Market culture	Also values stability and control but is more focused on external rather than internal issues. This culture values profit, productivity, competitive advantage and achievement
Clan culture	Focuses on internal issues and flexibility and discretion rather than seeking stability and control. It values team-spirit, participation, consensus and mutual support
Adhocracy culture	Focuses on external issues and values flexibility. Its values are adaptability and innovation

This categorization is not clear-cut: all organizations have aspects of all four cultures. An 'adhocracy', for example, which is intent on creativity and flexibility, still needs to contain some 'hierarchy' values if it is not to run out of control; a 'market' culture may be so focused on making profit that individuals – and their health – may become secondary to the whole operation; a 'clan' culture may allow for so much uncontrolled individualism that the company's tasks become secondary. However, over time, one type of culture tends to predominate. High performance entails, therefore, balancing conflicting and competing demands.

The elements in the competing values framework, as well as the language used, can be used to discuss organizational culture and change. As such, the framework serves as a basis for diagnosing the predominant culture of an organization and for assessing whether it is responding appropriately to the challenges and changes in the environment. Equally important, the framework helps in the diagnosis and management of the interrelationships, congruencies and contradictions in the organization. Altogether, the framework helps leaders to improve in a comprehensive way the organization's performance and value creation.

MINI-CASE 18.2

GM and Chrysler steer different paths to recovery

By Bernard Simon in Toronto

Detroit's two embattled carmakers, General Motors and Chrysler, have been a study in contrasts since their emergence from court-supervised restructurings in recent months. The 'new' GM has galloped out of the gate with a slew of announcements on management shuffles, new vehicles and other initiatives. Meanwhile, Chrysler has been relatively silent apart from run-of-the-mill sales promotions.

Fritz Henderson, GM's chief executive, has hosted numerous webchats and media conferences lately, in an attempt to persuade car buyers, especially Americans, that the dinosaur of old is managing to turn itself into a nimble, cutting-edge enterprise. He and his colleagues on Monday invited about 100 consumers, including some of GM's fiercest critics, to a face-to-face feedback session about the company and its vehicles.

This week, GM cemented a joint venture with Ebay to sell vehicles online, outlined plans for a new Cadillac model and trumpeted the fuel efficiency of its new Chevy Volt plug-in hybrid, to be launched at the end of next year.

'We're changing the culture of GM,' Mr Henderson said at the Volt briefing on Tuesday.

By contrast, Chrysler, now under the day-to-day control of Italy's Fiat, has discontinued its monthly sales data briefings. Its sole representative at a motor industry conference in Traverse City, Michigan, last week was a public affairs manager. Toyota's president, GM's vice-chairman and Ford Motor's chief financial officer were among other speakers present.

It is too early to judge which of the two companies is on the right track. Some outsiders question whether the flurry of activity at GM is more representative of style than substance.

Source: from GM and Chrysler steer different paths to recovery, *The Financial Times*, 14/08/2009 (Simon, B.), Copyright © The Financial Times Ltd.

Questions

1. Using Figure 18.1, describe how GM is attempting to bring about changes to the GM culture.
2. Which of Schein's 'mechanisms of change' do you think are being applied at GM?

The 'organizational culture assessment instrument' used to carry out the diagnosis is described in detail by Cameron and Quinn (1999). It takes the form of a questionnaire in which respondents complete questions covering six items. The questions are answered first in terms of the organization's current culture, then answered again in terms of what the respondents think should be developed in the culture to respond to future challenges. Once the present and future profiles of the organization have been drawn up, they can be examined from several angles:

- What type of culture is most heavily emphasized (what basic assumptions, styles and values are dominant)?
- What discrepancies are there between the present and future profiles (what needs to be done to close the gap)?
- What is the degree of congruence between the individual responses to the questions (to what degree are the values and assumptions shared)?

An organization's profile can also be measured against an average industry profile. Cameron and Quinn (1999) provide a range of these, mostly from the US but also in Europe, South America, Africa, Australasia and Asia. Comparing the two profiles allows insights to be developed concerning the cultural changes needed: is the organization out of line with the requirements of the sector's environment, or is the mismatch itself a source of competitive advantage?

> ### SPOTLIGHT 18.2
>
> #### Decision-making and competing values
>
> *Here is a short extract from an article written by John Kay, founding Director of the Said Business School at Oxford University, in which he examines the question of decision-making, the theory and the reality.*
>
> We do not solve problems in the way the concept of decision science implies because we can't. The achievement of the great statesman is not to reach the best decision fastest, but to mediate effectively among competing views and values. The achievement of the successful business leader is not to articulate visions of the far future, but to match continuously the capabilities of the firm to the changing market environment. The test of financial acumen is to navigate successfully through irresolvable uncertainties.
>
> ...
>
> Our approaches are iterative and adaptive. We make our choices from a limited range of options. Our knowledge of the relevant information and of what information is relevant, is imperfect. Different people make different judgments in the same situation, not just because they have different objectives, but because they observe different options, select different information, and assess that information differently; even with hindsight it will often not be possible to say who was right and who was wrong.
>
> Source: from Decision-making, John Kays' way, *The Financial Times*, 20/03/2010 (Kay, J.), Copyright © The Financial Times Ltd.

As a final point with regard to the competing values framework, it is worth returning to the survey by Despharde et al. (1997). Although the authors came to the conclusion that successful international companies were likely to foster very similar competitive, entrepreneurial values, they also noted differences of emphasis when it came to categorizing these companies according to the CV framework. They found, for example, that the Japanese companies under investigation fostered 'hierarchy' and 'clan' values while at the same time stressing competition and performance. English companies, although fostering values associated with 'adhocracy', also displayed 'clan' values of loyalty and cohesiveness. French companies embraced many values associated with 'hierarchy' cultures, but also embraced the virtues of entrepreneurship and innovation associated with the 'adhocracy' culture. These findings confirm the 'competing' nature of the framework, but also clearly imply that congruity between an organization's cultural values and national cultural values are a measure of a company's success.

Conclusion

Chapter 18 has described the role of culture in organizational change. It has outlined the cultural issues which, according to Schein, are prevalent at the various stages in a company's development, and it has summarized the actions he proposes as mechanisms of change.

One crucial factor in any change process is the extent to which a company is aware of its culture and of the operational environment. Using the competing values framework devised by Cameron and Quinn is one way of assessing whether a company and its employees are responding appropriately to the environment; this framework has been outlined in the chapter.

Chapter 18 has also shown that, even if the culture of a multinational organization needs to be changed, any transformation carried out will need to reflect the national culture while at the same time ensuring that the subsidiaries involved remain integral parts of the whole multinational.

Points for reflection

1. As the text indicates, companies tend not to give explicit attention to cultural issues when planning and implementing organizational change. Laurent advocates a dual approach to address this situation.

   What type of leader is required in this approach and what does that leader need to do? Where does this approach belong in Table 18.2 (Schein's 'mechanisms of cultural change')?

2. Concept 7.2 summarized a classification of the types of cultures, made by Deal and Kennedy (2000) on the basis of a study they made of various firms and their business environment.

   What are the similarities between this and the cultures defined in the competing values framework presented in Figure 18.1? What differences do your perceive between the two – and how do you account for these?

Further reading

Schein, E.H. (2004) *Organizational Culture and Leadership*, 3rd edn, San Francisco, CA: Jossey-Bass.
This is the third edition of the book published originally in 1985. Schein offers his readers considerable insight into the dynamics of organizations and change. Using the findings of contemporary research, as well as referring to many of the organizations with whom he has worked, Schein examines occupational cultures as well as the ways in which leaders apply the principles of culture to achieve organizational goals. He also addresses the question of cultural change within an organization, specifically the role of the leader in this process. One aspect that Schein considers indispensable – and which he says is almost completely ignored in most leadership books – is the question of organizational growth and the different role that culture plays during each stage of growth.

Cameron, K.S. and Quinn, R.E. (1999) *Diagnosing and Changing Organizational Culture*, Upper Saddle River, NJ: Prentice-Hall. This book provides an instrument for diagnosing organizational culture and a framework for understanding organizational culture. It then describes a step-by-step process for producing an organizational culture profile, identifying the ways in which the culture of the organization should change, and formulating a strategy for accomplishing that change. The book contains an assessment instrument that readers can use to determine their own cultural profile as leaders/managers/employees in an organization.

References

Adler, N.J. (2002) *International Dimension of Organizational Behaviour*, Cincinnati, OH: South-Western.

Cameron, K.S. and Quinn, R.E. (1999) *Diagnosing and Changing Organizational Culture*, Upper Saddle River, NJ: Prentice Hall.

Deal, T.E. and Kennedy, A.A. (2000) *Corporate Cultures: The Rites and Rituals of Corporate Life*, Cambridge, MA: Perseus.

Despharde, R., Farley, J.U. and Webster Jr., F.E. (1997) 'Factors affecting organizational performance: a five-country comparison.' *Harvard Business School Working Paper*, No. 98-027, 1997.

Laurent, A. (1989) 'A cultural view of organizational change', in Evans, P., Doz, Y. and Laurent, A. (eds), *Human Resource Management in International Firms*, London: Macmillan: 83–94.

Qi, L. (2005) 'Learn to agree to differ', *The Link*, Autumn 2005, Chinese Europe International Business School on its website (www.ceibs.edu/link/index.shtml).

Schein, E.H. (1989) 'Organizational culture: what it is and how to change it', in Evans, P., Doz, Y. and Laurent, A. (eds), *Human Resource Management in International Firms*, London: Macmillan: 56–82.

Schein, E.H. (2004) *Organizational Culture and Leadership*, 3rd edn, San Francisco, CA: Jossey-Bass.

Chapter 18 Activities

ACTIVITY 18.1

The summary of events given below concerning Michelin's joint venture in China is based on the detailed account given in the autumn 2005 issue of *The Link*, the learning interface of China European Business School, Shanghai, accessed 1 June 2008 (www.ceibs.edu/link/index.shtml).

Answer the questions that follow the summary.

Michelin in China implementing a human resources strategy

In 2001, Michelin, the world's leading tyre manufacturer and based in France, set up a joint venture in Shanghai, China, with Shanghai Tyre and Rubber Company. The Chinese tyre market was expected to almost treble within three years, so Michelin was happy to invest $200 million in the company.

The new company, in which Michelin had a 70 per cent stake, was mostly made up of employees from the Chinese partner plus a small team of expatriate managers and managers recruited from other international ventures in China. The expatriates were used to lay the foundation for future operations and to support the management team that had originally run the Chinese company. This team was kept in place to facilitate the integration process.

Michelin wished to implement its well-established personal management philosophy in the new company. This was the way to develop the personal and professional effectiveness of the workforce as well as help individuals develop their career in the company. The company badly needed managers who could work in a joint venture environment, so this active approach to human resource development compensated for the dearth of suitable managers available in China.

The management approach Michelin wished to have adopted was based on Michelin's five core values which were founded on respect for: customers, people, shareholders, the environment and facts. See the company's corporate website: http://www.michelin.com/corporate/front/templates/affich.jsp?codeRubrique=74&lang=EN.

These values were immediately recognizable and not difficult for the Chinese employees to accept. But were they aware of what the implementation of these values through the management approach entailed?

The personnel department in Shanghai, as well as its counterparts in other Michelin production plants, was responsible for creating and maintaining a strong, open and shared company culture, one that was a source of social cohesion and motivation. The department encouraged individual employees to advance themselves professionally according to their performance, skills and ambitions. Just as on other Michelin sites, the department was set apart from the business units. The personnel managers had no formal position in the hierarchy but worked closely with partners, the managers of the business units. During the employees' progress within the company there was continual evaluation and face-to-face dialogue involving the employee, the unit manager and the career manager from the personnel department.

In her analysis of the personnel situation in the Shanghai plant, the human resources director of Michelin China described the difficulties that the integration of this approach into the joint venture would cause (Qi, 2005). Clearly, this could not be done overnight. The concept of appraisal and the role of career managers did not fit into the concept that the Chinese have of management and the importance given to hierarchical relationships. Other elements of the HR approach that would be difficult for the Chinese to accept included the notion that support functions such as human resources were as important as functional departments and the expectation that employees should speak openly about themselves and the working environment.

The starting point of any integration needed to be for both sides to understand each other's ways of thinking. In this way initial fears and suspicions could be removed and the process of building mutual trust set in motion. The employees who had been recruited from other joint ventures and who had become familiar with Western practices acted as a bridge between the expatriates (who were mostly involved in the technical process) and the line managers (who were Chinese). In addition, considerable resources were dedicated to training courses and study abroad for (potential) managers.

Four years after the creation of the joint venture, the HR director saw some progress, but that integration was by no means complete. Although some employees were unable to adapt to the changing environment and left, the majority appeared to be willing to accept Michelin's approach to human resources. The career management system was 'taking shape' and the process of dialogue between employees, career managers and line managers was under way. At the same time, the expatriates had gained a deeper insight into how the Chinese culture works.

As the writer indicates, one core value of the Michelin culture – respect for people – lies at the core of the integration process. Respect by both sides of both sides. The process was therefore not about establishing the Michelin way, or the Chinese way; it was about establishing the Michelin China way.

Questions

1. Summarize what you believe to be the 'Michelin China way'.
2. Which of the values, as described in the competing values framework, do you recognize in the case with regard to Michelin and its Chinese partner? How do you account for any similarities or differences?

ACTIVITY 18.2

The article below describes the changes which an Asian company is attempting to bring to its R&D department in order to improve the company's position in the global market.

Read the article and answer the questions follow.

Samsung sows for the future with its garden of delights

By Anna Fifield

Samsung Electronics executives often feel uneasy when they enter the company's 'value innovation programme' (VIP) centre south of Seoul, where grass sprouts from the ceilings, the doors are covered with funfair mirrors and the walls covered with chalk drawings of ideas.

South Korean offices typically feature grey computers on grey desks inside grey walls, where workers adhere to strict Confucian traditions and would never dream of questioning a superior or making wacky suggestions. But here, in the Samsung idea incubator, they are encouraged to put on Viking and bumblebee hats, lie on the floor and throw round ideas without regard for rank, play with Elmo toys and inflatable dolphins, all the while taking polaroids of themselves. Such an environment might be commonplace in the information technology companies of California but it is revolutionary in Korea.

'Some people come here because their manager tells them to, and when they arrive they say "I can't work in this environment",' says Chung Sue-young, one of the 'VIP' centre coordinators. 'The engineers immediately start tidying up and stacking all the magazines in date order, the R&D people only want to talk with Americans, and the designers just stand there and don't say anything,' she says.

But this kind of change is crucial as Samsung, which has made a remarkable transformation from copy-cat manufacturer to become Asia's most valuable technology company, now finds itself in something of a rut. Many of its products – such as semiconductors and flat-screens – are becoming commodities, and it has yet to produce a killer product, as Sony did with the Walkman and Apple with the iPod.

So Samsung is increasingly sending employees to the VIP centre for weeks at a time, encouraging them to think outside the box, and outside the office. They go to department stores to watch people shopping, or to museums to think about space and light.

'In our Samsung culture, it looks like the people here are slacking off,' Ms Chung explains in one of the VIP centre rooms, which is incongruously housed in a run-down old dormitory at its main research and development centre. 'But there are more and more people who recognize the value of creative slacking,' she adds.

Chairman Lee Kun-hee recognizes the need for creativity if Samsung is going to make the next leap forward.

'An unexpected but tremendously rapid change will occur by 2010,' he said last year at the Samsung Electronics research centre. 'In all areas from design, marketing and R&D, we have to be prepared for the future by implementing creative management schemes.'

The value innovation programme – which essentially boils down to providing the things that a customer wants, at the lowest cost – is central to that drive. It was here that three engineers, a designer and a marketing specialist came up with the 'Bordeaux' flat screen television. With its focus on design – the speakers are hidden and the lines are supposed to be reminiscent of a wine glass – the Bordeaux became Samsung's first LCD television to sell more than 1m units.

'People often complain that the TV takes up lots of space and that it doesn't go with the other furniture. What the Bordeaux team did was simply to sit down and say, we're going to make the kind of pretty TV that customers want,' Ms Chung explains. 'This is common sense but when you work with technology and are very product oriented, sometimes you are too specialist to see these kinds of things,' she says.

While the VIP centre is a kind of hotbed for creative thinking, Samsung is trying to develop a more creative culture across its R&D centre, which is now home to more than 39,000 employees.

'Traditionally we have been workaholics, spending very long hours in the office, but now the emphasis is moving to efficiency and the number of people coming in at weekends has drastically decreased,' says Eugene Pak, vice-president of the technology planning team.

In Mr. Pak's department, executives are gathering for morning '10-minute talks', chatting about things such as their hobbies or current events – topics that would be water-cooler talk in other countries but which could be deemed frivolous here.

Samsung is also changing its recruiting priorities.

'Before, we looked for loyalty but these days we are increasingly also looking for creativity and a knack for doing something unique, something a little bit crazy. We now look for people that have that extra dimension,' Mr. Pak says.

'We have good talent but we are maybe 2 per cent short – we just need the extra push to make it to the top,' he says. 'We need that extra insight that I think we can get from bringing people from abroad to help change the corporate culture.'

Source: adapted from Samsung sows for the future with its garden of delights, *The Financial Times*, 04/01/2008 (Fifield, A.), Copyright © The Financial Times Ltd.

Questions

1. How does the environment of the 'idea incubator' encourage those working there to change their behaviour?
2. Using the Competing Values framework outlined in Concept 18.1, describe the changes that Samsung is attempting to bring to the R&D department.
3. The author of the article refers to Samsung as having once been a 'copy-cat' manufacturer. To what extent to you consider the creation of the VIP centre to be an example of 'copy-cat' behaviour?